Android Programming

THE BIG NERD RANCH GUIDE

Bill Phillips, Chris Stewart, Brian Hardy & Kristin Marsicano

Big Nerd
Ranch

Android Programming: The Big Nerd Ranch Guide

by Bill Phillips, Chris Stewart, Brian Hardy and Kristin Marsicano

Big Nerd Ranch, LLC.
200 Arizona Ave NE
Atlanta, GA 30307
(770) 817-6373
http://www.bignerdranch.com/
book-comments@bignerdranch.com

The 10-gallon hat with propeller logo is a trademark of Big Nerd Ranch, Inc.

Exclusive worldwide distribution of the English edition of this book by

Pearson Technology Group
800 East 96th Street
Indianapolis, IN 46240 USA
http://www.informit.com

The authors and publisher have taken care in writing and printing this book but make no expressed or implied warranty of any kind and assume no responsibility for errors or omissions. No liability is assumed for incidental or consequential damages in connection with or arising out of the use of the information or programs contained herein.

Many of the designations used by manufacturers and sellers to distinguish their products are claimed as trademarks. Where those designations appear in this book, and the publisher was aware of a trademark claim, the designations have been printed with initial capital letters or in all capitals.

ISBN-10 0134171454
ISBN-13 978-0134171456

Second edition, first printing, August 2015

Dedication

To God, or to whatever it is that you personally have faith in. Reader, I hope that you find the many explanations in this book useful. Please don't ask me how they got here, though. I once thought that I was responsible. Fortunately for you, I was wrong.

— B.P.

To my dad, David, for teaching me the value of hard work. To my mom, Lisa, for pushing me to always do the right thing.

— C.S.

For Donovan. May he live a life filled with activities and know when to use fragments.

— B.H.

To my dad, Dave Vadas, for inspiring and encouraging me to pursue a career in computing. And to my mom, Joan Vadas, for cheering me on through all the ups and downs (and for reminding me that watching an episode of The Golden Girls always makes things better).

— K.M.

Acknowledgments

We feel a bit sheepish having our names on the cover of this book. The truth is that without an army of collaborators, this book could never have happened. We owe them all a debt of gratitude.

- Our co-instructors and members of our Android development team, Andrew Lunsford, Bolot Kerimbaev, Brian Gardner, David Greenhalgh, Jason Atwood, Josh Skeen, Kurt Nelson, Matt Compton, Paul Turner, and Sean Farrell. We thank them for their patience in teaching work-in-progress material, as well as their suggestions and corrections. If we could give ourselves additional brains to do with as we pleased, we would not. We would just put the new brains in a big pile, and share them with our colleagues. We trust them at least as much as we trust our own selves.

- Special thanks to Sean Farrell for graciously updating many screen shots as Android Studio evolved, and to Matt Compton for publishing all of our sample apps to the Google Play Store.

- Kar Loong Wong and Zack Simon, members of Big Nerd Ranch's amazing design team. Kar made BeatBox look intimidating and polished, and provided advice and imagery for the material design chapter. Zack took time out of his schedule to design MockWalker for us. Kar and Zack's design abilities seem like unknowable superpowers to us. We thank them, and bid them fond returns to their home planet.

- Our technical reviewers, Frank Robles and Roy Kravitz, who helped us find and fix flaws.

- Thanks to Aaron Hillegass. Aaron's faith in people is one of the great and terrifying forces of nature. Without it, we would never have had the opportunity to write this book, nor would we ever have completed it. (He also gave us money, which was very friendly of him.)

- Our editor, Elizabeth Holaday, who many times saved us from going down rabbit holes. She kept our writing focused on what our readers actually care about and spared you all from confusing, boring, and irrelevant detours. Thank you, Liz, for being organized and patient, and for being a constant supportive presence, even though you live many miles away.

- Ellie Volckhausen, who designed our cover.

- Simone Payment, our copy-editor, who found and smoothed rough spots.

- Chris Loper at IntelligentEnglish.com, who designed and produced the print book and the EPUB and Kindle versions. His DocBook toolchain made life much easier, too.

Finally, thanks to our students. We wish that we had room to thank every single student who gave us a correction or opinion on the book as it was shaping up. It is your curiosity we have worked to satisfy, your confusions we have worked to clarify. Thank you.

Table of Contents

Learning Android

As a beginning Android programmer, you face a steep learning curve. Learning Android is like moving to a foreign city. Even if you speak the language, it will not feel like home at first. Everyone around you seems to understand things that you are missing. Things you already knew turn out to be dead wrong in this new context.

Android has a culture. That culture speaks Java, but knowing Java is not enough. Getting your head around Android requires learning many new ideas and techniques. It helps to have a guide through unfamiliar territory.

That's where we come in. At Big Nerd Ranch, we believe that to be an Android programmer, you must:

- *write* Android applications

- *understand* what you are writing

This guide will help you do both. We have trained hundreds of professional Android programmers using it. We lead you through writing several Android applications, introducing concepts and techniques as needed. When there are rough spots, when some things are tricky or obscure, you will face them head on, and we will do our best to explain why things are the way they are.

This approach allows you to put what you have learned into practice in a working app right away rather than learning a lot of theory and then having to figure out how to apply it all later. You will come away with the experience and understanding you need to get going as an Android developer.

Prerequisites

To use this book, you need to be familiar with Java, including classes and objects, interfaces, listeners, packages, inner classes, anonymous inner classes, and generic classes.

If these ideas do not ring a bell, you will be in the weeds by page 2. Start instead with an introductory Java book and return to this book afterward. There are many excellent introductory books available, so you can choose one based on your programming experience and learning style.

If you are comfortable with object-oriented programming concepts, but your Java is a little rusty, you will probably be OK. We will provide some brief reminders about Java specifics (like interfaces and anonymous inner classes). Keep a Java reference handy in case you need more support as you go through the book.

What's New in the Second Edition?

This second edition shows how to use the Android Studio integrated development environment to write practical applications for Android 5.1 (Lollipop) that are backwards-compatible through Android 4.1 (Jelly Bean). It includes updated coverage of the fundamentals of Android programming as well as new Lollipop tools like the toolbar and material design. It also covers new tools from the support libraries, like **RecyclerView** and Google Play Services, plus some key standard library tools, like **SoundPool**, animations, and assets.

How to Use This Book

This book is not a reference book. Its goal is to get you over the initial hump to where you can get the most out of the reference and recipe books available. It is based on our five-day class at Big Nerd Ranch. As such, it is meant to be worked through from the beginning. Chapters build on each other and skipping around is unproductive.

In our classes, students work through these materials, but they also benefit from the right environment – a dedicated classroom, good food and comfortable board, a group of motivated peers, and an instructor to answer questions.

As a reader, you want your environment to be similar. That means getting a good night's rest and finding a quiet place to work. These things can help, too:

- Start a reading group with your friends or coworkers.

- Arrange to have blocks of focused time to work on chapters.

- Participate in the forum for this book at `http://forums.bignerdranch.com`.

- Find someone who knows Android to help you out.

How This Book is Organized

As you work through this book, you will write eight Android apps. A couple are very simple and take only a chapter to create. Others are more complex. The longest app spans 11 chapters. All are designed to teach you important concepts and techniques and give you direct experience using them.

GeoQuiz	In your first app, you will explore the fundamentals of Android projects, activities, layouts, and explicit intents.
CriminalIntent	The largest app in the book, CriminalIntent lets you keep a record of your colleagues' lapses around the office. You will learn to use fragments, master-detail interfaces, list-backed interfaces, menus, the camera, implicit intents, and more.
BeatBox	Intimidate your foes with this app while you learn more about fragments, media playback, themes, and drawables.
NerdLauncher	Building this custom launcher will give you insight into the intent system and tasks.
PhotoGallery	A Flickr client that downloads and displays photos from Flickr's public feed, this app will take you through services, multithreading, accessing web services, and more.

DragAndDraw   In this simple drawing app, you will learn about handling touch events and creating custom views.

Sunset   In this toy app, you will create a beautiful representation of a sunset over open water while learning about animations.

Locatr   This app lets you query Flickr for pictures around your current location and display them on a map. In it, you will learn how to use location services and maps.

Challenges

Most chapters have a section at the end with exercises for you to work through. This is your opportunity to use what you have learned, explore the documentation, and do some problem solving on your own.

We strongly recommend that you do the challenges. Going off the beaten path and finding your way will solidify your learning and give you confidence with your own projects.

If you get lost, you can always visit `http://forums.bignerdranch.com` for some assistance.

Are you more curious?

There are also sections at the ends of chapters labeled "For the More Curious." These sections offer deeper explanations or additional information about topics presented in the chapter. The information in these sections is not absolutely essential, but we hope you will find it interesting and useful.

Code Style

There are two areas where our choices differ from what you might see elsewhere in the Android community:

We use anonymous inner classes for listeners.

This is mostly a matter of opinion. We find it makes for cleaner code in the applications in this book because it puts the listener's method implementations right where you want to see them. In high-performance contexts or large applications, anonymous inner classes may cause problems, but for most circumstances they work fine.

After we introduce fragments in Chapter 7, we use them for all user interfaces.

Fragments are not an absolutely necessary tool but we find that, when used correctly, they are a valuable tool in any Android developer's toolkit. Once you get comfortable with fragments, they are not that difficult to work with. Fragments have clear advantages over activities that make them worth the effort, including flexibility in building and presenting your user interfaces.

Typographical Conventions

To make this book easier to read, certain items appear in certain fonts. Variables, constants, and types appear in a fixed-width font. Class names, interface names, and method names appear in a bold, fixed-width font.

All code and XML listings are in a fixed-width font. Code or XML that you need to type in is always bold. Code or XML that should be deleted is struck through. For example, in the following method implementation, you are deleting the call to `makeText(…)` and adding the call to `checkAnswer(true)`.

```
@Override
public void onClick(View v) {
    Toast.makeText(QuizActivity.this, R.string.incorrect_toast,
                   Toast.LENGTH_SHORT).show();
    checkAnswer(true);
}
```

Android Versions

This book teaches Android development for all widely used versions of Android. As of this writing, that is Android 4.1 (Jelly Bean) - Android 5.1 (Lollipop). While there is a small amount of market-share on older versions of Android, we find that for most developers the amount of effort required to support those versions is not worth the reward. For more info on the support of versions of Android earlier than 4.1 (in particular, Android 2.2 and Android 2.3), see the first edition of this book.

As Android releases new versions, the techniques you learn in this book will continue to work thanks to Android's backwards compatibility support (see Chapter 6 for details). We will keep track of changes at `http://forums.bignerdranch.com` and offer notes on using this book with the latest version.

The Necessary Tools

To get started with this book, you will need Android Studio. Android Studio is an integrated development environment used for Android development that is based off of the popular IntelliJ IDEA.

An install of Android Studio includes:

Android SDK

> the latest version of the Android SDK

Android SDK tools and platform-tools

> tools for debugging and testing your apps

A system image for the Android emulator

> lets you create and test your apps on different virtual devices

As of this writing, Android Studio is under active development and is frequently updated. Be aware that you may find differences between your version of Android Studio and what you see in this book. Visit `http://forums.bignerdranch.com` for help with these differences.

Downloading and Installing Android Studio

Android Studio is available from Android's developer site at `https://developer.android.com/sdk/`.

If you do not already have it installed, you will need to install the Java Development Kit (JDK7), which you can download from `http://www.oracle.com`.

If you are still having problems, return to `https://developer.android.com/sdk/` for more information.

Downloading Earlier SDK Versions

Android Studio provides the SDK and the emulator system image from the latest platform. However, you may want to test your apps on earlier versions of Android.

You can get components for each platform using the Android SDK Manager. In Android Studio, select Tools → Android → SDK Manager. (You will only see the Tools menu if you have a project open. If you have not created a project yet, you can instead access the SDK Manager from the Android Setup Wizard screen. Under the Quick Start section, select Configure → SDK Manager, as shown in Figure 1.)

Figure 1 Android SDK Manager

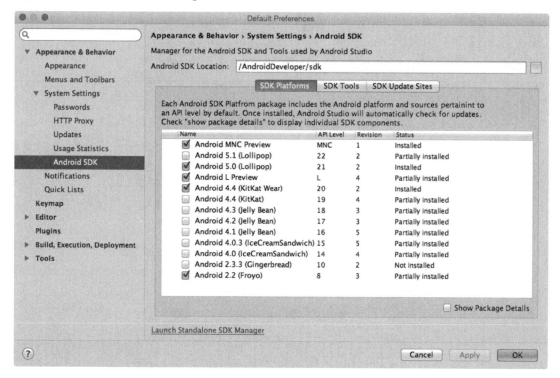

Select and install each version of Android that you want to test with. Note that downloading these components may take a while.

The Android SDK Manager is also how to get Android's latest releases, like a new platform or an update of the tools.

An Alternative Emulator

The speed of the Android emulator has improved significantly over time and it is a reasonable way to run the code that you write in this book.

As an alternative, Genymotion is a popular, third-party Android emulator. You will occasionally see references to the Genymotion emulator in this book. For more information on Genymotion, visit `http://genymotion.com/`.

A Hardware Device

The emulator and Genymotion are useful for testing apps. However, they are no substitute for an actual Android device when measuring performance. If you have a hardware device, we recommend using that device at times when working through this book.

1

Your First Android Application

This first chapter is full of new concepts and moving parts required to build an Android application. It is OK if you do not understand everything by the end of this chapter. You will be revisiting these ideas again and in greater detail as you proceed through the book.

The application you are going to create is called GeoQuiz. GeoQuiz tests the user's knowledge of geography. The user presses True or False to answer the question on screen, and GeoQuiz provides instant feedback.

Figure 1.1 shows the result of a user pressing the False button:

Figure 1.1 (It's Istanbul, not Constantinople)

App Basics

Your GeoQuiz application will consist of an *activity* and a *layout*:

- An *activity* is an instance of **Activity**, a class in the Android SDK. An activity is responsible for managing user interaction with a screen of information.

  You write subclasses of **Activity** to implement the functionality that your app requires. A simple application may need only one subclass; a complex application can have many.

  GeoQuiz is a simple app, so it will have a single **Activity** subclass named **QuizActivity**. **QuizActivity** will manage the user interface shown in Figure 1.1.

- A *layout* defines a set of user interface objects and their position on the screen. A layout is made up of definitions written in XML. Each definition is used to create an object that appears on screen, like a button or some text.

  GeoQuiz will include a layout file named activity_quiz.xml. The XML in this file will define the user interface shown in Figure 1.1.

The relationship between **QuizActivity** and activity_quiz.xml is diagrammed in Figure 1.2.

Figure 1.2 **QuizActivity** manages what activity_quiz.xml defines

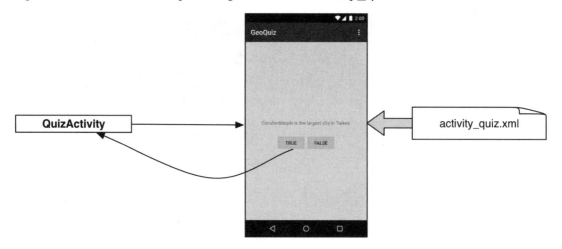

With those ideas in mind, let's build an app.

Creating an Android Project

The first step is to create an Android *project*. An Android project contains the files that make up an application. To create a new project, first open Android Studio.

If this is your first time running Android Studio, you will see the Welcome dialog, as in Figure 1.3.

Figure 1.3 Welcome to Android Studio

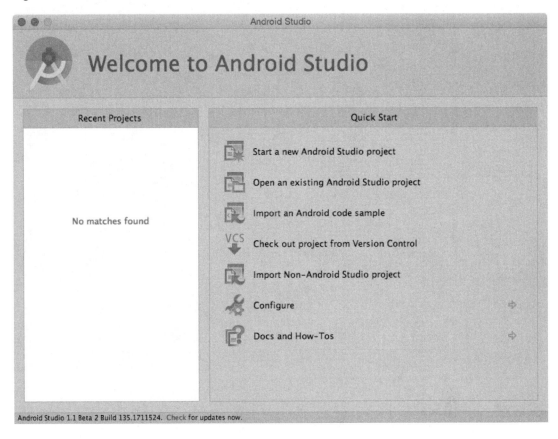

From the dialog, choose Start a new Android Studio project. If you do not see the dialog, you may have created projects before. In this case, choose File → New Project....

You should see the new project wizard. In the first screen of the wizard, enter GeoQuiz as the application name (Figure 1.4). For the Company Domain, enter android.bignerdranch.com. As you do this, you will see the generated Package name change to com.bignerdranch.android.geoquiz. For the Project location, you can use any location on your filesystem that you want.

Figure 1.4 Creating a new application

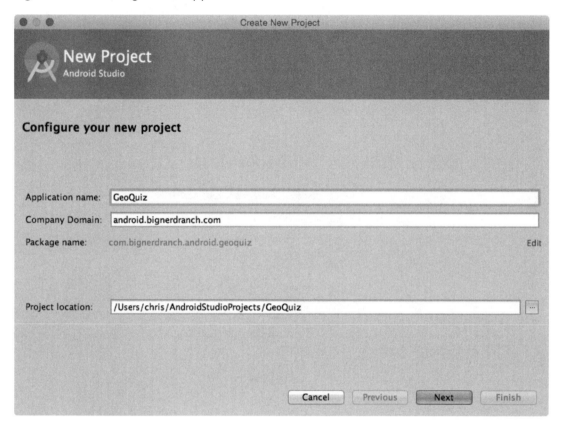

Notice that the package name uses a "reverse DNS" convention in which the domain name of your organization is reversed and suffixed with further identifiers. This convention keeps package names unique and distinguishes applications from each other on a device and on Google Play.

Click Next. The next screen allows you to specify details about which devices you want to support. GeoQuiz will only support phones, so just check Phone and Tablet. Select a Minimum SDK version of API 16: Android 4.1 (Jelly Bean) (Figure 1.5). You will learn about the different versions of Android in Chapter 6.

Figure 1.5 Specifying device support

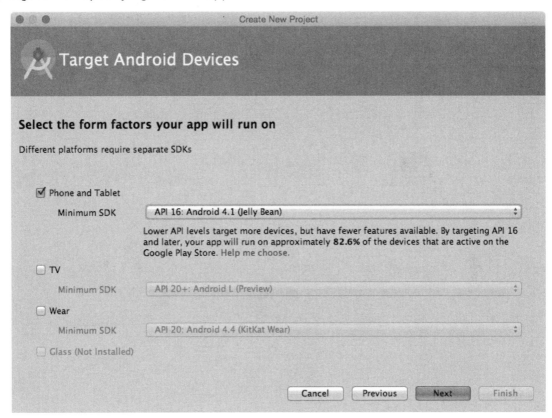

(Android Studio updates regularly, so your wizard may look slightly different from what we are showing you. This is usually not a problem; the choices should be similar. If your wizard looks very different, then the tools have changed more drastically. Do not panic. Head to this book's forum at forums.bignerdranch.com and we will help you navigate the latest version.)

Click Next.

In the next screen, you are prompted to choose a template for the first screen of GeoQuiz (Figure 1.6). Choose Blank Activity and click Next.

Figure 1.6 Choosing a type of Activity

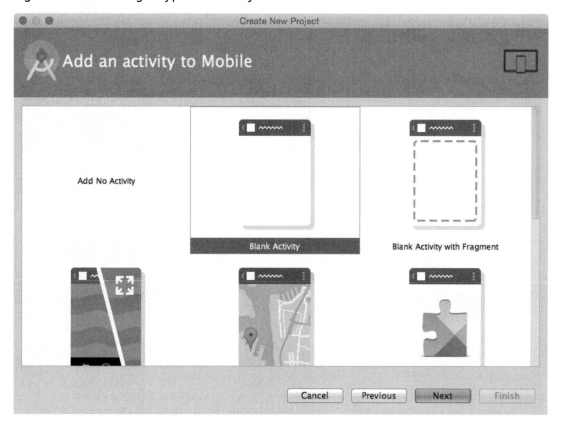

In the final dialog of this wizard, name the activity subclass **QuizActivity** (Figure 1.7). Notice the **Activity** suffix on the class name. This is not required, but it is an excellent convention to follow.

Figure 1.7 Configuring the new activity

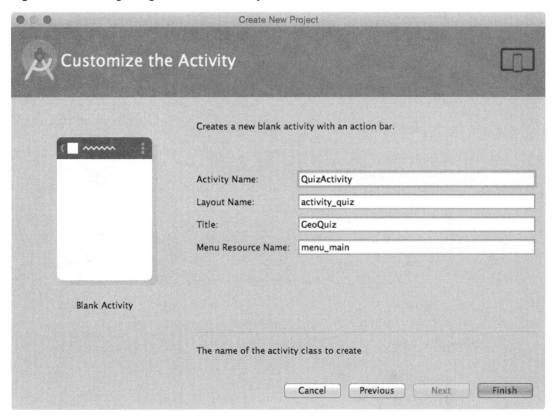

The layout name will automatically update to activity_quiz to reflect the activity's new name. The layout name reverses the order of the activity name, is all lowercase, and has underscores between words. This naming style is recommended for layouts as well as other resources that you will learn about later.

For the Title, enter GeoQuiz to match the name of the app. Leave the Menu Resource Name as is and click Finish. Android Studio will create and open your new project.

Navigating in Android Studio

Android Studio opens your project in a window, as shown in Figure 1.8.

The different panes of the project window are called *Tool Windows*.

The lefthand view is the *project tool window*. From here, you can view and manage the files associated with your project.

The middle view is the *editor*. To get you started, Android Studio has opened activity_quiz.xml in the editor. (If you see an image in the editor, click the Text tab at the bottom.) You can also see a preview of that file on the righthand side.

Figure 1.8 A fresh project window

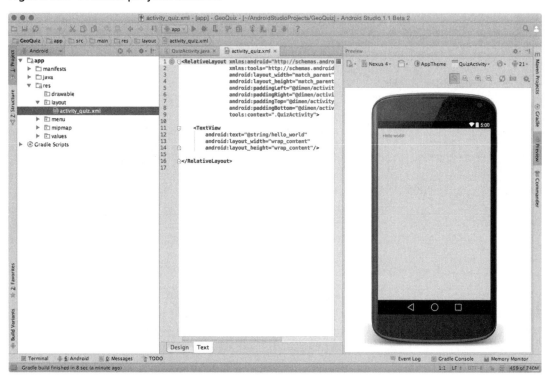

You can toggle the visibility of the various tool windows by clicking on their names in the strip of tool buttons on the left, right, or bottom of the screen. There are keyboard shortcuts for many of these as well. If you do not see the tool button strips, click the gray square button in the lower left corner of the main window or choose View → Tool Buttons.

Laying Out the User Interface

Currently, `activity_quiz.xml` defines the default activity layout. The defaults change frequently, but the XML will look something like Listing 1.1.

Listing 1.1 Default activity layout (`activity_quiz.xml`)

```xml
<RelativeLayout xmlns:android="http://schemas.android.com/apk/res/android"
    xmlns:tools="http://schemas.android.com/tools"
    android:layout_width="match_parent"
    android:layout_height="match_parent"
    android:paddingLeft="@dimen/activity_horizontal_margin"
    android:paddingRight="@dimen/activity_horizontal_margin"
    android:paddingTop="@dimen/activity_vertical_margin"
    android:paddingBottom="@dimen/activity_vertical_margin"
    tools:context=".QuizActivity">

    <TextView
        android:text="@string/hello_world"
        android:layout_width="wrap_content"
        android:layout_height="wrap_content" />

</RelativeLayout>
```

The default activity layout defines two *widgets*: a **RelativeLayout** and a **TextView**.

Widgets are the building blocks you use to compose a user interface. A widget can show text or graphics, interact with the user, or arrange other widgets on the screen. Buttons, text input controls, and checkboxes are all types of widgets.

The Android SDK includes many widgets that you can configure to get the appearance and behavior you want. Every widget is an instance of the **View** class or one of its subclasses (such as **TextView** or **Button**).

Figure 1.9 shows how the **RelativeLayout** and **TextView** defined in Listing 1.1 would appear on screen.

Figure 1.9 Default widgets as seen on screen

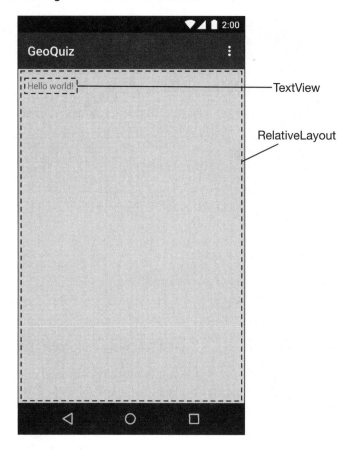

But these are not the widgets you are looking for. The interface for **QuizActivity** requires five widgets:

- a vertical **LinearLayout**

- a **TextView**

- a horizontal **LinearLayout**

- two **Button**s

Figure 1.10 shows how these widgets compose **QuizActivity**'s interface.

Figure 1.10 Planned widgets as seen on screen

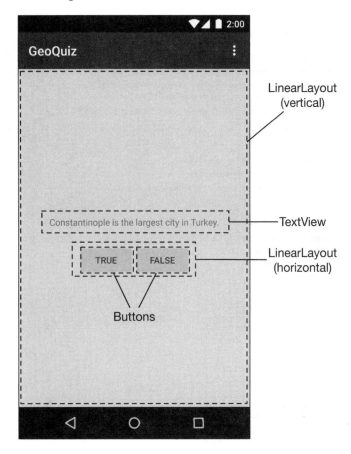

Now you need to define these widgets in activity_quiz.xml.

In activity_quiz.xml, make the changes shown in Listing 1.2. The XML that you need to delete is struck through, and the XML that you need to add is in a bold font. This is the pattern we will use throughout the book.

Do not worry about understanding what you are typing; you will learn how it works next. However, do be careful. Layout XML is not validated, and typos will cause problems sooner or later.

Depending on your version of the tools, you might get errors on the three lines that start with android:text. Ignore these errors for now; you will fix them soon.

Listing 1.2 Defining widgets in XML (`activity_quiz.xml`)

```
<RelativeLayout xmlns:android="http://schemas.android.com/apk/res/android"
    xmlns:tools="http://schemas.android.com/tools"
    android:layout_width="match_parent"
    android:layout_height="match_parent"
    android:paddingLeft="@dimen/activity_horizontal_margin"
    android:paddingRight="@dimen/activity_horizontal_margin"
    android:paddingTop="@dimen/activity_vertical_margin"
    android:paddingBottom="@dimen/activity_vertical_margin"
    tools:context=".QuizActivity">

    <TextView
        android:text="@string/hello_world"
        android:layout_width="wrap_content"
        android:layout_height="wrap_content" />

</RelativeLayout>

<LinearLayout xmlns:android="http://schemas.android.com/apk/res/android"
  android:layout_width="match_parent"
  android:layout_height="match_parent"
  android:gravity="center"
  android:orientation="vertical" >

  <TextView
    android:layout_width="wrap_content"
    android:layout_height="wrap_content"
    android:padding="24dp"
    android:text="@string/question_text" />

  <LinearLayout
    android:layout_width="wrap_content"
    android:layout_height="wrap_content"
    android:orientation="horizontal" >

    <Button
      android:layout_width="wrap_content"
      android:layout_height="wrap_content"
      android:text="@string/true_button" />

    <Button
      android:layout_width="wrap_content"
      android:layout_height="wrap_content"
      android:text="@string/false_button" />

  </LinearLayout>

</LinearLayout>
```

Compare your XML with the user interface shown in Figure 1.10. Every widget has a corresponding XML element. The name of the element is the type of the widget.

Each element has a set of XML *attributes*. Each *attribute* is an instruction about how the widget should be configured.

To understand how the elements and attributes work, it helps to look at the layout from a hierarchical perspective.

The view hierarchy

Your widgets exist in a hierarchy of **View** objects called the *view hierarchy*. Figure 1.11 shows the view hierarchy that corresponds to the XML in Listing 1.2.

Figure 1.11 Hierarchical layout of widgets and attributes

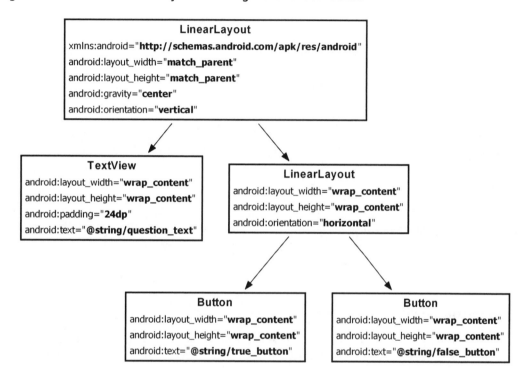

The root element of this layout's view hierarchy is a **LinearLayout**. As the root element, the **LinearLayout** must specify the Android resource XML namespace at http://schemas.android.com/apk/res/android.

LinearLayout inherits from a subclass of **View** named **ViewGroup**. A **ViewGroup** is a widget that contains and arranges other widgets. You use a **LinearLayout** when you want widgets arranged in a single column or row. Other **ViewGroup** subclasses are **FrameLayout**, **TableLayout**, and **RelativeLayout**.

When a widget is contained by a **ViewGroup**, that widget is said to be a *child* of the **ViewGroup**. The root **LinearLayout** has two children: a **TextView** and another **LinearLayout**. The child **LinearLayout** has two **Button** children of its own.

Widget attributes

Let's go over some of the attributes that you have used to configure your widgets.

android:layout_width and android:layout_height

The `android:layout_width` and `android:layout_height` attributes are required for almost every type of widget. They are typically set to either `match_parent` or `wrap_content`:

`match_parent`	view will be as big as its parent
`wrap_content`	view will be as big as its contents require

(You may see `fill_parent` in some places. This deprecated value is equivalent to `match_parent`.)

For the root **LinearLayout**, the value of both the height and width attributes is `match_parent`. The **LinearLayout** is the root element, but it still has a parent – the view that Android provides for your app's view hierarchy to live in.

The other widgets in your layout have their widths and heights set to `wrap_content`. You can see in Figure 1.10 how this determines their sizes.

The **TextView** is slightly larger than the text it contains due to its `android:padding="24dp"` attribute. This attribute tells the widget to add the specified amount of space to its contents when determining its size. You are using it to get a little breathing room between the question and the buttons. (Wondering about the dp units? These are density-independent pixels that you will learn about in Chapter 8.)

android:orientation

The `android:orientation` attribute on the two **LinearLayout** widgets determines whether their children will appear vertically or horizontally. The root **LinearLayout** is vertical; its child **LinearLayout** is horizontal.

The order in which children are defined determines the order in which they appear on screen. In a vertical **LinearLayout**, the first child defined will appear topmost. In a horizontal **LinearLayout**, the first child defined will be leftmost. (Unless the language of the device is a language that runs right-to-left, such as Arabic or Hebrew. In that case, the first child will be rightmost.)

android:text

The **TextView** and **Button** widgets have `android:text` attributes. This attribute tells the widget what text to display.

Notice that the values of these attributes are not literal strings. They are references to *string resources*.

A *string resource* is a string that lives in a separate XML file called a *strings file*. You can give a widget a hard-coded string, like `android:text="True"`, but it is usually not a good idea. Placing strings into a separate file and then referencing them is better because it makes localization easy.

The string resources you are referencing in `activity_quiz.xml` do not exist yet. Let's fix that.

Creating string resources

Every project includes a default strings file named `strings.xml`.

In the Project tool window, find the `app/res/values` directory, reveal its contents, and open `strings.xml`.

The template has already added a few string resources for you. Remove the unused string named `hello_world` and add the three new strings that your layout requires.

Listing 1.3 Adding string resources (`strings.xml`)

```
<resources>
    <string name="app_name">GeoQuiz</string>

    <string name="hello_world">Hello world!</string>
    <string name="question_text">
        Constantinople is the largest city in Turkey.
    </string>
    <string name="true_button">True</string>
    <string name="false_button">False</string>
    <string name="action_settings">Settings</string>
</resources>
```

(Do not delete the `action_settings` string. Your project came with a menu already prepared. Deleting `action_settings` will cause cascading errors in other files related to the menu.)

Now, whenever you refer to `@string/false_button` in any XML file in the GeoQuiz project, you will get the literal string "False" at runtime.

Save `strings.xml`. If you had errors in `activity_quiz.xml` about the missing string resources, they should now be gone. (If you still have errors, check both files for typos.)

Although the default strings file is named `strings.xml`, you can name a strings file anything you want. You can also have multiple strings files in a project. As long as the file is located in `res/values/`, has a `resources` root element, and contains child `string` elements, your strings will be found and used appropriately.

Previewing the layout

Your layout is now complete, and you can preview the layout in the graphical layout tool (Figure 1.12). First, make sure that your files are saved and error free. Then return to `activity_quiz.xml` and open the Preview tool window (if it is not already open) using the tab to the right of the editor.

Figure 1.12 Preview in graphical layout tool (`activity_quiz.xml`)

From Layout XML to View Objects

How do XML elements in `activity_quiz.xml` become **View** objects? The answer starts in the **QuizActivity** class.

When you created the GeoQuiz project, a subclass of **Activity** named **QuizActivity** was created for you. The class file for **QuizActivity** is in the app/java directory of your project. The java directory is where the Java code for your project lives.

In the Project tool window, reveal the contents of the app/java directory and then the contents of the com.bignerdranch.android.geoquiz package. Open the QuizActivity.java file and take a look at its contents (Listing 1.4).

Listing 1.4 Default class file for **QuizActivity** (QuizActivity.java)

```
package com.bignerdranch.android.geoquiz;

import android.support.v7.app.AppCompatActivity;
import android.os.Bundle;
import android.view.Menu;
import android.view.MenuItem;


public class QuizActivity extends AppCompatActivity {

    @Override
    protected void onCreate(Bundle savedInstanceState) {
        super.onCreate(savedInstanceState);
        setContentView(R.layout.activity_quiz);
    }

    @Override
    public boolean onCreateOptionsMenu(Menu menu) {
        getMenuInflater().inflate(R.menu.quiz, menu);
        return true;
    }

    @Override
    public boolean onOptionsItemSelected(MenuItem item) {
        int id = item.getItemId();
        if (id == R.id.action_settings) {
            return true;
        }
        return super.onOptionsItemSelected(item);
    }
}
```

(Wondering what **AppCompatActivity** is? It is a subclass of Android's **Activity** class that provides compatibility support for older versions of Android. You will learn much more about **AppCompatActivity** in Chapter 13.)

If you are not seeing all of the import statements, click the symbol to the left of the first import statement to reveal the others.

This file has three **Activity** methods: **onCreate(Bundle)**, **onCreateOptionsMenu(Menu)**, and **onOptionsItemSelected(MenuItem)**.

Ignore **onCreateOptionsMenu(Menu)** and **onOptionsItemSelected(MenuItem)** for now. You will return to menus in detail in Chapter 13.

The **onCreate(Bundle)** method is called when an instance of the activity subclass is created. When an activity is created, it needs a user interface to manage. To get the activity its user interface, you call the following **Activity** method:

```
public void setContentView(int layoutResID)
```

This method *inflates* a layout and puts it on screen. When a layout is *inflated*, each widget in the layout file is instantiated as defined by its attributes. You specify which layout to inflate by passing in the layout's resource ID.

Resources and resource IDs

A layout is a *resource*. A *resource* is a piece of your application that is not code – things like image files, audio files, and XML files.

Resources for your project live in a subdirectory of the app/res directory. In the Project tool window, you can see that activity_quiz.xml lives in res/layout/. Your strings file, which contains string resources, lives in res/values/.

To access a resource in code, you use its *resource ID*. The resource ID for your layout is R.layout.activity_quiz.

To see the current resource IDs for GeoQuiz, you must first change your project view. By default, Android Studio uses the Android project view (Figure 1.13). This view hides away the true directory structure of your Android project so that you can focus on the files and folders that you need most often.

Figure 1.13 Changing the project view

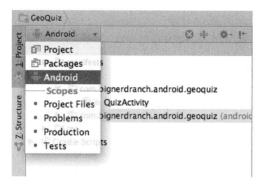

Locate the dropdown at the top of the Project tool window and change from the Android project view to the Project view. The Project view will show you the files and folders in your project as they actually are.

To see the resources for GeoQuiz, reveal the contents of the app/build/generated/source/r/debug directory. In this directory, find your project's package name and open R.java within that package. Because this file is generated by the Android build process, you should not change it, as you are subtly warned at the top of the file.

After making a change to your resources, you may not see this file instantly update. Android Studio maintains a hidden R.java that your code builds against. The R.java file that you are looking at here is the one that is generated for your app just before it is installed on a device or emulator. You will see this file update when you run your app.

Listing 1.5 Current GeoQuiz resource IDs (R.java)

```
/* AUTO-GENERATED FILE.  DO NOT MODIFY.
 *
 * This class was automatically generated by the
 * aapt tool from the resource data it found.  It
 * should not be modified by hand.
 */

package com.bignerdranch.android.geoquiz;

public final class R {
    public static final class anim {
        ...
    }

    ...

    public static final class id {
        ...
    }
    public static final class layout {
        ...
        public static final int activity_quiz=0x7f030017;
    }
    public static final class mipmap {
        public static final int ic_launcher=0x7f030000;
    }
    public static final class string {
        ...
        public static final int app_name=0x7f0a0010;
        public static final int correct_toast=0x7f0a0011;
        public static final int false_button=0x7f0a0012;
        public static final int incorrect_toast=0x7f0a0013;
        public static final int question_text=0x7f0a0014;
        public static final int true_button=0x7f0a0015;
    }
}
```

The R.java file can be large and much of this file is omitted from Listing 1.5.

This is where the R.layout.activity_quiz comes from – it is an integer constant named activity_quiz within the **layout** inner class of **R**.

Your strings also have resource IDs. You have not yet referred to a string in code, but if you did, it would look like this:

```
setTitle(R.string.app_name);
```

Android generated a resource ID for the entire layout and for each string, but it did not generate IDs for the individual widgets in activity_quiz.xml. Not every widget needs a resource ID. In this chapter, you will only interact with the two buttons in code, so only they need resource IDs.

Before generating the resource IDs, switch back to the Android project view. Throughout this book, the Android project view will be used – but feel free to use the Project version if you prefer.

To generate a resource ID for a widget, you include an android:id attribute in the widget's definition. In activity_quiz.xml, add an android:id attribute to each button.

Listing 1.6 Adding IDs to **Button**s (`activity_quiz.xml`)

```xml
<LinearLayout xmlns:android="http://schemas.android.com/apk/res/android"
... >

  <TextView
    android:layout_width="wrap_content"
    android:layout_height="wrap_content"
    android:padding="24dp"
    android:text="@string/question_text" />

  <LinearLayout
    android:layout_width="wrap_content"
    android:layout_height="wrap_content"
    android:orientation="horizontal">

    <Button
      android:id="@+id/true_button"
      android:layout_width="wrap_content"
      android:layout_height="wrap_content"
      android:text="@string/true_button" />

    <Button
      android:id="@+id/false_button"
      android:layout_width="wrap_content"
      android:layout_height="wrap_content"
      android:text="@string/false_button" />

  </LinearLayout>

</LinearLayout>
```

Notice that there is a + sign in the values for `android:id` but not in the values for `android:text`. This is because you are *creating* the IDs and only *referencing* the strings.

Wiring Up Widgets

Now that the buttons have resource IDs, you can access them in **QuizActivity**. The first step is to add two member variables.

Type the following code into `QuizActivity.java`. (Do not use code completion; type it in yourself.) After you save the file, it will report two errors.

Listing 1.7 Adding member variables (`QuizActivity.java`)

```java
public class QuizActivity extends AppCompatActivity {

    private Button mTrueButton;
    private Button mFalseButton;

    @Override
    protected void onCreate(Bundle savedInstanceState) {
        super.onCreate(savedInstanceState);
        setContentView(R.layout.activity_quiz);
    }

...
}
```

You will fix the errors in just a second. First, notice the m prefix on the two member (instance) variable names. This prefix is an Android naming convention that we will follow throughout this book.

Now mouse over the red error indicators. They report the same problem: Cannot resolve symbol 'Button'.

These errors are telling you that you need to import the **android.widget.Button** class into QuizActivity.java. You could type the following import statement at the top of the file:

```
import android.widget.Button;
```

Or you can do it the easy way and let Android Studio do it for you. Just press Option+Return (or Alt +Enter) to let the IntelliJ magic under the hood amaze you. The new import statement now appears with the others at the top of the file. This shortcut is generally useful when something is not correct with your code. Try it often!

This should get rid of the errors. (If you still have errors, check for typos in your code and XML.)

Now you can wire up your button widgets. This is a two-step process:

- get references to the inflated **View** objects

- set listeners on those objects to respond to user actions

Getting references to widgets

In an activity, you can get a reference to an inflated widget by calling the following **Activity** method:

```
public View findViewById(int id)
```

This method accepts a resource ID of a widget and returns a **View** object.

In QuizActivity.java, use the resource IDs of your buttons to retrieve the inflated objects and assign them to your member variables. Note that you must cast the returned **View** to **Button** before assigning it.

Listing 1.8 Getting references to widgets (QuizActivity.java)

```
public class QuizActivity extends AppCompatActivity {

    private Button mTrueButton;
    private Button mFalseButton;

    @Override
    protected void onCreate(Bundle savedInstanceState) {
        super.onCreate(savedInstanceState);
        setContentView(R.layout.activity_quiz);

        mTrueButton = (Button) findViewById(R.id.true_button);
        mFalseButton = (Button) findViewById(R.id.false_button);
    }

    ...
}
```

Setting listeners

Android applications are typically *event driven*. Unlike command-line programs or scripts, event-driven applications start and then wait for an event, such as the user pressing a button. (Events can also be initiated by the OS or another application, but user-initiated events are the most obvious.)

When your application is waiting for a specific event, we say that it is "listening for" that event. The object that you create to respond to an event is called a *listener*, and the *listener* implements a *listener interface* for that event.

The Android SDK comes with listener interfaces for various events, so you do not have to write your own. In this case, the event you want to listen for is a button being pressed (or "clicked"), so your listener will implement the **View.OnClickListener** interface.

Start with the True button. In QuizActivity.java, add the following code to **onCreate(…)** just after the variable assignment.

Listing 1.9 Set listener for True button (`QuizActivity.java`)

```
...

@Override
protected void onCreate(Bundle savedInstanceState) {
    super.onCreate(savedInstanceState);
    setContentView(R.layout.activity_quiz);

    mTrueButton = (Button) findViewById(R.id.true_button);
    mTrueButton.setOnClickListener(new View.OnClickListener() {
        @Override
        public void onClick(View v) {
            // Does nothing yet, but soon!
        }
    });

    mFalseButton = (Button) findViewById(R.id.false_button);
}
}
```

(If you have a View cannot be resolved to a type error, try using Option+Return (Alt+Enter) to import the **View** class.)

In Listing 1.9, you set a listener to inform you when the **Button** known as mTrueButton has been pressed. The **setOnClickListener(OnClickListener)** method takes a listener as its argument. In particular, it takes an object that implements **OnClickListener**.

Using anonymous inner classes

This listener is implemented as an *anonymous inner class*. The syntax is a little tricky, but it helps to remember that everything within the outermost set of parentheses is passed into **setOnClickListener(OnClickListener)**. Within these parentheses, you create a new, nameless class and pass its entire implementation.

```
mTrueButton.setOnClickListener(new View.OnClickListener() {
    @Override
    public void onClick(View v) {
        // Does nothing yet, but soon!
    }
});
```

All of the listeners in this book will be implemented as anonymous inner classes. Doing so puts the implementations of the listeners' methods right where you want to see them. And there is no need for the overhead of a named class because the class will be used in one place only.

Because your anonymous class implements **OnClickListener**, it must implement that interface's sole method, **onClick(View)**. You have left the implementation of **onClick(View)** empty for now, and the compiler is OK with that. A listener interface requires you to implement **onClick(View)**, but it makes no rules about *how* to implement it.

(If your knowledge of anonymous inner classes, listeners, or interfaces is rusty, you may want to review some Java before continuing or at least keep a reference nearby.)

Set a similar listener for the False button.

Listing 1.10 Set listener for False button (`QuizActivity.java`)

```
    ...
        mTrueButton.setOnClickListener(new View.OnClickListener() {
            @Override
            public void onClick(View v) {
                // Does nothing yet, but soon!
            }
        });

        mFalseButton = (Button) findViewById(R.id.false_button);
        mFalseButton.setOnClickListener(new View.OnClickListener() {
            @Override
            public void onClick(View v) {
                // Does nothing yet, but soon!
            }
        });
    }
```

Making Toasts

Now to make the buttons fully armed and operational. You are going to have a press of each button trigger a pop-up message called a *toast*. A *toast* is a short message that informs the user of something but does not require any input or action. You are going to make toasts that announce whether the user answered correctly or incorrectly (Figure 1.14).

Figure 1.14 A toast providing feedback

First, return to `strings.xml` and add the string resources that your toasts will display.

Listing 1.11 Adding toast strings (`strings.xml`)

```
<resources>
  <string name="app_name">GeoQuiz</string>

  <string name="question_text">Constantinople is the largest city in Turkey.</string>
  <string name="true_button">True</string>
  <string name="false_button">False</string>
  <string name="correct_toast">Correct!</string>
  <string name="incorrect_toast">Incorrect!</string>
  <string name="action_settings">Settings</string>
</resources>
```

To create a toast, you call the following method from the **Toast** class:

```
public static Toast makeText(Context context, int resId, int duration)
```

The **Context** parameter is typically an instance of **Activity** (**Activity** is a subclass of **Context**). The second parameter is the resource ID of the string that the toast should display. The **Context** is needed by the **Toast** class to be able to find and use the string's resource ID. The third parameter is one of two **Toast** constants that specify how long the toast should be visible.

After you have created a toast, you call **Toast.show()** on it to get it on screen.

In **QuizActivity**, you are going to call **makeText(…)** in each button's listener (Listing 1.12). Instead of typing everything in, try using Android Studio's code completion feature to add these calls.

Using code completion

Code completion can save you a lot of time, so it is good to become familiar with it early.

Start typing the code addition shown in Listing 1.12. When you get to the period after the **Toast** class, a pop-up window will appear with a list of suggested methods and constants from the **Toast** class.

To choose one of the suggestions, use the up and down arrow keys to select it. (If you wanted to ignore code completion, you could just keep typing. It will not complete anything for you if you do not press the Tab key, press the Return/Enter key, or click on the pop-up window.)

From the list of suggestions, select **makeText(Context context, int resID, int duration)**. Code completion will add the complete method call for you.

Fill in the parameters for the **makeText** method until you have added the code shown in Listing 1.12.

Listing 1.12 Making toasts (`QuizActivity.java`)

```
...
mTrueButton.setOnClickListener(new View.OnClickListener() {
    @Override
    public void onClick(View v) {
        Toast.makeText(QuizActivity.this,
                       R.string.incorrect_toast,
                       Toast.LENGTH_SHORT).show();
        // Does nothing yet, but soon!
    }
});

mFalseButton.setOnClickListener(new View.OnClickListener() {
    @Override
    public void onClick(View v) {
        Toast.makeText(QuizActivity.this,
                       R.string.correct_toast,
                       Toast.LENGTH_SHORT).show();
        // Does nothing yet, but soon!
    }
});
```

In **makeText(…)**, you pass the instance of **QuizActivity** as the **Context** argument. However, you cannot simply pass the variable this as you might expect. At this point in the code, you are defining the anonymous class where this refers to the **View.OnClickListener**.

Because you used code completion, you do not have to do anything to import the **Toast** class. When you accept a code completion suggestion, the necessary classes are imported automatically.

Save your work, and let's see your new app in action.

Running on the Emulator

To run an Android application, you need a device – either a hardware device or a *virtual device*. Virtual devices are powered by the Android emulator, which ships with the developer tools.

To create an Android virtual device (AVD), choose Tools → Android → AVD Manager. When the AVD Manager appears, click the Create Virtual Device... button on the lefthand side of the window.

In the dialog that appears, you are offered many options for configuring a virtual device. For your first AVD, choose to emulate a Nexus 5, as shown in Figure 1.15. Click Next.

Figure 1.15 Choosing a virtual device

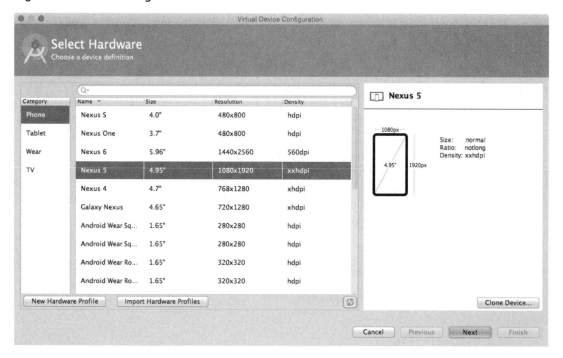

On the next screen, choose a system image that your emulator is based on. For this emulator, select an x86 Lollipop emulator and select Next (Figure 1.16).

Figure 1.16 Choosing a system image

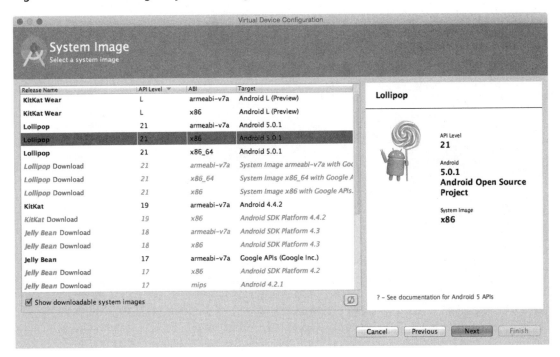

Finally, you can review and tweak properties of the emulator. You can also edit the properties of an existing emulator later on. For now, name your emulator something that will help you to identify it later on and click Finish (Figure 1.17).

Figure 1.17 Updating emulator properties

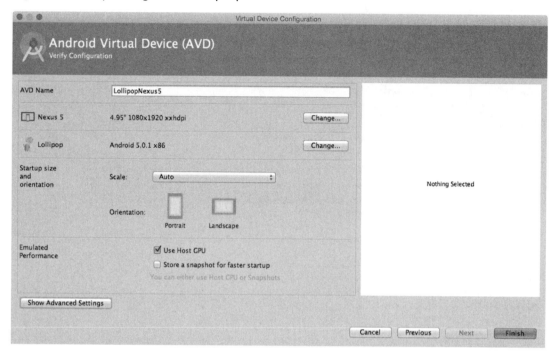

Once you have an AVD, you can run GeoQuiz on it. From the Android Studio toolbar, click the Run button (it looks like a green "play" symbol) or press Control+R. Android Studio will find the virtual device you created, start it, install the application package on it, and run the app.

Starting up the emulator can take a while, but eventually your GeoQuiz app will launch on the AVD that you created. Press buttons and admire your toasts. (Note that if the app launches and you are not around, you may have to unlock the AVD when you come back. The AVD works like a real device, and it will lock itself after a time.)

If GeoQuiz crashes when launching or when you press a button, useful information will appear in the LogCat view in the Android DDMS tool window. (If LogCat did not open automatically when you ran GeoQuiz, you can open it by clicking the Android button at the bottom of the Android Studio window.) Look for exceptions in the log; they will be an eye-catching red color, as shown in Figure 1.18.

Figure 1.18 An example **NullPointerException** at line 21

```
Text
at dalvik.system.NativeStart.main(Native Method)
Caused by: java.lang.NullPointerException
at com.bignerdranch.android.geoquiz.QuizActivity.onCreate(QuizActivity.java:21)
at android.app.Activity.performCreate(Activity.java:5008)
at android.app.Instrumentation.callActivityOnCreate(Instrumentation.java:1079)
```

Compare your code with the code in the book to try to find the cause of the problem. Then try running again. (You will learn more about LogCat and debugging in the next two chapters.)

Keep the emulator running; you do not want to wait for it to launch on every run. You can stop the app by pressing the Back button (the arrow that is making a U-turn). Then re-run the app from Android Studio to test changes.

The emulator is useful, but testing on a real device gives more accurate results. In Chapter 2, you will run GeoQuiz on a hardware device. You will also give GeoQuiz more geography questions with which to test the user.

For the More Curious: Android Build Process

By now, you probably have some burning questions about how the Android build process works. You have already seen that Android Studio builds your project automatically as you modify it rather than on command. During the build process, the Android tools take your resources, code, and the `AndroidManifest.xml` file (which contains meta-data about the application) and turn them into an `.apk` file. This file is then signed with a debug key, which allows it to run on the emulator. (To distribute your `.apk` to the masses, you have to sign it with a release key. There is more information about this process in the Android developer documentation at `http://developer.android.com/tools/publishing/preparing.html`.)

Figure 1.19 shows the complete build process.

Figure 1.19 Building GeoQuiz

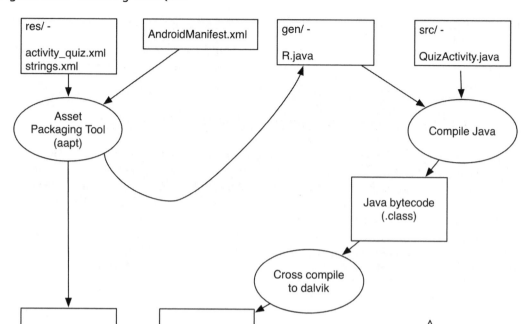

How do the contents of activity_quiz.xml turn into **View** objects in an application? As part of the build process, aapt (Android Asset Packaging Tool) compiles layout file resources into a more compact format. These compiled resources are packaged into the .apk file. Then, when **setContentView(…)** is called in the **QuizActivity**'s **onCreate(…)** method, the **QuizActivity** uses the **LayoutInflater** class to instantiate each of the **View** objects as defined in the layout file (Figure 1.20).

Figure 1.20 Inflating `activity_quiz.xml`

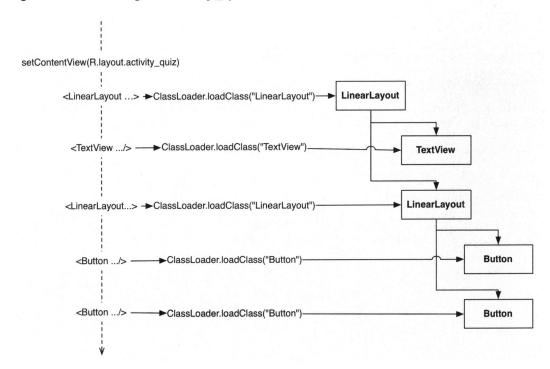

(You can also create your view classes programmatically in the activity instead of defining them in XML. But there are benefits to separating your presentation from the logic of the application. The main one is taking advantage of configuration changes built into the SDK, which you will learn more about in Chapter 3.)

For more details on how the different XML attributes work and how views display themselves on the screen, see Chapter 8.

Android build tools

All of the builds you have seen so far have been executed from within Android Studio. This build is integrated into the IDE – it invokes standard Android build tools like `aapt`, but the build process itself is managed by Android Studio.

You may, for your own reasons, want to perform builds from outside of Android Studio. The easiest way to do this is to use a command-line build tool. The modern Android build system uses a tool called Gradle.

(You will know if this section applies to you. If it does not, feel free to read along but do not be concerned if you are not sure of why you might want to do this or if the commands below do not seem to work. Coverage of the ins and outs of using the command line is beyond the scope of this book.)

To use Gradle from the command line, navigate to your project's directory and run the following command:

```
$ ./gradlew tasks
```

On Windows, your command will look a little different:

```
> gradlew.bat tasks
```

This will show you a list of available tasks you can execute. The one you want is called "installDebug". Make it so with a command like this:

```
$ ./gradlew installDebug
```

Or, on Windows:

```
> gradlew.bat installDebug
```

This will install your app on whatever device is connected. However, it will not run the app. For that, you will need to pull up the launcher and launch the app by hand.

2

Android and Model-View-Controller

In this chapter, you are going to upgrade GeoQuiz to present more than one question, as shown in Figure 2.1.

Figure 2.1 More questions!

To make this happen, you are going to add a class named **Question** to the GeoQuiz project. An instance of this class will encapsulate a single true-false question.

Then, you will create an array of **Question** objects for **QuizActivity** to manage.

Creating a New Class

In the Project tool window, right-click the com.bignerdranch.android.geoquiz package and select New → Java Class. Name the class **Question** and click OK (Figure 2.2).

Figure 2.2 Creating the **Question** class

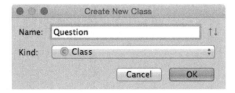

In Question.java, add two member variables and a constructor.

Listing 2.1 Adding to **Question** class (Question.java)

```java
public class Question {

    private int mTextResId;
    private boolean mAnswerTrue;

    public Question(int textResId, boolean answerTrue) {
        mTextResId = textResId;
        mAnswerTrue = answerTrue;
    }
}
```

The **Question** class holds two pieces of data: the question text and the question answer (true or false).

Why is mTextResId an int and not a String? The mTextResId variable will hold the resource ID (always an int) of a string resource for the question. You will create the question string resources in a later section.

These variables need getter and setter methods. Rather than typing them in yourself, you can have Android Studio generate the implementations for you.

Generating getters and setters

The first step is to configure Android Studio to recognize the m prefix for member variables.

Open Android Studio's preferences (from the Android Studio menu on Mac and from File → Settings on Windows). Expand Editor and then expand Code Style. Select Java, then choose the Code Generation tab.

In the Naming table, select the Field row (Figure 2.3) and add m as the Name prefix for fields. Then add s as the Name prefix for static fields. (You will not be using the s prefix in the GeoQuiz project, but it will be useful in later projects.)

Figure 2.3 Setting Java code style preferences

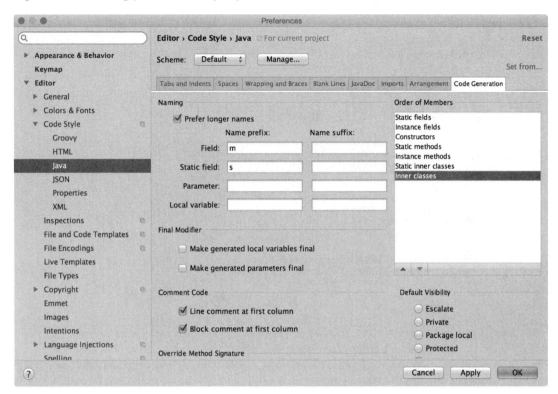

Click OK.

What is the point of setting these prefixes? Now, when you ask Android Studio to generate a getter for mTextResId, it will create **getTextResId()** rather than **getMTextResId()** and **isAnswerTrue()** rather than **isMAnswerTrue()**.

Back in Question.java, right-click after the constructor and select Generate... and then Getter and Setter. Select mTextResId and mAnswerTrue and click OK to create a getter and setter for each variable.

Listing 2.2 Generated getters and setters (`Question.java`)

```java
public class Question {

    private int mTextResId;
    private boolean mAnswerTrue;

    ...

    public int getTextResId() {
        return mTextResId;
    }

    public void setTextResId(int textResId) {
        mTextResId = textResId;
    }

    public boolean isAnswerTrue() {
        return mAnswerTrue;
    }

    public void setAnswerTrue(boolean answerTrue) {
        mAnswerTrue = answerTrue;
    }

}
```

Your **Question** class is now complete. In a moment, you will modify **QuizActivity** to work with **Question**. First, let's take a look at how the pieces of GeoQuiz will work together. You are going to have **QuizActivity** create an array of **Question** objects. It will then interact with the **TextView** and the three **Button**s to display questions and provide feedback. Figure 2.4 diagrams these relationships.

Figure 2.4 Object diagram for GeoQuiz

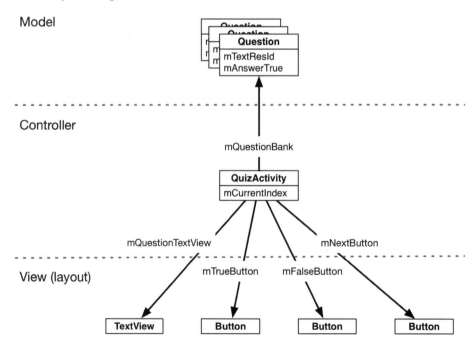

Model-View-Controller and Android

Notice that the objects in Figure 2.4 are separated into three sections labeled Model, Controller, and View. Android applications are designed around an architecture called Model-View-Controller, or MVC for short. In MVC, all objects in your application must be a *model object*, a *view object*, or a *controller object*.

- A *model object* holds the application's data and "business logic." Model classes are typically designed to *model* the things your app is concerned with, such as a user, a product in a store, a photo on a server, or a television show. Or a true-false question. Model objects have no knowledge of the user interface; their sole purpose is holding and managing data.

  In Android applications, model classes are generally custom classes you create. All of the model objects in your application compose its *model layer*.

  GeoQuiz's model layer consists of the **Question** class.

- *View objects* know how to draw themselves on the screen and how to respond to user input, like touches. A simple rule of thumb is that if you can see it on screen, then it is a view.

  Android provides a wealth of configurable view classes. You can also create custom view classes. An application's view objects make up its *view layer*.

  GeoQuiz's view layer consists of the widgets that are inflated from `activity_quiz.xml`.

- *Controller objects* tie the view and model objects together. They contain "application logic." Controllers are designed to respond to various events triggered by view objects and to manage the flow of data to and from model objects and the view layer.

  In Android, a controller is typically a subclass of **Activity**, **Fragment**, or **Service**. (You will learn about fragments in Chapter 7 and services in Chapter 26.)

  GeoQuiz's controller layer, at present, consists solely of **QuizActivity**.

Figure 2.5 shows the flow of control between objects in response to a user event, like a press of a button. Notice that model and view objects do not talk to each other directly; controllers sit squarely in the middle of everything, receiving messages from some objects and dispatching instructions to others.

Figure 2.5 MVC flow with user input

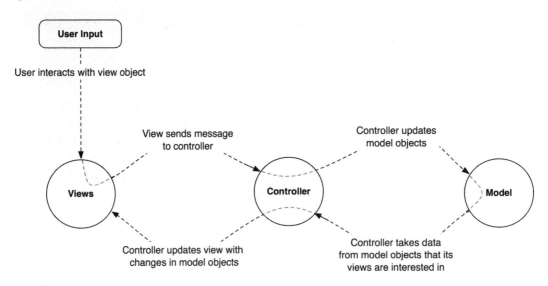

Benefits of MVC

An application can accumulate features until it is too complicated to understand. Separating code into classes helps you design and understand the application as a whole; you can think in terms of classes instead of individual variables and methods.

Similarly, separating classes into model, view, and controller layers helps you design and understand an application; you can think in terms of layers instead of individual classes.

Although GeoQuiz is not a complicated app, you can still see the benefits of keeping layers separate. In a moment, you are going to update GeoQuiz's view layer to include a Next button. When you do that, you will not need to remember a single thing about the **Question** class you just created.

MVC also makes classes easier to reuse. A class with restricted responsibilities is more reusable than one with its fingers in every pie.

For instance, your model class, **Question**, knows nothing about the widgets used to display a true-false question. This makes it easy to use **Question** throughout your app for different purposes. For example, if you wanted to display a list of all the questions at once, you could use the same object that you use here to display just one question at a time.

Updating the View Layer

Now that you have been introduced to MVC, you are going to update GeoQuiz's view layer to include a Next button.

In Android, objects in the view layer are typically inflated from XML within a layout file. The sole layout in GeoQuiz is defined in `activity_quiz.xml`. This layout needs to be updated as shown in Figure 2.6. (Note that to save space we are not showing the attributes of unchanged widgets.)

Figure 2.6 New button!

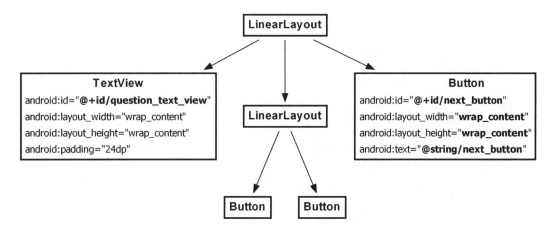

So the changes you need to make to the view layer are:

- Remove the `android:text` attribute from the **TextView**. You no longer want a hard-coded question to be part of its definition.

- Give the **TextView** an `android:id` attribute. This widget will need a resource ID so that you can set its text in **QuizActivity**'s code.

- Add the new **Button** widget as a child of the root **LinearLayout**.

Return to `activity_quiz.xml` and make it happen.

Listing 2.3 New button... and changes to the text view (`activity_quiz.xml`)

```
<LinearLayout
  ... >

  <TextView
    android:id="@+id/question_text_view"
    android:layout_width="wrap_content"
    android:layout_height="wrap_content"
    android:padding="24dp"
    android:text="@string/question_text"
    />

  <LinearLayout
    ... >

    ...

  </LinearLayout>

  <Button
    android:id="@+id/next_button"
    android:layout_width="wrap_content"
    android:layout_height="wrap_content"
    android:text="@string/next_button" />

</LinearLayout>
```

Save `activity_quiz.xml`, and you may see a familiar error pop up to alert you about a missing string resource.

Return to `res/values/strings.xml`. Remove the question string and add a string for the new button.

Listing 2.4 Updating strings (`strings.xml`)

```
...

  <string name="app_name">GeoQuiz</string>
  <string name="question_text">Constantinople is the largest city in Turkey.</string>
  <string name="true_button">True</string>
  <string name="false_button">False</string>
  <string name="next_button">Next</string>
  <string name="correct_toast">Correct!</string>

  ...
```

While you have `strings.xml` open, go ahead and add the strings for the set of geography questions that will be shown to the user.

Listing 2.5 Adding question strings in advance (strings.xml)

...

```
<string name="incorrect_toast">Incorrect!</string>
<string name="action_settings">Settings</string>
<string name="question_oceans">The Pacific Ocean is larger than
    the Atlantic Ocean.</string>
<string name="question_mideast">The Suez Canal connects the Red Sea
    and the Indian Ocean.</string>
<string name="question_africa">The source of the Nile River is in Egypt.</string>
<string name="question_americas">The Amazon River is the longest river
    in the Americas.</string>
<string name="question_asia">Lake Baikal is the world\'s oldest and deepest
    freshwater lake.</string>
...
```

Notice that you use the escape sequence \' in the last value to get an apostrophe in your string. You can use all the usual escape sequences in your string resources, such as \n for a new line.

Save your files. Then return to activity_quiz.xml and preview your layout changes in the graphical layout tool.

That is all for now for GeoQuiz's view layer. Time to wire everything up in your controller class, **QuizActivity**.

Updating the Controller Layer

In the previous chapter, there was not much happening in GeoQuiz's one controller, **QuizActivity**. It displayed the layout defined in activity_quiz.xml. It set listeners on two buttons and wired them to make toasts.

Now that you have multiple questions to retrieve and display, **QuizActivity** will have to work harder to tie GeoQuiz's model and view layers together.

Open QuizActivity.java. Add variables for the **TextView** and the new **Button**. Also, create an array of **Question** objects and an index for the array.

Listing 2.6 Adding variables and a **Question** array (QuizActivity.java)

```
public class QuizActivity extends AppCompatActivity {

    private Button mTrueButton;
    private Button mFalseButton;
    private Button mNextButton;
    private TextView mQuestionTextView;

    private Question[] mQuestionBank = new Question[] {
        new Question(R.string.question_oceans, true),
        new Question(R.string.question_mideast, false),
        new Question(R.string.question_africa, false),
        new Question(R.string.question_americas, true),
        new Question(R.string.question_asia, true),
    };

    private int mCurrentIndex = 0;
    ...
```

Here you call the **Question** constructor several times and create an array of **Question** objects.

(In a more complex project, this array would be created and stored elsewhere. In later apps, you will see better options for storing model data. For now, we are keeping it simple and just creating the array within your controller.)

You are going to use mQuestionBank, mCurrentIndex, and the accessor methods in **Question** to get a parade of questions on screen.

First, get a reference for the **TextView** and set its text to the question at the current index.

Listing 2.7 Wiring up the **TextView** (QuizActivity.java)

```
public class QuizActivity extends AppCompatActivity {

    ...

    @Override
    protected void onCreate(Bundle savedInstanceState) {
        super.onCreate(savedInstanceState);
        setContentView(R.layout.activity_quiz);

        mQuestionTextView = (TextView) findViewById(R.id.question_text_view);
        int question = mQuestionBank[mCurrentIndex].getTextResId();
        mQuestionTextView.setText(question);

        mTrueButton = (Button) findViewById(R.id.true_button);
        ...
    }
}
```

Save your files and check for any errors. Then run GeoQuiz. You should see the first question in the array appear in the **TextView**.

Now let's see about the Next button. First, get a reference to the button. Then set a **View.OnClickListener** on it. This listener will increment the index and update the **TextView**'s text.

Listing 2.8 Wiring up the new button (`QuizActivity.java`)

```java
public class QuizActivity extends AppCompatActivity {

    ...

    @Override
    protected void onCreate(Bundle savedInstanceState) {
        super.onCreate(savedInstanceState);
        setContentView(R.layout.activity_quiz);

        mQuestionTextView = (TextView) findViewById(R.id.question_text_view);
        int question = mQuestionBank[mCurrentIndex].getTextResId();
        mQuestionTextView.setText(question);

        ...

        mFalseButton.setOnClickListener(new View.OnClickListener() {
            @Override
            public void onClick(View v) {
                Toast.makeText(QuizActivity.this,
                        R.string.correct_toast,
                        Toast.LENGTH_SHORT).show();
            }
        });

        mNextButton = (Button) findViewById(R.id.next_button);
        mNextButton.setOnClickListener(new View.OnClickListener() {
            @Override
            public void onClick(View v) {
                mCurrentIndex = (mCurrentIndex + 1) % mQuestionBank.length;
                int question = mQuestionBank[mCurrentIndex].getTextResId();
                mQuestionTextView.setText(question);
            }
        });
        ...
    }
}
```

You now have code in two separate places that updates the mQuestionTextView variable. Take a moment to put this code into a private method instead, as shown in Listing 2.9. Then call that method in the mNextButton's listener and at the end of **onCreate(Bundle)** to initially set the text in the activity's view.

Listing 2.9 Encapsulating with **updateQuestion()** (QuizActivity.java)

```java
public class QuizActivity extends AppCompatActivity {

    ...

    private void updateQuestion() {
        int question = mQuestionBank[mCurrentIndex].getTextResId();
        mQuestionTextView.setText(question);
    }

    @Override
    protected void onCreate(Bundle savedInstanceState) {
        ...

        mQuestionTextView = (TextView) findViewById(R.id.question_text_view);
        int question = mQuestionBank[mCurrentIndex].getTextResId();
        mQuestionTextView.setText(question);

    ...

        mNextButton.setOnClickListener(new View.OnClickListener() {
            @Override
            public void onClick(View v) {
                mCurrentIndex = (mCurrentIndex + 1) % mQuestionBank.length;
                int question = mQuestionBank[mCurrentIndex].getTextResId();
                mQuestionTextView.setText(question);
                updateQuestion();
            }
        });

        updateQuestion();
    ...
    }
}
```

Run GeoQuiz and test your new Next button.

Now that you have the questions behaving appropriately, it is time to turn to the answers. At the moment, GeoQuiz thinks that the answer to every question is "False." Let's rectify that. Here again, you will implement a private method to encapsulate code rather than writing similar code in two places.

The method that you are going to add to **QuizActivity** is:

```java
private void checkAnswer(boolean userPressedTrue)
```

This method will accept a boolean variable that identifies whether the user pressed True or False. Then, it will check the user's answer against the answer in the current **Question** object. Finally, after determining whether the user answered correctly, it will make a **Toast** that displays the appropriate message to the user.

In QuizActivity.java, add the implementation of **checkAnswer(boolean)** shown in Listing 2.10.

Listing 2.10 Adding **checkAnswer(boolean)** (QuizActivity.java)

```java
public class QuizActivity extends AppCompatActivity {

    ...

    private void updateQuestion() {
        int question = mQuestionBank[mCurrentIndex].getTextResId();
        mQuestionTextView.setText(question);
    }

    private void checkAnswer(boolean userPressedTrue) {
        boolean answerIsTrue = mQuestionBank[mCurrentIndex].isAnswerTrue();

        int messageResId = 0;

        if (userPressedTrue == answerIsTrue) {
            messageResId = R.string.correct_toast;
        } else {
            messageResId = R.string.incorrect_toast;
        }

        Toast.makeText(this, messageResId, Toast.LENGTH_SHORT)
            .show();
    }

    @Override
    protected void onCreate(Bundle savedInstanceState) {
        ...

    }
}
```

Within the button's listeners, call **checkAnswer(boolean)**, as shown in Listing 2.11.

Listing 2.11 Calling **checkAnswer(boolean)** (QuizActivity.java)

```
public class QuizActivity extends AppCompatActivity {

    ...

    @Override
    protected void onCreate(Bundle savedInstanceState) {
        ...

        mTrueButton = (Button) findViewById(R.id.true_button);
        mTrueButton.setOnClickListener(new View.OnClickListener() {

            @Override
            public void onClick(View v) {
                Toast.makeText(QuizActivity.this,
                        R.string.incorrect_toast,
                        Toast.LENGTH_SHORT).show();
                checkAnswer(true);
            }
        });

        mFalseButton = (Button) findViewById(R.id.false_button);
        mFalseButton.setOnClickListener(new View.OnClickListener() {
            @Override
            public void onClick(View v) {
                Toast.makeText(QuizActivity.this,
                        R.string.correct_toast,
                        Toast.LENGTH_SHORT).show();
                checkAnswer(false);
            }
        });

        mNextButton = (Button) findViewById(R.id.next_button);
        ...

    }
}
```

GeoQuiz is ready to run again. Let's get it running on a real device.

Running on a Device

In this section, you will set up your system, device, and application to get GeoQuiz running on your hardware device.

Connecting your device

First, plug the device into your system. If you are developing on a Mac, your system should recognize the device right away. On Windows, you may need to install the adb (Android Debug Bridge) driver. If Windows cannot find the adb driver, then download one from the device manufacturer's website.

Configuring your device for development

To test apps on your device, you need to enable USB debugging on the device.

- On devices running Android 4.2 or later, Developer options is not visible by default. To enable it, go to Settings → About Tablet/Phone and press Build Number 7 times. Then you can return to Settings, see Developer options, and enable USB debugging.

- On devices running Android 4.0 or 4.1, go to Settings → Developer options instead.

- On devices running versions of Android earlier than 4.0, go to Settings → Applications → Development and find the option to enable USB debugging.

As you can see, the options vary considerably across devices. If you are having problems enabling your device, visit http://developer.android.com/tools/device.html for more help.

You can confirm that your device is recognized by opening the Devices view. The quickest way to the Devices view is to select the Android tool window near the bottom of Android Studio. Inside of this window, you will see a drop-down list of connected devices (Figure 2.7). You should see your AVD and your hardware device listed.

Figure 2.7 Viewing connected devices

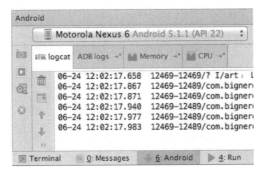

If you are having trouble getting your device recognized, verify that your device is turned on and the developer options are enabled.

If you are still unable to see your device in the Devices view, you can find more help on the Android developers' site. Start at http://developer.android.com/tools/device.html. Or visit this book's forum at forums.bignerdranch.com for more troubleshooting help.

Run GeoQuiz as before. Android Studio will offer a choice between running on the virtual device or the hardware device plugged into your system. Select the hardware device and continue. GeoQuiz will launch on your device.

If Android Studio defaults to your emulator without offering a choice of device to run the app on, recheck the steps above and make sure your device is plugged in. Next, ensure that your run configuration is correct. To modify the run configuration, select the app drop-down list near the top of the window, as shown in Figure 2.8.

Figure 2.8 Run configurations

Choose Edit Configurations and you will be presented with a new window with details about your run configuration (Figure 2.9). Select app in the left pane and verify that your Target Device is set to Show chooser dialog. Select OK and re-run the app. You will now be presented with a choice of device to launch the app on.

Figure 2.9 Run configuration properties

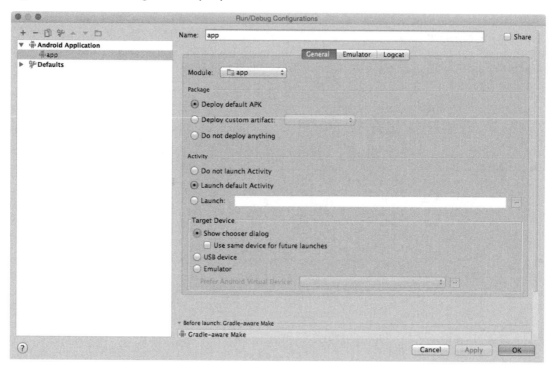

Adding an Icon

GeoQuiz is now up and running, but the user interface would be spiffier if the Next button also displayed a right-pointing arrow icon.

You can find such an arrow in the solutions file for this book. The solutions file is a collection of Android Studio projects for each chapter of this book. The solutions are hosted here:

```
https://www.bignerdranch.com/solutions/AndroidProgramming2e.zip
```

Download this file and open the `02_MVC/GeoQuiz/app/src/main/res` directory. Within this directory, locate the `drawable-hdpi`, `res/drawable-mdpi`, `drawable-xhdpi`, and `drawable-xxhdpi` directories.

The suffixes on these directory names refer to the screen pixel density of a device:

`mdpi`	medium-density screens (~160dpi)
`hdpi`	high-density screens (~240dpi)
`xhdpi`	extra-high-density screens (~320dpi)
`xxhdpi`	extra-extra-high-density screens (~480dpi)

(There are a few other density categories that are omitted from the solutions, including ldpi and xxxhdpi.)

Within each directory, you will find two image files – `arrow_right.png` and `arrow_left.png`. These files have been customized for the screen pixel density specified in the directory's name.

You are going to include all the image files from the solutions in GeoQuiz. When it runs, the OS will choose the best image file for the specific device running the app. Note that by duplicating the images multiple times, you increase the size of your application. In this case, this is not a problem because GeoQuiz is a simple app.

If an app runs on a device that has a screen density not included in any of the application's screen density qualifiers, Android will automatically scale the available image to the appropriate size for the device. Thanks to this feature, it is not necessary to provide images for all of the pixel density buckets. To reduce the size of your application, you can focus on one or a few of the higher resolution buckets and selectively optimize for lower resolutions when Android's automatic scaling provides an image with artifacts on those lower resolution devices.

(For alternatives to duplicating images at different densities and an explanation of your `mipmap` directory, see Chapter 21.)

Adding resources to a project

The next step is to add the image files to GeoQuiz's resources.

First, confirm that you have the necessary drawable folders. Make sure the project tools window is displaying the **Project** view (select **Project** from the dropdown at the top of the project tools window, as shown in Figure 1.13 in Chapter 1). Expand the contents of `GeoQuiz/app/src/main/res`. You should see folders named `drawable-hdpi`, `drawable-mdpi`, `drawable-xhdpi`, and `drawable-xxhdpi`, as shown in Figure 2.10. (You will likely see other folders as well. Ignore those for now.)

Figure 2.10 Verifying existence of drawable directories

If you are missing any of the drawable folders listed above, you will need to add them before you can add the image resources. Right-click on your res directory and select New → Directory. Give your directory the name of whichever directory is missing, such as drawable-mdpi and click OK (Figure 2.11).

Figure 2.11 Creating a drawable directory

After creating the drawable-mdpi directory, you should see it appear in the Project view in the project tools window. (If you do not see the new directory, you are probably still using the Android view. Switch to the Project view, as suggested earlier.)

Repeat the process to create the drawable-hdpi, drawable-xhdpi, and drawable-xxhdpi directories.

Once you have all of the drawable directories, for each of the drawable directories in the solutions file, copy the arrow_left.png and arrow_right.png files and paste them into your project's corresponding drawable directory.

After copying all of the images, you will see the new arrow_left.png and arrow_right.png files in the project tool window (as shown in Figure 2.12).

Figure 2.12 Arrow icons in GeoQuiz `drawable` directories

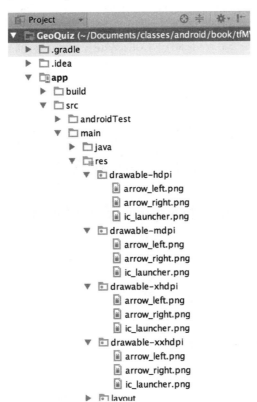

If you switch the project tools window back to the Android view, you will see the newly added drawable files summarized (as shown in Figure 2.13).

Figure 2.13 Summary of arrow icons in GeoQuiz `drawable` directories

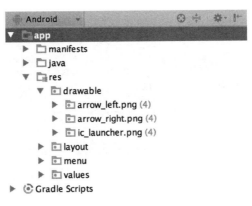

Including images in your app is as simple as that. Any `.png`, `.jpg`, or `.gif` file you add to a `res/` `drawable` folder will be automatically assigned a resource ID. (Note that filenames must be lowercase and not have any spaces.)

These resource IDs are not qualified by screen density. So you do not need to determine the device's screen density at runtime. All you have to do is use this resource ID in your code. When the app is run, the OS will determine the appropriate image to display on that particular device.

You will learn more about how the Android resource system works starting in Chapter 3. For now, let's put that right arrow to work.

Referencing resources in XML

You use resource IDs to reference resources in code. But you want to configure the Next button to display the arrow in the layout definition. How do you reference a resource from XML?

With a slightly different syntax. Open `activity_quiz.xml` and add two attributes to the **Button** widget definition.

Listing 2.12 Adding an icon to the Next button (`activity_quiz.xml`)

```
<LinearLayout
  ... >

  ...

  <LinearLayout
    ... >

    ...

  </LinearLayout>

  <Button
    android:id="@+id/next_button"
    android:layout_width="wrap_content"
    android:layout_height="wrap_content"
    android:text="@string/next_button"
    android:drawableRight="@drawable/arrow_right"
    android:drawablePadding="4dp"
    />

</LinearLayout>
```

In an XML resource, you refer to another resource by its resource type and name. A reference to a string resource begins with @string/. A reference to a drawable resource begins with @drawable/.

You will learn more about naming resources and working in the res directory structure starting in Chapter 3.

Save and run GeoQuiz. Admire your button's new appearance. Then test it to make sure it still works as before.

GeoQuiz does, however, have a bug. While GeoQuiz is running, press the Next button to show another question. Then rotate the device. (If you are running on the emulator, press Fn+Control+F12/Ctrl+F12 to rotate.)

After you rotate, you will be looking at the first question again. How did this happen, and how can you fix it?

The answers to those questions have to do with the activity lifecycle, which is the topic of Chapter 3.

Challenges

Challenges are exercises at the end of the chapter for you to do on your own. Some are easy and provide practice doing the same thing you have done in the chapter. Other challenges are harder and require more problem solving.

We cannot encourage you enough to take on these challenges. Tackling them cements what you have learned, builds confidence in your skills, and bridges the gap between us teaching you Android programming and you being able to do Android programming on your own.

If you get stuck while working on a challenge, take a break and come back and try again fresh. If that does not help, check out the forum for this book at forums.bignerdranch.com. In the forum, you can review questions and solutions that other readers have posted as well as ask questions and post solutions of your own.

To protect the integrity of your current project, we recommend you make a copy and work on challenges in the new copy.

In your computer's file explorer, navigate to the root directory of your project. Copy the GeoQuiz folder and Paste a new copy next to the original (on OS X, use the Duplicate feature). Rename the new folder GeoQuiz Challenge. Back in Android Studio, select File → Import Project.... Inside the import window, navigate to GeoQuiz Challenge and select OK. The copied project will then appear in a new window ready for work.

Challenge: Add a Listener to the TextView

Your Next button is nice, but you could also make it so that a user could press the TextView itself to see the next question.

Hint: You can use the View.OnClickListener listener for the TextView that you have used with the Buttons, because TextView also inherits from View.

Challenge: Add a Previous Button

Add a button that the user can press to go back one question. The UI should look something like Figure 2.14.

Figure 2.14 Now with a previous button!

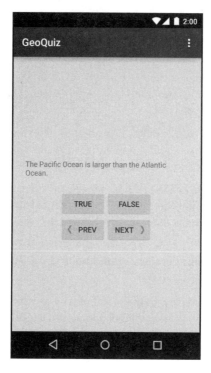

This is a great challenge. It requires you to retrace many of the steps in these two chapters.

Challenge: From Button to ImageButton

Perhaps the user interface would look even better if the next and previous buttons showed *only* icons, as in Figure 2.15.

Figure 2.15 Icon-only buttons

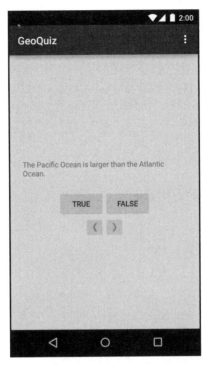

To accomplish this challenge, these two widgets must become **ImageButton**s instead of regular **Button**s.

ImageButton is a widget that inherits from **ImageView**. **Button**, on the other hand, inherits from **TextView**. Figure 2.16 shows their different inheritance hierarchies.

Figure 2.16 Inheritance diagram for **ImageButton** and **Button**

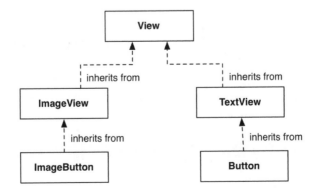

You can replace the text and drawable attributes on the Next button with a single **ImageView** attribute:

```
<Button ImageButton
    android:id="@+id/next_button"
    android:layout_width="wrap_content"
    android:layout_height="wrap_content"
    android:text="@string/next_button"
    android:drawableRight="@drawable/arrow_right"
    android:drawablePadding="4dp"
    android:src="@drawable/arrow_right"
    />
```

Of course, you will need to modify **QuizActivity** to work with **ImageButton**.

After you have changed these buttons to **ImageButton**s, Android Studio will warn you about a missing android:contentDescription attribute. This attribute supports accessibility for low-vision readers. You set the value to a string, and then that string is read aloud when users have the appropriate settings applied.

Finally, add an android:contentDescription attribute to each **ImageButton**.

3

The Activity Lifecycle

Every instance of **Activity** has a lifecycle. During this lifecycle, an activity transitions between three states: running, paused, and stopped. For each transition, there is an **Activity** method that notifies the activity of the change in its state. Figure 3.1 shows the activity lifecycle, states, and methods.

Figure 3.1 Activity state diagram

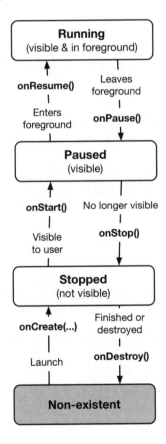

Subclasses of **Activity** can take advantage of the methods named in Figure 3.1 to get work done at critical transitions in the activity's lifecycle.

You are already acquainted with one of these methods – **onCreate(Bundle)**. The OS calls this method after the activity instance is created but before it is put on screen.

Typically, an activity overrides **onCreate(…)** to prepare the specifics of its user interface:

- inflating widgets and putting them on screen (in the call to (**setContentView(int)**))

- getting references to inflated widgets

- setting listeners on widgets to handle user interaction

- connecting to external model data

It is important to understand that you never call **onCreate(…)** or any of the other **Activity** lifecycle methods yourself. You override them in your activity subclasses, and Android calls them at the appropriate time.

Logging the Activity Lifecycle

In this section, you are going to override lifecycle methods to eavesdrop on **QuizActivity**'s lifecycle. Each implementation will simply log a message informing you that the method has been called.

Making log messages

In Android, the **android.util.Log** class sends log messages to a shared system-level log. **Log** has several methods for logging messages. Here is the one that you will use most often in this book:

```
public static int d(String tag, String msg)
```

The **d** stands for "debug" and refers to the level of the log message. (There is more about the **Log** levels in the final section of this chapter.) The first parameter identifies the source of the message, and the second is the contents of the message.

The first string is typically a TAG constant with the class name as its value. This makes it easy to determine the source of a particular message.

In QuizActivity.java, add a TAG constant to **QuizActivity**:

Listing 3.1 Adding TAG constant (QuizActivity.java)

```
public class QuizActivity extends AppCompatActivity {

    private static final String TAG = "QuizActivity";

    ...

}
```

Next, in **onCreate(…)**, call **Log.d(…)** to log a message.

Listing 3.2 Adding log statement to **onCreate(…)** (QuizActivity.java)

```java
public class QuizActivity extends AppCompatActivity {

    ...

    @Override
    protected void onCreate(Bundle savedInstanceState) {
        super.onCreate(savedInstanceState);
        Log.d(TAG, "onCreate(Bundle) called");
        setContentView(R.layout.activity_quiz);

        ...
    }
}
```

Now override five more methods in **QuizActivity** by adding the following after **onCreate(Bundle)** and before **onCreateOptionsMenu(Menu)**:

Listing 3.3 Overriding more lifecycle methods (QuizActivity.java)

```java
    @Override
    public void onStart() {
        super.onStart();
        Log.d(TAG, "onStart() called");
    }

    @Override
    public void onPause() {
        super.onPause();
        Log.d(TAG, "onPause() called");
    }

    @Override
    public void onResume() {
        super.onResume();
        Log.d(TAG, "onResume() called");
    }

    @Override
    public void onStop() {
        super.onStop();
        Log.d(TAG, "onStop() called");
    }

    @Override
    public void onDestroy() {
        super.onDestroy();
        Log.d(TAG, "onDestroy() called");
    }

    ...
}
```

Notice that you call the superclass implementations before you log your messages. These superclass calls are required. Calling the superclass implementation before you do anything else is critical in **onCreate(…)**; the order is less important in the other methods.

You may have been wondering about the @Override annotation. This asks the compiler to ensure that the class actually has the method that you are attempting to override. For example, the compiler would be able to alert you to the following misspelled method name:

```
public class QuizActivity extends AppCompatActivity {

    @Override
    public void onCreat(Bundle savedInstanceState) {
        super.onCreate(savedInstanceState);
        setContentView(R.layout.activity_quiz);
    }

    ...
```

The **Activity** class does not have an **onCreat(Bundle)** method, so the compiler will complain. Then you can fix the typo rather than accidentally implementing **QuizActivity.onCreat(Bundle)**.

Using LogCat

To access the log while the application is running, you can use LogCat, a log viewer included in the Android SDK tools.

When you run GeoQuiz, you should see LogCat appear at the bottom of Android Studio, as shown in Figure 3.2. If LogCat is not visible, select the Android tool window near the bottom of the screen and ensure that the Devices | logcat tab is selected.

Figure 3.2 Android Studio with LogCat

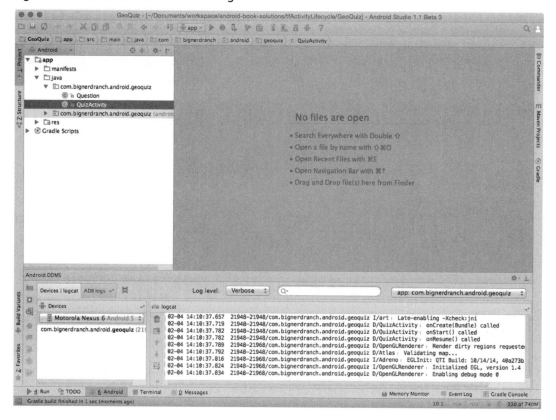

Run GeoQuiz and messages will start materializing in LogCat. By default, log statements that are generated with your app's package name are shown. You will see your own messages along with some system output.

To make your messages easier to find, you can filter the output using the TAG constant. In LogCat, click the filter drop-down box in the top right of the LogCat pane. Notice the existing filter, which is set up to show messages from only your app. Selecting No Filters will show log messages generated from all over the system.

In the filter dropdown, select Edit Filter Configuration. Use the + button to create a brand-new filter. Name the filter **QuizActivity** and enter **QuizActivity** in the by Log Tag: field (Figure 3.3).

Figure 3.3 Creating a filter in LogCat

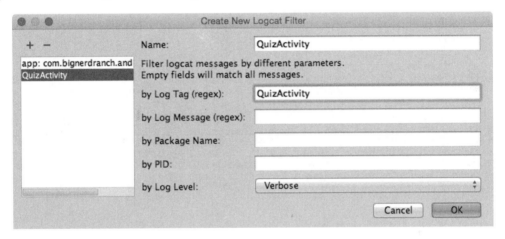

Click OK, and only messages tagged **QuizActivity** will be visible (Figure 3.4).

Three lifecycle methods were called after GeoQuiz was launched and the initial instance of **QuizActivity** was created.

Figure 3.4 Launching GeoQuiz creates, starts, and resumes an activity

```
logcat
08-04 17:51:02.316  16366-16366/com.bignerdranch.android.geoquiz D/QuizActivity: onCreate() called
08-04 17:51:02.347  16366-16366/com.bignerdranch.android.geoquiz D/QuizActivity: onStart() called
08-04 17:51:02.347  16366-16366/com.bignerdranch.android.geoquiz D/QuizActivity: onResume() called
```

(If you are not seeing the filtered list, select the QuizActivity filter from LogCat's filter dropdown.)

Now let's have some fun. Press the Back button on the device and then check LogCat. Your activity received calls to **onPause()**, **onStop()**, and **onDestroy()** (Figure 3.5).

Figure 3.5 Pressing the Back button destroys the activity

```
logcat
08-04 17:51:02.316  16366-16366/com.bignerdranch.android.geoquiz D/QuizActivity: onCreate() called
08-04 17:51:02.347  16366-16366/com.bignerdranch.android.geoquiz D/QuizActivity: onStart() called
08-04 17:51:02.347  16366-16366/com.bignerdranch.android.geoquiz D/QuizActivity: onResume() called
08-04 17:54:35.463  16366-16366/com.bignerdranch.android.geoquiz D/QuizActivity: onPause() called
08-04 17:54:35.811  16366-16366/com.bignerdranch.android.geoquiz D/QuizActivity: onStop() called
08-04 17:54:35.811  16366-16366/com.bignerdranch.android.geoquiz D/QuizActivity: onDestroy() called
```

When you pressed the Back button, you told Android, "I'm done with this activity, and I won't need it anymore." Android then destroyed your activity. This is Android's way of being frugal with your device's limited resources.

Relaunch GeoQuiz. Press the Home button and then check LogCat. Your activity received calls to **onPause()** and **onStop()**, but not **onDestroy()** (Figure 3.6).

Figure 3.6 Pressing the Home button stops the activity

```
logcat
08-04 17:56:05.477  18475-18475/com.bignerdranch.android.geoquiz D/QuizActivity: onCreate() called
08-04 17:56:05.533  18475-18475/com.bignerdranch.android.geoquiz D/QuizActivity: onStart() called
08-04 17:56:05.533  18475-18475/com.bignerdranch.android.geoquiz D/QuizActivity: onResume() called
08-04 17:56:10.851  18475-18475/com.bignerdranch.android.geoquiz D/QuizActivity: onPause() called
08-04 17:56:11.191  18475-18475/com.bignerdranch.android.geoquiz D/QuizActivity: onStop() called
```

On the device, pull up the task manager: On newer devices, press the Recents button next to the Home button (Figure 3.7). On devices without a Recents button, long-press the Home button.

Figure 3.7 Home, Back, and Recents buttons

In the task manager, press GeoQuiz and then check LogCat. The activity was started and resumed, but it did not need to be created.

Pressing the Home button tells Android, "I'm going to go look at something else, but I might come back." Android pauses and stops your activity but tries not to destroy it in case you come back.

However, a stopped activity's survival is not guaranteed. When the system needs to reclaim memory, it will destroy stopped activities.

Another situation that pauses an activity is when it is obscured from the user, such as by a pop-up window. Even if the window only partially covers the activity, the activity is paused and cannot be interacted with. The activity resumes when the pop-up window is dismissed.

As you continue through the book, you will override the different activity lifecycle methods to do real things for your application. When you do, you will learn more about the uses of each method.

Rotation and the Activity Lifecycle

Let's get back to the bug you found at the end of Chapter 2. Run GeoQuiz, press the Next button to reveal the second question, and then rotate the device. (On the emulator, press Fn+Control+F12/Ctrl +F12 to rotate.)

After rotating, GeoQuiz will display the first question again. Check LogCat to see what has happened. Your output should look like Figure 3.8.

Figure 3.8 **QuizActivity** is dead. Long live **QuizActivity**!

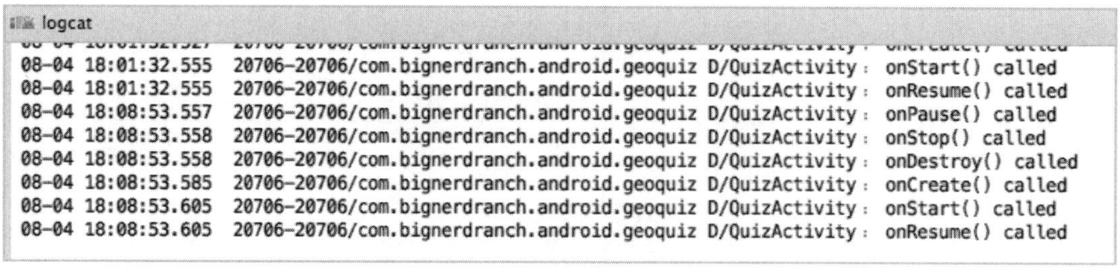

When you rotated the device, the instance of **QuizActivity** that you were looking at was destroyed, and a new one was created. Rotate the device again to witness another round of destruction and rebirth.

This is the source of your bug. Each time a new **QuizActivity** is created, mCurrentIndex is initialized to 0, and the user starts over at the first question. You will fix this bug in a moment. First, let's take a closer look at why this happens.

Device configurations and alternative resources

Rotating the device changes the *device configuration*. The *device configuration* is a set of characteristics that describe the current state of an individual device. The characteristics that make up the configuration include screen orientation, screen density, screen size, keyboard type, dock mode, language, and more.

Typically, applications provide alternative resources to match different device configurations. You saw an example of this when you added multiple arrow icons to your project for different screen densities.

Screen density is a fixed component of the device configuration; it cannot change at runtime. On the other hand, some components, like screen orientation, *can* change at runtime.

When a *runtime configuration change* occurs, there may be resources that are a better match for the new configuration. To see this in action, let's create an alternative resource for Android to find and use when the device's screen orientation changes to landscape.

Creating a landscape layout

In the Project tool window, right-click the res directory and select New → Android resource directory. You should see a window similar to Figure 3.9 that lists the resource types and qualifiers for those types. Select layout in the Resource type drop-down box. Leave the Source set option set to main. Next, you will choose how the layout resources will be qualified. Select Orientation in the Available qualifiers list and click the >> button to move Orientation to the Chosen qualifiers section.

Figure 3.9 Creating a new resource directory

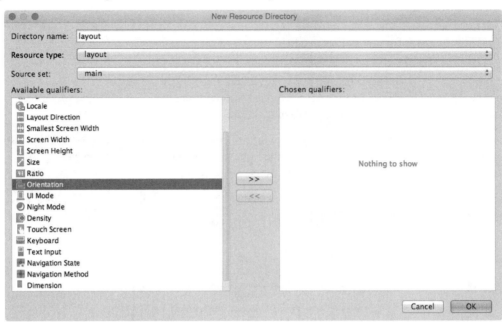

Finally, ensure that Landscape is selected in the Screen Orientation dropdown, as shown in Figure 3.10. Verify that the Directory name now indicates that your directory is called layout-land. While this window looks fancy, its purpose is just to set the name of your directory. Click OK and Android Studio will create the res/layout-land/ folder.

Figure 3.10 Creating res/layout-land

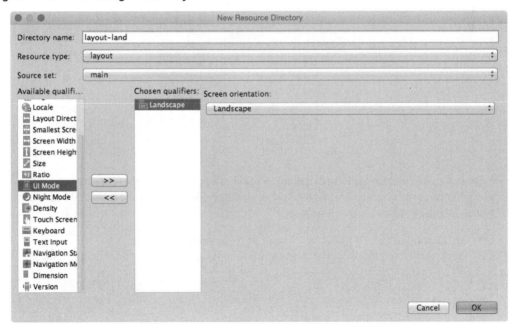

The -land suffix is another example of a configuration qualifier. Configuration qualifiers on res subdirectories are how Android identifies which resources best match the current device configuration. You can find the list of configuration qualifiers that Android recognizes and the pieces of the device configuration that they refer to at http://developer.android.com/guide/topics/resources/providing-resources.html.

When the device is in landscape orientation, Android will find and use resources in the res/layout-land directory. Otherwise, it will stick with the default in res/layout/. However, at the moment there are no resources in the res/layout-land directory. Let's fix that.

Copy the activity_quiz.xml file from res/layout/ to res/layout-land/. You now have a landscape layout and a default layout. Keep the filename the same. The two layout files must have the same filename so that they can be referenced with the same resource ID.

Now make some changes to the landscape layout so that it is different from the default. Figure 3.11 shows the changes that you are going to make.

Figure 3.11 An alternative landscape layout

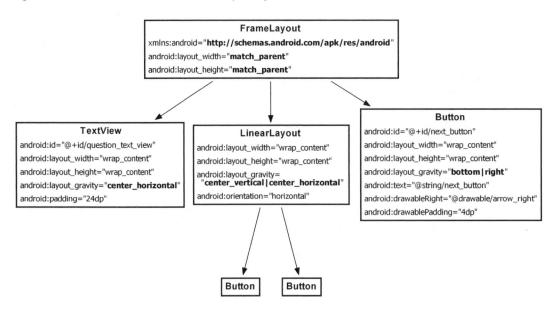

The **FrameLayout** will replace the **LinearLayout**. **FrameLayout** is the simplest **ViewGroup** and does not arrange its children in any particular manner. In this layout, child views will be arranged according to their android:layout_gravity attributes.

The **TextView**, **LinearLayout**, and **Button** children of the **FrameLayout** need android:layout_gravity attributes. The **Button** children of the **LinearLayout** will stay exactly the same.

Open layout-land/activity_quiz.xml and make the necessary changes using Figure 3.11. You can use Listing 3.4 to check your work.

Listing 3.4 Tweaking the landscape layout (`layout-land/activity_quiz.xml`)

```xml
<LinearLayout xmlns:android="http://schemas.android.com/apk/res/android"
  android:layout_width="match_parent"
  android:layout_height="match_parent"
  android:gravity="center"
  android:orientation="vertical" >

<FrameLayout xmlns:android="http://schemas.android.com/apk/res/android"
  android:layout_width="match_parent"
  android:layout_height="match_parent" >

  <TextView
    android:id="@+id/question_text_view"
    android:layout_width="wrap_content"
    android:layout_height="wrap_content"
    android:layout_gravity="center_horizontal"
    android:padding="24dp" />

  <LinearLayout
    android:layout_width="wrap_content"
    android:layout_height="wrap_content"
    android:layout_gravity="center_vertical|center_horizontal"
    android:orientation="horizontal" >

    ...

  </LinearLayout>

  <Button
    android:id="@+id/next_button"
    android:layout_width="wrap_content"
    android:layout_height="wrap_content"
    android:layout_gravity="bottom|right"
    android:text="@string/next_button"
    android:drawableRight="@drawable/arrow_right"
    android:drawablePadding="4dp"
    />

</LinearLayout>
</FrameLayout>
```

Run GeoQuiz again. Rotate the device to landscape to see the new layout (Figure 3.12). Of course, this is not just a new layout – it is a new **QuizActivity** as well.

Figure 3.12 QuizActivity in landscape orientation

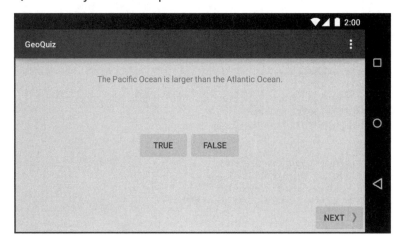

Rotate back to portrait to see the default layout and yet another new **QuizActivity**.

Android does the work of determining the best resource for you, but it has to create a new activity from scratch to do it. For a **QuizActivity** to display a different layout, **setContentView(R.layout.activity_quiz)** must be called again. And this will not happen unless **QuizActivity.onCreate(…)** is called again. Thus, Android destroys the current **QuizActivity** on rotation and starts fresh to ensure that it has the resources that best match the new configuration.

Note that Android destroys the current activity and creates a new one whenever any runtime configuration change occurs. A change in keyboard availability or language could also occur at runtime, but a change in screen orientation is the runtime change that occurs most frequently.

Saving Data Across Rotation

Android does a great job of providing alternative resources at the right time. However, destroying and re-creating activities on rotation can cause headaches, too, like GeoQuiz's bug of reverting back to the first question when the device is rotated.

To fix this bug, the post-rotation **QuizActivity** needs to know the old value of mCurrentIndex. You need a way to save this data across a runtime configuration change, like rotation. One way to do this is to override the **Activity** method:

```
protected void onSaveInstanceState(Bundle outState)
```

This method is normally called by the system before **onPause()**, **onStop()**, and **onDestroy()**.

The default implementation of **onSaveInstanceState(…)** directs all of the activity's views to save their state as data in the **Bundle** object. A **Bundle** is a structure that maps string keys to values of certain limited types.

You have seen this **Bundle** before. It is passed into **onCreate(Bundle)**:

```
@Override
public void onCreate(Bundle savedInstanceState) {
    super.onCreate(savedInstanceState);
    ...
}
```

When you override **onCreate(…)**, you call **onCreate(…)** on the activity's superclass and pass in the bundle you just received. In the superclass implementation, the saved state of the views is retrieved and used to re-create the activity's view hierarchy.

Overriding onSaveInstanceState(Bundle)

You can override **onSaveInstanceState(…)** to save additional data to the bundle and then read that data back in **onCreate(…)**. This is how you are going to save the value of mCurrentIndex across rotation.

First, in QuizActivity.java, add a constant that will be the key for the key-value pair that will be stored in the bundle.

Listing 3.5 Adding a key for the value (QuizActivity.java)

```
public class QuizActivity extends AppCompatActivity {

    private static final String TAG = "QuizActivity";
    private static final String KEY_INDEX = "index";

    private Button mTrueButton;
    ...
```

Next, override **onSaveInstanceState(…)** to write the value of mCurrentIndex to the bundle with the constant as its key.

Listing 3.6 Overriding **onSaveInstanceState(…)** (QuizActivity.java)

```
        mNextButton.setOnClickListener(new View.OnClickListener() {
            @Override
            public void onClick(View v) {
                mCurrentIndex = (mCurrentIndex + 1) % mQuestionBank.length;
                updateQuestion();
            }
        });

        updateQuestion();
    }

    @Override
    public void onSaveInstanceState(Bundle savedInstanceState) {
        super.onSaveInstanceState(savedInstanceState);
        Log.i(TAG, "onSaveInstanceState");
        savedInstanceState.putInt(KEY_INDEX, mCurrentIndex);
    }
```

Finally, in **onCreate(…)**, check for this value. If it exists, assign it to mCurrentIndex.

Listing 3.7 Checking bundle in **onCreate(…)** (QuizActivity.java)

```
...

if (savedInstanceState != null) {
    mCurrentIndex = savedInstanceState.getInt(KEY_INDEX, 0);
}

updateQuestion();
}
```

Run GeoQuiz and press Next. No matter how many device rotations you perform, the newly minted **QuizActivity** will "remember" what question you were on.

Note that the types that you can save to and restore from a **Bundle** are primitive types and classes that implement the **Serializable** or **Parcelable** interfaces. It is usually a bad practice to put objects of custom types into a **Bundle**, however, because the data might be stale when you get it back out. It is a better choice to use some other kind of storage for the data and put a primitive identifier into the **Bundle** instead.

Testing the implementation of **onSaveInstanceState(…)** is a good idea – especially if you are saving and restoring objects. Rotation is easy to test; testing low-memory situations is harder. There is information at the end of this chapter about how to simulate your activity being destroyed by Android to reclaim memory.

The Activity Lifecycle, Revisited

Overriding **onSaveInstanceState(Bundle)** is not just for handling rotation. An activity can also be destroyed if the user navigates away for a while and Android needs to reclaim memory.

Android will never destroy a running activity to reclaim memory – the activity must be in the paused or stopped state to be destroyed. If an activity is paused or stopped, then its **onSaveInstanceState(…)** method has been called.

When **onSaveInstanceState(…)** is called, the data is saved to the **Bundle** object. That **Bundle** object is then stuffed into your activity's *activity record* by the OS.

To understand the activity record, let's add a *stashed* state to the activity lifecycle (Figure 3.13).

Figure 3.13 The complete activity lifecycle

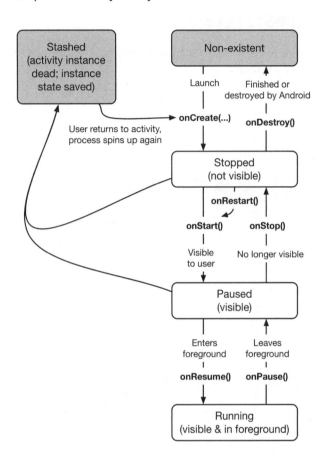

When your activity is stashed, an **Activity** object does not exist, but the activity record object lives on in the OS. The OS can reanimate the activity using the activity record when it needs to.

Note that your activity can pass into the stashed state without **onDestroy()** being called. However, you can always rely on **onPause()** and **onSaveInstanceState(…)** to be called. Typically, you override **onSaveInstanceState(…)** to stash small, transient states that belong to the current activity in your **Bundle** and **onPause()** for anything else that needs to be done.

Under some situations, Android will not only kill your activity but also completely shut down your application's process. This will only happen if the user is not currently looking at your application, but it can (and does) happen. Even in this case, the activity record will live on and enable a quick restart of your activity if the user returns.

So when does the activity record get snuffed? When the user presses the Back button, your activity really gets destroyed, once and for all. At that point, your activity record is discarded. Activity records are also typically discarded on reboot and may also be discarded if they are not used for a long time.

For the More Curious: Testing onSaveInstanceState(Bundle)

If you are overriding **onSaveInstanceState(Bundle)**, you should test that your state is being saved and restored as expected. This is easy to do on the emulator.

Start up a virtual device. Within the list of applications on the device, find the Settings app (Figure 3.14). This app is included with most system images used on the emulator.

Figure 3.14 Finding the Settings app

Launch Settings and select Developer options. Here you will see many possible settings. Turn on the setting labeled Don't keep activities, as shown in Figure 3.15.

Figure 3.15 Don't keep activities selected

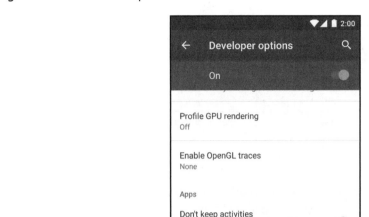

Now run your app and press the Home button. Pressing Home causes the activity to be paused and stopped. Then the stopped activity will be destroyed just as if the Android OS had reclaimed it for its memory. Then you can restore the app to see if your state was saved as you expected. *Be sure to turn this setting off when you are done testing, as it will cause a performance decrease and some apps will perform poorly.*

Pressing the Back button instead of the Home button will always destroy the activity, regardless of whether you have this development setting on. Pressing the Back button tells the OS that the user is done with the activity.

To run the same test on a hardware device, you must install Dev Tools on the device. For more information, visit http://developer.android.com/tools/debugging/debugging-devtools.html.

For the More Curious: Logging Levels and Methods

When you use the **android.util.Log** class to send log messages, you control not only the content of a message, but also a *level* that specifies how important the message is. Android supports five log levels, shown in Figure 3.16. Each level has a corresponding method in the **Log** class. Sending output to the log is as simple as calling the corresponding **Log** method.

Figure 3.16 Log levels and methods

Log Level	Method	Notes
ERROR	Log.e(...)	Errors
WARNING	Log.w(...)	Warnings
INFO	Log.i(...)	Informational messages
DEBUG	Log.d(...)	Debug output; may be filtered out
VERBOSE	Log.v(...)	For development only!

In addition, each of the logging methods has two signatures: one which takes a *tag* string and a message string and a second that takes those two arguments plus an instance of **Throwable**, which makes it easy to log information about a particular exception that your application might throw. Listing 3.8 shows some sample log method signatures. Use regular Java string concatenation to assemble your message string, or **String.format** if you have fancier needs.

Listing 3.8 Different ways of logging in Android

```
// Log a message at "debug" log level
Log.d(TAG, "Current question index: " + mCurrentIndex);

Question question;
try {
    question = mQuestionBank[mCurrentIndex];
} catch (ArrayIndexOutOfBoundsException ex) {
    // Log a message at "error" log level, along with an exception stack trace
    Log.e(TAG, "Index was out of bounds", ex);
}
```

4

Debugging Android Apps

In this chapter, you will find out what to do when apps get buggy. You will learn how to use LogCat, Android Lint, and the debugger that comes with Android Studio.

To practice debugging, the first step is to break something. In QuizActivity.java, comment out the code in **onCreate(Bundle)** where you pull out mQuestionTextView.

Listing 4.1 Comment out a crucial line (QuizActivity.java)

```
@Override
protected void onCreate(Bundle savedInstanceState) {
    super.onCreate(savedInstanceState);
    Log.d(TAG, "onCreate() called");
    setContentView(R.layout.activity_quiz);

    mQuestionTextView = (TextView)findViewById(R.id.question_text_view);
    // mQuestionTextView = (TextView)findViewById(R.id.question_text_view);

    mTrueButton = (Button)findViewById(R.id.true_button);
    mTrueButton.setOnClickListener(new View.OnClickListener() {
        ...
    });

    ...
}
```

Run GeoQuiz and see what happens. Figure 4.1 shows the message that appears when your app crashes and burns. Different versions of Android will have slightly different messages, but they all mean the same thing.

Figure 4.1 GeoQuiz is about to E.X.P.L.O.D.E.

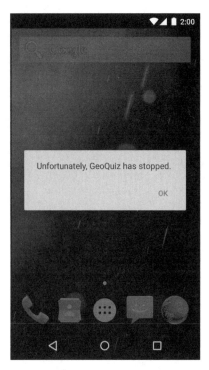

Of course, you know what is wrong with your app, but if you did not, it might help to look at your app from a new perspective.

Exceptions and Stack Traces

Expand the Android DDMS tool window so that you can see what has happened. If you scroll up and down in LogCat, you should eventually find an expanse of red, as shown in Figure 4.2. This is a standard AndroidRuntime exception report. If you are unable to see this exception in LogCat, you may need to tweak LogCat's filters. Select the No Filters option in the filter dropdown. You can also adjust the Log Level to Error, which will show only the most severe log messages.

Figure 4.2 Exception and stack trace in LogCat

```
09-03 12:44:08.523    5458-5458/? E/AndroidRuntime: FATAL EXCEPTION: main
    Process: com.bignerdranch.android.geoquiz, PID: 5458
    java.lang.RuntimeException: Unable to start activity ComponentInfo{com.bignerdranch.android.ge
            at android.app.ActivityThread.performLaunchActivity(ActivityThread.java:2184)
            at android.app.ActivityThread.handleLaunchActivity(ActivityThread.java:2233)
            at android.app.ActivityThread.access$800(ActivityThread.java:135)
            at android.app.ActivityThread$H.handleMessage(ActivityThread.java:1196)
            at android.os.Handler.dispatchMessage(Handler.java:102)
            at android.os.Looper.loop(Looper.java:136)
            at android.app.ActivityThread.main(ActivityThread.java:5001)
            at java.lang.reflect.Method.invokeNative(Native Method) <1 internal calls>
            at com.android.internal.os.ZygoteInit$MethodAndArgsCaller.run(ZygoteInit.java:785)
            at com.android.internal.os.ZygoteInit.main(ZygoteInit.java:601)
            at dalvik.system.NativeStart.main(Native Method)
     Caused by: java.lang.NullPointerException
            at com.bignerdranch.android.geoquiz.QuizActivity.updateQuestion(QuizActivity.java:35)
            at com.bignerdranch.android.geoquiz.QuizActivity.onCreate(QuizActivity.java:90)
            at android.app.Activity.performCreate(Activity.java:5231)
            at android.app.Instrumentation.callActivityOnCreate(Instrumentation.java:1087)
            at android.app.ActivityThread.performLaunchActivity(ActivityThread.java:2148)
            at android.app.ActivityThread.handleLaunchActivity(ActivityThread.java:2233)
            at android.app.ActivityThread.access$800(ActivityThread.java:135)
            at android.app.ActivityThread$H.handleMessage(ActivityThread.java:1196)
            at android.os.Handler.dispatchMessage(Handler.java:102)
            at android.os.Looper.loop(Looper.java:136)
            at android.app.ActivityThread.main(ActivityThread.java:5001)
            at java.lang.reflect.Method.invokeNative(Native Method)
            at java.lang.reflect.Method.invoke(Method.java:515) <3 more...>
```

The report tells you the top-level exception and its stack trace, then the exception that caused that exception and *its* stack trace, and so on and so forth until it finds an exception with no cause.

In most of the code you will write, that last exception with no cause is the interesting one. Here the exception without a cause is a java.lang.NullPointerException. The line just below this exception is the first line in its stack trace. This line tells you the class and method where the exception occurred as well as what file and line number the exception occurred on. Click the blue link, and Android Studio will take you to that line in your source code.

The line to which you are taken is the first use of the mQuestionTextView variable, inside **updateQuestion()**. The name NullPointerException gives you a hint to the problem: this variable was not initialized.

Uncomment the line initializing mQuestionTextView to fix the bug.

When you encounter runtime exceptions, remember to look for the last exception in LogCat and the first line in its stack trace that refers to code that you have written. That is where the problem occurs, and it is the best place to start looking for answers.

If a crash occurs while a device is not plugged in, all is not lost. The device will store the latest lines written to the log. The length and expiration of the stored log depends on the device, but you can usually count on retrieving log results within 10 minutes. Just plug in the device and select your device in the Devices view. LogCat will fill itself with the stored log.

Diagnosing misbehaviors

Problems with your apps will not always be crashes. In some cases, they will be misbehaviors. For example, suppose that every time you pressed the Next button, nothing happened. That would be a noncrashing, misbehaving bug.

In `QuizActivity.java`, make a change to the `mNextButton` listener to comment out the code that increments `mCurrentIndex`.

Listing 4.2 Forget a critical line of code (`QuizActivity.java`)

```
@Override
protected void onCreate(Bundle savedInstanceState) {
    super.onCreate(savedInstanceState);

    ...

    mNextButton = (Button)findViewById(R.id.next_button);
    mNextButton.setOnClickListener(new View.OnClickListener() {
        @Override
        public void onClick(View v) {
            mCurrentIndex = (mCurrentIndex + 1) % mQuestionBank.length;
            // mCurrentIndex = (mCurrentIndex + 1) % mQuestionBank.length;
            updateQuestion();
        }
    });

    ...
}
```

Run GeoQuiz and press the Next button. You should see no effect.

This bug is trickier than the last bug. It is not throwing an exception, so fixing the bug is not a simple matter of making the exception go away. On top of that, this misbehavior could be caused in two different ways: the index might not be changed, or **updateQuestion()** might not be called.

If you had no idea what was causing the problem, you would need to track down the culprit. In the next few sections, you will see two ways to do this: diagnostic logging of a stack trace and using the debugger to set a breakpoint.

Logging stack traces

In **QuizActivity**, add a log statement to **updateQuestion()**.

Listing 4.3 **Exception** for fun and profit (`QuizActivity.java`)

```
public class QuizActivity extends AppCompatActivity {
    ...

    private void updateQuestion() {
        Log.d(TAG, "Updating question text for question #" + mCurrentIndex,
            new Exception());
        int question = mQuestionBank[mCurrentIndex].getTextResId();
        mQuestionTextView.setText(question);
    }
```

The **Log.d(String, String, Throwable)** version of **Log.d** logs the entire stack trace just like with the AndroidRuntime exception you saw earlier. The stack trace will tell you where the call to **updateQuestion()** was made.

The exception that you pass to **Log.d(…)** does not have to be a thrown exception that you caught. You can create a brand new **Exception** and pass it to the method without ever throwing it, and you will get a report of where the exception was created.

Run GeoQuiz, press the Next button, and then check the output in LogCat (Figure 4.3).

Figure 4.3 The results

```
09-04 12:47:37.733  30612-30612/com.bignerdranch.android.geoquiz D/QuizActivity: Updating question text
    java.lang.Exception
            at com.bignerdranch.android.geoquiz.QuizActivity.updateQuestion(QuizActivity.java:34)
            at com.bignerdranch.android.geoquiz.QuizActivity.access$100(QuizActivity.java:12)
            at com.bignerdranch.android.geoquiz.QuizActivity$3.onClick(QuizActivity.java:83)
            at android.view.View.performClick(View.java:4438)
            at android.view.View$PerformClick.run(View.java:18422)
            at android.os.Handler.handleCallback(Handler.java:733)
            at android.os.Handler.dispatchMessage(Handler.java:95)
            at android.os.Looper.loop(Looper.java:136)
            at android.app.ActivityThread.main(ActivityThread.java:5001)
            at java.lang.reflect.Method.invokeNative(Native Method) <1 internal calls>
            at com.android.internal.os.ZygoteInit$MethodAndArgsCaller.run(ZygoteInit.java:785)
            at com.android.internal.os.ZygoteInit.main(ZygoteInit.java:601)
            at dalvik.system.NativeStart.main(Native Method)
```

The top line in the stack trace is the line where you logged out the **Exception**. Two lines after that you can see where **updateQuestion()** was called from within your **onClick(…)** implementation. Click the link on this line, and you will be taken to where you commented out the line to increment your question index. But do not get rid of the bug; you are going to use the debugger to find it again in a moment.

Logging out stack traces is a powerful tool, but it is also a verbose one. Leave a bunch of these hanging around, and soon LogCat will be an unmanageable mess. Also, a competitor might steal your ideas by reading your stack traces to understand what your code is doing.

On the other hand, sometimes a stack trace showing what your code does is exactly what you need. If you are seeking help with a problem at http://stackoverflow.com or forums.bignerdranch.com, it often helps to include a stack trace. You can copy and paste lines directly from LogCat.

Before continuing, delete the log statement in QuizActivity.java.

Listing 4.4 Farewell, old friend (`QuizActivity.java`)

```java
public class QuizActivity extends AppCompatActivity {

    ...

    private void updateQuestion() {
        Log.d(TAG, "Updating question text for question #" + mCurrentIndex,
            new Exception());
        int question = mQuestionBank[mCurrentIndex].getTextResId();
        mQuestionTextView.setText(question);
    }
}
```

Setting breakpoints

Now you will use the debugger that comes with Android Studio to track down the same bug. You will set a *breakpoint* on **updateQuestion()** to see whether it was called. A breakpoint pauses execution before the line executes and allows you to examine line by line what happens next.

In QuizActivity.java, return to the **updateQuestion()** method. In the first line of this method, click the gray bar in the lefthand margin. You should now see a red circle in the gray bar like the one shown in Figure 4.4. This is a breakpoint.

Figure 4.4 A breakpoint

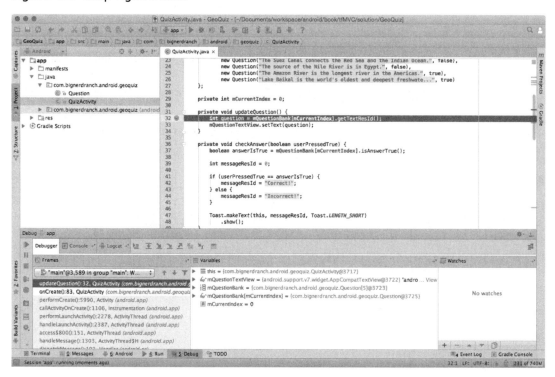

To engage the debugger and trigger your breakpoint, you need to debug your app instead of running it. To debug your app, click the debug button (represented by a green bug), next to the run button. Alternatively, you can navigate to Run → Debug 'app' in the menu bar. Your device will report that it is waiting for the debugger to attach, and then it will proceed normally.

Once your app is up and running with the debugger attached, it will pause. Firing up GeoQuiz called **QuizActivity.onCreate(Bundle)**, which called **updateQuestion()**, which hit your breakpoint.

In Figure 4.5, you can see that this editor has opened QuizActivity.java and highlighted the line with the breakpoint where execution has paused.

Figure 4.5 Stop right there!

The Debug tool window at the bottom of the screen is now visible and contains the Frames and Variables views (Figure 4.6).

Figure 4.6 The Debug tool window

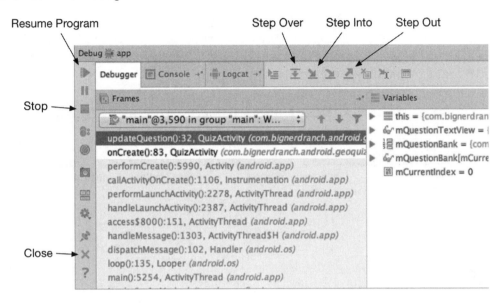

You can use the arrow buttons at the top of the view to step through your program. You can see from the stack trace that **updateQuestion()** has been called from inside **onCreate(Bundle)**. But you are interested in investigating the Next button's behavior, so click the Resume Program button to continue execution. Then press the Next button in GeoQuiz to see if your breakpoint is hit and execution is stopped (it should be).

Now that you are stopped at an interesting point of execution, you can take a look around. The Variables view allows you to examine the values of the objects in your program. You should see the variables that you have created in **QuizActivity** as well as an additional value: this (the **QuizActivity** instance itself).

You could expand the this variable to see all the variables declared in **QuizActivity**'s superclass, **Activity**, in **Activity**'s superclass, in its super-superclass, and so on. But for now, focus on the variables that you created.

You are only interested in one value: mCurrentIndex. Scroll down in the variables view until you see mCurrentIndex. Sure enough, it still has a value of 0.

This code looks perfectly fine. To continue your investigation, you need to step out of this method. Click the Step Out button.

Check the editor view. It has now jumped you over to your mNextButton's **OnClickListener**, right after **updateQuestion()** was called. Pretty nifty.

You will want to fix this implementation, but before you make any changes to code, you should stop debugging your app. You can do this in two ways: you can either stop the program, or you can simply disconnect the debugger. To stop the program, click the Stop button shown in Figure 4.6. Usually it is easier to simply disconnect the debugger. To do that, click the Close button also labeled in Figure 4.6.

Now return your **OnClickListener** to its former glory.

Listing 4.5 Returning to normalcy (QuizActivity.java)

```
@Override
protected void onCreate(Bundle savedInstanceState) {
    super.onCreate(savedInstanceState);
    ...

    mNextButton = (Button)findViewById(R.id.next_button);
    mNextButton.setOnClickListener(new View.OnClickListener() {
        @Override
        public void onClick(View v) {
            // mCurrentIndex = (mCurrentIndex + 1) % mQuestionBank.length;
            mCurrentIndex = (mCurrentIndex + 1) % mQuestionBank.length;
            updateQuestion();
        }
    });

    ...
}
```

You have tried out two ways of tracking down a misbehaving line of code: stack trace logging and setting a breakpoint in the debugger. Which is better? Each has its uses, and one or the other will probably end up being your favorite.

Logging out stack traces has the advantage that you can see stack traces from multiple places in one log. The downside is that to learn something new you have to add new log statements, rebuild, deploy, and navigate through your app to see what happened. The debugger is more convenient. If you run your app with the debugger attached, then you can set a breakpoint while the application is still running and poke around to get information about multiple issues.

Using exception breakpoints

As if that were not enough choices, you can also use the debugger to catch exceptions. Return to **QuizActivity**'s **onCreate** method and comment out a line of code that will cause the app to crash.

Listing 4.6 Making GeoQuiz crash again (QuizActivity.java)

```
@Override
protected void onCreate(Bundle savedInstanceState) {
super.onCreate(savedInstanceState);
    ...

    mNextButton = (Button) findViewById(R.id.next_button);
    // mNextButton = (Button) findViewById(R.id.next_button);
    mNextButton.setOnClickListener(new View.OnClickListener() {
        @Override
        public void onClick(View view) {
            mCurrentIndex = (mCurrentIndex + 1) % mQuestionBank.length;
            updateQuestion();
        }
    });

    ...
}
```

Now select Run → View Breakpoints... to pull up the breakpoints dialog, as shown in Figure 4.7.

Figure 4.7 Setting an exception breakpoint

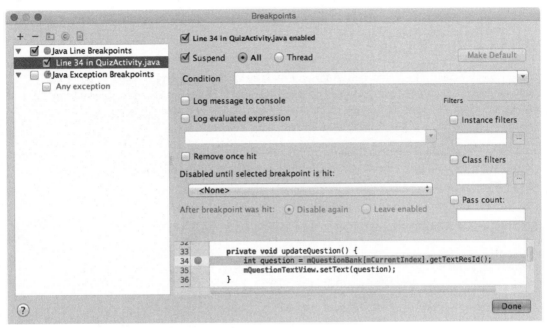

This dialog shows all of your currently set breakpoints. Remove the breakpoint you added earlier by highlighting it and clicking the Remove button (shaped like a minus sign).

The breakpoints dialog also allows you to set a breakpoint that is triggered when an exception is thrown, wherever it might happen. You can limit it to only uncaught exceptions, or apply it to both caught and uncaught exceptions.

Click the Add button (shaped like a plus sign) to add a new breakpoint. Choose Java Exception Breakpoints in the drop-down list. You can now select the type of exception that you want to catch. Type in **RuntimeException** and choose RuntimeException (java.lang) from the suggestions. **RuntimeException** is the superclass of **NullPointerException**, **ClassCastException**, and other runtime problems, so it makes a nice catch-all.

Click Done and launch GeoQuiz with the debugger attached. This time, your debugger will jump right to the line where the exception was thrown as soon as it happens. Exquisite.

Now, this is a fairly big hammer. If you leave this breakpoint on while debugging, you can expect it to stop on some framework code or in other places you do not expect. So you may want to turn it off when you are not using it. Go ahead and remove the breakpoint now by returning to Run → View Breakpoints....

Undo the change from Listing 4.6 to get GeoQuiz back to a good state.

Android-Specific Debugging

Most Android debugging is just like Java debugging. However, you will run into issues with Android-specific parts, such as resources, that the Java compiler knows nothing about.

Using Android Lint

This is where Android Lint comes in. Android Lint is a *static analyzer* for Android code. A static analyzer is a program that examines your code to find defects without running it. Android Lint uses its knowledge of the Android frameworks to look deeper into your code and find problems that the compiler cannot. In most cases, Android Lint's advice is worth taking.

In Chapter 6, you will see Android Lint warn you about compatibility problems. Android Lint can also perform type-checking for objects that are defined in XML. Make the following casting mistake in **QuizActivity**:

Listing 4.7 A simple mix-up (`QuizActivity.java`)

```
@Override
protected void onCreate(Bundle savedInstanceState) {
    super.onCreate(savedInstanceState);
    Log.d(TAG, "onCreate() called");
    setContentView(R.layout.activity_quiz);

    mQuestionTextView = (TextView)findViewById(R.id.question_text_view);

    mTrueButton = (Button)findViewById(R.id.true_button);
    mTrueButton = (Button)findViewById(R.id.question_text_view);

    ...
}
```

Because you used the wrong resource ID, this code will attempt to cast a **TextView** as a **Button** at runtime. This will cause an improper cast exception. The Java compiler sees no problem with this code, but Android Lint will catch this error. You should see Lint immediately highlight this line of code indicating that there is a problem.

You can manually run Lint to see all of the potential issues in your project, including those that are not as serious as the one above. Select Analyze → Inspect Code... from the menu bar. You will be asked which parts of your project you would like to inspect. Choose Whole project. Android Studio will now run Lint as well as a few other static analyzers on your code.

Once the scan is complete, you will see a few categories of potential issues. Expand the Android Lint category to see Lint's information about your project (Figure 4.8).

Figure 4.8 Lint warnings

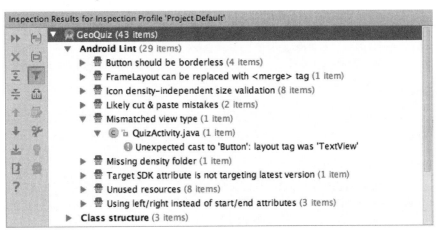

You can select an issue in this list to see more detailed information and its location in your project.

The Mismatched view type warning is the one that you created above. Go ahead and correct the cast in `onCreate(Bundle)`.

Listing 4.8 Fixing that simple mix-up (`QuizActivity.java`)

```
@Override
protected void onCreate(Bundle savedInstanceState) {
    super.onCreate(savedInstanceState);
    Log.d(TAG, "onCreate() called");
    setContentView(R.layout.activity_quiz);

    mQuestionTextView = (TextView)findViewById(R.id.question_text_view);

    mTrueButton = (Button)findViewById(R.id.question_text_view);
    mTrueButton = (Button)findViewById(R.id.true_button);

    ...
}
```

Run GeoQuiz once more and confirm that the app is back to normal.

Issues with the R class

You are familiar with build errors that occur when you reference resources before adding them or delete resources that other files refer to. Usually, resaving the files once the resource is added or the references are removed will cause Android Studio to rebuild without any fuss.

Sometimes, however, these build errors will persist or appear seemingly out of nowhere. If this happens to you, here are some things you can try:

Recheck the validity of the XML in your resource files

If your R.java file was not generated for the last build, you will see errors in your project wherever you reference a resource. Often, this is caused by an XML typo in one of your XML files. Layout XML is not always validated, so typos in these files may not be pointedly brought to your attention. Finding the typo and resaving the file should cause R.java to regenerate.

Clean your project

Select Build → Clean Project. Android Studio will rebuild the project from scratch, which often results in an error-free build. We can all use a deep clean every now and then.

Sync your project with Gradle

If you make changes to your build.gradle file, you will need to sync those changes to update your project's build settings. Select Tools → Android → Sync Project with Gradle Files. Android Studio will rebuild the project from scratch with the correct project settings, which can help to resolve issues after changing your Gradle configuration.

Run Android Lint

Pay close attention to the warnings from Android Lint. You will often discover unexpected issues with this tool.

If you are still having problems with resources (or having different problems), give the error messages and your layout files a fresh look. It is easy to miss mistakes in the heat of the moment. Check out any Android Lint errors and warnings as well. A cool-headed reconsideration of the error messages may turn up a bug or typo.

Finally, if you are stuck or having other issues with Android Studio, check the archives at http://stackoverflow.com or visit the forum for this book at http://forums.bignerdranch.com.

5

Your Second Activity

In this chapter, you will add a second activity to GeoQuiz. An activity controls a screen of information, and this activity will add a second screen that offers users a chance to see the answer to the current question. Figure 5.1 shows the new activity.

Figure 5.1 **CheatActivity** offers the chance to peek at the answer

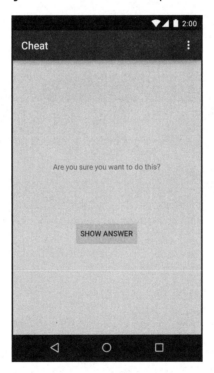

If the user chooses to view the answer and then returns to the **QuizActivity** and answers the question, he or she will get a new message, shown in Figure 5.2.

Figure 5.2 **QuizActivity** knows if you've been cheating

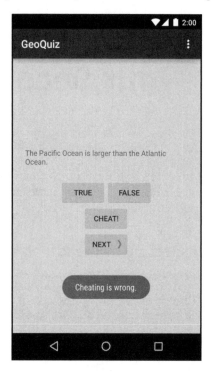

Why is this a good Android programming exercise? You will learn how to:

- Create a new activity and a new layout for it.

- Start an activity from another activity. *Starting* an activity means asking the OS to create an activity instance and call its **onCreate(Bundle)** method.

- Pass data between the parent (starting) activity and the child (started) activity.

Setting Up a Second Activity

There is a lot to do in this chapter. Fortunately, some of the grunt work can be done for you by Android Studio's New Activity wizard.

But before you invoke the magic, open strings.xml and add all the strings you will need for this chapter.

Listing 5.1 Adding strings (`strings.xml`)

```
<?xml version="1.0" encoding="utf-8"?>
<resources>

    ...
    <string name="question_asia">Lake Baikal is the world\'s oldest and deepest
      freshwater lake.</string>
    <string name="warning_text">Are you sure you want to do this?</string>
    <string name="show_answer_button">Show Answer</string>
    <string name="cheat_button">Cheat!</string>
    <string name="judgment_toast">Cheating is wrong.</string>

</resources>
```

Creating a new activity

Creating an activity typically involves touching at least three files: the Java class file, an XML layout, and the application manifest. If you touch those files in the wrong ways, Android can get mad. To ensure that you do it right, you should use Android Studio's New Activity wizard.

Launch the New Activity wizard by right-clicking on your `com.bignerdranch.android.geoquiz` package in the Project Tool Window. Choose New → Activity → Blank Activity as shown in Figure 5.3.

Figure 5.3 The New Activity Wizard menu

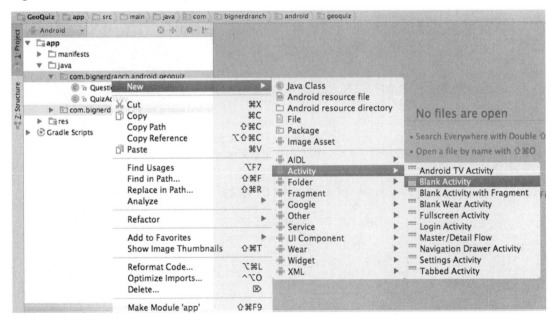

You should then see a dialog like Figure 5.4. Set Activity Name to **CheatActivity**. This is the name of your **Activity** subclass. Layout Name should be automatically set to `activity_cheat`. This will be the base name of the layout file the wizard creates. Title will be set to "CheatActivity" for you, but since this is a string the user will see, change it to simply "Cheat".

The defaults for the remaining fields should be fine, but take care to ensure that the package name is what you expect. This determines where `CheatActivity.java` will live on the filesystem. Click the Finish button to make the magic happen.

Figure 5.4 The New Blank Activity wizard

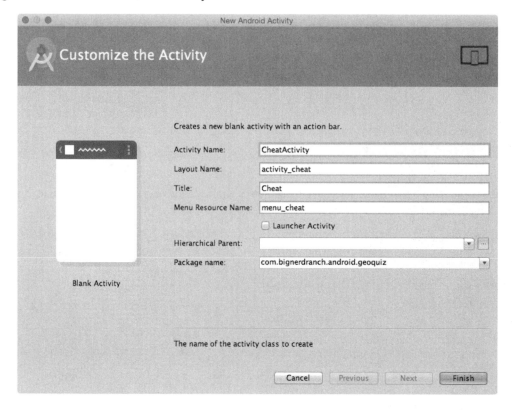

Now it is time to make the user interface look good. The screenshot at the beginning of the chapter shows you what **CheatActivity**'s view should look like. Figure 5.5 shows the widget definitions.

Figure 5.5 Diagram of layout for CheatActivity

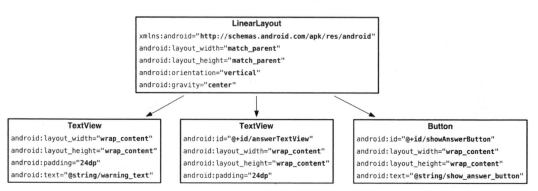

After the wizard completes its work, it should open `activity_cheat.xml` in the `layout` directory. If it did not, go ahead and open it now, and switch to the Text (XML) view.

Try creating the XML for the layout using Figure 5.5 as a guide. Replace the sample layout with a new **LinearLayout** and so on down the tree. After Chapter 8, we will only show layout diagrams like Figure 5.5 instead of long passages of XML, so it is a good idea to start using them now to create your layout XML. You can check your work against Listing 5.2.

Listing 5.2 Filling out the second activity's layout (`activity_cheat.xml`)

```xml
<LinearLayout xmlns:android="http://schemas.android.com/apk/res/android"
              xmlns:tools="http://schemas.android.com/tools"
              android:layout_width="match_parent"
              android:layout_height="match_parent"
              android:gravity="center"
              android:orientation="vertical"
              tools:context="com.bignerdranch.android.geoquiz.CheatActivity">

    <TextView
        android:layout_width="wrap_content"
        android:layout_height="wrap_content"
        android:padding="24dp"
        android:text="@string/warning_text"/>

    <TextView
        android:id="@+id/answer_text_view"
        android:layout_width="wrap_content"
        android:layout_height="wrap_content"
        android:padding="24dp"
        tools:text="Answer"/>

    <Button
        android:id="@+id/show_answer_button"
        android:layout_width="wrap_content"
        android:layout_height="wrap_content"
        android:text="@string/show_answer_button"/>

</LinearLayout>
```

Notice the special XML namespace for `tools` and the `tools:text` attribute on the **TextView** widget where the answer will appear. This namespace allows you to override any attribute on a widget for the purpose of displaying it differently in the Android Studio preview. Since **TextView** has a text attribute, you can provide a literal dummy value for it to help you know what it will look like at runtime. The value "Answer" will never show up in the real app. Handy!

You will not be creating a landscape alternative for `activity_cheat.xml`, but there is a way to preview how the default layout will appear in landscape.

In the Preview tool window, find the button in the toolbar above the preview pane that looks like a device with a curved arrow. Click this button to change the orientation of the preview (Figure 5.6).

Figure 5.6 Previewing `activity_cheat.xml` in landscape

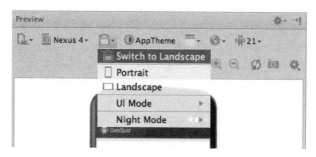

The default layout works well enough in both orientations, so let's move on to fleshing out the activity subclass.

A new activity subclass

In the Project tool window, find the `com.bignerdranch.android.geoquiz` Java package and open the `CheatActivity` class, which is in the `CheatActivity.java` file.

This class already includes a basic implementation of `onCreate(…)` that passes the resource ID of the layout defined in `activity_cheat.xml` to `setContentView(…)`.

`CheatActivity` will eventually do more in its `onCreate(…)` method. For now, let's take a look at another thing the New Activity wizard did for you: declaring `CheatActivity` in the application's manifest.

Declaring activities in the manifest

The *manifest* is an XML file containing metadata that describes your application to the Android OS. The file is always named `AndroidManifest.xml`, and it lives in the `app/manifests` directory of your project.

In the Project tool window, find and open `AndroidManifest.xml`. You can also use Android Studio's Quick Open dialog by pressing Command+Shift+O (Ctrl+Shift+N) and starting to type the filename. Once it has guessed the right file, press Return (Enter) to open it.

Every activity in an application must be declared in the manifest so that the OS can access it.

When you used the New Application wizard to create `QuizActivity`, the wizard declared the activity for you. Likewise, the New Activity wizard declared `CheatActivity` by adding the XML highlighted in Listing 5.3.

Listing 5.3 Declaring **CheatActivity** in the manifest (AndroidManifest.xml)

```xml
<?xml version="1.0" encoding="utf-8"?>
<manifest xmlns:android="http://schemas.android.com/apk/res/android"
    package="com.bignerdranch.android.geoquiz" >

    <application
        android:allowBackup="true"
        android:icon="@mipmap/ic_launcher"
        android:label="@string/app_name"
        android:theme="@style/AppTheme" >
        <activity
            android:name=".QuizActivity"
            android:label="@string/app_name" >
            <intent-filter>
                <action android:name="android.intent.action.MAIN" />

                <category android:name="android.intent.category.LAUNCHER" />
            </intent-filter>
        </activity>
        <activity
            android:name=".CheatActivity"
            android:label="@string/title_activity_cheat" >
        </activity>
    </application>

</manifest>
```

The android:name attribute is required, and the dot at the start of this attribute's value tells the OS that this activity's class is in the package specified in the package attribute in the manifest element at the top of the file.

You will sometimes see a fully qualified android:name attribute:
android:name="com.bignerdranch.android.geoquiz.CheatActivity". The long-form notation is identical to the version in Listing 5.3.

There are many interesting things in the manifest, but for now, let's stay focused on getting **CheatActivity** up and running. You will learn about the different parts of the manifest in later chapters.

Adding a Cheat! button to QuizActivity

The plan is for the user to press a button in **QuizActivity** to get an instance of **CheatActivity** on screen. So you need new buttons in layout/activity_quiz.xml and layout-land/ activity_quiz.xml.

In the default layout, add the new button as a direct child of the root **LinearLayout**. Its definition should come right before the Next button.

Listing 5.4 Adding a Cheat! button to the default layout (layout/ activity_quiz.xml)

```
    ...
  </LinearLayout>

    <Button
        android:id="@+id/cheat_button"
        android:layout_width="wrap_content"
        android:layout_height="wrap_content"
        android:text="@string/cheat_button"/>

    <Button
        android:id="@+id/next_button"
        android:layout_width="wrap_content"
        android:layout_height="wrap_content"
        android:text="@string/next_button"
        android:drawableRight="@drawable/arrow_right"
        android:drawablePadding="4dp"/>

</LinearLayout>
```

In the landscape layout, have the new button appear at the bottom and center of the root **FrameLayout**.

Listing 5.5 Adding a Cheat! button to the landscape layout (layout-land/ activity_quiz.xml)

```
    ...
  </LinearLayout>

  <Button
    android:id="@+id/cheat_button"
    android:layout_width="wrap_content"
    android:layout_height="wrap_content"
    android:layout_gravity="bottom|center"
    android:text="@string/cheat_button" />

  <Button
    android:id="@+id/next_button"
    android:layout_width="wrap_content"
    android:layout_height="wrap_content"
    android:layout_gravity="bottom|right"
    android:text="@string/next_button"
    android:drawableRight="@drawable/arrow_right"
    android:drawablePadding="4dp" />

</FrameLayout>
```

Save your layout files and reopen QuizActivity.java. Add a variable, get a reference, and set a **View.OnClickListener** stub for the Cheat! button.

Listing 5.6 Wiring up the Cheat! button (QuizActivity.java)

```java
public class QuizActivity extends AppCompatActivity {

    ...

    private Button mNextButton;
    private Button mCheatButton;

    ...

    @Override
    protected void onCreate(Bundle savedInstanceState) {

        ...

        mCheatButton = (Button)findViewById(R.id.cheat_button);
        mCheatButton.setOnClickListener(new View.OnClickListener() {
            @Override
            public void onClick(View v) {
                // Start CheatActivity
            }
        });

        if (savedInstanceState != null) {
            mCurrentIndex = savedInstanceState.getInt(KEY_INDEX, 0);
        }

        updateQuestion();
    }

    ...

}
```

Now you can get to the business of starting **CheatActivity**.

Starting an Activity

The simplest way one activity can start another is with the **Activity** method:

```java
public void startActivity(Intent intent)
```

You might guess that **startActivity(…)** is a static method that you call on the **Activity** subclass that you want to start. But it is not. When an activity calls **startActivity(…)**, this call is sent to the OS.

In particular, it is sent to a part of the OS called the **ActivityManager**. The **ActivityManager** then creates the **Activity** instance and calls its **onCreate(…)** method, as shown in Figure 5.7.

Figure 5.7 Starting an activity

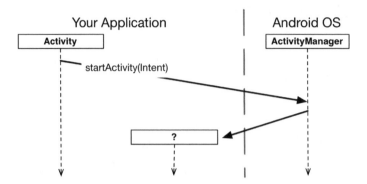

How does the **ActivityManager** know which **Activity** to start? That information is in the **Intent** parameter.

Communicating with intents

An *intent* is an object that a *component* can use to communicate with the OS. The only components you have seen so far are activities, but there are also services, broadcast receivers, and content providers.

Intents are multi-purpose communication tools, and the **Intent** class provides different constructors depending on what you are using the intent to do.

In this case, you are using an intent to tell the **ActivityManager** which activity to start, so you will use this constructor:

```
public Intent(Context packageContext, Class<?> cls)
```

The **Class** argument specifies the activity class that the **ActivityManager** should start. The **Context** argument tells the **ActivityManager** which application package the activity class can be found in (Figure 5.8).

Figure 5.8 The intent: telling **ActivityManager** what to do

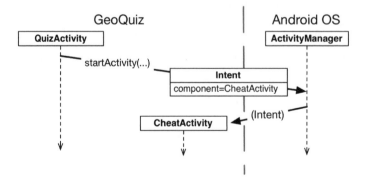

Within mCheatButton's listener, create an **Intent** that includes the **CheatActivity** class. Then pass the intent into **startActivity(Intent)** (Listing 5.7).

Listing 5.7 Starting **CheatActivity** (QuizActivity.java)

```
...

mCheatButton = (Button)findViewById(R.id.cheat_button);
mCheatButton.setOnClickListener(new View.OnClickListener() {

    @Override
    public void onClick(View v) {
        // Start CheatActivity
        Intent i = new Intent(QuizActivity.this, CheatActivity.class);
        startActivity(i);
    }
});

...
```

Before starting the activity, the **ActivityManager** checks the package's manifest for a declaration with the same name as the specified **Class**. If it finds a declaration, it starts the activity, and all is well. If it does not, you get a nasty ActivityNotFoundException, which can crash your app. This is why all of your activities must be declared in the manifest.

Run GeoQuiz. Press the Cheat! button, and an instance of your new activity will appear on screen. Now press the Back button. This will destroy the **CheatActivity** and return you to the **QuizActivity**.

Explicit and implicit intents

When you create an **Intent** with a **Context** and a **Class** object, you are creating an *explicit intent*. You use explicit intents to start activities within your application.

It may seem strange that two activities within your application must communicate via the **ActivityManager**, which is outside of your application. However, this pattern makes it easy for an activity in one application to work with an activity in another application.

When an activity in your application wants to start an activity in another application, you create an *implicit intent*. You will use implicit intents in Chapter 15.

Passing Data Between Activities

Now that you have a **QuizActivity** and a **CheatActivity**, you can think about passing data between them. Figure 5.9 shows what data you will pass between the two activities.

Figure 5.9 The conversation between **QuizActivity** and **CheatActivity**

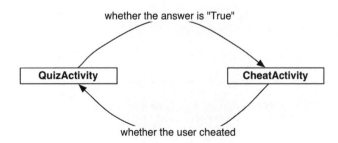

The **QuizActivity** will inform the **CheatActivity** of the answer to the current question when the **CheatActivity** is started.

When the user presses the Back button to return to the **QuizActivity**, the **CheatActivity** will be destroyed. In its last gasp, it will send data to the **QuizActivity** about whether the user cheated.

You will start with passing data from **QuizActivity** to **CheatActivity**.

Using intent extras

To inform the **CheatActivity** of the answer to the current question, you will pass it the value of

```
mQuestionBank[mCurrentIndex].isAnswerTrue()
```

You will send this value as an *extra* on the **Intent** that is passed into **startActivity(Intent)**.

Extras are arbitrary data that the calling activity can include with an intent. You can think of them like constructor arguments, even though you cannot use a custom constructor with an activity subclass (Android creates activity instances and is responsible for their lifecycle). The OS forwards the intent to the recipient activity, which can then access the extras and retrieve the data, as shown in Figure 5.10.

Figure 5.10 Intent extras: communicating with other activities

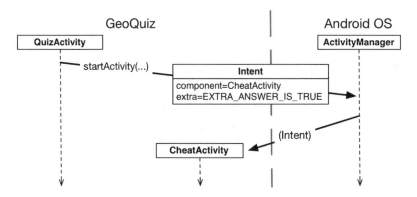

An extra is structured as a key-value pair, like the one you used to save out the value of mCurrentIndex in **QuizActivity.onSaveInstanceState(Bundle)**.

To add an extra to an intent, you use **Intent.putExtra(…)**. In particular, you will be calling

```
public Intent putExtra(String name, boolean value)
```

Intent.putExtra(…) comes in many flavors, but it always has two arguments. The first argument is always a **String** key, and the second argument is the value, whose type will vary. It returns the **Intent** itself, so you can chain multiple calls if you need to.

In CheatActivity.java, add a key for the extra.

Listing 5.8 Adding extra constant (CheatActivity.java)

```java
public class CheatActivity extends AppCompatActivity {

    private static final String EXTRA_ANSWER_IS_TRUE =
        "com.bignerdranch.android.geoquiz.answer_is_true";

    ...
```

An activity may be started from several different places, so you should define keys for extras on the activities that retrieve and use them. Using your package name as a qualifier for your extra, as shown in Listing 5.8, prevents name collisions with extras from other apps.

Now you could return to **QuizActivity** and put the extra on the intent, but there is a better approach. There is no reason for **QuizActivity**, or any other code in your app, to know the implementation details of what **CheatActivity** expects as extras on its **Intent**. Instead, you can encapsulate that work into a **newIntent(…)** method.

Create this method in **CheatActivity** now:

Listing 5.9 A **newIntent(…)** method for **CheatActivity** (CheatActivity.java)

```java
public class CheatActivity extends AppCompatActivity {

    private static final String EXTRA_ANSWER_IS_TRUE =
            "com.bignerdranch.android.geoquiz.answer_is_true";

    public static Intent newIntent(Context packageContext, boolean answerIsTrue) {
        Intent i = new Intent(packageContext, CheatActivity.class);
        i.putExtra(EXTRA_ANSWER_IS_TRUE, answerIsTrue);
        return i;
    }

    ...
```

This static method allows us to create an **Intent** properly configured with the extras **CheatActivity** will need. The answerIsTrue argument, a boolean, is put into the intent with a private name using the EXTRA_ANSWER_IS_TRUE constant. You will extract this value momentarily. Using a **newIntent(…)** method like this for your activity subclasses will make it easy for other code to properly configure their launching intents.

Speaking of other code, use this new method in **CheatActivity**'s cheat button listener now.

Listing 5.10 Launching **CheatActivity** with an extra (QuizActivity.java)

```java
        ...
        mCheatButton.setOnClickListener(new View.OnClickListener() {
            @Override
            public void onClick(View v) {
                // Start CheatActivity
                Intent i = new Intent(QuizActivity.this, CheatActivity.class);
                boolean answerIsTrue = mQuestionBank[mCurrentIndex].isAnswerTrue();
                Intent i = CheatActivity.newIntent(QuizActivity.this, answerIsTrue);
                startActivity(i);
            }
        });

        updateQuestion();
    }
```

You only need one extra, but you can put multiple extras on an **Intent** if you need to. If you do, add more arguments to your **newIntent(…)** method to stay consistent with the pattern.

To retrieve the value from the extra, you will use:

```
public boolean getBooleanExtra(String name, boolean defaultValue)
```

The first argument is the name of the extra. The second argument of **getBooleanExtra(…)** is a default answer if the key is not found.

In **CheatActivity**, retrieve the value from the extra in **onCreate(Bundle)** and store it in a member variable.

Listing 5.11 Using an extra (CheatActivity.java)

```
public class CheatActivity extends AppCompatActivity {

    private static final String EXTRA_ANSWER_IS_TRUE =
            "com.bignerdranch.android.geoquiz.answer_is_true";

    private boolean mAnswerIsTrue;

    ...

    @Override
    protected void onCreate(Bundle savedInstanceState) {
        super.onCreate(savedInstanceState);
        setContentView(R.layout.activity_cheat);

        mAnswerIsTrue = getIntent().getBooleanExtra(EXTRA_ANSWER_IS_TRUE, false);
    }

    ...
}
```

Note that **Activity.getIntent()** always returns the **Intent** that started the activity. This is what you sent when calling **startActivity(Intent)**.

Finally, wire up the answer **TextView** and the Show Answer button to use the retrieved value.

Listing 5.12 Enabling cheating (CheatActivity.java)

```java
public class CheatActivity extends AppCompatActivity {

    ...

    private boolean mAnswerIsTrue;

    private TextView mAnswerTextView;
    private Button mShowAnswer;

    ...

    @Override
    protected void onCreate(Bundle savedInstanceState) {
        super.onCreate(savedInstanceState);
        setContentView(R.layout.activity_cheat);

        mAnswerIsTrue = getIntent().getBooleanExtra(EXTRA_ANSWER_IS_TRUE, false);

        mAnswerTextView = (TextView) findViewById(R.id.answer_text_view);

        mShowAnswer = (Button) findViewById(R.id.show_answer_button);
        mShowAnswer.setOnClickListener(new View.OnClickListener() {
            @Override
            public void onClick(View v) {
                if (mAnswerIsTrue) {
                    mAnswerTextView.setText(R.string.true_button);
                } else {
                    mAnswerTextView.setText(R.string.false_button);
                }
            }
        });
    }

}
```

This code is pretty straightforward. You set the **TextView**'s text using **TextView.setText(int)**. **TextView.setText(…)** has many variations, and here you use the one that accepts the resource ID of a string resource.

Run GeoQuiz. Press Cheat! to get to **CheatActivity**. Then press Show Answer to reveal the answer to the current question.

Getting a result back from a child activity

At this point, the user can cheat with impunity. Let's fix that by having the **CheatActivity** tell the **QuizActivity** whether the user chose to view the answer.

When you want to hear back from the child activity, you call the following **Activity** method:

```java
public void startActivityForResult(Intent intent, int requestCode)
```

The first parameter is the same intent as before. The second parameter is the *request code*. The *request code* is a user-defined integer that is sent to the child activity and then received back by the parent. It is used when an activity starts more than one type of child activity and needs to know who is reporting back. **QuizActivity** will only ever start one type of child activity, but using a constant for the request code is a best practice that will set you up well for future changes.

In **QuizActivity**, modify mCheatButton's listener to call **startActivityForResult(Intent, int)**.

Listing 5.13 Calling **startActivityForResult(…)** (QuizActivity.java)

```
public class QuizActivity extends AppCompatActivity {
    private static final String TAG = "QuizActivity";
    private static final String KEY_INDEX = "index";
    private static final int REQUEST_CODE_CHEAT = 0;

    @Override
    protected void onCreate(Bundle savedInstanceState) {

        ...

        mCheatButton.setOnClickListener(new View.OnClickListener() {
            @Override
            public void onClick(View v) {
                boolean answerIsTrue = mQuestionBank[mCurrentIndex].isAnswerTrue();
                Intent i = CheatActivity.newIntent(QuizActivity.this, answerIsTrue);
                startActivity(i);
                startActivityForResult(i, REQUEST_CODE_CHEAT);
            }
        });

        ...
```

Setting a result

There are two methods you can call in the child activity to send data back to the parent:

```
public final void setResult(int resultCode)
public final void setResult(int resultCode, Intent data)
```

Typically, the *result code* is one of two predefined constants: Activity.RESULT_OK or Activity.RESULT_CANCELED. (You can use another constant, RESULT_FIRST_USER, as an offset when defining your own result codes.)

Setting result codes is useful when the parent needs to take different action depending on how the child activity finished.

For example, if a child activity had an OK button and a Cancel button, the child activity would set a different result code depending on which button was pressed. Then the parent activity would take different action depending on the result code.

Calling **setResult(…)** is not required of the child activity. If you do not need to distinguish between results or receive arbitrary data on an intent, then you can let the OS send a default result code. A result code is always returned to the parent if the child activity was started with **startActivityForResult(…)**. If **setResult(…)** is not called, then when the user presses the Back button the parent will receive Activity.RESULT_CANCELED.

Sending back an intent

In this implementation, you are interested in passing some specific data back to **QuizActivity**. So you are going to create an **Intent**, put an extra on it, and then call **Activity.setResult(int, Intent)** to get that data into **QuizActivity**'s hands.

In **CheatActivity**, add a constant for the extra's key and a private method that does this work. Then call this method in the Show Answer button's listener.

Listing 5.14 Setting a result (CheatActivity.java)

```java
public class CheatActivity extends AppCompatActivity {

    private static final String EXTRA_ANSWER_IS_TRUE =
        "com.bignerdranch.android.geoquiz.answer_is_true";
    private static final String EXTRA_ANSWER_SHOWN =
        "com.bignerdranch.android.geoquiz.answer_shown";

    ...

    @Override
    protected void onCreate(Bundle savedInstanceState) {
        ...

        mShowAnswer.setOnClickListener(new View.OnClickListener() {
            @Override
            public void onClick(View v) {
                if (mAnswerIsTrue) {
                    mAnswerTextView.setText(R.string.true_button);
                } else {
                    mAnswerTextView.setText(R.string.false_button);
                }
                setAnswerShownResult(true);
            }
        });
    }

    private void setAnswerShownResult(boolean isAnswerShown) {
        Intent data = new Intent();
        data.putExtra(EXTRA_ANSWER_SHOWN, isAnswerShown);
        setResult(RESULT_OK, data);
    }

}
```

When the user presses the Show Answer button, the **CheatActivity** packages up the result code and the intent in the call to **setResult(int, Intent)**.

Then, when the user presses the Back button to return to the **QuizActivity**, the **ActivityManager** calls the following method on the parent activity:

```java
protected void onActivityResult(int requestCode, int resultCode, Intent data)
```

The parameters are the original request code from **QuizActivity** and the result code and intent passed into **setResult(…)**.

Figure 5.11 shows this sequence of interactions.

Figure 5.11 Sequence diagram for GeoQuiz

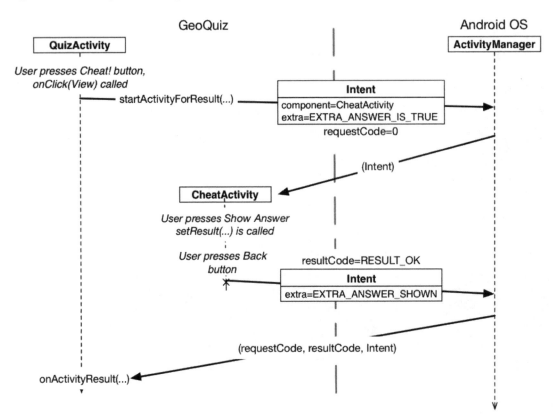

The final step is to override **onActivityResult(int, int, Intent)** in **QuizActivity** to handle the result. However, because the contents of the result **Intent** are also an implementation detail of **CheatActivity**, add another method to help decode the extra into something **QuizActivity** can use.

Listing 5.15 Decoding the result intent (CheatActivity.java)

```java
public static Intent newIntent(Context packageContext, boolean answerIsTrue) {
    Intent i = new Intent(packageContext, CheatActivity.class);
    i.putExtra(EXTRA_ANSWER_IS_TRUE, answerIsTrue);
    return i;
}

public static boolean wasAnswerShown(Intent result) {
    return result.getBooleanExtra(EXTRA_ANSWER_SHOWN, false);
}

@Override
protected void onCreate(Bundle savedInstanceState) {
    ...
}
```

Handling a result

In QuizActivity.java, add a new member variable to hold the value that **CheatActivity** is passing back. Then override **onActivityResult(…)** to retrieve it, checking the request code and result code to be sure they are what you expect. This, again, is a best practice to make future maintenance easier.

Listing 5.16 Implementing **onActivityResult(…)** (QuizActivity.java)

```java
public class QuizActivity extends AppCompatActivity {

    ...

    private int mCurrentIndex = 0;
    private boolean mIsCheater;

    ...

    @Override
    protected void onCreate(Bundle savedInstanceState) {
        ...
    }

    @Override
    protected void onActivityResult(int requestCode, int resultCode, Intent data) {
        if (resultCode != Activity.RESULT_OK) {
            return;
        }

        if (requestCode == REQUEST_CODE_CHEAT) {
            if (data == null) {
                return;
            }
            mIsCheater = CheatActivity.wasAnswerShown(data);
        }
    }

    ...
}
```

Finally, modify the **checkAnswer(boolean)** method in **QuizActivity** to check whether the user cheated and to respond appropriately.

Listing 5.17 Changing toast message based on value of `mIsCheater` (QuizActivity.java)

```java
private void checkAnswer(boolean userPressedTrue) {
    boolean answerIsTrue = mQuestionBank[mCurrentIndex].isAnswerTrue();

    int messageResId = 0;

    if (mIsCheater) {
        messageResId = R.string.judgment_toast;
    } else {
        if (userPressedTrue == answerIsTrue) {
            messageResId = R.string.correct_toast;
        } else {
            messageResId = R.string.incorrect_toast;
        }
    }

    Toast.makeText(this, messageResId, Toast.LENGTH_SHORT)
        .show();
}

@Override
protected void onCreate(Bundle savedInstanceState) {
    ...

    mNextButton = (Button)findViewById(R.id.next_button);
    mNextButton.setOnClickListener(new View.OnClickListener() {
        @Override
        public void onClick(View v) {
            mCurrentIndex = (mCurrentIndex + 1) % mQuestionBank.length;
            mIsCheater = false;
            updateQuestion();
        }
    });

    ...
}
```

Run GeoQuiz. Cheat and see what happens.

How Android Sees Your Activities

Let's look at what is going on OS-wise as you move between activities. First, when you click on the GeoQuiz app in the launcher, the OS does not start the application; it starts an activity in the application. More specifically, it starts the application's *launcher activity*. For GeoQuiz, **QuizActivity** is the launcher activity.

When the New Application wizard created the GeoQuiz application and **QuizActivity**, it made **QuizActivity** the launcher activity by default. Launcher activity status is specified in the manifest by the intent-filter element in **QuizActivity**'s declaration (Listing 5.18).

Listing 5.18 **QuizActivity** declared as launcher activity (AndroidManifest.xml)

```xml
<?xml version="1.0" encoding="utf-8"?>
<manifest xmlns:android="http://schemas.android.com/apk/res/android"
  ... >

  ...

  <application
    ... >
    <activity
      android:name="com.bignerdranch.android.geoquiz.QuizActivity"
      android:label="@string/app_name" >
      <intent-filter>
        <action android:name="android.intent.action.MAIN" />
        <category android:name="android.intent.category.LAUNCHER" />
      </intent-filter>
    </activity>
    <activity
      android:name=".CheatActivity"
      android:label="@string/app_name" />
  </application>

</manifest>
```

After the instance of **QuizActivity** is on screen, the user can press the Cheat! button. When this happens, an instance of **CheatActivity** is started – on top of the **QuizActivity**. These activities exist in a stack (Figure 5.12).

Pressing the Back button in **CheatActivity** pops this instance off the stack, and the **QuizActivity** resumes its position at the top, as shown in Figure 5.12.

Figure 5.12 GeoQuiz's back stack

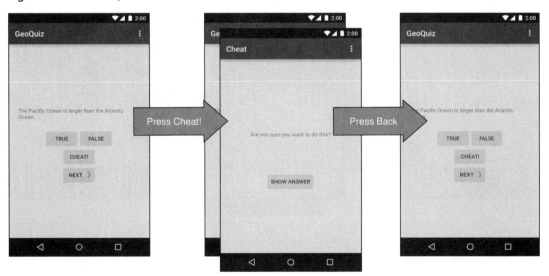

A call to **Activity.finish()** in **CheatActivity** would also pop the **CheatActivity** off the stack.

If you run GeoQuiz and press Back from the **QuizActivity**, the **QuizActivity** will be popped off the stack and you will return to the last screen you were viewing before running GeoQuiz (Figure 5.13).

Figure 5.13 Looking at Home screen

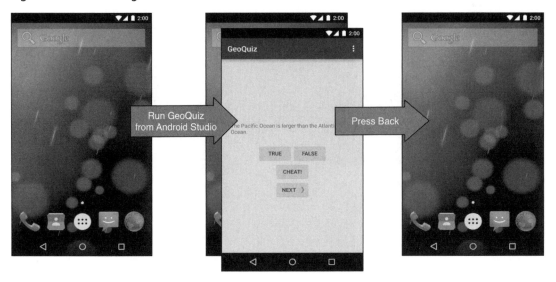

If you started GeoQuiz from the launcher application, pressing the Back button from **QuizActivity** will return you to the launcher (Figure 5.14).

Figure 5.14 Running GeoQuiz from launcher

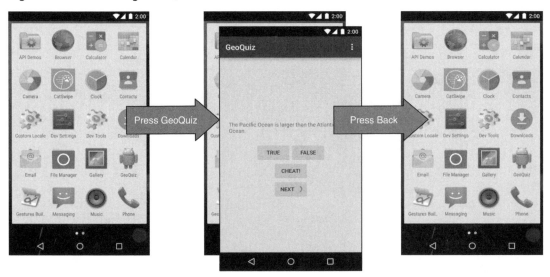

Pressing the Back button from the launcher will return you to the screen you were looking at before you opened the launcher.

What you are seeing here is that the **ActivityManager** maintains a *back stack* and that this back stack is not just for your application's activities. Activities for all applications share the back stack, which is one reason the **ActivityManager** is involved in starting your activities and lives with the OS and not your application. The stack represents the use of the OS and device as a whole rather than the use of a single application.

(Wondering about the "Up" button? We will discuss how to implement and configure this button in Chapter 13.)

Challenge

Cheaters never win. Unless, of course, they persistently circumvent your anticheating measures. Which they probably will. Because they are cheaters.

GeoQuiz has a few major loopholes. For this challenge, you will busy yourself with closing them. Here are the loopholes in ascending order, from easiest to hardest to close:

- Users can rotate **CheatActivity** after they cheat to clear out the cheating result.

- Once they get back, users can rotate **QuizActivity** to clear out mIsCheater.

- Users can press Next until the question they cheated on comes back around.

Good luck!

6

Android SDK Versions and Compatibility

Now that you have gotten your feet wet with GeoQuiz, let's review some background material about the different versions of Android. The information in this chapter is important to have under your belt as you continue with the book and develop more complex and realistic apps.

Android SDK Versions

Table 6.1 shows the SDK versions, the associated versions of the Android firmware, and the percentage of devices running them as of June 2015.

Table 6.1 Android API levels, firmware versions, and percent of devices in use

API level	Codename	Device firmware version	% of devices in use
22	Lollipop	5.1	0.8
21	Lollipop	5.0	11.6
19	KitKat	4.4	39.2
18	Jelly Bean	4.3	5.2
17	Jelly Bean	4.2	17.5
16	Jelly Bean	4.1	14.7
15	Ice Cream Sandwich (ICS)	4.0.3, 4.0.4	5.1
10	Gingerbread	2.3.3 - 2.3.7	5.6
8	Froyo	2.2	0.3

Note that versions of Android with less than 0.1% distribution are omitted from this table.

Each "codenamed" release is followed by incremental releases. For instance, Ice Cream Sandwich was initially released as Android 4.0 (API level 14). It was almost immediately replaced with incremental releases culminating in Android 4.0.3 and 4.0.4 (API level 15).

The percentage of devices using each version changes constantly, of course, but the figures do reveal an important trend: Android devices running older versions are not immediately upgraded or replaced when a newer version is available. As of June 2015, more than 10% of devices are still running Ice Cream Sandwich or Gingerbread. Android 4.0.4 (the last ICS update) was released in March 2012.

(If you are curious, the data in Table 6.1 is kept current at `http://developer.android.com/about/ dashboards/index.html`.)

Why do so many devices still run older versions of Android? Most of it has to do with heavy competition among Android device manufacturers and US carriers. Carriers want features and phones that no other network has. Device manufacturers feel this pressure, too – all of their phones are based on the same OS, but they want to stand out from the competition. The combination of pressures from the market and the carriers means that there is a bewildering array of devices with proprietary, one-off modifications of Android.

A device with a proprietary version of Android is not able to run a new version of Android released by Google. Instead, it must wait for a compatible proprietary upgrade. That upgrade might not be available until months after Google releases its version, if it is ever available at all. Manufacturers often choose to spend resources on newer devices rather than keeping older ones up to date.

Compatibility and Android Programming

The delay in upgrades combined with regular new releases makes compatibility an important issue in Android programming. To reach a broad market, Android developers must create apps that perform well on devices running Jelly Bean, KitKat, Lollipop, and any more recent versions of Android, as well as on different device form factors.

Targeting different sizes of devices is easier than you might think. Phone screens are a variety of sizes, but the Android layout system does a good job at adapting. Tablets require more work, but in that case you can use configuration qualifiers to do the job (as you will see in Chapter 17). However, for Android TV and Android Wear devices (both of which also run Android) the differences in UI are large enough that you need to rethink the user interaction patterns and design of your app.

A sane minimum

The oldest version of Android that the exercises in this book support is API level 16 (Jelly Bean). There are references to legacy versions of Android, but the focus is on what we consider to be modern versions (API level 16+). With the distribution of Froyo, Gingerbread, and Ice Cream Sandwich dropping month by month, the amount of work required to support those older versions eclipses the value they can provide.

Incremental releases cause little problem with backward compatibility. Major versions are a different story. The work required to support only 4.x devices is not terribly significant. If you also need to support 2.x devices, you will have to spend time working through the differences in those versions. (For detailed information about support for 2.x versions of Android, check out the first edition of this very book.) Some effort is required to support Android 5.0 (Lollipop) along with 4.x versions, but Google has provided libraries to ease the pain. You will learn about these libraries in later chapters.

Why is there so much effort required to support 2.x devices? The release of Honeycomb, Android 3.0, was a major shift that introduced a new UI and new architectural components. Honeycomb was released only for tablets, so it was not until Ice Cream Sandwich that these new developments were widely available. Since then, new releases have been more incremental.

Android has provided help for maintaining backward compatibility. There are also third-party libraries that can help. But maintaining compatibility does complicate learning Android programming.

When you created the GeoQuiz project, you set a minimum SDK version within the New Application wizard, as shown in Figure 6.1. (Note that Android uses the terms "SDK version" and "API level" interchangeably.)

Figure 6.1 Remember me?

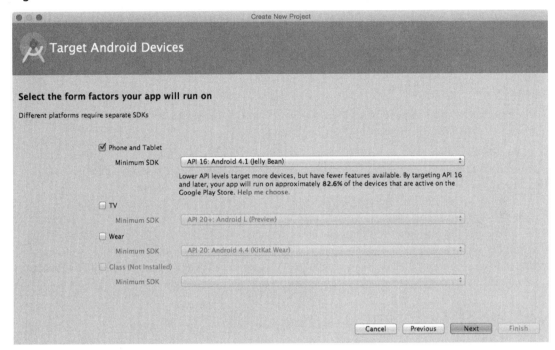

In addition to the minimum supported version, you can also set the target version and the build version. Let's explain the default choices and see how to change them.

All of these properties are set in the build.gradle file in your app module. The build version lives exclusively in this file. The minimum SDK version and target SDK version are set in the build.gradle file, but are used to overwrite or set values in your AndroidManifest.xml.

Open the build.gradle file that exists in your app module. Notice the values for compileSdkVersion, minSdkVersion, and targetSdkVersion.

Listing 6.1 Examining the build configuration (app/build.gradle)

```
...

compileSdkVersion 22
buildToolsVersion "23.0.0"

defaultConfig {
    applicationId "com.bignerdranch.android.geoquiz"
    minSdkVersion 16
    targetSdkVersion 22
    ...
}

...
```

Minimum SDK version

The `minSdkVersion` value is a hard floor below which the OS should refuse to install the app.

By setting this version to API level 16 (Jelly Bean), you give Android permission to install GeoQuiz on devices running Jelly Bean or higher. Android will refuse to install GeoQuiz on a device running, say, Froyo.

Looking again at Table 6.1, you can see why API 16 is a good choice for a minimum SDK version: it allows your app to be installed on over 88% of devices in use.

Target SDK version

The `targetSdkVersion` value tells Android which API level your app was *designed* to run on. Most often this will be the latest Android release.

When would you lower the target SDK? New SDK releases can change how your app appears on a device or even how the OS behaves behind the scenes. If you have already designed an app, you should confirm that it works as expected on new releases. Check the documentation at `http://developer.android.com/reference/android/os/Build.VERSION_CODES.html` to see where problems might arise. Then you can modify your app to work with the new behavior or lower the target SDK. Not increasing the target SDK when a new version of Android is released ensures that your app will still run with the appearance and behavior of the targeted version on which it worked well. This option exists for compatibility with newer versions of Android, as changes in subsequent releases are ignored until the `targetSdkVersion` is increased.

Compile SDK version

The last SDK setting is labeled compileSdkVersion in Listing 6.1. This setting is not used to update the `AndroidManifest.xml` file. Whereas the minimum and target SDK versions are placed in the manifest when you build your app, in order to advertise those values to the OS, the compile SDK version is private information between you and the compiler.

Android's features are exposed through the classes and methods in the SDK. The compile SDK version, or *build target*, specifies which version to use when building your own code. When Android Studio is looking to find the classes and methods you refer to in your imports, the build target determines which SDK version it checks against.

The best choice for a build target is the latest API level (currently 21, Lollipop). However, you can change the build target of an existing application if you need to. For instance, you might want to update the build target when yet another version of Android is released so that you can make use of the new methods and classes introduced in that version of Android.

You can modify the minimum SDK version, target SDK version, and compile SDK version in your `build.gradle` file, but note that modification of this file requires that you sync your project with the gradle changes before they will be reflected. You can select Tools → Android → Sync Project with Gradle Files. This will trigger a fresh build of your project with the updated values.

Adding code from later APIs safely

The difference between GeoQuiz's minimum SDK version and build SDK version leaves you with a compatibility gap to manage. For example, in GeoQuiz, what happens if you call code from an SDK version that is later than the minimum SDK of Jelly Bean (API level 16)? When your app is installed and run on a Jelly Bean device, it will crash.

This used to be a testing nightmare. However, thanks to improvements in Android Lint, potential problems caused by calling newer code on older devices can be caught at compile time. If you use code from a higher version than your minimum SDK, Android Lint will report build errors.

Right now, all of GeoQuiz's simple code was introduced in API level 16 or earlier. Let's add some code from API level 21 (Lollipop) and see what happens.

Open CheatActivity.java. In the **OnClickListener** for the Show Answer button, add the following code to present a fancy circular animation while hiding the button:

Listing 6.2 Adding activity animation code (CheatActivity.java)

```
mShowAnswer.setOnClickListener(new View.OnClickListener() {
    @Override
    public void onClick(View v) {
        if (mAnswerIsTrue) {
            mAnswerTextView.setText(R.string.true_button);
        } else {
            mAnswerTextView.setText(R.string.false_button);
        }
        setAnswerShownResult(true);

        int cx = mShowAnswer.getWidth() / 2;
        int cy = mShowAnswer.getHeight() / 2;
        float radius = mShowAnswer.getWidth();
        Animator anim = ViewAnimationUtils
                .createCircularReveal(mShowAnswer, cx, cy, radius, 0);
        anim.addListener(new AnimatorListenerAdapter() {
            @Override
            public void onAnimationEnd(Animator animation) {
                super.onAnimationEnd(animation);
                mAnswerTextView.setVisibility(View.VISIBLE);
                mShowAnswer.setVisibility(View.INVISIBLE);
            }
        });
        anim.start();
    }
});
```

The **createCircularReveal** method creates an **Animator** from a few parameters. First, you specify the **View** that will be hidden or shown based on the animation. Next, a center position for the animation as well as the start radius and end radius of the animation. You are hiding the Show Answer button, so the radius moves from the width of the button to 0.

Before the newly created animation is started, you set a listener which allows you to know when the animation is complete. Once complete, you will show the answer and hide the button.

Finally, the animation is started and the circular reveal animation will begin. You will learn much more about animation in Chapter 30.

The **ViewAnimationUtils** and its **createCircularReveal** method were both added to the Android SDK in API level 21, so this code would crash on a device running a lower version than that.

After you enter the code in Listing 6.2, Android Lint should immediately present you with a warning that the code is not safe on your minimum SDK version. If you do not see a warning, you can manually trigger Lint by selecting Analyze → Inspect Code.... Because your build SDK version is API level 21, the compiler itself has no problem with this code. Android Lint, on the other hand, knows about your minimum SDK version and will complain loudly.

The error messages read something like Call requires API level 21 (Current min is 16). You can still run the code with this warning, but Lint knows it is not safe.

How do you get rid of these errors? One option is to raise the minimum SDK version to 21. However, raising the minimum SDK version is not really dealing with this compatibility problem as much as ducking it. If your app cannot be installed on API level 16 and older devices, then you no longer have a compatibility problem.

A better option is to wrap the higher API code in a conditional statement that checks the device's version of Android.

Listing 6.3 Checking the device's build version first

```
mShowAnswer.setOnClickListener(new View.OnClickListener() {
    @Override
    public void onClick(View v) {
        if (mAnswerIsTrue) {
            mAnswerTextView.setText(R.string.true_button);
        } else {
            mAnswerTextView.setText(R.string.false_button);
        }
        setAnswerShownResult(true);

        if (Build.VERSION.SDK_INT >= Build.VERSION_CODES.LOLLIPOP) {
            int cx = mShowAnswer.getWidth() / 2;
            int cy = mShowAnswer.getHeight() / 2;
            float radius = mShowAnswer.getWidth();
            Animator anim = ViewAnimationUtils
                    .createCircularReveal(mShowAnswer, cx, cy, radius, 0);
            anim.addListener(new AnimatorListenerAdapter() {
                @Override
                public void onAnimationEnd(Animator animation) {
                    super.onAnimationEnd(animation);
                    mAnswerTextView.setVisibility(View.VISIBLE);
                    mShowAnswer.setVisibility(View.INVISIBLE);
                }
            });
            anim.start();
        } else {
            mAnswerTextView.setVisibility(View.VISIBLE);
            mShowAnswer.setVisibility(View.INVISIBLE);
        }
    }
});
```

The Build.VERSION.SDK_INT constant is the device's version of Android. You then compare that version with the constant that stands for the Lollipop release. (Version codes are listed at http://developer.android.com/reference/android/os/Build.VERSION_CODES.html.)

Now your circular reveal code will only be called when the app is running on a device with API level 21 or higher. You have made your code safe for API level 16, and Android Lint should now be content.

Run GeoQuiz on a Lollipop or higher device and check out your new animation when starting the `CheatActivity`.

You can also run GeoQuiz on a Jelly Bean or KitKat device (virtual or otherwise). It will not have the circular animation, but you can confirm that the app still runs safely.

Using the Android Developer Documentation

Android Lint errors will tell you what API level your incompatible code is from. But you can also find out which API level particular classes and methods belong to in Android's developer documentation.

It is a good idea to get comfortable using the developer documentation right away. There is far too much in the Android SDKs to keep in your head, and, with new versions appearing regularly, you will need to learn what is new and how to use it.

The Android developer documentation is an excellent and voluminous source of information. The main page of the documentation is `http://developer.android.com/`. It is split into three parts: Design, Develop, and Distribute. The Design section of the documentation includes patterns and principles for the UI design of your apps. The Develop section contains documentation and training. The Distribute section shows you how to prepare and publish your apps on Google Play or through open distribution. It is all worth perusing when you get a chance.

The Develop section is further divided into six areas:

Training	Beginning and advanced developer training modules, including downloadable sample code
API Guides	Topic-based descriptions of app components, features, and best practices
Reference	Searchable, linked documentation of every class, method, interface, attribute constant, etc. in the SDK
Tools	Descriptions and links to developer tools
Google Services	Information about Google's proprietary APIs, including Google Maps and Google Cloud Messaging
Samples	Sample code demonstrating some examples of how to use the APIs

You do not have to be online to have access to the documentation. If you navigate on your filesystem to where you have downloaded the SDKs, there is a `docs` directory that contains the complete documentation.

To determine what API level `ViewAnimationUtils` belongs to, search for this class using the search bar at the top-right of the browser. You will see results from a few different categories. Make sure that you select a result that is from the reference section (there is a filter on the left).

Select the first result, and you will be sent to the `ViewAnimationUtils` class reference page shown in Figure 6.2. At the top of this page are links to its different sections.

Figure 6.2 **ViewAnimationUtils** reference page

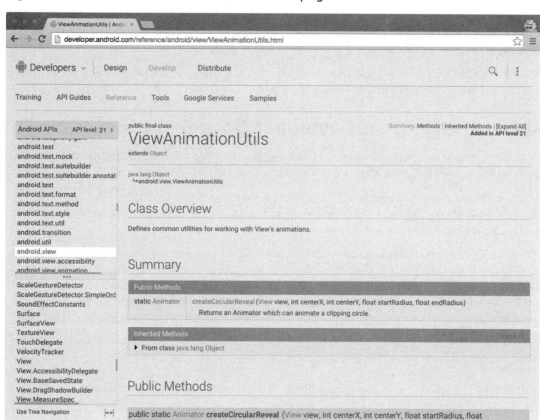

Scroll down, find the **createCircularReveal(…)** method, and click on the method name to see a description. To the right of the method signature, you can see that **createCircularReveal(…)** was introduced in API level 21.

If you want to see which **ViewAnimationUtils** methods are available in, say, API level 16, you can filter the reference by API level. On the lefthand side of the page where the classes are indexed by package, find where it says API level: 21. Click the adjacent control and select 16 from the list. In most cases, everything that Android has introduced after API level 16 will be grayed-out. In this case, **ViewAnimationUtils** was introduced in API level 21, so you will see a warning indicating that this entire class is not available at all on API level 16.

The API level filter is much more useful for a class that is available at the API level that you are using. Search for the reference page on the **Activity** class in the documentation. Change the API level filter back down to API level 16 and notice that many methods have been added since API 16, such as **onEnterAnimationComplete**, which is an addition to the SDK in Lollipop that allows you to provide interesting transitions between activities.

As you continue through this book, be sure to visit the developer documentation often. You will certainly need the documentation to tackle the challenge exercises, but also consider exploring it whenever you get curious about particular classes, methods, or other topics. Android is constantly updating and improving the documentation, so there is always something new to learn.

Challenge: Reporting the Build Version

Add a **TextView** widget to the GeoQuiz layout that reports to the user what API level the device is running. Figure 6.3 shows what the final result should look like.

Figure 6.3 Finished challenge

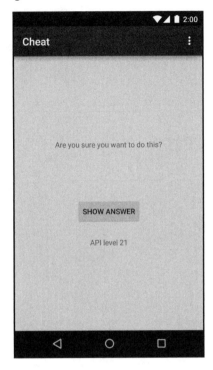

You cannot set this **TextView**'s text in the layout because you will not know the device's build version until runtime. Find the **TextView** method for setting text in the **TextView** reference page in Android's documentation. You are looking for a method that accepts a single argument – a string (or a **CharSequence**).

Use other XML attributes listed in the **TextView** reference to adjust the size or typeface of the text.

7
UI Fragments and the Fragment Manager

In this chapter, you will start building an application named CriminalIntent. CriminalIntent records the details of "office crimes" – things like leaving dirty dishes in the breakroom sink or walking away from an empty shared printer after documents have printed.

With CriminalIntent, you can make a record of a crime including a title, a date, and a photo. You can also identify a suspect from your contacts and lodge a complaint via email, Twitter, Facebook, or another app. After documenting and reporting a crime, you can proceed with your work free of resentment and ready to focus on the business at hand.

CriminalIntent is a complex app that will take thirteen chapters to complete. It will have a list-detail interface: The main screen will display a list of recorded crimes. Users will be able to add new crimes or select an existing crime to view and edit its details (Figure 7.1).

Figure 7.1 CriminalIntent, a list-detail app

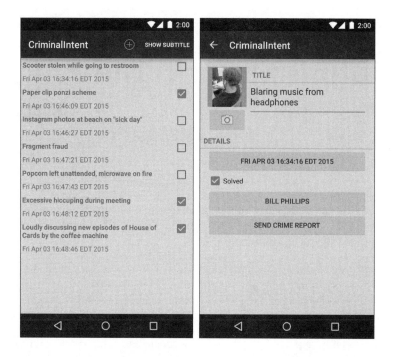

The Need for UI Flexibility

You might imagine that a list-detail application consists of two activities: one managing the list and the other managing the detail view. Clicking a crime in the list would start an instance of the detail activity. Pressing the Back button would destroy the detail activity and return you to the list where you could select another crime.

That would work, but what if you wanted more sophisticated presentation and navigation between screens?

- Imagine that your user is running CriminalIntent on a tablet. Tablets and some larger phones have screens large enough to show the list and detail at the same time – at least in landscape orientation (Figure 7.2).

Figure 7.2 Ideal list-detail interface for phone and tablet

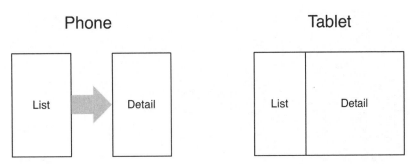

- Imagine the user is viewing a crime on a phone and wants to see the next crime in the list. It would be better if the user could swipe to see the next crime without having to return to the list. Each swipe should update the detail view with information for the next crime.

What these scenarios have in common is UI flexibility: the ability to compose and recompose an activity's view at runtime depending on what the user or the device requires.

Activities were not built to provide this flexibility. An activity's views may change at runtime, but the code to control those views must live inside the activity. As a result, activities are tightly coupled to a particular screen used by the user.

Introducing Fragments

You can get around the letter of the Android law by moving the app's UI management from the activity to one or more *fragments*.

A *fragment* is a controller object that an activity can deputize to perform tasks. Most commonly, the task is managing a user interface. The user interface can be an entire screen or just one part of the screen.

A fragment managing a user interface is known as a *UI fragment*. A UI fragment has a view of its own that is inflated from a layout file. The fragment's view contains the interesting UI elements that the user wants to see and interact with.

The activity's view contains a spot where the fragment's view will be inserted. Or it might have several spots for the views of several fragments.

You can use the fragment(s) associated with the activity to compose and re-compose the screen as your app and users require. The activity's view technically stays the same throughout its lifetime, and no laws of Android are violated.

Let's see how this would work in a list-detail application to display the list and detail together. You would compose the activity's view from a list fragment and a detail fragment. The detail view would show the details of the selected list item.

Selecting another item should display a new detail view. This is easy with fragments; the activity will replace the detail fragment with another detail fragment (Figure 7.3). No activities need to die for this major view change to happen.

Figure 7.3 Detail fragment is swapped out

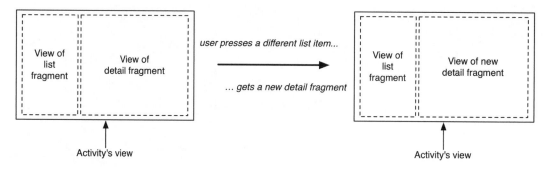

Using UI fragments separates the UI of your app into building blocks, which is useful for more than just list-detail applications. Working with individual blocks, it is easy to build tab interfaces, tack on animated sidebars, and more.

Achieving this UI flexibility comes at a cost: more complexity, more moving parts, and more code. You will reap the benefits of using fragments in Chapter 11 and Chapter 17. The complexity, however, starts now.

Starting CriminalIntent

In this chapter, you are going to start on the detail part of CriminalIntent. Figure 7.4 shows you what CriminalIntent will look like at the end of this chapter.

It may not seem like a very exciting goal to shoot for. Just keep in mind that this chapter is about laying the foundation for the bigger things that are coming.

Figure 7.4 CriminalIntent at the end of this chapter

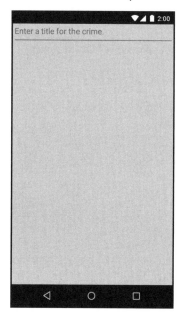

The screen shown in Figure 7.4 will be managed by a UI fragment named **CrimeFragment**. An instance of **CrimeFragment** will be *hosted* by an activity named **CrimeActivity**.

For now, think of hosting as the activity providing a spot in its view hierarchy where the fragment can place its view (Figure 7.5). A fragment is incapable of getting a view on screen itself. Only when it is placed in an activity's hierarchy will its view appear.

Figure 7.5 **CrimeActivity** hosting a **CrimeFragment**

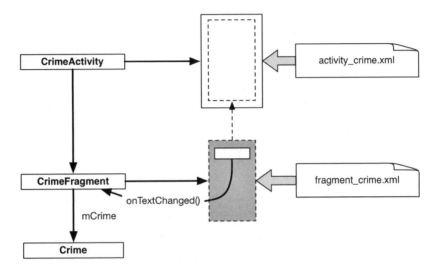

CriminalIntent will be a large project, and one way to keep your head wrapped around a project is with an object diagram. Figure 7.6 gives you the big picture of CriminalIntent. You do not have to memorize these objects and their relationships, but it is good to have an idea of where you are heading before you start.

You can see that **CrimeFragment** will do the sort of work that your activities did in GeoQuiz: create and manage the user interface and interact with the model objects.

Figure 7.6 Object diagram for CriminalIntent (for this chapter)

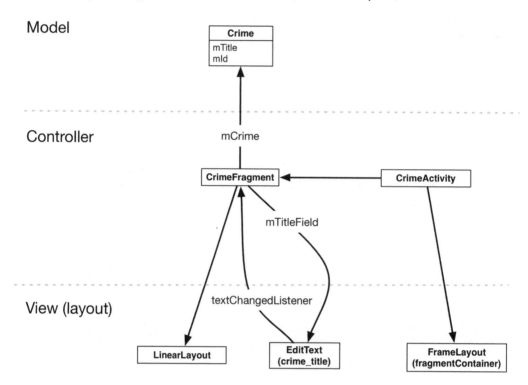

Three of the classes shown in Figure 7.6 are classes that you will write: **Crime**, **CrimeFragment**, and **CrimeActivity**.

An instance of **Crime** will represent a single office crime. In this chapter, a crime will have only a title and an ID. The title is a descriptive name, like "Toxic sink dump" or "Someone stole my yogurt!" The ID will uniquely identify an instance of **Crime**.

For this chapter, you will keep things very simple and use a single instance of **Crime**. **CrimeFragment** will have a member variable (mCrime) to hold this isolated incident.

CrimeActivity's view will consist of a **FrameLayout** that defines the spot where the **CrimeFragment**'s view will appear.

CrimeFragment's view will consist of a **LinearLayout** and an **EditText**. **CrimeFragment** will have a member variable for the **EditText** (mTitleField) and will set a listener on it to update the model layer when the text changes.

Creating a new project

Enough talk; time to build a new app. Create a new Android application (File → New Project...). Name the application CriminalIntent and name the package com.bignerdranch.android.criminalintent, as shown in Figure 7.7.

Figure 7.7 Creating the CriminalIntent application

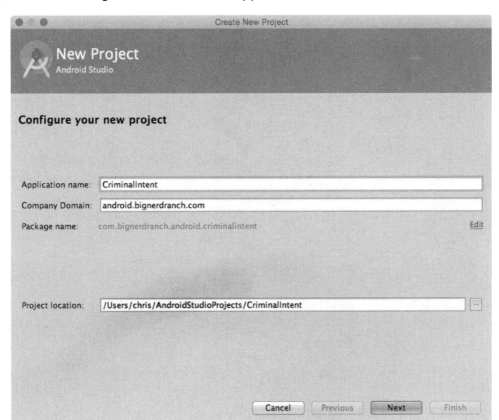

Click Next and specify a minimum SDK of API 16: Android 4.1. Also ensure that only the Phone and Tablet application type is checked.

Click Next again to select the type of Activity to add. Choose Blank Activity and continue along in the wizard.

In the final step of the New Project wizard, name the activity **CrimeActivity** and click Finish (Figure 7.8).

Figure 7.8 Configuring **CrimeActivity**

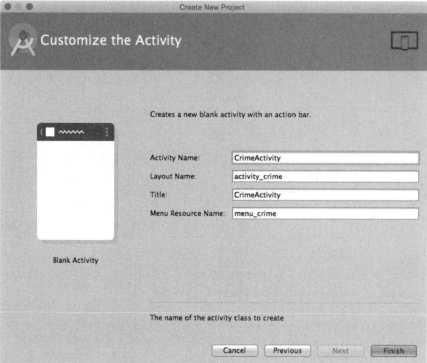

Fragments and the support library

Fragments were introduced in API level 11 along with the first Android tablets and the sudden need for UI flexibility. In the old days of Android development, which you can see in the first edition of this book, many developers supported devices running API level 8 and newer. Luckily, those developers were still able to use fragments because of Android's *support library*.

The *support library* includes a complete implementation of fragments that work all the way back to API level 4. In this book, we will use the support implementation of fragments rather than the implementation built into the Android OS. This is a good idea because the support library is quickly updated when new features are added to the fragments API. To use those new features, you can update your project with the latest version of the support library. Detailed reasoning for this decision is laid out at the end of the chapter in the section called "For the More Curious: Why Support Fragments are Superior".

Note that when you use a support library class, it is not just used on older versions where no native class is available; it is also used on newer versions instead of the native class.

There are two key classes that we will use from the *support library*: the **Fragment** class (**android.support.v4.app.Fragment**) and the **FragmentActivity** class (**android.support.v4.app.FragmentActivity**). Using fragments requires activities that know how to manage fragments. The **FragmentActivity** class knows how to manage the support version of fragments.

Figure 7.9 shows you the name of each of these classes and where they live. Since the support library (and **android.support.v4.app.Fragment**) lives with your application, it is safe to use no matter where your app is running.

Figure 7.9 Where the different fragment classes live

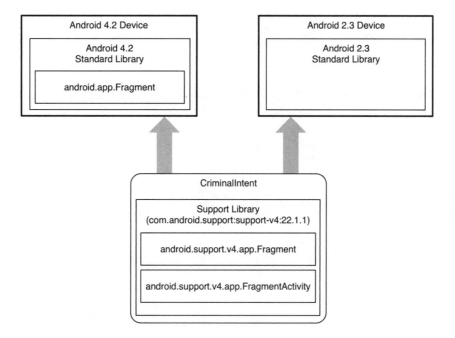

Adding dependencies in Android Studio

To use the support library, your project must list it as a dependency. Open the build.gradle file located in your app module. Your project will come with two build.gradle files, one for the project as a whole and one for your app module. We will edit the one located at app/build.gradle.

Listing 7.1 Gradle dependencies (app/build.gradle)

```
apply plugin: 'com.android.application'

android {
    ...
}

dependencies {
    compile fileTree(dir: 'libs', include: ['*.jar'])
}
```

In the current dependencies section of your build.gradle file, you should see something similar to Listing 7.1 that specifies that the project depends on all of the jar files in the project's libs directory.

Gradle also allows for the specification of dependencies that you have not copied into your project. When your app is compiled, Gradle will find, download, and include the dependencies for you. All you have to do is specify an exact string incantation and Gradle will do the rest.

Nobody can remember these incantations, though, so Android Studio maintains a list of common libraries for you. Navigate to the project structure for your project (File → Project Structure...).

Select the app module on the left and the Dependencies tab in the app module. The dependencies for the app module are listed here. (You may have other dependencies already specified here, such as the AppCompat dependency shown in Figure 7.10. If you have other dependencies, do not remove them. You will learn about the AppCompat library in Chapter 13.)

Figure 7.10 App dependencies

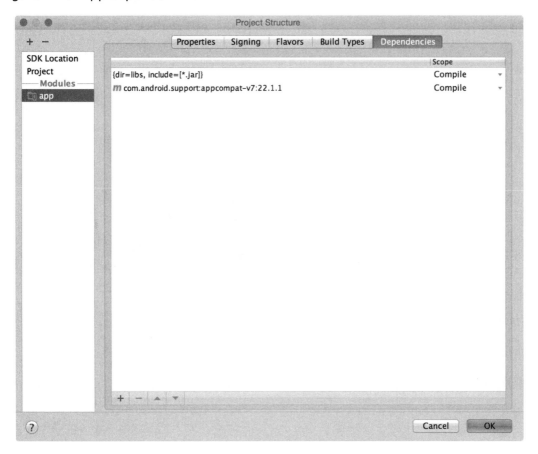

You may have additional dependencies specified here, such as the AppCompat dependency. If you have other dependencies, do not remove them. You will learn about the AppCompat library in Chapter 13.

Use the + button and choose Library dependency to add a new dependency (Figure 7.11). Choose the support-v4 library from the list and click OK.

Figure 7.11 A collection of dependencies

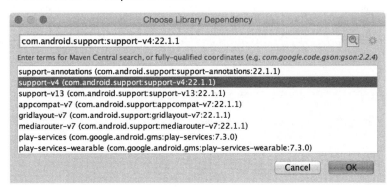

Navigate back to the editor window showing app/build.gradle and you should see a new addition, as shown in Listing 7.2.

Listing 7.2 Updated Gradle dependencies (app/build.gradle)

```
...

dependencies {
    compile fileTree(dir: 'libs', include: ['*.jar'])
    compile 'com.android.support:support-v4:22.1.1'
}
```

(If you modify this file manually, outside of the project structure window, you will need to sync your project with the Gradle file for your project to reflect any updates that you have made. This sync asks Gradle to update the build based on your changes by either downloading or removing dependencies. Changes within the project structure window will trigger this sync automatically. To manually perform this sync, navigate to Tools → Android → Sync Project with Gradle Files.)

The shaded dependency string in Listing 7.2 uses the following Maven coordinates format: groupId:artifactId:version. (Maven is a dependency management tool. You can learn more about Maven at https://maven.apache.org/.)

The groupId is the unique identifier for a set of libraries available on the Maven repository. Often the library's base package name is used as the groupId, which is com.android.support in this case.

The artifactId is the name of a specific library within the package. In this case, the name of the library you are referring to is support-v4. There are different libraries available within com.android.support, such as support-v13, appcompat-v7, and gridlayout-v7. Google uses the naming convention basename-vX for their support libraries, where -vX represents the minimum API level the library supports. So, for example, appcompat-v7 is Google's compatibility library that works on devices running Android API version 7 and higher.

Last but not least, the version represents which revision number of the library. CriminalIntent depends on the 22.1.1 version of the support-v4 library. Version 22.1.1 is the latest version as of this writing, but any version newer than that should work for this project. In fact, it is a good idea to use the latest version of the support library so that you can use newer APIs and receive the latest bug fixes. If Android Studio added a newer version of the library for you, do not roll it back to the version shown above.

Now that the support library is a dependency in the project, it is time to use it. In the package explorer, find and open CrimeActivity.java. Change **CrimeActivity**'s superclass to **FragmentActivity**. While you are there, remove the template's implementation of **onCreateOptionsMenu(Menu)** and **onOptionsItemSelected(MenuItem)**. (You will be creating an options menu for CriminalIntent from scratch in Chapter 13.)

Listing 7.3 Tweaking template code (CrimeActivity.java)

```java
public class CrimeActivity extends AppCompatActivity FragmentActivity {

    @Override
    protected void onCreate(Bundle savedInstanceState) {
        super.onCreate(savedInstanceState);
        setContentView(R.layout.activity_crime);
    }

    @Override
    public boolean onCreateOptionsMenu(Menu menu) {
        getMenuInflater().inflate(R.menu.crime, menu);
        return true;
    }

    @Override
    public boolean onOptionsItemSelected(MenuItem item) {
        int id = item.getItemId();
        if (id == R.id.action_settings) {
            return true;
        }
        return super.onOptionsItemSelected(item);
    }
}
```

Before proceeding further with **CrimeActivity**, let's create the model layer for CriminalIntent by writing the **Crime** class.

Creating the Crime class

In the project tool window, right-click the com.bignerdranch.android.criminalintent package and select New → Java Class. Name the class **Crime** and click OK.

In Crime.java, add the following code:

Listing 7.4 Adding to **Crime** class (Crime.java)

```java
public class Crime {

    private UUID mId;
    private String mTitle;

    public Crime() {
        // Generate unique identifier
        mId = UUID.randomUUID();
    }
}
```

Next, you want to generate only a getter for the read-only mId and both a getter and setter for mTitle. Right-click after the constructor and select Generate... → Getter and select the mId variable. Then, generate the getter and setter for mTitle by repeating the process, but selecting Getter and Setter in the Generate... menu.

Listing 7.5 Generated getters and setter (Crime.java)

```java
public class Crime {
    private UUID mId;

    private String mTitle;

    public Crime() {
        mId = UUID.randomUUID();
    }

    public UUID getId() {
        return mId;
    }

    public String getTitle() {
        return mTitle;
    }

    public void setTitle(String title) {
        mTitle = title;
    }
}
```

That is all you need for the **Crime** class and for CriminalIntent's model layer in this chapter.

At this point, you have created the model layer and an activity that is capable of hosting a support fragment. Now you will get into the details of how the activity performs its duties as host.

Hosting a UI Fragment

To host a UI fragment, an activity must:

- define a spot in its layout for the fragment's view

- manage the lifecycle of the fragment instance

The fragment lifecycle

Figure 7.12 shows the fragment lifecycle. It is similar to the activity lifecycle: it has stopped, paused, and running states, and it has methods you can override to get things done at critical points – many of which correspond to activity lifecycle methods.

Figure 7.12 Fragment lifecycle diagram

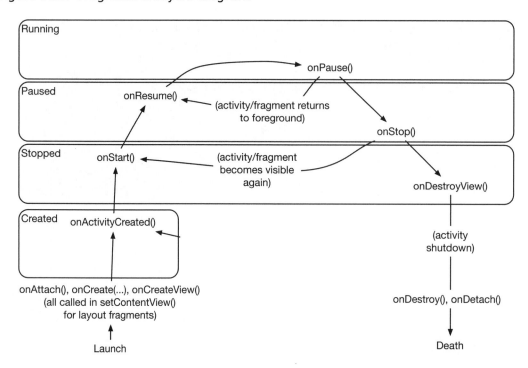

The correspondence is important. Because a fragment works on behalf of an activity, its state should reflect the activity's state. Thus, it needs corresponding lifecycle methods to handle the activity's work.

One critical difference between the fragment lifecycle and the activity lifecycle is that fragment lifecycle methods are called by the hosting activity, not the OS. The OS knows nothing about the fragments that an activity is using to manage things. Fragments are the activity's internal business.

You will see more of the fragment lifecycle methods as you continue building CriminalIntent.

Two approaches to hosting

You have two options when it comes to hosting a UI fragment in an activity:

- add the fragment to the activity's *layout*

- add the fragment in the activity's *code*

The first approach is known as using a *layout fragment*. It is simple but inflexible. If you add the fragment to the activity's layout, you hardwire the fragment and its view to the activity's view and cannot swap out that fragment during the activity's lifetime.

The second approach, adding the fragment to the activity's code, is more complex. But it is the only way to have control at runtime over your fragments. You determine when the fragment is added to the activity and what happens to it after that. You can remove the fragment, replace it with another, and then add the first fragment back again.

Thus, to achieve real UI flexibility you must add your fragment in code. This is the approach you will use for **CrimeActivity**'s hosting of a **CrimeFragment**. The code details will come later in the chapter. First, you are going to define **CrimeActivity**'s layout.

Defining a container view

You will be adding a UI fragment in the hosting activity's code, but you still need to make a spot for the fragment's view in the activity's view hierarchy. In **CrimeActivity**'s layout, this spot will be the **FrameLayout** shown in Figure 7.13.

Figure 7.13 Fragment-hosting layout for **CrimeActivity**

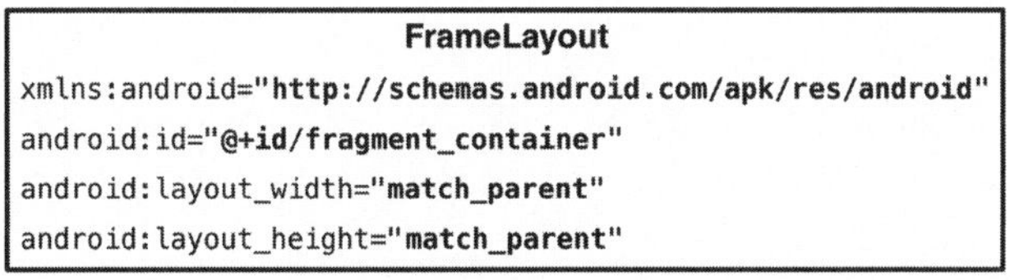

```
                          FrameLayout
xmlns:android="http://schemas.android.com/apk/res/android"
android:id="@+id/fragment_container"
android:layout_width="match_parent"
android:layout_height="match_parent"
```

This **FrameLayout** will be the *container view* for a **CrimeFragment**. Notice that the container view is completely generic; it does not name the **CrimeFragment** class. You can and will use this same layout to host other fragments.

Locate **CrimeActivity**'s layout at res/layout/activity_crime.xml. Open this file and replace the default layout with the **FrameLayout** diagrammed in Figure 7.13. Your XML should match that in Listing 7.6.

Listing 7.6 Create fragment container layout (`activity_crime.xml`)

```xml
<FrameLayout xmlns:android="http://schemas.android.com/apk/res/android"
  android:id="@+id/fragment_container"
  android:layout_width="match_parent"
  android:layout_height="match_parent"
  />
```

Note that while activity_crime.xml consists solely of a container view for a single fragment, an activity's layout can be more complex and define multiple container views as well as widgets of its own.

You can preview your layout file or run CriminalIntent to check your code. You will only see an empty **FrameLayout** because the **CrimeActivity** is not yet hosting a fragment (Figure 7.14).

Figure 7.14 An empty **FrameLayout**

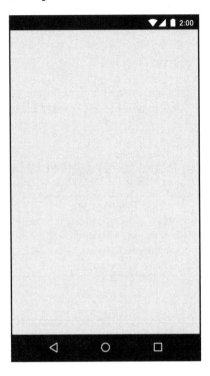

Later, you will write code that puts a fragment's view inside this **FrameLayout**. But first you need to create a fragment.

Creating a UI Fragment

The steps to creating a UI fragment are the same as those you followed to create an activity:

- compose a user interface by defining widgets in a layout file

- create the class and set its view to be the layout that you defined

- wire up the widgets inflated from the layout in code

Defining CrimeFragment's layout

CrimeFragment's view will display the information contained within an instance of **Crime**. Eventually, the **Crime** class and **CrimeFragment**'s view will include many interesting pieces, but for this chapter you just need a text field to contain the crime's title.

Figure 7.15 shows the layout for **CrimeFragment**'s view. It consists of a vertical **LinearLayout** that contains an **EditText**. **EditText** is a widget that presents an area where the user can add or edit text.

Figure 7.15 Initial layout for **CrimeFragment**

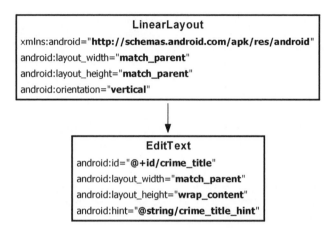

To create a layout file, right-click the res/layout folder in the project tool window and select New → Layout resource file. Name this file fragment_crime.xml and enter **LinearLayout** as the root element. Click OK and Android Studio will generate the file for you.

When the file opens, navigate to the XML. The wizard has added the **LinearLayout** for you. Using Figure 7.15 as a guide, make the necessary changes to fragment_crime.xml. You can use Listing 7.7 to check your work.

Listing 7.7 Layout file for fragment's view (fragment_crime.xml)

```
<LinearLayout xmlns:android="http://schemas.android.com/apk/res/android"
  android:layout_width="match_parent"
  android:layout_height="match_parent"
  android:orientation="vertical"
  >
  <EditText android:id="@+id/crime_title"
    android:layout_width="match_parent"
    android:layout_height="wrap_content"
    android:hint="@string/crime_title_hint"
    />
</LinearLayout>
```

Open res/values/strings.xml and add a crime_title_hint string resource.

Listing 7.8 Adding a string (res/values/strings.xml)

```
<?xml version="1.0" encoding="utf-8"?>
<resources>
    <string name="app_name">CriminalIntent</string>
    <string name="hello_world">Hello world!</string>
    <string name="action_settings">Settings</string>
    <string name="crime_title_hint">Enter a title for the crime.</string>
</resources>
```

Save your files. Navigate back to fragment_crime.xml to see a preview of your fragment's view.

Creating the CrimeFragment class

Right-click the com.bignerdranch.android.criminalintent package and select New → Java Class. Name the class **CrimeFragment** and click OK to generate the class.

Now, turn this class into a fragment. Update **CrimeFragment** to subclass the **Fragment** class.

Listing 7.9 Subclass the **Fragment** class (CrimeFragment.java)

```
public class CrimeFragment extends Fragment {

}
```

As you subclass the **Fragment** class, you will notice that Android Studio finds two classes with the **Fragment** name. You will see **Fragment (android.app)** and **Fragment (android.support.v4.app)**. The android.app **Fragment** is the version of fragments that are built into the Android OS. We will use the support library version, so be sure to select the android.support.v4.app version of the **Fragment** class when you see the dialog, as shown in Figure 7.16.

Figure 7.16 Choosing the support library's **Fragment** class

Your code should match Listing 7.10.

Listing 7.10 Support **Fragment** import (CrimeFragment.java)

```
package com.bignerdranch.android.criminalintent;

import android.support.v4.app.Fragment;

public class CrimeFragment extends Fragment {

}
```

If you do not see this dialog or the wrong fragment class was imported, you can manually import the correct class. If you have an import for **android.app.Fragment**, remove that line of code. Import the correct **Fragment** class with the Option+Return (or Alt+Enter) shortcut. Be sure to select the support version of the **Fragment** class.

Implementing fragment lifecycle methods

CrimeFragment is a controller that interacts with model and view objects. Its job is to present the details of a specific crime and update those details as the user changes them.

In GeoQuiz, your activities did most of their controller work in activity lifecycle methods. In CriminalIntent this work will be done by fragments in fragment lifecycle methods. Many of these methods correspond to the **Activity** methods you already know, such as **onCreate(Bundle)**.

In CrimeFragment.java, add a member variable for the **Crime** instance and an implementation of **Fragment.onCreate(Bundle)**.

Listing 7.11 Overriding **Fragment.onCreate(Bundle)** (CrimeFragment.java)

```java
public class CrimeFragment extends Fragment {
    private Crime mCrime;

    @Override
    public void onCreate(Bundle savedInstanceState) {
        super.onCreate(savedInstanceState);
        mCrime = new Crime();
    }

}
```

There are a couple of things to notice in this implementation. First, **Fragment.onCreate(Bundle)** is a public method whereas **Activity.onCreate(Bundle)** is protected. **Fragment.onCreate(…)** and other **Fragment** lifecycle methods must be public because they will be called by whatever activity is hosting the fragment.

Second, similar to an activity, a fragment has a bundle to which it saves and retrieves its state. You can override **Fragment.onSaveInstanceState(Bundle)** for your own purposes just like with **Activity.onSaveInstanceState(Bundle)**.

Also, note what does *not* happen in **Fragment.onCreate(…)**: you do not inflate the fragment's view. You configure the fragment instance in **Fragment.onCreate(…)**, but you create and configure the fragment's view in another fragment lifecycle method:

```java
    public View onCreateView(LayoutInflater inflater, ViewGroup container,
        Bundle savedInstanceState)
```

This method is where you inflate the layout for the fragment's view and return the inflated **View** to the hosting activity. The **LayoutInflater** and **ViewGroup** parameters are necessary to inflate the layout. The **Bundle** will contain data that this method can use to recreate the view from a saved state.

139

In `CrimeFragment.java`, add an implementation of **onCreateView(…)** that inflates `fragment_crime.xml`.

Listing 7.12 Overriding **onCreateView(…)** (CrimeFragment.java)

```
public class CrimeFragment extends Fragment {
    private Crime mCrime;

    @Override
    public void onCreate(Bundle savedInstanceState) {
        super.onCreate(savedInstanceState);
        mCrime = new Crime();
    }

    @Override
    public View onCreateView(LayoutInflater inflater, ViewGroup container,
            Bundle savedInstanceState) {
        View v = inflater.inflate(R.layout.fragment_crime, container, false);
        return v;
    }

}
```

Within **onCreateView(…)**, you explicitly inflate the fragment's view by calling **LayoutInflater.inflate(…)** and passing in the layout resource ID. The second parameter is your view's parent, which is usually needed to configure the widgets properly. The third parameter tells the layout inflater whether to add the inflated view to the view's parent. You pass in `false` because you will add the view in the activity's code.

Wiring widgets in a fragment

The **onCreateView(…)** method is also the place to wire up the **EditText** to respond to user input. After the view is inflated, get a reference to the **EditText** and add a listener.

Listing 7.13 Wiring up the **EditText** widget (`CrimeFragment.java`)

```java
public class CrimeFragment extends Fragment {
    private Crime mCrime;
    private EditText mTitleField;

    ...

    @Override
    public View onCreateView(LayoutInflater inflater, ViewGroup container,
            Bundle savedInstanceState) {
        View v = inflater.inflate(R.layout.fragment_crime, container, false);

        mTitleField = (EditText)v.findViewById(R.id.crime_title);
        mTitleField.addTextChangedListener(new TextWatcher() {
            @Override
            public void beforeTextChanged(
                CharSequence s, int start, int count, int after) {
                // This space intentionally left blank
            }

            @Override
            public void onTextChanged(
                CharSequence s, int start, int before, int count) {
                mCrime.setTitle(s.toString());
            }

            @Override
            public void afterTextChanged(Editable s) {
                // This one too
            }
        });

        return v;
    }
}
```

Getting references in **Fragment.onCreateView(…)** works nearly the same as in
Activity.onCreate(…). The only difference is that you call **View.findViewById(int)** on the
fragment's view. The **Activity.findViewById(int)** method that you used before is a convenience
method that calls **View.findViewById(int)** behind the scenes. The **Fragment** class does not have a
corresponding convenience method, so you have to call the real thing.

Setting listeners in a fragment works exactly the same as in an activity. In Listing 7.13, you create an
anonymous class that implements the **TextWatcher** listener interface. **TextWatcher** has three methods,
but you only care about one: **onTextChanged(…)**.

In **onTextChanged(…)**, you call **toString()** on the **CharSequence** that is the user's input. This method
returns a string, which you then use to set the **Crime**'s title.

Your code for **CrimeFragment** is now complete. It would be great if you could run CriminalIntent now
and play with the code you have written. But you cannot. Fragments cannot put their views on screen.
To realize your efforts, you first have to add a **CrimeFragment** to **CrimeActivity**.

Adding a UI Fragment to the FragmentManager

When the **Fragment** class was introduced in Honeycomb, the **Activity** class was changed to include a piece called the **FragmentManager**. The **FragmentManager** is responsible for managing your fragments and adding their views to the activity's view hierarchy (Figure 7.17).

The **FragmentManager** handles two things: a list of fragments and a back stack of fragment transactions (which you will learn about shortly).

Figure 7.17 The **FragmentManager**

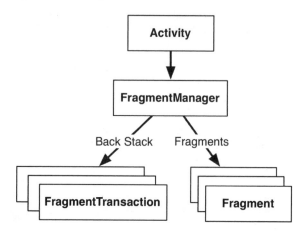

For CriminalIntent, you will only be concerned with the **FragmentManager**'s list of fragments.

To add a fragment to an activity in code, you make explicit calls to the activity's **FragmentManager**. The first step is to get the **FragmentManager** itself. In CrimeActivity.java, add the following code to **onCreate(…)**.

Listing 7.14 Getting the **FragmentManager** (CrimeActivity.java)

```java
public class CrimeActivity extends FragmentActivity {

    @Override
    protected void onCreate(Bundle savedInstanceState) {
        super.onCreate(savedInstanceState);
        setContentView(R.layout.activity_crime);

        FragmentManager fm = getSupportFragmentManager();
    }
}
```

If you see an error after adding this line of code, check the import statements to make sure that the support version of the **FragmentManager** class was imported.

You call **getSupportFragmentManager()** because you are using the support library and the **FragmentActivity** class. If you were not interested in using the support library, then you would subclass **Activity** and call **getFragmentManager()**.

Fragment transactions

Now that you have the **FragmentManager**, add the following code to give it a fragment to manage. (We will step through this code afterward. Just get it in for now.)

Listing 7.15 Adding a **CrimeFragment** (CrimeActivity.java)

```java
public class CrimeActivity extends FragmentActivity {

    @Override
    protected void onCreate(Bundle savedInstanceState) {
        super.onCreate(savedInstanceState);
        setContentView(R.layout.activity_crime);

        FragmentManager fm = getSupportFragmentManager();
        Fragment fragment = fm.findFragmentById(R.id.fragment_container);

        if (fragment == null) {
            fragment = new CrimeFragment();
            fm.beginTransaction()
                .add(R.id.fragment_container, fragment)
                .commit();
        }
    }
}
```

The best place to start understanding the code that you added in Listing 7.15 is not at the beginning. Instead, find the **add(…)** operation and the code around it. This code creates and commits a *fragment transaction*.

```java
        if (fragment == null) {
            fragment = new CrimeFragment();
            fm.beginTransaction()
                .add(R.id.fragment_container, fragment)
                .commit();
```

Fragment transactions are used to add, remove, attach, detach, or replace fragments in the fragment list. They are the heart of how you use fragments to compose and recompose screens at runtime. The **FragmentManager** maintains a back stack of fragment transactions that you can navigate.

The **FragmentManager.beginTransaction()** method creates and returns an instance of **FragmentTransaction**. The **FragmentTransaction** class uses a *fluent interface* - methods that configure **FragmentTransaction** return a **FragmentTransaction** instead of void, which allows you to chain them together. So the code highlighted above says, "Create a new fragment transaction, include one add operation in it, and then commit it."

The **add(…)** method is the meat of the transaction. It has two parameters: a container view ID and the newly created **CrimeFragment**. The container view ID should look familiar. It is the resource ID of the **FrameLayout** that you defined in activity_crime.xml.

A container view ID serves two purposes:

- It tells the **FragmentManager** where in the activity's view the fragment's view should appear.

- It is used as a unique identifier for a fragment in the **FragmentManager**'s list.

When you need to retrieve the **CrimeFragment** from the **FragmentManager**, you ask for it by container view ID:

```
FragmentManager fm = getSupportFragmentManager();
Fragment fragment = fm.findFragmentById(R.id.fragment_container);

if (fragment == null) {
    fragment = new CrimeFragment();
    fm.beginTransaction()
        .add(R.id.fragment_container, fragment)
        .commit();
}
```

It may seem odd that the **FragmentManager** identifies the **CrimeFragment** using the resource ID of a **FrameLayout**. But identifying a UI fragment by the resource ID of its container view is built into how the **FragmentManager** operates. If you are adding multiple fragments to an activity, you would typically create separate containers with separate IDs for each of those fragments.

Now we can summarize the code you added in Listing 7.15 from start to finish.

First, you ask the **FragmentManager** for the fragment with a container view ID of R.id.fragment_container. If this fragment is already in the list, the **FragmentManager** will return it.

Why would a fragment already be in the list? The call to **CrimeActivity.onCreate(…)** could be in response to **CrimeActivity** being *re-created* after being destroyed on rotation or to reclaim memory. When an activity is destroyed, its **FragmentManager** saves out its list of fragments. When the activity is re-created, the new **FragmentManager** retrieves the list and re-creates the listed fragments to make everything as it was before.

On the other hand, if there is no fragment with the given container view ID, then fragment will be null. In this case, you create a new **CrimeFragment** and a new fragment transaction that adds the fragment to the list.

CrimeActivity is now hosting a **CrimeFragment**. Run CriminalIntent to prove it. You should see the view defined in fragment_crime.xml, as shown in Figure 7.18.

Figure 7.18 **CrimeFragment**'s view hosted by **CrimeActivity**

A single widget on screen may not seem like much of a reward for all the work you have done in this chapter. But you have laid down a solid foundation to do greater things with CriminalIntent in the chapters ahead.

The FragmentManager and the fragment lifecycle

Now that you know about the **FragmentManager**, let's take another look at the fragment lifecycle (Figure 7.19).

Figure 7.19 The fragment lifecycle, again

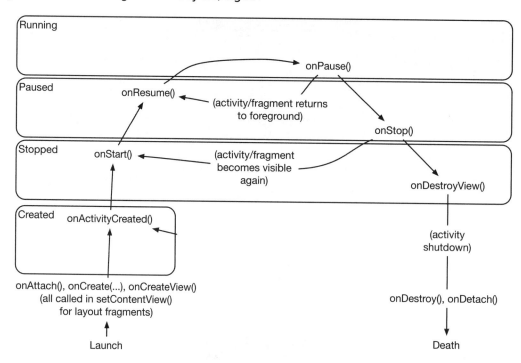

The **FragmentManager** of an activity is responsible for calling the lifecycle methods of the fragments in its list. The **onAttach(Activity)**, **onCreate(Bundle)**, and **onCreateView(…)** methods are called when you add the fragment to the **FragmentManager**.

The **onActivityCreated(…)** method is called after the hosting activity's **onCreate(…)** method has executed. You are adding the **CrimeFragment** in **CrimeActivity.onCreate(…)**, so this method will be called after the fragment has been added.

What happens if you add a fragment while the activity is already running? In that case, the **FragmentManager** immediately walks the fragment through whatever steps are necessary to get it caught up to the activity's state. For example, as a fragment is added to an activity that is already running, that fragment gets calls to **onAttach(Activity)**, **onCreate(Bundle)**, **onCreateView(…)**, **onActivityCreated(Bundle)**, **onStart()**, and then **onResume()**.

Once the fragment's state is caught up to the activity's state, the hosting activity's **FragmentManager** will call further lifecycle methods around the same time it receives the corresponding calls from the OS to keep the fragment's state aligned with that of the activity.

Application Architecture with Fragments

Designing your app with fragments the right way is supremely important. Many developers, after first learning about fragments, try to use them for every reusable component in their application. This is the wrong way to use fragments.

Fragments are intended to encapsulate major components in a reusable way. A major component in this case would be on the level of an entire screen of your application. If you have a significant number of fragments on screen at once, your code will be littered with fragment transactions and unclear responsibility. A better architectural solution for reuse with smaller components is to extract them into a custom view (a class that subclasses `View` or one of its subclasses).

Use fragments responsibly. A good rule of thumb is to have no more than two or three fragments on the screen at a time (Figure 7.20).

Figure 7.20 Less is more

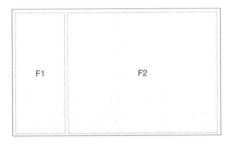
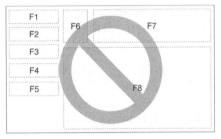

The reason all our activities will use fragments

From here on, all of the apps in this book will use fragments – no matter how simple. This may seem like overkill. Many of the examples you will see in following chapters could be written without fragments. The user interfaces could be created and managed from activities, and doing so might even be less code.

However, we believe it is better for you to become comfortable with the pattern you will most likely use in real life.

You might think it would be better to begin a simple app without fragments and add them later, when (or if) necessary. There is an idea in Extreme Programming methodology called YAGNI. YAGNI stands for "You Aren't Gonna Need It," and it urges you not to write code if you think you *might* need it later. Why? Because YAGNI. It is tempting to say "YAGNI" to fragments.

Unfortunately, adding fragments later can be a minefield. Changing an activity to an activity hosting a UI fragment is not difficult, but there are swarms of annoying gotchas. Keeping some interfaces managed by activities and having others managed by fragments only makes things worse because you have to keep track of this meaningless distinction. It is far easier to write your code using fragments from the beginning and not worry about the pain and annoyance of reworking it later, or having to remember which style of controller you are using in each part of your application.

Therefore, when it comes to fragments, we have a different principle: AUF, or "Always Use Fragments." You can kill a lot of brain cells deciding whether to use a fragment or an activity, and it is just not worth it. AUF!

For the More Curious: Why Support Fragments are Superior

This book uses the support library implementation of fragments over the implementation built into the Android OS, which may seem like an unusual choice. After all, the support library implementation of fragments was initially created so that developers could use fragments on old versions of Android that do not support the API. Today, most developers can exclusively work with versions of Android that do include support for fragments.

We still prefer support fragments. Why? Support fragments are superior because you can update the version of the support library in your application and ship a new version of your app at any time. New releases of the support library come out multiple times a year. When a new feature is added to the fragment API, that feature is also added to the support library fragment API along with any available bug fixes. To use this new goodness, just update the version of the support library in your application.

As an example, official support for fragment nesting (hosting a fragment in a fragment) was added in Android 4.2. If you are using the Android OS implementation of fragments and supporting Android 4.0 and newer, you cannot use this API on all devices that your app supports. If you are using the support library, you can update the version of the library in your app and nest fragments until you run out of memory on the device.

There are no significant downsides to using the support library's fragments. The implementation of fragments is nearly identical in the support library as it is in the OS. The only real downside is that you have to include the support library in your project and it has a nonzero size. However, it is currently under a megabyte – and you will likely use the support library for some of its other features as well.

We take a practical approach in this book and in our own application development. The support library is king.

For the More Curious: Using Built-In Fragments

If you are strong-willed and do not believe in the advice above, you can use the fragment implementation built into the Android OS.

To use standard library fragments, you would make three changes to the project:

- Subclass the standard library **Activity** class (**android.app.Activity**) instead of **FragmentActivity**. Activities have support for fragments out of the box on API level 11 or higher.

- Subclass **android.app.Fragment** instead of **android.support.v4.app.Fragment**.

- To get the **FragmentManager**, call **getFragmentManager()** instead of **getSupportFragmentManager()**.

8

Creating User Interfaces with Layouts and Widgets

In this chapter, you will learn more about layouts and widgets while adding a crime's date and status to CriminalIntent.

Upgrading Crime

Open Crime.java and add two new fields. The **Date** field represents the date a crime occurred. The **boolean** field represents whether the crime has been solved.

Listing 8.1 Adding more fields to **Crime** (Crime.java)

```java
public class Crime {
    private UUID mId;
    private String mTitle;
    private Date mDate;
    private boolean mSolved;

    public Crime() {
        mId = UUID.randomUUID();
        mDate = new Date();
    }

    ...
}
```

Android Studio may find two classes with the name **Date**. Use the Option+Return (or Alt+Enter) shortcut to manually import the class. When asked which version of the **Date** class to import, choose the **java.util.Date** version.

Initializing the **Date** variable using the default **Date** constructor sets mDate to the current date. This will be the default date for a crime.

Next, generate getters and setters for your new fields (right-click in the file and choose Generate..., then Getter and Setter).

Listing 8.2 Generated getters and setters (`Crime.java`)

```
public class Crime {
    ...

    public void setTitle(String title) {
            mTitle = title;
    }


    public Date getDate() {
        return mDate;
    }
    public void setDate(Date date) {
        mDate = date;
    }

    public boolean isSolved() {
        return mSolved;
    }
    public void setSolved(boolean solved) {
        mSolved = solved;
    }
}
```

Your next steps will be updating the layout in `fragment_crime.xml` with new widgets and wiring up those widgets in `CrimeFragment.java`.

Updating the Layout

Figure 8.1 shows what **CrimeFragment**'s view will look like by the end of this chapter.

Figure 8.1 CriminalIntent, episode 2

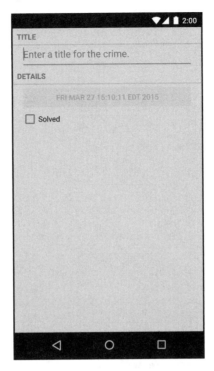

To get this on screen, you are going to add four widgets to **CrimeFragment**'s layout: two **TextView** widgets, a **Button**, and a **CheckBox**.

Open `fragment_crime.xml` and make the changes shown in Listing 8.3. You may get errors from missing string resources; you will create them in a moment.

Listing 8.3 Adding new widgets (fragment_crime.xml)

```xml
<?xml version="1.0" encoding="utf-8"?>
<LinearLayout xmlns:android="http://schemas.android.com/apk/res/android"
    android:layout_width="match_parent"
    android:layout_height="wrap_content"
    android:orientation="vertical"
    >
    <TextView
        android:layout_width="match_parent"
        android:layout_height="wrap_content"
        android:text="@string/crime_title_label"
        style="?android:listSeparatorTextViewStyle"
        />
    <EditText android:id="@+id/crime_title"
        android:layout_width="match_parent"
        android:layout_height="wrap_content"
        android:layout_marginLeft="16dp"
        android:layout_marginRight="16dp"
        android:hint="@string/crime_title_hint"
        />
    <TextView
        android:layout_width="match_parent"
        android:layout_height="wrap_content"
        android:text="@string/crime_details_label"
        style="?android:listSeparatorTextViewStyle"
        />
    <Button android:id="@+id/crime_date"
        android:layout_width="match_parent"
        android:layout_height="wrap_content"
        android:layout_marginLeft="16dp"
        android:layout_marginRight="16dp"
        />
    <CheckBox android:id="@+id/crime_solved"
        android:layout_width="match_parent"
        android:layout_height="wrap_content"
        android:layout_marginLeft="16dp"
        android:layout_marginRight="16dp"
        android:text="@string/crime_solved_label"
        />
</LinearLayout>
```

Notice that you did not give the **Button** an android:text attribute. This button will display the date of the **Crime** being displayed, and its text will be set in code.

Why display the date on a **Button**? You are preparing for the future. For now, a crime's date defaults to the current date and cannot be changed. In Chapter 12, you will wire up the button so that a press presents a **DatePicker** widget from which the user can set the date.

There are some new things in this layout to discuss, such as the style attribute and the margin attributes. But first let's get CriminalIntent up and running with the new widgets.

Open res/values/strings.xml and add the necessary string resources.

Listing 8.4 Adding string resources (`strings.xml`)

```
<resources>
    <string name="app_name">CriminalIntent</string>
    <string name="hello_world">Hello world!</string>
    <string name="action_settings">Settings</string>
    <string name="crime_title_hint">Enter a title for the crime.</string>
    <string name="crime_title_label">Title</string>
    <string name="crime_details_label">Details</string>
    <string name="crime_solved_label">Solved</string>
</resources>
```

Check for typos and save your files.

Wiring Widgets

Next, you are going to make the **CheckBox** display whether a **Crime** has been solved. You also need to update the **Crime**'s mSolved field when a user toggles the **CheckBox**.

For now, all the new **Button** needs to do is display the date in the **Crime**'s mDate field.

In `CrimeFragment.java`, add two new instance variables.

Listing 8.5 Adding widget instance variables (`CrimeFragment.java`)

```
public class CrimeFragment extends Fragment {
    private Crime mCrime;
    private EditText mTitleField;
    private Button mDateButton;
    private CheckBox mSolvedCheckBox;

    @Override
    public void onCreate(Bundle savedInstanceState) {
    ...
```

Next, in **onCreateView(…)**, get a reference to the new button, set its text as the date of the crime, and disable it for now.

Listing 8.6 Setting **Button** text (`CrimeFragment.java`)

```
@Override
public View onCreateView(LayoutInflater inflater, ViewGroup parent,
        Bundle savedInstanceState) {
    View v = inflater.inflate(R.layout.fragment_crime, parent, false);

    ...

    mTitleField.addTextChangedListener(new TextWatcher() {
        ...
    });

    mDateButton = (Button)v.findViewById(R.id.crime_date);
    mDateButton.setText(mCrime.getDate().toString());
    mDateButton.setEnabled(false);

    return v;
}
```

Disabling the button ensures that it will not respond in any way to the user pressing it. It also changes its appearance to advertise its disabled state. In Chapter 12, you will enable the button when you set its listener.

Moving on to the **CheckBox**, get a reference and set a listener that will update the mSolved field of the **Crime**.

Listing 8.7 Listening for **CheckBox** changes (CrimeFragment.java)

```
...
mDateButton = (Button)v.findViewById(R.id.crime_date);
mDateButton.setText(mCrime.getDate().toString());
mDateButton.setEnabled(false);

mSolvedCheckBox = (CheckBox)v.findViewById(R.id.crime_solved);
mSolvedCheckBox.setOnCheckedChangeListener(new OnCheckedChangeListener() {
    @Override
    public void onCheckedChanged(CompoundButton buttonView, boolean isChecked) {
        // Set the crime's solved property
        mCrime.setSolved(isChecked);
    }
});

return v;
}
```

When creating the **OnCheckedChangeListener**, you will see two import options. Be sure to choose the **android.widget.CompoundButton** version.

Run CriminalIntent. Toggle the new **CheckBox** and admire your disabled **Button** that displays the date.

More on XML Layout Attributes

Let's go back over some of the attributes you added in fragment_crime.xml and answer some lingering questions you might have about widgets and attributes.

Styles, themes, and theme attributes

A *style* is an XML resource that contains attributes that describe how a widget should look and behave. For example, the following is a style resource that configures a widget with a larger-than-normal text size.

```
<style name="BigTextStyle">
  <item name="android:textSize">20sp</item>
  <item name="android:padding">3dp</item>
</style>
```

You can create your own styles (and you will in Chapter 20). You add them to a styles file in res/values/ and refer to them in layouts like this: @style/my_own_style.

Take another look at the **TextView** widgets in fragment_crime.xml; each has a style attribute that refers to a style created by Android. This particular style makes the **TextView**s look like list separators and comes from the app's *theme*. A *theme* is a collection of styles. Structurally, a theme is itself a style resource whose attributes point to other style resources.

Android provides platform themes that your apps can use. When you created CriminalIntent, the wizard set up a theme for the app that is referenced on the `application` tag in the manifest.

You can apply a style from the app's theme to a widget using a *theme attribute reference*. This is what you are doing in `fragment_crime.xml` when you use the value `?android:listSeparatorTextViewStyle`.

In a theme attribute reference, you tell Android's runtime resource manager, "Go to the app's theme and find the attribute named `listSeparatorTextViewStyle`. This attribute points to another style resource. Put the value of that resource here."

Every Android theme will include an attribute named `listSeparatorTextViewStyle`, but its definition will be different depending on the overall look and feel of the particular theme. Using a theme attribute reference ensures that the **TextView**s will have the correct look and feel for your app.

You will learn more about how styles and themes work in Chapter 20.

Screen pixel densities and dp and sp

In `fragment_crime.xml`, you specify the margin attribute values in terms of dp units. You have seen these units in layouts before; now it is time to learn what they are.

Sometimes you need to specify values for view attributes in terms of specific sizes (usually in pixels but sometimes points, millimeters, or inches). You see this most commonly with attributes for text size, margins, and padding. Text size is the pixel height of the text on the device's screen. Margins specify the distances between views, and padding specifies the distance between a view's outside edges and its content.

As you saw in the section called "Adding an Icon" in Chapter 2, Android automatically scales images to different screen pixel densities using density qualified drawable folders (such as `drawable-xhdpi`). But what happens when your images scale, but your margins do not? Or what happens when the user configures a larger-than-default text size?

To solve these problems, Android provides density-independent dimension units that you can use to get the same size on different screen densities. Android translates these units into pixels at runtime, so there is no tricky math for you to do (Figure 8.2).

Figure 8.2 Dimension units in action on **TextView** (left: MDPI; middle: HDPI; right: HDPI with large text)

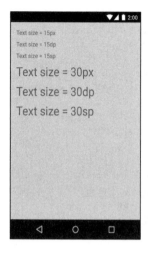
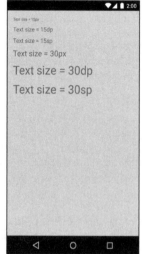

dp (or dip)	Short for *density-independent pixel* and usually pronounced "dip." You typically use this for margins, padding, or anything else for which you would otherwise specify size with a pixel value. When your display is a higher density, density-independent pixels will expand to fill a larger number of screen pixels. One dp is always 1/160th of an inch on a device's screen. You get the same size regardless of screen density.
sp	Short for *scale-independent pixel*. Scale-independent pixels are density-independent pixels that also take into account the user's font size preference. You will almost always use sp to set display text size.
pt, mm, in	These are scaled units like dp that allow you to specify interface sizes in points (1/72 of an inch), millimeters, or inches. However, we do not recommend using them: not all devices are correctly configured for these units to scale correctly.

In practice and in this book, you will use dp and sp almost exclusively. Android will translate these values into pixels at runtime.

Android's design guidelines

Notice that for your margins, you use a 16dp value in Listing 8.3. This value follows Android's material design guideline. You can find all of the Android design guidelines at http://developer.android.com/design/index.html.

Modern Android apps should follow these guidelines as closely as possible. The guidelines rely heavily on newer Android SDK functionality that is not always available or easy to achieve on older devices. Many of the design recommendations can be followed using the AppCompat library, which you can read about in Chapter 13.

Layout parameters

By now, you have probably noticed that some attribute names begin with layout_ (android:layout_marginLeft) and others do not (android:text).

Attributes whose names do *not* begin with layout_ are directions to the widget. When it is inflated, the widget calls a method to configure itself based on each of these attributes and their values.

When an attribute's name begins with layout_, that attribute is a direction to that widget's *parent*. These attributes are known as *layout parameters*, and they tell the parent layout how to arrange the child element within the parent.

Even when a layout object like **LinearLayout** is the root element of a layout, it is still a widget with a parent and has layout parameters. When you defined the **LinearLayout** in fragment_crime.xml, you gave it attributes for android:layout_width and android:layout_height. These attributes will be used by the **LinearLayout**'s parent layout when it is inflated. In this case, the **LinearLayout**'s layout parameters will be used by the **FrameLayout** in **CrimeActivity**'s content view.

Margins vs. padding

In fragment_crime.xml, you have given widgets margin and padding attributes. Beginning developers sometimes get confused between these attributes. Now that you understand what a layout parameter is, the difference is easier to explain. Margin attributes are layout parameters. They determine the distance between widgets. Given that a widget can only know about itself, margins must be the responsibility of the widget's parent.

Padding, on the other hand, is not a layout parameter. The android:padding attribute tells the widget how much bigger than its contents it should draw itself. For example, say you wanted the date button to be spectacularly large without changing its text size (Figure 8.3). You could add the following attribute to the **Button**, save your layout, and run again.

Listing 8.8 Padding in action (fragment_crime.xml)

```
<Button android:id="@+id/crime_date"
  android:layout_width="match_parent"
  android:layout_height="wrap_content"
  android:layout_marginLeft="16dp"
  android:layout_marginRight="16dp"
  android:padding="80dp"
  />
```

Figure 8.3 I like big buttons and I cannot lie...

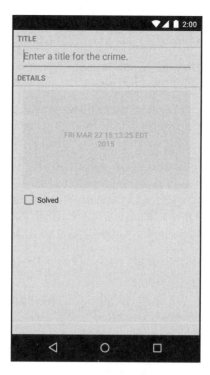

Alas, you should probably remove this attribute before continuing.

Using the Graphical Layout Tool

So far, you have created layouts by typing XML. In this section, you will use the graphical layout tool. In particular, you are going to make an alternative landscape layout for **CrimeFragment**.

Most built-in layout classes, like **LinearLayout**, will automatically stretch and resize themselves and their children on rotation. Sometimes, however, the default resizing does not make the best use of the available space.

Run CriminalIntent and rotate the device to see the **CrimeFragment** layout in landscape orientation (Figure 8.4).

Figure 8.4 **CrimeFragment** in landscape mode

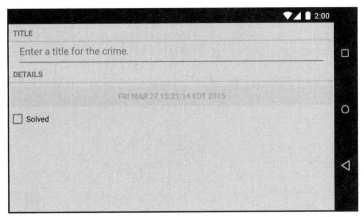

The date button becomes oddly long; it would be better if the landscape layout had the button and checkbox side by side.

To make these changes, switch to the graphical layout tool. Open fragment_crime.xml and select the Design tab at the bottom of the file.

In the middle of the graphical layout tool is the preview you have already seen. On the lefthand side is the *palette*. This view contains all the widgets you could wish for, organized by category (Figure 8.5).

Figure 8.5 Views in the graphical layout tool

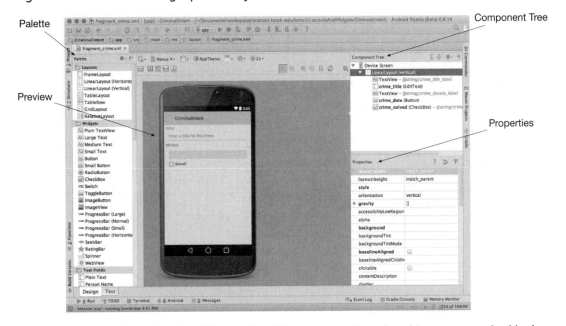

The *component tree* is to the right of the preview. The tree shows how the widgets are organized in the layout.

Beneath the component tree is the *properties view*. In this view, you can view and edit the attributes of the widget selected in the component tree.

Creating a landscape layout

The graphical layout editor can generate the landscape version of a layout file for you. Locate the button that looks like a piece of paper with an Android in the bottom right, as shown in Figure 8.6. Click that button and select Create Landscape Variation.

Figure 8.6 Creating an alternative layout in the graphical layout editor

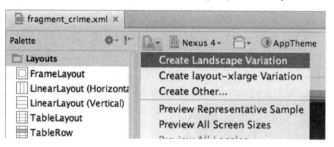

A new layout appears. Behind the scenes, the res/layout-land directory was created for you and the existing fragment_crime.xml layout file was copied to that new directory.

Now let's consider what changes to make to this landscape layout. Take a look at Figure 8.7.

Figure 8.7 Landscape layout for **CrimeFragment**

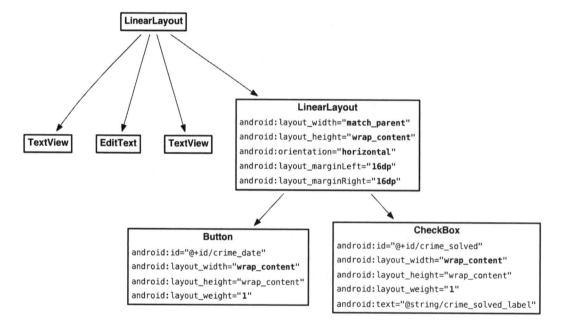

The changes can be broken into four parts:

- add a new **LinearLayout** widget to the layout
- edit the attributes of the **LinearLayout**

- make the **Button** and **CheckBox** widgets children of the **LinearLayout**

- update the layout parameters of the **Button** and **CheckBox**

Adding a new widget

You can add a widget by selecting it in the palette and then dragging to the component tree. Click the Layouts category in the palette if it is not already expanded. Select LinearLayout (Horizontal) and drag it to the component tree. Drop this **LinearLayout** just above the date button. Ensure that the new **LinearLayout** is a child of the root **LinearLayout**, as shown in Figure 8.8.

Figure 8.8 **LinearLayout** added to fragment_crime.xml

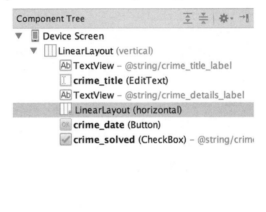

You can add widgets by dragging from the palette to the preview, too. However, layout widgets are often empty or obscured by other views, so it can be hard to see exactly where to drop a widget in the preview to get the hierarchy you want. Dragging to the component tree makes this much easier.

Editing attributes in properties view

Select the new **LinearLayout** in the component tree to display its attributes in the properties view. Examine the layout:width and layout:height attributes.

Modify the layout:width attribute to match_parent and the layout:height attribute to wrap_content, as shown in Figure 8.9. Now, the **LinearLayout** will fill the available width and take up as much height as it needs to display the **CheckBox** and **Button**.

Figure 8.9 Changing **LinearLayout**'s width and height

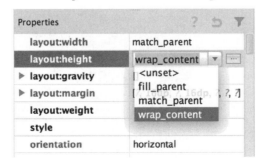

161

You also want to update the **LinearLayout**'s margins to match your other widgets. Expand the layout:margin attribute. Select the field next to Left and type 16dp. Do the same for the right margin (Figure 8.10).

Figure 8.10 Margins set in properties view

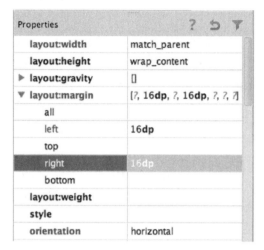

Save your layout file and switch to the XML by selecting the text tab at the bottom of the preview. You should see a **LinearLayout** element with the size and margin attributes you just added.

Reorganizing widgets in the component tree

The next step is to make the **Button** and **CheckBox** children of the new **LinearLayout**. Return to the graphical layout tool, and, in the component tree, select the **Button** and drag it on top of the **LinearLayout**.

The component tree should reflect that the **Button** is now a child of the new **LinearLayout** (Figure 8.11). Do the same for the **CheckBox**.

Figure 8.11 **Button** and **CheckBox** are now children of the new **LinearLayout**

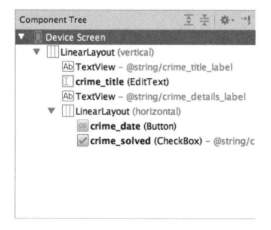

If widget children are out of order, you can reorder them in the component tree by dragging. You can also delete widgets from the layout in the component tree, but be careful: deleting a widget also deletes its children.

Back in the preview, the **CheckBox** seems to be missing. The **Button** is obscuring it. The **LinearLayout** considered the width (match_parent) of its first child (the **Button**) and gave the first child all of the space, leaving nothing for the **CheckBox** (Figure 8.12).

Figure 8.12 The first-defined **Button** child obscures the **CheckBox**

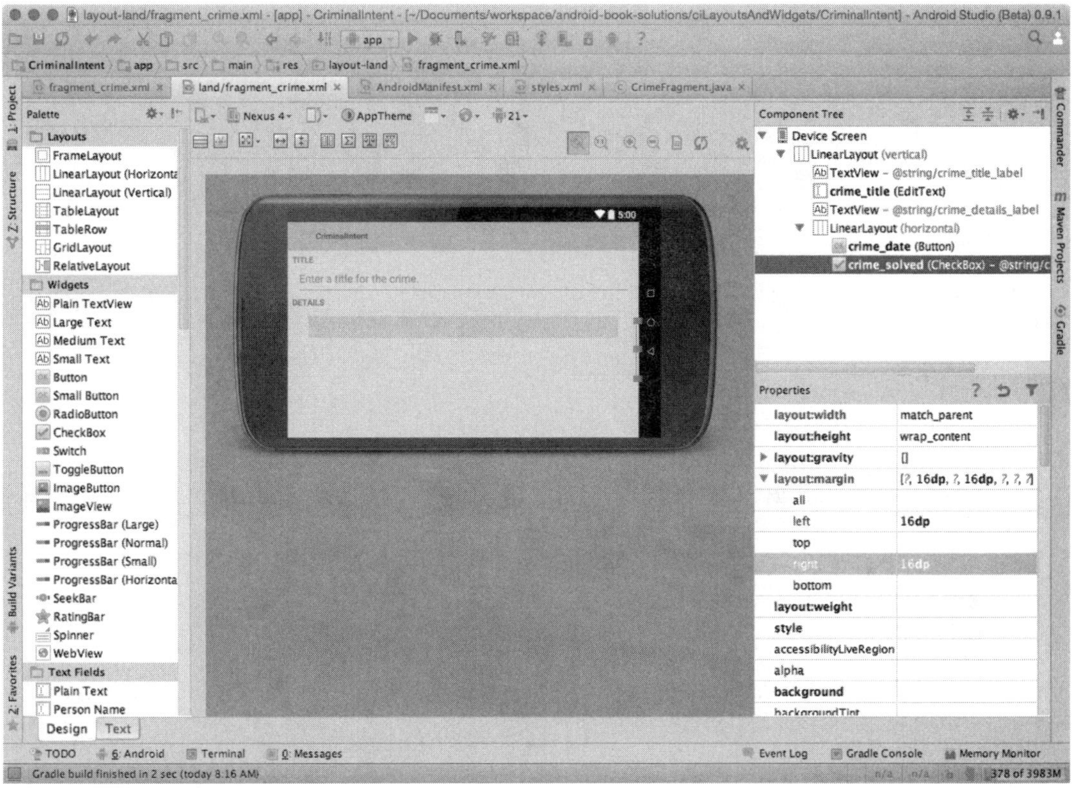

You can introduce some equity in the **LinearLayout**'s parenting by adjusting the layout parameters of its children.

Updating child layout parameters

First, select the date button in the component tree. In the properties view, click on the current layout:width value and change it to wrap_content.

Next, delete both of the button's 16dp margin values. The button will not need these margins now that it is inside the **LinearLayout**.

Finally, find the layout:weight field and set its value to 1. This field corresponds to the android:layout_weight attribute shown in Figure 8.7.

Select the **CheckBox** in the component tree and make the same attribute changes: layout:width should be wrap_content, the margins should be empty, and layout:weight should be 1.

Check the preview to confirm that both widgets are now visible. Then save your file and return to the XML to confirm your changes. Listing 8.9 shows the relevant XML.

Listing 8.9 XML for the graphically created layout (`layout-land/fragment_crime.xml`)

```
...

<TextView
    android:layout_width="match_parent"
    android:layout_height="wrap_content"
    android:text="@string/crime_details_label"
    style="?android:listSeparatorTextViewStyle"
    />
<LinearLayout
    android:layout_width="match_parent"
    android:layout_height="wrap_content"
    android:layout_marginLeft="16dp"
    android:layout_marginRight="16dp" >
    <Button
        android:id="@+id/crime_date"
        android:layout_width="wrap_content"
        android:layout_height="wrap_content"
        android:layout_weight="1" />
    <CheckBox
        android:id="@+id/crime_solved"
        android:layout_width="wrap_content"
        android:layout_height="wrap_content"
        android:layout_weight="1"
        android:text="@string/crime_solved_label" />
  </LinearLayout>
</LinearLayout>
```

Run CriminalIntent, rotate to landscape, and pat yourself on the back for optimizing the layout for a new configuration of the device.

How android:layout_weight works

The android:layout_weight attribute tells the **LinearLayout** how to distribute its children. You have given both widgets the same value, but that does not necessarily make them the same width on screen. To determine the width of its child views, **LinearLayout** uses a mixture of the layout_width and layout_weight parameters.

LinearLayout makes two passes to set the width of a view. In the first pass, **LinearLayout** looks at layout_width (or layout_height, for vertical orientation). The value for layout_width for both the **Button** and **CheckBox** is now wrap_content, so each view will get only enough space to draw itself (Figure 8.13).

(It is hard to see how layout weights work in the preview because your button's contents are not part of the layout itself. The following figures show what the **LinearLayout** would look like if the button already had its contents.)

Figure 8.13 Pass 1: space given out based on `layout_width`

In the next pass, **LinearLayout** allocates any extra space based on the values for `layout_weight` (Figure 8.14).

Figure 8.14 Pass 2: extra space given out based on 1:1 `layout_weight`

In your layout, the **Button** and **CheckBox** have the same value for `layout_weight`, so they split the extra space 50/50. If you set the weight for your **Button** to 2, then it would receive 2/3 of the extra space, leaving 1/3 for the **CheckBox** (Figure 8.15).

Figure 8.15 Extra space divided unevenly based on 2:1 `layout_weight`

Any floating point number can be a valid weight. Programmers have different conventions for the kinds of weights they use. In `fragment_crime.xml`, you are using a "cocktail recipe" style weighting. Another common convention is to have weights add up to 1.0 or 100, which would make the weight for the button in the last example 0.66 or 66, respectively.

What if you want the **LinearLayout** to allocate exactly 50% of its width to each view? You simply skip the first pass by setting the `layout_width` of each widget to `0dp` instead of `wrap_content`. This leaves `layout_weight` the sole component in the **LinearLayout**'s decision making (Figure 8.16).

Figure 8.16 When `layout_width="0dp"`, only `layout_weight` values matter

The graphical layout tool and you

The graphical layout tool is useful, and it is improving with every Android Studio release. However, it can be buggy at times and may be hard to use with complex layouts. You can switch between making changes in the graphical layout tool and in the XML directly at any time.

Feel free to use the graphical layout tool to create layouts in this book. From now on, we will show you a diagram like Figure 8.7 when you need to create a layout. You can decide how to create it – XML, graphical layout tool, or some of each.

Widget IDs and multiple layouts

The two layouts that you have created for CriminalIntent do not vary significantly, but there may be times when your layouts will. When this is the case, you should ensure that widgets actually exist before you access them in code.

If you have a widget in one layout and not another, use null-checking in the code to determine if the widget is present in the current orientation before calling methods on it:

```
Button landscapeOnlyButton = (Button)v.findViewById(R.id.landscapeOnlyButton);
if (landscapeOnlyButton != null) {
    // Set it up
}
```

Finally, remember that a widget must have the *same* android:id attribute in every layout in which it appears so that your code can find it.

Challenge: Formatting the Date

The **Date** object is more of a timestamp than a conventional date. A timestamp is what you see when you call **toString()** on a **Date**, so that is what you have on your button. While timestamps make for good documentation, it might be nicer if the button just displayed the date as humans think of it – like "Jul 22, 2015." You can do this with an instance of the **android.text.format.DateFormat** class. The place to start is the reference page for this class in the Android documentation.

You can use methods in the **DateFormat** class to get a common format. Or you can prepare your own format string. For a more advanced challenge, create a format string that will display the day of the week as well – for example, "Wednesday, Jul 22, 2015."

9

Displaying Lists with RecyclerView

CriminalIntent's model layer currently consists of a single instance of **Crime**. In this chapter, you will update CriminalIntent to work with a list of crimes. The list will display each **Crime**'s title and date and whether the case has been solved, as shown in Figure 9.1.

Figure 9.1 A list of crimes

Figure 9.2 shows the overall plan for CriminalIntent in this chapter.

Figure 9.2 CriminalIntent with a list of crimes

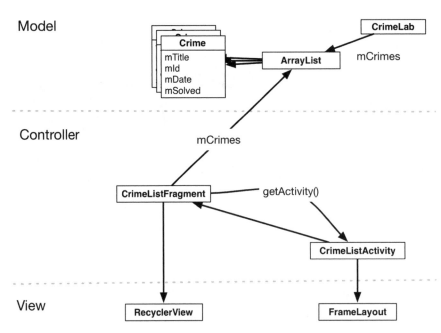

In the model layer, you have a new object, **CrimeLab**, that will be a centralized data stash for **Crime** objects.

Displaying a list of crimes requires a new activity and a new fragment in CriminalIntent's controller layer: **CrimeListActivity** and **CrimeListFragment**.

(Where are **CrimeActivity** and **CrimeFragment** in Figure 9.2? They are part of the detail view, so we are not showing them here. In Chapter 10, you will connect the list and the detail parts of CriminalIntent.)

In Figure 9.2, you can also see the view objects associated with **CrimeListActivity** and **CrimeListFragment**. The activity's view will consist of a fragment-containing **FrameLayout**. The fragment's view will consist of a **RecyclerView**. You will learn more about the **RecyclerView** class later in the chapter.

Updating CriminalIntent's Model Layer

The first step is to upgrade CriminalIntent's model layer from a single **Crime** object to a **List** of **Crime** objects.

Singletons and centralized data storage

You are going to store the **List** of crimes in a *singleton*. A *singleton* is a class that allows only one instance of itself to be created.

A singleton exists as long as the application stays in memory, so storing the list in a singleton will keep the crime data available throughout any lifecycle changes in your activities and fragments. Be careful with singleton classes, as they will be destroyed when Android removes your application from memory. The **CrimeLab** singleton is not a solution for long-term storage of data, but it does allow the app to have one owner of the crime data and provides a way to easily pass that data between controller classes.

(See the For the More Curious section at the end of this chapter for more about singleton classes.)

To create a singleton, you create a class with a private constructor and a **get()** method. If the instance already exists, then **get()** simply returns the instance. If the instance does not exist yet, then **get()** will call the constructor to create it.

Right-click the com.bignerdranch.android.criminalintent package and choose New → Java Class. Name this class **CrimeLab** and click Finish.

In CrimeLab.java, implement **CrimeLab** as a singleton with a private constructor and a **get()** method.

Listing 9.1 Setting up the singleton (CrimeLab.java)

```java
public class CrimeLab {
    private static CrimeLab sCrimeLab;

    public static CrimeLab get(Context context) {
        if (sCrimeLab == null) {
            sCrimeLab = new CrimeLab(context);
        }
        return sCrimeLab;
    }

    private CrimeLab(Context context) {

    }
}
```

There are a few interesting things in this **CrimeLab** implementation. First, notice the s prefix on the sCrimeLab variable. You are using this Android convention to make it clear that sCrimeLab is a static variable.

Also, notice the private constructor on the **CrimeLab**. Other classes will not be able to create a **CrimeLab**, bypassing the **get()** method.

Finally, in the **get()** method on **CrimeLab**, you pass in a **Context** object. You are not currently using this **Context** object but you will make use of it in Chapter 14.

Let's give **CrimeLab** some **Crime** objects to store. In **CrimeLab**'s constructor, create an empty **List** of **Crime**s. Also add two methods: a **getCrimes()** method that returns the **List** and a **getCrime(UUID)** that returns the **Crime** with the given ID.

Listing 9.2 Setting up the **List** of **Crime** objects (CrimeLab.java)

```java
public class CrimeLab {
    private static CrimeLab sCrimeLab;

    private List<Crime> mCrimes;

    public static CrimeLab get(Context context) {
        ...
    }

    private CrimeLab(Context context) {
        mCrimes = new ArrayList<>();
    }

    public List<Crime> getCrimes() {
        return mCrimes;
    }

    public Crime getCrime(UUID id) {
        for (Crime crime : mCrimes) {
            if (crime.getId().equals(id)) {
                return crime;
            }
        }
        return null;
    }
}
```

List<E> is an interface that supports an ordered list of objects of a given type. It defines methods for retrieving, adding, and deleting elements. A commonly used implementation of **List** is **ArrayList**, which uses a regular Java array to store the list elements.

Since mCrimes holds an **ArrayList**, and **ArrayList** is also a **List**, both **ArrayList** and **List** are valid types for mCrimes. In situations like this, we recommend using the interface type for the variable declaration: **List**. That way, if you ever need to use a different kind of **List** implementation – like **LinkedList**, for example – you can do so easily.

The mCrimes instantiation line uses *diamond notation*, <>, which was introduced in Java 7. This shorthand notation tells the compiler to infer the type of items the **List** will contain based on the generic argument passed in the variable declaration. Here, the compiler will infer that the **ArrayList** contains **Crime**s because the variable declaration, private List<Crime> mCrimes;, specifies **Crime** for the generic argument. (The more verbose equivalent, which developers were required to use prior to Java 7, is mCrimes = new ArrayList<Crime>();.)

Eventually, the **List** will contain user-created **Crime**s that can be saved and reloaded. For now, populate the **List** with 100 boring **Crime** objects.

Listing 9.3 Generating crimes (`CrimeLab.java`)

```
private CrimeLab(Context context) {
    mCrimes = new ArrayList<>();
    for (int i = 0; i < 100; i++) {
        Crime crime = new Crime();
        crime.setTitle("Crime #" + i);
        crime.setSolved(i % 2 == 0); // Every other one
        mCrimes.add(crime);
    }
}
```

Now you have a fully loaded model layer with 100 crimes.

An Abstract Activity for Hosting a Fragment

In a moment, you will create the **CrimeListActivity** class that is designed to host a **CrimeListFragment**. First, you are going to set up a view for **CrimeListActivity**.

A generic fragment-hosting layout

For **CrimeListActivity**, you can simply reuse the layout defined in `activity_crime.xml` (Listing 9.4). This layout provides a **FrameLayout** as a container view for a fragment, which is then named in the activity's code.

Listing 9.4 `activity_crime.xml` is already generic

```
<?xml version="1.0" encoding="utf-8"?>
<FrameLayout xmlns:android="http://schemas.android.com/apk/res/android"
    android:id="@+id/fragment_container"
    android:layout_width="match_parent"
    android:layout_height="match_parent"
    />
```

Because `activity_crime.xml` does not name a particular fragment, you can use it for any activity hosting a single fragment. Rename it `activity_fragment.xml` to reflect its larger scope.

In the Project tool window, right-click res/layout/activity_crime.xml. (Be sure to right-click activity_crime.xml and not fragment_crime.xml.)

From the context menu, select Refactor → Rename.... Rename this layout `activity_fragment.xml`. When you rename a resource, the references to it are updated automatically.

Android Studio should automatically update the references to the new `activity_fragment.xml` file. If you see an error in `CrimeActivity.java`, then you need to manually update the reference in **CrimeActivity**, as shown in Listing 9.5.

Listing 9.5 Update layout file for **CrimeActivity** (CrimeActivity.java)

```java
public class CrimeActivity extends FragmentActivity {
    /** Called when the activity is first created. */
    @Override
    public void onCreate(Bundle savedInstanceState) {
        super.onCreate(savedInstanceState);
        setContentView(R.layout.activity_crime);
        setContentView(R.layout.activity_fragment);

        FragmentManager fm = getSupportFragmentManager();
        Fragment fragment = fm.findFragmentById(R.id.fragment_container);

        if (fragment == null) {
            fragment = new CrimeFragment();
            fm.beginTransaction()
                .add(R.id.fragment_container, fragment)
                .commit();
        }
    }
}
```

An abstract Activity class

To create the **CrimeListActivity** class, you could reuse **CrimeActivity**'s code. Look back at the code you wrote for **CrimeActivity** (Listing 9.5). It is simple and almost generic. In fact, the only nongeneric code is the instantiation of the **CrimeFragment** before it is added to the **FragmentManager**.

Listing 9.6 **CrimeActivity** is almost generic (CrimeActivity.java)

```java
public class CrimeActivity extends FragmentActivity {
    /** Called when the activity is first created. */
    @Override
    public void onCreate(Bundle savedInstanceState) {
        super.onCreate(savedInstanceState);
        setContentView(R.layout.activity_fragment);

        FragmentManager fm = getSupportFragmentManager();
        Fragment fragment = fm.findFragmentById(R.id.fragment_container);

        if (fragment == null) {
            fragment = new CrimeFragment();
            fm.beginTransaction()
                .add(R.id.fragment_container, fragment)
                .commit();
        }
    }
}
```

Nearly every activity you will create in this book will require the same code. To avoid typing it again and again, you are going to stash it in an abstract class.

Create a new class named **SingleFragmentActivity** in CriminalIntent's package. Make this class a subclass of **FragmentActivity** and make the class an abstract class.

Listing 9.7 Creating an abstract Activity (`SingleFragmentActivity.java`)

```java
public abstract class SingleFragmentActivity extends FragmentActivity {

}
```

Now, add the following code to `SingleFragmentActivity.java`. Except for the highlighted portions, it is identical to your old **CrimeActivity** code.

Listing 9.8 Add a generic superclass (`SingleFragmentActivity.java`)

```java
public abstract class SingleFragmentActivity extends FragmentActivity {

    protected abstract Fragment createFragment();

    @Override
    public void onCreate(Bundle savedInstanceState) {
        super.onCreate(savedInstanceState);
        setContentView(R.layout.activity_fragment);

        FragmentManager fm = getSupportFragmentManager();
        Fragment fragment = fm.findFragmentById(R.id.fragment_container);

        if (fragment == null) {
            fragment = createFragment();
            fm.beginTransaction()
                .add(R.id.fragment_container, fragment)
                .commit();
        }
    }
}
```

In this code, you set the activity's view to be inflated from `activity_fragment.xml`. Then you look for the fragment in the **FragmentManager** in that container, creating and adding it if it does not exist.

The only difference between the code in Listing 9.8 and the code in **CrimeActivity** is an abstract method named **createFragment()** that you use to instantiate the fragment. Subclasses of **SingleFragmentActivity** will implement this method to return an instance of the fragment that the activity is hosting.

Using an abstract class

Try it out with **CrimeActivity**. Change **CrimeActivity**'s superclass to **SingleFragmentActivity**, remove the implementation of **onCreate(Bundle)**, and implement the **createFragment()** method as shown in Listing 9.9.

Listing 9.9 Clean up **CrimeActivity** (CrimeActivity.java)

```
public class CrimeActivity extends FragmentActivity SingleFragmentActivity {
    /** Called when the activity is first created. */
    @Override
    public void onCreate(Bundle savedInstanceState) {
        super.onCreate(savedInstanceState);
        setContentView(R.layout.activity_fragment);
        FragmentManager fm = getSupportFragmentManager();
        Fragment fragment = fm.findFragmentById(R.id.fragment_container);

        if (fragment == null) {
            fragment = new CrimeFragment();
            fm.beginTransaction()
                .add(R.id.fragment_container, fragment)
                .commit();
        }
    }

    @Override
    protected Fragment createFragment() {
        return new CrimeFragment();
    }
}
```

Creating the new controllers

Now, you will create the two new controller classes: **CrimeListActivity** and **CrimeListFragment**.

Right-click on the **com.bignerdranch.android.criminalintent** package, select New → Java Class, and name the class **CrimeListActivity**.

Modify the new **CrimeListActivity** class to also subclass **SingleFragmentActivity** and implement the **createFragment()** method.

Listing 9.10 Implement **CrimeListActivity** (CrimeListActivity.java)

```
public class CrimeListActivity extends SingleFragmentActivity {

    @Override
    protected Fragment createFragment() {
        return new CrimeListFragment();
    }

}
```

If you have other methods in your **CrimeListActivity**, such as **onCreate**, remove them. Let **SingleFragmentActivity** do its job and keep **CrimeListActivity** simple.

The **CrimeListFragment** class has not yet been created. Let's remedy that.

Right-click on the **com.bignerdranch.android.criminalintent** package again, select New → Java Class, and name the class **CrimeListFragment**.

Listing 9.11 Implement **CrimeListFragment** (CrimeListFragment.java)

```
public class CrimeListFragment extends Fragment {

    // Nothing yet

}
```

For now, **CrimeListFragment** will be an empty shell of a fragment. You will work with this fragment later in the chapter.

SingleFragmentActivity will save you a lot of typing and time as you proceed through the book. And now your activity code is nice and tidy.

Declaring CrimeListActivity

Now that you have created **CrimeListActivity**, you must declare it in the manifest. In addition, you want the list of crimes to be the first screen that the user sees when CriminalIntent is launched, so **CrimeListActivity** should be the launcher activity.

In the manifest, declare **CrimeListActivity** and move the launcher intent filter from **CrimeActivity**'s declaration to **CrimeListActivity**'s.

Listing 9.12 Declaring **CrimeListActivity** as the launcher activity (AndroidManifest.xml)

```
...
<application
    android:allowBackup="true"
    android:icon="@mipmap/ic_launcher"
    android:label="@string/app_name"
    android:theme="@style/AppTheme" >
    <activity android:name=".CrimeListActivity">
        <intent-filter>
            <action android:name="android.intent.action.MAIN" />
            <category android:name="android.intent.category.LAUNCHER" />
        </intent-filter>
    </activity>
    <activity android:name=".CrimeActivity"
        android:label="@string/app_name">
        <intent-filter>
            <action android:name="android.intent.action.MAIN" />
            <category android:name="android.intent.category.LAUNCHER" />
        </intent-filter>
    </activity>

</application>

</manifest>
```

CrimeListActivity is now the launcher activity. Run CriminalIntent, and you will see **CrimeListActivity**'s **FrameLayout** hosting an empty **CrimeListFragment**, as shown in Figure 9.3.

Figure 9.3 Blank **CrimeListActivity** screen

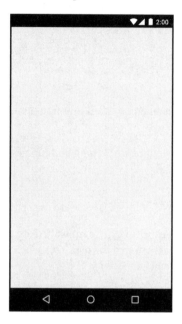

RecyclerView, Adapter, and ViewHolder

Now, you want **CrimeListFragment** to display a list of crimes to the user. To do this, you will use a **RecyclerView**.

RecyclerView is a subclass of **ViewGroup**. It displays a list of child **View** objects, one for each item in your list of items. Depending on the complexity of what you need to display, these child **View**s can be complex or very simple.

Your first implementation of providing list items for display will be simple: a list item will only display the title of a **Crime**, and the **View** object will be a simple **TextView**, as shown in Figure 9.4.

Figure 9.4 A **RecyclerView** with child **TextView**s

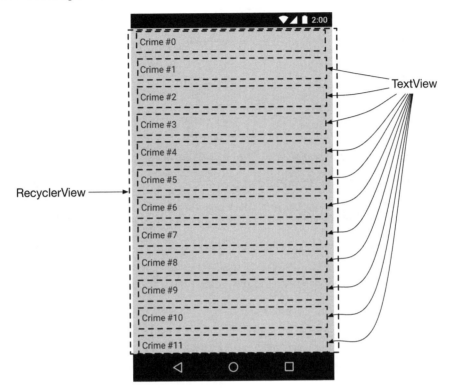

Figure 9.4 shows 12 **TextView**s. Later you will be able to run CriminalIntent and swipe to scroll through 100 **TextView**s to see all of your **Crime**s. Does that mean that you have 100 **TextView**s? Thanks to your **RecyclerView**, no.

Creating a **TextView** for every item in the list could easily become unworkable. As you can imagine, a list can have far more than 100 items, and **TextView**s can be much more involved than your simple implementation here. Also, a **Crime** only needs a **View** when it is on the screen, so there is no need to have 100 **View**s ready and waiting. It would make far more sense to create view objects only as you need them.

RecyclerView does just that. Instead of creating 100 **View**s, it creates 12 – enough to fill the screen. When a view is scrolled off the screen, **RecyclerView** reuses it rather than throwing it away. In short, it lives up to its name: it recycles views over and over.

ViewHolders and Adapters

The **RecyclerView**'s only responsibilities are recycling **TextView**s and positioning them on the screen. To get the **TextView**s in the first place, it works with two classes that you will build in a moment: an **Adapter** subclass and a **ViewHolder** subclass.

The **ViewHolder**'s job is small, so let's talk about it first. The **ViewHolder** does one thing: it holds on to a **View** (Figure 9.5).

Figure 9.5 The lowly **ViewHolder**

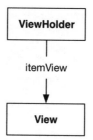

A small job, but that is what **ViewHolder**s do. A typical **ViewHolder** subclass looks like this:

Listing 9.13 A typical **ViewHolder** subclass

```
public class ListRow extends RecyclerView.ViewHolder {
    public ImageView mThumbnail;

    public ListRow(View view) {
        super(view);

        mThumbnail = (ImageView) view.findViewById(R.id.thumbnail);
    }
}
```

You can then create a **ListRow** and access both mThumbnail, which you created yourself, and itemView, a field which your superclass **RecyclerView.ViewHolder** assigns for you. The itemView field is your **ViewHolder**'s reason for existing: it holds a reference to the entire **View** you passed in to **super(view)**.

Listing 9.14 Typical usage of a **ViewHolder**

```
ListRow row = new ListRow(inflater.inflate(R.layout.list_row, parent, false));
View view = row.itemView;
ImageView thumbnailView = row.mThumbnail;
```

A **RecyclerView** never creates **View**s by themselves. It always creates **ViewHolder**s, which bring their itemViews along for the ride (Figure 9.6).

Figure 9.6 A **RecyclerView** with its **ViewHolder**s

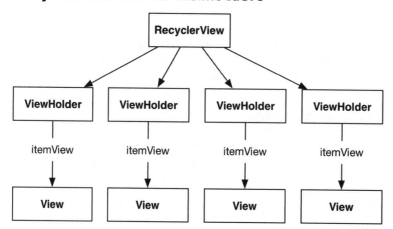

When the **View** is simple, **ViewHolder** has few responsibilities. For more complicated **View**s, the **ViewHolder** makes wiring up the different parts of itemView to a **Crime** simpler and more efficient. You will see how this works later on in this chapter, when you build a complex **View** yourself.

Adapters

Figure 9.6 is somewhat simplified. **RecyclerView** does not create **ViewHolder**s itself. Instead, it asks an *adapter*. An *adapter* is a controller object that sits between the **RecyclerView** and the data set that the **RecyclerView** should display.

The adapter is responsible for

- creating the necessary **ViewHolder**s

- binding **ViewHolder**s to data from the model layer

To build an adapter, you first define a subclass of **RecyclerView.Adapter**. Your adapter subclass will wrap the list of crimes you get from **CrimeLab**.

When the **RecyclerView** needs a view object to display, it will have a conversation with its adapter. Figure 9.7 shows an example of a conversation that a **RecyclerView** might initiate.

Figure 9.7 A scintillating **RecyclerView**-**Adapter** conversation

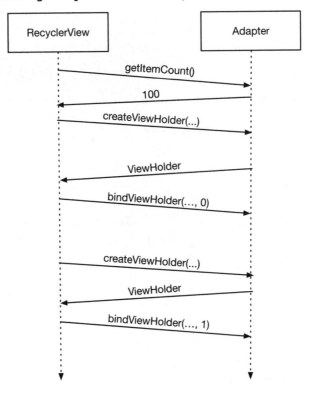

First, the **RecyclerView** asks how many objects are in the list by calling the adapter's **getItemCount()** method.

Then the **RecyclerView** calls the adapter's **createViewHolder(ViewGroup, int)** method to create a new **ViewHolder**, along with its juicy payload: a **View** to display.

Finally, the **RecyclerView** calls **onBindViewHolder(ViewHolder, int)**. The **RecyclerView** will pass a **ViewHolder** into this method along with the position. The adapter will look up the model data for that position and *bind* it to the **ViewHolder**'s **View**. To bind it, the adapter fills in the **View** to reflect the data in the model object.

After this process is complete, **RecyclerView** will place a list item on the screen. Note that **createViewHolder(ViewGroup, int)** will happen a lot less often than **onBindViewHolder(ViewHolder, int)**. Once a sufficient number of **ViewHolder**s have been created, **RecyclerView** stops calling **createViewHolder(…)**. Instead, it saves time and memory by recycling old **ViewHolder**s.

Using a RecyclerView

Enough talk; time for the implementation. The **RecyclerView** class lives in one of Google's many support libraries. The first step to using a **RecyclerView** is to add the RecyclerView library as a dependency.

Navigate to your project structure window with File → Project Structure.... Select the app module on the left, then the Dependencies tab. Use the + button and choose Library dependency to add a dependency.

Find and select the recyclerview-v7 library and click OK to add the library as a dependency, as shown in Figure 9.8.

Figure 9.8 Adding the RecyclerView dependency

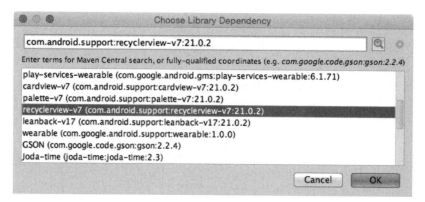

Your **RecyclerView** will live in **CrimeListFragment**'s layout file. First, you must create the layout file. Right-click on the **res/layout** directory and select New → Layout resource file. Name the file `fragment_crime_list` and click OK to create the file.

Open the new `fragment_crime_list` file and modify the root view to be a **RecyclerView** and to give it an ID attribute.

Listing 9.15 Adding **RecyclerView** to a layout file (fragment_crime_list.xml)

```xml
<android.support.v7.widget.RecyclerView
    xmlns:android="http://schemas.android.com/apk/res/android"
    android:id="@+id/crime_recycler_view"
    android:layout_width="match_parent"
    android:layout_height="match_parent"/>
```

Now that **CrimeListFragment**'s view is set up, hook up the view to the fragment. Modify **CrimeListFragment** to use this layout file and to find the **RecyclerView** in the layout file, as shown in Listing 9.16.

Listing 9.16 Setting up the view for **CrimeListFragment** (CrimeListFragment.java)

```java
public class CrimeListFragment extends Fragment {

    private RecyclerView mCrimeRecyclerView;

    @Override
    public View onCreateView(LayoutInflater inflater, ViewGroup container,
        Bundle savedInstanceState) {
        View view = inflater.inflate(R.layout.fragment_crime_list, container, false);

        mCrimeRecyclerView = (RecyclerView) view
                .findViewById(R.id.crime_recycler_view);
        mCrimeRecyclerView.setLayoutManager(new LinearLayoutManager(getActivity()));

        return view;
    }

}
```

Note that as soon as you create your **RecyclerView**, you give it another object called a **LayoutManager**. **RecyclerView** requires a **LayoutManager** to work. If you forget to give it one, it will crash.

We said earlier that **RecyclerView**'s only responsibilities are recycling **TextView**s and positioning them on the screen. But **RecyclerView** does not do the job of positioning items on the screen itself. It delegates that out to the **LayoutManager**. The **LayoutManager** handles the positioning of items and also defines the scrolling behavior. So if the **LayoutManager** is not there, **RecyclerView** will just fall over and die when it tries to do those things. This may change in the future, but that is the case for now.

There are a few built-in **LayoutManager**s to choose from, and you can find more as third-party libraries. You will use the **LinearLayoutManager**, which will position the items in the list vertically. Later on in this book, you will use **GridLayoutManager** to arrange items in a grid instead.

Run the app and you should again see a blank screen, but now you are looking at an empty **RecyclerView**. You will not see any **Crime**s represented on the screen until the **Adapter** and **ViewHolder** implementations are defined.

Implementing an Adapter and ViewHolder

Start by defining the **ViewHolder** as an inner class in **CrimeListFragment**.

Listing 9.17 A simple **ViewHolder** (CrimeListFragment.java)

```
public class CrimeListFragment extends Fragment {
    ...

    private class CrimeHolder extends RecyclerView.ViewHolder {

        public TextView mTitleTextView;

        public CrimeHolder(View itemView) {
            super(itemView);

            mTitleTextView = (TextView) itemView;
        }
    }
}
```

As it is now, this **ViewHolder** maintains a reference to a single view: the title **TextView**. This code expects for the itemView to be a **TextView**, and will crash if it is not. Later in the chapter, **CrimeHolder** will be given more responsibilities.

With the **ViewHolder** defined, create the adapter.

Listing 9.18 The beginnings of an adapter (CrimeListFragment.java)

```
public class CrimeListFragment extends Fragment {
    ...

    private class CrimeAdapter extends RecyclerView.Adapter<CrimeHolder> {

        private List<Crime> mCrimes;

        public CrimeAdapter(List<Crime> crimes) {
            mCrimes = crimes;
        }
    }
}
```

(The code in Listing 9.18 will not compile. You will fix this in a moment.)

The **RecyclerView** will communicate with this adapter when a **ViewHolder** needs to be created or connected with a **Crime** object. The **RecyclerView** itself will not know anything about the **Crime** object, but the **Adapter** will know all of **Crime**'s intimate and personal details.

Next, implement three methods in **CrimeAdapter**.

Listing 9.19 **CrimeAdapter** filled out (CrimeListFragment.java)

```java
private class CrimeAdapter extends RecyclerView.Adapter<CrimeHolder> {

    ...

    @Override
    public CrimeHolder onCreateViewHolder(ViewGroup parent, int viewType) {
        LayoutInflater layoutInflater = LayoutInflater.from(getActivity());
        View view = layoutInflater
            .inflate(android.R.layout.simple_list_item_1, parent, false);
        return new CrimeHolder(view);
    }

    @Override
    public void onBindViewHolder(CrimeHolder holder, int position) {
        Crime crime = mCrimes.get(position);
        holder.mTitleTextView.setText(crime.getTitle());
    }

    @Override
    public int getItemCount() {
        return mCrimes.size();
    }
}
```

There are a few things to unpack with this code. Let's start with the **onCreateViewHolder** implementation.

onCreateViewHolder is called by the **RecyclerView** when it needs a new **View** to display an item. In this method, you create the **View** and wrap it in a **ViewHolder**. The **RecyclerView** does not expect that you will hook it up to any data yet.

For the **View**, you inflate a layout from the Android standard library called simple_list_item_1. This layout contains a single **TextView**, styled to look nice in a list. Later in the chapter, you will make a more advanced **View** for the list items.

Next, **onBindViewHolder**: This method will bind a **ViewHolder**'s **View** to your model object. It receives the **ViewHolder** and a position in your data set. To bind your **View**, you use that position to find the right model data. Then you update the **View** to reflect that model data.

In your implementation, that position is the index of the **Crime** in your array. Once you pull it out, you bind that **Crime** to your **View** by sending its title to your **ViewHolder**'s **TextView**.

Now that you have an **Adapter**, your final step is to connect it to your **RecyclerView**. Implement a method called **updateUI** that sets up **CrimeListFragment**'s user interface. For now it will create a **CrimeAdapter** and set it on the **RecyclerView**.

Listing 9.20 Setting an **Adapter** (CrimeListFragment.java)

```
public class CrimeListFragment extends Fragment {

    private RecyclerView mCrimeRecyclerView;
    private CrimeAdapter mAdapter;

    @Override
    public View onCreateView(LayoutInflater inflater, ViewGroup container,
                             Bundle savedInstanceState) {
        View view = inflater.inflate(R.layout.fragment_crime_list, container, false);

        mCrimeRecyclerView = (RecyclerView) view
                .findViewById(R.id.crime_recycler_view);
        mCrimeRecyclerView.setLayoutManager(new LinearLayoutManager(getActivity()));

        updateUI();

        return view;
    }

    private void updateUI() {
        CrimeLab crimeLab = CrimeLab.get(getActivity());
        List<Crime> crimes = crimeLab.getCrimes();

        mAdapter = new CrimeAdapter(crimes);
        mCrimeRecyclerView.setAdapter(mAdapter);
    }

    ...
}
```

In later chapters, you will add more to **updateUI()** as configuring your user interface gets more involved.

Run CriminalIntent and scroll through your new **RecyclerView**, which should look like Figure 9.9.

Figure 9.9 A beautiful list of **Crime**s

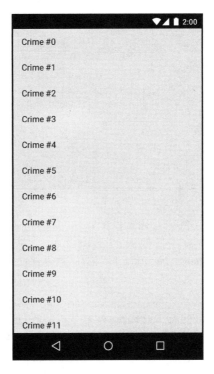

Customizing List Items

So far, each of your list items only displays the title of a **Crime** using a simple **TextView**.

What do you do when you want to display more information in each list item? What if you want to customize the design of each list item? Moving your item view to a separate layout file will allow you to do both of these things while also cleaning up the code.

Creating the list item layout

For CriminalIntent, a list item's layout should include the crime's title, its date, and whether the case has been solved (Figure 9.10). This layout calls for two **TextView**s and a **CheckBox**.

Figure 9.10 A handful of custom list items

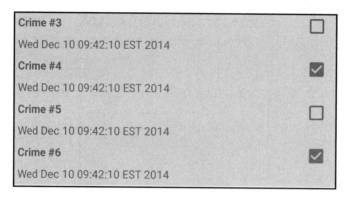

You create a new layout for a list item view the same way you do for the view of an activity or a fragment. In the Project tool window, right-click the res/layout directory and choose New → Layout resource file. In the dialog that appears, name the file list_item_crime. Set the Root element to RelativeLayout and click OK.

In a RelativeLayout, you use layout parameters to arrange child views relative to the root layout and to each other. You are going to have the CheckBox align itself to the right-hand side of the RelativeLayout. The two TextViews will align themselves relative to the CheckBox.

Figure 9.11 shows the widgets for the custom list item layout. The CheckBox child should be defined first even though it will appear on the right-hand side of the layout. This is because the TextViews will use the ID of the CheckBox as an attribute value. For the same reason, the title TextView is defined before the date TextView. In a layout file, an ID must be defined with an @+id before other widgets can use that ID in their own definitions with @id.

Figure 9.11 Custom list item layout (`list_item_crime.xml`)

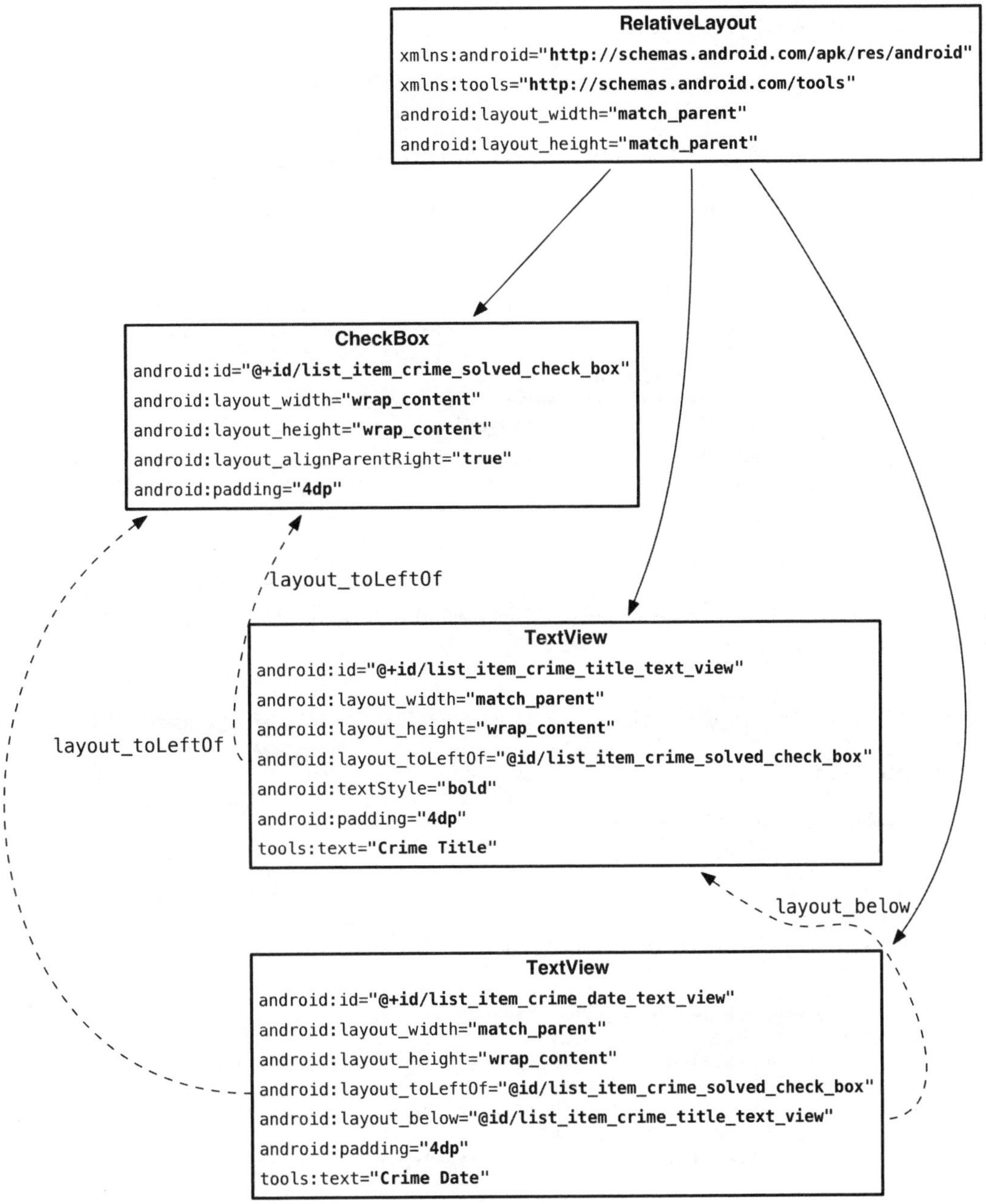

RelativeLayout
xmlns:android="**http://schemas.android.com/apk/res/android**"
xmlns:tools="**http://schemas.android.com/tools**"
android:layout_width="**match_parent**"
android:layout_height="**match_parent**"

CheckBox
android:id="**@+id/list_item_crime_solved_check_box**"
android:layout_width="**wrap_content**"
android:layout_height="**wrap_content**"
android:layout_alignParentRight="**true**"
android:padding="**4dp**"

layout_toLeftOf

TextView
android:id="**@+id/list_item_crime_title_text_view**"
android:layout_width="**match_parent**"
android:layout_height="**wrap_content**"
android:layout_toLeftOf="**@id/list_item_crime_solved_check_box**"
android:textStyle="**bold**"
android:padding="**4dp**"
tools:text="**Crime Title**"

layout_toLeftOf

layout_below

TextView
android:id="**@+id/list_item_crime_date_text_view**"
android:layout_width="**match_parent**"
android:layout_height="**wrap_content**"
android:layout_toLeftOf="**@id/list_item_crime_solved_check_box**"
android:layout_below="**@id/list_item_crime_title_text_view**"
android:padding="**4dp**"
tools:text="**Crime Date**"

Notice that when you use a widget's ID in another widget's definition, you do not include the +. The + sign is used to create the ID when it first appears in a layout file – typically in an android:id attribute. You can use + to create the ID in another place if necessary, but layout files are usually easier to read when you include the IDs in the widget's android:id attribute.

Your custom list item layout is complete, and you can turn to the next step – updating your adapter.

Using a custom item view

Now, update the **CrimeAdapter** to use the new list_item_crime layout file.

Listing 9.21 Inflating a custom layout (CrimeListFragment.java)

```
private class CrimeAdapter extends RecyclerView.Adapter<CrimeHolder> {

    ...

    @Override
    public CrimeHolder onCreateViewHolder(ViewGroup parent, int viewType) {
        LayoutInflater layoutInflater = LayoutInflater.from(getActivity());
        View view = layoutInflater
            .inflate(android.R.layout.simple_list_item_1
                     R.layout.list_item_crime, parent, false);
        return new CrimeHolder(view);
    }

    ...

}
```

Next, it is finally time to give **CrimeHolder** more responsibility. Modify **CrimeHolder** to find the title **TextView**, date **TextView**, and solved **CheckBox**.

Listing 9.22 Finding views in the **CrimeHolder** (CrimeListFragment.java)

```
private class CrimeHolder extends RecyclerView.ViewHolder {

    public TextView mTitleTextView;
    private TextView mTitleTextView;
    private TextView mDateTextView;
    private CheckBox mSolvedCheckBox;

    public CrimeHolder(View itemView) {
        super(itemView);

        mTitleTextView = (TextView) itemView;
        mTitleTextView = (TextView)
            itemView.findViewById(R.id.list_item_crime_title_text_view);
        mDateTextView = (TextView)
            itemView.findViewById(R.id.list_item_crime_date_text_view);
        mSolvedCheckBox = (CheckBox)
            itemView.findViewById(R.id.list_item_crime_solved_check_box);
    }
}
```

This is where your **ViewHolder** starts to flourish. Calls to **findViewById(int)** are often expensive. They go door to door throughout your entire itemView looking for your **View**: "Hey, are you list_item_crime_title_text_view? No? Oh, sorry for troubling you." This takes time to do, and you have to walk all over your memory neighborhood to do it.

ViewHolder can relieve a lot of this pain. By stashing the results of these **findViewById(int)** calls, you only have to spend that time in **createViewHolder(…)**. When **onBindViewHolder(…)** is called, the work is already done. Which is nice, because **onBindViewHolder(…)** is called much more often than **onCreateViewHolder(…)**.

However, that binding process is a little more complicated now. Add a **bindCrime(Crime)** method to **CrimeHolder** to clean things up a bit.

Listing 9.23 Binding views in the **CrimeHolder** (CrimeListFragment.java)

```
private class CrimeHolder extends RecyclerView.ViewHolder {

    private Crime mCrime;

    ...

    public void bindCrime(Crime crime) {
        mCrime = crime;
        mTitleTextView.setText(mCrime.getTitle());
        mDateTextView.setText(mCrime.getDate().toString());
        mSolvedCheckBox.setChecked(mCrime.isSolved());
    }
}
```

When given a **Crime**, **CrimeHolder** will now update the title **TextView**, date **TextView**, and solved **CheckBox** to reflect the state of the **Crime**.

The **CrimeHolder** has everything it needs to do its job. The **CrimeAdapter** just needs to use the new **bindCrime** method.

Listing 9.24 Connecting the **CrimeAdapter** to the **CrimeHolder** (CrimeListFragment.java)

```
private class CrimeAdapter extends RecyclerView.Adapter<CrimeHolder> {

    ...

    @Override
    public void onBindViewHolder(CrimeHolder holder, int position) {
        Crime crime = mCrimes.get(position);
        holder.mTitleTextView.setText(crime.getTitle());
        holder.bindCrime(crime);
    }

    ...
}
```

Run CriminalIntent to see the new list_item_crime layout file in action (Figure 9.12).

Figure 9.12 Now with custom list items!

Responding to Presses

As icing on the **RecyclerView** cake, CriminalIntent should also respond to a press on these list items. In Chapter 10, you will launch the detail view for a **Crime** when the user presses on that **Crime** in the list. For now, show a **Toast** when the user takes action on a **Crime**.

As you may have noticed, **RecyclerView**, while powerful and capable, has precious few real responsibilities. (May it be an example to us all.) The same goes here: handling touch events is mostly up to you. If you need them, **RecyclerView** can forward along raw touch events. Most of the time, though, this is not necessary.

Instead, you can handle them like you normally do: by setting an **OnClickListener**. Since each **View** has an associated **ViewHolder**, you can make your **ViewHolder** the **OnClickListener** for its **View**.

Modify the **CrimeHolder** to handle presses for the entire row.

Listing 9.25 Detecting presses in **CrimeHolder** (CrimeListFragment.java)

```java
private class CrimeHolder extends RecyclerView.ViewHolder
        implements View.OnClickListener {

    ...
    public CrimeHolder(View itemView) {
        super(itemView);
        itemView.setOnClickListener(this);

        ...
    }

    ...

    @Override
    public void onClick(View v) {
        Toast.makeText(getActivity(),
                mCrime.getTitle() + " clicked!", Toast.LENGTH_SHORT)
                .show();
    }
}
```

In Listing 9.25, the **CrimeHolder** itself is implementing the **OnClickListener** interface. On the **itemView**, which is the **View** for the entire row, the **CrimeHolder** is set as the receiver of click events.

Run CriminalIntent and press on an item in the list. You should see a **Toast** indicating that the item was clicked.

For the More Curious: ListView and GridView

The core Android OS includes **ListView**, **GridView**, and **Adapter** classes. Until the release of Android 5.0, these were the preferred ways to create lists or grids of items.

The API for these components is very similar to that of a **RecyclerView**. The **ListView** or **GridView** class is responsible for scrolling a collection of items, but does not know much about each of those items. The **Adapter** is responsible for creating each of the **View**s in the list. However, **ListView** and **GridView** do not enforce that you use the **ViewHolder** pattern (though you can – and should – use it).

These old implementations are replaced by the **RecyclerView** implementation because of the complexity required to alter the behavior of a **ListView** or **GridView**.

Creating a horizontally scrolling **ListView**, for example, is not included in the **ListView** API and requires a lot of work. Creating custom layout and scrolling behavior with a **RecyclerView** is still a lot of work, but **RecyclerView** was built to be extended, so it is not quite so bad.

Another key feature of **RecyclerView** is the animation of items in the list. Animating the addition or removal of items in a **ListView** or **GridView** is a complex and error-prone task. **RecyclerView** makes this much easier, includes a few built-in animations, and allows for easy customization of these animations.

For example, if you found out that the crime at position 0 moved to position 5, you could animate that change like so:

```java
mRecyclerView.getAdapter().notifyItemMoved(0, 5);
```

For the More Curious: Singletons

The singleton pattern, as used in the `CrimeLab`, is very common on Android. Singletons get a bad rap because they can be misused in a way that makes an app hard to maintain.

Singletons are often used in Android because they outlive a single fragment or activity. A singleton will still exist across rotation and will exist as you move between activities and fragments in your application.

Singletons make a convenient owner of your model objects. Imagine a more complex CriminalIntent application that had many activities and fragments modifying crimes. When one controller modifies a crime, how would you make sure that updated crime was sent over to the other controllers? If the `CrimeLab` is the owner of crimes and all modifications to crimes pass through the `CrimeLab`, propagating changes is much easier. As you transition between controllers, you can pass the crime ID as an identifier for a particular crime and have each controller pull the full crime object from the `CrimeLab` using that ID.

However, singletons do have a few downsides. For example, while they allow for an easy place to stash data with a longer lifetime than a controller, singletons do have a lifetime. Singletons will be destroyed, along with all of their instance variables, as Android reclaims memory at some point after you switch out of an application. Singletons are not a long-term storage solution. (Writing the files to disk or sending them to a web server is.)

Singletons can also make your code hard to unit test. There is not a great way to replace the `CrimeLab` instance in this chapter with a mock version of itself because the code is calling a static method directly on the `CrimeLab` object. In practice, Android developers usually solve this problem using a tool called a *dependency injector*. This tool allows for objects to be shared as singletons, while still making it possible to replace them when needed.

Singletons also have the potential to be misused. The temptation is to use singletons for everything, since they are convenient – you can get to them wherever you are, and store whatever information you need to get at later. But when you do that, you are avoiding answering important questions: Where is this data used? Where is this method important?

A singleton does not answer those questions. So whoever comes after you will open up your singleton and find something that looks like somebody's disorganized junk drawer: batteries, zip ties, old photographs? What is all this here for? Make sure that anything in your singleton is truly global and has a strong reason for being there.

On balance, however, singletons are a key component of a well-architected Android app – when used correctly.

10

Using Fragment Arguments

In this chapter, you will get the list and the detail parts of CriminalIntent working together. When a user presses an item in the list of crimes, a new **CrimeActivity** hosting a **CrimeFragment** will appear and display the details for a particular instance of **Crime** (Figure 10.1).

Figure 10.1 Starting **CrimeActivity** from **CrimeListActivity**

In GeoQuiz, you had one activity (**QuizActivity**) start another activity (**CheatActivity**). In CriminalIntent, you are going to start the **CrimeActivity** from a fragment. In particular, you will have **CrimeListFragment** start an instance of **CrimeActivity**.

Starting an Activity from a Fragment

Starting an activity from a fragment works nearly the same as starting an activity from another activity. You call the **Fragment.startActivity(Intent)** method, which calls the corresponding **Activity** method behind the scenes.

In **CrimeListFragment**'s **CrimeHolder**, replace the toast with code that starts an instance of **CrimeActivity**.

Listing 10.1 Starting **CrimeActivity** (CrimeListFragment.java)

```java
private class CrimeHolder extends RecyclerView.ViewHolder
        implements View.OnClickListener {
    ...

    @Override
    public void onClick(View v) {
        Toast.makeText(getActivity(),
                mCrime.getTitle() + " clicked!", Toast.LENGTH_SHORT)
                .show();

        Intent intent = new Intent(getActivity(), CrimeActivity.class);
        startActivity(intent);
    }
}
```

Here **CrimeListFragment** creates an explicit intent that names the **CrimeActivity** class. **CrimeListFragment** uses the **getActivity()** method to pass its hosting activity as the **Context** object that the **Intent** constructor requires.

Run CriminalIntent. Press any list item, and you will see a new **CrimeActivity** hosting a **CrimeFragment** (Figure 10.2).

Figure 10.2 A blank **CrimeFragment**

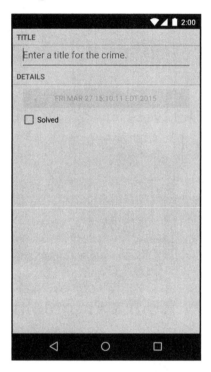

The **CrimeFragment** does not yet display the data for a specific **Crime** because you have not told it which **Crime** to display.

Putting an extra

You can tell **CrimeFragment** which **Crime** to display by passing the crime ID as an **Intent** extra when **CrimeActivity** is started.

Start by creating a **newIntent** method in **CrimeActivity**.

Listing 10.2 Creating a **newIntent** method (`CrimeActivity.java`)

```java
public class CrimeActivity extends SingleFragmentActivity {

    public static final String EXTRA_CRIME_ID =
            "com.bignerdranch.android.criminalintent.crime_id";

    public static Intent newIntent(Context packageContext, UUID crimeId) {
        Intent intent = new Intent(packageContext, CrimeActivity.class);
        intent.putExtra(EXTRA_CRIME_ID, crimeId);
        return intent;
    }

    ...

}
```

After creating an explicit intent, you call **putExtra(…)** and pass in a string key and the value the key maps to (the `crimeId`). In this case, you are calling **putExtra(String, Serializable)** because **UUID** is a **Serializable** object.

Now, update the **CrimeHolder** to use the **newIntent** method while passing in the crime ID.

Listing 10.3 Stashing and passing a **Crime** (`CrimeListFragment.java`)

```java
private class CrimeHolder extends RecyclerView.ViewHolder
        implements View.OnClickListener {

    ...

    @Override
    public void onClick(View v) {
        Intent intent = new Intent(getActivity(), CrimeActivity.class);
        Intent intent = CrimeActivity.newIntent(getActivity(), mCrime.getId());
        startActivity(intent);
    }
}
```

Retrieving an extra

The crime ID is now safely stashed in the intent that belongs to **CrimeActivity**. However, it is the **CrimeFragment** class that needs to retrieve and use that data.

There are two ways a fragment can access data in its activity's intent: an easy, direct shortcut and a complex, flexible implementation. First, you are going to try out the shortcut. Then you will implement the complex and flexible solution that involves *fragment arguments*.

In the shortcut, **CrimeFragment** will simply use the **getActivity()** method to access the **CrimeActivity**'s intent directly. Return to **CrimeFragment** and retrieve the extra from **CrimeActivity**'s intent and use it to fetch the **Crime**.

Listing 10.4 Retrieving the extra and fetching the **Crime** (CrimeFragment.java)

```java
public class CrimeFragment extends Fragment {

    ...

    public void onCreate(Bundle savedInstanceState) {
        super.onCreate(savedInstanceState);
        mCrime = new Crime();
        UUID crimeId = (UUID) getActivity().getIntent()
                .getSerializableExtra(CrimeActivity.EXTRA_CRIME_ID);
        mCrime = CrimeLab.get(getActivity()).getCrime(crimeId);
    }

    ...
}
```

In Listing 10.4, other than the call to **getActivity()**, the code is the same as if you were retrieving the extra from the activity's code. The **getIntent()** method returns the **Intent** that was used to start **CrimeActivity**. You call **getSerializableExtra(String)** on the **Intent** to pull the **UUID** out into a variable.

After you have retrieved the ID, you use it to fetch the **Crime** from **CrimeLab**.

Updating CrimeFragment's view with Crime data

Now that **CrimeFragment** fetches a **Crime**, its view can display that **Crime**'s data. Update **onCreateView(…)** to display the **Crime**'s title and solved status. (The code for displaying the date is already in place.)

Listing 10.5 Updating view objects (CrimeFragment.java)

```java
@Override
public View onCreateView(LayoutInflater inflater, ViewGroup parent,
        Bundle savedInstanceState) {
    ...

    mTitleField = (EditText)v.findViewById(R.id.crime_title);
    mTitleField.setText(mCrime.getTitle());
    mTitleField.addTextChangedListener(new TextWatcher() {
        ...
    });

    ...

    mSolvedCheckBox = (CheckBox)v.findViewById(R.id.crime_solved);
    mSolvedCheckBox.setChecked(mCrime.isSolved());
    mSolvedCheckBox.setOnCheckedChangeListener(new OnCheckedChangeListener() {
        ...
    });

    ...

    return v;
}
```

Run CriminalIntent. Select Crime #4 and watch a **CrimeFragment** instance with the correct crime data appear (Figure 10.3).

Figure 10.3 The crime that you wanted to see

The downside to direct retrieval

Having the fragment access the intent that belongs to the hosting activity makes for simple code. However, it costs you the encapsulation of your fragment. **CrimeFragment** is no longer a reusable building block because it expects that it will always be hosted by an activity whose **Intent** defines an extra named com.bignerdranch.android.criminalintent.crime_id.

This may be a reasonable expectation on **CrimeFragment**'s part, but it means that **CrimeFragment**, as currently written, cannot be used with just any activity.

A better solution is to stash the crime ID someplace that belongs to **CrimeFragment** rather than keeping it in **CrimeActivity**'s personal space. The **CrimeFragment** could then retrieve this data without relying on the presence of a particular extra in the activity's intent. The "someplace" that belongs to a fragment is known as its *arguments* bundle.

Fragment Arguments

Every fragment instance can have a **Bundle** object attached to it. This bundle contains key-value pairs that work just like the intent extras of an **Activity**. Each pair is known as an *argument*.

To create fragment arguments, you first create a **Bundle** object. Next, you use type-specific "put" methods of **Bundle** (similar to those of **Intent**) to add arguments to the bundle:

```
Bundle args = new Bundle();
args.putSerializable(EXTRA_MY_OBJECT, myObject);
args.putInt(EXTRA_MY_INT, myInt);
args.putCharSequence(EXTRA_MY_STRING, myString);
```

Attaching arguments to a fragment

To attach the arguments bundle to a fragment, you call **Fragment.setArguments(Bundle)**. Attaching arguments to a fragment must be done after the fragment is created but before it is added to an activity.

To hit this window, Android programmers follow a convention of adding a static method named **newInstance()** to the **Fragment** class. This method creates the fragment instance and bundles up and sets its arguments.

When the hosting activity needs an instance of that fragment, you have it call the **newInstance()** method rather than calling the constructor directly. The activity can pass in any required parameters to **newInstance(…)** that the fragment needs to create its arguments.

In **CrimeFragment**, write a **newInstance(UUID)** method that accepts a **UUID**, creates an arguments bundle, creates a fragment instance, and then attaches the arguments to the fragment.

Listing 10.6 Writing a **newInstance(UUID)** method (CrimeFragment.java)

```
public class CrimeFragment extends Fragment {

    private static final String ARG_CRIME_ID = "crime_id";

    private Crime mCrime;
    private EditText mTitleField;
    private Button mDateButton;
    private CheckBox mSolvedCheckbox;

    public static CrimeFragment newInstance(UUID crimeId) {
        Bundle args = new Bundle();
        args.putSerializable(ARG_CRIME_ID, crimeId);

        CrimeFragment fragment = new CrimeFragment();
        fragment.setArguments(args);
        return fragment;
    }

    ...
}
```

Now **CrimeActivity** should call **CrimeFragment.newInstance(UUID)** when it needs to create a **CrimeFragment**. It will pass in the **UUID** it retrieved from its extra. Return to **CrimeActivity** and, in **createFragment()**, retrieve the extra from **CrimeActivity**'s intent and pass it into **CrimeFragment.newInstance(UUID)**.

You can now also make **EXTRA_CRIME_ID** private since no other class will access that extra. (Note that while we have struck through and replaced the complete line for clarity, in reality you only have to replace "public" with "private" for the first change shown.)

Listing 10.7 Using **newInstance(UUID)** (CrimeActivity.java)

```java
public class CrimeActivity extends SingleFragmentActivity {

    public static final String EXTRA_CRIME_ID =
            "com.bignerdranch.android.criminalintent.crime_id";

    private static final String EXTRA_CRIME_ID =
            "com.bignerdranch.android.criminalintent.crime_id";

    ...

    @Override
    protected Fragment createFragment() {
        return new CrimeFragment();
        UUID crimeId = (UUID) getIntent()
                .getSerializableExtra(EXTRA_CRIME_ID);
        return CrimeFragment.newInstance(crimeId);
    }

}
```

Notice that the need for independence does not go both ways. **CrimeActivity** has to know plenty about **CrimeFragment**, including that it has a **newInstance(UUID)** method. This is fine. Hosting activities should know the specifics of how to host their fragments, but fragments should not have to know specifics about their activities. At least, not if you want to maintain the flexibility of independent fragments.

Retrieving arguments

When a fragment needs to access its arguments, it calls the **Fragment** method **getArguments()** and then one of the type-specific "get" methods of **Bundle**.

Back in **CrimeFragment.onCreate(…)**, replace your shortcut code with retrieving the **UUID** from the fragment arguments.

Listing 10.8 Getting crime ID from the arguments (CrimeFragment.java)

```java
@Override
public void onCreate(Bundle savedInstanceState) {
    super.onCreate(savedInstanceState);

    UUID crimeId = (UUID) getActivity().getIntent()
            .getSerializableExtra(CrimeActivity.EXTRA_CRIME_ID);
    UUID crimeId = (UUID) getArguments().getSerializable(ARG_CRIME_ID);

    mCrime = CrimeLab.get(getActivity()).getCrime(crimeId);

}
```

Run CriminalIntent. The app will behave the same, but you should feel all warm and fuzzy inside for maintaining **CrimeFragment**'s independence. You are also well prepared for the next chapter, where you will implement more sophisticated navigation in CriminalIntent.

Reloading the List

There is one more detail to take care of. Run CriminalIntent, press a list item, and then modify that **Crime**'s details. These changes are saved to the model, but when you return to the list, the **RecyclerView** is unchanged.

The **RecyclerView**'s **Adapter** needs to be informed that the data has changed (or may have changed) so that it can refetch the data and reload the list. You can work with the **ActivityManager**'s back stack to reload the list at the right moment.

When **CrimeListFragment** starts an instance of **CrimeActivity**, the **CrimeActivity** is put on top of the stack. This pauses and stops the instance of **CrimeListActivity** that was initially on top.

When the user presses the Back button to return to the list, the **CrimeActivity** is popped off the stack and destroyed. At that point, the **CrimeListActivity** is started and resumed (Figure 10.4).

Figure 10.4 CriminalIntent's back stack

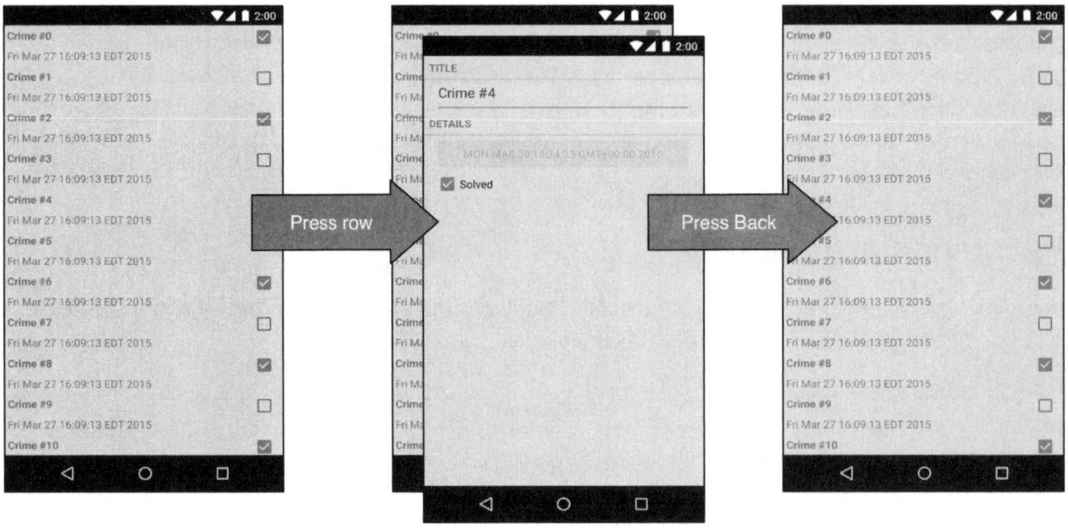

When the **CrimeListActivity** is resumed, it receives a call to **onResume()** from the OS. When **CrimeListActivity** receives this call, its **FragmentManager** calls **onResume()** on the fragments that the activity is currently hosting. In this case, the only fragment is **CrimeListFragment**.

In **CrimeListFragment**, override **onResume()** and trigger a call to **updateUI()** to reload the list. Modify the **updateUI()** method to call **notifyDataSetChanged()** if the **CrimeAdapter** is already set up.

Listing 10.9 Reloading the list in **onResume()** (CrimeListFragment.java)

```java
@Override
public View onCreateView(LayoutInflater inflater, ViewGroup container,
                         Bundle savedInstanceState) {
    ...
}

@Override
public void onResume() {
    super.onResume();
    updateUI();
}

private void updateUI() {
    CrimeLab crimeLab = CrimeLab.get(getActivity());
    List<Crime> crimes = crimeLab.getCrimes();

    if (mAdapter == null) {
        mAdapter = new CrimeAdapter(crimes);
        mCrimeRecyclerView.setAdapter(mAdapter);
    } else {
        mAdapter.notifyDataSetChanged();
    }
}
```

Why override **onResume()** to update the **RecyclerView** and not **onStart()**? You cannot assume that your activity will be stopped when another activity is in front of it. If the other activity is transparent, your activity may just be paused. If your activity is paused and your update code is in **onStart()**, then the list will not be reloaded. In general, **onResume()** is the safest place to take action to update a fragment's view.

Run CriminalIntent. Select a crime and change its details. When you return to the list, you will immediately see your changes.

You have made progress with CriminalIntent in the last two chapters. Let's take a look at an updated object diagram (Figure 10.5).

Figure 10.5 Updated object diagram for CriminalIntent

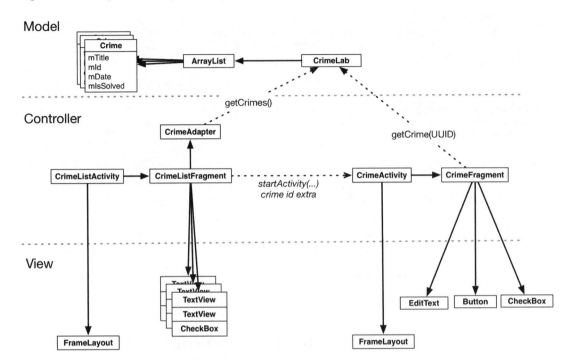

Getting Results with Fragments

In this chapter, you did not need a result back from the started activity. What if you did? Your code would look a lot like it did in GeoQuiz. Instead of using the **Activity**'s **startActivityForResult(…)** method, you would use **Fragment.startActivityForResult(…)**. Instead of overriding **Activity.onActivityResult(…)**, you would override **Fragment.onActivityResult(…)**:

```
public class CrimeListFragment extends Fragment {

    private static final int REQUEST_CRIME = 1;

    ...

    private class CrimeHolder extends RecyclerView.ViewHolder
            implements View.OnClickListener {

        ...

        @Override
        public void onClick(View v) {
            Intent intent = CrimeActivity.newIntent(getActivity(), mCrime.getId());
            startActivityForResult(intent, REQUEST_CRIME);
        }
    }

    @Override
    public void onActivityResult(int requestCode, int resultCode, Intent data) {
        if (requestCode == REQUEST_CRIME) {
            // Handle result
        }
    }

    ...
}
```

Fragment.startActivityForResult(Intent, int) is similar to the **Activity** method with the same name. It includes some additional code to route the result to your fragment from its host activity.

Returning results from a fragment is a bit different. A fragment can receive a result from an activity, but it cannot have its own result. Only activities have results. So while **Fragment** has its own **startActivityForResult(…)** and **onActivityResult(…)** methods, it does not have any **setResult(…)** methods.

Instead, you tell the *host activity* to return a value. Like this:

```
public class CrimeFragment extends Fragment {
    ...

    public void returnResult() {
        getActivity().setResult(Activity.RESULT_OK, null);
    }
}
```

Challenge: Efficient RecyclerView Reloading

The **notifyDataSetChanged** method on your **Adapter** is a handy way to ask the **RecyclerView** to reload all of the items that are currently visible.

The use of this method in CriminalIntent is wildly inefficient because at most one **Crime** will have changed when returning to the **CrimeListFragment**.

Use the **RecyclerView.Adapter**'s **notifyItemChanged(int)** method to reload a single item in the list. Modifying the code to call that method is easy. The challenge is discovering which position has changed and reloading the correct item.

For the More Curious: Why Use Fragment Arguments?

This all seems so complicated. Why not just set an instance variable on the **CrimeFragment** when it is created?

Because it would not always work. When the OS re-creates your fragment, either across a configuration change or when the user has switched out of your app and the OS reclaims memory, all of your instance variables will be lost. Also, remember that there is no way to cheat low-memory death, no matter how hard you try.

If you want something that works in all cases, you have to persist your arguments.

One option is to use the saved instance state mechanism. You can store the crime ID as a normal instance variable, save the crime ID in **onSaveInstanceState(Bundle)**, and snag it from the **Bundle** in **onCreate(Bundle)**. This will work in all situations.

However, that solution is hard to maintain. If you revisit this fragment in a few years and add another argument, you may not remember to save the argument in **onSaveInstanceState(Bundle)**. Going this route is less explicit.

Android developers prefer the fragment arguments solution because it is very explicit and clear in its intentions. In a few years, you will come back and know that the crime ID is an argument and is safely shuttled along to new instances of this fragment. If you add another argument, you will know to stash it in the arguments bundle.

11

Using ViewPager

In this chapter, you will create a new activity to host **CrimeFragment**. This activity's layout will consist of an instance of **ViewPager**. Adding a **ViewPager** to your UI lets users navigate between list items by swiping across the screen to "page" forward or backward through the crimes (Figure 11.1).

Figure 11.1 Swiping to page through crimes

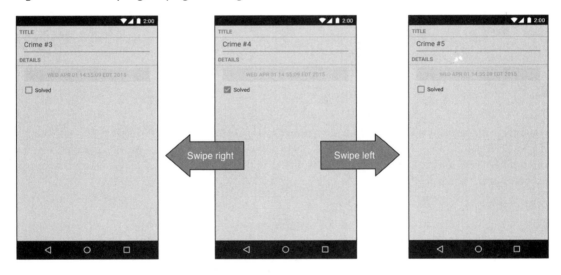

Figure 11.2 shows an updated diagram for CriminalIntent. The new activity will be named **CrimePagerActivity** and will take the place of **CrimeActivity**. Its layout will consist of a **ViewPager**.

Figure 11.2 Object diagram for **CrimePagerActivity**

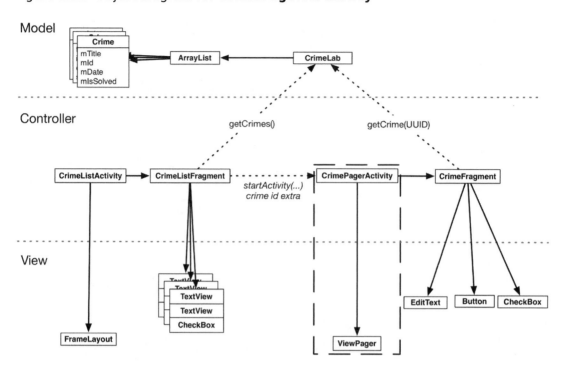

The only new objects you need to create are within the dashed rectangle in the diagram above. Nothing else in CriminalIntent needs to change to implement paging between detail views. In particular, you will not have to touch the **CrimeFragment** class thanks to the work you did in Chapter 10 to ensure **CrimeFragment**'s independence.

Here are the tasks ahead in this chapter:

- create the **CrimePagerActivity** class

- define a view hierarchy that consists of a **ViewPager**

- wire up the **ViewPager** and its adapter in **CrimePagerActivity**

- modify **CrimeHolder.onClick(...)** to start **CrimePagerActivity** instead of **CrimeActivity**

Creating CrimePagerActivity

CrimePagerActivity will be a subclass of **FragmentActivity**. It will create and manage the **ViewPager**.

Create a new class named **CrimePagerActivity**. Make its superclass **FragmentActivity** and set up the view for the activity.

Listing 11.1 Set up **ViewPager** (CrimePagerActivity.java)

```
public class CrimePagerActivity extends FragmentActivity {

    @Override
    protected void onCreate(Bundle savedInstanceState) {
        super.onCreate(savedInstanceState);
        setContentView(R.layout.activity_crime_pager);
    }
}
```

The layout file does not yet exist. Create a new layout file in res/layout/ and name it activity_crime_pager. Make its root view a **ViewPager** and give it the attributes shown in Figure 11.3. Notice that you must use **ViewPager**'s full package name (**android.support.v4.view.ViewPager**).

Figure 11.3 **CrimePagerActivity**'s **ViewPager** (activity_crime_pager.xml)

android.support.v4.view.ViewPager
xmlns:android="**http://schemas.android.com/apk/res/android**"
android:id="**@+id/activity_crime_pager_view_pager**"
android:layout_width="**match_parent**"
android:layout_height="**match_parent**"

You use **ViewPager**'s full package name when adding it to the layout file because the **ViewPager** class is from the support library. Unlike **Fragment**, **ViewPager** is only available in the support library; there is not a "standard" **ViewPager** class in a later SDK.

ViewPager and PagerAdapter

A **ViewPager** is like a **RecyclerView** in some ways. A **RecyclerView** requires an **Adapter** to provide views. A **ViewPager** requires a **PagerAdapter**.

However, the conversation between **ViewPager** and **PagerAdapter** is much more involved than the conversation between **RecyclerView** and **Adapter**. Luckily, you can use **FragmentStatePagerAdapter**, a subclass of **PagerAdapter**, to take care of many of the details.

FragmentStatePagerAdapter will boil down the conversation to two simple methods: **getCount()** and **getItem(int)**. When your **getItem(int)** method is called for a position in your array of crimes, it will return a **CrimeFragment** configured to display the crime at that position.

In **CrimePagerActivity**, set the **ViewPager**'s pager adapter and implement its **getCount()** and **getItem(int)** methods.

Listing 11.2 Setting up pager adapter (`CrimePagerActivity.java`)

```java
public class CrimePagerActivity extends FragmentActivity {

    private ViewPager mViewPager;
    private List<Crime> mCrimes;

    @Override
    protected void onCreate(Bundle savedInstanceState) {
        super.onCreate(savedInstanceState);
        setContentView(R.layout.activity_crime_pager);

        mViewPager = (ViewPager) findViewById(R.id.activity_crime_pager_view_pager);

        mCrimes = CrimeLab.get(this).getCrimes();
        FragmentManager fragmentManager = getSupportFragmentManager();
        mViewPager.setAdapter(new FragmentStatePagerAdapter(fragmentManager) {

            @Override
            public Fragment getItem(int position) {
                Crime crime = mCrimes.get(position);
                return CrimeFragment.newInstance(crime.getId());
            }

            @Override
            public int getCount() {
                return mCrimes.size();
            }
        });
    }
}
```

Let's go through this code. After finding the **ViewPager** in the activity's view, you get your data set
from **CrimeLab** – the **List** of crimes. Next, you get the activity's instance of **FragmentManager**.

Then you set the adapter to be an unnamed instance of **FragmentStatePagerAdapter**.
Creating the **FragmentStatePagerAdapter** requires the **FragmentManager**. Remember that
FragmentStatePagerAdapter is your agent managing the conversation with **ViewPager**. For your agent
to do its job with the fragments that **getItem(int)** returns, it needs to be able to add them to your
activity. That is why it needs your **FragmentManager**.

(What exactly is your agent doing? The short story is that it is adding the fragments you return to your
activity and helping **ViewPager** identify the fragments' views so that they can be placed correctly. More
details are in the For the More Curious section at the end of the chapter.)

The pager adapter's two methods are straightforward. The **getCount()** method returns the number of
items in the array list. The **getItem(int)** method is where the magic happens. It fetches the **Crime**
instance for the given position in the dataset. It then uses that **Crime**'s ID to create and return a properly
configured **CrimeFragment**.

Integrating CrimePagerActivity

Now you can begin the process of decommissioning **CrimeActivity** and putting **CrimePagerActivity**
in its place.

First add a **newIntent** method to **CrimePagerActivity** along with an extra for the crime ID.

Listing 11.3 Creating **newIntent** (CrimePagerActivity.java)

```java
public class CrimePagerActivity extends FragmentActivity {
    private static final String EXTRA_CRIME_ID =
            "com.bignerdranch.android.criminalintent.crime_id";

    private ViewPager mViewPager;
    private List<Crime> mCrimes;

    public static Intent newIntent(Context packageContext, UUID crimeId) {
        Intent intent = new Intent(packageContext, CrimePagerActivity.class);
        intent.putExtra(EXTRA_CRIME_ID, crimeId);
        return intent;
    }

    @Override
    protected void onCreate(Bundle savedInstanceState) {
        super.onCreate(savedInstanceState);
        setContentView(R.layout.activity_crime_pager);

        UUID crimeId = (UUID) getIntent()
                .getSerializableExtra(EXTRA_CRIME_ID);
        ...
    }
}
```

Now, you want pressing a list item in **CrimeListFragment** to start an instance of **CrimePagerActivity** instead of **CrimeActivity**.

Return to CrimeListFragment.java and modify **CrimeHolder.onClick(…)** to start a **CrimePagerActivity**.

Listing 11.4 Firing it up (CrimeListFragment.java)

```java
private class CrimeHolder extends RecyclerView.ViewHolder
        implements View.OnClickListener {

    ...

    @Override
    public void onClick(View v) {
        Intent intent = CrimeActivity.newIntent(getActivity(), mCrime.getId());
        Intent intent = CrimePagerActivity.newIntent(getActivity(), mCrime.getId());
        startActivity(intent);
    }
}
```

You also need to add **CrimePagerActivity** to the manifest so that the OS can start it. While you are in the manifest, remove **CrimeActivity**'s declaration. To accomplish this, you can just rename the **CrimeActivity** to **CrimePagerActivity** in the manifest.

Listing 11.5 Adding **CrimePagerActivity** to manifest (AndroidManifest.xml)

```xml
<?xml version="1.0" encoding="utf-8"?>
<manifest ...>
  ...
  <application ...>
    ...

    <activity
      android:name=".CrimeActivity"
      android:name=".CrimePagerActivity"
      android:label="@string/app_name" >
    </activity>

    ...
  </application>

</manifest>
```

Finally, to keep your project tidy, delete CrimeActivity.java from the project tool window.

Run CriminalIntent. Press Crime #0 to view its details. Then swipe left and right to browse more crimes. Notice that the paging is smooth and there is no delay in loading. By default, **ViewPager** loads the item currently on screen plus one neighboring page in each direction so that the response to a swipe is immediate. You can tweak how many neighboring pages are loaded by calling **setOffscreenPageLimit(int)**.

But all is not yet perfect with your **ViewPager**. Press Back to return to the list of crimes and press a different item. You will see the first crime displayed again instead of the crime that you asked for.

By default, the **ViewPager** shows the first item in its **PagerAdapter**. You can have it show the crime that was selected by setting the **ViewPager**'s current item to the index of the selected crime.

At the end of **CrimePagerActivity.onCreate(…)**, find the index of the crime to display by looping through and checking each crime's ID. When you find the **Crime** instance whose mId matches the crimeId in the intent extra, set the current item to the index of that **Crime**.

Listing 11.6 Setting initial pager item (CrimePagerActivity.java)

```java
public class CrimePagerActivity extends FragmentActivity {
    @Override
    public void onCreate(Bundle savedInstanceState) {
        ...

        FragmentManager fragmentManager = getSupportFragmentManager();
        mViewPager.setAdapter(new FragmentStatePagerAdapter(fragmentManager) {
            ...
        });

        for (int i = 0; i < mCrimes.size(); i++) {
            if (mCrimes.get(i).getId().equals(crimeId)) {
                mViewPager.setCurrentItem(i);
                break;
            }
        }
    }
}
```

Run CriminalIntent. Selecting any list item should display the details of the correct **Crime**. And that is it. Your **ViewPager** is now fully armed and operational.

FragmentStatePagerAdapter vs. FragmentPagerAdapter

There is another **PagerAdapter** type that you can use called **FragmentPagerAdapter**. **FragmentPagerAdapter** is used exactly like **FragmentStatePagerAdapter**. It only differs in how it unloads your fragments when they are no longer needed (Figure 11.4).

Figure 11.4 **FragmentStatePagerAdapter**'s fragment management

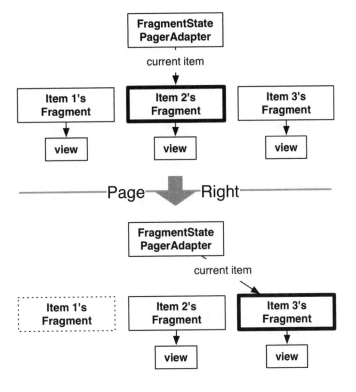

With **FragmentStatePagerAdapter**, your unneeded fragment is destroyed. A transaction is committed to completely remove the fragment from your activity's **FragmentManager**. The "state" in **FragmentStatePagerAdapter** comes from the fact that it will save out your fragment's **Bundle** from **onSaveInstanceState(Bundle)** when it is destroyed. When the user navigates back, the new fragment will be restored using that instance state.

FragmentPagerAdapter handles things differently. When your fragment is no longer needed, **FragmentPagerAdapter** calls **detach(Fragment)** on the transaction, instead of **remove(Fragment)**. This destroys the fragment's view, but leaves the fragment instance alive in the **FragmentManager**. So the fragments created by **FragmentPagerAdapter** are never destroyed (Figure 11.5).

Figure 11.5 **FragmentPagerAdapter**'s fragment management

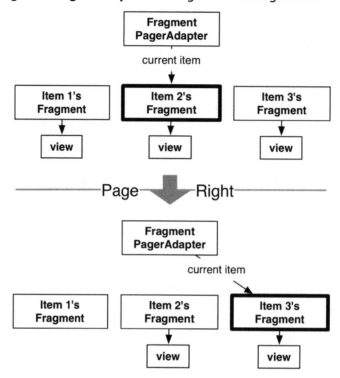

Which kind of adapter you want to use depends on your application. In general, **FragmentStatePagerAdapter** is more frugal with memory. CriminalIntent is displaying what could be a long list of crimes, each of which will eventually include a photo. You do not want to keep all that information in memory, so you use **FragmentStatePagerAdapter**.

On the other hand, if your interface has a small, fixed number of fragments, **FragmentPagerAdapter** is safe and appropriate. The most common example of this scenario is a tabbed interface. Some detail views have enough details to require two screens, so the details are split across multiple tabs. Adding a swipeable **ViewPager** to this interface makes the app tactile. Keeping these fragments in memory can make your controller code easier to manage, and because this style of interface usually has only two or three fragments per activity there is little danger of running low on memory.

For the More Curious: How ViewPager Really Works

The **ViewPager** and **PagerAdapter** classes handle many things for you behind the scenes. This section will supply more details about what is going on back there.

A caveat before we get into this discussion: you do not need to understand the nitty-gritty details in most cases.

But if you need to implement the **PagerAdapter** interface yourself, you will need to know how the **ViewPager**-**PagerAdapter** relationship differs from an ordinary **RecyclerView**-**Adapter** relationship.

When would you need to implement the **PagerAdapter** interface yourself? When you want **ViewPager** to host something other than **Fragment**s. If you want to host normal **View** objects in a **ViewPager**, like a few images, you implement the raw **PagerAdapter** interface.

So why is **ViewPager** not a **RecyclerView**?

Using a **RecyclerView** in this case would be a lot of work because you could not use your existing **Fragment**. An **Adapter** expects you to provide a **View** instantly. However, your **FragmentManager** determines when your fragment's view is created, not you. So when **RecyclerView** comes knocking at your **Adapter**'s door for your fragment's view, you will not be able to create the fragment *and* provide its view immediately.

This is the reason **ViewPager** exists. Instead of an **Adapter**, it uses a class called **PagerAdapter**. **PagerAdapter** is more complicated than **Adapter** because it does more of the work of managing views than **Adapter** does. Here are the basics.

Instead of an **onBindViewHolder(…)** method that returns a view holder and its corresponding view, **PagerAdapter** has the following methods:

```
public Object instantiateItem(ViewGroup container, int position)
public void destroyItem(ViewGroup container, int position, Object object)
public abstract boolean isViewFromObject(View view, Object object)
```

PagerAdapter.instantiateItem(ViewGroup, int) tells the pager adapter to create an item view for a given position and add it to a container **ViewGroup**, and **destroyItem(ViewGroup, int, Object)** tells it to destroy that item. Note that **instantiateItem(ViewGroup, int)** does not say to create the view *right now*. The **PagerAdapter** could create the view at any time after that.

Once the view has been created, **ViewPager** will notice it at some point. To figure out which item's view it is, it calls **isViewFromObject(View, Object)**. The **Object** parameter is an object received from a call to **instantiateItem(ViewGroup, int)**. So if **ViewPager** calls **instantiateItem(ViewGroup, 5)** and receives object A, **isViewFromObject(View, A)** should return true if the **View** passed in is for item 5, and false otherwise.

This is a complicated process for the **ViewPager**, but it is less complicated for the **PagerAdapter**, which only needs to be able to create views, destroy views, and identify which object a view comes from. This loose requirement gives a **PagerAdapter** implementation enough wiggle room to create and add a new fragment inside **instantiateItem(ViewGroup, int)** and return the fragment as the **Object** to keep track of. Then **isViewFromObject(View, Object)** looks like this:

```
@Override
public boolean isViewFromObject(View view, Object object) {
    return ((Fragment)object).getView() == view;
}
```

Implementing all those **PagerAdapter** overrides would be a pain to do every time you needed to use **ViewPager**. Thank goodness for **FragmentPagerAdapter** and **FragmentStatePagerAdapter**.

For the More Curious: Laying Out Views in Code

Throughout the book, you have been creating your views in layout files. It is also possible to create your views in code.

In fact, you could have defined your **ViewPager** in code without a layout file at all.

```
@Override
protected void onCreate(Bundle savedInstanceState) {
    super.onCreate(savedInstanceState);
    ViewPager viewPager = new ViewPager(this);
    setContentView(viewPager);

    ...
}
```

No magic is necessary to create a view: just call its constructor, passing in a **Context** as the parameter. You can programmatically create an entire view hierarchy instead of using layout files.

However, creating views in code should be avoided, because layout files provide a few benefits.

One benefit of layout files is that they help to provide a clear separation between your controller and view objects in your app. The view exists in XML and the controller exists in Java code. This separation makes your code easier to maintain by limiting the amount of changes in your controller when you change your view and vice versa.

Another benefit to views defined in XML is that you can use Android's resource qualification system to automatically choose the appropriate version of that XML file based on the properties of the device.

As you saw in Chapter 3, this system makes it easy to change your layout file depending on the orientation of the device (as well as other configurations).

So what are the downsides to using layout files? Well, you do have to go to the trouble of creating an XML file and inflating it. If you are creating a single view, sometimes you may not want to go to the trouble.

Otherwise, though, there are no downsides worth speaking of – the Android team has never recommended constructing view hierarchies programmatically, even back in the old days when developers had to be even more conscious of performance than they are now. Even if you need something as small as an ID on your view (which is often necessary, even with a programmatically created view), it is simpler to have a layout file.

12

Dialogs

Dialogs demand attention and input from the user. They are useful for presenting a choice or important information. In this chapter, you will add a dialog in which users can change the date of a crime. Pressing the date button in **CrimeFragment** will present this dialog on Lollipop (Figure 12.1).

Figure 12.1 A dialog for picking the date of a crime

The dialog in Figure 12.1 is an instance of **AlertDialog**, a subclass of **Dialog**. **AlertDialog** is the all-purpose **Dialog** subclass that you will use most often.

When Lollipop was released, dialogs were given a visual makeover. **AlertDialog**s on Lollipop automatically use this new style. On earlier versions of Android, **AlertDialog** will fall back to the older style as seen on the left in Figure 12.2.

Figure 12.2 Old vs new

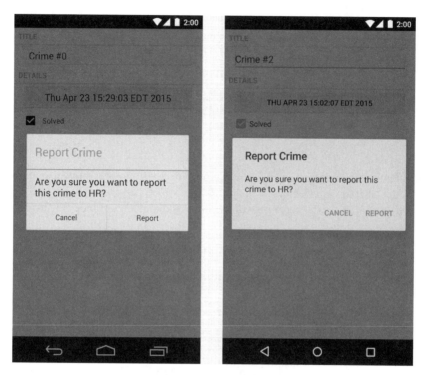

Rather than displaying the crusty old dialog style, it would be nice to always show the new dialog style, no matter which version of Android the user's device is on. You can do this with the *AppCompat* library.

The AppCompat library is a compatibility library provided by Google that back ports some features of recent versions of Android to older devices. In this chapter, you will use the AppCompat library to create a consistent dialog experience on all of your supported versions of Android. In Chapter 13 and Chapter 20, you will use some of the other features of the AppCompat library.

The AppCompat Library

To use the AppCompat library, you must first add it as a dependency. Depending on how your project was created, you may already have the AppCompat dependency.

Open the Project Structure window (File → Project Structure...), then select the app module and click on the Dependencies tab. If you do not see the AppCompat library listed, add it by clicking the + button and selecting the appcompat-v7 dependency from the list, as shown in Figure 12.3.

Figure 12.3 Selecting the AppCompat dependency

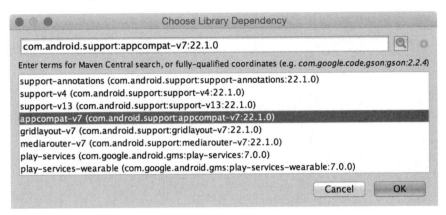

The AppCompat library includes its own **AlertDialog** class that you will use. This version of **AlertDialog** is very similar to the one included in the Android OS. The trick to using the right one is to make sure that you import the correct version of **AlertDialog**. You will use **android.support.v7.app.AlertDialog**.

Creating a DialogFragment

When using an **AlertDialog**, it is a good idea to wrap it in an instance of **DialogFragment**, a subclass of **Fragment**. It is possible to display an **AlertDialog** without a **DialogFragment**, but it is not recommended. Having the dialog managed by the **FragmentManager** gives you more options for presenting the dialog.

In addition, a bare **AlertDialog** will vanish if the device is rotated. On the other hand, if the **AlertDialog** is wrapped in a fragment, then the dialog will be re-created and put on screen after rotation.

For CriminalIntent, you are going to create a **DialogFragment** subclass named **DatePickerFragment**. Within **DatePickerFragment**, you will create and configure an instance of **AlertDialog** that displays a **DatePicker** widget. **DatePickerFragment** will be hosted by **CrimePagerActivity**.

Figure 12.4 shows you an overview of these relationships.

Figure 12.4 Object diagram for two fragments hosted by **CrimePagerActivity**

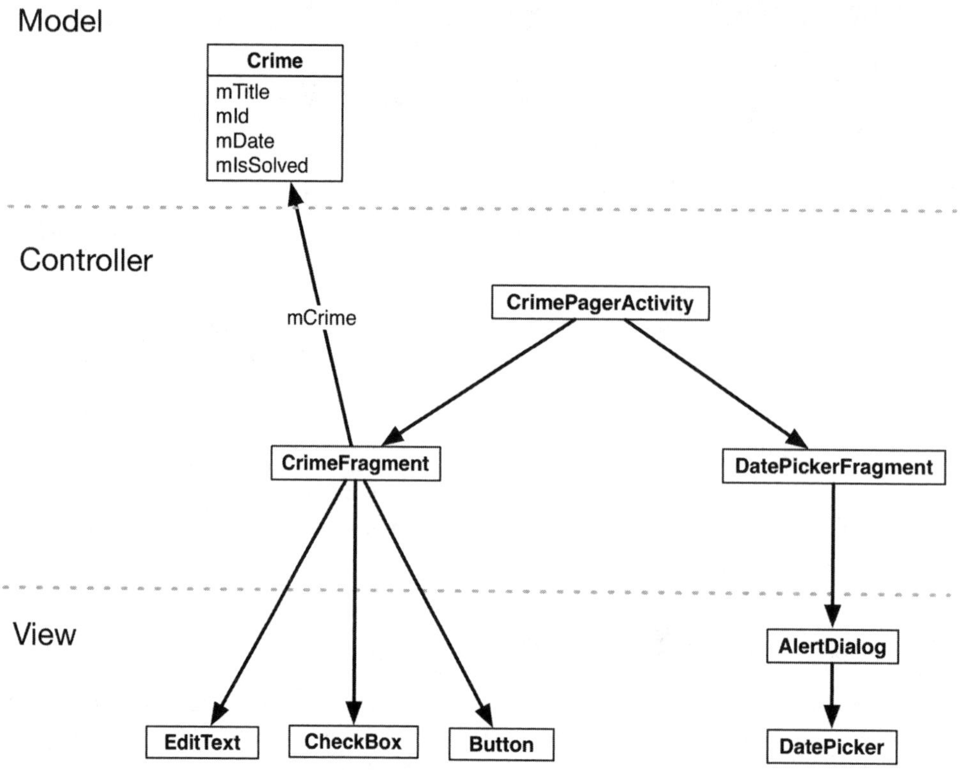

Your first tasks are:

- creating the **DatePickerFragment** class

- building an **AlertDialog**

- getting the dialog on screen via the **FragmentManager**

Later in the chapter, you will wire up the **DatePicker** and pass the necessary data between **CrimeFragment** and **DatePickerFragment**.

Before you get started, add the string resource shown in Listing 12.1.

Listing 12.1 Adding string for dialog title (`values/strings.xml`)

```
<resources>

    ...
    <string name="crime_solved_label">Solved</string>
    <string name="date_picker_title">Date of crime:</string>

</resources>
```

Create a new class named **DatePickerFragment** and make its superclass **DialogFragment**. Be sure to choose the support library's version of **DialogFragment**: **android.support.v4.app.DialogFragment**.

DialogFragment includes the following method:

```
public Dialog onCreateDialog(Bundle savedInstanceState)
```

The **FragmentManager** of the hosting activity calls this method as part of putting the **DialogFragment** on screen.

In DatePickerFragment.java, add an implementation of **onCreateDialog(…)** that builds an **AlertDialog** with a title and one OK button. (You will add the **DatePicker** widget later.)

Be sure that the version of **AlertDialog** that you import is the AppCompat version: **android.support.v7.app.AlertDialog**.

Listing 12.2 Creating a **DialogFragment** (DatePickerFragment.java)

```java
public class DatePickerFragment extends DialogFragment {
    @Override
    public Dialog onCreateDialog(Bundle savedInstanceState) {
        return new AlertDialog.Builder(getActivity())
            .setTitle(R.string.date_picker_title)
            .setPositiveButton(android.R.string.ok, null)
            .create();
    }
}
```

In this implementation, you use the **AlertDialog.Builder** class that provides a fluent interface for constructing an **AlertDialog** instance.

First, you pass a **Context** into the **AlertDialog.Builder** constructor, which returns an instance of **AlertDialog.Builder**.

Next, you call two **AlertDialog.Builder** methods to configure your dialog:

```java
public AlertDialog.Builder setTitle(int titleId)
public AlertDialog.Builder setPositiveButton(int textId,
    DialogInterface.OnClickListener listener)
```

This **setPositiveButton(…)** method accepts a string resource and an object that implements **DialogInterface.OnClickListener**. In Listing 12.2, you pass in an Android constant for OK and null for the listener parameter. You will implement a listener later in the chapter.

(A *positive* button is what the user should press to accept what the dialog presents or to take the dialog's primary action. There are two other buttons that you can add to an **AlertDialog**: a *negative* button and a *neutral* button. These designations determine the positions of the buttons in the dialog.)

Finally, you finish building the dialog with a call to **AlertDialog.Builder.create()**, which returns the configured **AlertDialog** instance.

There is more that you can do with **AlertDialog** and **AlertDialog.Builder**, and the details are well covered in the developer documentation. For now, let's move on to the mechanics of getting your dialog on screen.

Showing a DialogFragment

Like all fragments, instances of **DialogFragment** are managed by the **FragmentManager** of the hosting activity.

To get a **DialogFragment** added to the **FragmentManager** and put on screen, you can call the following methods on the fragment instance:

```
public void show(FragmentManager manager, String tag)
public void show(FragmentTransaction transaction, String tag)
```

The string parameter uniquely identifies the **DialogFragment** in the **FragmentManager**'s list. Whether you use the **FragmentManager** or **FragmentTransaction** version is up to you. If you pass in a **FragmentTransaction**, you are responsible for creating and committing that transaction. If you pass in a **FragmentManager**, a transaction will automatically be created and committed for you.

Here, you will pass in a **FragmentManager**.

In **CrimeFragment**, add a constant for the **DatePickerFragment**'s tag. Then, in **onCreateView(…)**, remove the code that disables the date button and set a **View.OnClickListener** that shows a **DatePickerFragment** when the date button is pressed.

Listing 12.3 Showing your **DialogFragment** (CrimeFragment.java)

```java
public class CrimeFragment extends Fragment {

    private static final String ARG_CRIME_ID = "crime_id";
    private static final String DIALOG_DATE = "DialogDate";

    ...

    @Override
    public View onCreateView(LayoutInflater inflater, ViewGroup container,
        Bundle savedInstanceState) {
        ...

        mDateButton = (Button) v.findViewById(R.id.crime_date);
        mDateButton.setText(mCrime.getDate().toString());
        mDateButton.setEnabled(false);
        mDateButton.setOnClickListener(new View.OnClickListener() {
            @Override
            public void onClick(View v) {
                FragmentManager manager = getFragmentManager();
                DatePickerFragment dialog = new DatePickerFragment();
                dialog.show(manager, DIALOG_DATE);
            }
        });

        mSolvedCheckBox = (CheckBox) v.findViewById(R.id.crime_solved);
        ...

        return v;
    }

    ...
}
```

Run CriminalIntent and press the date button to see the dialog (Figure 12.5).

Figure 12.5 An **AlertDialog** with a title and a button

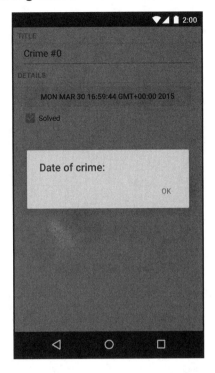

Setting a dialog's contents

Next, you are going to add a **DatePicker** widget to your **AlertDialog** using the following **AlertDialog.Builder** method:

```
public AlertDialog.Builder setView(View view)
```

This method configures the dialog to display the passed-in **View** object between the dialog's title and its button(s).

In the Project tool window, create a new layout resource file named dialog_date.xml and make its root element **DatePicker**. This layout will consist of a single **View** object – a **DatePicker** – that you will inflate and pass into **setView(…)**.

Configure the **DatePicker** as shown in Figure 12.6.

Figure 12.6 **DatePicker** layout (layout/dialog_date.xml)

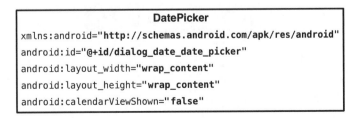

In **DatePickerFragment.onCreateDialog(…)**, inflate this view and then set it on the dialog.

Listing 12.4 Adding **DatePicker** to **AlertDialog** (DatePickerFragment.java)

```
@Override
public Dialog onCreateDialog(Bundle savedInstanceState) {
    View v = LayoutInflater.from(getActivity())
        .inflate(R.layout.dialog_date, null);

    return new AlertDialog.Builder(getActivity())
        .setView(v)
        .setTitle(R.string.date_picker_title)
        .setPositiveButton(android.R.string.ok, null)
        .create();
}
```

Run CriminalIntent. Press the date button to confirm that the dialog now presents a **DatePicker**. If you are running Lollipop, you will see a calendar picker (Figure 12.7).

Figure 12.7 Lollipop **DatePicker**

The calendar picker in Figure 12.7 was introduced along with Material design. This version of the **DatePicker** widget ignores the calendarViewShown attribute you set in your layout. If you are running a previous version of Android, however, you will see the old spinner-based **DatePicker** version which respects that attribute (Figure 12.8).

Figure 12.8 An **AlertDialog** with a **DatePicker**

Either version works fine. The newer one sure is pretty, though.

You may be wondering why you went to the trouble of defining and inflating a layout when you could have created the **DatePicker** object in code, like this:

```
@Override
public Dialog onCreateDialog(Bundle savedInstanceState) {
    DatePicker datePicker = new DatePicker(getActivity());

    return new AlertDialog.Builder(getActivity())
        .setView(datePicker)
        ...
        .create();
}
```

Using a layout makes modifications easy if you change your mind about what the dialog should present. For instance, what if you wanted a **TimePicker** next to the **DatePicker** in this dialog? If you are already inflating a layout, you can simply update the layout file, and the new view will appear.

Also, notice that the selected date in the **DatePicker** is automatically preserved across rotation. (With the dialog open, select a date other than the default and press Fn+Control+F12/Ctrl+F1 to see this in action.) How does this happen? Remember that **View**s can save state across configuration changes, but only if they have an ID attribute. When you created the **DatePicker** in dialog_date.xml you also asked the build tools to generate a unique ID value for that **DatePicker**.

If you created the **DatePicker** in code, you would have to programmatically set an ID on the **DatePicker** for its state saving to work.

Your dialog is on screen and looks good. In the next section, you will wire it up to present the **Crime**'s date and allow the user to change it.

Passing Data Between Two Fragments

You have passed data between two activities, and you have passed data between two fragment-based activities. Now you need to pass data between two fragments that are hosted by the same activity – **CrimeFragment** and **DatePickerFragment** (Figure 12.9).

Figure 12.9 Conversation between **CrimeFragment** and **DatePickerFragment**

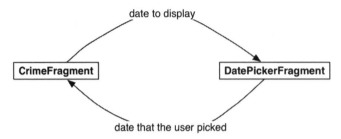

To get the **Crime**'s date to **DatePickerFragment**, you are going to write a **newInstance(Date)** method and make the **Date** an argument on the fragment.

To get the new date back to the **CrimeFragment** so that it can update the model layer and its own view, you will package up the date as an extra on an **Intent** and pass this **Intent** in a call to **CrimeFragment.onActivityResult(…)**, as shown in Figure 12.10.

Figure 12.10 Sequence of events between **CrimeFragment** and **DatePickerFragment**

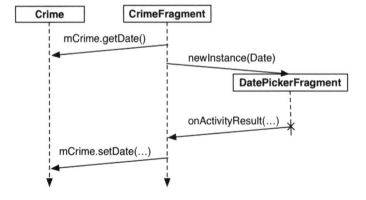

It may seem strange to call **Fragment.onActivityResult(…)**, given that the hosting activity receives no call to **Activity.onActivityResult(…)** in this interaction. However, using **onActivityResult(…)** to pass data back from one fragment to another not only works, but it also offers some flexibility in how you present a dialog fragment, as you will see later in the chapter.

Passing data to DatePickerFragment

To get data into your **DatePickerFragment**, you are going to stash the date in **DatePickerFragment**'s arguments bundle, where the **DatePickerFragment** can access it.

Creating and setting fragment arguments is typically done in a **newInstance()** method that replaces the fragment constructor. In DatePickerFragment.java, add a **newInstance(Date)** method.

Listing 12.5 Adding a **newInstance(Date)** method (DatePickerFragment.java)

```java
public class DatePickerFragment extends DialogFragment {

    private static final String ARG_DATE = "date";

    private DatePicker mDatePicker;

    public static DatePickerFragment newInstance(Date date) {
        Bundle args = new Bundle();
        args.putSerializable(ARG_DATE, date);

        DatePickerFragment fragment = new DatePickerFragment();
        fragment.setArguments(args);
        return fragment;
    }

    ...
}
```

In **CrimeFragment**, remove the call to the **DatePickerFragment** constructor and replace it with a call to **DatePickerFragment.newInstance(Date)**.

Listing 12.6 Adding call to **newInstance()** (CrimeFragment.java)

```java
@Override
public View onCreateView(LayoutInflater inflater,
        ViewGroup parent, Bundle savedInstanceState) {
    ...

    mDateButton = (Button)v.findViewById(R.id.crime_date);
    mDateButton.setOnClickListener(new View.OnClickListener() {
        public void onClick(View v) {
            FragmentManager manager = getActivity()
                    .getSupportFragmentManager();
            DatePickerFragment dialog = new DatePickerFragment();
            DatePickerFragment dialog = DatePickerFragment
                .newInstance(mCrime.getDate());
            dialog.show(manager, DIALOG_DATE);
        }
    });

    return v;
}
```

225

DatePickerFragment needs to initialize the **DatePicker** using the information held in the **Date**. However, initializing the **DatePicker** requires integers for the month, day, and year. **Date** is more of a timestamp and cannot provide integers like this directly.

To get the integers you need, you must create a **Calendar** object and use the **Date** to configure the **Calendar**. Then you can retrieve the required information from the **Calendar**.

In **onCreateDialog(…)**, get the **Date** from the arguments and use it and a **Calendar** to initialize the **DatePicker**.

Listing 12.7 Extracting the date and initializing **DatePicker** (DatePickerFragment.java)

```java
@Override
public Dialog onCreateDialog(Bundle savedInstanceState) {
    Date date = (Date) getArguments().getSerializable(ARG_DATE);

    Calendar calendar = Calendar.getInstance();
    calendar.setTime(date);
    int year = calendar.get(Calendar.YEAR);
    int month = calendar.get(Calendar.MONTH);
    int day = calendar.get(Calendar.DAY_OF_MONTH);

    View v = LayoutInflater.from(getActivity())
            .inflate(R.layout.dialog_date, null);

    mDatePicker = (DatePicker) v.findViewById(R.id.dialog_date_date_picker);
    mDatePicker.init(year, month, day, null);

    return new AlertDialog.Builder(getActivity())
            .setView(v)
            .setTitle(R.string.date_picker_title)
            .setPositiveButton(android.R.string.ok, null)
            .create();
}
```

Now **CrimeFragment** is successfully telling **DatePickerFragment** what date to show. You can run CriminalIntent and make sure that everything works as before.

Returning data to CrimeFragment

To have **CrimeFragment** receive the date back from **DatePickerFragment**, you need a way to keep track of the relationship between the two fragments.

With activities, you call **startActivityForResult(…)**, and the **ActivityManager** keeps track of the parent-child activity relationship. When the child activity dies, the **ActivityManager** knows which activity should receive the result.

Setting a target fragment

You can create a similar connection by making **CrimeFragment** the *target fragment* of **DatePickerFragment**. This connection is automatically reestablished after both **CrimeFragment** and

DatePickerFragment are destroyed and re-created by the OS. To create this relationship, you call the following **Fragment** method:

```
public void setTargetFragment(Fragment fragment, int requestCode)
```

This method accepts the fragment that will be the target and a request code just like the one you send in **startActivityForResult(…)**. The target fragment can use the request code later to identify which fragment is reporting back.

The **FragmentManager** keeps track of the target fragment and request code. You can retrieve them by calling **getTargetFragment()** and **getTargetRequestCode()** on the fragment that has set the target.

In CrimeFragment.java, create a constant for the request code and then make **CrimeFragment** the target fragment of the **DatePickerFragment** instance.

Listing 12.8 Setting target fragment (CrimeFragment.java)

```
public class CrimeFragment extends Fragment {

    private static final String ARG_CRIME_ID = "crime_id";
    private static final String DIALOG_DATE = "DialogDate";

    private static final int REQUEST_DATE = 0;

    ...

    @Override
    public View onCreateView(LayoutInflater inflater, ViewGroup parent,
            Bundle savedInstanceState) {
        ...

        mDateButton.setOnClickListener(new View.OnClickListener() {
            public void onClick(View v) {
                FragmentManager manager = getFragmentManager();
                DatePickerFragment dialog = DatePickerFragment
                        .newInstance(mCrime.getDate());
                dialog.setTargetFragment(CrimeFragment.this, REQUEST_DATE);
                dialog.show(manager, DIALOG_DATE);
            }
        });

        return v;
    }

    ...
}
```

Sending data to the target fragment

Now that you have a connection between **CrimeFragment** and **DatePickerFragment**, you need to send the date back to **CrimeFragment**. You are going to put the date on an **Intent** as an extra.

What method will you use to send this intent to the target fragment? Oddly enough, you will have **DatePickerFragment** pass it into **CrimeFragment.onActivityResult(int, int, Intent)**.

Activity.onActivityResult(…) is the method that the **ActivityManager** calls on the parent activity after the child activity dies. When dealing with activities, you do not call

Activity.onActivityResult(…) yourself; that is the **ActivityManager**'s job. After the activity has received the call, the activity's **FragmentManager** then calls **Fragment.onActivityResult(…)** on the appropriate fragment.

When dealing with two fragments hosted by the same activity, you can borrow **Fragment.onActivityResult(…)** and call it directly on the target fragment to pass back data. It has exactly what you need:

- a request code that matches the code passed into **setTargetFragment(…)** to tell the target what is returning the result

- a result code to determine what action to take

- an **Intent** that can have extra data

In **DatePickerFragment**, create a private method that creates an intent, puts the date on it as an extra, and then calls **CrimeFragment.onActivityResult(…)**.

Listing 12.9 Calling back to your target (DatePickerFragment.java)

```java
public class DatePickerFragment extends DialogFragment {

    public static final String EXTRA_DATE =
            "com.bignerdranch.android.criminalintent.date";

    private static final String ARG_DATE = "date";

    ...

    @Override
    public Dialog onCreateDialog(Bundle savedInstanceState) {
        ...
    }

    private void sendResult(int resultCode, Date date) {
        if (getTargetFragment() == null) {
            return;
        }

        Intent intent = new Intent();
        intent.putExtra(EXTRA_DATE, date);

        getTargetFragment()
                .onActivityResult(getTargetRequestCode(), resultCode, intent);
    }
}
```

Now it is time to make use of this new **sendResult** method. When the user presses the positive button in the dialog, you want to retrieve the date from the **DatePicker** and send the result back to **CrimeFragment**. In **onCreateDialog(…)**, replace the null parameter of **setPositiveButton(…)** with an implementation of **DialogInterface.OnClickListener** that retrieves the selected date and calls **sendResult**.

Listing 12.10 Are you OK? (DatePickerFragment.java)

```java
@Override
public Dialog onCreateDialog(Bundle savedInstanceState) {
    ...

    return new AlertDialog.Builder(getActivity())
        .setView(v)
        .setTitle(R.string.date_picker_title)
        .setPositiveButton(android.R.string.ok, null);
        .setPositiveButton(android.R.string.ok,
                new DialogInterface.OnClickListener() {
                    @Override
                    public void onClick(DialogInterface dialog, int which) {
                        int year = mDatePicker.getYear();
                        int month = mDatePicker.getMonth();
                        int day = mDatePicker.getDayOfMonth();
                        Date date = new GregorianCalendar(year, month, day).getTime();
                        sendResult(Activity.RESULT_OK, date);
                    }
                }
        })
        .create();
}
```

In **CrimeFragment**, override **onActivityResult(…)** to retrieve the extra, set the date on the **Crime**, and refresh the text of the date button.

Listing 12.11 Responding to the dialog (CrimeFragment.java)

```java
public class CrimeFragment extends Fragment {

    ...

    @Override
    public View onCreateView(LayoutInflater inflater, ViewGroup container,
                             Bundle savedInstanceState) {
        ...
    }

    @Override
    public void onActivityResult(int requestCode, int resultCode, Intent data) {
        if (resultCode != Activity.RESULT_OK) {
            return;
        }

        if (requestCode == REQUEST_DATE) {
            Date date = (Date) data
                    .getSerializableExtra(DatePickerFragment.EXTRA_DATE);
            mCrime.setDate(date);
            mDateButton.setText(mCrime.getDate().toString());
        }
    }
}
```

The code that sets the button's text is identical to code you call in **onCreateView(…)**. To avoid setting the text in two places, encapsulate this code in a private **updateDate()** method and then call it in **onCreateView(…)** and **onActivityResult(…)**.

You could do this by hand or you can have Android Studio do it for you. Highlight the entire line of code that sets **mDateButton**'s text. Right-click and select Refactor → Extract → Method... (Figure 12.11).

Figure 12.11 Extracting a method with Android Studio

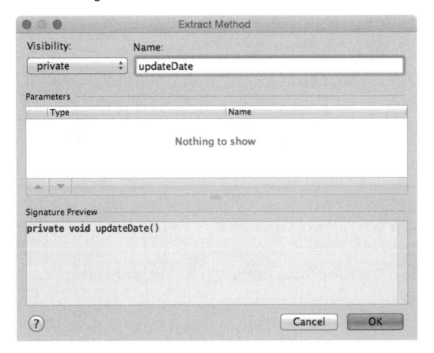

Make the method private and name it **updateDate**. Click OK and Android Studio will tell you that it has found one other place where this line of code was used. Click Yes to allow Android Studio to update the other reference, then verify that your code is now extracted to a single **updateDate** method as shown in Listing 12.12.

Listing 12.12 Cleaning up with **updateDate()** (CrimeFragment.java)

```java
public class CrimeFragment extends Fragment {

    ...

    @Override
    public View onCreateView(LayoutInflater inflater, ViewGroup container,
                            Bundle savedInstanceState) {
        View v = inflater.inflate(R.layout.fragment_crime, container, false);

        ...

        mDateButton = (Button) v.findViewById(R.id.crime_date);
        updateDate();
        ...
    }

    @Override
    public void onActivityResult(int requestCode, int resultCode, Intent data) {
        if (resultCode != Activity.RESULT_OK) {
            return;
        }

        if (requestCode == REQUEST_DATE) {
            Date date = (Date) data
                    .getSerializableExtra(DatePickerFragment.EXTRA_DATE);
            mCrime.setDate(date);
            updateDate();
        }
    }

    private void updateDate() {
        mDateButton.setText(mCrime.getDate().toString());
    }
}
```

Now the circle is complete. The dates must flow. He who controls the dates controls time itself. Run CriminalIntent to ensure that you can, in fact, control the dates. Change the date of a **Crime** and confirm that the new date appears in **CrimeFragment**'s view. Then return to the list of crimes and check the **Crime**'s date to ensure that the model layer was updated.

More flexibility in presenting a DialogFragment

Using **onActivityResult(…)** to send data back to a target fragment is especially nice when you are writing an app that needs lots of input from the user and more room to ask for it – and you want the app working well on phones and tablets.

On a phone, you do not have much screen real estate, so you would likely use an activity with a full-screen fragment to ask the user for input. This child activity would be started by a fragment of the parent activity calling **startActivityForResult(…)**. On the death of the child activity, the parent activity would receive a call to **onActivityResult(…)**, which would be forwarded to the fragment that started the child activity (Figure 12.12).

Figure 12.12 Inter-activity communication on phones

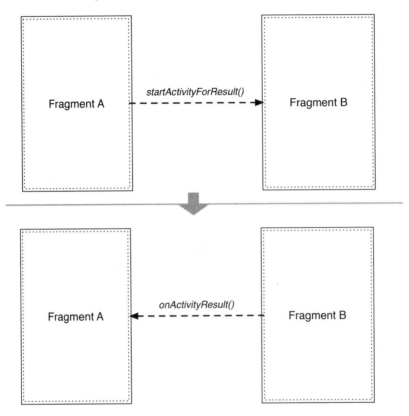

On a tablet, where you have plenty of room, it is often better to present a **DialogFragment** to the user to get the same input. In this case, you set the target fragment and call **show(…)** on the dialog fragment. When dismissed, the dialog fragment calls **onActivityResult(…)** on its target (Figure 12.13).

Figure 12.13 Inter-fragment communication on tablets

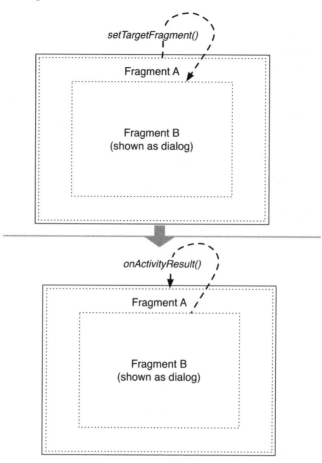

The fragment's **onActivityResult(…)** will always be called, whether the fragment started an activity or showed a dialog. So you can use the same code for different presentations.

When setting things up to use the same code for a full-screen fragment or a dialog fragment, you can override **DialogFragment.onCreateView(…)** instead of **onCreateDialog(…)** to prepare for both presentations.

Challenge: More Dialogs

Write another dialog fragment named **TimePickerFragment** that allows the user to select what time of day the crime occurred using a **TimePicker** widget. Add another button to **CrimeFragment** that will display a **TimePickerFragment**.

Challenge: A Responsive DialogFragment

For a more involved challenge, modify the presentation of the **DatePickerFragment**.

The first stage of this challenge is to supply the **DatePickerFragment**'s view by overriding **onCreateView** instead of **onCreateDialog**. When setting up a **DialogFragment** in this way, your dialog will not be presented with the built-in title area and button area on the top and bottom of the dialog. You will need to create your own OK button in `dialog_date.xml`.

Once **DatePickerFragment**'s view is created in **onCreateView**, you can present **DatePickerFragment** as a dialog or embedded in an activity. For the second stage of this challenge, create a new subclass of **SingleFragmentActivity** and host **DatePickerFragment** in that activity.

When presenting **DatePickerFragment** in this way, you will use the **startActivityForResult** mechanism to pass the date back to **CrimeFragment**. In **DatePickerFragment**, if the target fragment does not exist, use the **setResult(int, intent)** method on the hosting activity to send the date back to the fragment.

For the final step of this challenge, modify CriminalIntent to present the **DatePickerFragment** as a full-screen activity when running on a phone. When running on a tablet, present the **DatePickerFragment** as a dialog. You may need to read ahead in Chapter 17 for details on how to optimize your app for multiple screen sizes.

13

The Toolbar

A key component of any well-designed Android app is the toolbar. The toolbar includes actions that the user can take, a new mechanism for navigation, and also provides design consistency and branding.

In this chapter, you will create a menu for CriminalIntent that will be displayed in the toolbar. This menu will have an *action item* that lets users add a new crime. You will also enable the Up button in the toolbar (Figure 13.1).

Figure 13.1 CriminalIntent's toolbar

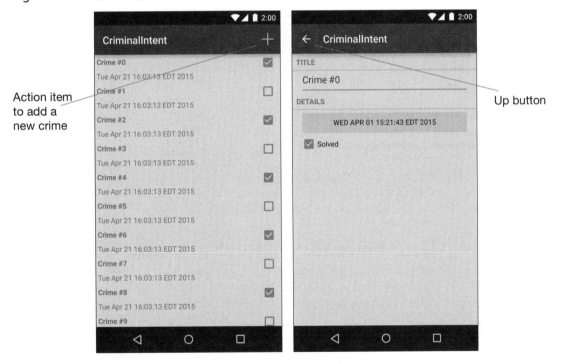

AppCompat

The toolbar component is a new addition to Android as of Android 5.0 (Lollipop). Prior to Lollipop, the *action bar* was the recommended component for navigation and actions within an app.

The action bar and toolbar are very similar components. The toolbar builds on top of the action bar. It has a tweaked user interface and is more flexible in the ways that you can use it.

CriminalIntent supports API 16+, which means that you cannot use the native toolbar on all supported versions of Android. Luckily, the toolbar has been back-ported to the AppCompat library. The AppCompat library allows you to provide a Lollipop'd toolbar on any version of Android back to API 7 (Android 2.1).

Using the AppCompat library

In Chapter 12 you added the AppCompat dependency to Criminal Intent. There are a few additional steps to fully integrate with the AppCompat library. Some of these steps may already be complete depending on how your project was created.

The following adjustments are required to use the AppCompat library:

- add the AppCompat dependency

- use one of the AppCompat themes

- ensure that all activities are a subclass of **AppCompatActivity**

Updating the theme

Since you already have the AppCompat dependency, the next step is to ensure that you are using one of AppCompat's themes. The AppCompat library comes with three themes:

- **Theme.AppCompat** – a dark theme

- **Theme.AppCompat.Light** – a light theme

- **Theme.AppCompat.Light.DarkActionBar** – a light theme with a dark toolbar

The theme for your application is specified at the application level and optionally per activity in your AndroidManifest.xml. Open AndroidManifest.xml and look at the **application** tag. Notice the android:theme attribute. You should see something similar to Listing 13.1.

Listing 13.1 The stock manifest (AndroidManifest.xml)

```
...

<application
    android:allowBackup="true"
    android:icon="@mipmap/ic_launcher"
    android:label="@string/app_name"
    android:theme="@style/AppTheme" >

...
```

The **AppTheme** is defined in res/values/styles.xml. Depending on how your initial project was created, you may have multiple versions of **AppTheme** in multiple styles.xml files. These files are resource-qualified for different versions of Android. When using the AppCompat library, there is no need to switch themes based on the version of Android, because you will provide a consistent experience on all platforms.

If you have multiple versions of the styles.xml file, delete the extra files. You should have a single styles.xml file that is located at res/values/styles.xml (Figure 13.2).

Figure 13.2 An extra `styles.xml`

```
▼  📁 styles.xml (2)
        📄 styles.xml
        📄 styles.xml (v21)
```

After cleaning up any extra files, open res/values/styles.xml and ensure that the parent theme of your AppTheme matches the shaded portion below.

Listing 13.2 Using an AppCompat theme (`res/values/styles.xml`)

```xml
<resources>

    <style name="AppTheme" parent="Theme.AppCompat.Light.DarkActionBar">
    </style>

</resources>
```

You will learn much more about styles and themes in Chapter 20.

Using AppCompatActivity

The final step in your AppCompat conversion is to change all of the activities in CriminalIntent to be subclasses of **AppCompatActivity**. Up until this point, all of your activities have been a subclass of **FragmentActivity**, which allows you to use the support library's fragment implementation.

AppCompatActivity itself is a subclass of **FragmentActivity**. This means that you can still use support fragments in **AppCompatActivity**, which makes this a simple change in CriminalIntent.

Update **SingleFragmentActivity** and **CrimePagerActivity** to be subclasses of **AppCompatActivity**.

(Why not **CrimeListActivity**? Because it is a subclass of **SingleFragmentActivity**.)

Listing 13.3 Converting to **AppCompatActivity** (`SingleFragmentActivity.java`)

```java
public abstract class SingleFragmentActivity extends FragmentActivity {
public abstract class SingleFragmentActivity extends AppCompatActivity {
    ...
}
```

Listing 13.4 Converting to **AppCompatActivity** (`CrimePagerActivity.java`)

```java
public class CrimePagerActivity extends FragmentActivity AppCompatActivity {
    ...
}
```

Run CriminalIntent and ensure that the app does not crash. You should see something similar to Figure 13.3.

Figure 13.3 The new **Toolbar**

Now that CriminalIntent uses the AppCompat toolbar, you can add actions to the toolbar.

Menus

The top-right area of the toolbar is reserved for the toolbar's menu. The menu consists of *action items* (sometimes also referred to as *menu items*), which can perform an action on the current screen or to the app as a whole. You will add an action item to allow the user to create a new crime.

Your menu will require a few string resources. Add them to `strings.xml` (Listing 13.5) now. These strings may seem mysterious at this point, but it is good to get them taken care of. When you need them later, they will already be in place, and you will not have to stop what you are doing to add them.

Listing 13.5 Adding strings for menus (`res/values/strings.xml`)

```
<resources>
  ...
  <string name="date_picker_title">Date of crime:</string>
  <string name="new_crime">New Crime</string>
  <string name="show_subtitle">Show Subtitle</string>
  <string name="hide_subtitle">Hide Subtitle</string>
  <string name="subtitle_format">%1$s crimes</string>
</resources>
```

Defining a menu in XML

Menus are a type of resource similar to layouts. You create an XML description of a menu and place the file in the res/menu directory of your project. Android generates a resource ID for the menu file that you then use to inflate the menu in code.

In the project tool window, right-click on the res directory and select New → Android resource file. Change the Resource type to Menu, name the menu resource fragment_crime_list, and click OK. Android Studio will generate res/menu/fragment_crime_list.xml (Figure 13.4).

Figure 13.4 Creating a menu file

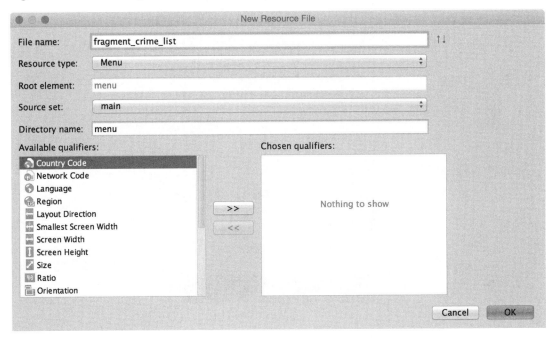

In the new fragment_crime_list.xml file, add an item element as shown in Listing 13.6.

Listing 13.6 Creating a menu resource for **CrimeListFragment** (fragment_crime_list.xml)

```xml
<?xml version="1.0" encoding="utf-8"?>
<menu xmlns:android="http://schemas.android.com/apk/res/android"
      xmlns:app="http://schemas.android.com/apk/res-auto">
    <item
        android:id="@+id/menu_item_new_crime"
        android:icon="@android:drawable/ic_menu_add"
        android:title="@string/new_crime"
        app:showAsAction="ifRoom|withText"/>
</menu>
```

The showAsAction attribute refers to whether the item will appear in the toolbar itself or in the *overflow menu*. You have piped together two values, ifRoom and withText, so the item's icon and text

239

will appear in the toolbar if there is room. If there is room for the icon but not the text, then only the icon will be visible. If there is no room for either, then the item will be relegated to the overflow menu.

The overflow menu is accessed by the three dots on the far-right side of the toolbar, as shown in Figure 13.5.

Figure 13.5 Overflow menu in the toolbar

Other options for showAsAction include always and never. Using always is not recommended; it is better to use ifRoom and let the OS decide. Using never is a good choice for less-common actions. In general, you should only put action items that users will use frequently in the toolbar to avoid cluttering the screen.

The app namespace

Notice that fragment_crime_list.xml uses the xmlns tag to define a new namespace, app, which is separate from the usual android namespace declaration. This app namespace is then used to specify the showAsAction attribute.

This unusual namespace declaration exists for legacy reasons with the AppCompat library. The action bar APIs were first added in Android 3.0. Originally, the AppCompat library was created to bundle a compatibility version of the action bar into apps supporting earlier versions of Android, so that the action bar would exist on any device, even those that did not support the native action bar. On devices running Android 2.3 or older, menus and their corresponding XML did exist, but the android:showAsAction attribute was only added with the release of the action bar.

The AppCompat library defines its own custom showAsAction attribute and does not look for the native showAsAction attribute.

Using Android Asset Studio

In the android:icon attribute, the value @android:drawable/ic_menu_add references a *system icon*. A *system icon* is one that is found on the device rather than in your project's resources.

In a prototype, referencing a system icon works fine. However, in an app that will be released, it is better to be sure of what your user will see instead of leaving it up to each device. System icons can change drastically across devices and OS versions, and some devices might have system icons that do not fit with the rest of your app's design.

One alternative is to create your own icons from scratch. You will need to prepare versions for each screen density and possibly for other device configurations. For more information, visit Android's Icon Design Guidelines at http://developer.android.com/design/style/iconography.html.

A second alternative is to find system icons that meet your app's needs and copy them directly into your project's drawable resources.

System icons can be found in your Android SDK directory. On a Mac, this is typically /Users/*user*/Library/Android/sdk. On Windows, the default location is \Users*user*\sdk. You can also verify your SDK location by opening the Project Structure window and selecting the SDK Location option.

In your SDK directory, you will find Android's resources, including ic_menu_add. These resources are found in /platforms/android–21/data/res where 21 represents the API level of the Android version.

The third and easiest alternative is to use the Android Asset Studio, which is included in Android Studio. The Asset Studio allows you to create and customize an image to use in the Toolbar.

Right-click on your drawable directory in the Project Tool window and select New → Image Asset to bring up the Asset Studio (Figure 13.6).

Figure 13.6 Asset Studio

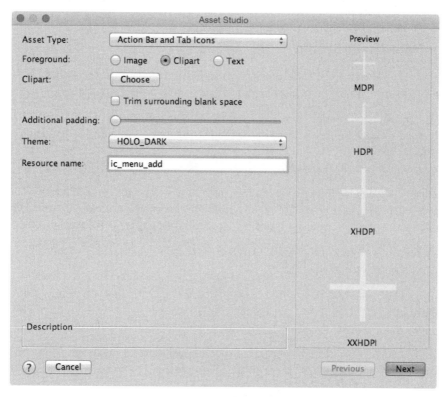

Here, you can generate a few types of icons. In the Asset Type: field, choose Action Bar and Tab Icons. Next, change the Foreground option to Clipart and select Choose to pick your clipart.

In the clipart window, choose the image that looks like a plus sign (Figure 13.7).

Figure 13.7 Clipart options – Where is that plus sign?

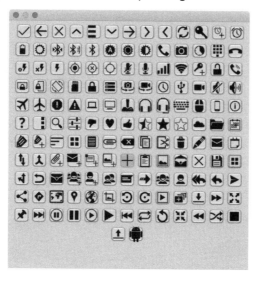

Finally, name your asset: ic_menu_add and select next (Figure 13.8).

Figure 13.8 Asset Studio's generated files

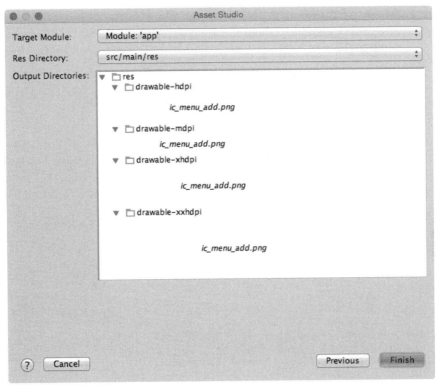

Next, the Asset Studio will ask you which module and directory to add the image to. Stick to the defaults to add this image to your app module. This window also provides a preview of the work that Asset Studio will do. Notice that an mdpi, hdpi, xhdpi, and xxhdpi icon will be created for you. Jim-dandy.

Select Finish to generate the images. Then, in your layout file, modify your icon attribute to reference the new resource in your own project.

Listing 13.7 Referencing a local resource (menu/fragment_crime_list.xml)

```
<item
    android:id="@+id/menu_item_new_crime"
    android:icon="@android:drawable/ic_menu_add"
    android:icon="@drawable/ic_menu_add"
    android:title="@string/new_crime"
    app:showAsAction="ifRoom|withText"/>
```

Creating the menu

In code, menus are managed by callbacks from the **Activity** class. When the menu is needed, Android calls the **Activity** method **onCreateOptionsMenu(Menu)**.

However, your design calls for code to be implemented in a fragment, not an activity. **Fragment** comes with its own set of menu callbacks, which you will implement in **CrimeListFragment**. The methods for creating the menu and responding to the selection of an action item are:

```
public void onCreateOptionsMenu(Menu menu, MenuInflater inflater)
public boolean onOptionsItemSelected(MenuItem item)
```

In CrimeListFragment.java, override **onCreateOptionsMenu(Menu, MenuInflater)** to inflate the menu defined in fragment_crime_list.xml.

Listing 13.8 Inflating a menu resource (CrimeListFragment.java)

```java
@Override
public void onResume() {
    super.onResume();
    updateUI();
}

@Override
public void onCreateOptionsMenu(Menu menu, MenuInflater inflater) {
    super.onCreateOptionsMenu(menu, inflater);
    inflater.inflate(R.menu.fragment_crime_list, menu);
}
```

Within this method, you call **MenuInflater.inflate(int, Menu)** and pass in the resource ID of your menu file. This populates the **Menu** instance with the items defined in your file.

Notice that you call through to the superclass implementation of **onCreateOptionsMenu(…)**. This is not required, but we recommend calling through as a matter of convention. That way, any menu functionality defined by the superclass will still work. However, it is only a convention – the base **Fragment** implementation of this method does nothing.

The **FragmentManager** is responsible for calling **Fragment.onCreateOptionsMenu(Menu, MenuInflater)** when the activity receives its **onCreateOptionsMenu(…)** callback from the OS. You must explicitly tell the **FragmentManager** that your fragment should receive a call to **onCreateOptionsMenu(…)**. You do this by calling the following method:

```
public void setHasOptionsMenu(boolean hasMenu)
```

Define **CrimeListFragment.onCreate(…)** and let the **FragmentManager** know that **CrimeListFragment** needs to receive menu callbacks.

Listing 13.9 Receiving menu callbacks (`CrimeListFragment.java`)

```
...

private RecyclerView mCrimeRecyclerView;
private CrimeAdapter mAdapter;

@Override
public void onCreate(Bundle savedInstanceState) {
    super.onCreate(savedInstanceState);
    setHasOptionsMenu(true);
}

@Override
public View onCreateView(LayoutInflater inflater, ViewGroup container,
...
```

You can run CriminalIntent now to see your menu (Figure 13.9).

Figure 13.9 Icon for the add crime action item directly in the toolbar

Where is the action item's text? Most phones have enough room only for the icon in portrait orientation. You can long-press an icon in the toolbar to reveal its title (Figure 13.10).

Figure 13.10 Long-pressing an icon in the toolbar shows the title

In landscape orientation, there is room in the toolbar for the icon and the text (Figure 13.11).

Figure 13.11 Icon and text in the toolbar

Responding to menu selections

To respond to the user pressing the New Crime action item, you need a way to add a new **Crime** to your list of crimes. In CrimeLab.java, add the following method that adds a **Crime** to the list.

Listing 13.10 Adding a new crime (`CrimeLab.java`)

```
...

public void addCrime(Crime c) {
    mCrimes.add(c);
}

public List<Crime> getCrimes() {
    return mCrimes;
}

...
```

In this brave new world where you will be able to add crimes yourself, the 100 programmatically generated crimes are no longer necessary. Remove the code that generates these crimes from `CrimeLab.java`.

Listing 13.11 Goodbye, random crimes! (`CrimeLab.java`)

```
private CrimeLab(Context context) {
    mCrimes = new ArrayList<>();
    for (int i = 0; i < 100; i++) {
        Crime crime = new Crime();
        crime.setTitle("Crime #" + i);
        crime.setSolved(i % 2 == 0);
        mCrimes.add(crime);
    }
}
```

When the user presses an action item, your fragment receives a callback to the method **onOptionsItemSelected(MenuItem)**. This method receives an instance of **MenuItem** that describes the user's selection.

Although your menu only contains one action item, menus often have more than one. You can determine which action item has been selected by checking the ID of the **MenuItem** and then respond appropriately. This ID corresponds to the ID you assigned to the **MenuItem** in your menu file.

In `CrimeListFragment.java`, implement **onOptionsItemSelected(MenuItem)** to respond to selection of the **MenuItem**. You will create a new **Crime**, add it to **CrimeLab**, and then start an instance of **CrimePagerActivity** to edit the new **Crime**.

Listing 13.12 Responding to menu selection (`CrimeListFragment.java`)

```java
@Override
public void onCreateOptionsMenu(Menu menu, MenuInflater inflater) {
    super.onCreateOptionsMenu(menu, inflater);
    inflater.inflate(R.menu.fragment_crime_list, menu);
}

@Override
public boolean onOptionsItemSelected(MenuItem item) {
    switch (item.getItemId()) {
        case R.id.menu_item_new_crime:
            Crime crime = new Crime();
            CrimeLab.get(getActivity()).addCrime(crime);
            Intent intent = CrimePagerActivity
                    .newIntent(getActivity(), crime.getId());
            startActivity(intent);
            return true;
        default:
            return super.onOptionsItemSelected(item);
    }
}
```

Notice that this method returns a boolean value. Once you have handled the **MenuItem**, you should return `true` to indicate that no further processing is necessary. The default case calls the superclass implementation if the item ID is not in your implementation.

Run CriminalIntent and try out your new menu. Add a few crimes and edit them afterward. (The empty list that you see before you add any crimes can be disconcerting. At the end of this chapter there is a challenge to present a helpful clue when the list is empty.)

Enabling Hierarchical Navigation

So far, CriminalIntent relies heavily on the Back button to navigate around the app. Using the Back button is *temporal navigation*. It takes you to where you were last. *Hierarchical navigation*, on the other hand, takes you up the app hierarchy. (It is sometimes called *ancestral navigation*.)

In hierarchical navigation, the user navigates up by pressing the Up button on the left side of the toolbar. Prior to Jelly Bean (API level 16), developers had to manually show the Up button and manually handle presses on the Up button. As of Jelly Bean, there is a much easier way to add this functionality.

Enable hierarchical navigation in CriminalIntent by adding a `parentActivityName` attribute in the `AndroidManifest.xml` file.

Listing 13.13 Turn on the Up button (`AndroidManifest.xml`)

```xml
...
<activity
    android:name=".CrimePagerActivity"
    android:label="@string/app_name"
    android:parentActivityName=".CrimeListActivity">
</activity>
...
```

Run the app and create a new crime. Notice the Up button, as shown in Figure 13.12. Pressing the Up button will take you up one level in CriminalIntent's hierarchy to CrimeListActivity.

Figure 13.12 CrimePagerActivity's Up button

How hierarchical navigation works

In CriminalIntent, navigating with the Back button and navigating with the Up button perform the same task. Pressing either of those from within the CrimePagerActivity will take the user back to the CrimeListActivity. Even though they accomplish the same result, behind the scenes they are doing very different things. This is important because, depending on the application, navigating up may pop the user back multiple activities in the back stack.

When the user navigates up from **CrimeActivity**, an intent like the following is created:

```
Intent intent = new Intent(this, CrimeListActivity.class);
intent.addFlags(Intent.FLAG_ACTIVITY_CLEAR_TOP);
startActivity(intent);
finish();
```

FLAG_ACTIVITY_CLEAR_TOP tells Android to look for an existing instance of the activity in the stack, and if there is one, pop every other activity off the stack so that the activity being started will be top-most (Figure 13.13).

Figure 13.13 FLAG_ACTIVITY_CLEAR_TOP at work

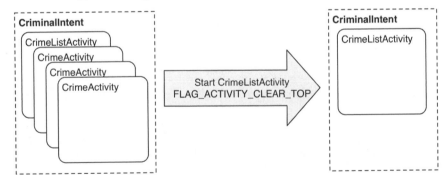

An Alternative Action Item

In this section, you will use what you have learned about menu resources to add an action item that lets users show and hide the subtitle of **CrimeListActivity**'s toolbar.

In res/menu/fragment_crime_list.xml, add an action item that will read Show Subtitle and will appear in the toolbar if there is room.

Listing 13.14 Adding Show Subtitle action item (res/menu/fragment_crime_list.xml)

```xml
<?xml version="1.0" encoding="utf-8"?>
<menu xmlns:android="http://schemas.android.com/apk/res/android"
      xmlns:app="http://schemas.android.com/apk/res-auto">
    <item
        android:id="@+id/menu_item_new_crime"
        android:icon="@android:drawable/ic_menu_add"
        android:title="@string/new_crime"
        app:showAsAction="ifRoom|withText"/>

    <item
        android:id="@+id/menu_item_show_subtitle"
        android:title="@string/show_subtitle"
        app:showAsAction="ifRoom"/>
</menu>
```

The subtitle will display the number of crimes in CriminalIntent. Create a new method, updateSubtitle(), that will set the subtitle of the toolbar.

Listing 13.15 Setting the toolbar's subtitle (CrimeListFragment.java)

```java
@Override
public boolean onOptionsItemSelected(MenuItem item) {
    ...
}

private void updateSubtitle() {
    CrimeLab crimeLab = CrimeLab.get(getActivity());
    int crimeCount = crimeLab.getCrimes().size();
    String subtitle = getString(R.string.subtitle_format, crimeCount);

    AppCompatActivity activity = (AppCompatActivity) getActivity();
    activity.getSupportActionBar().setSubtitle(subtitle);
}
```

updateSubtitle first generates the subtitle string using the getString(int resId, Object… formatArgs) method, which accepts replacement values for the placeholders in the string resource.

Next, the activity that is hosting the **CrimeListFragment** is cast to an **AppCompatActivity**. CriminalIntent uses the AppCompat library, so all activities will be a subclass of **AppCompatActivity**, which allows you to access the toolbar. For legacy reasons, the toolbar is still referred to as "action bar" in many places within the AppCompat library.

Now that updateSubtitle is defined, call the method when the user presses on the new action item.

Listing 13.16 Responding to Show Subtitle action item (CrimeListFragment.java)

```java
@Override
public boolean onOptionsItemSelected(MenuItem item) {
    switch (item.getItemId()) {
        case R.id.menu_item_new_crime:
            ...
        case R.id.menu_item_show_subtitle:
            updateSubtitle();
            return true;
        default:
            return super.onOptionsItemSelected(item);
    }
}
```

Run CriminalIntent, press the Show Subtitle item, and confirm that you can see the number of crimes in the subtitle.

Toggling the action item title

Now the subtitle is visible, but the action item still reads Show Subtitle. It would be better if the action item toggled its title and function to show or hide the subtitle.

When **onOptionsItemSelected(MenuItem)** is called, you are given the **MenuItem** that the user pressed as a parameter. You could update the text of the Show Subtitle item in this method, but the subtitle change would be lost as you rotate the device and the toolbar is re-created.

A better solution is to update the Show Subtitle **MenuItem** in **onCreateOptionsMenu(…)** and trigger a re-creation of the toolbar when the user presses on the subtitle item. This allows you to share the code for updating the action item in the case that the user selects an action item or the toolbar is re-created.

First, add a member variable to keep track of the subtitle visibility.

Listing 13.17 Keeping subtitle visibility state (CrimeListFragment.java)

```java
public class CrimeListFragment extends Fragment {

    private RecyclerView mCrimeRecyclerView;
    private CrimeAdapter mAdapter;
    private boolean mSubtitleVisible;

    ...
```

Next, modify the subtitle in **onCreateOptionsMenu(…)** and trigger a re-creation of the action items when the user presses on the Show Subtitle action item.

Listing 13.18 Updating a **MenuItem** (CrimeListFragment.java)

```
@Override
public void onCreateOptionsMenu(Menu menu, MenuInflater inflater) {
    super.onCreateOptionsMenu(menu, inflater);
    inflater.inflate(R.menu.fragment_crime_list, menu);

    MenuItem subtitleItem = menu.findItem(R.id.menu_item_show_subtitle);
    if (mSubtitleVisible) {
        subtitleItem.setTitle(R.string.hide_subtitle);
    } else {
        subtitleItem.setTitle(R.string.show_subtitle);
    }
}

@Override
public boolean onOptionsItemSelected(MenuItem item) {
    switch (item.getItemId()) {
        case R.id.menu_item_new_crime:
            ...
        case R.id.menu_item_show_subtitle:
            mSubtitleVisible = !mSubtitleVisible;
            getActivity().invalidateOptionsMenu();
            updateSubtitle();
            return true;
        default:
            return super.onOptionsItemSelected(item);
    }
}
```

Finally, respect the mSubtitleVisible member variable when showing or hiding the subtitle in the toolbar.

Listing 13.19 Showing or hiding the subtitle (CrimeListFragment.java)

```
private void updateSubtitle() {
    CrimeLab crimeLab = CrimeLab.get(getActivity());
    int crimeCount = crimeLab.getCrimes().size();
    String subtitle = getString(R.string.subtitle_format, crimeCount);

    if (!mSubtitleVisible) {
        subtitle = null;
    }

    AppCompatActivity activity = (AppCompatActivity) getActivity();
    activity.getSupportActionBar().setSubtitle(subtitle);
}
```

Run CriminalIntent and modify the subtitle visibility in the toolbar. Notice that the action item text reflects the existence of the subtitle.

"Just one more thing..."

Programming in Android is often like being questioned by the TV detective Columbo. You think you have the angles covered and are home free. But Android always turns at the door and says, "Just one more thing..."

Here, there are actually two more things. First, when creating a new crime and then returning to **CrimeListActivity** with the Back button, the number of crimes in the subtitle will not update to reflect the new number of crimes. Second, the visibility of the subtitle is lost across rotation.

Tackle the update issue first. The solution to this problem is to update the subtitle text when returning to **CrimeListActivity**. Trigger a call to **updateSubtitle** in **onResume**. Your **updateUI** method is already called in **onResume** and **onCreate**. Add a call to **updateSubtitle** to the **updateUI** method.

Listing 13.20 Showing the most recent state (`CrimeListFragment.java`)

```java
private void updateUI() {
    CrimeLab crimeLab = CrimeLab.get(getActivity());
    List<Crime> crimes = crimeLab.getCrimes();

    if (mAdapter == null) {
        mAdapter = new CrimeAdapter(crimes);
        mCrimeRecyclerView.setAdapter(mAdapter);
    } else {
        mAdapter.notifyDataSetChanged();
    }

    updateSubtitle();
}
```

Run CriminalIntent, show the subtitle, create a new crime, and press the Back button on the device to return to **CrimeListActivity**. The number of crimes in the toolbar will be correct.

Now repeat these steps, but instead of using the Back button use the Up button. The visibility of the subtitle will be reset. Why does this happen?

An unfortunate side effect of the way hierarchical navigation is implemented in Android is that the activity that you navigate up to will be completely re-created from scratch. This means that any instance variables will be lost and it also means that any saved instance state will be lost as well. This parent activity is seen as a completely new activity.

There is not an easy way to ensure that the subtitle stays visible when navigating up. One option is to override the mechanism that navigates up. In CriminalIntent, you could call **finish** on the **CrimePagerActivity** to pop back to the previous activity. This would work perfectly well in CriminalIntent but would not work in apps with a more realistic hierarchy, as this would only pop back one activity.

Another option is to pass information about the subtitle visibility as an extra to **CrimePagerActivity** when it is started. Then, override the **getParentActivityIntent()** method in **CrimePagerActivity** to add an extra to the intent that is used to re-create the **CrimeListActivity**. This solution requires **CrimePagerActivity** to know the details of how its parent works.

Both of these solutions are less than ideal, and there is not a great alternative.

Now that the subtitle always displays the correct number of crimes, solve the rotation issue. To fix this problem, save the mSubtitleVisible instance variable across rotation with the saved instance state mechanism.

Listing 13.21 Saving subtitle visibility (`CrimeListFragment.java`)

```java
public class CrimeListFragment extends Fragment {

    private static final String SAVED_SUBTITLE_VISIBLE = "subtitle";

    ...

    @Override
    public View onCreateView(LayoutInflater inflater, ViewGroup container,
                             Bundle savedInstanceState) {
        ...

        if (savedInstanceState != null) {
            mSubtitleVisible = savedInstanceState.getBoolean(SAVED_SUBTITLE_VISIBLE);
        }

        updateUI();

        return view;
    }

    @Override
    public void onResume() {
        ...
    }

    @Override
    public void onSaveInstanceState(Bundle outState) {
        super.onSaveInstanceState(outState);
        outState.putBoolean(SAVED_SUBTITLE_VISIBLE, mSubtitleVisible);
    }
}
```

Run CriminalIntent. Show the subtitle and then rotate. The subtitle should appear as expected in the re-created view.

For the More Curious: Toolbar vs Action Bar

What is the difference between the toolbar and the action bar?

The most obvious difference between the two is the updated visual design of the toolbar. The toolbar no longer includes an icon on the left side and decreases some of the spacing between the action items on the right side. Another major visual change is the Up button. In the action bar, this button was much more subtle and was just an accessory next to the icon in the action bar.

Aside from the visual differences, the main goal of the toolbar is to be more flexible than the action bar. The action bar has many constraints. It will always appear at the top of the screen. There can only be one action bar. The size of the action bar is fixed and should not be changed. The toolbar does not have these constraints.

In this chapter, you used a toolbar that was provided by one of the AppCompat themes. Alternatively, you can manually include a toolbar as a normal view in your activity or fragment's layout file. You can place this toolbar anywhere you like and you can even include multiple toolbars on the screen at the same time. This flexibility allows for interesting designs; for example, imagine if each fragment that you use maintains its own toolbar. When you host multiple fragments on the screen at the same time, each of them can bring along their own toolbar instead of sharing a single toolbar at the top of the screen.

Another interesting addition with the toolbar is the ability to place **View**s inside of the toolbar and to also adjust the height of the toolbar. This allows for much more flexibility in the way that your app works.

Challenge: Deleting Crimes

Once a crime has been created in CriminalIntent, there is no way to erase that crime from the official record. For this challenge, add a new action item to the **CrimeFragment** that allows the user to delete the current crime. Once the user presses the new delete action item, be sure to pop the user back to the previous activity with a call to the **finish** method on the **CrimeFragment**'s hosting activity.

Challenge: Plural String Resources

The subtitle is not grammatically correct when there is a single crime. "1 crimes" just does not show the right amount of attention to detail for your taste. For this challenge, correct this subtitle text.

You could have two different strings and determine which one to use in code, but this will quickly fall apart when you localize your app for different languages. A better option is to use plural string resources (sometimes also called quantity strings).

First, define a plural string in your strings.xml file.

```
<plurals name="subtitle_plural">
    <item quantity="one">%1$s crime</item>
    <item quantity="other">%1$s crimes</item>
</plurals>
```

Then, use the **getQuantityString** method to correctly pluralize the string.

```
int crimeSize = crimeLab.getCrimes().size();
String subtitle = getResources()
    .getQuantityString(R.plurals.subtitle_plural, crimeSize, crimeSize);
```

Challenge: An Empty View for the RecyclerView

Currently, when CriminalIntent launches it displays an empty **RecyclerView** – a big white void. You should give users something to interact with when there are no items in the list.

For this challenge, display a message like, "There are no crimes" and add a button to the view that will trigger the creation of a new crime.

Use the **setVisibility** method that exists on any **View** class to show and hide this new placeholder view when appropriate.

14

SQLite Databases

Almost every application needs a place to save data for the long term, longer than savedInstanceState will keep it around. Android provides a place to do this for you: a local filesystem on your phone or tablet's flash memory storage.

Each application on an Android device has a directory in its *sandbox*. Keeping files in the sandbox protects them from being accessed by other applications or even the prying eyes of users (unless the device has been "rooted," in which case the user can get to whatever he or she likes).

Each application's sandbox directory is a child of the device's /data/data directory named after the application package. For CriminalIntent, the full path to the sandbox directory is /data/data/ com.bignerdranch.android.criminalintent.

However, most application data is not stored in plain old files. Here is why: say that you had a file with all of your **Crime**s written out. To change the title on a **Crime** at the beginning of the file, you would have to read in the entire file and write out a whole new version. With a lot of **Crime**s, that would take a long time.

This is where SQLite comes in. SQLite is an open source relational database, like MySQL or Postgresql. Unlike other databases, though, SQLite stores its data in simple files, which you can read and write using the SQLite library. Android includes this SQLite library in its standard library, along with some additional Java helper classes.

This chapter will not cover everything SQLite. For that, you will want to visit http:// www.sqlite.org, which has complete documentation of SQLite itself. Here you will see how Android's basic SQLite helper classes work. These will let you open, read, and write to SQLite databases in your application sandbox, without necessarily knowing where that is.

Defining a Schema

Before you create a database, you have to decide what will be in that database. CriminalIntent stores a single list of crimes, so you will define one table named **crimes** (Figure 14.1).

Figure 14.1 The **crimes** table

_id	uuid	title	date	solved
1	13090636733242	Stolen yogurt	13090636733242	0
2	13090732131909	Dirty sink	13090732131909	1

People do this kind of thing in a lot of different ways in the programming world. They are all trying to achieve the same thing: to DRY up their code. DRY means "Don't Repeat Yourself," and refers to a rule of thumb when writing a program: if you write something down, write it down in one authoritative place. That way, instead of repeating yourself all over the place, you are always referring to the one authoritative place for that information.

Doing this with databases can be involved. There are even complex tools called object-relational mappers (or ORMs for short) that let you use your model objects (like **Crime**) as your One True Definition. In this chapter, you will take the simpler route of defining a simplified *database schema* in Java code that says what your table is named and what its columns are.

Start by creating a class to put your schema in. You will call this class **CrimeDbSchema**, but in the New Class dialog, enter **database.CrimeDbSchema**. This will put the CrimeDbSchema.java file in its own database package, which you will use to organize all your database-related code.

Inside **CrimeDbSchema**, define an inner class called **CrimeTable** to describe your table.

Listing 14.1 Defining **CrimeTable** (CrimeDbSchema.java)

```
public class CrimeDbSchema {
    public static final class CrimeTable {
        public static final String NAME = "crimes";
    }
}
```

The **CrimeTable** class only exists to define the **String** constants needed to describe the moving pieces of your table definition. The first piece of that definition is the name of the table in your database, CrimeTable.NAME.

Next, describe the columns.

Listing 14.2 Defining your table columns (CrimeDbSchema.java)

```
public class CrimeDbSchema {
    public static final class CrimeTable {
        public static final String NAME = "crimes";

        public static final class Cols {
            public static final String UUID = "uuid";
            public static final String TITLE = "title";
            public static final String DATE = "date";
            public static final String SOLVED = "solved";
        }
    }
}
```

With that, you will be able to refer to the column named "title" in a Java-safe way: CrimeTable.Cols.TITLE. That makes it much safer to change your program if you ever need to change the name of that column or add additional data to the table.

Building Your Initial Database

With your schema defined, you are ready to create the database itself. Android provides some low-level methods on **Context** to open a database file into an instance of **SQLiteDatabase**: **openOrCreateDatabase(…)** and **databaseList()**.

However, in practice you will always need to follow a few basic steps:

1. Check to see if the database already exists.

2. If it does not, create it and create the tables and initial data it needs.

3. If it does, open it up and see what version of your **CrimeDbSchema** it has. (You may want to add or remove things in future versions of **CriminalIntent**.)

4. If it is an old version, run code to upgrade it to a newer version.

Android provides the **SQLiteOpenHelper** class to handle all of this for you. Create a class called **CrimeBaseHelper** in your database package.

Listing 14.3 Creating **CrimeBaseHelper** (CrimeBaseHelper.java)

```java
public class CrimeBaseHelper extends SQLiteOpenHelper {
    private static final int VERSION = 1;
    private static final String DATABASE_NAME = "crimeBase.db";

    public CrimeBaseHelper(Context context) {
        super(context, DATABASE_NAME, null, VERSION);
    }

    @Override
    public void onCreate(SQLiteDatabase db) {

    }

    @Override
    public void onUpgrade(SQLiteDatabase db, int oldVersion, int newVersion) {

    }
}
```

A **SQLiteOpenHelper** is a class designed to get rid of the grunt work of opening a **SQLiteDatabase**. Use it inside of **CrimeLab** to create your crime database.

Listing 14.4 Opening a **SQLiteDatabase** (CrimeLab.java)

```java
public class CrimeLab {
    private static CrimeLab sCrimeLab;

    private List<Crime> mCrimes;
    private Context mContext;
    private SQLiteDatabase mDatabase;

    ...

    private CrimeLab(Context context) {
      mContext = context.getApplicationContext();
      mDatabase = new CrimeBaseHelper(mContext)
              .getWritableDatabase();
      mCrimes = new ArrayList<>();
    }

    ...
```

(Wondering why the context is stored in an instance variable? **CrimeLab** will make use of it in Chapter 16.)

When you call **getWritableDatabase()** here, **CrimeBaseHelper** will do the following:

1. Open up /data/data/com.bignerdranch.android.criminalintent/databases/crimeBase.db, creating a new database file if it does not already exist.

2. If this is the first time the database has been created, call **onCreate(SQLiteDatabase)**, then save out the latest version number.

3. If this is not the first time, check the version number in the database. If the version number in **CrimeOpenHelper** is higher, call **onUpgrade(SQLiteDatabase, int, int)**.

The upshot is this: you put your code to create the initial database in **onCreate(SQLiteDatabase)**, your code to handle any upgrades in **onUpgrade(SQLiteDatabase, int, int)**, and it just works.

For now, CriminalIntent will only have one version, so you can ignore **onUpgrade(…)**. You only need to create your database tables in **onCreate(…)**. To do that, you will refer to the **CrimeTable** inner class of **CrimeDbSchema**.

The import is a two-step process. First, write the initial part of your SQL creation code, as shown here:

Listing 14.5 Writing first part of **onCreate(…)** (CrimeBaseHelper.java)

```
@Override
public void onCreate(SQLiteDatabase db) {
    db.execSQL("create table " + CrimeDbSchema.CrimeTable.NAME);
}
```

Put your cursor on the word **CrimeTable** and key in Option+Return (Alt+Enter). Then select the first item, Add import for 'com.bignerdranch.android.criminalintent.database.CrimeDbSchema.CrimeTable' as shown in Figure 14.2.

Figure 14.2 Adding a **CrimeTable** import

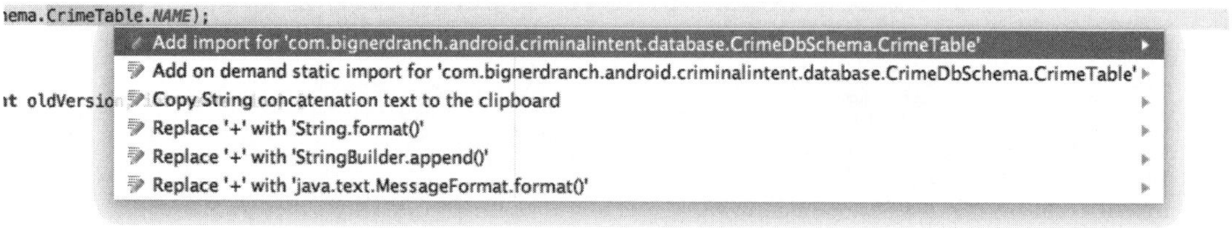

Android Studio will generate an import like this for you:

```
...

import com.bignerdranch.android.criminalintent.database.CrimeDbSchema.CrimeTable;

public class CrimeBaseHelper extends SQLiteOpenHelper {
    ...
```

That will let you refer to the **String** constants in **CrimeDbSchema.CrimeTable**
by typing in CrimeTable.Cols.UUID, rather than typing out the entirety of
CrimeDbSchema.CrimeTable.Cols.UUID. Use that to finish filling out your table definition code.

Listing 14.6 Creating crime table (`CrimeBaseHelper.java`)

```java
@Override
public void onCreate(SQLiteDatabase db) {
    db.execSQL("create table " + CrimeTable.NAME + "(" +
            " _id integer primary key autoincrement, " +
            CrimeTable.Cols.UUID + ", " +
            CrimeTable.Cols.TITLE + ", " +
            CrimeTable.Cols.DATE + ", " +
            CrimeTable.Cols.SOLVED +
            ")"
    );
}
```

Creating a table in SQLite requires less ceremony than in other databases: you do not have to specify
the type of a column at creation time. It is a good idea to do that, but here you will save a bit of labor
by doing without it.

Run CriminalIntent, and your database will be created (Figure 14.3). If you are running on an emulator
or a rooted device, you can look at it directly. (Not on a real device, though – it is saved in private
storage, which is secret.) Just pull up Tools → Android → Android Device Monitor, and look in /data/
data/com.bignerdranch.android.criminalintent/databases/.

Figure 14.3 Your database

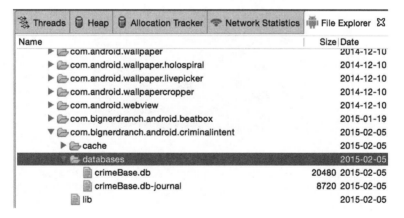

Debugging database issues

When writing code dealing with a SQLite database, you will sometimes need to tweak the layout of
the database. For example, in an upcoming chapter you will add a suspect for each crime. This will
require an additional column on the crime table. The "right" way to do this is to write code in your
SQLiteOpenHelper to bump the version number, and then update the tables inside **onUpgrade(…)**.

Well, the "right" way involves a fair amount of code – code that is ridiculous to write when you are only trying to get version 1 or 2 of the database right. In practice, the best thing to do is destroy the database and start over, so that **SQLiteOpenHelper.onCreate(…)** is called again.

The easiest way to destroy your database is to delete the app off your device. And the easiest way to delete the app on stock Android is to go to the application browser and drag CriminalIntent's icon up to where it says Uninstall at the top of screen. (The process may be different if your version of Android is different from stock Android.) Then you will see a screen similar to the one shown in Figure 14.4.

Figure 14.4 Deleting an app

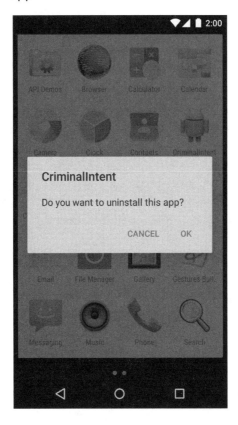

Remember this trick if you run into any issues with your database tables in this chapter.

Gutting CrimeLab

Now that you have a database, your next step is to change a lot of code inside of **CrimeLab**, swapping it to use mDatabase for storage instead of mCrimes.

Start out by doing some demolition. Strip out all the code related to mCrimes in **CrimeLab**.

Listing 14.7 Tearing down some walls (`CrimeLab.java`)

```java
public class CrimeLab {
    private static CrimeLab sCrimeLab;

    private List<Crime> mCrimes;
    private Context mContext;
    private SQLiteDatabase mDatabase;

    public static CrimeLab get(Context context) {
        ...
    }

    private CrimeLab(Context context) {
        mContext = context.getApplicationContext();
        mDatabase = new CrimeBaseHelper(mContext)
                .getWritableDatabase();
        mCrimes = new ArrayList<>();
    }

    public void addCrime(Crime c) {
        mCrimes.add(c);
    }

    public List<Crime> getCrimes() {
        return mCrimes;
        return new ArrayList<>();
    }

    public Crime getCrime(UUID id) {
        for (Crime crime : mCrimes) {
            if (crime.getId().equals(id)) {
                return crime;
            }
        }
        return null;
    }
}
```

This will leave CriminalIntent in a state where it is not really working; you can see an empty list of crimes, but if you add a crime it will show an empty **CrimePagerActivity**. This is irritating, but fine for now.

Writing to the Database

The first step in using your **SQLiteDatabase** is to write data to it. You will need to insert new rows into the crime table as well as update rows that are already there when **Crime**s are changed.

Using ContentValues

Writes and updates to databases are done with the assistance of a class called **ContentValues**. **ContentValues** is a key-value store class, like Java's **HashMap** or the **Bundle**s you have been using so far. However, unlike **HashMap** or **Bundle** it is specifically designed to store the kinds of data SQLite can hold.

You will be creating **ContentValues** instances from **Crime**s a few times in **CrimeLab**. Add a private method to take care of shuttling a **Crime** into a **ContentValues**. (Remember to use the same two-step trick from above to add an import of **CrimeTable**: when you get to CrimeTable.Cols.UUID, type Option+Return (Alt+Enter) and choose Add import for 'com.bignerdranch.android.criminalintent.database.CrimeDbSchema.CrimeTable'.)

Listing 14.8 Creating a **ContentValues** (CrimeLab.java)

```
    public getCrime(UUID id) {
        return null;
    }

    private static ContentValues getContentValues(Crime crime) {
        ContentValues values = new ContentValues();
        values.put(CrimeTable.Cols.UUID, crime.getId().toString());
        values.put(CrimeTable.Cols.TITLE, crime.getTitle());
        values.put(CrimeTable.Cols.DATE, crime.getDate().getTime());
        values.put(CrimeTable.Cols.SOLVED, crime.isSolved() ? 1 : 0);

        return values;
    }
}
```

For the keys, you use your column names. These are not arbitrary names; they specify the columns that you want to insert or update. If they are misspelled or typo'd compared to what is in the database, your insert or update will fail. Every column is specified here except for _id, which is automatically created for you as a unique row ID.

Inserting and updating rows

Now that you have a **ContentValues**, time to add rows to the database. Fill out **addCrime(Crime)** with a new implementation.

Listing 14.9 Inserting a row (CrimeLab.java)

```
public void addCrime(Crime c) {
    ContentValues values = getContentValues(c);

    mDatabase.insert(CrimeTable.NAME, null, values);
}
```

The **insert(String, String, ContentValues)** method has two important arguments, and one that is rarely used. The first argument is the table you want to insert into – here, CrimeTable.NAME. The last argument is the data you want to put in.

And the second argument? The second argument is called nullColumnHack. And what does it do?

Well, say that you decided to call **insert(…)** with an empty **ContentValues**. SQLite does not allow this, so your **insert(…)** call would fail.

If you passed in a value of uuid for nullColumnHack, though, it would ignore that empty **ContentValues**. Instead, it would pass in a **ContentValues** with uuid set to null. This would allow your **insert(…)** to succeed and create a new row.

Handy? Perhaps someday. Not today, though. Now you know about it, at least.

Continue applying **ContentValues** by writing a method to update rows in the database.

Listing 14.10 Updating a **Crime** (CrimeLab.java)

```java
public Crime getCrime(UUID id) {
    return null;
}

public void updateCrime(Crime crime) {
    String uuidString = crime.getId().toString();
    ContentValues values = getContentValues(crime);

    mDatabase.update(CrimeTable.NAME, values,
            CrimeTable.Cols.UUID + " = ?",
            new String[] { uuidString });
}

private static ContentValues getContentValues(Crime crime) {
    ContentValues values = new ContentValues();
    values.put(CrimeTable.Cols.UUID, crime.getId().toString());
    ...
```

The **update(String, ContentValues, String, String[])** method starts off similarly to **insert(…)** – you pass in the table name you want to update and the **ContentValues** you want to assign to each row you update. However, the last bit is different, because now you have to specify *which* rows get updated. You do that by building a where clause (the third argument), and then specifying values for the arguments in the where clause (the final **String[]** array).

You may be wondering why you are not putting uuidString directly into the where clause. That would be a bit simpler than using ? and passing it in as a **String[]**, after all.

The answer is that in some cases your **String** might itself contain SQL code. If you put that **String** directly in your query, that code could change the meaning of your query, or even alter your database. This is called a SQL injection attack, and it is a bad thing indeed.

If you use ?, though, your code will do what you intended: treat it as a **String** value, not code. So it is best to be safe and use ? as a matter of habit, which will always do what you intend no matter what the **String** contains.

Crime instances get modified in **CrimeFragment**, and will need to be written out when **CrimeFragment** is done. So add an override to **CrimeFragment.onPause()** that updates **CrimeLab**'s copy of your **Crime**.

Listing 14.11 Pushing updates (CrimeFragment.java)

```java
@Override
public void onCreate(Bundle savedInstanceState) {
    super.onCreate(savedInstanceState);
    UUID crimeId = (UUID) getArguments().getSerializable(ARG_CRIME_ID);
    mCrime = CrimeLab.get(getActivity()).getCrime(crimeId);
}

@Override
public void onPause() {
    super.onPause();

    CrimeLab.get(getActivity())
            .updateCrime(mCrime);
}
```

Sadly, you have no way of verifying that this code works. That will need to wait until you can read in the crimes you updated. To make sure that everything compiles correctly, run CriminalIntent one more time before moving on to the next section. You should see a blank list.

Reading from the Database

Reading in data from SQLite is done using the **query(…)** method. **SQLiteDatabase.query(…)** has quite a lot going on. There are a few different overloads of this method. The one you will be using looks like this:

```
public Cursor query(
    String table,
    String[] columns,
    String where,
    String[] whereArgs,
    String groupBy,
    String having,
    String orderBy,
    String limit)
```

If you have dealt with SQL before, then most of these will be familiar to you as arguments of the select statement. If you have not, then you only need to worry about the ones you will be using:

```
public Cursor query(
    String table,
    String[] columns,
    String where,
    String[] whereArgs,
    String groupBy,
    String having,
    String orderBy,
    String limit)
```

The table argument is the table to query. The columns argument names which columns you want values for and what order you want to receive them in. And then where and whereArgs do the same thing they do in **update(…)**.

Use **query(…)** in a convenience method to call this on your **CrimeTable**.

Listing 14.12 Querying for **Crime**s (CrimeLab.java)

```
...
    values.put(CrimeTable.Cols.DATE, crime.getDate().getTime());
    values.put(CrimeTable.Cols.SOLVED, crime.isSolved() ? 1 : 0);

    return values;
}

private Cursor queryCrimes(String whereClause, String[] whereArgs) {
    Cursor cursor = mDatabase.query(
            CrimeTable.NAME,
            null, // Columns - null selects all columns
            whereClause,
            whereArgs,
            null, // groupBy
            null, // having
            null  // orderBy
    );

    return cursor;
}
```

Using a CursorWrapper

A **Cursor** leaves a lot to be desired as a way to look at a table. All it does is give you raw column values. Pulling data out of a **Cursor** looks like this:

```
String uuidString = cursor.getString(
    cursor.getColumnIndex(CrimeTable.Cols.UUID));
String title = cursor.getString(
    cursor.getColumnIndex(CrimeTable.Cols.TITLE));
long date = cursor.getLong(
    cursor.getColumnIndex(CrimeTable.Cols.DATE));
int isSolved = cursor.getInt(
    cursor.getColumnIndex(CrimeTable.Cols.SOLVED));
```

Every time you pull a **Crime** out of a cursor, you need to write this code one more time. (And that does not include the code to create a **Crime** instance with those values!)

Remember the DRY rule of thumb: Don't Repeat Yourself. Instead of writing this code each time you need to read data from a **Cursor**, you can create your own **Cursor** subclass that takes care of this in one place. The easiest way to write a **Cursor** subclass is to use **CursorWrapper**. A **CursorWrapper** lets you wrap a **Cursor** you received from another place and add new methods on top of it.

Create a new class in the database package called **CrimeCursorWrapper**.

Listing 14.13 Creating **CrimeCursorWrapper** (CrimeCursorWrapper.java)

```
public class CrimeCursorWrapper extends CursorWrapper {
    public CrimeCursorWrapper(Cursor cursor) {
        super(cursor);
    }
}
```

That creates a thin wrapper around a **Cursor**. It has all the same methods as the **Cursor** it wraps, and calling those methods does the exact same thing. This would be pointless, except that it makes it possible to add new methods that operate on the underlying **Cursor**.

Add a **getCrime()** method that pulls out relevant column data. (Remember to use the two-step import trick for **CrimeTable** here, as you did earlier.)

Listing 14.14 Adding **getCrime()** method (CrimeCursorWrapper.java)

```
public class CrimeCursorWrapper extends CursorWrapper {
    public CrimeCursorWrapper(Cursor cursor) {
        super(cursor);
    }

    public Crime getCrime() {
        String uuidString = getString(getColumnIndex(CrimeTable.Cols.UUID));
        String title = getString(getColumnIndex(CrimeTable.Cols.TITLE));
        long date = getLong(getColumnIndex(CrimeTable.Cols.DATE));
        int isSolved = getInt(getColumnIndex(CrimeTable.Cols.SOLVED));

        return null;
    }
}
```

You will need to return a **Crime** with an appropriate **UUID** from this method. Add another constructor to **Crime** to do this.

Listing 14.15 Adding **Crime** constructor (Crime.java)

```
public Crime() {
    this(UUID.randomUUID());
    mId = UUID.randomUUID();
    mDate = new Date();
}

public Crime(UUID id) {
    mId = id;
    mDate = new Date();
}
```

And then finish up **getCrime()**.

Listing 14.16 Finishing up **getCrime()** (CrimeCursorWrapper.java)

```
public Crime getCrime() {
    String uuidString = getString(getColumnIndex(CrimeTable.Cols.UUID));
    String title = getString(getColumnIndex(CrimeTable.Cols.TITLE));
    long date = getLong(getColumnIndex(CrimeTable.Cols.DATE));
    int isSolved = getInt(getColumnIndex(CrimeTable.Cols.SOLVED));

    Crime crime = new Crime(UUID.fromString(uuidString));
    crime.setTitle(title);
    crime.setDate(new Date(date));
    crime.setSolved(isSolved != 0);

    return crime;
    return null;
}
```

(Android Studio will ask you to choose between **java.util.Date** and **java.sql.Date**. Even though you are dealing with databases, **java.util.Date** is the right choice here.)

Converting to model objects

With **CrimeCursorWrapper**, vending out a **List<Crime>** from **CrimeLab** will be straightforward. You need to wrap the cursor you get back from your query in a **CrimeCursorWrapper**, then iterate over it calling **getCrime()** to pull out its **Crime**s.

For the first part, **queryCrimes(…)** to use **CrimeCursorWrapper**.

Listing 14.17 Vending cursor wrapper (CrimeLab.java)

```
private Cursor queryCrimes(String whereClause, String[] whereArgs) {
private CrimeCursorWrapper queryCrimes(String whereClause, String[] whereArgs) {
    Cursor cursor = mDatabase.query(
            CrimeTable.NAME,
            null, // Columns - null selects all columns
            whereClause,
            whereArgs,
            null, // groupBy
            null, // having
            null  // orderBy
    );

    return cursor;
    return new CrimeCursorWrapper(cursor);
}
```

Then get **getCrimes()** into shape. Add code to query for all crimes, walk the cursor, and populate a **Crime** list.

Listing 14.18 Returning crime list (CrimeLab.java)

```
public List<Crime> getCrimes() {
    return new ArrayList<>();
    List<Crime> crimes = new ArrayList<>();

    CrimeCursorWrapper cursor = queryCrimes(null, null);

    try {
        cursor.moveToFirst();
        while (!cursor.isAfterLast()) {
            crimes.add(cursor.getCrime());
            cursor.moveToNext();
        }
    } finally {
        cursor.close();
    }

    return crimes;
}
```

Database cursors are called cursors because they always have their finger on a particular place in a query. So to pull the data out of a cursor, you move it to the first element by calling **moveToFirst()**, and then reading in row data. Each time you want to advance to a new row, you call **moveToNext()**, until finally **isAfterLast()** tells you that your pointer is off the end of the dataset.

The last important thing to do is to call **close()** on your **Cursor**. This bit of housekeeping is important. If you do not do it, your Android device will spit out nasty error logs to berate you. Even worse, if you make a habit out of it, you will eventually run out of open file handles and crash your app. So: close your cursors.

`CrimeLab.getCrime(UUID)` will look similar to `getCrimes()`, except it will only need to pull the first item, if it is there.

Listing 14.19 Rewriting `getCrime(UUID)` (`CrimeLab.java`)

```
public Crime getCrime(UUID id) {
    return null;
    CrimeCursorWrapper cursor = queryCrimes(
            CrimeTable.Cols.UUID + " = ?",
            new String[] { id.toString() }
    );

    try {
        if (cursor.getCount() == 0) {
            return null;
        }

        cursor.moveToFirst();
        return cursor.getCrime();
    } finally {
        cursor.close();
    }
}
```

That completes a few moving pieces:

- You can insert crimes, so the code that adds **Crime** to **CrimeLab** when you press the New Crime action item now works.

- You can successfully query the database, so **CrimePagerActivity** can see all the **Crime**s in **CrimeLab**, too.

- **CrimeLab.getCrime(UUID)** works, too, so each **CrimeFragment** displayed in **CrimePagerActivity** is showing the real **Crime**.

Now you should be able to press New Crime and see the new **Crime** displayed in **CrimePagerActivity**. Run CriminalIntent and verify that you can do this. If you cannot, double-check your implementations from this chapter so far.

Refreshing model data

You are not quite done. Your crimes are persistently stored to the database, but the persistent data is not read back in. So if you press the Back button after editing your new **Crime**, it will not show up in **CrimeListActivity**.

This is because **CrimeLab** now works a little differently. Before, there was only one **List<Crime>**, and one object for each **Crime**: the one in the **List<Crime>**. That was because mCrimes was the only authority for which **Crime**s your app knew about.

Things have changed now. mCrimes is gone. So the **List<Crime>** returned by `getCrimes()` is a snapshot of the **Crime**s at one point in time. To refresh **CrimeListActivity**, you need to update that snapshot.

Most of the moving pieces to do this are already in place. **CrimeListActivity** already calls **updateUI()** to refresh other parts of its interface. All you need to do is have it refresh its view of **CrimeLab**, too.

First, add a **setCrimes(List<Crime>)** method to **CrimeAdapter** to swap out the crimes it displays.

Listing 14.20 Adding **setCrimes(List<Crime>)** (CrimeListFragment.java)

```
private class CrimeAdapter extends RecyclerView.Adapter<CrimeHolder> {
    ...

    @Override
    public int getItemCount() {
        return mCrimes.size();
    }

    public void setCrimes(List<Crime> crimes) {
        mCrimes = crimes;
    }
}
```

Then call **setCrimes(List<Crime>)** in **updateUI()**.

Listing 14.21 Calling **setCrimes(List<>)** (CrimeListFragment.java)

```
private void updateUI() {
    CrimeLab crimeLab = CrimeLab.get(getActivity());
    List<Crime> crimes = crimeLab.getCrimes();

    if (mAdapter == null) {
        mAdapter = new CrimeAdapter(crimes);
        mCrimeRecyclerView.setAdapter(mAdapter);
    } else {
        mAdapter.setCrimes(crimes);
        mAdapter.notifyDataSetChanged();
    }

    updateSubtitle();
}
```

Now everything should work correctly. Run CriminalIntent and verify that you can add a crime, press the Back button, and see that crime in **CrimeListActivity**.

This is also a good time to test that calls to **updateCrime(Crime)** in **CrimeFragment** work, too. Press a **Crime** and edit its title inside **CrimePagerActivity**. Press the Back button and make sure that the new title is reflected in the list.

For the More Curious: More Databases

For the sake of space and simplicity, we do not go into all the details you might see in a professional app's application database here. There is a reason people resort to tools like ORMs: this stuff can get complicated.

For a more substantial application you will want to look into adding the following to your database and your description of it:

- Data types on columns. Technically, SQLite does not have typed columns, so you can get by without them. Giving SQLite hints is kinder, though.

- Indexes. Queries against columns with appropriate indexes are much faster than columns without them.

- Foreign keys. Your database here only has one table, but associated data would need foreign key constraints, too.

There are also deeper performance considerations to dive into. Your app creates a new list of all-new **Crime** objects every time you query the database. A high-performance app would optimize this by recycling instances of **Crime** or by treating them like an in-memory object store (like you did before this chapter). That ends up being quite a bit more code, so this is another problem ORMs often try to solve.

For the More Curious: The Application Context

Earlier in this chapter, you used the *Application Context* in the constructor of the **CrimeLab**.

```
private CrimeLab(Context context) {
  mContext = context.getApplicationContext();
  ...
}
```

What makes the Application Context special? When should you use the application context over an activity as a context?

It's important to think about the lifetime of each of these objects. If any of your activities exist, Android will have also created an *Application* object. Activities come and go as the user navigates through your application but the application object will still exist. It has a much longer lifetime than any one activity.

The **CrimeLab** is a singleton, which means that once it is created, it will not be destroyed until your entire application process is destroyed. The **CrimeLab** maintains a reference to its **mContext** object. If you store an activity as the **mContext** object, that activity will never be cleaned up by the garbage collector because the **CrimeLab** has a reference to it. Even if the user has navigated away from that activity, it will never be cleaned up.

To avoid this wasteful situation, you use the application context so that your activities can come and go and the **CrimeLab** can maintain a reference to a **Context** object. Always think about the lifetime of your activities as you keep a reference to them.

Challenge: Deleting Crimes

If you added a Delete Crime action item earlier, this challenge builds off of that by adding the ability to delete crimes from your database by calling a **deleteCrime(Crime)** method on **CrimeLab**, which will call **mDatabase.delete(…)** to finish the job.

And if you do not have a Delete Crime? Well, go ahead and add it! Add an action item to **CrimeFragment**'s toolbar that calls **CrimeLab.deleteCrime(Crime)** and **finish()**es its **Activity**.

15

Implicit Intents

In Android, you can start an activity in another application on the device using an *implicit intent*. In an explicit intent, you specify the class of the activity to start, and the OS will start it. In an implicit intent, you describe the job that you need done, and the OS will start an activity in an appropriate application for you.

In CriminalIntent, you will use implicit intents to enable picking a suspect for a **Crime** from the user's list of contacts and sending a text-based report of a crime. The user will choose a suspect from whatever contacts app is installed on the device and will be offered a choice of apps to send the crime report (Figure 15.1).

Figure 15.1 Opening contacts app and a text-sending app

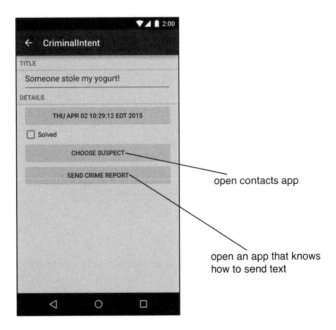

Using implicit intents to harness other applications is far easier than writing your own implementations for common tasks. Users also appreciate being able to use apps they already know and like in conjunction with your app.

Before you can create these implicit intents, there is some setup to do in CriminalIntent:

- add Choose Suspect and Send Crime Report buttons to **CrimeFragment**'s layouts

- add an mSuspect field to the **Crime** class that will hold the name of a suspect

- create a crime report using a set of format resource strings

Adding Buttons

You are going to start by updating **CrimeFragment**'s layouts to include new buttons for accusation and tattling: namely, a suspect button and a report button. First, add the strings that these buttons will display.

Listing 15.1 Adding button strings (strings.xml)

```
...
    <string name="subtitle_format">%1$s crimes</string>
    <string name="crime_suspect_text">Choose Suspect</string>
    <string name="crime_report_text">Send Crime Report</string>
</resources>
```

In layout/fragment_crime.xml, add two button widgets, as shown in Figure 15.2. Notice that in this diagram we are not showing the first **LinearLayout** and all of its children so that you can focus on the new and interesting parts of the diagram on the right.

Figure 15.2 Adding suspect and crime report buttons (layout/fragment_crime.xml)

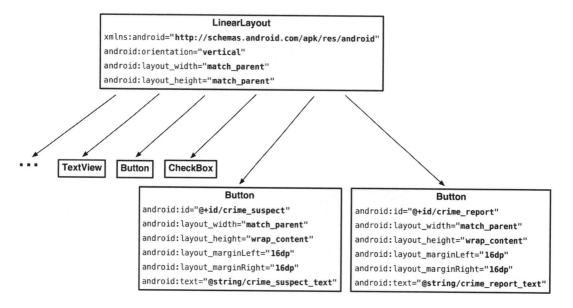

In the landscape layout, you are going to make these new buttons children of a new horizontal **LinearLayout** below the one that contains the date button and the checkbox. Figure 15.3 shows the new layout.

Figure 15.3 New landscape layout

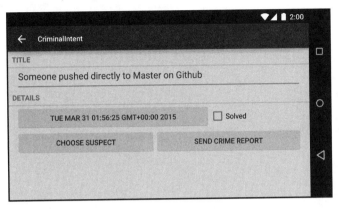

In layout-land/fragment_crime.xml, add the **LinearLayout** and two button widgets, as shown in Figure 15.4.

Figure 15.4 Adding suspect and crime report buttons (layout-land/ fragment_crime.xml)

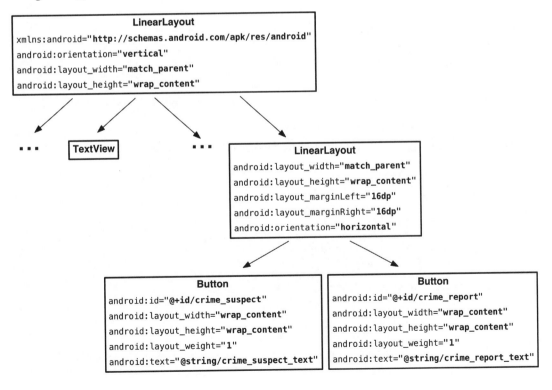

At this point, you can preview the layouts or run CriminalIntent to confirm that your new buttons are in place.

Adding a Suspect to the Model Layer

Next, open Crime.java and add a new member variable to give **Crime** a field that will hold the name of a suspect.

Listing 15.2 Adding suspect field (Crime.java)

```java
public class Crime {

    ...
    private boolean mSolved;
    private String mSuspect;

    public Crime() {
        this(UUID.randomUUID());
    }

    ...

    public void setSolved(boolean solved) {
        mSolved = solved;
    }

    public String getSuspect() {
        return mSuspect;
    }

    public void setSuspect(String suspect) {
        mSuspect = suspect;
    }
}
```

Now you need to add an additional field to your crime database. First, add a suspect column to **CrimeDbSchema**.

Listing 15.3 Adding suspect column (CrimeDbSchema.java)

```java
public class CrimeDbSchema {
    public static final class CrimeTable {
        public static final String NAME = "crimes";

        public static final class Cols {
            public static final String UUID = "uuid";
            public static final String TITLE = "title";
            public static final String DATE = "date";
            public static final String SOLVED = "solved";
            public static final String SUSPECT = "suspect";
        }
    }
}
```

Add the column in **CrimeBaseHelper**, also. (Notice that the new code begins with a comma after CrimeTable.Cols.SOLVED.)

Listing 15.4 Adding suspect column again (`CrimeBaseHelper.java`)

```java
@Override
public void onCreate(SQLiteDatabase db) {

    db.execSQL("create table " + CrimeTable.NAME + "(" +
            " _id integer primary key autoincrement, " +
            CrimeTable.Cols.UUID + ", " +
            CrimeTable.Cols.TITLE + ", " +
            CrimeTable.Cols.DATE + ", " +
            CrimeTable.Cols.SOLVED + ", " +
            CrimeTable.Cols.SUSPECT +
            ")"
    );
}
```

Next, write to the new column in **CrimeLab.getContentValues(Crime)**.

Listing 15.5 Writing to suspect column (`CrimeLab.java`)

```java
...
private static ContentValues getContentValues(Crime crime) {
    ContentValues values = new ContentValues();
    values.put(CrimeTable.Cols.UUID, crime.getId().toString());
    values.put(CrimeTable.Cols.TITLE, crime.getTitle());
    values.put(CrimeTable.Cols.DATE, crime.getDate().getTime());
    values.put(CrimeTable.Cols.SOLVED, crime.isSolved() ? 1 : 0);
    values.put(CrimeTable.Cols.SUSPECT, crime.getSuspect());

    return values;
}
...
```

Now read from it in **CrimeCursorWrapper**.

Listing 15.6 Reading from suspect column (`CrimeCursorWrapper.java`)

```java
    ...
    public Crime getCrime() {
        String uuidString = getString(getColumnIndex(CrimeTable.Cols.UUID));
        String title = getString(getColumnIndex(CrimeTable.Cols.TITLE));
        long date = getLong(getColumnIndex(CrimeTable.Cols.DATE));
        int isSolved = getInt(getColumnIndex(CrimeTable.Cols.SOLVED));
        String suspect = getString(getColumnIndex(CrimeTable.Cols.SUSPECT));

        Crime crime = new Crime(UUID.fromString(uuidString));
        crime.setTitle(title);
        crime.setDate(new Date(date));
        crime.setSolved(isSolved != 0);
        crime.setSuspect(suspect);

        return crime;
    }
}
```

If CriminalIntent is already installed on your device, your existing database will not have the suspect column, and your new onCreate(SQLiteDatabase) will not be run to add the new column, either. The easiest solution is to wipe out your old database in favor of a new one. (This happens a lot in app development.)

First, uninstall the CriminalIntent app by opening the app launcher screen and dragging the CriminalIntent icon to the top of the screen. All your sandbox storage will get blown away, along with the out-of-date database schema, as part of the uninstall process. Next, run CriminalIntent from Android Studio. A new database will be created with the new column as part of the app installation process.

Using a Format String

The last preliminary is to create a template crime report that can be configured with the specific crime's details. Because you will not know a crime's details until runtime, you must use a format string with placeholders that can be replaced at runtime. Here is the format string you will use:

```
<string name="crime_report">%1$s! The crime was discovered on %2$s. %3$s, and %4$s
```

The %1$s, %2$s, etc. are placeholders that expect string arguments. In code, you will call getString(…) and pass in the format string and four other strings in the order in which they should replace the placeholders.

First, in strings.xml, add the strings shown in Listing 15.7.

Listing 15.7 Adding string resources (strings.xml)

```
<string name="crime_suspect_text">Choose Suspect</string>
<string name="crime_report_text">Send Crime Report</string>
<string name="crime_report">%1$s!
  The crime was discovered on %2$s. %3$s, and %4$s
</string>
<string name="crime_report_solved">The case is solved</string>
<string name="crime_report_unsolved">The case is not solved</string>
<string name="crime_report_no_suspect">there is no suspect.</string>
<string name="crime_report_suspect">the suspect is %s.</string>
<string name="crime_report_subject">CriminalIntent Crime Report</string>
<string name="send_report">Send crime report via</string>

</resources>
```

In CrimeFragment.java, add a method that creates four strings and then pieces them together and returns a complete report.

Listing 15.8 Adding **getCrimeReport()** method (CrimeFragment.java)

```
...
private void updateDate() {
    mDateButton.setText(mCrime.getDate().toString());
}

private String getCrimeReport() {
    String solvedString = null;
    if (mCrime.isSolved()) {
        solvedString = getString(R.string.crime_report_solved);
    } else {
        solvedString = getString(R.string.crime_report_unsolved);
    }

    String dateFormat = "EEE, MMM dd";
    String dateString = DateFormat.format(dateFormat, mCrime.getDate()).toString();

    String suspect = mCrime.getSuspect();
    if (suspect == null) {
        suspect = getString(R.string.crime_report_no_suspect);
    } else {
        suspect = getString(R.string.crime_report_suspect, suspect);
    }

    String report = getString(R.string.crime_report,
        mCrime.getTitle(), dateString, solvedString, suspect);

    return report;
}
```

(Note that there are two **DateFormat** classes: **android.text.format.DateFormat**, and **java.text.DateFormat**. Use **android.text.format.DateFormat**.)

Now the preliminaries are complete, and you can turn to implicit intents.

Using Implicit Intents

An **Intent** is an object that describes to the OS something that you want it to do. With the *explicit* intents that you have created thus far, you explicitly name the activity that you want the OS to start.

```
Intent intent = new Intent(getActivity(), CrimePagerActivity.class);
intent.putExtra(EXTRA_CRIME_ID, crimeId);
startActivity(intent);
```

With an *implicit* intent, you describe to the OS the job that you want done. The OS then starts the activity that has advertised itself as capable of doing that job. If the OS finds more than one capable activity, then the user is offered a choice.

Parts of an implicit intent

Here are the critical parts of an intent that you can use to define the job you want done:

the *action* that you are trying to perform

These are typically constants from the **Intent** class. If you want to view a URL, you can use Intent.ACTION_VIEW for your action. To send something, you use Intent.ACTION_SEND.

the location of any *data*

This can be something outside the device, like the URL of a web page, but it can also be a URI to a file or a *content URI* pointing to a record in a **ContentProvider**.

the *type* of data that the action is for

This is a MIME type, like text/html or audio/mpeg3. If an intent includes a location for data, then the type can usually be inferred from that data.

optional *categories*

If the action is used to describe *what* to do, the category usually describes *where*, *when*, or *how* you are trying to use an activity. Android uses the category android.intent.category.LAUNCHER to indicate that an activity should be displayed in the top-level app launcher. The android.intent.category.INFO category, on the other hand, indicates an activity that shows information about a package to the user but should not show up in the launcher.

A simple implicit intent for viewing a website would include an action of Intent.ACTION_VIEW and a data **Uri** that is the URL of a website.

Based on this information, the OS will launch the appropriate activity of an appropriate application. (If it finds more than one candidate, the user gets a choice.)

An activity would advertise itself as an appropriate activity for ACTION_VIEW via an intent filter in the manifest. If you wanted to write a browser app, for instance, you would include the following intent filter in the declaration of the activity that should respond to ACTION_VIEW:

```
<activity
  android:name=".BrowserActivity"
  android:label="@string/app_name" >
  <intent-filter>
    <action android:name="android.intent.action.VIEW" />
    <category android:name="android.intent.category.DEFAULT" />
    <data android:scheme="http" android:host="www.bignerdranch.com" />
  </intent-filter>
</activity>
```

To respond to implicit intents, a DEFAULT category must be set explicitly in an intent filter. The action element in the intent filter tells the OS that the activity is capable of performing the job, and the DEFAULT category tells the OS that this activity should be considered for the job when the OS is asking for volunteers. This DEFAULT category is implicitly added to every implicit intent. (In Chapter 22, you will see that this is not the case when Android is not asking for a volunteer.)

Implicit intents can also include extras just like explicit intents. Any extras on an implicit intent, however, are not used by the OS to find an appropriate activity.

Note that the action and data parts of an intent can also be used in conjunction with an explicit intent. That would be the equivalent of telling a particular activity to do something specific.

Sending a crime report

Let's see how this works by creating an implicit intent to send a crime report in CriminalIntent. The job you want done is sending plain text; the crime report is a string. So the implicit intent's action will be ACTION_SEND. It will not point to any data or have any categories, but it will specify a type of text/plain.

In CrimeFragment.onCreateView(…), get a reference to the Send Crime Report button and set a listener on it. Within the listener's implementation, create an implicit intent and pass it into startActivity(Intent).

Listing 15.9 Sending a crime report (CrimeFragment.java)

```java
private Crime mCrime;
private EditText mTitleField;
private Button mDateButton;
private CheckBox mSolvedCheckbox;
private Button mReportButton;

...

public View onCreateView(LayoutInflater inflater, ViewGroup container,
        Bundle savedInstanceState) {
    ...

    mReportButton = (Button) v.findViewById(R.id.crime_report);
    mReportButton.setOnClickListener(new View.OnClickListener() {
        public void onClick(View v) {
            Intent i = new Intent(Intent.ACTION_SEND);
            i.setType("text/plain");
            i.putExtra(Intent.EXTRA_TEXT, getCrimeReport());
            i.putExtra(Intent.EXTRA_SUBJECT,
                    getString(R.string.crime_report_subject));
            startActivity(i);
        }
    });

    return v;
}
```

Here you use the **Intent** constructor that accepts a string that is a constant defining the action. There are other constructors that you can use depending on what kind of implicit intent you need to create. You can find them all on the **Intent** reference page in the documentation. There is no constructor that accepts a type, so you set it explicitly.

You include the text of the report and the string for the subject of the report as extras. Note that these extras use constants defined in the **Intent** class. Any activity responding to this intent will know these constants and what to do with the associated values.

Run CriminalIntent and press the Send Crime Report button. Because this intent will likely match many activities on the device, you will probably see a list of activities presented in a chooser (Figure 15.5).

Figure 15.5 Activities volunteering to send your crime report

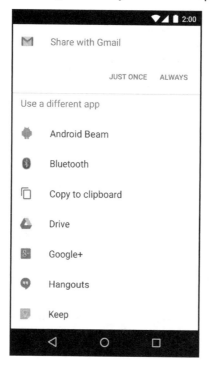

If you are offered a choice, make a selection. You will see your crime report loaded into the app that you chose. All you have to do is address and send it.

If, on the other hand, you do not see a chooser, that means one of two things. Either you have already set a default app for an identical implicit intent, or your device has only a single activity that can respond to this intent.

Often, it is best to go with the user's default app for an action. In CriminalIntent, however, you always want the user to have a choice for ACTION_SEND. Today a user might want to be discreet and email the crime report, but tomorrow he or she may prefer public shaming via Twitter.

You can create a chooser to be shown every time an implicit intent is used to start an activity. After you create your implicit intent as before, you call the following **Intent** method and pass in the implicit intent and a string for the chooser's title:

```
public static Intent createChooser(Intent target, String title)
```

Then you pass the intent returned from **createChooser(…)** into **startActivity(…)**.

In CrimeFragment.java, create a chooser to display the activities that respond to your implicit intent.

Listing 15.10 Using a chooser (`CrimeFragment.java`)

```java
public void onClick(View v) {
    Intent i = new Intent(Intent.ACTION_SEND);
    i.setType("text/plain");
    i.putExtra(Intent.EXTRA_TEXT, getCrimeReport());
    i.putExtra(Intent.EXTRA_SUBJECT,
            getString(R.string.crime_report_subject));
    i = Intent.createChooser(i, getString(R.string.send_report));
    startActivity(i);
}
```

Run CriminalIntent and press the Send Crime Report button. As long as you have more than one activity that can handle your intent, you will be offered a list to choose from (Figure 15.6).

Figure 15.6 Sending text with a chooser

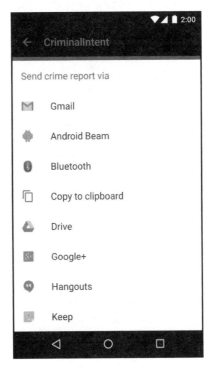

Asking Android for a contact

Now you are going to create another implicit intent that enables users to choose a suspect from their contacts. This implicit intent will have an action and a location where the relevant data can be found. The action will be `Intent.ACTION_PICK`. The data for contacts is at `ContactsContract.Contacts.CONTENT_URI`. In short, you are asking Android to help pick an item in the contacts database.

You expect a result back from the started activity, so you will pass the intent via `startActivityForResult(…)` along with a request code. In `CrimeFragment.java`, add a constant for the request code and a member variable for the button.

Listing 15.11 Adding field for suspect button (CrimeFragment.java)

```
...
private static final int REQUEST_DATE = 0;
private static final int REQUEST_CONTACT = 1;

...

private CheckBox mSolvedCheckbox;
private Button mSuspectButton;

...
```

At the end of **onCreateView(…)**, get a reference to the button and set a listener on it. Within the listener's implementation, create the implicit intent and pass it into **startActivityForResult(…)**. Also, once a suspect is assigned show the name on the suspect button.

Listing 15.12 Sending an implicit intent (CrimeFragment.java)

```
public View onCreateView(LayoutInflater inflater, ViewGroup container,
        Bundle savedInstanceState) {
    ...

    final Intent pickContact = new Intent(Intent.ACTION_PICK,
            ContactsContract.Contacts.CONTENT_URI);
    mSuspectButton = (Button) v.findViewById(R.id.crime_suspect);
    mSuspectButton.setOnClickListener(new View.OnClickListener() {
        public void onClick(View v) {
            startActivityForResult(pickContact, REQUEST_CONTACT);
        }
    });

    if (mCrime.getSuspect() != null) {
        mSuspectButton.setText(mCrime.getSuspect());
    }

    return v;
}
```

You will be using pickContact one more time in a bit, which is why you put it outside mSuspectButton's **OnClickListener**.

Run CriminalIntent and press the Choose Suspect button. You should see a list of contacts (Figure 15.7).

Figure 15.7 A list of possible suspects

If you have a different contacts app installed, your screen will look different. Again, this is one of the benefits of implicit intents. You do not have to know the name of the contacts application to use it from your app. Users can install whatever app they like best, and the OS will find and launch it.

Getting the data from the contact list

Now you need to get a result back from the contacts application. Contacts information is shared by many applications, so Android provides an in-depth API for working with contacts information through a **ContentProvider**. Instances of this class wrap databases and make it available to other applications. You can access a **ContentProvider** through a **ContentResolver**.

Because you started the activity for a result with ACTION_PICK, you will receive an intent via **onActivityResult(…)**. This intent includes a data URI. The URI is a locator that points at the single contact the user picked.

In CrimeFragment.java, add the following code to your **onActivityResult(…)** implementation in **CrimeFragment**.

Listing 15.13 Pulling contact name out (`CrimeFragment.java`)

```java
@Override
public void onActivityResult(int requestCode, int resultCode, Intent data) {
    if (resultCode != Activity.RESULT_OK) {
        return;
    }

    if (requestCode == REQUEST_DATE) {
        ...
        updateDate();

    } else if (requestCode == REQUEST_CONTACT && data != null) {
        Uri contactUri = data.getData();
        // Specify which fields you want your query to return
        // values for.
        String[] queryFields = new String[] {
                ContactsContract.Contacts.DISPLAY_NAME
        };
        // Perform your query - the contactUri is like a "where"
        // clause here
        Cursor c = getActivity().getContentResolver()
                .query(contactUri, queryFields, null, null, null);

        try {
            // Double-check that you actually got results
            if (c.getCount() == 0) {
                return;
            }

            // Pull out the first column of the first row of data -
            // that is your suspect's name.
            c.moveToFirst();
            String suspect = c.getString(0);
            mCrime.setSuspect(suspect);
            mSuspectButton.setText(suspect);
        } finally {
            c.close();
        }
    }
}
```

In Listing 15.13, you create a query that asks for all the display names of the contacts in the returned data. Then you query the contacts database and get a **Cursor** object to work with. Because you know that the cursor only contains one item, you move to the first item and get it as a string. This string will be the name of the suspect, and you use it to set the **Crime**'s suspect and the text of the Choose Suspect button.

(The contacts database is a large topic in itself. We will not cover it here. If you would like to know more, read the Contacts Provider API guide: `http://developer.android.com/guide/topics/providers/contacts-provider.html`.)

Go ahead and run your app. Some devices may not have a contacts app for you to use. If that is the case, use an emulator to test this code.

Contacts permissions

How are you getting permission to read from the contacts database? The contacts app is extending its permissions to you. The contacts app has full permissions to the contacts database. When the contacts app returns a data URI in an **Intent** to the parent activity, it also adds the flag Intent.FLAG_GRANT_READ_URI_PERMISSION. This flag signals to Android that the parent activity in CriminalIntent should be allowed to use this data one time. This works well because you do not really need access to the entire contacts database. You only need access to one contact inside that database.

Checking for responding activities

The first implicit intent you created in this chapter will always be responded to in some way – there may be no way to send a report, but the chooser will still display properly. However, that is not the case for the second example: some devices or users may not have a contacts app, and if the OS cannot find a matching activity, then the app will crash.

The fix is to check with part of the OS called the **PackageManager** first. Do this in **onCreateView(…)**.

Listing 15.14 Guarding against no contacts app (CrimeFragment.java)

```java
public View onCreateView(LayoutInflater inflater, ViewGroup container,
        Bundle savedInstanceState) {
    ...

    if (mCrime.getSuspect() != null) {
        mSuspectButton.setText(mCrime.getSuspect());
    }

    PackageManager packageManager = getActivity().getPackageManager();
    if (packageManager.resolveActivity(pickContact,
            PackageManager.MATCH_DEFAULT_ONLY) == null) {
        mSuspectButton.setEnabled(false);
    }

    return v;
}
```

PackageManager knows about all the components installed on your Android device, including all of its activities. (You will run into the other components later on in this book.) By calling **resolveActivity(Intent, int)**, you ask it to find an activity that matches the **Intent** you gave it. The MATCH_DEFAULT_ONLY flag restricts this search to activities with the CATEGORY_DEFAULT flag, just like **startActivity(Intent)** does.

If this search is successful, it will return an instance of **ResolveInfo** telling you all about which activity it found. On the other hand, if the search returns null, the game is up – no contacts app. So you disable the useless suspect button.

If you would like to verify that your filter works, but do not have a device without a contacts application, temporarily add an additional category to your intent. This category does nothing, but it will prevent any contacts applications from matching your intent.

Listing 15.15 Dummy code to verify filter (`CrimeFragment.java`)

```
...

final Intent pickContact = new Intent(Intent.ACTION_PICK,
        ContactsContract.Contacts.CONTENT_URI);
pickContact.addCategory(Intent.CATEGORY_HOME);
mSuspectButton = (Button)v.findViewById(R.id.crime_suspect);
mSuspectButton.setOnClickListener(new View.OnClickListener() {
    public void onClick(View v) {
        startActivityForResult(pickContact, REQUEST_CONTACT);
    }
});

...
```

Now you should see the suspect button disabled (Figure 15.8).

Figure 15.8 Disabled suspect button

Delete the dummy code once you are done verifying this behavior.

Listing 15.16 Deleting dummy code (`CrimeFragment.java`)

```
...

    final Intent pickContact = new Intent(Intent.ACTION_PICK,
            ContactsContract.Contacts.CONTENT_URI);
    pickContact.addCategory(Intent.CATEGORY_HOME);
    mSuspectButton = (Button)v.findViewById(R.id.crime_suspect);
    mSuspectButton.setOnClickListener(new View.OnClickListener() {
        public void onClick(View v) {
            startActivityForResult(pickContact, REQUEST_CONTACT);
        }
    });

...
```

Challenge: ShareCompat

Your first challenge is an easy one. Android's support library provides a class called **ShareCompat**, with an inner class called **IntentBuilder**. **ShareCompat.IntentBuilder** makes it a bit easier to build the exact kind of **Intent** you used for your report button.

So your first challenge is this: in mReportButton's **OnClickListener**, use **ShareCompat.IntentBuilder** to build your **Intent** instead of doing it by hand.

Challenge: Another Implicit Intent

Instead of sending a crime report, an angry user may prefer a phone confrontation with the suspect. Add a new button that calls the named suspect.

You will need the phone number out of the contacts database. This will require you to query another table in the **ContactsContract** database called **CommonDataKinds.Phone**. Check out the documentation for **ContactsContract** and **ContactsContract.CommonDataKinds.Phone** for more information on how to query for this information.

A couple of tips: to query for additional data, you can use the android.permission.READ_CONTACTS permission. With that permission in hand, you can read the ContactsContract.Contacts._ID to get a contact ID on your original query. You can then use that ID to query the **CommonDataKinds.Phone** table.

Once you have the phone number, you can create an implicit intent with a telephone URI:

```
Uri number = Uri.parse("tel:5551234");
```

The action can be Intent.ACTION_DIAL or Intent.ACTION_CALL. ACTION_CALL pulls up the phone app and immediately calls the number sent in the intent; ACTION_DIAL just dials the number and waits for the user to initiate the call.

We recommend using ACTION_DIAL. ACTION_CALL may be restricted and will definitely require a permission. Your user may also appreciate the chance to cool down before pressing the Call button.

16

Taking Pictures with Intents

Now that you know how to work with implicit intents, you can document your crimes in even more detail. With a picture of the crime, you can share the gory details with everyone.

Taking a picture will involve a couple of new tools, used in combination with a tool you recently got to know: the implicit intent. An implicit intent can be used to start up the user's favorite camera application and receive a new picture from it.

An implicit intent can get you a picture, but where do you put it? And once the picture comes in, how do you display it? In this chapter, you will answer both of those questions.

A Place for Your Photo

The first step is to build out a place for your photo to live. You will need two new **View** objects: an **ImageView** to display the photo and a **Button** to press to take a new photo (Figure 16.1).

Figure 16.1 New user interface

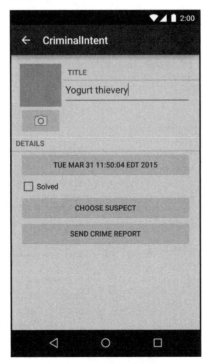

Dedicating an entire row to a thumbnail and a button would make your app look clunky and unprofessional. You do not want that, so you will arrange things nicely.

Including layout files

Your arrangement will include a large section that is the same in both layout and landscape versions of fragment_crime.xml. You can accomplish this by simply having this large section appear in both res/layout/fragment_crime.xml and res/layout-land/fragment_crime.xml. This is usually the right choice, but it is not the only choice. You can also use an *include*.

An *include* allows you to include one layout file in another. You are going to use one here for the common elements. The first step is to make a layout file that displays only the section of the view shown in Figure 16.2.

Figure 16.2 Camera and title

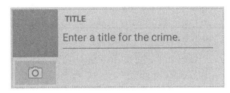

Now to make the layout file. Call it view_camera_and_title.xml. Build out the left-hand side first (Figure 16.3).

Figure 16.3 Camera view layout (res/layout/view_camera_and_title.xml)

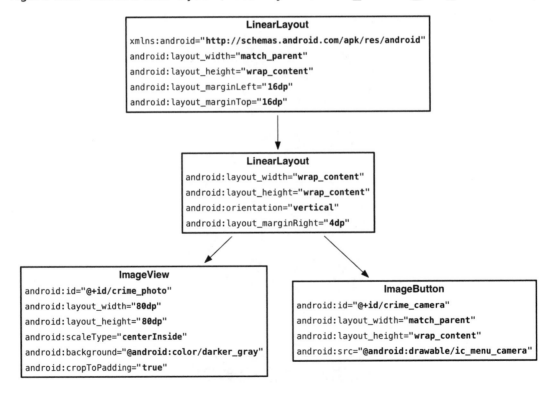

And then the right-hand side (Figure 16.4).

Figure 16.4 Title layout (res/layout/view_camera_and_title.xml)

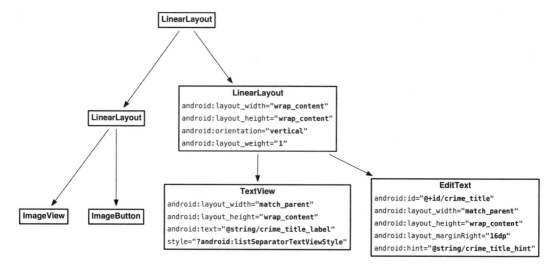

Use the design view to verify that your layout file looks like Figure 16.2.

Now you can use include tags to include this layout in your other layout files. When using the include tag, take note that the layout attribute does not use the normal android prefix.

Modify your main layout file first (Figure 16.5).

Figure 16.5 Including camera layout (portrait) (res/layout/
fragment_crime.xml)

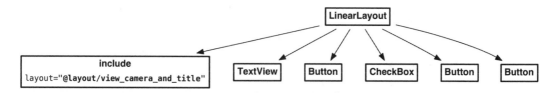

And then your landscape layout (Figure 16.6).

Figure 16.6 Including camera layout (landscape) (res/layout-land/
fragment_crime.xml)

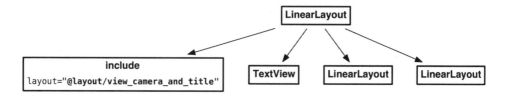

Run CriminalIntent, and you should see your new user interface looking just like Figure 16.1.

Looks great, but to respond to presses on your **ImageButton** and to control the content of your **ImageView**, you need instance variables referring to each of them. No special steps are required to find views inside included layouts. Call **findViewById(int)** as usual on your inflated fragment_crime.xml and you will find views from view_camera_and_title.xml, too.

Listing 16.1 Adding instance variables (CrimeFragment.java)

```
...
private CheckBox mSolvedCheckbox;
private Button mSuspectButton;
private ImageButton mPhotoButton;
private ImageView mPhotoView;

...

@Override
public View onCreateView(LayoutInflater inflater, ViewGroup container,
                         Bundle savedInstanceState) {
    ...

    PackageManager packageManager = getActivity().getPackageManager();
    if (packageManager.resolveActivity(pickContact,
            PackageManager.MATCH_DEFAULT_ONLY) == null) {
        mSuspectButton.setEnabled(false);
    }

    mPhotoButton = (ImageButton) v.findViewById(R.id.crime_camera);
    mPhotoView = (ImageView) v.findViewById(R.id.crime_photo);

    return v;
}

...
```

And with that, you are done with the user interface for the time being. (You will wire those buttons up in a minute or two.)

External Storage

Your photo needs more than a place on the screen. Full-size pictures are too large to stick inside a SQLite database, much less an **Intent**. They will need a place to live on your device's filesystem.

Normally, you would put them in your private storage. Recall that you used your private storage to save your SQLite database. With methods like **Context.getFileStreamPath(String)** and **Context.getFilesDir()**, you can do the same thing with regular files, too (which will live in a subfolder adjacent to the databases subfolder your SQLite database lives in).

Table 16.1 Basic file and directory methods in `Context`

Method	Purpose
`File getFilesDir()`	Returns a handle to the directory for private application files.
`FileInputStream openFileInput(String name)`	Opens an existing file for input (relative to the files directory).
`FileOutputStream openFileOutput(String name, int mode)`	Opens a file for output, possibly creating it (relative to the files directory).
`File getDir(String name, int mode)`	Gets (and possibly creates) a subdirectory within the files directory.
`String[] fileList()`	Gets a list of file names in the main files directory, such as for use with `openFileInput(String)`.
`File getCacheDir()`	Returns a handle to a directory you can use specifically for storing cache files. You should take care to keep this directory tidy and use as little space as possible.

If you are storing files that *only your current application* needs to use, these methods are exactly what you need.

On the other hand, if you need another application to write to those files, you are out of luck: while there is a `Context.MODE_WORLD_READABLE` flag you can pass in to `openFileOutput(String, int)`, it is deprecated, and not completely reliable in its effects on newer devices. If you are storing files to share with other apps or receiving files from other apps (files like stored pictures), you need to store them on *external storage* instead.

There are two kinds of external storage: primary, and everything else. All Android devices have at least one location for external storage: the primary location, which is located in the folder returned by `Environment.getExternalStorageDirectory()`. This may be an SD card, but nowadays it is more commonly integrated into the device itself. Some devices may have additional external storage. That would fall under "everything else."

`Context` provides quite a few methods for getting at external storage, too. These methods provide easy ways to get at your primary external storage, and kinda-sorta-easy ways to get at everything else. *All* of these methods store files in publicly available places, too, so be careful with them.

Table 16.2 External file and directory methods in **Context**

Method	Purpose
File getExternalCacheDir()	Returns a handle to a cache folder in primary external storage. Treat it like you do **getCacheDir()**, except a little more carefully. Android is even less likely to clean up this folder than the private storage one.
File[] getExternalCacheDirs()	Returns cache folders for multiple external storage locations.
File getExternalFilesDir(String)	Returns a handle to a folder on primary external storage in which to store regular files. If you pass in a type **String**, you can access a specific subfolder dedicated to a particular type of content. Type constants are defined in **Environment**, where they are prefixed with DIRECTORY_. For example, pictures go in Environment.DIRECTORY_PICTURES.
File[] getExternalFilesDirs(String)	Same as **getExternalFilesDir(String)**, but returns all possible file folders for the given type.
File[] getExternalMediaDirs()	Returns handles to all the external folders Android makes available for storing media – pictures, movies, and music. What makes this different from calling **getExternalFilesDir(Environment.DIRECTORY_PICTURES)** is that the media scanner automatically scans this folder. The media scanner makes files available to applications that play music, or browse movies and photos, so anything that you put in a folder returned by **getExternalMediaDirs()** will automatically appear in those apps.

Technically, the external folders provided above may not be available, since some devices use a removable SD card for external storage. In practice this is rarely an issue, because almost all modern devices have nonremovable internal storage for their "external" storage. So it is not worth going to extreme lengths to account for it. But we do recommended including simple code to guard against the possibility, which you will do in a moment.

Designating a picture location

Time to give your pictures a place to live. First, add a method to **Crime** to get a well-known filename.

Listing 16.2 Adding filename-derived property (`Crime.java`)

```
...

    public void setSuspect(String suspect) {
        mSuspect = suspect;
    }

    public String getPhotoFilename() {
        return "IMG_" + getId().toString() + ".jpg";
    }
}
```

Crime.getPhotoFilename() will not know what folder the photo will be stored in. However, the filename will be unique, since it is based on the **Crime**'s ID.

Next, find where the photos should live. **CrimeLab** is responsible for everything related to persisting data in CriminalIntent, so it is a natural owner for this idea. Add a **getPhotoFile(Crime)** method to **CrimeLab** that does this.

Listing 16.3 Finding photo file location (`CrimeLab.java`)

```
public class CrimeLab {
    ...

    public Crime getCrime(UUID id) {
        ...
    }

    public File getPhotoFile(Crime crime) {
        File externalFilesDir = mContext
                .getExternalFilesDir(Environment.DIRECTORY_PICTURES);

        if (externalFilesDir == null) {
            return null;
        }

        return new File(externalFilesDir, crime.getPhotoFilename());
    }

    ...
```

This code does not create any files on the filesystem. It only returns **File** objects that point to the right locations. It does perform one check: it verifies that there is external storage to save them to. If there is no external storage, **getExternalFilesDir(String)** will return `null`. And so will this method.

Using a Camera Intent

The next step is to actually take the picture. This is the easy part: you get to use an implicit intent again.

Start by stashing the location of the photo file. (You will use it a few more times, so this will save a bit of work.)

Listing 16.4 Grabbing photo file location (`CrimeFragment.java`)

```
...

private Crime mCrime;
private File mPhotoFile;
private EditText mTitleField;
...

@Override
public void onCreate(Bundle savedInstanceState) {
    super.onCreate(savedInstanceState);
    UUID crimeId = (UUID) getArguments().getSerializable(ARG_CRIME_ID);
    mCrime = CrimeLab.get(getActivity()).getCrime(crimeId);
    mPhotoFile = CrimeLab.get(getActivity()).getPhotoFile(mCrime);
}

...
```

Next you will hook up the camera button to actually take the picture. The camera intent is defined in **MediaStore**, Android's lord and master of all things media related. You will send an intent with an action of `MediaStore.ACTION_IMAGE_CAPTURE`, and Android will fire up a camera activity and take a picture for you.

But hold that thought for one minute.

External storage permission

In general, you need a *permission* to write or read from external storage. Permissions are well-known string values you put in your manifest using the <uses-permission> tag. They tell Android that you want to do something that Android wants you to ask permission for.

Here, Android expects you to ask permission because it wants to enforce some accountability. You tell Android that you need to access external storage, and Android will then tell the user that this is one of the things your application does when they try to install it. That way, nobody is surprised when you start saving things to their SD card.

In Android 4.4, KitKat, they loosened this restriction. Since `Context.getExternalFilesDir(String)` returns a folder that is specific to your app, it makes sense that you would want to be able to read and write files that live there. So on Android 4.4 (API 19) and up, you do not need this permission for this folder. (But you still need it for other kinds of external storage.)

Add a line to your manifest that requests the permission to read external storage, but only up to API 18.

Listing 16.5 Requesting external storage permission (`AndroidManifest.xml`)

```
<manifest xmlns:android="http://schemas.android.com/apk/res/android"
    package="com.bignerdranch.android.criminalintent" >

    <uses-permission android:name="android.permission.READ_EXTERNAL_STORAGE"
                     android:maxSdkVersion="18"
        />
    ...
```

The `maxSdkVersion` attribute makes it so that your app only asks for this permission on versions of Android that are older than API 19, Android KitKat.

Note that you are only asking to read external storage. There is also a `WRITE_EXTERNAL_STORAGE` permission, but you do not need it. You will not be writing anything to external storage: The camera app will do that for you.

Firing the intent

Now you are ready to fire the camera intent. The action you want is called `ACTION_CAPTURE_IMAGE`, and it is defined in the **MediaStore** class. **MediaStore** defines the public interfaces used in Android for interacting with common media – images, videos, and music. This includes the image capture intent, which fires up the camera.

By default, `ACTION_CAPTURE_IMAGE` will dutifully fire up the camera application and take a picture, but it will not be a full-resolution picture. Instead, it will take a small resolution thumbnail picture, and stick the whole thing inside the **Intent** object returned in **onActivityResult(…)**.

For a full-resolution output, you need to tell it where to save the image on the filesystem. This can be done by passing a **Uri** pointing to where you want to save the file in `MediaStore.EXTRA_OUTPUT`.

Write an implicit intent to ask for a new picture to be taken into the location saved in `mPhotoFile`. Add code to ensure that the button is disabled if there is no camera app, or if there is no location at which to save the photo. (To determine whether there is a camera app available, you will query **PackageManager** for activities that respond to your camera implicit intent. Querying the **PackageManager** is discussed in more detail in the section called "Checking for responding activities" in Chapter 15.)

Listing 16.6 Firing a camera intent (`CrimeFragment.java`)

```
...

private static final int REQUEST_DATE = 0;
private static final int REQUEST_CONTACT = 1;
private static final int REQUEST_PHOTO= 2;

...

@Override
public View onCreateView(LayoutInflater inflater, ViewGroup container,
                         Bundle savedInstanceState) {
    ...

    mPhotoButton = (ImageButton) v.findViewById(R.id.crime_camera);
    final Intent captureImage = new Intent(MediaStore.ACTION_IMAGE_CAPTURE);

    boolean canTakePhoto = mPhotoFile != null &&
            captureImage.resolveActivity(packageManager) != null;
    mPhotoButton.setEnabled(canTakePhoto);

    if (canTakePhoto) {
        Uri uri = Uri.fromFile(mPhotoFile);
        captureImage.putExtra(MediaStore.EXTRA_OUTPUT, uri);
    }

    mPhotoButton.setOnClickListener(new View.OnClickListener() {
        @Override
        public void onClick(View v) {
            startActivityForResult(captureImage, REQUEST_PHOTO);
        }
    });

    mPhotoView = (ImageView) v.findViewById(R.id.crime_photo);

    return v;
}
```

Run CriminalIntent and press the camera button to run your camera app (Figure 16.7).

Figure 16.7 [Insert your camera app here]

Scaling and Displaying Bitmaps

With that, you are successfully taking pictures. Your image will be saved to a file on the filesystem for you to use.

Your next step will be to take this file, load it up, and show it to the user. To do this, you need to load it into a reasonably sized **Bitmap** object. To get a **Bitmap** from a file, all you need to do is use the **BitmapFactory** class:

```
Bitmap bitmap = BitmapFactory.decodeFile(mPhotoFile.getPath());
```

There has to be a catch, though, right? Otherwise we would have put that in bold, you would have typed it in, and you would be done.

Here is the catch: when we say "reasonably sized," we mean it. A **Bitmap** is a simple object that stores literal pixel data. That means that even if the original file was compressed, there is no compression in the **Bitmap** itself. So a 16 megapixel 24-bit camera image which might only be a 5 Mb JPG would blow up to 48 Mb loaded into a **Bitmap** object (!).

You can get around this, but it does mean that you will need to scale the bitmap down by hand. You can do this by first scanning the file to see how big it is, next figuring out how much you need to scale it by to fit it in a given area, and finally rereading the file to create a scaled-down **Bitmap** object.

Create a new class called PictureUtils.java for this new method, and add a static method to it called **getScaledBitmap(String, int, int)**.

Listing 16.7 Creating **getScaledBitmap(…)** (PictureUtils.java)

```java
public class PictureUtils {
    public static Bitmap getScaledBitmap(String path, int destWidth, int destHeight) {
        // Read in the dimensions of the image on disk
        BitmapFactory.Options options = new BitmapFactory.Options();
        options.inJustDecodeBounds = true;
        BitmapFactory.decodeFile(path, options);

        float srcWidth = options.outWidth;
        float srcHeight = options.outHeight;

        // Figure out how much to scale down by
        int inSampleSize = 1;
        if (srcHeight > destHeight || srcWidth > destWidth) {
            if (srcWidth > srcHeight) {
                inSampleSize = Math.round(srcHeight / destHeight);
            } else {
                inSampleSize = Math.round(srcWidth / destWidth);
            }
        }

        options = new BitmapFactory.Options();
        options.inSampleSize = inSampleSize;

        // Read in and create final bitmap
        return BitmapFactory.decodeFile(path, options);
    }
}
```

The key parameter above is inSampleSize. This determines how big each "sample" should be for each pixel – a sample size of 1 has one final horizontal pixel for each horizontal pixel in the original file, and a sample size of 2 has one horizontal pixel for every two horizontal pixels in the original file. So when inSampleSize is 2, the image has a quarter of the number of pixels of the original.

One more bit of bad news: when your fragment initially starts up, you will not know how big **PhotoView** is. Until a layout pass happens, views do not have dimensions on screen. The first layout pass happens after **onCreate(…)**, **onStart()**, and **onResume()** initially run, which is why **PhotoView** does not know how big it is.

There are two solutions to this problem: either you can wait until a layout pass happens, or you can use a conservative estimate. The conservative estimate approach is less efficient, but more straightforward. Write another static method called **getScaledBitmap(String, Activity)** to scale a **Bitmap** for a particular **Activity**'s size.

Listing 16.8 Writing conservative scale method (PictureUtils.java)

```java
public class PictureUtils {
    public static Bitmap getScaledBitmap(String path, Activity activity) {
        Point size = new Point();
        activity.getWindowManager().getDefaultDisplay()
                .getSize(size);

        return getScaledBitmap(path, size.x, size.y);
    }

    ...
```

This method checks to see how big the screen is, and then scales the image down to that size. The **ImageView** you load into will always be smaller than this size, so this is a very conservative estimate.

Next, to load this **Bitmap** into your **ImageView** add a method to **CrimeFragment** to update mPhotoView.

Listing 16.9 Updating mPhotoView (`CrimeFragment.java`)

```
...

private String getCrimeReport() {
    ...
}

private void updatePhotoView() {
    if (mPhotoFile == null || !mPhotoFile.exists()) {
        mPhotoView.setImageDrawable(null);
    } else {
        Bitmap bitmap = PictureUtils.getScaledBitmap(
                mPhotoFile.getPath(), getActivity());
        mPhotoView.setImageBitmap(bitmap);
    }
}
}
```

Then call that method from inside **onCreateView(…)** and **onActivityResult(…)**.

Listing 16.10 Calling **updatePhotoView()** (`CrimeFragment.java`)

```
    mPhotoButton.setOnClickListener(new View.OnClickListener() {
        @Override
        public void onClick(View v) {
            startActivityForResult(captureImage, REQUEST_PHOTO);
        }
    });

    mPhotoView = (ImageView) v.findViewById(R.id.crime_photo);
    updatePhotoView();

    return v;
}

@Override
public void onActivityResult(int requestCode, int resultCode, Intent data) {
    if (resultCode != Activity.RESULT_OK) {
        return;
    }

    if (requestCode == REQUEST_DATE) {
        ...
    } else if (requestCode == REQUEST_CONTACT && data != null) {
        ...

    } else if (requestCode == REQUEST_PHOTO) {
        updatePhotoView();
    }
}
```

Run again, and you should see your image displayed in the thumbnail view.

Declaring Features

Your camera implementation works great now. One more task remains: tell potential users about it. When your app uses a feature like the camera, or NFC, or any other feature that may vary from device to device, it is strongly recommended that you tell Android about it. This allows other apps (like the Google Play store) to refuse to install your app if it uses a feature the device does not support.

To declare that you use the camera, add a `<uses-feature>` tag to your `AndroidManifest.xml`:

Listing 16.11 Adding uses-feature tag (`AndroidManifest.xml`)

```xml
<?xml version="1.0" encoding="utf-8"?>
<manifest xmlns:android="http://schemas.android.com/apk/res/android"
    package="com.bignerdranch.android.criminalintent" >

    <uses-permission android:name="android.permission.READ_EXTERNAL_STORAGE"
                     android:maxSdkVersion="18"
        />
    <uses-feature android:name="android.hardware.camera"
                  android:required="false"
        />

    ...
```

You include the optional attribute `android:required` here. Why? By default, declaring that you use a feature means that your app will not work correctly at all without that feature. This is not the case for CriminalIntent. You call **resolveActivity(…)** to check for a working camera app, then gracefully disable that button if you do not find one.

Passing in `android:required="false"` handles this situation correctly. You tell Android that your app can work fine without the camera, but that some parts will be disabled as a result.

For the More Curious: Using Includes

In this chapter, you used an include so that you would not have to repeat a large portion of your layout file across both landscape and portrait orientations. From that example, you can see how includes can be handy: they reduce typing and they help you follow the Don't Repeat Yourself principle. But that does not mean that you should use them every time you have common layout items in landscape and portrait.

First, a detail about how includes work. In this chapter, you used an include tag without any `android` attributes. When you do that, the view you include gets all of the attributes it had in its original layout file.

However, you do not have to limit yourself to this. You can also add additional attributes. If you do, these attributes will be added directly to the root view you inflate. They will overwrite the original values of those attributes, too. This means that if you want to change the value of `layout_width`, you can.

The next thing we want to say about includes is cautionary. In this case, they have saved you some time and complexity, which is nice. But includes are not a perfect tool.

CriminalIntent's views duplicate some **Button**s as well. You might be wondering why you did not get rid of that duplication with an include. The answer is: because this is not something we recommend.

One of the nice things about layout files is that they are authoritative: you can go to the layout file and see exactly how the view is supposed to be structured. Include files break this. You have to look at the layout file *and* all the files it includes to understand what is going on. This can quickly get irritating.

Visuals are often the part of an app that changes the most. When that is the case, perfectly following the DRY principle can mean that you end up worrying more about preserving your DRYitude than about actually building your interface. So try hard to be judicious, thoughtful, intentional, and restrained in how you apply includes in your view layer.

Challenge: Detail Display

While you can certainly see the image you display here, you cannot see it very well.

For this first challenge, create a new **DialogFragment** that displays a zoomed-in version of your crime scene photo. When you press on the thumbnail, it should pull up the zoomed-in **DialogFragment**.

Challenge: Efficient Thumbnail Load

In this chapter, you had to use a crude estimate of the size you should scale down to. This is not ideal, but it works and is quick to implement.

With the out-of-the-box APIs you can use a tool called **ViewTreeObserver**. **ViewTreeObserver** is an object that you can get from any view in your **Activity**'s hierarchy:

```
ViewTreeObserver observer = mImageView.getViewTreeObserver();
```

You can register a variety of listeners on a **ViewTreeObserver**, including **OnGlobalLayoutListener**. This listener fires an event whenever a layout pass happens.

For this challenge, adjust your code so that it uses the dimensions of mPhotoView when they are valid, and waits until a layout pass before initially calling **updatePhotoView()**.

17

Two-Pane Master-Detail Interfaces

In this chapter, you will create a tablet interface for CriminalIntent that allows users to see and interact with the list of crimes and the details of an individual crime at the same time. Figure 17.1 shows this list-detail interface, which is also commonly referred to as a *master-detail interface*.

Figure 17.1 Master and detail sharing the spotlight

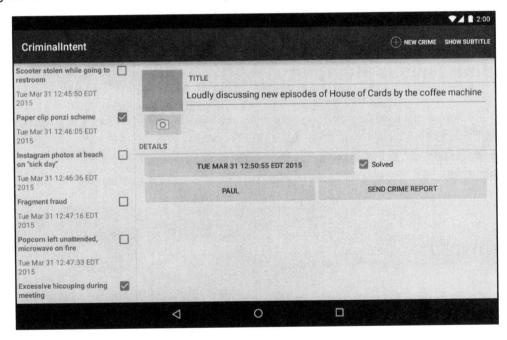

You will need a tablet device or AVD for testing in this chapter. To create a tablet AVD, select Tools → Android → Android Virtual Device Manager. Click Create Virtual Device... and select the Tablet category on the left. Select your favorite hardware profile, click Next, and choose an API level of at least 21 (Figure 17.2).

Figure 17.2 Device selections for a tablet AVD

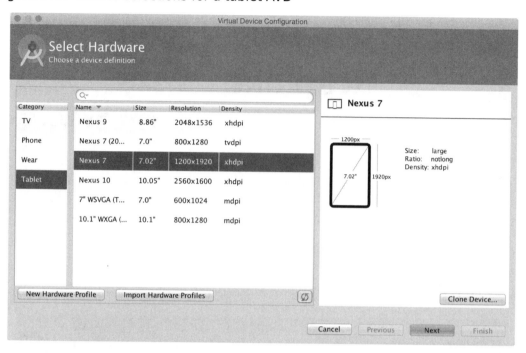

Adding Layout Flexibility

On a phone, you want **CrimeListActivity** to inflate a single-pane layout, as it currently does. On a tablet, you want it to inflate a two-pane layout that is capable of displaying the master and detail views at the same time.

In the two-pane layout, **CrimeListActivity** will host both a **CrimeListFragment** and a **CrimeFragment**, as shown in Figure 17.3.

Figure 17.3 Different types of layouts

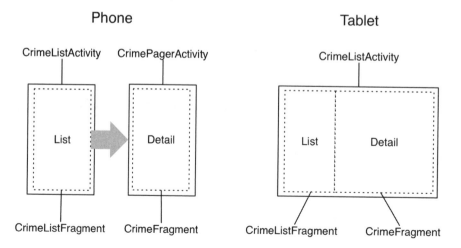

To make this happen, you are going to:

- modify **SingleFragmentActivity** so that the layout that gets inflated is not hardcoded

- create a new layout that consists of two fragment containers

- modify **CrimeListActivity** so that it will inflate a single-container layout on phones and a two-container layout on tablets

Modifying SingleFragmentActivity

CrimeListActivity is a subclass of **SingleFragmentActivity**. Currently, **SingleFragmentActivity** is set up to always inflate activity_fragment.xml. To make **SingleFragmentActivity** more flexible, you are going to enable a subclass to provide its own resource ID for the layout instead.

In SingleFragmentActivity.java, add a protected method that returns the ID of the layout that the activity will inflate.

Listing 17.1 Making **SingleFragmentActivity** flexible
(SingleFragmentActivity.java)

```java
public abstract class SingleFragmentActivity extends AppCompatActivity {
    protected abstract Fragment createFragment();

    @LayoutRes
    protected int getLayoutResId() {
        return R.layout.activity_fragment;
    }

    @Override
    public void onCreate(Bundle savedInstanceState) {
        super.onCreate(savedInstanceState);
        setContentView(R.layout.activity_fragment);
        setContentView(getLayoutResId());
        FragmentManager fm = getSupportFragmentManager();
        Fragment fragment = fm.findFragmentById(R.id.fragment_container);

        if (fragment == null) {
            fragment = createFragment();
            fm.beginTransaction()
                .add(R.id.fragment_container, fragment)
                .commit();
        }
    }
}
```

The default implementation of **SingleFragmentActivity** will work the same as before, but now its subclasses can choose to override **getLayoutResId()** to return a layout other than activity_fragment.xml. You annotate **getLayoutResId()** with @LayoutRes to tell Android Studio that any implementation of this method should return a valid layout resource ID.

Creating a layout with two fragment containers

In the Project tool window, right-click res/layout/ and create a new Android XML file. Ensure that the resource type is Layout, name the file activity_twopane.xml, and give it a **LinearLayout** root element.

Use Figure 17.4 to write the XML for the two-pane layout.

Figure 17.4 A layout with two fragment containers (`layout/activity_twopane.xml`)

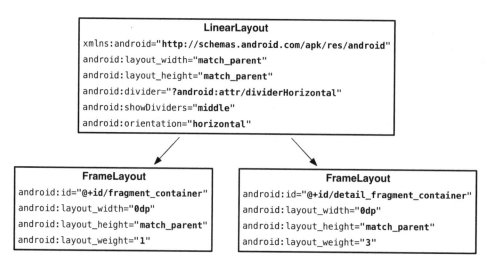

Note that the first **FrameLayout** has a fragment_container layout ID, so the code in **SingleFragmentActivity.onCreate(…)** can work as before. When the activity is created, the fragment that is returned in **createFragment()** will appear in the lefthand pane.

Test this layout in **CrimeListActivity** by overriding **getLayoutResId()** to return R.layout.activity_twopane.

Listing 17.2 Changing to two-pane layout file (`CrimeListActivity.java`)

```java
public class CrimeListActivity extends SingleFragmentActivity {

    @Override
    protected Fragment createFragment() {
        return new CrimeListFragment();
    }

    @Override
    protected int getLayoutResId() {
        return R.layout.activity_twopane;
    }
}
```

Run CriminalIntent on a tablet device and confirm that you have two panes (Figure 17.5). Note that the larger detail pane is empty and that pressing a list item will not display the crime's details. You will hook up the detail container later in the chapter.

Figure 17.5 Two-pane layout on a tablet

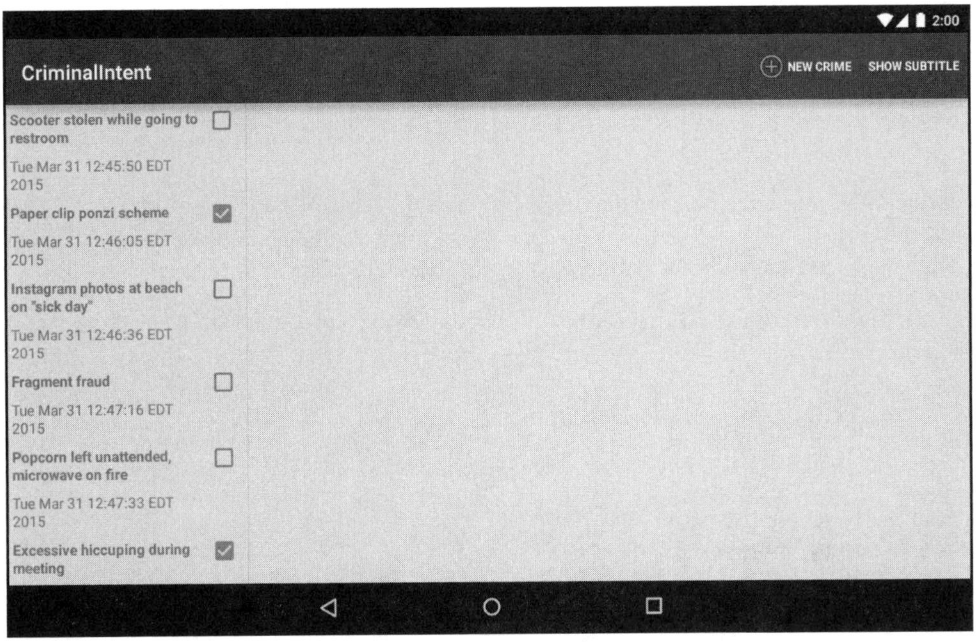

As currently written, **CrimeListActivity** will also inflate the two-pane interface when running on a phone. In the next section, you will fix that using an alias resource.

Using an alias resource

An *alias resource* is a resource that points to another resource. Alias resources live in res/values/ and, by convention, are defined in a refs.xml file.

Your next job will be to have **CrimeListActivity** show a different layout file depending on whether it is on a tablet or a phone. You do this the same way you show a different layout for landscape and portrait: by using a resource qualifier.

Doing that with files in res/layout works, but has some drawbacks. Each layout file has to contain a complete copy of the layout you want to show. This can result in a lot of redundancy. If you wanted an activity_masterdetail.xml layout file, you would have to copy all of activity_fragment.xml into res/layout/activity_masterdetail.xml and all of activity_twopane.xml into res/layout-sw600dp/activity_masterdetail.xml. (You will see what sw600dp does in a moment.)

Instead of doing that, you will use an alias resource. In this section, you will create an alias resource that points to the activity_fragment.xml layout on phones and the activity_twopane.xml layout on tablets.

In the Project tool window, right-click the res/values directory and create a new values resource file. Name the file refs.xml and the directory values. It should have no qualifiers. Click Finish. Then add the item shown in Listing 17.3.

Listing 17.3 Creating a default alias resource value (`res/values/refs.xml`)

```
<resources>

  <item name="activity_masterdetail" type="layout">@layout/activity_fragment</item>

</resources>
```

This resource's value is a reference to the single-pane layout. It also has a resource ID: `R.layout.activity_masterdetail`. Note that the alias's `type` attribute is what determines the inner class of the ID. Even though the alias itself is in `res/values/`, its ID is in `R.layout`.

You can now use this resource ID in place of `R.layout.activity_fragment`. Make that change in **CrimeListActivity**.

Listing 17.4 Switching layout again (`CrimeListActivity.java`)

```
@Override
protected int getLayoutResId() {
    return R.layout.activity_twopane;
    return R.layout.activity_masterdetail;
}
```

Run CriminalIntent to confirm that your alias is working properly. **CrimeListActivity** should inflate the single-pane layout again.

Creating tablet alternatives

Because your alias is in `res/values/`, it is the default alias. So, by default, **CrimeListActivity** inflates the single-pane layout.

Now you are going to create an alternative resource so that the `activity_masterdetail` alias will point to `activity_twopane.xml` on larger devices.

In the Project tool window, right-click `res/values/` and create a new values resource file. Name it `refs.xml` and name its directory `values` again. But this time, select Smallest Screen Width under Available qualifiers and click the >> button to move it over to the right (Figure 17.6).

Figure 17.6 Adding a qualifier

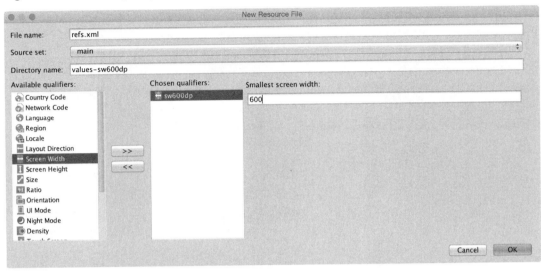

This qualifier is a bit different. It asks you to specify a value for the smallest screen width. Type in 600 here, and click OK. Once it opens your new resource file, add the activity_masterdetail alias to this file, too, pointing at a different layout file.

Listing 17.5 Alternative alias for larger devices (res/values-sw600dp/ refs.xml)

```xml
<resources>

  <item name="activity_masterdetail" type="layout">@layout/activity_twopane</item>

</resources>
```

Let's explain what you are doing here. Your goal is to have logic that works like this:

- For devices that are under a specified size, use activity_fragment.xml.

- For devices that are over a specified size, use activity_twopane.xml.

Android does not provide a way to use a resource only when a device is under a particular size, but it does provide the next best thing. The -sw600dp configuration qualifier lets you provide resources only when a device is above a certain size. The sw stands for "smallest width," but refers to the screen's smallest *dimension*, and thus is independent of the device's current orientation.

With a -sw600dp qualifier, you are saying, "Use this resource on any device whose smallest dimension is 600dp or greater." This is a good rule of thumb for specifying a tablet-sized screen.

What about the other part, where you want to use activity_fragment.xml on smaller devices? Smaller devices will not match your -sw600dp resource, so the default will be used: activity_fragment.xml.

Run CriminalIntent on a phone and on a tablet. Confirm that the single- and two-pane layouts appear where you expect them.

Activity: Fragment Boss

Now that your layouts are behaving properly, you can turn to adding a **CrimeFragment** to the detail fragment container when **CrimeListActivity** is sporting a two-pane layout.

You might think to simply write an alternative implementation of **CrimeHolder.onClick(View)** for tablets. Instead of starting a new **CrimePagerActivity**, **onClick(View)** would get **CrimeListActivity**'s **FragmentManager** and commit a fragment transaction that adds a **CrimeFragment** to the detail fragment container.

The code in your **CrimeListFragment.CrimeHolder** would look like this:

```
public void onClick(View v) {
    // Stick a new CrimeFragment in the activity's layout
    Fragment fragment = CrimeFragment.newInstance(mCrime.getId());
    FragmentManager fm = getActivity().getSupportFragmentManager();
    fm.beginTransaction()
        .add(R.id.detail_fragment_container, fragment)
        .commit();
}
```

This works, but it is not how stylish Android programmers do things. Fragments are intended to be standalone, composable units. If you write a fragment that adds fragments to the activity's **FragmentManager**, then that fragment is making assumptions about how the hosting activity works, and your fragment is no longer a standalone, composable unit.

For example, in the code above **CrimeListFragment** adds a **CrimeFragment** to **CrimeListActivity** and assumes that **CrimeListActivity** has a detail_fragment_container in its layout. This is business that should be handled by **CrimeListFragment**'s hosting activity instead of **CrimeListFragment**.

To maintain the independence of your fragments, you will delegate work back to the hosting activity by defining callback interfaces in your fragments. The hosting activities will implement these interfaces to perform fragment-bossing duties and layout-dependent behavior.

Fragment callback interfaces

To delegate functionality back to the hosting activity, a fragment typically defines a callback interface named **Callbacks**. This interface defines work that the fragment needs done by its boss, the hosting activity. Any activity that will host the fragment must implement this interface.

With a callback interface, a fragment is able to call methods on its hosting activity without having to know anything about which activity is hosting it.

Implementing CrimeListFragment.Callbacks

To implement a **Callbacks** interface, you first define a member variable that holds an object that implements **Callbacks**. Then you cast the hosting activity to **Callbacks** and assign it to that variable.

You assign the activity in the **Fragment** lifecycle method:

```
public void onAttach(Activity activity)
```

This method is called when a fragment is attached to an activity, whether it was retained or not.

Similarly, you will set the variable to null in the corresponding waning lifecycle method:

```
public void onDetach()
```

You set the variable to null here because afterward you cannot access the activity or count on the activity continuing to exist.

In CrimeListFragment.java, add a **Callbacks** interface to **CrimeListFragment**. Also add an mCallbacks variable and override **onAttach(Activity)** and **onDetach()** to set and unset it.

Listing 17.6 Adding callback interface (`CrimeListFragment.java`)

```java
public class CrimeListFragment extends Fragment {

    ...
    private boolean mSubtitleVisible;
    private Callbacks mCallbacks;

    /**
     * Required interface for hosting activities.
     */
    public interface Callbacks {
        void onCrimeSelected(Crime crime);
    }

    @Override
    public void onAttach(Activity activity) {
        super.onAttach(activity);
        mCallbacks = (Callbacks) activity;
    }

    @Override
    public void onCreate(Bundle savedInstanceState) {
        super.onCreate(savedInstanceState);
        setHasOptionsMenu(true);
    }

    ...

    @Override
    public void onSaveInstanceState(Bundle outState) {
        super.onSaveInstanceState(outState);
        outState.putBoolean(SAVED_SUBTITLE_VISIBLE, mSubtitleVisible);
    }

    @Override
    public void onDetach() {
        super.onDetach();
        mCallbacks = null;
    }
```

Now **CrimeListFragment** has a way to call methods on its hosting activity. It does not matter which activity is doing the hosting. As long as the activity implements **CrimeListFragment.Callbacks**, everything in **CrimeListFragment** can work the same.

Note that **CrimeListFragment** performs an unchecked cast of its activity to **CrimeListFragment.Callbacks**. This means that the hosting activity *must* implement **CrimeListFragment.Callbacks**. That is not a bad dependency to have, but it is important to document it.

Next, in **CrimeListActivity**, implement **CrimeListFragment.Callbacks**. Leave **onCrimeSelected(Crime)** empty for now.

Listing 17.7 Implementing callbacks (`CrimeListActivity.java`)

```java
public class CrimeListActivity extends SingleFragmentActivity
    implements CrimeListFragment.Callbacks {

    @Override
    protected Fragment createFragment() {
        return new CrimeListFragment();
    }

    @Override
    protected int getLayoutResId() {
        return R.layout.activity_masterdetail;
    }

    @Override
    public void onCrimeSelected(Crime crime) {
    }
}
```

Eventually, **CrimeListFragment** will call this method in **CrimeHolder.onClick(…)**
and also when the user chooses to create a new crime. First, let's figure out
CrimeListActivity.onCrimeSelected(Crime)'s implementation.

When **onCrimeSelected(Crime)** is called, **CrimeListActivity** needs to do one of two things:

- if using the phone interface, start a new **CrimePagerActivity**

- if using the tablet interface, put a **CrimeFragment** in detail_fragment_container

To determine which interface was inflated, you could check for a certain layout ID. But it is better to
check whether the layout has a detail_fragment_container. Checking a layout's capabilities is a
more precise test of what you need. Filenames can change, and you do not really care what file the
layout was inflated from; you just need to know whether it has a detail_fragment_container to put
your **CrimeFragment** in.

If the layout does have a detail_fragment_container, then you are going to create a fragment
transaction that removes the existing **CrimeFragment** from detail_fragment_container (if there is
one in there) and adds the **CrimeFragment** that you want to see.

In CrimeListActivity.java, implement **onCrimeSelected(Crime)** to handle the selection of a crime
in either interface.

Listing 17.8 Conditional **CrimeFragment** startup (`CrimeListActivity.java`)

```java
@Override
public void onCrimeSelected(Crime crime) {
    if (findViewById(R.id.detail_fragment_container) == null) {
        Intent intent = CrimePagerActivity.newIntent(this, crime.getId());
        startActivity(intent);
    } else {
        Fragment newDetail = CrimeFragment.newInstance(crime.getId());

        getSupportFragmentManager().beginTransaction()
                .replace(R.id.detail_fragment_container, newDetail)
                .commit();
    }
}
```

Finally, in **CrimeListFragment**, you are going to call **onCrimeSelected(Crime)** in the places where you currently start a new **CrimePagerActivity**.

In CrimeListFragment.java, modify **CrimeHolder.onClick(View)** and **onOptionsItemSelected(MenuItem)** to call **Callbacks.onCrimeSelected(Crime)**.

Listing 17.9 Calling all callbacks! (CrimeListFragment.java)

```java
@Override
public boolean onOptionsItemSelected(MenuItem item) {
    switch (item.getItemId()) {
        case R.id.menu_item_new_crime:
            Crime crime = new Crime();
            CrimeLab.get(getActivity()).addCrime(crime);
            Intent intent = CrimePagerActivity
                    .newIntent(getActivity(), crime.getId());
            startActivity(intent);
            updateUI();
            mCallbacks.onCrimeSelected(crime);
            return true;
        case R.id.menu_item_show_subtitle:
            mSubtitleVisible = !mSubtitleVisible;
            getActivity().invalidateOptionsMenu();
            updateSubtitle();
            return true;
        default:
            return super.onOptionsItemSelected(item);
    }
}

...

private class CrimeHolder extends RecyclerView.ViewHolder
        implements View.OnClickListener {

    ...

    @Override
    public void onClick(View v) {
        Intent intent = CrimePagerActivity.newIntent(getActivity(), mCrime.getId());
        startActivity(intent);
        mCallbacks.onCrimeSelected(mCrime);
    }
}
```

When you call back in **onOptionsItemSelected(…)**, you also reload the list immediately upon adding a new crime. This is necessary because, on tablets, the list will remain visible after adding a new crime. Before, you were guaranteed that the detail screen would appear in front of it.

Run CriminalIntent on a tablet. Create a new crime, and a **CrimeFragment** will be added and shown in the detail_fragment_container. Then view an old crime to see the **CrimeFragment** being swapped out for a new one (Figure 17.7).

Figure 17.7 Master and detail now wired up

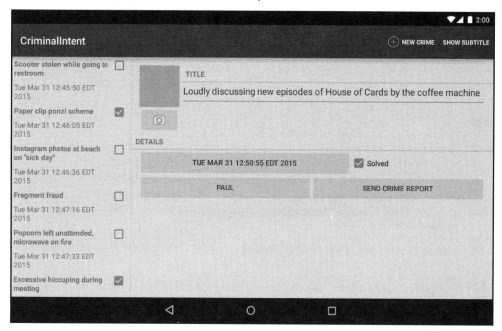

Looks great! One small problem, though: If you make changes to a crime, the list will not update to reflect them. Right now, you only reload the list immediately after adding a crime and in `CrimeListFragment.onResume()`. But on a tablet, `CrimeListFragment` stays visible alongside the `CrimeFragment`. The `CrimeListFragment` is not paused when the `CrimeFragment` appears, so it is never resumed. Thus, the list is not reloaded.

You can fix this problem with another callback interface – this one in `CrimeFragment`.

Implementing CrimeFragment.Callbacks

`CrimeFragment` will define the following interface:

```
public interface Callbacks {
    void onCrimeUpdated(Crime crime);
}
```

For `CrimeFragment` to push updates to a peer `Fragment`, it will need to do two things. First, since CriminalIntent's single source of truth is its SQLite database, it will need to save its `Crime` to `CrimeLab`. Then `CrimeFragment` will call `onCrimeUpdated(Crime)` on its hosting activity. `CrimeListActivity` will implement `onCrimeUpdated(Crime)` to reload `CrimeListFragment`'s list, which will pull the latest data from the database and display it.

Before you start with `CrimeFragment`'s interface, change the visibility of `CrimeListFragment.updateUI()` so that it can be called from `CrimeListActivity`.

Listing 17.10 Changing **updateUI()**'s visibility (CrimeListFragment.java)

```
private public void updateUI() {
    ...
}
```

Then, in `CrimeFragment.java`, add the callback interface along with an `mCallbacks` variable and implementations of `onAttach(…)` and `onDetach()`.

Listing 17.11 Adding **CrimeFragment** callbacks (CrimeFragment.java)

```java
...
private ImageButton mPhotoButton;
private ImageView mPhotoView;
private Callbacks mCallbacks;

/**
 * Required interface for hosting activities.
 */
public interface Callbacks {
    void onCrimeUpdated(Crime crime);
}

public static CrimeFragment newInstance(UUID crimeId) {
    ...
}

@Override
public void onAttach(Activity activity) {
    super.onAttach(activity);
    mCallbacks = (Callbacks)activity;
}

@Override
public void onCreate(Bundle savedInstanceState) {
    ...
}

@Override
public void onPause() {
    ...
}

@Override
public void onDetach() {
    super.onDetach();
    mCallbacks = null;
}
```

Now implement **CrimeFragment.Callbacks** in **CrimeListActivity** to reload the list in `onCrimeUpdated(Crime)`.

Listing 17.12 Refreshing crime list (CrimeListActivity.java)

```java
public class CrimeListActivity extends SingleFragmentActivity
        implements CrimeListFragment.Callbacks, CrimeFragment.Callbacks {

    ...

    public void onCrimeUpdated(Crime crime) {
        CrimeListFragment listFragment = (CrimeListFragment)
                getSupportFragmentManager()
                        .findFragmentById(R.id.fragment_container);
        listFragment.updateUI();
    }
}
```

CrimeFragment.Callbacks must be implemented in all activities that host **CrimeFragment**. So provide an empty implementation in **CrimePagerActivity**, too.

Listing 17.13 Providing empty callbacks implementation (CrimePagerActivity.java)

```java
public class CrimePagerActivity extends AppCompatActivity
        implements CrimeFragment.Callbacks {
    ...

    @Override
    public void onCrimeUpdated(Crime crime) {

    }
}
```

CrimeFragment will be doing a Time Warp two-step a lot internally: Jump to the left, save mCrime to **CrimeLab**. Step to the right, call **mCallbacks.onCrimeUpdated(Crime)**. Add a method to make it more convenient to do this jig.

Listing 17.14 Adding **updateCrime()** method (CrimeFragment.java)

```java
...

@Override
public void onActivityResult(int requestCode, int resultCode, Intent data) {
    ...
}

private void updateCrime() {
    CrimeLab.get(getActivity()).updateCrime(mCrime);
    mCallbacks.onCrimeUpdated(mCrime);
}

private void updateDate() {
    mDateButton.setText(mCrime.getDate().toString());
}

...
```

Then add calls in CrimeFragment.java to **updateCrime()** when a **Crime**'s title or solved status has changed.

Listing 17.15 Calling **onCrimeUpdated(Crime)** (CrimeFragment.java)

```java
@Override
public View onCreateView(LayoutInflater inflater, ViewGroup container,
                         Bundle savedInstanceState) {
    ...
    mTitleField.addTextChangedListener(new TextWatcher() {
        ...

        @Override
        public void onTextChanged(CharSequence s, int start, int before, int count) {
            mCrime.setTitle(s.toString());
            updateCrime();
        }

        ...
    });

    ...
    mSolvedCheckbox.setOnCheckedChangeListener(new OnCheckedChangeListener() {
        @Override
        public void onCheckedChanged(CompoundButton buttonView, boolean isChecked) {
            mCrime.setSolved(isChecked);
            updateCrime();
        }
    });

    ...
}
```

You also need to call **onCrimeUpdated(Crime)** in **onActivityResult(…)**, where the **Crime**'s date, photo, and suspect can be changed. Currently, the photo and suspect do not appear in the list item's view, but **CrimeFragment** should still be neighborly and report those updates.

Listing 17.16 Calling **onCrimeUpdated(Crime)** again (CrimeFragment.java)

```
@Override
public void onActivityResult(int requestCode, int resultCode, Intent data) {
    ...

    if (requestCode == REQUEST_DATE) {
        Date date = (Date) data
                .getSerializableExtra(DatePickerFragment.EXTRA_DATE);
        mCrime.setDate(date);
        updateCrime();
        updateDate();
    } else if (requestCode == REQUEST_CONTACT && data != null) {
        ...

        try {
            ...

            String suspect = c.getString(0);
            mCrime.setSuspect(suspect);
            updateCrime();
            mSuspectButton.setText(suspect);
        } finally {
            c.close();
        }
    } else if (requestCode == REQUEST_PHOTO) {
        updateCrime();
        updatePhotoView();
    }
}
```

Run CriminalIntent on a tablet and confirm that your **RecyclerView** updates when changes are made in **CrimeFragment** (Figure 17.8). Then run it on a phone to confirm that the app works as before.

Figure 17.8 List reflects changes made in detail

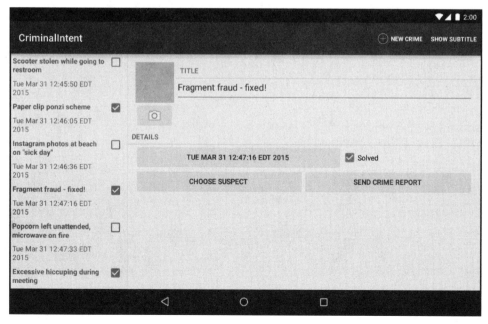

You have reached the end of your time with CriminalIntent. In 11 chapters, you created a complex application that uses fragments, talks to other apps, takes pictures, and stores data. Why not celebrate with a piece of cake?

Just be sure to clean up after yourself. You never know who might be watching.

For the More Curious: More on Determining Device Size

Before Android 3.2, the screen size qualifier was used to provide alternative resources based the size of a device. Screen size is a qualifier that groups different devices into four broad categories – small, normal, large, and xlarge.

Table 17.1 shows the minimum screen sizes for each qualifier:

Table 17.1 Screen size qualifiers

Name	Minimum screen size
small	320x426dp
normal	320x470dp
large	480x640dp
xlarge	720x960dp

Screen size qualifiers were deprecated in Android 3.2 in favor of qualifiers that allow you to test for the dimensions of the device. Table 17.2 shows these new qualifiers.

Table 17.2 Discrete screen dimension qualifiers

Qualifier format	description
wXXXdp	Available width: width is greater than or equal to XXX dp
hXXXdp	Available height: height greater than or equal to XXX dp
swXXXdp	Smallest width: width or height (whichever is smaller) greater than or equal to XXX dp

Let's say that you wanted to specify a layout that would only be used if the display were at least 300dp wide. In that case, you could use an available width qualifier and put your layout file in res/layout-w300dp (the "w" is for "width"). You can do the same thing for height by using an "h" (for "height").

However, the height and width may swap depending on the orientation of the device. To detect a particular size of screen, you can use sw, which stands for *smallest width*. This specifies the smallest dimension of your screen. Depending on the device's orientation, this can be either width or height. If the screen is 1024x800, then sw is 800. If the screen is 800x1024, sw is still 800.

18
Assets

So far, you have dealt with the main way Android gives you to ship images, XML, and other such non-Java things: the resources system. In this chapter, you will learn about another way of packaging content to ship with your app: *assets*.

This chapter also starts a new application, BeatBox (Figure 18.1). BeatBox is not a box for musical beats. It is a box that helps you beat people up. It does not help with the easy part, though: the part where you wave your arms around dangerously, bruising and hurting another human being. It helps with the hard part: yelling in a manner calculated to frighten your opponent into submission.

Figure 18.1 BeatBox at the end of this chapter

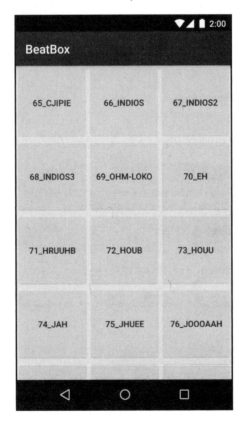

Why Assets, Not Resources

Resources can store sounds. Just stash a file like 79_long_scream.wav in res/raw, and you can get at it with the ID R.raw.79_long_scream. With sounds stored as resources, you can do all the usual resource things, like having different sounds for different orientations, languages, versions of Android, and so on.

However, BeatBox will have a lot of sounds: more than 20 different files. Dealing with them all one by one in the resources system would be cumbersome. It would be nice to just ship them all out in one big folder, but resources do not let you do this, nor do they allow you to give your resources anything other than a totally flat structure.

This is exactly what the assets system is great for. Assets are like a little file system that ships with your packaged application. With assets, you can use whatever folder structure you want. Since they give you this kind of organizational ability, assets are commonly used for loading graphics and sound in applications that have a lot of those things, like games.

Creating BeatBox

Time to get started. The first step is to create your BeatBox app. In Android Studio, select File → New Project... to create a new project. Call it BeatBox, and give it a company domain of android.bignerdranch.com. Use API 16 for your minimum SDK, and start with one Blank Activity called **BeatBoxActivity**. Leave the defaults as they are.

You will be using **RecyclerView** again, so open your project preferences and add the com.android.support:recyclerview-v7 dependency.

Now, let's build out the basics of the app. The main screen will show a grid of buttons, each of which plays a sound. So, you will need two layout files: one for the grid and one for the buttons.

Create your layout file for the **RecyclerView** first. You will not need res/layout/activity_beat_box.xml, so go ahead and rename it fragment_beat_box.xml. Then fill it up like so:

Listing 18.1 Create main layout file (res/layout/fragment_beat_box.xml)

```xml
<?xml version="1.0" encoding="utf-8"?>
<android.support.v7.widget.RecyclerView
  xmlns:android="http://schemas.android.com/apk/res/android"
  android:id="@+id/fragment_beat_box_recycler_view"
  android:layout_width="match_parent"
  android:layout_height="match_parent"
  />
```

Next, create the layout for the buttons, res/layout/list_item_sound.xml.

Listing 18.2 Create sound layout (res/layout/list_item_sound.xml)

```xml
<?xml version="1.0" encoding="utf-8"?>
<Button
  xmlns:android="http://schemas.android.com/apk/res/android"
  xmlns:tools="http://schemas.android.com/tools"
  android:id="@+id/list_item_sound_button"
  android:layout_width="match_parent"
  android:layout_height="120dp"
  tools:text="Sound name"/>
```

Now create a new **Fragment** called **BeatBoxFragment** in com.bignerdranch.android.beatbox, and hook it up to the layout you just created.

Listing 18.3 Create **BeatBoxFragment** (BeatBoxFragment.java)

```
public class BeatBoxFragment extends Fragment {
    public static BeatBoxFragment newInstance() {
        return new BeatBoxFragment();
    }

    @Override
    public View onCreateView(LayoutInflater inflater, ViewGroup container,
                             Bundle savedInstanceState) {
        View view = inflater.inflate(R.layout.fragment_beat_box, container, false);

        RecyclerView recyclerView = (RecyclerView)view
            .findViewById(R.id.fragment_beat_box_recycler_view);
        recyclerView.setLayoutManager(new GridLayoutManager(getActivity(), 3));

        return view;
    }
}
```

Notice that you use a different implementation of **LayoutManager** here than you did in Chapter 9. This **LayoutManager** lays out items in a grid, so that there are multiple items on each line. You passed in 3 here, to indicate that there are three columns in your grid.

Create a **ViewHolder** wired up to list_item_sound.xml.

Listing 18.4 Create **SoundHolder** (BeatBoxFragment.java)

```
public class BeatBoxFragment extends Fragment {
    ...

    @Override
    public View onCreateView(LayoutInflater inflater, ViewGroup container,
                             Bundle savedInstanceState) {
        ...
    }

    private class SoundHolder extends RecyclerView.ViewHolder {
        private Button mButton;

        public SoundHolder(LayoutInflater inflater, ViewGroup container) {
            super(inflater.inflate(R.layout.list_item_sound, container, false));

            mButton = (Button)itemView.findViewById(R.id.list_item_sound_button);
        }
    }
}
```

Next, create an **Adapter** hooked up to **SoundHolder**. (If you put your cursor on **RecyclerView.Adapter** before typing in any of the methods below and hit Option+Return (Alt+Enter), Android Studio will enter most of this code for you.)

Listing 18.5 Create **SoundAdapter** (BeatBoxFragment.java)

```java
public class BeatBoxFragment extends Fragment {

    ...

    private class SoundHolder extends RecyclerView.ViewHolder {
        ...
    }

    private class SoundAdapter extends RecyclerView.Adapter<SoundHolder> {
        @Override
        public SoundHolder onCreateViewHolder(ViewGroup parent, int viewType) {
            LayoutInflater inflater = LayoutInflater.from(getActivity());
            return new SoundHolder(inflater, parent);
        }

        @Override
        public void onBindViewHolder(SoundHolder soundHolder, int position) {

        }

        @Override
        public int getItemCount() {
            return 0;
        }
    }
}
```

Now wire up **SoundAdapter** in **onCreateView(…)**.

Listing 18.6 Wiring up **SoundAdapter** (BeatBoxFragment.java)

```java
@Override
public View onCreateView(LayoutInflater inflater, ViewGroup container,
                         Bundle savedInstanceState) {
    View view = inflater.inflate(R.layout.fragment_beat_box, container, false);

    RecyclerView recyclerView = (RecyclerView)view
        .findViewById(R.id.fragment_beat_box_recycler_view);
    recyclerView.setLayoutManager(new GridLayoutManager(getActivity(), 3));
    recyclerView.setAdapter(new SoundAdapter());

    return view;
}
```

Finally, hook up **BeatBoxFragment** in **BeatBoxActivity**. You will use the same
SingleFragmentActivity architecture you used in CriminalIntent.

First, copy SingleFragmentActivity.java from CriminalIntent into app/java/
com.bignerdranch.android.beatbox, and then copy activity_fragment.xml into app/src/res/
layout. (You can either pull these files out of your own CriminalIntent folder, or from the solutions.
For information on how to access the solutions files, refer back to the section called "Adding an Icon"
in Chapter 2.)

Next, delete everything in the body of **BeatBoxActivity**, change it to a subclass of
SingleFragmentActivity, and override **createFragment()**, like so:

Listing 18.7 Filling out **BeatBoxActivity** (BeatBoxActivity.java)

```java
public class BeatBoxActivity extends SingleFragmentActivity {
    @Override
    protected Fragment createFragment() {
        return BeatBoxFragment.newInstance();
    }
}
```

That should be enough to get your skeleton up and running. Your **BeatBoxFragment** implementation does not display anything yet, but go ahead and run your app to make sure that everything is wired up correctly (Figure 18.2).

Figure 18.2 Empty BeatBox

Importing Assets

Now to import your assets. Create an assets folder inside your project by right-clicking on your app module and selecting New → Folder → Assets Folder (Figure 18.3). Leave the Change Folder Location checkbox unchecked, and leave the Target Source Set set to main.

Figure 18.3 Creating the assets folder

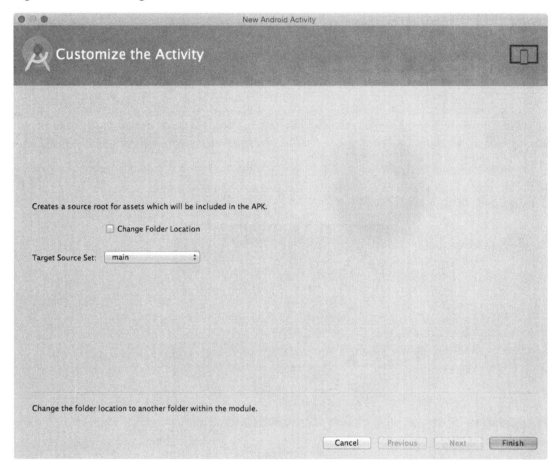

Click Finish to create your assets folder.

Next, right-click on assets to create a subfolder for your sounds by selecting New → Directory. Enter sample_sounds for the directory name (Figure 18.4).

Figure 18.4 Create sample_sounds folder

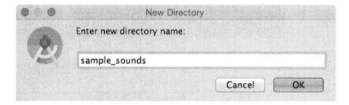

Everything inside of the assets folder is deployed with your app. For the sake of convenience and organization, you created a subfolder called sample_sounds. Unlike with resources, though, this is not something you have to do.

So where can you find the sounds? You will be using a Creative Commons licensed sound set we initially found provided by the user plagasul at http://www.freesound.org/people/plagasul/packs/3/. We have put them up in one zip file for you at the following location:

```
https://www.bignerdranch.com/solutions/sample_sounds.zip
```

Download the zip file and unzip its contents into assets/sample_sounds (Figure 18.5).

Figure 18.5 Imported assets

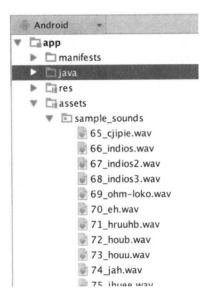

(Make sure only .wav files are in there, by the way – not the .zip file you got them from.)

Rebuild your app to make sure everything is hunky-dory. The next step will be to list out those assets and show them to the user.

Getting at Assets

BeatBox will end up doing a lot of work related to asset management: finding assets, keeping track of them, and eventually playing them as sounds. To manage all this, create a new class called **BeatBox** in com.bignerdranch.android.beatbox. Go ahead and add a couple of constants: one for logging and one to remember which folder you saved your wrestling grunts in.

Listing 18.8 New **BeatBox** class (BeatBox.java)

```java
public class BeatBox {
    private static final String TAG = "BeatBox";

    private static final String SOUNDS_FOLDER = "sample_sounds";
}
```

Assets are accessed using the **AssetManager** class. You can get an **AssetManager** from any **Context**. Since **BeatBox** will need one, give it a constructor that takes in a **Context** as a dependency, pulls out an **AssetManager**, and stashes it away.

Listing 18.9 Stash an **AssetManager** for safekeeping (BeatBox.java)

```java
public class BeatBox {
    private static final String TAG = "BeatBox";

    private static final String SOUNDS_FOLDER = "sample_sounds";

    private AssetManager mAssets;

    public BeatBox(Context context) {
        mAssets = context.getAssets();
    }
}
```

When getting at assets, in general you do not need to worry about which **Context** you are using. In every situation you are likely to encounter in practice, every **Context**'s **AssetManager** will be wired up to the same set of assets.

To get a listing of what you have in your assets, you can use the **list(String)** method. Write a method called **loadSounds()** that looks in your assets with **list(String)**.

Listing 18.10 Look at assets (BeatBox.java)

```java
public BeatBox(Context context) {
    mAssets = context.getAssets();
    loadSounds();
}

private void loadSounds() {
    String[] soundNames;
    try {
        soundNames = mAssets.list(SOUNDS_FOLDER);
        Log.i(TAG, "Found " + soundNames.length + " sounds");
    } catch (IOException ioe) {
        Log.e(TAG, "Could not list assets", ioe);
        return;
    }
}
```

AssetManager.list(String) lists filenames contained in the folder path you pass in. So by passing in your sounds folder, you should see every .wav file you put in there.

To verify that this is working correctly, create an instance of **BeatBox** in **BeatBoxFragment**.

Listing 18.11 Create **BeatBox** instance (BeatBoxFragment.java)

```java
public class BeatBoxFragment extends Fragment {

    private BeatBox mBeatBox;

    public static BeatBoxFragment newInstance() {
        return new BeatBoxFragment();
    }

    @Override
    public void onCreate(Bundle savedInstanceState) {
        super.onCreate(savedInstanceState);

        mBeatBox = new BeatBox(getActivity());
    }

    ...
}
```

Run your app and you should see some log output telling you how many sound files were found. We provided 22 .wav files, so if you used our files, you should see:

```
...1823-1823/com.bignerdranch.android.beatbox I/BeatBox: Found 22 sounds
```

Wiring Up Assets for Use

Now that you have your asset filenames, you should present them to the user. Eventually, you will want the files to be played, so it makes sense to have an object responsible for keeping track of the filename, the name the user should see, and any other information related to that sound.

Create a **Sound** class to hold all of this. (Remember to let Android Studio generate your getters.)

Listing 18.12 Create **Sound** object (Sound.java)

```java
public class Sound {
    private String mAssetPath;
    private String mName;

    public Sound(String assetPath) {
        mAssetPath = assetPath;
        String[] components = assetPath.split("/");
        String filename = components[components.length - 1];
        mName = filename.replace(".wav", "");
    }

    public String getAssetPath() {
        return mAssetPath;
    }

    public String getName() {
        return mName;
    }
}
```

In the constructor, you do a little work to make a presentable name for your sound. First, you split off the filename using **String.split(String)**. Once you have done that, you use **String.replace(String, String)** to strip off the file extension, too.

Next, build up a list of **Sound**s in **BeatBox.loadSounds()**.

Listing 18.13 Create **Sound**s (BeatBox.java)

```java
public class BeatBox {
    ...

    private AssetManager mAssets;
    private List<Sound> mSounds = new ArrayList<>();

    public BeatBox(Context context) {
        ...
    }

    private void loadSounds() {
        String[] soundNames;
        try {
            ...
        } catch (IOException ioe) {
            ...
        }

        for (String filename : soundNames) {
            String assetPath = SOUNDS_FOLDER + "/" + filename;
            Sound sound = new Sound(assetPath);
            mSounds.add(sound);
        }
    }

    public List<Sound> getSounds() {
        return mSounds;
    }
}
```

Then, back in **BeatBoxFragment**, add code in **SoundHolder** to bind to a **Sound**.

Listing 18.14 Bind to **Sound** (BeatBoxFragment.java)

```java
private class SoundHolder extends RecyclerView.ViewHolder {
    private Button mButton;
    private Sound mSound;

    public SoundHolder(LayoutInflater inflater, ViewGroup container) {
        ...
    }

    public void bindSound(Sound sound) {
        mSound = sound;
        mButton.setText(mSound.getName());
    }
}
```

Wire up **SoundAdapter** to a **List** of **Sound**s.

Listing 18.15 Hook up to **Sound** list (BeatBoxFragment.java)

```
private class SoundAdapter extends RecyclerView.Adapter<SoundHolder> {
    private List<Sound> mSounds;

    public SoundAdapter(List<Sound> sounds) {
        mSounds = sounds;
    }

    ...

    @Override
    public void onBindViewHolder(SoundHolder soundHolder, int position) {
        Sound sound = mSounds.get(position);
        soundHolder.bindSound(sound);
    }

    @Override
    public int getItemCount() {
        return 0;
        return mSounds.size();
    }
}
```

And then pass in **BeatBox**'s sounds in **onCreateView(…)**.

Listing 18.16 Pass in **Sound**s to adapter (BeatBoxFragment.java)

```
@Override
public View onCreateView(LayoutInflater inflater, ViewGroup container,
                         Bundle savedInstanceState) {
    View view = inflater.inflate(R.layout.fragment_beat_box, container, false);

    RecyclerView recyclerView = (RecyclerView)view
        .findViewById(R.id.fragment_beat_box_recycler_view);
    recyclerView.setLayoutManager(new GridLayoutManager(getActivity(), 3));
    recyclerView.setAdapter(new SoundAdapter());
    recyclerView.setAdapter(new SoundAdapter(mBeatBox.getSounds()));

    return view;
}
```

With that, you should see a grid of sound files when you run BeatBox (Figure 18.6).

Figure 18.6 Finished BeatBox interface

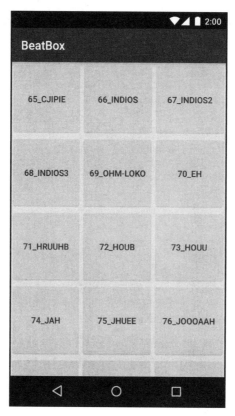

Accessing Assets

You have finished all the work for this chapter. You will develop BeatBox to actually use the content of your assets in the next chapter.

Before you do, though, let's discuss a bit more about how assets work.

Your **Sound** object has an asset file path defined on it. Asset file paths will not work if you try to open them with a **File**; you must use them with an **AssetManager**:

```
String assetPath = sound.getAssetPath();
InputStream soundData = mAssets.open(assetPath);
```

This gives you a standard **InputStream** for the data, which you can use like any other **InputStream** in Java.

Some APIs require **FileDescriptor**s instead. (This is what you will use with **SoundPool** in the next chapter.) If you need that, you can call **AssetManager.openFd(String)** instead:

```
String assetPath = sound.getAssetPath();
// AssetFileDescriptors are different from FileDescriptors,
AssetFileDescriptor assetFd = mAssets.openFd(assetPath);
// but you get can a regular FileDescriptor easily if you need to.
FileDescriptor fd = assetFd.getFileDescriptor();
```

For the More Curious: Non-Assets?

AssetManager has methods called **openNonAssetFd(…)**. You might reasonably ask why a class dedicated to assets would concern itself with non-assets. We might reasonably answer, "These aren't the droids you're looking for," so that you might go on believing that you never heard of **openNonAssetFd(…)** in the first place.

There is no reason that we know of to ever use this method, so there is no real reason to learn about it.

You did buy our book, though. So we might as well throw this answer out there for fun:

Remember that earlier we said that Android has two systems, assets and resources? Well, the resources system has a nice big lookup system. But some big resources are too big to fit inside that system. So these big resources – images and raw sound files, usually – are actually stored in the assets system. Under the hood, Android opens these things itself using the **openNonAsset** methods, not all of which are publicly available.

When would you need to use these? As far as we know, never. And now you know, too.

19
Audio Playback with SoundPool

Now that you are ready to go with your assets, it is time to actually play all these .wav files. Android's audio APIs are fairly low level for the most part, but there is a tool practically tailor-made for the app you are writing: **SoundPool**.

SoundPool can load a large set of sounds into memory and control the maximum number of sounds that are playing back at any one time. So if your app's user gets a bit too excited and mashes all the buttons at the same time, it will not break your app or overtax your phone.

Ready? Time to get started.

Creating a SoundPool

The first step is to create a **SoundPool** object.

Listing 19.1 Creating a **SoundPool** (BeatBox.java)

```java
public class BeatBox {
    private static final String TAG = "BeatBox";

    private static final String SOUNDS_FOLDER = "sample_sounds";
    private static final int MAX_SOUNDS = 5;

    private AssetManager mAssets;
    private List<Sound> mSounds;
    private SoundPool mSoundPool;

    public BeatBox(Context context) {
        mAssets = context.getAssets();
        // This old constructor is deprecated, but we need it for
        // compatibility.
        mSoundPool = new SoundPool(MAX_SOUNDS, AudioManager.STREAM_MUSIC, 0);
        loadSounds();
    }

    ...
}
```

Lollipop introduced a new way of creating a **SoundPool** using a **SoundPool.Builder**. However, since **SoundPool.Builder** is not available on your minimum-supported API 16, you are using the older **SoundPool(int, int, int)** constructor instead.

The first parameter specifies how many sounds can play at any given time. Here, you pass in 5. If five sounds are playing and you try to play a sixth one, the **SoundPool** will stop playing the oldest one.

The second parameter determines the kind of audio stream your **SoundPool** will play on. Android has a variety of different audio streams, each of which has its own independent volume settings. This is why turning down the music does not also turn down your alarms. Check out the documentation for the AUDIO_* constants in **AudioManager** to see the other options. STREAM_MUSIC will put you on the same volume setting as music and games on the device.

And the last parameter? It specifies the quality for the sample rate converter. The documentation says it is ignored, so you just pass in 0.

Loading Sounds

The next thing to do with your **SoundPool** is to load it up with sounds. The main benefit of using a **SoundPool** over some other methods of playing audio is that **SoundPool** is responsive: when you tell it to play a sound, it will play the sound immediately, with no lag.

The trade-off for that is that you have to load sounds into your **SoundPool** before you play them. Each sound you load will get its own integer ID. So go ahead and add a mSoundId field to **Sound** and a generated getter and setter to keep track of this.

Listing 19.2 Adding sound ID field (Sound.java)

```java
public class Sound {
    private String mAssetPath;
    private String mName;
    private Integer mSoundId;

    ...

    public String getName() {
        return mName;
    }

    public Integer getSoundId() {
        return mSoundId;
    }

    public void setSoundId(Integer soundId) {
        mSoundId = soundId;
    }
}
```

By making mSoundId an **Integer** instead of an int, you make it possible to represent the state where a **Sound** has no value for mSoundId by assigning it a null value.

Now to load your sounds in. Add a **load(Sound)** method to **BeatBox** to load a **Sound** into your **SoundPool**.

Listing 19.3 Loading sounds into **SoundPool** (BeatBox.java)

```
private void loadSounds() {
    ...
}

private void load(Sound sound) throws IOException {
    AssetFileDescriptor afd = mAssets.openFd(sound.getAssetPath());
    int soundId = mSoundPool.load(afd, 1);
    sound.setSoundId(soundId);
}
}
```

Calling **mSoundPool.load(AssetFileDescriptor, int)** loads a file into your **SoundPool** for later playback. To keep track of the sound and play it back again (or unload it), **mSoundPool.load(…)** returns an int ID, which you stash in the mSoundId field you just defined. And since calling **openFd(String)** throws **IOException**, **load(Sound)** throws **IOException**, too.

Now load up all your sounds by calling **load(Sound)** inside **BeatBox.loadSounds()**.

Listing 19.4 Loading up all your sounds (BeatBox.java)

```
private void loadSounds() {
    ...

    mSounds = new ArrayList<Sound>();
    for (String filename : soundNames) {
        try {
            String assetPath = SOUNDS_FOLDER + "/" + filename;
            Sound sound = new Sound(assetPath);
            load(sound);
            mSounds.add(sound);
        } catch (IOException ioe) {
            Log.e(TAG, "Could not load sound " + filename, ioe);
        }
    }
}
```

Run BeatBox to make sure that all the sounds loaded correctly. If they did not, you will see red exception logs in LogCat.

Playing Sounds

One last step: playing the sounds back. Add the **play(Sound)** method to **BeatBox**.

Listing 19.5 Playing sounds back (BeatBox.java)

```
    mSoundPool = new SoundPool(MAX_SOUNDS, AudioManager.STREAM_MUSIC, 0);
    loadSounds();
}

public void play(Sound sound) {
    Integer soundId = sound.getSoundId();
    if (soundId == null) {
        return;
    }
    mSoundPool.play(soundId, 1.0f, 1.0f, 1, 0, 1.0f);
}

public List<Sound> getSounds() {
    return mSounds;
}
```

Before playing your soundId, you check to make sure it is not null. This might happen if the **Sound** failed to load.

Once you are sure you have a non-null value, play the sound by calling **SoundPool.play(int, float, float, int, int, float)**. Those parameters are, respectively: the sound ID, volume on the left, volume on the right, priority (which is ignored), whether the audio should loop, and playback rate. For full volume and normal playback rate, you pass in 1.0. Passing in 0 for the looping value says "do not loop." (You can pass in –1 if you want it to loop forever. We speculate that this would be incredibly annoying.)

With that method written, you can play the sound each time one of the buttons is pressed.

Listing 19.6 Playing sound on button press (BeatBoxFragment.java)

```
private class SoundHolder extends RecyclerView.ViewHolder
        implements View.OnClickListener {
    private Button mButton;
    private Sound mSound;

    public SoundHolder(LayoutInflater inflater, ViewGroup container) {
        super(inflater.inflate(R.layout.list_item_sound, parent, false));

        mButton = (Button)itemView.findViewById(R.id.button);
        mButton.setOnClickListener(this);
    }

    public void bindSound(Sound sound) {
        mSound = sound;
        mButton.setText(mSound.getName());
    }

    @Override
    public void onClick(View v) {
        mBeatBox.play(mSound);
    }
}
```

Press a button, as shown in Figure 19.1, and you should hear a sound played.

Figure 19.1 A functioning sound bank

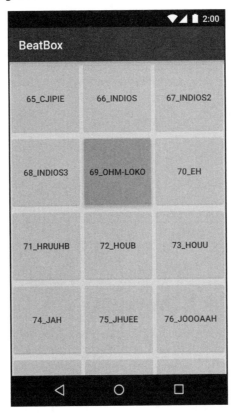

Unloading Sounds

The app works, but you still have some cleanup to do. To be a good citizen, you should clean up your **SoundPool** by calling **SoundPool.release()** when you are done with it. Add a matching **BeatBox.release()** method.

Listing 19.7 Releasing your **SoundPool** (BeatBox.java)

```java
public class BeatBox {
    ...

    public void play(Sound sound) {
        ...
    }

    public void release() {
        mSoundPool.release();
    }

    ...
}
```

Then, clean it up when you are done with it in **BeatBoxFragment**.

Listing 19.8 Releasing your BeatBox (BeatBoxFragment.java)

```java
public class BeatBoxFragment extends Fragment {

    ...

    @Override
    public View onCreateView(LayoutInflater inflater, ViewGroup container,
                             Bundle savedInstanceState) {
        ...
    }

    @Override
    public void onDestroy() {
        super.onDestroy();
        mBeatBox.release();
    }

    ...
}
```

Go ahead and run your app to make sure it works correctly with your new **release()** method.

Rotation and Object Continuity

Now you are a good citizen, which is nice. Unfortunately, your app no longer handles rotation correctly. Try playing the 69_ohm-loko sound and rotating the screen: the sound will stop abruptly. (If it does not, make sure you have built and run the app with your recent **onDestroy()** implementation.)

Here is the problem: on rotation, the **BeatBoxActivity** is destroyed. As this happens, the **FragmentManager** destroys your **BeatBoxFragment**, too. In doing that, it calls **BeatBoxFragment**'s waning lifecycle methods: **onPause()**, **onStop()**, and **onDestroy()**. In **BeatBoxFragment.onDestroy()**, you call **BeatBox.release()**, which releases the **SoundPool** and stops sound playback.

You have seen how **Activity** and **Fragment** instances die on rotation before, and you have solved these issues using **onSaveInstanceState(Bundle)**. However, that solution will not work this time, because it relies on saving data out and restoring it using **Parcelable** data inside a **Bundle**.

Parcelable, like **Serializable**, is an API for saving an object out to a stream of bytes. Objects may elect to implement the **Parcelable** interface if they are what we will call "stashable" here. Objects are stashed in Java by putting them in a **Bundle**, or by marking them **Serializable** so that they can be serialized, or by implementing the **Parcelable** interface. Whichever way you do it, the same idea applies: you should not be using any of these tools unless your object is stashable.

To illustrate what we mean by "stashable," imagine watching a television program with a friend. You could write down the channel you are watching, the volume level, and even the TV you are watching the program on. Once you do that, even if a fire alarm goes off and the power goes out, you can look at what you wrote down and get back to watching TV just like you were before.

So the configuration of your TV watching time is stashable. The time you spend watching TV is not, though: once the fire alarm goes off and the power goes out, that session is gone. You can return and create a new session just like it, but you will experience an interruption no matter what you do. So the session is *not* stashable.

Some parts of **BeatBox** are stashable: everything contained in **Sound** is stashable, for example. **SoundPool** is more like your TV watching session, though. Yes, you can create a new **SoundPool** that has all the same sounds as an older one. You can even start playing again right where you left off. You will always experience a brief interruption, though, no matter what you do. That means that **SoundPool** is not stashable.

Non-stashability tends to be contagious. If a non-stashable object is critical to another object's mission, that other object is probably not stashable, either. Here, **BeatBox** has the same mission as **SoundPool**: to play back sounds. Therefore, ipso facto, Q.E.D.: **BeatBox** is not stashable. (Sorry.)

The regular savedInstanceState mechanism preserves stashable data for you, but **BeatBox** is not stashable. You need your **BeatBox** instance to be continuously available as your **Activity** is created and destroyed.

What to do?

Retaining a fragment

Fortunately, fragments have a feature that you can use to keep the **BeatBox** instance alive across a configuration change: retainInstance. Override **BeatBoxFragment.onCreate(…)** and set a property of the fragment.

Listing 19.9 Calling **setRetainInstance(true)** (BeatBoxFragment.java)

```
...

public static BeatBoxFragment newInstance() {
    return new BeatBoxFragment();
}

@Override
public void onCreate(Bundle savedInstanceState) {
    super.onCreate(savedInstanceState);
    setRetainInstance(true);

    mBeatBox = new BeatBox(getActivity());
}

@Override
public View onCreateView(LayoutInflater inflater, ViewGroup container,
                         Bundle savedInstanceState) {
    ...
```

By default, the retainInstance property of a fragment is false. This means it is not *retained*, and it is destroyed and re-created on rotation along with the activity that hosts it. Calling setRetainInstance(true) *retains* the fragment. When a fragment is *retained*, the fragment is not destroyed with the activity. Instead, it is preserved and passed along intact to the new activity.

When you retain a fragment, you can count on all of its instance variables (like mBeatBox) to keep the same values. When you reach for them, they are simply there.

Run BeatBox again. Play the 69_ohm-loko sound, rotate the device, and confirm that playback continues unimpeded.

Rotation and retained fragments

Let's take a closer look at how retained fragments work. Retained fragments take advantage of the fact that a fragment's view can be destroyed and re-created without having to destroy the fragment itself.

During a configuration change, the **FragmentManager** first destroys the views of the fragments in its list. Fragment views always get destroyed and re-created on a configuration change for the same reasons that activity views are destroyed and re-created: If you have a new configuration, then you might need new resources. Just in case better matching resources are now available, you rebuild the view from scratch.

Next, the **FragmentManager** checks the retainInstance property of each fragment. If it is false, which it is by default, then the **FragmentManager** destroys the fragment instance. The fragment and its view will be re-created by the new **FragmentManager** of the new activity "on the other side" (Figure 19.2).

Figure 19.2 Default rotation with a UI fragment

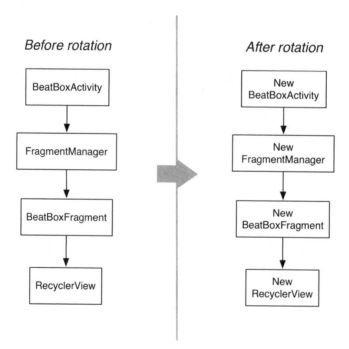

On the other hand, if retainInstance is true, then the fragment's view is destroyed but the fragment itself is not. When the new activity is created, the new **FragmentManager** finds the retained fragment and re-creates its view (Figure 19.3).

Figure 19.3 Rotation with a retained UI fragment

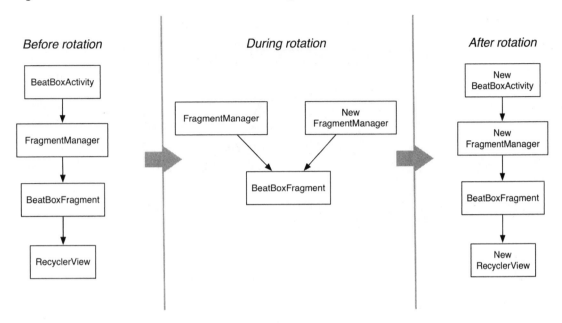

A retained fragment is not destroyed, but it is *detached* from the dying activity. This puts the fragment in a *retained* state. The fragment still exists, but it is not hosted by any activity (Figure 19.4).

Figure 19.4 Fragment lifecycle

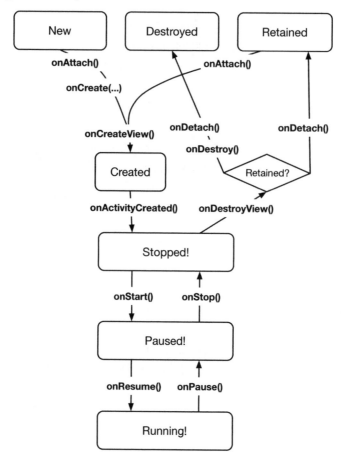

The retained state is only entered into when two conditions are met:

- **setRetainInstance(true)** has been called on the fragment.

- The hosting activity is being destroyed for a configuration change (typically rotation).

A fragment is only in the retained state for an extremely brief interval – the time between being detached from the old activity and being reattached to the new activity that is immediately created.

For the More Curious: Whether to Retain

Retained fragments: pretty nifty, right? Yes! They are indeed nifty. They appear to solve all the problems that pop up from activities and fragments being destroyed on rotation. When the device configuration changes, you get the most appropriate resources by creating a brand-new view, and you have an easy way to retain data and objects.

You may wonder why you would not retain every fragment or why fragments are not retained by default. In general, we do not recommend using this mechanism unless you absolutely need to, for a couple of reasons.

The first reason is simply that retained fragments are more complicated than unretained fragments. When something goes wrong with them, it takes longer to get to the bottom of what went wrong. Programs are always more complicated than you want them to be, so if you can get by without this complication, you are better off.

The other reason is that fragments that handle rotation using saved instance state handle all lifecycle situations, but retained fragments only handle the case when an activity is destroyed for a configuration change. If your activity is destroyed because the OS needs to reclaim memory, then all your retained fragments are destroyed, too, which may mean that you lose some data.

For the More Curious: More on Rotation Handling

The `onSaveInstanceState(Bundle)` is another tool you have used to handle rotation. In fact, if your app does not have any problems with rotation, it is because the default behavior of `onSaveInstanceState(…)` is working.

Your CriminalIntent app is a good example. `CrimeFragment` is not retained, but if you make changes to the crime's title or toggle the checkbox, the new states of these `View` objects are automatically saved out and restored after rotation. This is what `onSaveInstanceState(…)` was designed to do – save out and restore the UI state of your app.

The major difference between overriding `Fragment.onSaveInstanceState(…)` and retaining the fragment is how long the preserved data lasts. If it only needs to last long enough to survive configuration changes, then retaining the fragment is much less work. This is especially true when preserving an object; you do not have to worry about whether the object implements `Serializable`.

However, if you need the data to last longer, retaining the fragment is no help. If an activity is destroyed to reclaim memory after the user has been away for a while, then any retained fragments are destroyed just like their unretained brethren.

To make this difference clearer, think back to your GeoQuiz app. The rotation problem you faced was that the question index was being reset to zero on rotation. No matter what question the user was on, rotating the device sent them back to the first question. You saved out the index data and then read it back in to ensure the user would see the right question.

GeoQuiz did not use fragments, but imagine a redesigned GeoQuiz with a `QuizFragment` hosted by `QuizActivity`. Should you override `Fragment.onSaveInstanceState(…)` to save out the index or retain `QuizFragment` and keep the variable alive?

Figure 19.5 shows the three different lifetimes you have to work with: the life of the activity object (and its unretained fragments), the life of a retained fragment, and the life of the activity record.

Figure 19.5 Three lifetimes

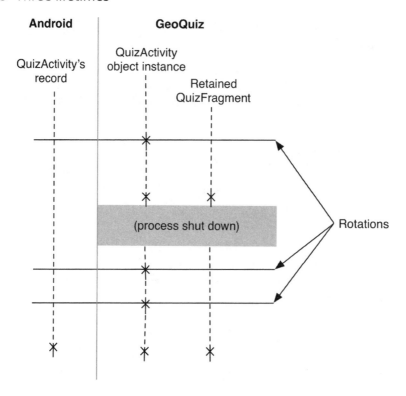

The lifetime of the activity object is too short. That is the source of the rotation problem. The index definitely needs to outlive the activity object.

If you retain **QuizFragment**, then the index will exist for the lifetime of this retained fragment. When GeoQuiz has only five questions, retaining **QuizFragment** is the easier choice and requires less code. You would initialize the index as a member variable and then call **setRetainInstance(true)** in **QuizFragment.onCreate(…)**.

Listing 19.10 Retaining of hypothetical **QuizFragment**

```
public class QuizFragment extends Fragment {

    ...

    private int mCurrentIndex = 0;

    ...

    @Override
    public void onCreate(Bundle savedInstanceState) {
        super.onCreate(savedInstanceState);
        setRetainInstance(true);
    }

    ...
}
```

By tying the index to the lifetime of the retained fragment, it survives the destruction of the activity object and solves the problem of resetting the index on rotation. However, as you can see in Figure 19.5, retaining **QuizFragment** does not preserve the value of the index across a process shutdown, which may happen if the user leaves the app for a while and the activity and the retained fragment are destroyed to reclaim memory.

For only five questions, having users start over may be an acceptable choice. But what if GeoQuiz had 100 questions? Users would rightly be irritated at returning to the app and having to start again at the first question. You need the state of the index to survive for the lifetime of the activity record. To make this happen, you would save out the index in **onSaveInstanceState(…)**. Then, if users left the app for a while, they would always be able to pick up where they left off.

Therefore, if you have something in your activity or fragment that should last a long time, then you should tie it to the activity record's lifetime by overriding **onSaveInstanceState(Bundle)** to save its state so that you can restore it later.

20

Styles and Themes

Now that BeatBox sounds intimidating, it is time to make it look intimidating, too.

So far, BeatBox sticks with the default user interface styles. The buttons are stock. The colors are stock. The app does not stand out. It does not have its own brand.

We can restyle it. We have the technology.

Figure 20.1 shows the better, stronger, faster – or at least more stylish – BeatBox.

Figure 20.1 A themed BeatBox

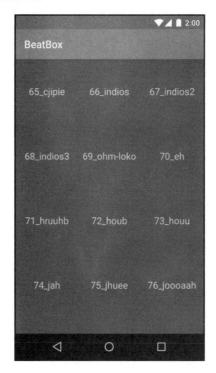

Color Resources

Begin by defining a few colors that you will use throughout the chapter. Create a colors.xml file in res/values.

Listing 20.1 Defining a few colors (`res/values/colors.xml`)

```
<resources>
  <color name="red">#F44336</color>
  <color name="dark_red">#C3352B</color>
  <color name="gray">#607D8B</color>
  <color name="soothing_blue">#0083BF</color>
  <color name="dark_blue">#005A8A</color>
</resources>
```

Color resources are a convenient way to specify color values in one place that you reference throughout your application.

Styles

Now, update the buttons in BeatBox with a *style*. A style is a set of attributes that you can apply to a widget.

Navigate to `res/values/styles.xml` and add a style named **BeatBoxButton**. (When you created BeatBox, your new project should have come with a built-in `styles.xml` file. If your project did not, create the file.)

Listing 20.2 Adding a style (`res/values/styles.xml`)

```
<resources>

  <style name="AppTheme" parent="Theme.AppCompat.Light.DarkActionBar">
  </style>

  <style name="BeatBoxButton">
      <item name="android:background">@color/dark_blue</item>
  </style>

</resources>
```

Here, you create a style called **BeatBoxButton**. This style defines a single attribute, **android:background**, and sets it to a dark blue color. You can apply this style to as many widgets as you like and then update the attributes of all of those widgets in this one place.

Now that the style is defined, apply **BeatBoxStyle** to your buttons in BeatBox.

Listing 20.3 Using a style (`res/layout/list_item_sound.xml`)

```
<Button xmlns:android="http://schemas.android.com/apk/res/android"
  xmlns:tools="http://schemas.android.com/tools"
  style="@style/BeatBoxButton"
  android:id="@+id/button"
  android:layout_width="match_parent"
  android:layout_height="120dp"
  tools:text="Sound name"/>
```

Run BeatBox and you will see that all of your buttons now have a dark blue background color (Figure 20.2).

Figure 20.2 BeatBox with button styles

You can create a style for any set of attributes that you want to reuse in your application. Pretty handy.

Style inheritance

Styles also support inheritance. A style can inherit and override attributes from some other style.

Create a new style called **BeatBoxButton.Strong** that inherits from **BeatBoxButton** but also bolds the text.

Listing 20.4 Inheriting from **BeatBoxButton** (res/layout/styles.xml)

```
...
<style name="BeatBoxButton">
    <item name="android:background">@color/dark_blue</item>
</style>

<style name="BeatBoxButton.Strong">
    <item name="android:textStyle">bold</item>
</style>

...
```

(While you could have added the **android:textStyle** attribute to the **BeatBoxButton** style directly, you created **BeatBoxButton.Strong** to demonstrate style inheritance.)

The naming convention here is a little strange. When you name your style **BeatBoxButton.Strong**, you are saying that your theme inherits attributes from **BeatBoxButton**.

There is also an alternative inheritance naming style. You can specify a **parent** when declaring the style:

```
<style name="BeatBoxButton">
    <item name="android:background">@color/dark_blue</item>
</style>

<style name="StrongBeatBoxButton" parent="@style/BeatBoxButton">
    <item name="android:textStyle">bold</item>
</style>
```

Stick with the **BeatBoxButton.Strong** style in BeatBox.

Update list_item_sound.xml to use your newer, stronger style.

Listing 20.5 Using a bolder style (res/layout/list_item_sound.xml)

```
<Button xmlns:android="http://schemas.android.com/apk/res/android"
  xmlns:tools="http://schemas.android.com/tools"
  style="@style/BeatBoxButton.Strong"
  android:id="@+id/button"
  android:layout_width="match_parent"
  android:layout_height="120dp"
  tools:text="Sound name"/>
```

Run BeatBox and verify that your button text is indeed bold, as in Figure 20.3.

Figure 20.3 A bolder BeatBox

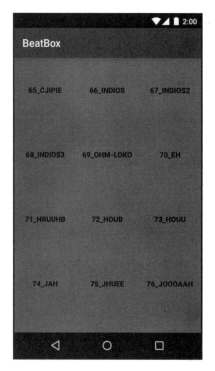

Themes

Styles are cool. They allow you to define a set of attributes in one place and then apply them to as many widgets as you want. The downside of styles is that you have to apply them to each and every widget, one at a time. What if you had a more complex app with lots of buttons in lots of layouts? Adding your BeatBoxButton style to them all could be a huge task.

That is where themes come in. Themes take styles a step further: they allow you to define a set of attributes in one place, like a style – but then those attributes are automatically applied throughout your app. Theme attributes can store a reference to concrete resources, such as colors, and they can also store a reference to styles. In a theme, you can say, for example, "I want all buttons to use this style." And you do not then need to find every button widget and tell it to use the theme.

Modifying the theme

When you created BeatBox, it was given a default theme. Navigate to the AndroidManifest.xml and look at the **theme** attribute on the **application** tag.

Listing 20.6 BeatBox's theme (AndroidManifest.xml)

```
<manifest xmlns:android="http://schemas.android.com/apk/res/android"
    package="com.bignerdranch.android.beatbox" >

    <application
        android:allowBackup="true"
        android:icon="@mipmap/ic_launcher"
        android:label="@string/app_name"
        android:theme="@style/AppTheme">
        ...
    </application>

</manifest>
```

The **theme** attribute is pointing to a theme called **AppTheme**. **AppTheme** was declared in the styles.xml file that you modified earlier.

As you can see, a theme is also a style. But themes specify different attributes than a style does (as you will see in a moment). Themes are also given superpowers by being declared in the manifest. This is what causes the theme to be applied across the entire app automatically.

Navigate to the definition of the **AppTheme** theme by Command-clicking (or Ctrl-clicking on Windows) on @style/AppTheme. Android Studio will take you to res/values/styles.xml.

Listing 20.7 BeatBox's **AppTheme** (res/values/styles.xml)

```
<resources>

    <style name="AppTheme" parent="Theme.AppCompat.Light.DarkActionBar">

    </style>

    <style name="BeatBoxButton">
        <item name="android:background">@color/dark_blue</item>
    </style>

    ...

</resources>
```

(As of this writing, when new projects are created in Android Studio, they are given an AppCompat theme. If you do not have an AppCompat theme in your solution, follow the instructions from Chapter 13 to convert BeatBox to use the AppCompat library.)

AppTheme is inheriting attributes from **Theme.AppCompat.Light.DarkActionBar**. Within **AppTheme**, you can add or override additional values from the parent theme.

The AppCompat library comes with three main themes:

- **Theme.AppCompat** – a dark theme

- **Theme.AppCompat.Light** – a light theme

- **Theme.AppCompat.Light.DarkActionBar** – a light theme with a dark toolbar

Change the parent theme to **Theme.AppCompat** to give BeatBox a dark theme as its base.

Listing 20.8 Changing to a dark theme (res/values/styles.xml)

```
<resources>

    <style name="AppTheme" parent="Theme.AppCompat.Light.DarkActionBar">

    </style>

    ...

</resources>
```

Run BeatBox to see your new dark theme (Figure 20.4).

Figure 20.4 A dark BeatBox

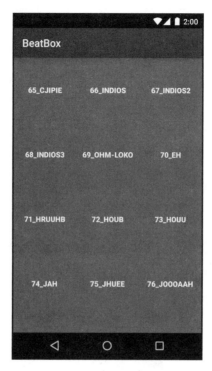

Adding Theme Colors

With the base theme squared away, it is time to customize the attributes of BeatBox's **AppTheme**.

In the styles.xml file, define three attributes on your theme.

Listing 20.9 Setting theme attributes (res/values/styles.xml)

```
<resources>

  <style name="AppTheme" parent="Theme.AppCompat.Light.DarkActionBar">
      <item name="colorPrimary">@color/red</item>
      <item name="colorPrimaryDark">@color/dark_red</item>
      <item name="colorAccent">@color/gray</item>
  </style>

  ...

</resources>
```

Here, you define three theme attributes. These theme attributes look similar to the style attributes that you set up earlier, but they specify different properties. Style attributes specify properties for an individual widget, such as the **textStyle** that you used to bold the button text. Theme attributes have a larger scope: they are properties that are set on the theme that any widget can access. For example, the toolbar will look at the **colorPrimary** attribute on the theme to set its background color.

These three attributes have a large impact. The **colorPrimary** attribute is the primary color for your app's brand. This color will be used as the toolbar's background as well as in a few other places.

colorPrimaryDark is used to color the status bar, which shows up at the top of the screen. Typically **colorPrimaryDark** will be a slightly darker version of your **colorPrimary** color. Status bar theming is a feature that was added to Android in Lollipop. Keep in mind that the status bar will be black on older devices (no matter what the theme specifies). Figure 20.5 shows the effect of these two theme attributes on BeatBox.

Figure 20.5 BeatBox with AppCompat color attributes

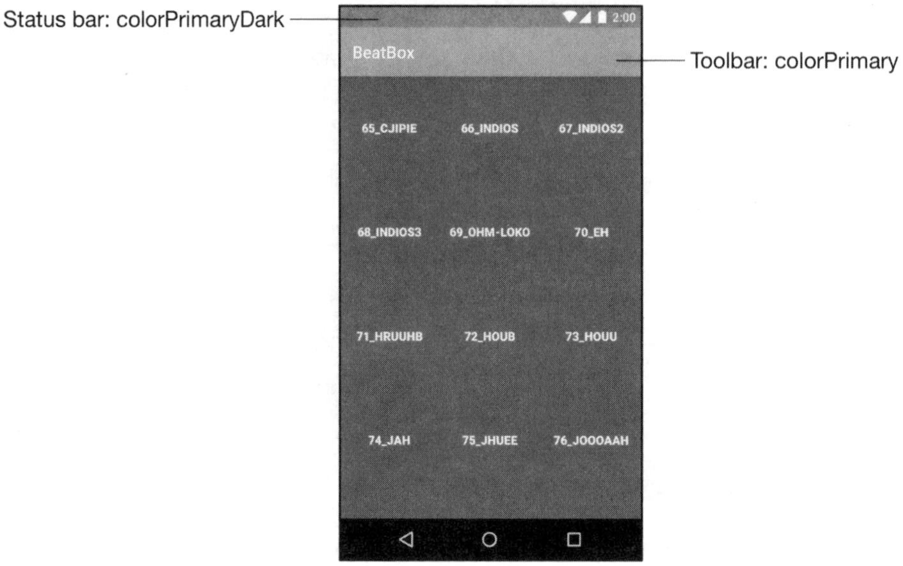

Finally, you set **colorAccent** to a gray color. **colorAccent** should contrast with your **colorPrimary** attribute; it is used to tint some widgets, such as an **EditText**.

You will not see the **colorAccent** attribute affect BeatBox because **Button**s do not support tinting. You still specify **colorAccent** because it is a good idea to think about these three color attributes together. These colors should mesh and the default **colorAccent** attribute from your parent theme may clash with the other colors that you specified. This sets you up well for any future additions.

Run BeatBox to see the new colors in action. Your app should look like Figure 20.5.

Overriding Theme Attributes

Now that the colors are worked out, it is time to dive in and see what theme attributes exist that you can override. Be warned, theme spelunking is tough. There is little to no documentation about which attributes exist, which ones you can override yourself, and even what the attributes do. You are going off the map here. It is a good thing you brought along your guide (this book).

Your first goal is to change the background color of BeatBox by altering the theme. While you could navigate to res/layout/fragment_beat_box.xml and manually set the **android:background** attribute on your **RecyclerView** – and then repeat the process in every other fragment and activity layout file that might exist – this would be wasteful. Wasteful of your time, obviously, but also wasteful of app effort.

The theme is always setting a background color. By setting another color on top of that, you are doing extra work. You are also writing code that is hard to maintain by duplicating the background attribute throughout the app.

Theme spelunking

Instead, you want to override the background color attribute on your theme. To discover the name of this attribute, take a look at how this attribute is set by your parent theme: **Theme.AppCompat**.

You might be thinking, "How will I know which attribute to override if I don't know its name?" You won't. You will read the names of the attributes and you will think, "That sounds right." Then you will override that attribute, run the app, and hope that you chose wisely.

What you want to do is find the ultimate ancestor of your theme: your theme's great-great-great … well, who-knows-how-great grandparent. To do this, you will keep on navigating up to one parent after another until you find a theme that is outside of the AppCompat library – maybe even a theme with no parent at all.

Open your **styles.xml** file and Command-click (or Ctrl-click on Windows) on **Theme.AppCompat**. Let's see how deep the rabbit hole goes.

(If you are unable to navigate through your theme attributes directly in Android Studio, or you want to do this outside of Android Studio, you can find Android's theme sources in: your-SDK-directory/platforms/android-21/data/res/values directory.)

At the time of this writing, you are brought to a very large file with a focus on this line:

```
<style name="Theme.AppCompat" parent="Base.Theme.AppCompat" />
```

The theme, **Theme.AppCompat** inherits attributes from **Base.Theme.AppCompat**. Interestingly, **Theme.AppCompat** does not override any attributes itself. It just points to its parent.

Command-click on **Base.Theme.AppCompat**. Android Studio will tell you that this theme is resource qualified. There are a few different versions of this theme depending on the version of Android that you are on.

Choose the values-v14/values.xml version and you will be brought to **Base.Theme.AppCompat**'s definition (Figure 20.6).

Figure 20.6 Choosing the v14 parent

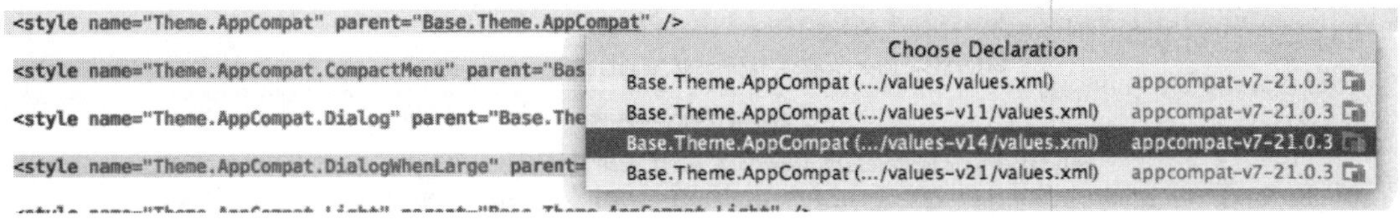

(You chose the v14 version because BeatBox supports API level 16 and higher. If you had chosen the v21 version, you might have come across features that were added in API level 21. See the challenge at the end of the chapter for more information about this.)

```
<style name="Base.Theme.AppCompat" parent="Base.V14.Theme.AppCompat">
  <item name="android:actionModeCutDrawable">?actionModeCutDrawable</item>
  <item name="android:actionModeCopyDrawable">?actionModeCopyDrawable</item>
  <item name="android:actionModePasteDrawable">?actionModePasteDrawable</item>
  <item name="android:actionModeSelectAllDrawable">?actionModeSelectAllDrawable</item>
  <item name="android:actionModeShareDrawable">?actionModeShareDrawable</item>
</style>
```

There are a few attributes in this theme but nothing looks like it will meet your goal: changing the background color. Navigate to **Base.V14.Theme.AppCompat**.

```
<style name="Base.V14.Theme.AppCompat" parent="Base.V11.Theme.AppCompat" />
```

Base.V14.Theme.AppCompat is another theme that exists only for its name and does not override any attributes. Continue along to its parent theme: **Base.V11.Theme.AppCompat**.

```
    <style name="Base.V11.Theme.AppCompat" parent="Base.V7.Theme.AppCompat" />
```

Another empty theme. Move to its parent.

```
<style name="Base.V7.Theme.AppCompat" parent="Platform.AppCompat">
  <item name="windowActionBar">true</item>
  <item name="windowActionBarOverlay">false</item>

  ...
</style>
```

You are getting closer. **Base.V7.Theme.AppCompat** has many attributes, but it is still not quite what you want. Once you break free of the AppCompat themes, you will find many more attributes. Navigate to **Platform.AppCompat**. You will see that this is resource qualified. Choose the values-v11/values.xml version.

```
<style name="Platform.AppCompat" parent="android:Theme.Holo">
  <item name="android:windowNoTitle">true</item>
  <item name="android:windowActionBar">false</item>
  <item name="buttonBarStyle">?android:attr/buttonBarStyle</item>
  <item name="buttonBarButtonStyle">?android:attr/buttonBarButtonStyle</item>
  <item name="selectableItemBackground">?android:attr/selectableItemBackground</item>
  ...
</style>
```

Finally, here you see that the parent of the **Platform.AppCompat** theme is **android:Theme.Holo**.

Notice that the Holo theme is not referenced just as **Theme.Holo**. Instead it has the **android** namespace in front of it.

You can think of the AppCompat library as something that lives within your own app. When you build your project, you include the AppCompat library and it brings along a bunch of Java and XML files. Those files are just like the files that you wrote yourself. If you want to refer to something in the AppCompat library, you do it directly. You would just write **Theme.AppCompat**, because those files exist in your app.

Themes that exist in the Android OS, like **Theme.Holo**, have to be declared with the namespace that points to their location. The AppCompat library uses **android:Theme.Holo** because the Holo theme exists in the Android OS.

Navigate to **android:Theme.Holo**.

```
<style name="Theme.Holo">
  <item name="colorForeground">@color/bright_foreground_holo_dark</item>
  <item name="colorForegroundInverse">…</item>
  <item name="colorBackground">@color/background_holo_dark</item>
  <item name="colorBackgroundCacheHint">…</item>
  <item name="disabledAlpha">0.5</item>
  <item name="backgroundDimAmount">0.6</item>
  ...
</style>
```

You have finally arrived. Here you see all of the attributes that you can override in your theme. You can of course navigate to **Theme.Holo**'s parent: **Theme**, but this is not necessary. The Holo theme overrides all of the attributes that you will need to use.

Right at the top, **colorBackground** is declared. It sounds like this attribute is the background color for the theme.

```
<style name="Theme.Holo">
  <item name="colorForeground">@color/bright_foreground_holo_dark</item>
  <item name="colorForegroundInverse">…</item>
  <item name="colorBackground">@color/background_holo_dark</item>

  ...
</style>
```

This is the attribute that you want to override in BeatBox. Navigate back to your styles.xml file and override the **colorBackground** attribute.

Listing 20.10 Setting the window background (res/values/styles.xml)

```
<style name="AppTheme" parent="Theme.AppCompat">
  <item name="colorPrimary">@color/red</item>
  <item name="colorPrimaryDark">@color/dark_red</item>
  <item name="colorAccent">@color/gray</item>

  <item name="android:colorBackground">@color/soothing_blue</item>
</style>
```

Notice that you must use the **android** namespace when overriding this attribute, because **colorBackground** is declared in the Android OS.

Run BeatBox, scroll down to the bottom of your recycler view and verify that the background, where it is not covered with a button, is a soothing blue, as in Figure 20.7.

Figure 20.7 BeatBox with a themed background

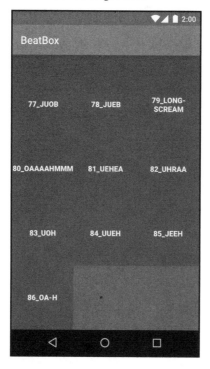

The steps that you just went through to find the **colorBackground** attribute are the same steps that every Android developer takes when modifying an app's theme. You will not find much documentation on these attributes. Most people go straight to the source to see what is available.

To recap, you navigated through the following themes:

- **Theme.AppCompat**

- **Base.Theme.AppCompat**

- **Base.V14.Theme.AppCompat**

- **Base.V11.Theme.AppCompat**

- **Base.V7.Theme.AppCompat**

- **Platform.AppCompat**

- **android:Theme.Holo**

You navigated through the theme hierarchy until you arrived at one of the Android OS's themes (outside of the AppCompat library). As you become more familiar with your theme options, you may opt to skip ahead to the appropriate Android theme in the future. But it is nice to follow the hierarchy so you can see your theme's roots.

Be aware that this theme hierarchy may change over time. But the task of walking the hierarchy will not. You follow your theme hierarchy until you find the attribute that you want to override.

Modifying Button Attributes

Earlier you customized the buttons in BeatBox by manually setting a **style** attribute in the res/layout/list_item_sound.xml file. If you have a more complex app, with buttons throughout many fragments, setting a **style** attribute on each and every button does not scale well. You can take your theme a step further by defining a style in your theme for every button in your app.

Before adding a button style to your theme, remove the **style** attribute from your res/layout/list_item_sound.xml file.

Listing 20.11 Be gone! We have a better way (res/layout/list_item_sound.xml)

```
<Button xmlns:android="http://schemas.android.com/apk/res/android"
  xmlns:tools="http://schemas.android.com/tools"
  style="@style/BeatBoxButton.Strong"
  android:id="@+id/button"
  android:layout_width="match_parent"
  android:layout_height="120dp"
  tools:text="Sound name"/>
```

Run BeatBox and verify that your buttons are back to the old, bland look.

Navigate back to the **Theme.Holo** definition and look for a group of button attributes.

```
<style name="Theme.Holo">
  ...

  <!-- Button styles -->
  <item name="buttonStyle">@style/Widget.Holo.Button</item>

  <item name="buttonStyleSmall">@style/Widget.Holo.Button.Small</item>
  <item name="buttonStyleInset">@style/Widget.Holo.Button.Inset</item>

  ...
</style>
```

Notice the attribute named **buttonStyle**. This is the style of any normal button within your app.

The **buttonStyle** attribute points to a style resource rather than a value. When you updated the **colorBackground** attribute, you passed in a value: the color. In this case, **buttonStyle** should point to a style. Navigate to **Widget.Holo.Button** to see the button style.

```
<style name="Widget.Holo.Button" parent="Widget.Button">
  <item name="background">@drawable/btn_default_holo_dark</item>
  <item name="textAppearance">?attr/textAppearanceMedium</item>
  <item name="textColor">@color/primary_text_holo_dark</item>
  <item name="minHeight">48dip</item>
  <item name="minWidth">64dip</item>
</style>
```

Every **Button** that you use in BeatBox is given these attributes.

Duplicate what happens in Android's own theme in BeatBox. Change the parent of **BeatBoxButton** to inherit from the existing button style. Also, remove your **BeatBoxButton.Strong** style from earlier.

Listing 20.12 Creating a button style (res/values/styles.xml)

```
<resources>

  <style name="AppTheme" parent="Theme.AppCompat">dark_blue
    <item name="colorPrimary">@color/red</item>
    <item name="colorPrimaryDark">@color/dark_red</item>
    <item name="colorAccent">@color/gray</item>

    <item name="android:colorBackground">@color/soothing_blue</item>
  </style>

  <style name="BeatBoxButton" parent="android:style/Widget.Holo.Button">
    <item name="android:background">@color/dark_blue</item>
  </style>

  <style name="BeatBoxButton.Strong">
    <item name="android:textStyle">bold</item>
  </style>

</resources>
```

You specified a parent of **android:style/Widget.Holo.Button**. You want your button to inherit all of the properties that a normal button would receive and then selectively modify attributes.

If you do not specify a parent theme for **BeatBoxButton**, you will notice that your buttons devolve into something that does not look like a button at all. Properties you expect to see, such as the text centered in the button, will be lost.

Now that you have fully defined **BeatBoxButton**, it is time to use it. Look back at the **buttonStyle** attribute that you found earlier when digging through Android's themes. Duplicate this attribute in your own theme.

Listing 20.13 Using the **BeatBoxButton** style (res/values/styles.xml)

```
<resources>

  <style name="AppTheme" parent="Theme.AppCompat">
    <item name="colorPrimary">@color/red</item>
    <item name="colorPrimaryDark">@color/dark_red</item>
    <item name="colorAccent">@color/gray</item>

    <item name="android:colorBackground">@color/soothing_blue</item>
    <item name="android:buttonStyle">@style/BeatBoxButton</item>
  </style>

  <style name="BeatBoxButton" parent="android:style/Widget.Holo.Button">
    <item name="android:background">@color/dark_blue</item>
  </style>

</resources>
```

You are now overriding the **buttonStyle** attribute from Android's themes and substituting your own style: **BeatBoxButton**.

Run BeatBox and notice that all of your buttons are dark blue (Figure 20.8). You changed the look of every normal button in BeatBox without modifying any layout files directly. Behold the power of theme attributes in Android!

Figure 20.8 The completely themed BeatBox

As you press the buttons, you will notice that the buttons do not change when you press them. There is no style change for the pressed state. In the next chapter, you will fix this issue and make these buttons really shine.

For the More Curious: More on Style Inheritance

The description of style inheritance earlier in the chapter does not explain the full story. You may have noticed a switch in inheritance style as you were exploring the theme hierarchy. The AppCompat themes used the name of the theme to indicate inheritance until you arrive at the **Platform.AppCompat** theme.

```
<style name="Platform.AppCompat" parent="android:Theme.Holo">
    ...
</style>
```

Here, the inheritance naming style changes to the more explicit **parent** attribute style. Why?

Specifying the parent theme in the theme name only works for themes that exist in the same package. So you will see the Android OS themes use the theme name inheritance style most of the time, and you will see the AppCompat library do the same. But once the AppCompat library crosses over to a parent outside of itself, the explicit **parent** attribute is used.

In your own applications, it is a good idea to follow the same convention. Specify your theme parent in the name of your theme if you are inheriting from one of your own themes. If you inherit from a style or theme in the Android OS, explicitly specify the **parent** attribute.

For the More Curious: Accessing Theme Attributes

Once attributes are declared in your theme, you can access them in XML or in code.

To access a theme attribute in XML, you use the notation that you saw on the **divider** attribute in Chapter 17. When referencing a concrete value in XML, such as a color, you use the @ notation. @color/gray points to a specific resource.

When referencing a resource in the theme, you use the ? notation.

```
<Button xmlns:android="http://schemas.android.com/apk/res/android"
  xmlns:tools="http://schemas.android.com/tools"
  android:id="@+id/button"
  android:layout_width="match_parent"
  android:layout_height="120dp"
  android:background="?attr/colorAccent"
  tools:text="Sound name"/>
```

The ? notation says to use the resource that the **colorAccent** attribute on your theme points to. In your case, this is the gray color that you defined in your colors.xml file.

You can also use theme attributes in code, although it is much more verbose.

```
Resources.Theme theme = getActivity().getTheme();
int[] attrsToFetch = { R.attr.colorAccent };
TypedArray a = theme.obtainStyledAttributes(R.style.AppTheme, attrsToFetch);
int accentColor = a.getInt(0, 0);
a.recycle();
```

On the **Theme** object, you ask to resolve the attribute R.attr.colorAccent that is defined in your **AppTheme**: R.style.AppTheme. This call returns a **TypedArray**, which holds your data. On the **TypedArray**, you ask for an int value to pull out the accent color. From here, you can use that color to change the background of a button, for example.

The toolbar and buttons in BeatBox are doing exactly this to style themselves based on your theme attributes.

Challenge: An Appropriate Base Theme

When you created **BeatBoxButton**, you inherited attributes from **android:style/ Widget.Holo.Button**. While inheriting from the Holo theme works, you are not taking advantage of the latest theme available.

In Android 5.0 (Lollipop), the material theme was released. This theme makes changes to various properties of your button, including the font size. It is a good idea to take advantage of this new look on a device that supports the material theme.

Your challenge is to create a resource-qualified version of your styles.xml file: values-v21/ styles.xml. Next, create two versions of your **BeatBoxButton** style. One should inherit attributes from **Widget.Holo.Button**, and the other from **Widget.Material.Button**.

21
XML Drawables

Now that BeatBox has been themed it is time to do something about those buttons.

Currently, the buttons do not show any kind of response when you press on them, and they are just blue boxes. In this chapter, you will use *XML drawables* to take BeatBox to the next level (Figure 21.1).

Figure 21.1 BeatBox makeover

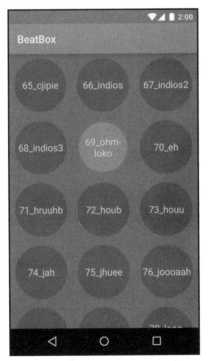

Android calls anything that is intended to be drawn to the screen a drawable, whether it is an abstract shape, a clever bit of code that subclasses the **Drawable** class, or a bitmap image. You have already seen one kind of drawable: **BitmapDrawable**, which wraps an image. In this chapter, you will see a few more kinds of drawables: *state list drawables*, *shape drawables*, and *layer list drawables*. All three are defined in XML files, so we group them together in the broader category of XML drawables.

Making Uniform Buttons

Before creating any XML drawables, modify list_item_sound.xml.

Listing 21.1 Spacing the buttons out (`res/layout/list_item_sound.xml`)

```
<Button xmlns:android="http://schemas.android.com/apk/res/android"
  xmlns:tools="http://schemas.android.com/tools"
  android:id="@+id/list_item_sound_button"
  android:layout_width="match_parent"
  android:layout_height="120dp"
  tools:text="Sound name"/>

<FrameLayout
  xmlns:android="http://schemas.android.com/apk/res/android"
  xmlns:tools="http://schemas.android.com/tools"
  android:layout_margin="8dp"
  android:layout_width="wrap_content"
  android:layout_height="wrap_content">

  <Button
    android:id="@+id/list_item_sound_button"
    android:layout_width="100dp"
    android:layout_height="100dp"
    android:layout_gravity="center"
    tools:text="Sound name"/>
</FrameLayout>
```

You gave each button a width and height of 100dp so that when the buttons are circles later on they will not be skewed.

Your recycler view will always show three columns, no matter what the screen size is. If there is extra room, the recycler view will stretch those columns to fit the device. You do not want the recycler view to stretch your buttons, so you wrapped your buttons in a frame layout. The frame layout will be stretched and the buttons will not.

Run BeatBox and you will see that your buttons are all the same size and have some space between them (Figure 21.2).

Figure 21.2 Spaced-out buttons

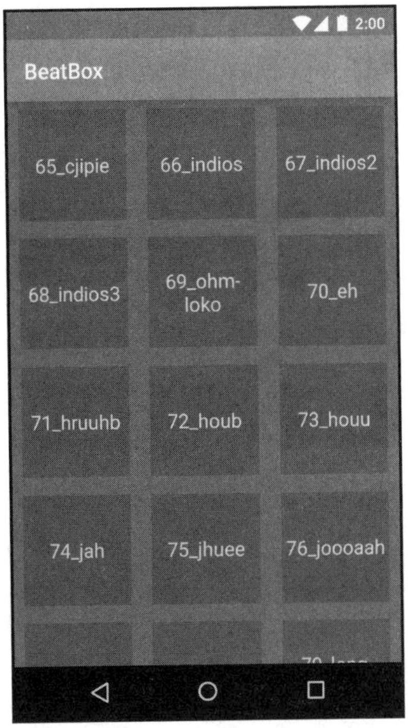

Shape Drawables

Now, make your buttons round with a **ShapeDrawable**. Since XML drawables are not density specific, they are placed in the default drawable folder instead of a density-specific one.

In the Project tool window, create a new file in `res/drawable` called `button_beat_box_normal.xml`. (Why is this one "normal"? Because soon it will have a not-so-normal friend.)

Listing 21.2 Making a round shape drawable (`res/drawable/` `button_beat_box_normal.xml`)

```
<shape xmlns:android="http://schemas.android.com/apk/res/android"
  android:shape="oval">

  <solid
    android:color="@color/dark_blue"/>

</shape>
```

This file creates an oval shape drawable that is filled in with a dark blue color. There are additional customization options with shape drawables, including rectangles, lines, and gradients. Check out the documentation at `http://developer.android.com/guide/topics/resources/drawable-resource.html` for details.

Apply `button_beat_box_normal` as the background for your buttons.

371

Listing 21.3 Modifying the background drawable (res/values/styles.xml)

```
<resources>

    <style name="AppTheme" parent="Theme.AppCompat">
        ...
    </style>

    <style name="BeatBoxButton" parent="android:style/Widget.Holo.Button">
        <item name="android:background">@color/dark_blue</item>
        <item name="android:background">@drawable/button_beat_box_normal</item>
    </style>

</resources>
```

Run BeatBox. Your buttons are now nice circles (Figure 21.3).

Figure 21.3 Circle buttons

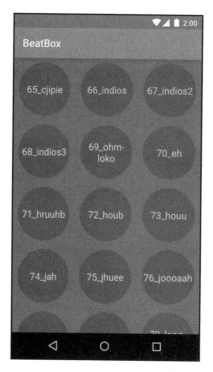

Press a button. You will hear the sound, but the button will not change its appearance. It would be better if the button looked different once it was pressed.

State List Drawables

To fix this, first define a new shape drawable that will be used for the pressed state of the button.

Create button_beat_box_pressed.xml in res/drawable. Make this pressed drawable the same as the normal version but with a red background color.

Listing 21.4 Defining a pressed shape drawable (`res/drawable/button_beat_box_pressed.xml`)

```xml
<shape xmlns:android="http://schemas.android.com/apk/res/android"
  android:shape="oval">

  <solid
    android:color="@color/red"/>

</shape>
```

Next, you are going to use this pressed version when the user presses the button. To do this, you will make use of a *state list drawable*.

A *state list drawable* is a drawable that points to other drawables based on the state of something. A button has a pressed and an unpressed state. You will use a state list drawable to specify one drawable as the background when pressed and a different drawable when not pressed.

Define a state list drawable in your `drawable` folder.

Listing 21.5 Creating a state list drawable (`res/drawable/button_beat_box.xml`)

```xml
<selector xmlns:android="http://schemas.android.com/apk/res/android">
  <item android:drawable="@drawable/button_beat_box_pressed"
        android:state_pressed="true"/>
  <item android:drawable="@drawable/button_beat_box_normal" />
</selector>
```

Now, modify your button style to use this new state list drawable as the button background.

Listing 21.6 Applying a state list drawable (`res/values/styles.xml`)

```xml
<resources>

    <style name="AppTheme" parent="Theme.AppCompat">
    ...
    </style>

    <style name="BeatBoxButton" parent="android:style/Widget.Holo.Button">
        <item name="android:background">@drawable/button_beat_box_normal</item>
        <item name="android:background">@drawable/button_beat_box</item>
    </style>

</resources>
```

When the state of the button is pressed, `button_beat_box_pressed` will be used as the background. Otherwise, `button_beat_box_normal` will be the background of the button.

Run BeatBox and press a button. The button's background changes (Figure 21.4). Pretty slick, right?

Figure 21.4 BeatBox, now with a pressed button state

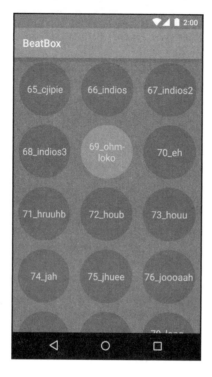

State list drawables are a handy customization tool. Many other states are also supported including disabled, focused, and activated. Check out the documentation at http://developer.android.com/guide/topics/resources/drawable-resource.html#StateList for details.

Layer List Drawables

BeatBox is looking good. You now have round buttons and they visually respond to presses. Time for something a little more advanced.

Layer list drawables allow you to combine two XML drawables into one. Armed with this tool, add a dark ring around your button when in the pressed state.

Listing 21.7 Using a layer list drawable (`res/drawable/button_beat_box_pressed.xml`)

```
<layer-list xmlns:android="http://schemas.android.com/apk/res/android">
  <item>
    <shape
        android:shape="oval">

        <solid
          android:color="@color/red"/>
    </shape>
  </item>
  <item>
    <shape
      android:shape="oval">

      <stroke
        android:width="4dp"
        android:color="@color/dark_red"/>

    </shape>
  </item>
</layer-list>
```

You specified two drawables in this layer list drawable. The first drawable is a red circle, as it was before this change. The second drawable will be drawn on top of the first. In the second drawable, you specified another oval with a stroke of 4dp. This will create a ring of dark red.

These two drawables combined form the layer list drawable. You can combine more than two drawables with a layer list to make something even more complex.

Run BeatBox and press on a button or two. You will see a nice ring around the pressed interface (Figure 21.5). Even slicker.

Figure 21.5 BeatBox complete

With the layer list drawable addition, BeatBox is now complete. Remember how plain BeatBox used to look? You now have something special and uniquely identifiable. Making your app a pleasure to look at makes it fun to use, and that will pay off in popularity.

For the More Curious: Why Bother with XML Drawables?

You will always want a pressed state for your buttons, so state list drawables are a critical component of any Android app. But what about shape drawables and layer list drawables? Should you use them?

XML drawables are flexible. You can use them for many purposes and you can easily update them in the future. With a combination of layer list drawables and shape drawables, you can create complex backgrounds without using an image editor. If you decide to change the color scheme in BeatBox, updating the colors in an XML drawable is easy.

In this chapter, you defined your XML drawables in the drawable directory with no resource qualifiers for the screen density. This is because XML drawables are density independent. With a standard background that is an image, you will typically create multiple versions of that same image in different densities so that the image will look crisp on most devices. XML drawables only need to be defined once and will look crisp at any screen density.

For the More Curious: 9-Patch Images

Sometimes (or maybe often), you will fall back to regular old image files for your button backgrounds. But what happens to those image files when your button can be displayed at many different sizes?

If the width of the button is greater than the width of its background image, the image just stretches, right? Is that always going to look good?

Uniformly stretching your background image will not always look right. Sometimes you need more control over how the image will stretch.

This section will convert BeatBox to use a 9-patch image as the background for the buttons. First, `list_item_sound.xml` should be modified to allow the button size to change based on the available space.

Listing 21.8 Let those buttons stretch (res/layout/`list_item_sound.xml`)

```
<FrameLayout
    xmlns:android="http://schemas.android.com/apk/res/android"
    xmlns:tools="http://schemas.android.com/tools"
    android:layout_margin="8dp"
    android:layout_width="wrap_content"
    android:layout_height="wrap_content">

    <Button
        android:id="@+id/list_item_sound_button"
        android:layout_width="match_parent"
        android:layout_height="match_parent"
        android:layout_gravity="center"
        tools:text="Sound name"/>
</FrameLayout>
```

Now the buttons will take up the available space, leaving an 8dp margin. The image in Figure 21.6, with a snazzy folded corner and shadow, will be used as the new button background for BeatBox.

Figure 21.6 A new button background image (res/drawable-xxhdpi/ ic_button_beat_box_default.png)

In the solutions for this chapter (see the section called "Adding an Icon" in Chapter 2), you can find this image along with a pressed version in the xxhdpi drawable folder. Copy these two images into your project's drawable-xxhdpi folder and apply them as your button background by modifying button_beat_box.xml.

Listing 21.9 Applying the new button background images (res/drawable/ button_beat_box.xml)

```
<selector xmlns:android="http://schemas.android.com/apk/res/android">
    <item android:drawable="@drawable/ic_button_beat_box_pressed"
          android:state_pressed="true"/>
    <item android:drawable="@drawable/ic_button_beat_box_default" />
</selector>
```

Running BeatBox, you will see the new button background (Figure 21.7).

Figure 21.7 BeastBox

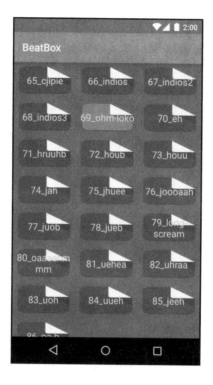

Whoa. That looks… bad.

Why does it look bad? Android is uniformly stretching ic_beat_box_button.png, including the dog-eared edge and the rounded corners. It would look better if you could specify which parts of the image to stretch and which parts not to stretch. Enter *9-patch* images.

A *9-patch* image file is specially formatted so that Android knows which portions can and cannot be scaled. Done properly, this ensures that the edges and corners of your background remain consistent with the image as it was created.

Why are they called 9-patches? A 9-patch breaks your image into a 3 x 3 grid – a grid with 9 sections, or patches. The corners of the grid remain unscaled, the sides are only scaled in one dimension, and the center is scaled in both dimensions, as shown in Figure 21.8.

Figure 21.8 How a 9-patch scales

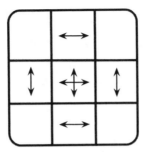

A 9-patch image is like a regular PNG image in everything except two aspects: its filename ends with
.9.png, and it has an additional one-pixel border around the edge. This border is used to specify the
location of the center square of the 9-patch. Border pixels are drawn black to indicate the center and
transparent to indicate the edges.

You can create a 9-patch using any image editor, with the draw9patch tool provided as part of the
Android SDK, or using Android Studio. As of this writing, Android Studio's 9-patch editor can be
flaky. If you need to use the draw9patch tool, you can find it in the tools directory of your SDK
installation.

First, convert your two new background images to 9-patch images by right-clicking on
ic_button_beat_box_default.png in the Project tool window and selecting Refactor → Rename...
to rename the file to: ic_button_beat_box_default.9.png. Then, repeat the process to rename the
pressed version to: ic_button_beat_box_pressed.9.png.

Next, double-click on the default image in the Project tool window to open it in Android Studio's built-
in 9-patch editor, as shown in Figure 21.9. (If Android Studio does not open the editor, try closing the
file and collapsing your drawable folder in the Project tool window. Then re-open the default image.)

In the 9-patch editor, fill in black pixels on the top and left borders to mark the stretchable regions of
the image, as shown.

Figure 21.9 Creating a 9-patch image

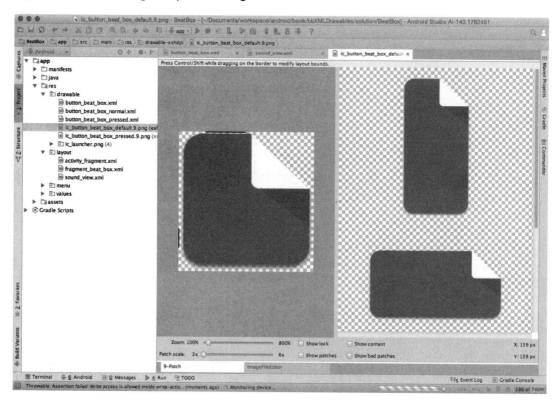

With these two lines, you are telling Android not to stretch the top-right area of the image and each corner if this file changes size. Repeat the process with the pressed version.

So the top and left lines indicate the areas of the image to stretch. What about the bottom and right borders? You use them to define an optional drawable region for the 9-patch image. The drawable region is the area where content (usually text) should be rendered. If you do not include a drawable region, it defaults to be the same as your stretchable region. This is what you want here – that is, you want the buttons' text to be on the stretchable region – so you will not define a separate drawable region.

Run BeatBox to see your new 9-patch image in action (Figure 21.10).

Figure 21.10 New and improved

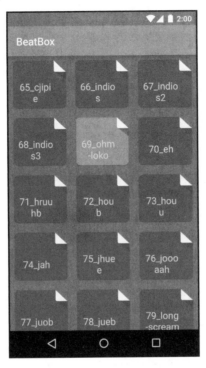

Try rotating to landscape. The images are even more stretched, but your button backgrounds still look good.

For the More Curious: Mipmap Images

Resource qualifiers and drawables are handy. When you need an image in your app, you generate the image at a few different sizes and add them to your resource-qualified folders: drawable-mdpi, drawable-hdpi, etc. Then, you reference the image by name and Android figures out which density to use based on the current device.

However, there is a downside to this system. The APK file that you release to the Google Play Store will contain all of the images in your drawable directories at each density that you added to your project – even though many of them will not be used. That is a lot of extra bloat.

To reduce this bloat, you can generate separate APKs for each screen density. You would have an mdpi APK of your app, an hdpi APK, and so on. (For more info on APK splitting, see the tools documentation: http://tools.android.com/tech-docs/new-build-system/user-guide/apk-splits.)

But, there is one exception. You want to maintain every density of your launcher icon.

A launcher on Android is a home screen application (you will learn much more about launchers in Chapter 22). When you press the Home button on your device, you are taken to the launcher.

Some newer launchers display app icons at a larger size than launchers have traditionally displayed them. To make this larger icon look nice, these launchers will take the icon from the next density

381

bucket up. If your device is an hdpi device, the launcher will use the xhdpi icon to represent your app. But if the xhdpi version has been stripped from your APK, the launcher will have to fall back to the lower resolution version.

Scaled-up low-res icons look fuzzy. You want your icon to look crisp.

The *mipmap* directory is Android's solution to this problem. As of this writing, new projects in Android studio are set up to use a mipmap resource for their launcher icon (Figure 21.11).

Figure 21.11 Mipmap icons

When APK splitting is enabled, mipmaps are not pruned from the APKs. Otherwise, mipmaps are identical to drawables.

So, we recommend putting just your launcher icon in the various `mipmap` directories. All other images belong in the `drawable` directories.

22

More About Intents and Tasks

In this chapter, you will use implicit intents to create a launcher app to replace Android's default launcher app. Figure 22.1 shows what this app, NerdLauncher, will look like.

Figure 22.1 NerdLauncher final product

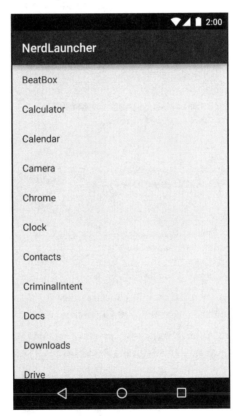

NerdLauncher will display a list of apps on the device. The user will press a list item to launch the app.

To get it working correctly, you will deepen your understanding of intents, intent filters, and how applications interact in the Android environment.

Setting Up NerdLauncher

Create a new Android application project named NerdLauncher. Select Phone and Tablet as the form factor and API 16: Android 4.1 (Jelly Bean) as the minimum SDK. Create a blank activity named **NerdLauncherActivity**.

NerdLauncherActivity will host a single fragment and in turn should be a subclass of **SingleFragmentActivity**. Copy SingleFragmentActivity.java and activity_fragment.xml into your NerdLauncher from the CriminalIntent project.

Open NerdLauncherActivity.java and change **NerdLauncherActivity**'s superclass to **SingleFragmentActivity**. Remove the template's code and override **createFragment()** to return a **NerdLauncherFragment**. (Bear with the error caused by the return line in **createFragment()**. This will be fixed in a moment when you create the **NerdLauncherFragment** class.)

Listing 22.1 Another **SingleFragmentActivity** (NerdLauncherActivity.java)

```java
public class NerdLauncherActivity extends SingleFragmentActivityAppCompatActivity {

    @Override
    protected Fragment createFragment() {
        return NerdLauncherFragment.newInstance();
    }

    @Override
    protected void onCreate(Bundle savedInstanceState) {
        /* Auto generated template code... */
    }

    @Override
    public boolean onCreateOptionsMenu(Menu menu) {
        /* Auto generated template code... */
    }

    @Override
    public boolean onOptionsItemSelected(MenuItem item) {
        /* Auto generated template code... */
    }
}
```

NerdLauncherFragment will display a list of application names in a **RecyclerView**. Add the RecyclerView library as a dependency, as you did in Chapter 9.

Rename layout/activity_nerd_launcher.xml to layout/fragment_nerd_launcher.xml to create a layout for the fragment. Replace its contents with the **RecyclerView** shown in Figure 22.2.

Figure 22.2 Create **NerdLauncherFragment** layout (layout/fragment_nerd_launcher.xml)

```
android.support.v7.widget.RecyclerView
xmlns:android="http://schemas.android.com/apk/res/android"
android:id="@+id/fragment_nerd_launcher_recycler_view"
android:layout_width="match_parent"
android:layout_height="match_parent"
```

Finally, add a new class named **NerdLauncherFragment** that extends from
android.support.v4.app.Fragment. Add a **newInstance()** method and override **onCreateView(…)**
to stash a reference to the **RecyclerView** object in a member variable. (You will hook data up to the
RecyclerView in just a bit.)

Listing 22.2 Basic **NerdLauncherFragment** implementation (NerdLauncherFragment.java)

```java
public class NerdLauncherFragment extends Fragment {

    private RecyclerView mRecyclerView;

    public static NerdLauncherFragment newInstance() {
        return new NerdLauncherFragment();
    }

    @Override
    public View onCreateView(LayoutInflater inflater, ViewGroup container,
                             Bundle savedInstanceState) {
        View v = inflater.inflate(R.layout.fragment_nerd_launcher, container, false);
        mRecyclerView = (RecyclerView) v
                    .findViewById(R.id.fragment_nerd_launcher_recycler_view);
        mRecyclerView.setLayoutManager(new LinearLayoutManager(getActivity()));

        return v;
    }
}
```

Run your app to make sure everything is hooked up correctly to this point. If so, you will be the proud
owner of an app titled NerdLauncher, displaying an empty **RecyclerView** (Figure 22.3).

Figure 22.3 NerdLauncher beginnings

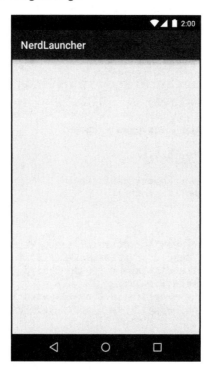

Resolving an Implicit Intent

NerdLauncher will show the user a list of launchable apps on the device. (A launchable app is an app the user can open by clicking an icon on the Home or launcher screen.) To do so, it will query the system (using the **PackageManager**) for launchable main activities. Launchable main activities are simply activities with intent filters that include a MAIN action and a LAUNCHER category. You have seen this intent filter in the AndroidManifest.xml file in your projects:

```
<intent-filter>
  <action android:name="android.intent.action.MAIN" />
  <category android:name="android.intent.category.LAUNCHER" />
</intent-filter>
```

In NerdLauncherFragment.java, add a method named **setupAdapter()** and call that method from **onCreateView(…)**. (Ultimately this method will create a **RecyclerView.Adapter** instance and set it on your **RecyclerView** object. For now, it will just generate a list of application data.) Also, create an implicit intent and get a list of activities that match the intent from the **PackageManager**. Log the number of activities that the **PackageManager** returns.

Listing 22.3 Querying the **PackageManager** (NerdLauncherFragment.java)

```java
public class NerdLauncherFragment extends Fragment {
    private static final String TAG = "NerdLauncherFragment";

    private RecyclerView mRecyclerView;

    public static NerdLauncherFragment newInstance() {
        return new NerdLauncherFragment();
    }

    @Override
    public View onCreateView(LayoutInflater inflater, ViewGroup container,
                             Bundle savedInstanceState) {
        ...
        setupAdapter();
        return v;
    }

    private void setupAdapter() {
        Intent startupIntent = new Intent(Intent.ACTION_MAIN);
        startupIntent.addCategory(Intent.CATEGORY_LAUNCHER);

        PackageManager pm = getActivity().getPackageManager();
        List<ResolveInfo> activities = pm.queryIntentActivities(startupIntent, 0);

        Log.i(TAG, "Found " + activities.size() + " activities.");
    }

}
```

Run NerdLauncher and check LogCat to see how many apps the **PackageManager** returned. (We got 42 the first time we tried it.)

In CriminalIntent, you used an implicit intent to send a crime report. You presented an activity chooser by creating an implicit intent, wrapping it in a chooser intent, and sending it to the OS with **startActivity(Intent)**:

```java
Intent i = new Intent(Intent.ACTION_SEND);
... // Create and put intent extras
i = Intent.createChooser(i, getString(R.string.send_report));
startActivity(i);
```

You may be wondering why you are not using that approach here. The short explanation is that the MAIN/LAUNCHER intent filter may or may not match a MAIN/LAUNCHER implicit intent that is sent via **startActivity(…)**.

It turns out that **startActivity(Intent)** does not mean "Start an activity matching this implicit intent." It means "Start the *default* activity matching this implicit intent." When you send an implicit intent via **startActivity(…)** (or **startActivityForResult(…)**), the OS secretly adds the Intent.CATEGORY_DEFAULT category to the intent.

Thus, if you want an intent filter to match implicit intents sent via **startActivity(…)**, you must include the DEFAULT category in that intent filter.

An activity that has the MAIN/LAUNCHER intent filter is the main entry point for the app that it belongs to. It only wants the job of main entry point for that application. It typically does not care about being the "default" main entry point, so it does not have to include the CATEGORY_DEFAULT category.

Because MAIN/LAUNCHER intent filters may not include CATEGORY_DEFAULT, you cannot reliably match them to an implicit intent sent via **startActivity(…)**. So, instead you use the intent to query the **PackageManager** directly for activities with the MAIN/LAUNCHER intent filter.

The next step is to display the labels of these activities in **NerdLauncherFragment**'s **RecyclerView**. An activity's *label* is its display name – something the user should recognize. Given that these activities are launcher activities, the label is most likely the application name.

You can find the labels for the activities, along with other metadata, in the **ResolveInfo** objects that the **PackageManager** returned.

First, sort the **ResolveInfo** objects returned from the **PackageManager** alphabetically by label using the **ResolveInfo.loadLabel(…)** method.

Listing 22.4 Sorting alphabetically (NerdLauncherFragment.java)

```java
public class NerdLauncherFragment extends Fragment {
    ...

    private void setupAdapter() {
        ...
        List<ResolveInfo> activities = pm.queryIntentActivities(startupIntent, 0);
        Collections.sort(activities, new Comparator<ResolveInfo>() {
            public int compare(ResolveInfo a, ResolveInfo b) {
                PackageManager pm = getActivity().getPackageManager();
                return String.CASE_INSENSITIVE_ORDER.compare(
                        a.loadLabel(pm).toString(),
                        b.loadLabel(pm).toString());
            }
        });
        Log.i(TAG, "Found " + activities.size() + " activities.");
    }
}
```

Now define a **ViewHolder** that displays an activity's label. Store the activity's **ResolveInfo** in a member variable (you will use it more than once later on).

Listing 22.5 **ViewHolder** implementation (NerdLauncherFragment.java)

```java
public class NerdLauncherFragment extends Fragment {
    ...

    private void setupAdapter() {
        ...
    }

    private class ActivityHolder extends RecyclerView.ViewHolder {
        private ResolveInfo mResolveInfo;
        private TextView mNameTextView;

        public ActivityHolder(View itemView) {
            super(itemView);
            mNameTextView = (TextView) itemView;
        }

        public void bindActivity(ResolveInfo resolveInfo) {
            mResolveInfo = resolveInfo;
            PackageManager pm = getActivity().getPackageManager();
            String appName = mResolveInfo.loadLabel(pm).toString();
            mNameTextView.setText(appName);
        }
    }
}
```

Next add a **RecyclerView.Adapter** implementation.

Listing 22.6 **RecyclerView.Adapter** implementation (NerdLauncherFragment.java)

```
public class NerdLauncherFragment extends Fragment {
    ...

    private class ActivityHolder extends RecyclerView.ViewHolder {
        ...
    }

    private class ActivityAdapter extends RecyclerView.Adapter<ActivityHolder> {
        private final List<ResolveInfo> mActivities;

        public ActivityAdapter(List<ResolveInfo> activities) {
            mActivities = activities;
        }

        @Override
        public ActivityHolder onCreateViewHolder(ViewGroup parent, int viewType) {
            LayoutInflater layoutInflater = LayoutInflater.from(getActivity());
            View view = layoutInflater
                    .inflate(android.R.layout.simple_list_item_1, parent, false);
            return new ActivityHolder(view);
        }

        @Override
        public void onBindViewHolder(ActivityHolder activityHolder, int position) {
            ResolveInfo resolveInfo = mActivities.get(position);
            activityHolder.bindActivity(resolveInfo);
        }

        @Override
        public int getItemCount() {
            return mActivities.size();
        }
    }
}
```

Last but not least, update **setupAdapter()** to create an instance of **ActivityAdapter** and set it as the **RecyclerView**'s adapter.

Listing 22.7 Set **RecyclerView**'s adapter (NerdLauncherFragment.java)

```
public class NerdLauncherFragment extends Fragment {
    ...

    private void setupAdapter() {
        ...
        Log.i(TAG, "Found " + activities.size() + " activities.");
        mRecyclerView.setAdapter(new ActivityAdapter(activities));
    }

    ...
}
```

Run NerdLauncher, and you will see a **RecyclerView** populated with activity labels (Figure 22.4).

Figure 22.4 All your activities are belong to us

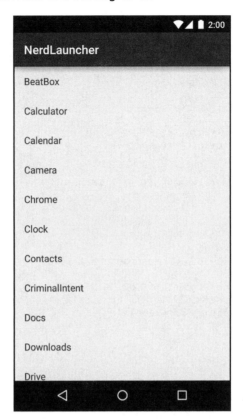

Creating Explicit Intents at Runtime

You used an implicit intent to gather the desired activities and present them in a list. The next step is to start the selected activity when the user presses its list item. You will start the activity using an explicit intent.

To create the explicit intent, you need to get the activity's package name and class name from the **ResolveInfo**. You can get this data from a part of the **ResolveInfo** called **ActivityInfo**. (You can learn what data is available in different parts of **ResolveInfo** from its reference page: http://developer.android.com/reference/android/content/pm/ResolveInfo.html.)

Update **ActivityHolder** to implement a click listener. When an activity in the list is pressed, use the **ActivityInfo** for that activity to create an explicit intent. Then use that explicit intent to launch the selected activity.

Listing 22.8 Launching pressed activity (NerdLauncherFragment.java)

...

```java
private class ActivityHolder extends RecyclerView.ViewHolder
        implements View.OnClickListener {
    private ResolveInfo mResolveInfo;
    private TextView mNameTextView;

    public ActivityHolder(View itemView) {
        super(itemView);
        mNameTextView = (TextView) itemView;
        mNameTextView.setOnClickListener(this);
    }

    public void bindActivity(ResolveInfo resolveInfo) {
        ...
    }

    @Override
    public void onClick(View v) {
        ActivityInfo activityInfo = mResolveInfo.activityInfo;

        Intent i = new Intent(Intent.ACTION_MAIN)
                .setClassName(activityInfo.applicationInfo.packageName,
                        activityInfo.name);

        startActivity(i);
    }
}
```

Notice that in this intent you are sending an action as part of an explicit intent. Most apps will behave the same whether you include the action or not. However, some may change their behavior. The same activity can display different interfaces depending on how it is started. As a programmer, it is best to declare your intentions clearly and let the activities you start do what they will.

In Listing 22.8, you get the package name and class name from the metadata and use them to create an explicit intent using the **Intent** method:

```java
public Intent setClassName(String packageName, String className)
```

This is different from how you have created explicit intents in the past. Before, you have used an **Intent** constructor that accepts a **Context** and a **Class** object:

```java
public Intent(Context packageContext, Class<?> cls)
```

This constructor uses its parameters to get what the **Intent** really needs – a **ComponentName**. A **ComponentName** is a package name and a class name stuck together. When you pass in an **Activity** and a **Class** to create an **Intent**, the constructor determines the fully qualified package name from the **Activity**.

You could also create a **ComponentName** yourself from the package and class names and use the following **Intent** method to create an explicit intent:

```java
public Intent setComponent(ComponentName component)
```

However, it is less code to use **setClassName(…)**, which creates the component name behind the scenes.

Run NerdLauncher and launch some apps.

Tasks and the Back Stack

Android uses tasks to keep track of the user's state within each running application. Each application opened from Android's default launcher app gets its own task. This is the desired behavior but, unfortunately for your NerdLauncher, it is not the default behavior. Before you foray into forcing applications to launch into their own tasks, let's discuss what tasks are and how they work.

A *task* is a stack of activities that the user is concerned with. The activity at the bottom of the stack is called the *base activity*, and whatever activity is on top is the activity that the user sees. When you press the Back button, you are popping the top activity off of this stack. If you are looking at the base activity and hit the Back button, it will send you to the Home screen.

By default, new activities are started in the current task. In CriminalIntent, whenever you started a new activity that activity was added to the current task (as shown in Figure 22.5). This was true even if the activity was not part of the CriminalIntent application, like when you started an activity to select a crime suspect.

Figure 22.5 CriminalIntent task

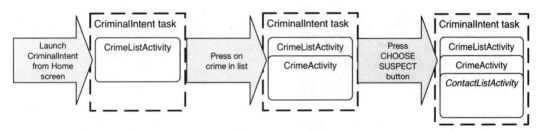

The benefit of adding an activity to the current task is that the user can navigate back through the task instead of the application hierarchy (as shown in Figure 22.6).

Figure 22.6 Pressing the Back button in CriminalIntent

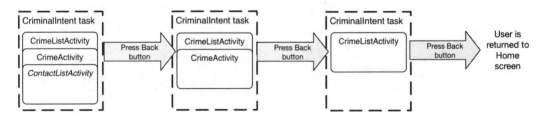

Switching between tasks

Using the *overview screen*, you can switch between tasks without affecting each task's state. For instance, if you start entering a new contact and switch to checking your Twitter feed, you will have two tasks started. If you switch back to editing contacts, your place in both tasks will be saved.

(The overview screen has many other names. You may hear it called the task manager, recents screen, recent apps screen, or recent tasks list.)

Try out the overview screen on your device or emulator. First, launch CriminalIntent from the Home screen or from your app launcher. (If your device or emulator no longer has CriminalIntent installed, open your CriminalIntent project in Android Studio and run it from there.) Select a crime from the crime list. Then push the Home button to return to the Home screen. Next, launch BeatBox from the Home screen or from your app launcher (or, if necessary, from Android Studio).

Open the overview screen. The method for doing so will vary depending on your device. Press the Recents button if the device has one. (The Recents button usually looks like a square or two overlapping rectangles and appears at the far right side of the navigation bar. You can see two examples of the Recents button in Figure 22.7.) Otherwise, try long-pressing the Home button. If that does not work, double-tap the Home button.

Figure 22.7 Overview screen versions

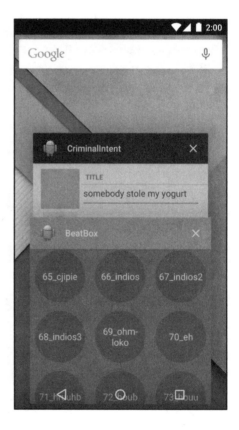

The overview screen displayed on the left in Figure 22.7 is what users will see if they are running KitKat. The overview screen displayed on the right is what users running Lollipop will see. In both cases, the entry displayed for each app (known as a *card* in Lollipop) represents the task for each app. A screenshot of the activity at the top of each task's back stack is displayed. Users can press on the BeatBox or CriminalIntent entry to return to the app (and to whatever activity they were interacting with in that app).

Users can clear an app's task by removing the card from the task list. Do this by swiping on the card entry. Clearing the task removes all activities from the application's back stack.

Try clearing CriminalIntent's task, then relaunch the app. You will see the list of crimes instead of the crime you were editing before you cleared the task.

Starting a new task

Sometimes, when you start an activity, you want the activity added to the current task. Other times, you want it started in a new task that is independent of the activity that started it.

Right now, any activity started from NerdLauncher is added to NerdLauncher's task, as depicted in Figure 22.8.

Figure 22.8 NerdLauncher's task contains CriminalIntent

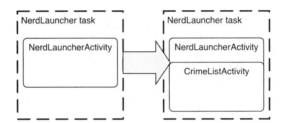

You can confirm this by clearing all the tasks displayed in the overview screen. Then start NerdLauncher and click on the CriminalIntent entry to launch the CriminalIntent app. Open the overview screen again. You will not see CriminalIntent listed anywhere. When `CrimeListActivity` was started, it was added to NerdLauncher's task (Figure 22.9). If you press the NerdLauncher task, you will be returned to whatever CriminalIntent screen you were looking at before starting the overview screen.

Figure 22.9 CriminalIntent not in its own task

Instead, you want NerdLauncher to start activities in new tasks (Figure 22.10). This way each application opened by pressing an item in the NerdLauncher list gets its own task, which will allow users to switch between running applications as they like (via the overview screen, NerdLauncher, or the Home screen).

Figure 22.10 Launching CriminalIntent into its own task

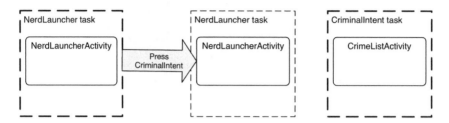

To start a new task when you start a new activity, add a flag to the intent in NerdLauncherFragment.java.

Listing 22.9 Adding new task flag to intent (NerdLauncherFragment.java)

```
public class NerdLauncherFragment extends Fragment {
    ...

    private class ActivityHolder extends RecyclerView.ViewHolder
            implements View.OnClickListener {
        ...

        @Override
        public void onClick(View v) {
            ...

            Intent i = new Intent(Intent.ACTION_MAIN)
                    .setClassName(activityInfo.applicationInfo.packageName,
                            activityInfo.name)
                    .addFlags(Intent.FLAG_ACTIVITY_NEW_TASK);

            startActivity(i);
        }
    }

    ...
}
```

Clear the tasks listed in your overview screen. Run NerdLauncher and start CriminalIntent. This time, when you pull up the overview screen you will see a separate task for CriminalIntent (Figure 22.11).

Figure 22.11 CriminalIntent now in its own task

If you start CriminalIntent from NerdLauncher again, you will not create a second CriminalIntent task. The `FLAG_ACTIVITY_NEW_TASK` flag by itself creates one task per activity. `CrimeListActivity` already has a task running, so Android will switch to that task instead of starting a new one.

Try this out. Open the detail screen for one of the crimes in CriminalIntent. Use the overview screen to switch to NerdLauncher. Press on CriminalIntent in the list. You will notice you are right back where you were in the CriminalIntent app, viewing details for a single crime.

Using NerdLauncher as a Home Screen

Who wants to start an app to start other apps? It would make more sense to offer NerdLauncher as a replacement for the device's Home screen. Open NerdLauncher's `AndroidManifest.xml` and add to its main intent filter.

Listing 22.10 Changing **NerdLauncherActivity**'s categories (AndroidManifest.xml)

```
<intent-filter>
  <action android:name="android.intent.action.MAIN" />
  <category android:name="android.intent.category.LAUNCHER" />
  <category android:name="android.intent.category.HOME" />
  <category android:name="android.intent.category.DEFAULT" />
</intent-filter>
```

By adding the HOME and DEFAULT categories, **NerdLauncherActivity** is asking to be offered as an option for the Home screen. Press the Home button, and NerdLauncher will be offered as an option (Figure 22.12).

Figure 22.12 Select Home app

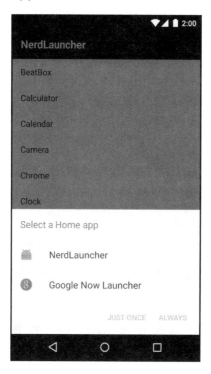

(If you make NerdLauncher the Home screen you can easily change it back later. Launch the Settings app from NerdLauncher. If you are running Lollipop, go to Settings → Apps. Select NerdLauncher from the app list. If you are running a pre-Lollipop version of Android, go to Settings → Applications → Manage Applications. Select All to find NerdLauncher. Once you have selected NerdLauncher, you should be on the App Info screen. Scroll down to Launch by default and press the CLEAR DEFAULTS button. The next time you press the Home button, you will be able to select another default.)

Challenge: Icons

You used **ResolveInfo.loadLabel(…)** in this chapter to present useful names in your launcher. **ResolveInfo** provides a similar method called **loadIcon()** that retrieves an icon to display for each application. For a small challenge, add an icon for each application to NerdLauncher.

For the More Curious: Processes vs. Tasks

All objects need memory and a virtual machine to live in. A *process* is a place created by the OS for your application's objects to live and for your application to run.

Processes may own resources managed by the OS, like memory, network sockets, and open files. Processes also have at least one, possibly many, threads of execution. On Android, your process will also always have exactly one *virtual machine* running.

While there are some obscure exceptions, in general every application component in Android is associated with exactly one process. Your application is created with its own process, and this is the default process for all components in your application.

(You can assign individual components to different processes, but we recommend sticking to the default process. If you think you need something running in a different process, you can usually achieve the same ends with multi-threading, which is more straightforward to program in Android than using multiple processes.)

Every activity instance lives in exactly one process and is referenced by exactly one task. But that is where the similarities between processes and tasks end. Tasks contain only activities and often consist of activities living in different application processes. Processes, on the other hand, contain all running code and objects for a single application.

It can be easy to confuse processes and tasks because there is some overlap between the two ideas and both are often referred to by an application name. For instance, when you launched CriminalIntent from NerdLauncher, the OS created a CriminalIntent process and a new task for which **CrimeListActivity** was the base activity. In the overview screen, this task was labeled CriminalIntent.

The task that an activity is referenced by can be different from the process it lives in. For example, consider the CriminalIntent and contact applications and walk through the following scenario.

Open CriminalIntent, select a crime from the list (or add a new crime), and then press CHOOSE SUSPECT. This launches the contacts application to choose a contact. The contact list activity is added to the CriminalIntent task. This means that when your user presses the Back button to navigate between different activities, he or she may be unknowingly switching between processes, which is nifty.

However, the contact list activity instance is actually created in the contacts app's process's memory space, and it runs on the virtual machine living in the contacts application's process. (The state of the activity instances and task references of this scenario are depicted in Figure 22.13.)

Figure 22.13 Tasks and processes

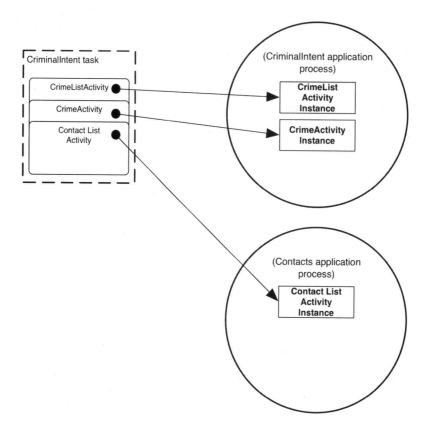

To explore the idea of processes vs. tasks further, leave CriminalIntent up and running on the contact list screen. (Make sure the contacts app itself is not listed on the overview screen. If so, clear the contacts app task.) Press the Home button. Launch the contacts app from the Home screen. Select a contact from the list of contacts (or select to add a new contact).

In doing this, new contact list activity and contact details instances will be created in the contact application's process. A new task will be created for the contacts application, and that task will reference the new contact list and contact details activity instances (as shown in Figure 22.14).

Figure 22.14 Tasks and processes

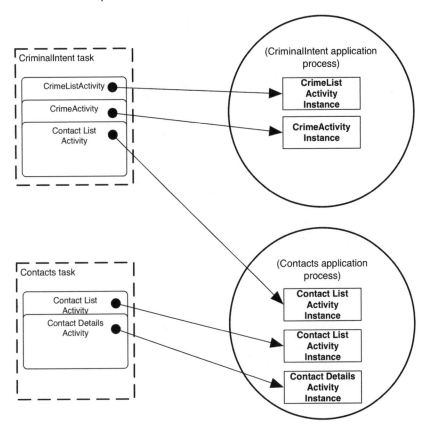

In this chapter, you created tasks and switched between them. What about replacing Android's default overview screen, as you are able to do with the Home screen? Unfortunately, Android does not provide a way to do this. Also, you should know that apps advertised on the Google Play store as "task killers" are, in fact, process killers. Such apps kill a particular process, which means you may be killing activities referenced by other applications' tasks.

For the More Curious: Concurrent Documents

If you are running your apps on a Lollipop device, you may have noticed some interesting behavior with respect to CriminalIntent and the overview screen. When you opt to send a crime report from CriminalIntent, the activity for the app you select from the chooser is added to its own separate task rather than to CriminalIntent's task (Figure 22.15).

Figure 22.15 Gmail launched into separate task

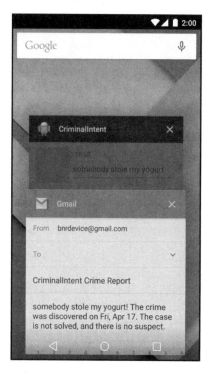

On Lollipop, the implicit intent chooser creates a new, separate task for activities launched with the android.intent.action.SEND or action.intent.action.SEND_MULTIPLE actions. (On older versions of Android, this does not happen, so Gmail's compose activity would have been added directly to CriminalIntent's task.)

This behavior uses a new notion in Lollipop called *concurrent documents*. Concurrent documents allow any number of tasks to be dynamically created for an app at runtime. Prior to Lollipop, apps could only have a predefined set of tasks, each of which had to be named in the manifest.

A prime example of concurrent documents in practice is the Google Drive app. You can open and edit multiple documents, each of which gets its own separate task in the Lollipop overview screen (Figure 22.16). If you were to take the same actions in Google Drive on a pre-Lollipop device, you would only see one task in the overview screen. This is because of the requirement on pre-Lollipop devices to define an app's tasks ahead of time in the manifest. It was not possible pre-Lollipop to generate a dynamic number of tasks for a single app.

Figure 22.16 Multiple Google Drive tasks on Lollipop

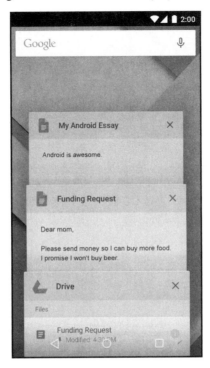

You can start multiple "documents" (tasks) from your own app running on a Lollipop device by either adding the **Intent.FLAG_ACTIVITY_NEW_DOCUMENT** flag to an intent before calling **startActivity(…)** or by setting the documentLaunchMode on the activity in the manifest like so:

```
<activity
    android:name=".CrimePagerActivity"
    android:label="@string/app_name"
    android:parentActivityName=".CrimeListActivity"
    android:documentLaunchMode="intoExisting" />
```

Using this approach, only one task per document will be created (so if you issue an intent with the same data as an already existing task, no new task is created). You can enforce a new task to always be created, even if one already exists for a given document, by either adding the Intent.FLAG_ACTIVITY_MULTIPLE_TASK flag along with the **Intent.FLAG_ACTIVITY_NEW_DOCUMENT** flag before issuing the intent, or by using always as the value for documentLaunchMode in your manifest.

To learn more about the overview screen and changes that were made to it with the Lollipop release, check out https://developer.android.com/guide/components/recents.html.

23

HTTP & Background Tasks

The apps that dominate the brains of users are networked apps. Those people fiddling with their phones instead of talking to each other at dinner? They are maniacally checking their newsfeeds, responding to text messages, or playing networked games.

To get started with networking in Android, you are going to create a new app called PhotoGallery. PhotoGallery is a client for the photo-sharing site Flickr. It will fetch and display the most recent public photos uploaded to Flickr. Figure 23.1 gives you an idea of what the app will look like.

Figure 23.1 Complete PhotoGallery

(We added a filter to our PhotoGallery implementation to show only photos listed on Flickr as having "no known copyright restrictions." Visit `https://www.flickr.com/commons/usage/` to learn more about unrestricted images. All other photos on Flickr are the property of the person who posted them and are subject to usage restrictions depending on the license specified by the owner. To read more about permissions for using third-party content that you retrieve from Flickr, visit `https://www.flickr.com/creativecommons/`.)

You will spend six chapters with PhotoGallery. It will take two chapters for you to get the basics of downloading and parsing JSON and displaying images up and running. Once that is done, in subsequent chapters you will add features that explore search, services, notifications, broadcast receivers, and web views.

In this chapter, you will learn how to use Android's high-level HTTP networking. Almost all day-to-day programming of web services these days is based on the HTTP networking protocol. By the end of the chapter, you will be fetching, parsing, and displaying photo captions from Flickr (Figure 23.2). (Retrieving and displaying photos will happen in Chapter 24.)

Figure 23.2 PhotoGallery at the end of the chapter

Creating PhotoGallery

Create a new Android application project. Configure the app as shown in Figure 23.3.

Figure 23.3 Creating PhotoGallery

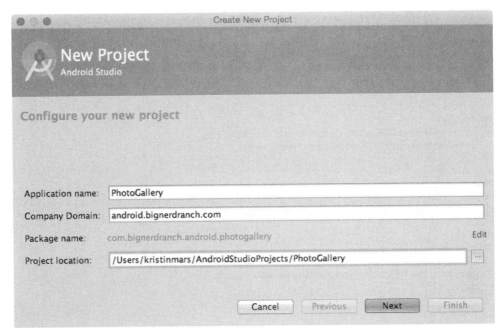

Click Next. When prompted, check Phone and Tablet as the target form factor and choose API 16: Android 4.1 (Jelly Bean) from the Minimum SDK dropdown.

Then have the wizard create a blank activity named **PhotoGalleryActivity**.

PhotoGallery will follow the same architecture you have been using so far. **PhotoGalleryActivity** will be a **SingleFragmentActivity** subclass and its view will be the container view defined in activity_fragment.xml. This activity will host a fragment – in particular, an instance of **PhotoGalleryFragment**, which you will create shortly.

Copy SingleFragmentActivity.java and activity_fragment.xml into your project from a previous project.

In PhotoGalleryActivity.java, set up **PhotoGalleryActivity** as a **SingleFragmentActivity** by deleting the code that the template generated and replacing it with an implementation of **createFragment()**. Have **createFragment()** return an instance of **PhotoGalleryFragment**. (Bear with the error that this code will cause for the moment. It will go away after you create the **PhotoGalleryFragment** class.)

Listing 23.1 Activity setup (PhotoGalleryActivity.java)

```java
public class PhotoGalleryActivity extends Activity SingleFragmentActivity {

    @Override
    protected void onCreate(Bundle savedInstanceState) {
        /* Auto-generated template code... */
    }


    @Override
    public boolean onCreateOptionsMenu(Menu menu) {
        /* Auto-generated template code... */
    }

    @Override
    public boolean onOptionsItemSelected(MenuItem item) {
        /* Auto-generated template code... */
    }

    @Override
    public Fragment createFragment() {
        return PhotoGalleryFragment.newInstance();
    }
}
```

PhotoGallery will display its results in a **RecyclerView**, using the built-in **GridLayoutManager** to arrange the items in a grid.

First, add the RecyclerView library as a dependency, as you did in Chapter 9. Open the Project Structure window and select the app module on the left. Select the Dependencies tab and click the + button. Select Library dependency from the drop-down menu that appears. Find and select the recyclerview-v7 library and click OK.

Rename layout/activity_photo_gallery.xml to layout/fragment_photo_gallery.xml to create a layout for the fragment. Then replace its contents with the **RecyclerView** shown in Figure 23.4.

Figure 23.4 A RecyclerView (layout/fragment_photo_gallery.xml)

```
android.support.v7.widget.RecyclerView
xmlns:android="http://schemas.android.com/apk/res/android"
android:id="@+id/fragment_photo_gallery_recycler_view"
android:layout_width="match_parent"
android:layout_height="match_parent"
```

Finally, create the **PhotoGalleryFragment** class. Retain the fragment, inflate the layout you just created, and initialize a member variable referencing the **RecyclerView** (Listing 23.2).

Listing 23.2 Some skeleton code (PhotoGalleryFragment.java)

```java
public class PhotoGalleryFragment extends Fragment {

    private RecyclerView mPhotoRecyclerView;

    public static PhotoGalleryFragment newInstance() {
        return new PhotoGalleryFragment();
    }

    @Override
    public void onCreate(Bundle savedInstanceState) {
        super.onCreate(savedInstanceState);
        setRetainInstance(true);
    }

    @Override
    public View onCreateView(LayoutInflater inflater, ViewGroup container,
            Bundle savedInstanceState) {
        View v = inflater.inflate(R.layout.fragment_photo_gallery, container, false);

        mPhotoRecyclerView = (RecyclerView) v
                .findViewById(R.id.fragment_photo_gallery_recycler_view);
        mPhotoRecyclerView.setLayoutManager(new GridLayoutManager(getActivity(), 3));

        return v;
    }
}
```

(Wondering why you are retaining the fragment? Hold that thought – we will explain later in the chapter. See the section called "Cleaning up AsyncTasks".)

Fire up PhotoGallery to make sure everything is wired up correctly before moving on. If all is well, you will be the proud owner of a blank screen.

Networking Basics

You are going to have one class handle the networking in PhotoGallery. Create a new Java class and, since you will be connecting to Flickr, name this class **FlickrFetchr**.

FlickrFetchr will start off small with only two methods: **getUrlBytes(String)** and **getUrlString(String)**. The **getUrlBytes(String)** method fetches raw data from a URL and returns it as an array of bytes. The **getUrlString(String)** method converts the result from **getUrlBytes(String)** to a **String**.

In FlickrFetchr.java, add implementations for **getUrlBytes(String)** and **getUrlString(String)** (Listing 23.3).

Listing 23.3 Basic networking code (FlickrFetchr.java)

```java
public class FlickrFetchr {
    public byte[] getUrlBytes(String urlSpec) throws IOException {
        URL url = new URL(urlSpec);
        HttpURLConnection connection = (HttpURLConnection)url.openConnection();

        try {
            ByteArrayOutputStream out = new ByteArrayOutputStream();
            InputStream in = connection.getInputStream();

            if (connection.getResponseCode() != HttpURLConnection.HTTP_OK) {
                throw new IOException(connection.getResponseMessage() +
                        ": with " +
                        urlSpec);
            }

            int bytesRead = 0;
            byte[] buffer = new byte[1024];
            while ((bytesRead = in.read(buffer)) > 0) {
                out.write(buffer, 0, bytesRead);
            }
            out.close();
            return out.toByteArray();
        } finally {
            connection.disconnect();
        }
    }

    public String getUrlString(String urlSpec) throws IOException {
        return new String(getUrlBytes(urlSpec));
    }
}
```

This code creates a **URL** object from a string – like, say, https://www.bignerdranch.com. Then it calls **openConnection()** to create a connection object pointed at the URL. **URL.openConnection()** returns a **URLConnection**, but because you are connecting to an http URL, you can cast it to **HttpURLConnection**. This gives you HTTP-specific interfaces for working with request methods, response codes, streaming methods, and more.

HttpURLConnection represents a connection, but it will not actually connect to your endpoint until you call **getInputStream()** (or **getOutputStream()** for POST calls). Until then, you cannot get a valid response code.

Once you create your URL and open a connection, you call **read()** repeatedly until your connection runs out of data. The **InputStream** will yield bytes as they are available. When you are done, you close it and spit out your **ByteArrayOutputStream**'s byte array.

While **getUrlBytes(String)** does the heavy lifting, **getUrlString(String)** is what you will actually use in this chapter. It converts the bytes fetched by **getUrlBytes(String)** into a **String**. Right now, it may seem strange to split this work into two methods. However, having two methods will be useful in the next chapter when you start downloading image data.

Asking permission to network

One other thing is required to get networking up and running: you have to ask permission. Just as users would not want you secretly taking their pictures, they also do not want you to secretly download ASCII pictures of farm animals.

To ask permission to network, add the following permission to your AndroidManifest.xml.

Listing 23.4 Adding networking permission to manifest (AndroidManifest.xml)

```
<manifest
    xmlns:android="http://schemas.android.com/apk/res/android"
    package="com.bignerdranch.android.photogallery" >

  <uses-permission android:name="android.permission.INTERNET" />

  <application
    ...
  </application>

</manifest>
```

When a user tries to download your app, a dialog showing these permissions is displayed. The user can then accept or deny installation.

This is not a great system. Your app may have a legitimate but not immediately obvious reason for requesting a permission. And if users do not like any particular permission request, their only option is to remove the entire app.

The upcoming Android M release has a fix for these problems. In M, you can ask permission at the time you first need it, not just when the app is installed. Also, users can revoke individual permissions at any time.

For permissions you cannot do without (like internet access in PhotoGallery), the old behavior is still best: prompt the user at app install. But for less obvious or less critical permissions, the newer style of request is much kinder.

Using AsyncTask to Run on a Background Thread

The next step is to call and test the networking code you just added. However, you cannot simply call **FlickrFetchr.getUrlString(String)** directly in **PhotoGalleryFragment**. Instead, you need to create a background thread and run your code there.

The easiest way to work with a background thread is with a utility class called **AsyncTask**. **AsyncTask** creates a background thread for you and runs the code in the **doInBackground(…)** method on that thread.

In PhotoGalleryFragment.java, add a new inner class called **FetchItemsTask** at the bottom of **PhotoGalleryFragment**. Override **AsyncTask.doInBackground(…)** to get data from a website and log it.

Listing 23.5 Writing an **AsyncTask**, part I (PhotoGalleryFragment.java)

```java
public class PhotoGalleryFragment extends Fragment {

    private static final String TAG = "PhotoGalleryFragment";

    private RecyclerView mPhotoRecyclerView;

    ...

    private class FetchItemsTask extends AsyncTask<Void,Void,Void> {
        @Override
        protected Void doInBackground(Void... params) {
            try {
                String result = new FlickrFetchr()
                        .getUrlString("https://www.bignerdranch.com");
                Log.i(TAG, "Fetched contents of URL: " + result);
            } catch (IOException ioe) {
                Log.e(TAG, "Failed to fetch URL: ", ioe);
            }
            return null;
        }
    }
}
```

Now, in **PhotoGalleryFragment.onCreate(…)**, call **execute()** on a new instance of **FetchItemsTask**.

Listing 23.6 Writing an **AsyncTask**, part II (PhotoGalleryFragment.java)

```java
public class PhotoGalleryFragment extends Fragment {

    private static final String TAG = "PhotoGalleryFragment";

    private RecyclerView mPhotoRecyclerView;

    @Override
    public void onCreate(Bundle savedInstanceState) {
        super.onCreate(savedInstanceState);
        setRetainInstance(true);
        new FetchItemsTask().execute();
    }

    ...
}
```

The call to **execute()** will start your **AsyncTask**, which will then fire up its background thread and call **doInBackground(…)**. Run your code and you should see the amazing Big Nerd Ranch home page HTML pop up in LogCat, as shown in Figure 23.5.

Figure 23.5 Big Nerd Ranch HTML in LogCat

Finding your log statements within the LogCat window can be tricky. It helps to search for something specific. In this case, enter "PhotoGalleryFragment" into the LogCat search box, as shown.

Now that you have created a background thread and run some networking code on it, let's take a closer look at threads in Android.

You and Your Main Thread

Networking does not happen immediately. A web server may take as long as a second or two to respond, and a file download can take even longer than that. Because networking can take so long, Android disallows all networking on the *main thread*. If you try to do it, Android will throw a NetworkOnMainThreadException.

Why? To understand that, you need to understand what a thread is, what the main thread is, and what the main thread does.

A thread is a single sequence of execution. Code running within a single thread will execute one step after another. Every Android app starts life with a *main thread*. The main thread, however, is not a preordained list of steps. Instead, it sits in an infinite loop and waits for events initiated by the user or the system. Then it executes code in response to those events as they occur (Figure 23.6).

Figure 23.6 Regular threads vs. the main thread

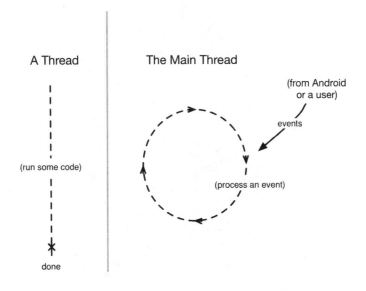

Imagine that your app is an enormous shoe store, and that you only have one employee – The Flash. (Who hasn't dreamed of that?) There are a lot of things to do in a store to keep the customers happy: arranging the merchandise, fetching shoes for customers, wielding the Brannock device. With The Flash as your salesperson, everyone is taken care of in a timely fashion, even though there is only one guy doing all the work.

For this situation to work, The Flash cannot spend too much time doing any one thing. What if a shipment of shoes goes missing? Someone will have to spend a lot of time on the phone straightening it out. Your customers will get mighty impatient waiting for shoes while The Flash is on hold.

The Flash is like the main thread in your application. It runs all the code that updates the UI. This includes the code executed in response to different UI-related events – activity startup, button presses, and so on. (Because the events are all related to the user interface in some way, the main thread is sometimes called the *UI thread*.)

The event loop keeps the UI code in sequence. It makes sure that none of these operations step on each other while still ensuring that the code is executed in a timely fashion. So far, all of the code you have written (except for the code you just wrote with `AsyncTask`) has been executed on the main thread.

Beyond the main thread

Networking is a lot like a phone call to your shoe distributor: it takes a long time compared to other tasks. During that time, the user interface will be completely unresponsive, which might result in an *application not responding*, or *ANR*.

An ANR occurs when Android's watchdog determines that the main thread has failed to respond to an important event, like pressing the Back button. To the user, it looks like Figure 23.7.

Figure 23.7 Application not responding

In your store, you would solve the problem by (naturally) hiring a second Flash to call the shoe distributor. In Android, you do something similar – you create a *background thread* and access the network from there.

And what is the easiest way to work with a background thread? Why, `AsyncTask`.

You will get to see other things `AsyncTask` can do later this chapter. Before you do that, you will want to do some real work with your networking code.

Fetching JSON from Flickr

JSON stands for JavaScript Object Notation, a format that has become popular in recent years, particularly for web services. Android includes the standard `org.json` package, which has classes that provide simple access to creating and parsing JSON text. The Android developer documentation has information about `org.json`, and you can get more information about JSON as a format at `http://json.org`.

Flickr offers a fine JSON API. All the details you need are available in the documentation at `http://www.flickr.com/services/api/`. Pull it up in your favorite web browser and find the list of Request Formats. You will be using the simplest – REST. This tells you that the API endpoint is `https://api.flickr.com/services/rest/`. You can invoke the methods Flickr provides on this endpoint.

Back on the main page of the API documentation, find the list of API Methods. Scroll down to the photos section, then locate and click on flickr.photos.getRecent. The documentation will report that this method "Returns a list of the latest public photos uploaded to flickr." That is exactly what you need for PhotoGallery.

The only required parameter for the **getRecent** method is an API key. To get an API key, return to `http://www.flickr.com/services/api/` and follow the link for API keys. You will need a Yahoo ID to log in. Once you are logged in, request a new, noncommercial API key. This usually only takes a moment. Your API key will look something like `4f721bgafa75bf6d2cb9af54f937bb70`. (You do not need the "Secret," which is only used when an app will access user-specific information or images.)

Once you have a key, you have all you need to make a request to the Flickr web service. Your GET request URL will look something like this:

```
https://api.flickr.com/services/rest/?
method=flickr.photos.getRecent&api_key=xxx&format=json&nojsoncallback=1.
```

The Flickr response is in XML format by default. In order to get a valid JSON response you need to specify values for both the `format` and `nojsoncallback` parameters. Setting `nojsoncallback` to 1 tells Flickr to exclude the enclosing method name and parentheses from the response it sends back. This is necessary so that your Java code can more easily parse the response.

Copy the example URL into your browser, replacing the "xxx" value provided for the api_key with your actual API key. This will allow you to see an example of what the response data will look like, as shown in Figure 23.8.

Figure 23.8 Example JSON output

← → C 🔒 https://api.flickr.com/services/rest/? method=flickr.photos.getRecent&api_key=xxx&format=json&nojsoncallback=1 ≡

{"photos":{"page":1,"pages":1,"perpage":100,"total":"41","photo":
[{"id":"9452133594","owner":"44494372@N05","secret":"d6d20af93e","server":"7365","farm":8,"title":"Low and Wisoff at
Work","ispublic":1,"isfriend":0,"isfamily":0},
{"id":"16317817559","owner":"44494372@N05","secret":"137d97804f","server":"8683","farm":9,"title":"Challenger as seen
from SPAS","ispublic":1,"isfriend":0,"isfamily":0},
{"id":"15882247283","owner":"44494372@N05","secret":"31f4fae842","server":"8624","farm":9,"title":"FIDO Rover
Retracted Arm and Camera","ispublic":1,"isfriend":0,"isfamily":0},
{"id":"16501394292","owner":"44494372@N05","secret":"d9920b4d04","server":"8674","farm":9,"title":"FIDO
Rover","ispublic":1,"isfriend":0,"isfamily":0},
{"id":"7544561540","owner":"44494372@N05","secret":"ed09f6cbdf","server":"8288","farm":9,"title":"Two Hours Before
First Neptune Flyby","ispublic":1,"isfriend":0,"isfamily":0},
{"id":"15081066390","owner":"44494372@N05","secret":"c9395321ef","server":"3844","farm":4,"title":"STS-
88","ispublic":1,"isfriend":0,"isfamily":0},
{"id":"9458246017","owner":"44494372@N05","secret":"bc548a6979","server":"2875","farm":3,"title":"Hubble
Redeployment","ispublic":1,"isfriend":0,"isfamily":0},
{"id":"9465001813","owner":"44494372@N05","secret":"be2c6aa9a4","server":"5458","farm":6,"title":"NASA Robot Brain
Surgeon","ispublic":1,"isfriend":0,"isfamily":0},
{"id":"8981696202","owner":"44494372@N05","secret":"1447feb7af","server":"7441","farm":8,"title":"Mars Science

Time to start coding. First, add some constants to **FlickrFetchr**.

Listing 23.7 Adding constants (FlickrFetchr.java)

```
public class FlickrFetchr {

    private static final String TAG = "FlickrFetchr";

    private static final String API_KEY = "yourApiKeyHere";
    ...
}
```

Make sure to replace yourApiKeyHere with the API key you generated earlier.

Now use the constants to write a method that builds an appropriate request URL and fetches its contents.

Listing 23.8 Adding **fetchItems()** method (FlickrFetchr.java)

```
public class FlickrFetchr {

    ...

    String getUrlString(String urlSpec) throws IOException {
        return new String(getUrlBytes(urlSpec));
    }

    public void fetchItems() {
        try {
            String url = Uri.parse("https://api.flickr.com/services/rest/")
                    .buildUpon()
                    .appendQueryParameter("method", "flickr.photos.getRecent")
                    .appendQueryParameter("api_key", API_KEY)
                    .appendQueryParameter("format", "json")
                    .appendQueryParameter("nojsoncallback", "1")
                    .appendQueryParameter("extras", "url_s")
                    .build().toString();
            String jsonString = getUrlString(url);
            Log.i(TAG, "Received JSON: " + jsonString);
        } catch (IOException ioe) {
            Log.e(TAG, "Failed to fetch items", ioe);
        }
    }
}
```

Here you use a **Uri.Builder** to build the complete URL for your Flickr API request.
Uri.Builder is a convenience class for creating properly escaped parameterized URLs.
Uri.Builder.appendQueryParameter(String, String) will automatically escape query strings for you.

Notice you added values for the method, api_key, format, and nojsoncallback parameters. You also specified one extra parameter called extras, with a value of url_s. Specifying the url_s extra tells Flickr to include the URL for the small version of the picture if it is available.

Finally, modify the **AsyncTask** in **PhotoGalleryFragment** to call the new **fetchItems()** method.

Listing 23.9 Calling `fetchItems()` (PhotoGalleryFragment.java)

```java
public class PhotoGalleryFragment extends Fragment {

    ...

    private class FetchItemsTask extends AsyncTask<Void,Void,Void> {
        @Override
        protected Void doInBackground(Void... params) {
            try {
                String result = new FlickrFetchr()
                        .getUrlString("https://www.bignerdranch.com");
                Log.i(TAG, "Fetched contents of URL: " + result);
            } catch (IOException ioe) {
                Log.e(TAG, "Failed to fetch URL: ", ioe);
            }
            new FlickrFetchr().fetchItems();
            return null;
        }
    }
}
```

Run PhotoGallery and you should see rich, fertile Flickr JSON in LogCat, like Figure 23.9. (It will help to search for "FlickrFetchr" in the LogCat search box.)

Figure 23.9 Flickr JSON in LogCat

Unfortunately the Android Studio LogCat window does not wrap the output nicely as of this writing. Scroll to the right to see more of the extremely long JSON response string. (LogCat can be finicky. Do not panic if you do not get results like ours. Sometimes the connection to the emulator is not quite right and the log messages do not get printed out. Usually it clears up over time, but sometimes you have to rerun your application or even restart your emulator.)

Now that you have such fine JSON from Flickr, what should you do with it? You do what you do with all data – put it in one or more model objects. The model class you are going to create for PhotoGallery is called **GalleryItem**. Figure 23.10 shows an object diagram of PhotoGallery.

Figure 23.10 Object diagram of PhotoGallery

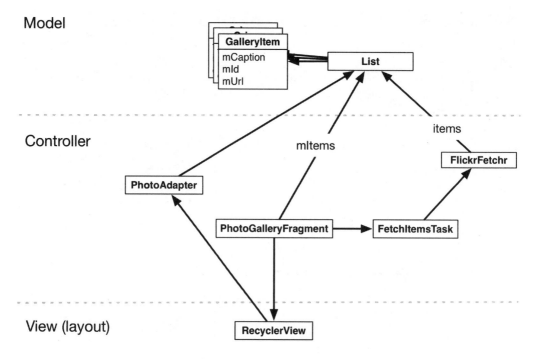

Note that Figure 23.10 does not show the hosting activity so that it can focus on the fragment and the networking code.

Create the **GalleryItem** class and add the following code:

Listing 23.10 Creating model object class (GalleryItem.java)

```java
public class GalleryItem {
    private String mCaption;
    private String mId;
    private String mUrl;

    @Override
    public String toString() {
        return mCaption;
    }
}
```

Have Android Studio generate getters and setters for mCaption, mId, and mUrl.

Now that you have made model objects, it is time to fill them with data from the JSON you got from Flickr.

Parsing JSON text

The JSON response displayed in your browser and LogCat window is hard to read. If you *pretty print* (format with white space) the response, it looks something like Figure 23.11.

Figure 23.11 JSON hierarchy

```
{
    "photos": {
        "page": 1,
        "pages": 10,
        "perpage": 100,
        "total": 1000,
        "photo": [
            {
                "id": "9452133594",
                "owner": "44494372@N05",
                "secret": "d6d20af93e",
                "server": "7365",
                "farm": 8,
                "title": "Low and Wisoff at Work",
                "ispublic": 1,
                "isfriend": 0,
                "isfamily": 0
            }, ...
            {
                "id": "16317817559",
                "owner": "44494372@N05",
                "secret": "137d97804f",
                "server": "8683",
                "farm": 9,
                "title": "Challenger as seen from SPAS",
                "ispublic": 1,
                "isfriend": 0,
                "isfamily": 0
            }
        ]
    },
    "stat": "ok"
}
```

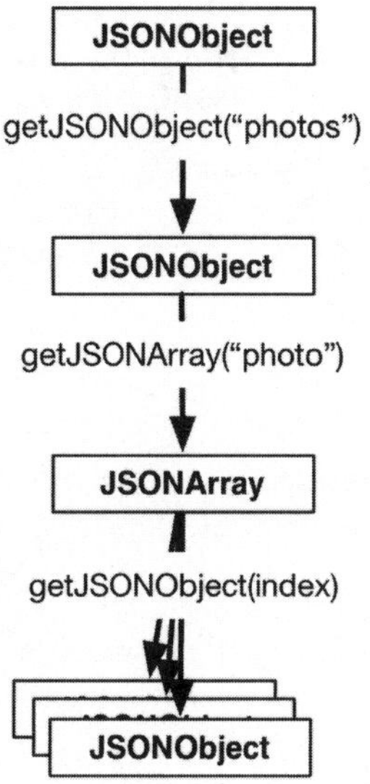

JSONObject

getJSONObject("photos")

JSONObject

getJSONArray("photo")

JSONArray

getJSONObject(index)

JSONObject

A JSON object is a set of name-value pairs enclosed between curly braces, { }. A JSON array is a comma-separated list of JSON objects enclosed in square brackets, [ ]. You can have objects nested within each other, resulting in a hierarchy.

The json.org API provides Java objects corresponding to JSON text, such as **JSONObject** and **JSONArray**. You can easily parse JSON text into corresponding Java objects using the **JSONObject(String)** constructor. Update **fetchItems()** to do just that.

Listing 23.11 Reading JSON string into **JSONObject** (FlickrFetchr.java)

```
public class FlickrFetchr {

    private static final String TAG = "FlickrFetchr";

    ...

    public void fetchItems() {
        try {
            ...
            Log.i(TAG, "Received JSON: " + jsonString);
            JSONObject jsonBody = new JSONObject(jsonString);
        } catch (JSONException je){
            Log.e(TAG, "Failed to parse JSON", je);
        } catch (IOException ioe) {
            Log.e(TAG, "Failed to fetch items", ioe);
        }
    }

}
```

The **JSONObject** constructor parses the JSON string you passed it, resulting in an object hierarchy that maps to the original JSON text. The object hierarchy for the JSON returned from Flickr is shown in Figure 23.11.

Here you have a top-level **JSONObject** that maps to the outermost curly braces in the original JSON text. This top-level object contains a nested **JSONObject** named photos. Within this nested **JSONObject** is a **JSONArray** named photo. This array contains a collection of **JSONObject**s, each representing metadata for a single photo.

Write a method that pulls out information for each photo. Make a **GalleryItem** for each photo and add it to a **List**.

Listing 23.12 Parsing Flickr photos (`FlickrFetchr.java`)

```java
public class FlickrFetchr {

    private static final String TAG = "FlickrFetchr";

    ...

    public void fetchItems() {
        ...
    }

    private void parseItems(List<GalleryItem> items, JSONObject jsonBody)
            throws IOException, JSONException {

        JSONObject photosJsonObject = jsonBody.getJSONObject("photos");
        JSONArray photoJsonArray = photosJsonObject.getJSONArray("photo");

        for (int i = 0; i < photoJsonArray.length(); i++) {
            JSONObject photoJsonObject = photoJsonArray.getJSONObject(i);

            GalleryItem item = new GalleryItem();
            item.setId(photoJsonObject.getString("id"));
            item.setCaption(photoJsonObject.getString("title"));

            if (!photoJsonObject.has("url_s")) {
                continue;
            }

            item.setUrl(photoJsonObject.getString("url_s"));
            items.add(item);
        }
    }

}
```

This code uses convenience methods such as **getJSONObject(String name)** and **getJSONArray(String name)** to navigate the **JSONObject** hierarchy. (These methods are also annotated on Figure 23.11.)

Flickr does not always return a url_s component for each image. You add a check here to ignore images that do not have an image url.

The **parseItems(…)** method needs a **List** and **JSONObject**. Update **fetchItems()** to call **parseItems(…)** and return a **List** of **GalleryItem**s.

Listing 23.13 Calling **parseItems(…)** (FlickrFetchr.java)

```java
public void List<GalleryItem> fetchItems() {

    List<GalleryItem> items = new ArrayList<>();

    try {
        String url = ...;
        String jsonString = getUrlString(url);
        Log.i(TAG, "Received JSON: " + jsonString);
        JSONObject jsonBody = new JSONObject(jsonString);
        parseItems(items, jsonBody);
    } catch (JSONException je) {
            Log.e(TAG, "Failed to parse JSON", je);
    } catch (IOException ioe) {
        Log.e(TAG, "Failed to fetch items", ioe);
    }

    return items;
}
```

Run PhotoGallery to test your JSON parsing code. PhotoGallery has no way of reporting the contents of your **List** right now, so you will need to set a breakpoint and use the debugger if you want to make sure everything worked correctly.

From AsyncTask Back to the Main Thread

To finish off, let's switch to the view layer and get **PhotoGalleryFragment**'s **RecyclerView** to display some captions.

First define a **ViewHolder** as an inner class.

Listing 23.14 Adding a **ViewHolder** implementation (PhotoGalleryFragment.java)

```java
public class PhotoGalleryFragment extends Fragment {

    private static final String TAG = "PhotoGalleryFragment";

    ...

    private class PhotoHolder extends RecyclerView.ViewHolder {
        private TextView mTitleTextView;

        public PhotoHolder(View itemView) {
            super(itemView);

            mTitleTextView = (TextView) itemView;
        }

        public void bindGalleryItem(GalleryItem item) {
            mTitleTextView.setText(item.toString());
        }
    }

    private class FetchItemsTask extends AsyncTask<Void,Void,Void> {
        ...
    }
}
```

Next, add a `RecyclerView.Adapter` to provide `PhotoHolder`s as needed based on a list of `GalleryItem`s.

Listing 23.15 Adding a **RecyclerView.Adapter** implementation (PhotoGalleryFragment.java)

```java
public class PhotoGalleryFragment extends Fragment {

    private static final String TAG = "PhotoGalleryFragment";

    ...

    private class PhotoHolder extends RecyclerView.ViewHolder {
        ...
    }

    private class PhotoAdapter extends RecyclerView.Adapter<PhotoHolder> {

        private List<GalleryItem> mGalleryItems;

        public PhotoAdapter(List<GalleryItem> galleryItems) {
            mGalleryItems = galleryItems;
        }

        @Override
        public PhotoHolder onCreateViewHolder(ViewGroup viewGroup, int viewType) {
            TextView textView = new TextView(getActivity());
            return new PhotoHolder(textView);
        }

        @Override
        public void onBindViewHolder(PhotoHolder photoHolder, int position) {
            GalleryItem galleryItem = mGalleryItems.get(position);
            photoHolder.bindGalleryItem(galleryItem);
        }

        @Override
        public int getItemCount() {
            return mGalleryItems.size();
        }
    }

    ...
}
```

Now that you have the appropriate nuts and bolts in place for `RecyclerView`, add code to set up and attach an adapter when appropriate.

Listing 23.16 Implementing **setupAdapter()** (PhotoGalleryFragment.java)

```java
public class PhotoGalleryFragment extends Fragment {

    private static final String TAG = "PhotoGalleryFragment";

    private RecyclerView mPhotoRecyclerView;
    private List<GalleryItem> mItems = new ArrayList<>();

    ...

    @Override
    public View onCreateView(LayoutInflater inflater, ViewGroup container,
                             Bundle savedInstanceState) {
        View v = inflater.inflate(R.layout.fragment_photo_gallery, container, false);
        mPhotoRecyclerView = (RecyclerView) v
            .findViewById(R.id.fragment_photo_gallery_recycler_view);
        mPhotoRecyclerView.setLayoutManager(new GridLayoutManager(getActivity(), 3));

        setupAdapter();

        return v;
    }

    private void setupAdapter() {
        if (isAdded()) {
            mPhotoRecyclerView.setAdapter(new PhotoAdapter(mItems));
        }
    }

    ...

}
```

The **setupAdapter()** method you just added looks at the current model state, namely the **List** of **GalleryItem**s, and configures the adapter appropriately on your **RecyclerView**. You call **setupAdapter()** in **onCreateView(…)** so that every time a new **RecyclerView** is created, it is reconfigured with an appropriate adapter. You also want to call it every time your set of model objects changes.

Notice that you check to see whether **isAdded()** is true before setting the adapter. This confirms that the fragment has been attached to an activity, and in turn that **getActivity()** will not be null.

Remember that fragments can exist unattached to any activity. Before now, this possibility has not come up because your method calls have been driven by callbacks from the framework. In this scenario, if a fragment is receiving callbacks, then it definitely is attached to an activity. No activity, no callbacks.

However, now that you are using an **AsyncTask** you are triggering some callbacks from a background thread. Thus you cannot assume that the fragment is attached to an activity. You must check to make sure that your fragment is still attached. If it is not, then operations that rely on that activity (like creating your **PhotoAdapter**, which in turn creates a **TextView** using the hosting activity as the context) will fail. This is why, in your code above, you check that **isAdded()** is true before setting the adapter.

Now you need to call **setupAdapter()** after data has been fetched from Flickr. Your first instinct might be to call **setupAdapter()** at the end of **FetchItemsTask**'s **doInBackground(…)**. This is not a good idea. Remember that you have two Flashes in the store now – one helping multiple customers, and one on the phone with Flickr. What will happen if the second Flash tries to help customers after hanging up the phone? Odds are good that the two Flashes will step on each other's toes.

On a computer, this toe-stepping-on results in objects in memory becoming corrupted. Because of this, you are not allowed to update the UI from a background thread, nor is it safe or advisable to do so.

What to do? **AsyncTask** has another method you can override called **onPostExecute(…)**. **onPostExecute(…)** is run after **doInBackground(…)** completes. More importantly, **onPostExecute(…)** is run on the main thread, not the background thread, so it is safe to update the UI within it.

Modify **FetchItemsTask** to update mItems and call **setupAdapter()** after fetching your photos to update the **RecyclerView**'s data source.

Listing 23.17 Adding adapter update code (PhotoGalleryFragment.java)

```
private class FetchItemsTask extends AsyncTask<Void,Void,Void List<GalleryItem>> {
    @Override
    protected Void List<GalleryItem> doInBackground(Void... params) {

        return new FlickrFetchr().fetchItems();
        return null;
    }

    @Override
    protected void onPostExecute(List<GalleryItem> items) {
        mItems = items;
        setupAdapter();
    }
}
```

You made three changes here. First, you changed the type of the **FetchItemsTask**'s third generic parameter. This parameter is the type of result produced by your **AsyncTask**. It sets the type of value returned by **doInBackground(…)** as well as the type of **onPostExecute(…)**'s input parameter.

Second, you modified **doInBackground(…)** to return your list of **GalleryItem**s. By doing this you fix your code so that it compiles properly. You also pass your list of items off so that it may be used from within **onPostExecute(…)**.

Finally, you added an implementation of **onPostExecute(…)**. This method accepts as input the list you fetched and returned inside **doInBackground(…)**, puts it in mItems, and updates your **RecyclerView**'s adapter.

With that, your work for this chapter is complete. Run, and you should see text displayed for each **GalleryItem** you downloaded (similar to Figure 23.2).

Cleaning Up AsyncTasks

In this chapter, your **AsyncTask** and other code was carefully structured so that you would not have to keep track of the **AsyncTask** instance. For example, you retained the fragment (called setRetainInstance(true)) so that rotation does not repeatedly fire off new **AsyncTask**s to fetch the JSON data. However, in other situations you will need to keep a handle on your **AsyncTask**s, even canceling and rerunning them at times.

For these more complicated uses, you will want to assign your **AsyncTask** to an instance variable. Once you have a handle on it, you can call **AsyncTask.cancel(boolean)**. This method allows you to cancel an ongoing **AsyncTask**.

AsyncTask.cancel(boolean) can work in a more rude or less rude fashion. If you call **cancel(false)**, it will be polite and simply set **isCancelled()** to true. The **AsyncTask** can then check **isCancelled()** inside of **doInBackground(…)** and elect to finish prematurely.

If you call **cancel(true)**, however, it will be impolite and interrupt the thread **doInBackground(…)** is on, if it is currently running. **AsyncTask.cancel(true)** is a more severe way of stopping the **AsyncTask**. If you can avoid it, you should.

When and where should you cancel your **AsyncTask**? It depends. First ask yourself, should the work the **AsyncTask** is doing stop if the fragment or activity is destroyed or goes out of view? If so, you should cancel the **AsyncTask** instance in either **onStop(…)** (to cancel the task when the view is no longer visible) or **onDestroy(…)** (to cancel the task when the fragment/activity instance is destroyed).

What if you want the work the **AsyncTask** is doing to survive the life of the fragment/activity and its view? You could just let the **AsyncTask** run to completion, without canceling. However, this has potential for memory leaks (e.g., the **Activity** instance being kept alive past when it should have been destroyed) or problems related to updating or accessing the UI when it is in an invalid state. If you have important work that must be completed regardless of what the user is doing, it is better to consider alternative options, such as launching a **Service** (you will learn more about this in Chapter 26).

For the More Curious: More on AsyncTask

In this chapter you saw how to use the last type parameter on **AsyncTask**, which specifies the return type. What about the other two?

The first type parameter allows you to specify the type of input parameters you will pass to the **execute()**, which in turn dictates the type of input parameters **doInBackground(…)** will receive. You would use it in the following way:

```
AsyncTask<String,Void,Void> task = new AsyncTask<String,Void,Void>() {
    public Void doInBackground(String... params) {
        for (String parameter : params) {
            Log.i(TAG, "Received parameter: " + parameter);
        }

        return null;
    }
};
```

Input parameters are passed in to the **execute(…)** method, which takes in a variable number of arguments:

```
task.execute("First parameter", "Second parameter", "Etc.");
```

Those variable arguments are then passed on to **doInBackground(…)**.

The second type parameter allows you to specify the type for sending progress updates. Here is what the code pieces look like:

```
final ProgressBar gestationProgressBar = /* A determinate progress bar */;
gestationProgressBar.setMax(42); /* max allowed gestation period */

AsyncTask<Void,Integer,Void> haveABaby = new AsyncTask<Void,Integer,Void>() {
    public Void doInBackground(Void... params) {
        while (!babyIsBorn()) {
            Integer weeksPassed = getNumberOfWeeksPassed();
            publishProgress(weeksPassed);
            patientlyWaitForBaby();
        }
    }

    public void onProgressUpdate(Integer... params) {
        int progress = params[0];
        gestationProgressBar.setProgress(progress);
    }
};

/* call when you want to execute the AsyncTask */
haveABaby.execute();
```

Progress updates usually happen in the middle of an ongoing background process. The problem is that you cannot make the necessary UI updates inside that background process. So **AsyncTask** provides **publishProgress(…)** and **onProgressUpdate(…)**.

Here is how it works: you call **publishProgress(…)** from **doInBackground(…)** in the background thread. This will make **onProgressUpdate(…)** be called on the UI thread. So you can do your UI updates in **onProgressUpdate(…)**, but control them from **doInBackground(…)** with **publishProgress(…)**.

For the More Curious: Alternatives to AsyncTask

If you use an **AsyncTask** to load data, you are responsible for managing its lifecycle during configuration changes, such as rotation, and stashing its data somewhere that lives through them. Often, this is simplified by using **setRetainInstance(true)** on a **Fragment** and storing the data there, but there are still situations where you have to intervene and code you have to write in order to ensure that everything happens correctly. Such situations include the user pressing the Back button while the **AsyncTask** is running, or the fragment that launched the **AsyncTask** getting destroyed during execution by the OS due to a low-memory situation.

Using a **Loader** is an alternative solution that takes some (but not all) of this responsibility off your hands. A loader is designed to load some kind of data (an object) from some source. The source could be a disk, a database, a **ContentProvider**, the network, or another process.

AsyncTaskLoader is an abstract **Loader** that uses an **AsyncTask** to move the work of loading data to another thread. Almost all useful loader classes you create will be a subclass of **AsyncTaskLoader**. The **AsyncTaskLoader** will do the job of fetching the data without blocking the main thread and delivering the results to whomever is interested.

Why would you use a loader instead of, say, an **AsyncTask** directly? Well, the most compelling reason is that the **LoaderManager** will keep your component's loaders alive, along with their data, between configuration changes like rotation. **LoaderManager** is responsible for starting, stopping, and maintaining the lifecycle of any **Loader**s associated with your component.

If, after a configuration change, you initialize a loader that has already finished loading its data, it can deliver that data immediately rather than trying to fetch it again. This works whether your fragment is retained or not, which can make your life easier because you do not have to consider the lifecycle complications that retained fragments can introduce.

Challenge: Gson

Deserializing JSON in Java objects, as you did in Listing 23.12, is a common task in app development regardless of the platform. Lots of smart people have created libraries to simplify the process of converting JSON text to Java objects and back again.

One such library is Gson (https://github.com/google/gson). Gson maps JSON data to Java objects for you automatically. This means you do not need to write any parsing code. For this reason, Gson is currently our favorite JSON parsing library.

For this challenge, simplify your JSON parsing code in **FlickrFetchr** by incorporating the Gson library into your app.

Challenge: Paging

By default, getRecent returns one page of 100 results. There is an additional parameter you can use called page that will let you return page two, three, and so on.

For this challenge, implement a **RecyclerView.OnScrollListener** that detects when you are at the end of your results and replaces the current page with the next page of results. For a slightly harder challenge, append subsequent pages to your results.

Challenge: Dynamically Adjusting the Number of Columns

Currently the number of columns displayed in the grid is fixed at three. Update your code to provide a dynamic number of columns so more columns appear in landscape and on larger devices.

A simple approach could involve providing an integer resource qualified for different orientations and/or screen sizes. This is similar to how you provided different layouts for different screen sizes in Chapter 17. Integer resources should be placed in the res/values folder(s). Check out the Android developer documentation for more details.

Providing qualified resources does not offer much in the way of granularity. For a more difficult challenge (and more flexible implementation), calculate and set the number of columns each time the fragment's view is created. Calculate the number of columns based on the current width of the **RecyclerView** and some predetermined constant column width.

There is only one catch: you cannot calculate the number of columns in **onCreateView()** because the **RecyclerView** will not be sized yet. Instead, implement a **ViewTreeObserver.OnGlobalLayoutListener** and put your column calculation code in **onGlobalLayout()**. Add the listener to your **RecyclerView** using **addOnGlobalLayoutListener()**.

24

Loopers, Handlers, and HandlerThread

Now that you have downloaded and parsed JSON from Flickr, your next task is to download and display images. In this chapter, you will learn how to use **Looper**, **Handler**, and **HandlerThread** to dynamically download and display photos in PhotoGallery.

Preparing RecyclerView to Display Images

The current **PhotoHolder** in **PhotoGalleryFragment** simply provides **TextView**s for the **RecyclerView**'s **GridLayoutManager** to display. Each **TextView** displays the caption of a **GalleryItem**.

To display photos, update **PhotoHolder** to provide **ImageView**s instead. Eventually, each **ImageView** will display a photo downloaded from the mUrl of a **GalleryItem**.

Start by creating a new layout file for your gallery items called gallery_item.xml. This layout will consist of a single **ImageView** (Figure 24.1).

Figure 24.1 Gallery item layout (res/layout/gallery_item.xml)

```
ImageView
xmlns:android="http://schemas.android.com/apk/res/android"
android:id="@+id/fragment_photo_gallery_image_view"
android:layout_width="match_parent"
android:layout_height="120dp"
android:layout_gravity="center"
android:scaleType="centerCrop"
```

These **ImageView**s will be managed by **RecyclerView**'s **GridLayoutManager**, which means that their width will vary. Their height, on the other hand, will remain fixed. To make the most of the **ImageView**'s space, you have set its scaleType to centerCrop. This setting centers the image and then scales it up so that the smaller dimension is equal to the view and the larger one is cropped on both sides.

Next, update **PhotoHolder** to hold an **ImageView** instead of a **TextView**. Replace **bindGalleryItem()** with a method to set the **ImageView**'s **Drawable**.

429

Listing 24.1 Updating **PhotoHolder** (PhotoGalleryFragment.java)

...

```
private class PhotoHolder extends RecyclerView.ViewHolder {
    private TextView mTitleTextView ImageView mItemImageView;

    public PhotoHolder(View itemView) {
        super(itemView);

        mTitleTextView = (TextView) itemView;
        mItemImageView = (ImageView) itemView
                .findViewById(R.id.fragment_photo_gallery_image_view);
    }

    public void bindGalleryItem(GalleryItem item) {
        mTitleTextView.setText(item.toString());
    }

    public void bindDrawable(Drawable drawable) {
        mItemImageView.setImageDrawable(drawable);
    }
}
```

...

Previously the **PhotoHolder** constructor assumed it would be passed a **TextView** directly. The new version instead expects a view hierarchy that contains an **ImageView** with the resource ID R.id.fragment_photo_gallery_image_view.

Update **PhotoAdapter**'s **onCreateViewHolder()** to inflate the gallery_item file you created and pass it to **PhotoHolder**'s constructor.

Listing 24.2 Updating **PhotoAdapter**'s **onCreateViewHolder()** (PhotoGalleryFragment.java)

```
public class PhotoGalleryFragment extends Fragment {
  ...

  private class PhotoAdapter extends RecyclerView.Adapter<PhotoHolder> {
      ...

      @Override
      public PhotoHolder onCreateViewHolder(ViewGroup viewGroup, int viewType) {
          TextView textView = new TextView(getActivity());
          return new PhotoHolder(textView);
          LayoutInflater inflater = LayoutInflater.from(getActivity());
          View view = inflater.inflate(R.layout.gallery_item, viewGroup, false);
          return new PhotoHolder(view);
      }

      ...
  }

  ...
}
```

430

Next, you will need a placeholder image for each **ImageView** to display until you download an image to replace it. Find `bill_up_close.jpg` in the solutions file and put it in `res/drawable`. (See the section called "Adding an Icon" in Chapter 2 for more on the solutions.)

Update **PhotoAdapter**'s **onBindViewHolder()** to set the placeholder image as the **ImageView**'s **Drawable**.

Listing 24.3 Binding default image (PhotoGalleryFragment.java)

```
public class PhotoGalleryFragment extends Fragment {
  ...

  private class PhotoAdapter extends RecyclerView.Adapter<PhotoHolder> {
      ...

      @Override
      public void onBindViewHolder(PhotoHolder photoHolder, int position) {
        GalleryItem galleryItem = mGalleryItems.get(position);
        photoHolder.bindGalleryItem(galleryItem);
        Drawable placeholder = getResources().getDrawable(R.drawable.bill_up_close);
        photoHolder.bindDrawable(placeholder);
      }

      ...
    }

  ...
}
```

Run PhotoGallery, and you should see an array of close-up Bills, as in Figure 24.2.

Figure 24.2 A Billsplosion

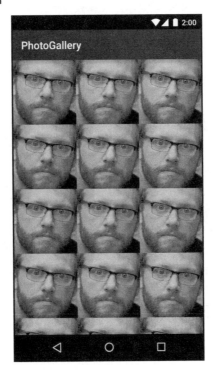

Downloading Lots of Small Things

Currently, PhotoGallery's networking works like this: **PhotoGalleryFragment** executes an **AsyncTask** that retrieves the JSON from Flickr on a background thread and parses the JSON into an array of **GalleryItem**s. Each **GalleryItem** now has a URL where a thumbnail-size photo lives.

The next step is to go and get those thumbnails. You might think that this additional networking code could simply be added to **FetchItemsTask**'s **doInBackground()** method. Your **GalleryItem** array has 100 URLs to download from. You would download the images one after another until you had all 100. When **onPostExecute(…)** executed, they would be displayed en masse in the **RecyclerView**.

However, downloading the thumbnails all at once causes two problems. The first is that it could take a while, and the UI would not be updated until the downloading was complete. On a slow connection, users would be staring at a wall of Bills for a long time.

The second problem is the cost of having to store the entire set of images. One hundred thumbnails will fit into memory easily. But what if it were 1000? What if you wanted to implement infinite scrolling? Eventually, you would run out of space.

Given these problems, real-world apps often download images only when they need to be displayed on screen. Downloading on demand puts the responsibility on the **RecyclerView** and its adapter. The adapter triggers the image downloading as part of its **onBindViewHolder(…)** implementation.

AsyncTask is the easiest way to get a background thread, but it is ill-suited for repetitive and long-running work. (You can read why in the For the More Curious section at the end of this chapter.)

Instead of using an **AsyncTask**, you are going to create a dedicated background thread. This is the most common way to implement downloading on an as-needed basis.

Communicating with the Main Thread

Your dedicated thread will download photos, but how will it work with the **RecyclerView**'s adapter to display them when it cannot directly access the main thread?

Think back to the shoe store with two Flashes. Background Flash has wrapped up his phone call to the distributor. He needs to tell Main Flash that the shoes are back in stock. If Main Flash is busy, Background Flash cannot do this right away. He would have to wait by the register to catch Main Flash at a spare moment. This would work, but it is not very efficient.

The better solution is to give each Flash an inbox. Background Flash writes a message about the shoes being in stock and puts it on top of Main Flash's inbox. Main Flash does the same thing when he wants to tell Background Flash that the stock of shoes has run out.

The inbox idea turns out to be really handy. The Flash may have something that needs to be done soon, but not right at the moment. In that case, he can put a message in his own inbox and then handle it when he has time.

In Android, the inbox that threads use is called a *message queue*. A thread that works by using a message queue is called a *message loop*; it loops again and again looking for new messages on its queue (Figure 24.3).

Figure 24.3 Flash dance

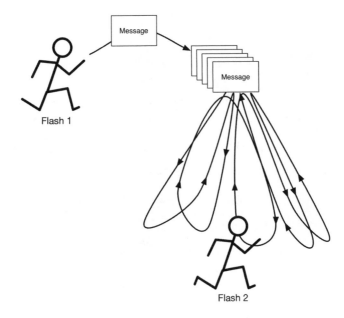

A message loop consists of a thread and a *looper*. The **Looper** is the object that manages a thread's message queue.

The main thread is a message loop and has a looper. Everything your main thread does is performed by its looper, which grabs messages off of its message queue and performs the task they specify.

You are going to create a background thread that is also a message loop. You will use a class called **HandlerThread** that prepares a **Looper** for you.

Assembling a Background Thread

Create a new class called **ThumbnailDownloader** that extends **HandlerThread**. Then give it a constructor and a stub implementation of a method called **queueThumbnail()** (Listing 24.4).

Listing 24.4 Initial thread code (ThumbnailDownloader.java)

```java
public class ThumbnailDownloader<T> extends HandlerThread {
    private static final String TAG = "ThumbnailDownloader";

    public ThumbnailDownloader() {
        super(TAG);
    }

    public void queueThumbnail(T target, String url) {
        Log.i(TAG, "Got a URL: " + url);
    }
}
```

Notice you gave the class a single generic argument, <T>. Your **ThumbnailDownloader**'s user, **PhotoGalleryFragment** in this case, will need to use some object to identify each download and to determine which UI element to update with the image once it is downloaded. Rather than locking the user into a specific type of object as the identifier, using a generic makes the implementation more flexible.

The **queueThumbnail()** method expects an object of type **T** to use as the identifier for the download and a **String** containing the URL to download. This is the method you will have **GalleryItemAdapter** call in its **onBindViewHolder(…)** implementation.

Open PhotoGalleryFragment.java. Give **PhotoGalleryFragment** a **ThumbnailDownloader** member variable. In **onCreate(…)**, create the thread and start it. Override **onDestroy()** to quit the thread.

Listing 24.5 Creating **ThumbnailDownloader** (PhotoGalleryFragment.java)

```java
public class PhotoGalleryFragment extends Fragment {

    private static final String TAG = "PhotoGalleryFragment";

    private RecyclerView mPhotoRecyclerView;
    private List<GalleryItem> mItems = new ArrayList<>();
    private ThumbnailDownloader<PhotoHolder> mThumbnailDownloader;

    ...

    @Override
    public void onCreate(Bundle savedInstanceState) {
        super.onCreate(savedInstanceState);
        setRetainInstance(true);
        new FetchItemsTask().execute();

        mThumbnailDownloader = new ThumbnailDownloader<>();
        mThumbnailDownloader.start();
        mThumbnailDownloader.getLooper();
        Log.i(TAG, "Background thread started");
    }

    @Override
    public View onCreateView(LayoutInflater inflater, ViewGroup container,
            Bundle savedInstanceState) {
        ...
    }

    @Override
    public void onDestroy() {
        super.onDestroy();
        mThumbnailDownloader.quit();
        Log.i(TAG, "Background thread destroyed");
    }
    ...
}
```

You can specify any type for **ThumbnailDownloader**'s generic argument. However, recall that this argument specifies the type of the object that will be used as the identifier for your download. In this case, the **PhotoHolder** makes for a convenient identifier as it is also the target where the downloaded images will eventually go.

A couple of safety notes. One: notice that you call **getLooper()** after calling **start()** on your **ThumbnailDownloader** (you will learn more about the **Looper** in a moment). This is a way to ensure that the thread's guts are ready before proceeding, to obviate a potential (though rarely occurring) race condition. Until you call **getLooper()**, there is no guarantee that **onLooperPrepared()** has been called, so there is a possibility that calls to **queueThumbnail(...)** will fail due to a null **Handler**.

Safety note number two: you call **quit()** to terminate the thread inside **onDestroy()**. This is critical. If you do not quit your **HandlerThread**s, they will never die. Like zombies. Or rock and roll.

Finally, within **PhotoAdapter.onBindViewHolder(...)**, call the thread's **queueThumbnail()** method and pass in the target **PhotoHolder** where the image will ultimately be placed and the **GalleryItem**'s URL to download from.

Listing 24.6 Hooking up **ThumbnailDownloader** (PhotoGalleryFragment.java)

```
public class PhotoGalleryFragment extends Fragment {

    ...

    private class PhotoAdapter extends RecyclerView.Adapter<PhotoHolder> {

        ...

        @Override
        public void onBindViewHolder(PhotoHolder photoHolder, int position) {
            GalleryItem galleryItem = mGalleryItems.get(position);
            Drawable placeholder = getResources().getDrawable(R.drawable.bill_up_close);
            photoHolder.bindDrawable(placeholder);
            mThumbnailDownloader.queueThumbnail(photoHolder, galleryItem.getUrl());
        }

        ...
    }

    ...
}
```

Run PhotoGallery and check out LogCat. When you scroll around the **RecyclerView**, you should see lines in LogCat signaling that **ThumbnailDownloader** is getting each one of your download requests.

Now that you have a **HandlerThread** up and running, the next step is to create a message with the information passed in to **queueThumbnail()** and put that message on the **ThumbnailDownloader**'s message queue.

Messages and Message Handlers

Before you create a message, you need to understand what a **Message** is and the relationship it has with its **Handler** (often called its *message handler*).

Message anatomy

Let's start by looking closely at messages. The messages that a Flash might put in an inbox (its own inbox or that of another Flash) are not supportive notes, like "You run very fast, Flash." They are tasks that need to be handled.

A message is an instance of **Message** and contains several fields. Three are relevant to your implementation:

what   a user-defined int that describes the message

obj   a user-specified object to be sent with the message

target   the **Handler** that will handle the message

The target of a **Message** is an instance of **Handler**. You can think of the name **Handler** as being short for "message handler." When you create a **Message**, it will automatically be attached to a **Handler**. And when your **Message** is ready to be processed, **Handler** will be the object in charge of making it happen.

Handler anatomy

To do any real work with messages, you will need an instance of **Handler** first. A **Handler** is not just a target for processing your **Message**s. A **Handler** is your interface for creating and posting **Message**s, too. Take a look at Figure 24.4.

Figure 24.4 **Looper**, **Handler**, **HandlerThread**, and **Message**s

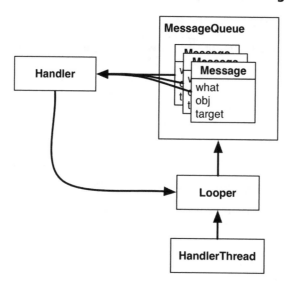

Messages must be posted and consumed on a **Looper**, because **Looper** owns the inbox of **Message** objects. So **Handler** always has a reference to its coworker, the **Looper**.

A **Handler** is attached to exactly one **Looper**, and a **Message** is attached to exactly one target **Handler**, called its *target*. A **Looper** has a whole queue of **Message**s. Multiple **Message**s can reference the same target **Handler** (Figure 24.5).

Figure 24.5 Multiple **Handlers**, one **Looper**

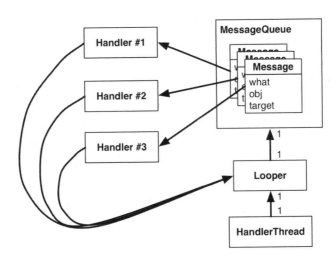

Multiple **Handler**s can be attached to one **Looper**. This means that your **Handler**'s **Message**s may be living side by side with another **Handler**'s messages.

Using handlers

Usually, you do not set a message's target **Handler** by hand. It is better to build the message by calling **Handler.obtainMessage(…)**. You pass the other message fields into this method, and it automatically sets the target to the **Handler** object the method was called on for you.

Handler.obtainMessage(…) pulls from a common recycling pool to avoid creating new **Message** objects, so it is also more efficient than creating new instances.

Once you have obtained a **Message**, you call **sendToTarget()** to send the **Message** to its **Handler**. The **Handler** will then put the **Message** on the end of **Looper**'s message queue.

In this case, you are going to obtain a message and send it to its target within the implementation of **queueThumbnail()**. The message's what will be a constant defined as MESSAGE_DOWNLOAD. The message's obj will be an object of type **T**, which will be used to identify the download. In this case, obj will be the **PhotoHolder** that the adapter passed in to **queueThumbnail()**.

When the looper pulls a **Message** from the queue, it gives the message to the message's target **Handler** to handle. Typically, the message is handled in the target's implementation of **Handler.handleMessage(…)**.

Figure 24.6 shows the object relationships involved.

Figure 24.6 Creating a **Message** and sending it

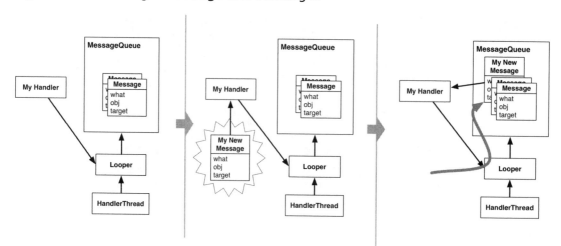

In this case, your implementation of **handleMessage(…)** will use **FlickrFetchr** to download bytes from the URL and then turn these bytes into a bitmap.

First, add the constant and member variables as shown in Listing 24.7.

Listing 24.7 Adding constant and member variables (ThumbnailDownloader.java)

```java
public class ThumbnailDownloader<T> extends HandlerThread {
    private static final String TAG = "ThumbnailDownloader";
    private static final int MESSAGE_DOWNLOAD = 0;

    private Handler mRequestHandler;
    private ConcurrentMap<T,String> mRequestMap = new ConcurrentHashMap<>();

    ...
}
```

MESSAGE_DOWNLOAD will be used to identify messages as download requests. (**ThumbnailDownloader** will set this as the what on any new download messages it creates.)

The newly added mRequestHandler will store a reference to the **Handler** responsible for queueing download requests as messages onto the **ThumbnailDownloader** background thread. This handler will also be in charge of processing download request messages when they are pulled off the queue.

The mRequestMap variable is a **ConcurrentHashMap**. A **ConcurrentHashMap** is a thread-safe version of **HashMap**. Here, using a download request's identifying object of type **T** as a key, you can store and retrieve the URL associated with a particular request. (In this case, the identifying object is a **PhotoHolder**, so the request response can be easily routed back to the UI element where the downloaded image should be placed.)

Next, add code to **queueThumbnail(…)** to update mRequestMap and to post a new message to the background thread's message queue.

Listing 24.8 Obtaining and sending a message (ThumbnailDownloader.java)

```java
public class ThumbnailDownloader<T> extends HandlerThread {
    private static final String TAG = "ThumbnailDownloader";
    private static final int MESSAGE_DOWNLOAD = 0;

    private Handler mRequestHandler;
    private ConcurrentMap<T,String> mRequestMap = new ConcurrentHashMap<>();

    public ThumbnailDownloader() {
        super(TAG);
    }

    public void queueThumbnail(T target, String url) {
        Log.i(TAG, "Got a URL: " + url);

        if (url == null) {
            mRequestMap.remove(target);
        } else {
            mRequestMap.put(target, url);
            mRequestHandler.obtainMessage(MESSAGE_DOWNLOAD, target)
                    .sendToTarget();
        }
    }
}
```

You obtain a message directly from mRequestHandler, which automatically sets the new **Message** object's target field to mRequestHandler. This means mRequestHandler will be in charge of processing the message when it is pulled off the message queue. The message's what field is set to MESSAGE_DOWNLOAD. Its obj field is set to the T target value (a **PhotoHolder** in this case) that is passed to **queueThumbnail(…)**.

The new message represents a download request for the specified T target (a **PhotoHolder** from the **RecyclerView**). Recall that **PhotoGalleryFragment**'s **RecyclerView**'s adapter implementation calls **queueThumbnail(…)** from **onBindViewHolder(…)**, passing along the **PhotoHolder** the image is being downloaded for and the URL location of the image to download.

Notice that the message itself does not include the URL. Instead you update **mRequestMap** with a mapping between the request identifier (**PhotoHolder**) and the URL for the request. Later you will pull the URL from mRequestMap to ensure that you are always downloading the most recently requested URL for a given **PhotoHolder** instance. (This is important because **ViewHolder** objects in **RecyclerView**s are recycled and reused.)

Finally, initialize mRequestHandler and define what that **Handler** will do when downloaded messages are pulled off the queue and passed to it.

Listing 24.9 Handling a message (ThumbnailDownloader.java)

```java
public class ThumbnailDownloader<T> extends HandlerThread {
    private static final String TAG = "ThumbnailDownloader";
    private static final int MESSAGE_DOWNLOAD = 0;

    private Handler mRequestHandler;
    private ConcurrentMap<T,String> mRequestMap = new ConcurrentHashMap<>();

    public ThumbnailDownloader(Handler responseHandler) {
        super(TAG);
    }

    @Override
    protected void onLooperPrepared() {
        mRequestHandler = new Handler() {
            @Override
            public void handleMessage(Message msg) {
                if (msg.what == MESSAGE_DOWNLOAD) {
                    T target = (T) msg.obj;
                    Log.i(TAG, "Got a request for URL: " + mRequestMap.get(target));
                    handleRequest(target);
                }
            }
        };
    }

    public void queueThumbnail(T target, String url) {
        ...
    }

    private void handleRequest(final T target) {
        try {
            final String url = mRequestMap.get(target);

            if (url == null) {
                return;
            }

            byte[] bitmapBytes = new FlickrFetchr().getUrlBytes(url);
            final Bitmap bitmap = BitmapFactory
                    .decodeByteArray(bitmapBytes, 0, bitmapBytes.length);
            Log.i(TAG, "Bitmap created");

        } catch (IOException ioe) {
            Log.e(TAG, "Error downloading image", ioe);
        }
    }
}
```

You implemented **Handler.handleMessage(…)** in your **Handler** subclass within **onLooperPrepared()**. **HandlerThread.onLooperPrepared()** is called before the **Looper** checks the queue for the first time. This makes it a good place to create your **Handler** implementation.

Within **Handler.handleMessage(…)**, you check the message type, retrieve the obj value (which will be of type **T** and serves as the identifier for the request), and then pass it to **handleRequest(…)**. (Recall that **Handler.handleMessage(…)** will get called when a download message is pulled off the queue and ready to be processed.)

The **handleRequest()** method is a helper method where the downloading happens. Here you check for the existence of a URL. Then you pass the URL to a new instance of your old friend **FlickrFetchr**. In particular, you use the **FlickrFetchr.getUrlBytes(…)** method that you created with such foresight in the last chapter.

Finally, you use **BitmapFactory** to construct a bitmap with the array of bytes returned from **getUrlBytes(…)**.

Run PhotoGallery and check LogCat for your confirming log statements.

Of course, the request will not be completely handled until you set the bitmap on the **PhotoHolder** that originally came from **PhotoAdapter**. However, this is UI work, so it must be done on the main thread.

Everything you have seen so far uses handlers and messages on a single thread – **ThumbnailDownloader** putting messages in **ThumbnailDownloader**'s own inbox. In the next section, you will see how **ThumbnailDownloader** can use a **Handler** to post requests to a separate thread (namely, the main thread).

Passing handlers

So far you are able to schedule work on the background thread from the main thread using **ThumbnailDownloader**'s mRequestHandler. This flow is shown in Figure 24.7.

Figure 24.7 Scheduling work on **ThumbnailDownloader** from the main thread

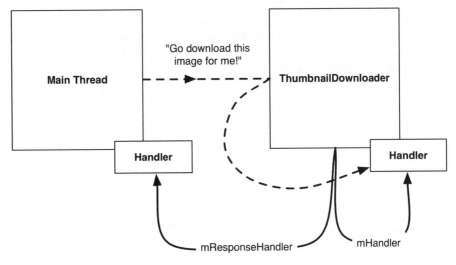

You can also schedule work on the main thread from the background thread using a **Handler** attached to the main thread. This flow looks like Figure 24.8.

Figure 24.8 Scheduling work on the main thread from **ThumbnailDownloader**'s thread

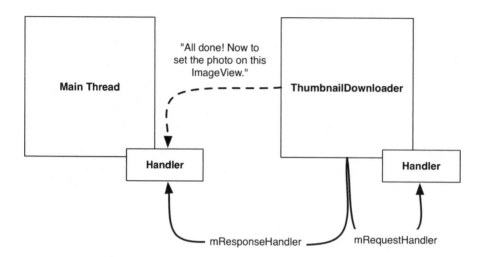

The main thread is a message loop with handlers and a **Looper**. When you create a **Handler** in the main thread, it will be associated with the main thread's **Looper**. You can then pass that **Handler** to another thread. The passed **Handler** maintains its loyalty to the **Looper** of the thread that created it. Any messages the **Handler** is responsible for will be handled on the main thread's queue.

In ThumbnailDownloader.java, add the mResponseHandler variable seen above to hold a **Handler** passed from the main thread. Then replace the constructor with one that accepts a **Handler** and sets the variable, and add a listener interface that will be used to communicate the responses (downloaded images) with the requester (the main thread).

Listing 24.10 Handling a message (ThumbnailDownloader.java)

```
public class ThumbnailDownloader<T> extends HandlerThread {
    private static final String TAG = "ThumbnailDownloader";
    private static final int MESSAGE_DOWNLOAD = 0;

    private Handler mRequestHandler;
    private ConcurrentMap<T,String> mRequestMap = new ConcurrentHashMap<>();
    private Handler mResponseHandler;
    private ThumbnailDownloadListener<T> mThumbnailDownloadListener;

    public interface ThumbnailDownloadListener<T> {
        void onThumbnailDownloaded(T target, Bitmap thumbnail);
    }

    public void setThumbnailDownloadListener(ThumbnailDownloadListener<T> listener) {
        mThumbnailDownloadListener = listener;
    }

    public ThumbnailDownloader(Handler responseHandler) {
        super(TAG);
        mResponseHandler = responseHandler;
    }

    ...
}
```

The **onThumbnailDownloaded(…)** method defined in your new **ThumbnailDownloadListener** interface will eventually be called when an image has been fully downloaded and is ready to be added to the UI. Using this listener delegates the responsibility of what to do with the downloaded image to a class other than **ThumbnailDownloader** (in this case, to **PhotoGalleryFragment**). Doing so separates the downloading task from the UI updating task (putting the images into **ImageView**s), so that **ThumbnailDownloader** could be used for downloading into other kinds of **View** objects as needed.

Next, modify **PhotoGalleryFragment** to pass a **Handler** attached to the main thread to **ThumbnailDownloader**. Also, set a **ThumbnailDownloadListener** to handle the downloaded image once it is complete.

Listing 24.11 Hooking up to response **Handler** (PhotoGalleryFragment.java)

...

```
@Override
public void onCreate(Bundle savedInstanceState) {
    super.onCreate(savedInstanceState);
    setRetainInstance(true);
    new FetchItemsTask().execute();

    Handler responseHandler = new Handler();
    mThumbnailDownloader = new ThumbnailDownloader<>(responseHandler);
    mThumbnailDownloader.setThumbnailDownloadListener(
        new ThumbnailDownloader.ThumbnailDownloadListener<PhotoHolder>() {
            @Override
            public void onThumbnailDownloaded(PhotoHolder photoHolder, Bitmap bitmap) {
                Drawable drawable = new BitmapDrawable(getResources(), bitmap);
                photoHolder.bindDrawable(drawable);
            }
        }
    );
    mThumbnailDownloader.start();
    mThumbnailDownloader.getLooper();
    Log.i(TAG, "Background thread started");
}
```

...

Remember that by default, the **Handler** will attach itself to the **Looper** for the current thread. Because this **Handler** is created in **onCreate(...)**, it will be attached to the main thread's **Looper**.

Now **ThumbnailDownloader** has access via mResponseHandler to a **Handler** that is tied to the main thread's **Looper**. It also has your **ThumbnailDownloadListener** to do the UI work with the returning **Bitmap**s. Specifically, the **onThumbnailDownloaded** implementation sets the **Drawable** of the originally requested **PhotoHolder** to the newly downloaded **Bitmap**.

You could send a custom **Message** back to the main thread requesting to add the image to the UI, similar to how you queued a request on the background thread to download the image. However, this would require another subclass of **Handler**, with an override of **handleMessage(...)**.

Instead, let's use another handy **Handler** method – **post(Runnable)**.

Handler.post(Runnable) is a convenience method for posting **Message**s that look like this:

```
Runnable myRunnable = new Runnable() {
    public void run() {
        /* Your code here */
    }
};
Message m = mHandler.obtainMessage();
m.callback = myRunnable;
```

When a **Message** has its callback field set, it is not routed to its target **Handler** when pulled off the message queue. Instead, the **run()** method of the **Runnable** stored in callback is executed directly.

In **ThumbnailDownloader.handleRequest()**, add the following code.

Listing 24.12 Downloading and displaying images (ThumbnailDownloader.java)

```
public class ThumbnailDownloader<T> extends HandlerThread {

    ...
    private Handler mResponseHandler;
    private ThumbnailDownloadListener<T> mThumbnailDownloadListener;

    ...

    private void handleRequest(final T target) {
        try {
            final String url = mRequestMap.get(target);

            if (url == null) {
                return;
            }

            byte[] bitmapBytes = new FlickrFetchr().getUrlBytes(url);
            final Bitmap bitmap = BitmapFactory
                    .decodeByteArray(bitmapBytes, 0, bitmapBytes.length);
            Log.i(TAG, "Bitmap created");

            mResponseHandler.post(new Runnable() {
                public void run() {
                    if (mRequestMap.get(target) != url) {
                        return;
                    }

                    mRequestMap.remove(target);
                    mThumbnailDownloadListener.onThumbnailDownloaded(target, bitmap);
                }
            });

        } catch (IOException ioe) {
            Log.e(TAG, "Error downloading image", ioe);
        }
    }
}
```

Because mResponseHandler is associated with the main thread's **Looper**, all of the code inside of **run()** will be executed on the main thread.

So what does this code do? First, you double-check the requestMap. This is necessary because the **RecyclerView** recycles its views. By the time **ThumbnailDownloader** finishes downloading the **Bitmap**, **RecyclerView** may have recycled the **PhotoHolder** and requested a different URL for it. This check ensures that each **PhotoHolder** gets the correct image, even if another request has been made in the meantime.

Finally, you remove the **PhotoHolder**-URL mapping from the requestMap and set the bitmap on the target **PhotoHolder**.

Before running PhotoGallery and seeing your hard-won images, there is one last danger you need to account for. If the user rotates the screen, **ThumbnailDownloader** may be hanging on to invalid **PhotoHolder**s. Bad things will happen if the corresponding **ImageView**s get pressed.

Write the following method to clean all the requests out of your queue.

Listing 24.13 Adding cleanup method (ThumbnailDownloader.java)

```java
public class ThumbnailDownloader<T> extends HandlerThread {

    ...

    public void queueThumbnail(T target, String url) {
        ...
    }

    public void clearQueue() {
        mRequestHandler.removeMessages(MESSAGE_DOWNLOAD);
    }

    private void handleRequest(final T target) {
        ...
    }
}
```

Then clean out your downloader in **PhotoGalleryFragment** when your view is destroyed.

Listing 24.14 Calling cleanup method (PhotoGalleryFragment.java)

```java
public class PhotoGalleryFragment extends Fragment {

    ...

    @Override
    public View onCreateView(LayoutInflater inflater, ViewGroup container,
                             Bundle savedInstanceState) {
        ...
    }

    @Override
    public void onDestroyView() {
        super.onDestroyView();
        mThumbnailDownloader.clearQueue();
    }

    @Override
    public void onDestroy() {
        ...
    }

    ...
}
```

With that, your work for this chapter is complete. Run PhotoGallery. Scroll around to see images dynamically loading.

PhotoGallery has achieved its basic goal of displaying images from Flickr. In the next few chapters, you will add more functionality, like searching for photos and opening each photo's Flickr page in a web view.

For the More Curious: AsyncTask vs. Threads

Now that you understand **Handler** and **Looper**, **AsyncTask** may not seem quite so magical. It is still less work than what you have done here. So why not use **AsyncTask** instead of a **HandlerThread**?

There are a few reasons. The most fundamental one is that **AsyncTask** is not designed for it. It is intended for work that is short lived and not repeated too often. Your code in the previous chapter is a place where **AsyncTask** shines. But if you are creating a lot of **AsyncTask**s or having them run for a long time, you are probably using the wrong class.

A more compelling technical reason is that in Android 3.2 **AsyncTask** changed its implementation in a significant way. Starting with Android 3.2, **AsyncTask** does not create a thread for each instance of **AsyncTask**. Instead, it uses something called an **Executor** to run background work for all **AsyncTask**s on a single background thread. That means that each **AsyncTask** will run one after the other. A long-running **AsyncTask** will hog the thread, preventing other **AsyncTask**s from getting any CPU time.

It is possible to safely run **AsyncTask**s in parallel by using a thread pool executor instead, but we do not recommend doing so. If you are considering doing this, it is usually better to do your own threading, using **Handler**s to communicate back to the main thread when necessary.

Challenge: Preloading and Caching

Users accept that not everything can be instantaneous. (Well, most users.) Even so, programmers strive toward perfection.

To approach instantaneity, most real-world apps augment the code you have here in two ways:

- adding a caching layer

- preloading images

A cache is a place to stash a certain number of **Bitmap** objects so that they stick around even when you are done using them. A cache can only hold so many items, so you need a strategy to decide what to keep when your cache runs out of room. Many caches use a strategy called LRU, or "least recently used." When you are out of room, the cache gets rid of the least recently used item.

The Android support library has a class called **LruCache** that implements an LRU strategy. For the first challenge, use **LruCache** to add a simple cache to **ThumbnailDownloader**. Whenever you download the **Bitmap** for a URL, you will stick it in the cache. Then, when you are about to download a new image, you will check the cache first to see if you already have it around.

Once you have built a cache, you can preload things into it. Preloading is loading items in the cache before you actually need them. That way, there is no delay for **Bitmap**s to download before displaying them.

Preloading is tricky to implement well, but it makes a huge difference for the user. For a second, harder challenge, for every **GalleryItem** you display, preload **Bitmap**s for the previous 10 and the next 10 **GalleryItem**s.

For the More Curious: Solving the Image Downloading Problem

This book is here to teach you about the tools in the standard Android library. If you are open to using third-party libraries, though, there are a few libraries that can save you a whole lot of time in various scenarios, including the image downloading work you implemented in PhotoGallery.

Admittedly, the solution you implemented in this chapter is far from perfect. When you start to need caching, transformations, and better performance, it is natural to ask if someone else has solved this problem before you. The answer is, of course: someone has. There are several libraries available that solve the image-loading problem. We currently use Picasso (http://square.github.io/picasso/) for image loading in our production applications.

Picasso lets you do everything from this chapter in one line:

```java
private class PhotoHolder extends RecyclerView.ViewHolder {
    ...

    public void bindGalleryItem(GalleryItem galleryItem) {
        Picasso.with(getActivity())
                .load(galleryItem.getUrl())
                .placeholder(R.drawable.bill_up_close)
                .into(mItemImageView);
    }

    ...
}
```

The fluent interface requires you specify a context using **with(Context)**. You can specify the URL of the image to download using **load(String)** and the **ImageView** object to load the result into using **into(ImageView)**. There are many other configurable options, such as specifying an image to display until the requested image is fully downloaded (using **placeholder(int)** or **placeholder(drawable)**).

In **PhotoAdapter.onBindViewHolder(…)**, you would replace the existing code with a call through to the new **bindGalleryItem(…)** method.

Picasso does all of the work of **ThumbnailDownloader** (along with the **ThumbnailDownloader.ThumbnailDownloadListener<T>** callback) and the image-related work of **FlickrFetchr**. This means you can remove **ThumbnailDownloader** if you use Picasso (you will still need **FlickrFetchr** for downloading the JSON data). In addition to simplifying your code, Picasso supports more advanced features such as image transformations and disk caching with minimal effort on your part.

You can add Picasso to your project as a library dependency using the Project Structure window, just as you did for other dependencies (like RecyclerView).

25
Search

Your next task with PhotoGallery is to search photos on Flickr. You will learn how to integrate search into your app the Android way. Or, as it turns out, one of the Android *ways*. Search has been integrated into Android from the very beginning, but it has changed a lot over time.

In this chapter you will implement search using `SearchView`.

The user will be able to submit a query using the `SearchView`, which will search Flickr using the query string and populate the `RecyclerView` with the search results (Figure 25.1). The query string submitted will be persisted to the filesystem. This means the user's last query will be accessible across restarts of the app and even the device.

Figure 25.1 App preview

Searching Flickr

Let's begin with the Flickr side of things. To search Flickr, you call the `flickr.photos.search` method. Here is what a GET request to search for the text "cat" looks like:

```
https://api.flickr.com/services/rest/?method=flickr.photos.search
&api_key=xxx&format=json&nojsoncallback=1&text=cat
```

The method is set to `flickr.photos.search`. A new parameter, `text`, is added and set to whatever string you are searching for ("cat," in this case).

While the search request URL differs from the one you used to request recent photos, the format of the JSON returned remains the same. This is good news, because it means you can use the same JSON parsing code you already wrote, regardless of whether you are searching or getting recent photos.

First, refactor some of your old **FlickrFetchr** code to reuse the parsing code across both scenarios. Start by adding constants for the reusable pieces of the URL, as shown in Listing 25.1. Cut the URI-building code from **fetchItems** and paste it as the value for ENDPOINT. However, make sure to only include the shaded parts. The constant ENDPOINT should not contain the method query parameter, and the build statement should not be converted to a string using **toString()**.

Listing 25.1 Adding URL constants (`FlickrFetchr.java`)

```java
public class FlickrFetchr {
    private static final String TAG = "FlickrFetchr";

    private static final String API_KEY = "yourApiKeyHere";
    private static final String FETCH_RECENTS_METHOD = "flickr.photos.getRecent";
    private static final String SEARCH_METHOD = "flickr.photos.search";
    private static final Uri ENDPOINT = Uri
            .parse("https://api.flickr.com/services/rest/")
            .buildUpon()
            .appendQueryParameter("api_key", API_KEY)
            .appendQueryParameter("format", "json")
            .appendQueryParameter("nojsoncallback", "1")
            .appendQueryParameter("extras", "url_s")
            .build();

    ...

    public List<GalleryItem> fetchItems() {

        List<GalleryItem> items = new ArrayList<>();

        try {
            String url = Uri.parse("https://api.flickr.com/services/rest/")
                    .buildUpon()
                    .appendQueryParameter("method", "flickr.photos.getRecent")
                    .appendQueryParameter("api_key", API_KEY)
                    .appendQueryParameter("format", "json")
                    .appendQueryParameter("nojsoncallback", "1")
                    .appendQueryParameter("extras", "url_s")
                    .build().toString();
            String jsonString = getUrlString(url);
            ...
        } catch (IOException ioe) {
            Log.e(TAG, "Failed to fetch items", ioe);
        } catch (JSONException je) {
            Log.e(TAG, "Failed to parse JSON", je);
        }

        return items;
    }

    ...
}
```

(The change you just made will result in an error in **fetchItems()**. You can ignore this error for now, as you are about to delete **fetchItems()** anyway.)

Rename **fetchItems()** to **downloadGalleryItems(String url)** to reflect its new, more general purpose. It no longer needs to be public, either, so change its visibility to private, too.

Listing 25.2 Refactoring Flickr code (FlickrFetchr.java)

```
public class FlickrFetchr {

    ...
    public List<GalleryItem> fetchItems() {
    private List<GalleryItem> downloadGalleryItems(String url) {
        List<GalleryItem> items = new ArrayList<>();

        try {
            String jsonString = getUrlString(url);
            Log.i(TAG, "Received JSON: " + jsonString);
            JSONObject jsonBody = new JSONObject(jsonString);
            parseItems(items, jsonBody);
        } catch (IOException ioe) {
            Log.e(TAG, "Failed to fetch items", ioe);
        } catch (JSONException je) {
            Log.e(TAG, "Failed to parse JSON", je);
        }

        return items;
    }

    ...
}
```

The new **downloadGalleryItems(String)** method takes a URL as input, so there is no need to build the URL inside. Instead, add a new method to build the URL based on method and query values.

Listing 25.3 Adding helper method to build URL (`FlickrFetchr.java`)

```java
public class FlickrFetchr {

    ...

    private List<GalleryItem> downloadGalleryItems(String url) {
        ...
    }

    private String buildUrl(String method, String query) {
        Uri.Builder uriBuilder = ENDPOINT.buildUpon()
                .appendQueryParameter("method", method);

        if (method.equals(SEARCH_METHOD)) {
            uriBuilder.appendQueryParameter("text", query);
        }

        return uriBuilder.build().toString();
    }

    private void parseItems(List<GalleryItem> items, JSONObject jsonBody)
            throws IOException, JSONException {
        ...
    }
}
```

The **buildUrl(…)** method appends the necessary parameters, just as the removed **fetchItems()** used to. But it dynamically fills in the method parameter value. Additionally, it appends a value for the text parameter only if the value specified for the method parameter is search.

Now add methods to kick off the download by building a URL and calling **downloadGalleryItems(String)**.

Listing 25.4 Adding methods to get recents and search (`FlickrFetchr.java`)

```java
public class FlickrFetchr {

    ...

    public String getUrlString(String urlSpec) throws IOException {
        return new String(getUrlBytes(urlSpec));
    }

    public List<GalleryItem> fetchRecentPhotos() {
        String url = buildUrl(FETCH_RECENTS_METHOD, null);
        return downloadGalleryItems(url);
    }

    public List<GalleryItem> searchPhotos(String query) {
        String url = buildUrl(SEARCH_METHOD, query);
        return downloadGalleryItems(url);
    }

    private List<GalleryItem> downloadGalleryItems(String url) {
        List<GalleryItem> items = new ArrayList<>();
        ...
        return items;
    }

    ...
}
```

FlickrFetchr is now equipped to handle both searching and getting recent photos. The **fetchRecentPhotos()** and **searchPhotos(String)** methods serve as the public interface for getting a list of **GalleryItem**s from the Flickr web service.

You need to update your fragment code to reflect the refactoring you just completed in **FlickrFetchr**. Open **PhotoGalleryFragment** and update **FetchItemsTask**.

Listing 25.5 Hardwired search query code (`PhotoGalleryFragment.java`)

```java
public class PhotoGalleryFragment extends Fragment {

    ...

    private class FetchItemsTask extends AsyncTask<Void,Void,List<GalleryItem>> {

        @Override
        protected List<GalleryItem> doInBackground(Void... params) {
            return new FlickrFetchr().fetchItems();
            String query = "robot"; // Just for testing

            if (query == null) {
                return new FlickrFetchr().fetchRecentPhotos();
            } else {
                return new FlickrFetchr().searchPhotos(query);
            }
        }

        @Override
        protected void onPostExecute(List<GalleryItem> items) {
            mItems = items;
            setupAdapter();
        }
    }

}
```

If the query string is not null (which for now is always the case), then **FetchItemsTask** will execute a Flickr search. Otherwise **FetchItemsTask** will default to fetching recent photos, just as it did before.

Hardcoding the query allows you to test out your new search code even though you have not yet provided a way to enter a query through the user interface.

Run PhotoGallery and see what you get. Hopefully, you will see a cool robot or two (Figure 25.2).

Figure 25.2 Hardcoded search results

Using SearchView

Now that **FlickrFetchr** supports searching, it is time to add a way for the user to enter a query and initiate a search. Do this by adding a **SearchView**.

SearchView is an *action view* – a view that may be included within the toolbar. **SearchView** allows your entire search interface to live within your application's toolbar.

First, confirm that a toolbar (containing your app title) appears at the top of your app. If not, follow the steps outlined in Chapter 13 to add a toolbar to your app.

Next, create a new menu XML file for **PhotoGalleryFragment** in res/menu/ fragment_photo_gallery.xml. This file will specify the items that should appear in the toolbar.

Listing 25.6 Adding menu XML file (res/menu/ fragment_photo_gallery.xml)

```xml
<?xml version="1.0" encoding="utf-8"?>
<menu xmlns:android="http://schemas.android.com/apk/res/android"
      xmlns:app="http://schemas.android.com/apk/res-auto">

    <item android:id="@+id/menu_item_search"
          android:title="@string/search"
          app:actionViewClass="android.support.v7.widget.SearchView"
          app:showAsAction="ifRoom" />

    <item android:id="@+id/menu_item_clear"
          android:title="@string/clear_search"
          app:showAsAction="never" />
</menu>
```

You will see a couple errors in the new XML, complaining that you have not yet defined the strings you are referencing for the android:title attributes. Ignore those for now. You will fix them in a bit.

The first item entry in Listing 25.6 tells the toolbar to display a **SearchView** by specifying the value android.support.v7.widget.SearchView for the app:actionViewClass attribute. (Notice the usage of the app namespace for the showAsAction and actionViewClass attributes. Please refer back to Chapter 13 if you are unsure of why this is used.)

SearchView (**android.widget.SearchView**) was originally introduced in API 11 (Honeycomb 3.0). However, **SearchView** was more recently included as part of the support library (**android.support.v7.widget.SearchView**). So which version of **SearchView** should you use? You have seen our answer in the code you just entered: the support library version. This may seem strange, as your app's minimum SDK is 16.

We recommend using the support library for the same reasons outlined in Chapter 7. As new features get added with each new release of Android, the features are often back-ported to the support library. A prime example is theming. With the release of API 21 (Lollipop 5.0), the native framework **SearchView** supports many options for customizing the **SearchView**'s appearance. The only way to get these fancy features on earlier versions of Android (down to API 7) is to use the support library version of **SearchView**.

The second item in Listing 25.6 will add a Clear Search option. This option will always display in the overflow menu because you set app:showAsAction to never. Later on you will configure this item so that, when pressed, the user's stored query will be erased from the disk. For now, you can ignore this item.

Now it is time to address the errors in your menu XML. Open strings.xml and add the missing strings:

Listing 25.7 Adding search strings (res/values/strings.xml)

```xml
<resources>
        ...
        <string name="search">Search</string>
        <string name="clear_search">Clear Search</string>

</resources>
```

Finally, open **PhotoGalleryFragment**. Add a call to **setHasOptionsMenu(true)** in **onCreate(…)** to register the fragment to receive menu callbacks. Override **onCreateOptionsMenu(…)** and inflate the menu XML file you created. This will add the items listed in your menu XML to the toolbar.

Listing 25.8 Overriding **onCreateOptionsMenu(…)** (PhotoGalleryFragment.java)

```java
public class PhotoGalleryFragment extends Fragment {

    ...

    @Override
    public void onCreate(Bundle savedInstanceState) {
        super.onCreate(savedInstanceState);
        setRetainInstance(true);
        setHasOptionsMenu(true);
        new FetchItemsTask().execute();

        ...
    }

    ...

    @Override
    public void onDestroy() {
        ...
    }

    @Override
    public void onCreateOptionsMenu(Menu menu, MenuInflater menuInflater) {
        super.onCreateOptionsMenu(menu, menuInflater);
        menuInflater.inflate(R.menu.fragment_photo_gallery, menu);
    }

    private void setupAdapter() {
        ...
    }

    ...
}
```

Fire up PhotoGallery and see what the **SearchView** looks like. Pressing the Search icon expands the view to display a text box where the user can enter a query (Figure 25.3).

Figure 25.3 SearchView collapsed and expanded

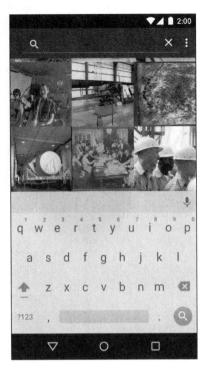

When the **SearchView** is expanded, a x icon appears on the right. Pressing the x icon one time clears out what you typed. Pressing the x again collapses the **SearchView** back to a single search icon.

If you try submitting a query, it will not do anything yet. Not to worry. You will make your **SearchView** more useful in just a moment.

Responding to SearchView user interactions

When the user submits a query, your app should execute a search against the Flickr web service and refresh the images the user sees with the search results. Fortunately, the **SearchView.OnQueryTextListener** interface provides a way to receive a callback when a query is submitted.

Update **onCreateOptionsMenu(…)** to add a **SearchView.OnQueryTextListener** to your **SearchView**.

Listing 25.9 Logging **SearchView.OnQueryTextListener** events (PhotoGalleryFragment.java)

```java
public class PhotoGalleryFragment extends Fragment {

    ...

    @Override
    public void onCreateOptionsMenu(Menu menu, MenuInflater menuInflater) {
        super.onCreateOptionsMenu(menu, menuInflater);
        menuInflater.inflate(R.menu.fragment_photo_gallery, menu);

        MenuItem searchItem = menu.findItem(R.id.menu_item_search);
        final SearchView searchView = (SearchView) searchItem.getActionView();

        searchView.setOnQueryTextListener(new SearchView.OnQueryTextListener() {
            @Override
            public boolean onQueryTextSubmit(String s) {
                Log.d(TAG, "QueryTextSubmit: " + s);
                updateItems();
                return true;
            }

            @Override
            public boolean onQueryTextChange(String s) {
                Log.d(TAG, "QueryTextChange: " + s);
                return false;
            }
        });
    }

    private void updateItems() {
        new FetchItemsTask().execute();
    }

    ...
}
```

In **onCreateOptionsMenu(…)**, you pull the **MenuItem** representing the search box from the menu and store it in searchItem. Then you pull the **SearchView** object from searchItem using the **getActionView()** method.

(Note: **MenuItem.getActionView()** was added in API 11. This is fine here as the minimum SDK for your app is API 16. However, if you need to make an app that goes back as far as the support library allows, you will need to take a different approach for getting access to the **SearchView** object.)

Once you have a reference to the **SearchView** you are able to set a **SearchView.OnQueryTextListener** using the **setOnQueryTextListener(…)** method. You must override two methods in the **SearchView.OnQueryTextListener** implementation: **onQueryTextSubmit(String)** and **onQueryTextChange(String)**.

The **onQueryTextChange(String)** callback is executed any time text in the **SearchView** text box changes. This means that it is called every time a single character changes. You will not do anything inside this callback for this app except log the input string.

The **onQueryTextSubmit(String)** callback is executed when the user submits a query. The query the user submitted is passed as input. Returning true signifies to the system that the search request

459

has been handled. This callback is where you will launch a **FetchItemsTask** to query for new results. (Right now **FetchItemsTask** still has a hardcoded query. You will refactor **FetchItemsTask** in a bit so that it uses a submitted query if there is one.)

The **updateItems()** does not seem terribly useful just yet. Later on you will have several places where you need to execute **FetchItemsTask**. The **updateItems()** method is a wrapper for doing just that.

As a last bit of cleanup, replace the line that creates and executes a **FetchItemsTask** with a call to **updateItems()** in the **onCreate(…)** method.

Listing 25.10 Cleaning up **onCreate(…)** (PhotoGalleryFragment.java)

```
public class PhotoGalleryFragment extends Fragment {

    ...

    @Override
    public void onCreate(Bundle savedInstanceState) {
        super.onCreate(savedInstanceState);
        setRetainInstance(true);
        setHasOptionsMenu(true);
        new FetchItemsTask().execute();
        updateItems();

        ...
        Log.i(TAG, "Background thread started");
    }

    ...
}
```

Run your app and submit a query. The search results will still be based on the hardcoded query in Listing 25.5, but you should see the images reload. You should also see log statements reflecting the fact that your **SearchView.OnQueryTextListener** callback methods have been executed.

Note: If you use the hardware keyboard (e.g., from your laptop) to submit your search query on an emulator, you will see the search executed two times, one after the other. It will look like the images start to load, then load all over again. This is because there is a small bug in **SearchView**. You can ignore this behavior because it is simply a side effect of using the emulator and will not affect your app when it runs on a real Android device.

Simple Persistence with Shared Preferences

The last piece of functionality you need to add is to actually use the query entered in the **SearchView** when the search request is submitted.

In your app, there will only be one active query at a time. That query should be persisted (remembered by the app) between restarts of the app (even after the user turns off the device). You will achieve this by writing the query string to *shared preferences*. Any time the user submits a query, you will first write the query to shared preferences, overwriting whatever query was there before. When a search is executed against Flickr, you will pull the query string from shared preferences and use it as the value for the text parameter.

Shared preferences are files on your filesystem that you read and edit using the **SharedPreferences** class. An instance of **SharedPreferences** acts like a key-value store, much like **Bundle**, except that it is backed by persistent storage. The keys are strings, and the values are atomic data types. If you look at them you will see that the files are simple XML, but **SharedPreferences** makes it easy to ignore that implementation detail. Shared preferences files are stored in your application's sandbox, so you should not store sensitive information (like passwords) there.

To get a specific instance of **SharedPreferences**, you can use the **Context.getSharedPreferences(String, int)** method. However, in practice, you will often not care too much about the specific instance, just that it is shared across the entire app. In that case, it is better to use the **PreferenceManager.getDefaultSharedPreferences(Context)** method, which returns an instance with a default name and private permissions (so that the preferences are only available from within your application).

Add a new class named **QueryPreferences**, which will serve as a convenient interface for reading and writing the query to and from shared preferences.

Listing 25.11 Adding class to manage stored query (QueryPreferences.java)

```java
public class QueryPreferences {
    private static final String PREF_SEARCH_QUERY = "searchQuery";

    public static String getStoredQuery(Context context) {
        return PreferenceManager.getDefaultSharedPreferences(context)
                .getString(PREF_SEARCH_QUERY, null);
    }

    public static void setStoredQuery(Context context, String query) {
        PreferenceManager.getDefaultSharedPreferences(context)
                .edit()
                .putString(PREF_SEARCH_QUERY, query)
                .apply();
    }
}
```

PREF_SEARCH_QUERY is used as the key for the query preference. You will use this key any time you read or write the query value.

The **getStoredQuery(Context)** method returns the query value stored in shared preferences. It does so by first acquiring the default **SharedPreferences** for the given context. (Because **QueryPreferences** does not have a **Context** of its own, the calling component will have to pass its context as input.)

Getting a value you previously stored is as simple as calling **SharedPreferences.getString(…)**, **getInt(…)**, or whichever method is appropriate for your data type. The second input to **SharedPreferences.getString(PREF_SEARCH_QUERY, null)** specifies the default return value that should be used if there is no entry for the **PREF_SEARCH_QUERY** key.

The **setStoredQuery(Context)** method writes the input query to the default shared preferences for the given context. In your code above, you call **SharedPreferences.edit()** to get an instance of **SharedPreferences.Editor**. This is the class you use to stash values in your **SharedPreferences**. It allows you to group sets of changes together in transactions, much like you do with **FragmentTransaction**. If you have a lot of changes, this will allow you to group them together into a single storage write operation.

Once you are done making all of your changes, you call **apply()** on your editor to make them visible to other users of that **SharedPreferences** file. The **apply()** method makes the change in memory immediately and then does the actual file writing on a background thread.

QueryPreferences is your entire persistence engine for PhotoGallery. Now that you have a way to easily store and access the user's most recent query, update **PhotoGalleryFragment** to read and write the query as necessary.

First, update the stored query whenever the user submits a new query.

Listing 25.12 Storing submitted query in shared preferences (PhotoGalleryFragment.java)

```java
public class PhotoGalleryFragment extends Fragment {

    ...

    @Override
    public void onCreateOptionsMenu(Menu menu, MenuInflater menuInflater) {
        ...

        searchView.setOnQueryTextListener(new SearchView.OnQueryTextListener() {
            @Override
            public boolean onQueryTextSubmit(String s) {
                Log.d(TAG, "QueryTextSubmit: " + s);
                QueryPreferences.setStoredQuery(getActivity(), s);
                updateItems();
                return true;
            }

            @Override
            public boolean onQueryTextChange(String s) {
                Log.d(TAG, "QueryTextChange: " + s);
                return false;
            }
        });
    }

    ...
}
```

Next, clear the stored query (set it to null) whenever the user selects the Clear Search item from the overflow menu.

Listing 25.13 Clearing stored query (`PhotoGalleryFragment.java`)

```java
public class PhotoGalleryFragment extends Fragment {

    ...

    @Override
    public void onCreateOptionsMenu(Menu menu, MenuInflater menuInflater) {
        ...
    }

    @Override
    public boolean onOptionsItemSelected(MenuItem item) {
        switch (item.getItemId()) {
            case R.id.menu_item_clear:
                QueryPreferences.setStoredQuery(getActivity(), null);
                updateItems();
                return true;
            default:
                return super.onOptionsItemSelected(item);
        }
    }

    ...
}
```

Note that you call **updateItems()** after you update the stored query, just as you did in Listing 25.12. This ensures that the images displayed in the **RecyclerView** reflect the most recent search query.

Last, but not least, update **FetchItemsTask** to use the stored query rather than a hardcoded string. Add a custom constructor to **FetchItemsTask** that accepts a query string as input and stashes it in a member variable. Update **updateItems()** to pull the stored query from shared preferences and use it to create a new instance of **FetchItemsTask**. All of these changes are shown in Listing 25.14.

Listing 25.14 Using stored query in **FetchItemsTask** (PhotoGalleryFragment.java)

```java
public class PhotoGalleryFragment extends Fragment {
    ...

    private void updateItems() {
        String query = QueryPreferences.getStoredQuery(getActivity());
        new FetchItemsTask(query).execute();
    }

    ...

    private class FetchItemsTask extends AsyncTask<Void,Void,List<GalleryItem>> {
        private String mQuery;

        public FetchItemsTask(String query) {
            mQuery = query;
        }

        @Override
        protected List<GalleryItem> doInBackground(Void... params) {
            String query = "robot"; // Just for testing

            if (querymQuery == null) {
                return new FlickrFetchr().fetchRecentPhotos();
            } else {
                return new FlickrFetchr().searchPhotos(querymQuery);
            }
        }

        @Override
        protected void onPostExecute(List<GalleryItem> items) {
            mItems = items;
            setupAdapter();
        }
    }

}
```

Search should now work like a charm. Run PhotoGallery, try searching for something, and see what you get.

Polishing Your App

For one last bit of polish, pre-populate the search text box with the saved query when the user presses on the search icon to expand the **SearchView**. **SearchView**'s **View.OnClickListener.onClick()** method is called when the user presses the search icon. Hook into this callback and set the **SearchView**'s query text when the view is expanded.

Listing 25.15 Pre-populating **SearchView** (PhotoGalleryFragment.java)

```java
public class PhotoGalleryFragment extends Fragment {

    ...

    @Override
    public void onCreateOptionsMenu(Menu menu, MenuInflater menuInflater) {
        ...

        searchView.setOnQueryTextListener(new SearchView.OnQueryTextListener() {
            ...
        });

        searchView.setOnSearchClickListener(new View.OnClickListener() {
            @Override
            public void onClick(View v) {
                String query = QueryPreferences.getStoredQuery(getActivity());
                searchView.setQuery(query, false);
            }
        });
    }

    ...
}
```

Run your app and play around with submitting a few searches. Revel at the polish your last bit of code added. Of course, there is always more polish you could add....

Challenge: Polishing Your App Some More

You may notice that, when you submit a query, there is a bit of a lag before the **RecyclerView** starts to refresh. For this challenge, make the response to the user's query submission feel more immediate. As soon as a query is submitted, hide the soft keyboard and collapse the **SearchView**.

As an extra challenge, clear the contents of the **RecyclerView** and display a loading indicator (indeterminate progress bar) as soon as a query is submitted. Get rid of the loading indicator once the JSON data has been fully downloaded. In other words, the loading indicator should not show once your code moves on to downloading individual images.

26

Background Services

All the code you have written so far has been hooked up to an activity, which means that it is associated with some screen for the user to look at.

But what if you do not need a screen? What if you need to do something out of sight and out of mind, like play music or check for new blog posts on an RSS feed? For this, you need a *service*.

In this chapter, you will add a new feature to PhotoGallery that will allow users to poll for new search results in the background. Whenever a new search result is available, the user will receive a notification in the status bar.

Creating an IntentService

Let's start by creating your service. In this chapter, you will use an **IntentService**. **IntentService** is not the only kind of service, but it is probably the most common. Create a subclass of **IntentService** called **PollService**. This will be the service you use to poll for search results.

Listing 26.1 Creating **PollService** (PollService.java)

```java
public class PollService extends IntentService {
    private static final String TAG = "PollService";

    public static Intent newIntent(Context context) {
        return new Intent(context, PollService.class);
    }

    public PollService() {
        super(TAG);
    }

    @Override
    protected void onHandleIntent(Intent intent) {
        Log.i(TAG, "Received an intent: " + intent);
    }
}
```

This is a very basic **IntentService**. What does it do? Well, it is sort of like an activity. It is a context (**Service** is a subclass of **Context**) and it responds to intents (as you can see in **onHandleIntent(Intent)**). As a matter of convention (and to be a good citizen) you added a **newIntent(Context)** method. Any component that wants to start this service should use **newIntent(…)**.

A service's intents are called *commands*. Each command is an instruction to the service to do something. Depending on the kind of service, that command could be serviced in a variety of ways.

An **IntentService** service pulls its commands off of a queue, as shown in Figure 26.1.

Figure 26.1 How **IntentService** services commands

1. Command Intent #1 Received
Service Created

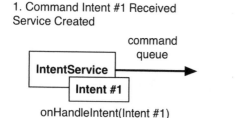

onHandleIntent(Intent #1)

2. Command Intent #2 Received

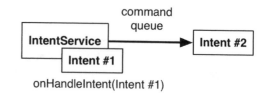

onHandleIntent(Intent #1)

3. Command Intent #3 Received

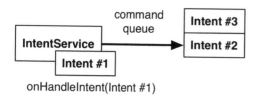

onHandleIntent(Intent #1)

4. Command Intent #1 Finished

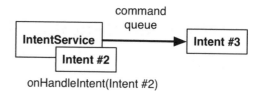

onHandleIntent(Intent #2)

5. Command Intent #2 Finished

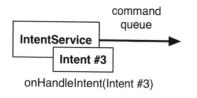

onHandleIntent(Intent #3)

6. Command Intent #3 Finished
Service Destroyed

When it receives its first command, the **IntentService** starts up, fires up a background thread, and puts the command on a queue.

The **IntentService** then services each command in sequence, calling **onHandleIntent(Intent)** on its background thread for each command. New commands that come in go to the back of the queue. When there are no commands left in the queue, the service stops and is destroyed.

This description only applies to **IntentService**. Later in the chapter, we will discuss the broader world of services and how commands work.

You might infer from what you just learned about how **IntentService** works that services respond to intents. That is true! And because services, like activities, respond to intents, they must also be declared in your AndroidManifest.xml. Add an element for **PollService** to your manifest.

Listing 26.2 Adding service to manifest (`AndroidManifest.xml`)

```xml
<manifest xmlns:android="http://schemas.android.com/apk/res/android"
        package="com.bignerdranch.android.photogallery" >

    <uses-permission android:name="android.permission.INTERNET" />

    <application
        ... >
        <activity
            android:name=".PhotoGalleryActivity"
            android:label="@string/app_name" >
            ...
        </activity>
        <service android:name=".PollService" />
    </application>

</manifest>
```

Then add code to start your service inside **PhotoGalleryFragment**.

Listing 26.3 Adding service startup code (`PhotoGalleryFragment.java`)

```java
public class PhotoGalleryFragment extends Fragment {
    private static final String TAG = "PhotoGalleryFragment";

    ...

    @Override
    public void onCreate(Bundle savedInstanceState) {
        ...

        updateItems();

        Intent i = PollService.newIntent(getActivity());
        getActivity().startService(i);

        Handler responseHandler = new Handler();
        mThumbnailDownloader = new ThumbnailDownloader<>(responseHandler);
        ...
    }

    ...
}
```

Fire this up and see what you get. You should see something like this in LogCat:

```
02-23 14:25:32.450    2692-2717/com.bignerdranch.android.photogallery I/PollService:
 Received an intent: Intent { cmp=com.bignerdranch.android.photogallery/.PollService }
```

What Services are For

OK, we admit it: looking at those LogCat statements was boring. But this code is really exciting! Why? What can you do with it?

Time to go back to the Land of Make Believe, where we are no longer programmers but work in retail shoe sales with superheroes who do our bidding.

Your Flash workers can work in two kinds of places in a store: the front of the store, where they talk to customers, and the back of the store, where they do not. The back of the store may be larger or smaller, depending on the store.

So far, all of your code has run in activities. Activities are your Android app's storefront. All this code is focused on a pleasant visual experience for your user, your customer.

Services are the back end of your Android app. Things can happen there that the user never needs to know about. Work can go on there long after the storefront has closed, when your activities are long gone.

OK, enough about stores. What can you do with a service that you cannot do with an activity? Well, for one, you can run a service while the user is occupied elsewhere.

Safe background networking

Your service is going to poll Flickr in the background. To perform networking in the background safely, some additional code is required. Android provides the ability for a user to turn off networking for backgrounded applications. If the user has a lot of power-hungry applications, this can be a big performance improvement.

This does mean, however, that if you are doing networking in the background, you need to verify with the ConnectivityManager that the network is available.

Add the code in Listing 26.4 to perform this check.

Listing 26.4 Checking for background network availability (PollService.java)

```java
public class PollService extends IntentService {
    private static final String TAG = "PollService";

    ...

    @Override
    protected void onHandleIntent(Intent intent) {
        if (!isNetworkAvailableAndConnected()) {
            return;
        }

        Log.i(TAG, "Received an intent: " + intent);
    }

    private boolean isNetworkAvailableAndConnected() {
        ConnectivityManager cm =
                (ConnectivityManager) getSystemService(CONNECTIVITY_SERVICE);

        boolean isNetworkAvailable = cm.getActiveNetworkInfo() != null;
        boolean isNetworkConnected = isNetworkAvailable &&
                cm.getActiveNetworkInfo().isConnected();

        return isNetworkConnected;
    }
}
```

The logic for checking network availability is in **isNetworkAvailableAndConnected()**. Toggling the background data setting to disallow downloading data in the background disables the network entirely for use by background services. In this case, **ConnectivityManager.getActiveNetworkInfo()** returns null, making it appear to the background service as if there is no active network available, even if there really is.

If the network is available to your background service, it gets an instance of **android.net.NetworkInfo** representing the current network connection. The code then checks whether the current network is fully connected by calling **NetworkInfo.isConnected()**.

If the app does not see a network available, or the device is not fully connected to a network, **onHandleIntent(…)** will return without executing the rest of the method (and in turn will not try to download data, once you have added the code to do so). This is good practice because your app cannot download any data if it is not connected to the network.

One more thing. To use **getActiveNetworkInfo()**, you also need to acquire the ACCESS_NETWORK_STATE permission. As you have seen, permissions are managed in your manifest.

Listing 26.5 Acquiring network state permission (`AndroidManifest.xml`)

```xml
<manifest xmlns:android="http://schemas.android.com/apk/res/android"
        package="com.bignerdranch.android.photogallery" >

    <uses-permission android:name="android.permission.INTERNET" />
    <uses-permission android:name="android.permission.ACCESS_NETWORK_STATE" />

    <application
        ... >
        ...
    </application>

</manifest>
```

Looking for New Results

Your service will be polling for new results, so it will need to know what the last result fetched was. This is a perfect job for another **SharedPreferences** entry.

Update **QueryPreferences** to store the ID of the most recently fetched photo.

Listing 26.6 Adding recent ID preference constant (QueryPreferences.java)

```java
public class QueryPreferences {

    private static final String PREF_SEARCH_QUERY = "searchQuery";
    private static final String PREF_LAST_RESULT_ID = "lastResultId";

    public static String getStoredQuery(Context context) {
        ...
    }

    public static void setStoredQuery(Context context, String query) {
        ...
    }

    public static String getLastResultId(Context context) {
        return PreferenceManager.getDefaultSharedPreferences(context)
                .getString(PREF_LAST_RESULT_ID, null);
    }

    public static void setLastResultId(Context context, String lastResultId) {
        PreferenceManager.getDefaultSharedPreferences(context)
                .edit()
                .putString(PREF_LAST_RESULT_ID, lastResultId)
                .apply();
    }
}
```

The next step is to fill out your service. Here is what you need to do:

1. Pull out the current query and the last result ID from the default **SharedPreferences**.

2. Fetch the latest result set with **FlickrFetchr**.

3. If there are results, grab the first one.

4. Check to see whether it is different from the last result ID.

5. Store the first result back in **SharedPreferences**.

Return to PollService.java and put this plan into action. Listing 26.7 shows a long swath of code, but it uses nothing you have not seen before.

Listing 26.7 Checking for new results (`PollService.java`)

```java
public class PollService extends IntentService {
    private static final String TAG = "PollService";

    ...

    @Override
    protected void onHandleIntent(Intent intent) {
        ...

        Log.i(TAG, "Received an intent: " + intent);
        String query = QueryPreferences.getStoredQuery(this);
        String lastResultId = QueryPreferences.getLastResultId(this);
        List<GalleryItem> items;

        if (query == null) {
            items = new FlickrFetchr().fetchRecentPhotos();
        } else {
            items = new FlickrFetchr().searchPhotos(query);
        }

        if (items.size() == 0) {
            return;
        }

        String resultId = items.get(0).getId();
        if (resultId.equals(lastResultId)) {
            Log.i(TAG, "Got an old result: " + resultId);
        } else {
            Log.i(TAG, "Got a new result: " + resultId);
        }

        QueryPreferences.setLastResultId(this, resultId);
    }

    ...
}
```

See each part we discussed above? Good.

Run PhotoGallery, and you should see your app getting new results initially. If you have a search query selected, you will probably see stale results when you subsequently start up the app.

Delayed Execution with AlarmManager

To actually use your service in the background, you will need some way to make things happen when none of your activities are running. Say, by making a timer that goes off every 5 minutes or so.

You could do this with a **Handler** by calling **Handler.sendMessageDelayed(…)** or **Handler.postDelayed(…)**. But this solution will probably fail if the user navigates away from all your activities. The process will shut down, and your **Handler** messages will go kaput with it.

So instead of **Handler**, you will use **AlarmManager**. **AlarmManager** is a system service that can send **Intent**s for you.

How do you tell **AlarmManager** what intents to send? You use a **PendingIntent**. You can use **PendingIntent** to package up a wish: "I want to start **PollService**." You can then send that wish to other components on the system, like **AlarmManager**.

Write a new method called **setServiceAlarm(Context, boolean)** inside **PollService** that turns an alarm on and off for you. You will write it as a static method. That keeps your alarm code with the other code in **PollService** that it is related to, but allows other components to invoke it. You will usually want to turn it on and off from frontend code in a fragment or other controller.

Listing 26.8 Adding alarm method (`PollService.java`)

```java
public class PollService extends IntentService {
    private static final String TAG = "PollService";

    private static final int POLL_INTERVAL = 1000 * 60; // 60 seconds

    public static Intent newIntent(Context context) {
        return new Intent(context, PollService.class);
    }

    public static void setServiceAlarm(Context context, boolean isOn) {
        Intent i = PollService.newIntent(context);
        PendingIntent pi = PendingIntent.getService(context, 0, i, 0);

        AlarmManager alarmManager = (AlarmManager)
                context.getSystemService(Context.ALARM_SERVICE);

        if (isOn) {
            alarmManager.setInexactRepeating(AlarmManager.ELAPSED_REALTIME,
                    SystemClock.elapsedRealtime(), POLL_INTERVAL, pi);
        } else {
            alarmManager.cancel(pi);
            pi.cancel();
        }
    }

    ...
}
```

The first thing you do in your method is construct your **PendingIntent** that starts **PollService**. You do this by calling **PendingIntent.getService(…)**. **PendingIntent.getService(…)** packages up an invocation of **Context.startService(Intent)**. It takes in four parameters: a **Context** with which to send the intent, a request code that you can use to distinguish this **PendingIntent** from others, the **Intent** object to send, and finally a set of flags that you can use to tweak how the **PendingIntent** is created. (You will use one of these in a moment.)

After that, you need to either set the alarm or cancel it.

To set the alarm, you call **AlarmManager.setInexactRepeating(…)**. This method also takes four parameters: a constant to describe the time basis for the alarm (about which more in a moment), the time at which to start the alarm, the time interval at which to repeat the alarm, and finally a **PendingIntent** to fire when the alarm goes off.

Because you used AlarmManager.ELAPSED_REALTIME as the time basis value, you specified the start time in terms of elapsed realtime: SystemClock.elapsedRealtime(). This triggers the alarm to go off when the specified amount of time has passed. If you had used `AlarmManager.RTC`, you would instead base the start time on "wall clock time" (e.g., `System.currentTimeMillis()`). This would trigger the alarm to go off at a fixed point in time.

Canceling the alarm is done by calling **`AlarmManager.cancel(PendingIntent)`**. You will also usually want to cancel the **`PendingIntent`**. In a moment, you will see how canceling the **`PendingIntent`** also helps you track the status of the alarm.

Add some quick test code to run your alarm from within **`PhotoGalleryFragment`**.

Listing 26.9 Adding alarm startup code (`PhotoGalleryFragment.java`)

```java
public class PhotoGalleryFragment extends Fragment {
    private static final String TAG = "PhotoGalleryFragment";

    ...

    @Override
    public void onCreate(Bundle savedInstanceState) {
        ...

        updateItems();

        Intent i = PollService.newIntent(getActivity());
        getActivity().startService(i);
        PollService.setServiceAlarm(getActivity(), true);

        Handler responseHandler = new Handler();
        mThumbnailDownloader = new ThumbnailDownloader<>(responseHandler);
        ...
    }

    ...
}
```

Finish typing in this code and run PhotoGallery. Then immediately hit the Back button and exit out of the app.

Notice anything in LogCat? **`PollService`** is faithfully chugging along, running again every 60 seconds. This is what **`AlarmManager`** is designed to do. Even if your process gets shut down, **`AlarmManager`** will keep on firing intents to start **`PollService`** again and again. (This behavior is, of course, extremely annoying. You may want to uninstall the app until we get it straightened out.)

(If you feel like 60 seconds is too long to wait, you can use a shorter interval. However, as of this writing, if you are running Android 5.1 the minimum interval allowed is 60 seconds. Any interval less than that minimum is rounded up to 60 seconds on Android 5.1.)

Being a good citizen: using alarms the right way

How exact do you need your repeating to be? Repeatedly executing work from your background service has the potential to eat up the user's battery power and data service allotment. Furthermore, waking the device from sleep (spinning up the CPU when the screen was off to do work on your behalf) is a costly operation. Luckily, you can configure your alarm to have a lighter usage footprint in terms of interval timing and wake requirements.

Inexact vs. exact repeating

There are two methods available for setting repeating alarms: `AlarmManager.setRepeating(…)` and `AlarmManager.setInexactRepeating(…)`.

If your interval requirements are flexible, as they are in this case, you should give the system flexibility to group your alarm with others. This is called "inexact repeating" and means your alarm will not occur at the exact interval you specify. Instead, the time between repetitions will vary. This allows the system to batch your alarm with others and minimize the amount of wake time needed.

Until API 19 (4.4 KitKat), `setRepeating(…)` set the alarm to repeat at exact intervals. And the `setInexactRepeating(…)` method set the alarm to be repeated in an inexact fashion. That is, unless you chose to specify a custom value for the interval. If you specified one of the provided interval constants (`INTERVAL_FIFTEEN_MINUTES`, `INTERVAL_HALF_HOUR`, `INTERVAL_HOUR`, `INTERVAL_HALF_DAY`, or `INTERVAL_DAY`), the alarm would repeat at inexact intervals, as you would expect. But if you specified a custom interval, the behavior degraded back to exact repeating.

Starting with API 19 (4.4 KitKat), the behavior of these methods changed. Both `setRepeating(…)` *and* `setInexactRepeating()` behave the same: they set the alarm for inexact repeating. Additionally, the restriction on using one of the predefined interval constants was removed. Using a custom interval with either of the methods still results in inexact repeating behavior.

In fact, the notion of exact repeating has been done away with in API 19 and higher. Instead you need to use one of the new methods, such as `AlarmManager.setWindow(…)` or `AlarmManager.setExact(…)`, which allow you to set an exact alarm to occur only once.

So what is a well-meaning Android developer to do when an app does not need an alarm with exact repeating? If your app supports only API 19 (KitKat) and up, call `setRepeating(…)` with whatever time interval you see fit. If your app supports pre-KitKat devices, call `setInexactRepeating(…)`. And, if at all possible, use one of the built-in interval constants to ensure you get inexact behavior on all devices.

Time basis options

Another important decision is which time basis value to specify. There are two main options: `AlarmManager.ELAPSED_REALTIME` and `AlarmManager.RTC`.

`AlarmManager.ELAPSED_REALTIME` uses the amount of time that has passed since the last boot of the device (including sleep time) as the basis for interval calculations. `ELAPSED_REALTIME` is the best choice for your alarm in PhotoGallery because it is based on the relative passage of time and thus does not depend on wall clock time. (Also, the documentation recommends you use `ELAPSED_REALTIME` instead of `RTC` if at all possible.)

`AlarmManager.RTC` uses "wall clock time" in terms of UTC. UTC should only be used for wall-clock basis alarms. However, UTC does not respect locale, whereas the user's idea of wall-clock time includes locale. Wall-clock basis alarms should respect locale somehow. This means you must implement your own locale handling in conjunction with using the `RTC` time basis if you want to set a wall-clock time alarm. Otherwise, use `ELAPSED_REALTIME` as the time basis.

If you use one of the time basis options outlined above, your alarm will not fire if the device is in sleep mode (the screen is turned off), even if the prescribed interval has passed. If you need your alarm to occur on a more precise interval or time, you can force the alarm to wake up the device by using one of the following time basis constants: AlarmManager.ELAPSED_REALTIME_WAKEUP and AlarmManager.RTC_WAKEUP. However, you should avoid using the wakeup options unless your alarm absolutely must occur at a specific time.

PendingIntent

Let's talk a little bit more about **PendingIntent**. A **PendingIntent** is a token object. When you get one here by calling **PendingIntent.getService(…)**, you say to the OS, "Please remember that I want to send this intent with **startService(Intent)**." Later on you can call **send()** on your **PendingIntent** token, and the OS will send the intent you originally wrapped up in exactly the way you asked.

The really nice thing about this is that when you give that **PendingIntent** token to someone else and they use it, it sends that token *as your application*. Also, because the **PendingIntent** itself lives in the OS, not in the token, you maintain control of it. If you wanted to be cruel, you could give someone else a **PendingIntent** object and then immediately cancel it, so that **send()** does nothing.

If you request a **PendingIntent** twice with the same intent, you will get the same **PendingIntent**. You can use this to test whether a **PendingIntent** already exists or to cancel a previously issued **PendingIntent**.

Managing alarms with PendingIntent

You can only register one alarm for each **PendingIntent**. That is how **setServiceAlarm(Context, boolean)** works when isOn is false: it calls **AlarmManager.cancel(PendingIntent)** to cancel the alarm for your **PendingIntent**, and then cancels your **PendingIntent**.

Because the **PendingIntent** is also cleaned up when the alarm is canceled, you can check whether that **PendingIntent** exists or not to see whether the alarm is active or not. This is done by passing in the PendingIntent.FLAG_NO_CREATE flag to **PendingIntent.getService(…)**. This flag says that if the **PendingIntent** does not already exist, return null instead of creating it.

Write a new method called **isServiceAlarmOn(Context)** that uses PendingIntent.FLAG_NO_CREATE to tell whether the alarm is on or not.

Listing 26.10 Adding **isServiceAlarmOn()** method (PollService.java)

```java
public class PollService extends IntentService {
    ...

    public static void setServiceAlarm(Context context, boolean isOn) {
        ...
    }

    public static boolean isServiceAlarmOn(Context context) {
        Intent i = PollService.newIntent(context);
        PendingIntent pi = PendingIntent
                .getService(context, 0, i, PendingIntent.FLAG_NO_CREATE);
        return pi != null;
    }

    ...
}
```

Because this **PendingIntent** is only used for setting your alarm, a null **PendingIntent** here means that your alarm is not set.

Controlling Your Alarm

Now that you can turn your alarm on and off (as well as tell whether it is on or off), let's add an interface to turn this thing on and off. Add another menu item to menu/fragment_photo_gallery.xml.

Listing 26.11 Adding service toggle (menu/fragment_photo_gallery.xml)

```
<menu xmlns:android="http://schemas.android.com/apk/res/android"
      xmlns:app="http://schemas.android.com/apk/res-auto">

    <item android:id="@+id/menu_item_search"
        ... />

    <item android:id="@+id/menu_item_clear"
        ... />

    <item android:id="@+id/menu_item_toggle_polling"
        android:title="@string/start_polling"
        app:showAsAction="ifRoom" />
</menu>
```

Then you need to add a few new strings – one to start polling and one to stop polling. (You will need a couple of other ones later, too, for a status bar notification. Go ahead and add those as well.)

Listing 26.12 Adding polling strings (res/values/strings.xml)

```
<resources>

    ...
    <string name="search">Search</string>
    <string name="clear_search">Clear Search</string>
    <string name="start_polling">Start polling</string>
    <string name="stop_polling">Stop polling</string>
    <string name="new_pictures_title">New PhotoGallery Pictures</string>
    <string name="new_pictures_text">You have new pictures in PhotoGallery.</string>

</resources>
```

Now delete your old debug code for starting the alarm and add an implementation for the menu item.

Listing 26.13 Toggle menu item implementation (PhotoGalleryFragment.java)

```
private static final String TAG = "PhotoGalleryFragment";

...

@Override
public void onCreate(Bundle savedInstanceState) {
    super.onCreate(savedInstanceState);
    ...
    updateItems();

    PollService.setServiceAlarm(getActivity(), true);

    Handler responseHandler = new Handler();
    ...
}

...

@Override
public boolean onOptionsItemSelected(MenuItem item) {
    switch (item.getItemId()) {
        case R.id.menu_item_clear:
            QueryPreferences.setStoredQuery(getActivity(), null);
            updateItems();
            return true;
        case R.id.menu_item_toggle_polling:
            boolean shouldStartAlarm = !PollService.isServiceAlarmOn(getActivity());
            PollService.setServiceAlarm(getActivity(), shouldStartAlarm);
            return true;
        default:
            return super.onOptionsItemSelected(item);
    }
}

...
```

With that, you should be able to toggle your alarm on and off. However, you will notice that the menu item for polling always says Start polling, even if the polling is currently on. You should instead toggle the menu item title as you did for Show Subtitle in the CriminalIntent app (Chapter 13).

In **onCreateOptionsMenu(…)**, check whether the alarm is on and change the text of menu_item_toggle_polling to show the appropriate label to the user.

Listing 26.14 Toggling the menu item (PhotoGalleryFragment.java)

```java
public class PhotoGalleryFragment extends Fragment {
    private static final String TAG = "PhotoGalleryFragment";

    ...

    @Override
    public void onCreateOptionsMenu(Menu menu, MenuInflater menuInflater) {
        super.onCreateOptionsMenu(menu, menuInflater);
        menuInflater.inflate(R.menu.fragment_photo_gallery, menu);

        MenuItem searchItem = menu.findItem(R.id.menu_item_search);
        final SearchView searchView = (SearchView) searchItem.getActionView();

        searchView.setOnQueryTextListener(…);

        searchView.setOnSearchClickListener(…);

        MenuItem toggleItem = menu.findItem(R.id.menu_item_toggle_polling);
        if (PollService.isServiceAlarmOn(getActivity())) {
            toggleItem.setTitle(R.string.stop_polling);
        } else {
            toggleItem.setTitle(R.string.start_polling);
        }
    }

    ...
}
```

Next, in **onOptionsItemSelected(MenuItem)**, tell **PhotoGalleryActivity** to update its toolbar options menu.

Listing 26.15 Invalidating your options menu (PhotoGalleryFragment.java)

```java
...

@Override
public boolean onOptionsItemSelected(MenuItem item) {
    switch (item.getItemId()) {
        case R.id.menu_item_clear:
            ...
        case R.id.menu_item_toggle_polling:
            boolean shouldStartAlarm = !PollService.isServiceAlarmOn(getActivity());
            PollService.setServiceAlarm(getActivity(), shouldStartAlarm);
            getActivity().invalidateOptionsMenu();
            return true;
        default:
            return super.onOptionsItemSelected(item);
    }
}

...
```

With that, your code to toggle the options menu contents should work great. And yet... there is something missing.

Notifications

Your service is now running and doing its thing in the background. But the user never knows a thing about it, so it is not worth much.

When your service needs to communicate something to the user, the proper tool is almost always a *notification*. Notifications are items that appear in the notifications drawer, which the user can access by dragging it down from the top of the screen.

To post a notification, you first need to create a **Notification** object. **Notification**s are created by using a builder object, much like **AlertDialog** was in Chapter 12. At a minimum, your **Notification** should have:

- *ticker text* to display in the status bar when the notification is first shown on pre-Lollipop devices (starting with Android 5.0 (Lollipop), ticker text is no longer displayed in the status bar but is still relevant for accessibility services)

- an *icon* to show in the status bar (the icon will appear after the ticker text goes away on pre-Lollipop devices)

- a *view* to show in the notification drawer to represent the notification itself

- a *PendingIntent* to fire when the user presses the notification in the drawer

Once you have created a **Notification** object, you can post it by calling **notify(int, Notification)** on the **NotificationManager** system service.

First you need to add some plumbing code, as shown in Listing 26.16. Open **PhotoGalleryActivity** and add a static **newIntent(Context)** method. This method will return an **Intent** instance that can be used to start **PhotoGalleryActivity**. (Eventually **PollService** will call **PhotoGalleryActivity.newIntent(…)**, wrap the resulting intent in a **PendingIntent**, and set that **PendingIntent** on a notification.)

Listing 26.16 Add **newIntent(…)** to **PhotoGalleryActivity** (PhotoGalleryActivity.java)

```java
public class PhotoGalleryActivity extends SingleFragmentActivity {

    public static Intent newIntent(Context context) {
        return new Intent(context, PhotoGalleryActivity.class);
    }

    @Override
    protected Fragment createFragment() {
        return PhotoGalleryFragment.newInstance();
    }
}
```

Make **PollService** notify the user that a new result is ready by adding the code in Listing 26.17, which creates a **Notification** and calls **NotificationManager.notify(int, Notification)**.

Listing 26.17 Adding a notification (`PollService.java`)

```
...

@Override
protected void onHandleIntent(Intent intent) {
    ...

    String resultId = items.get(0).getId();
    if (resultId.equals(lastResultId)) {
        Log.i(TAG, "Got an old result: " + resultId);
    } else {
        Log.i(TAG, "Got a new result: " + resultId);

        Resources resources = getResources();
        Intent i = PhotoGalleryActivity.newIntent(this);
        PendingIntent pi = PendingIntent.getActivity(this, 0, i, 0);

        Notification notification = new NotificationCompat.Builder(this)
                .setTicker(resources.getString(R.string.new_pictures_title))
                .setSmallIcon(android.R.drawable.ic_menu_report_image)
                .setContentTitle(resources.getString(R.string.new_pictures_title))
                .setContentText(resources.getString(R.string.new_pictures_text))
                .setContentIntent(pi)
                .setAutoCancel(true)
                .build();

        NotificationManagerCompat notificationManager =
                NotificationManagerCompat.from(this);
        notificationManager.notify(0, notification);
    }

    QueryPreferences.setLastResultId(this, resultId);
}

...
```

Let's go over this from top to bottom. First, you configure the ticker text and small icon by calling **setTicker(CharSequence)** and **setSmallIcon(int)**. (Note that the icon resource referenced is provided as part of the Android framework, denoted by the package name `android.R.drawable.some_drawable_resource_name`, so you do not have to pull the icon image into your resource folder.)

After that, you configure the appearance of your **Notification** in the drawer itself. It is possible to create a completely custom look and feel, but it is easier to use the standard look for a notification, which features an icon, a title, and a text area. It will use the value from **setSmallIcon(int)** for the icon. To set the title and text, you call **setContentTitle(CharSequence)** and **setContentText(CharSequence)**, respectively.

Next, you must specify what happens when the user presses your **Notification**. Like **AlarmManager**, this is done using a **PendingIntent**. The **PendingIntent** you pass in to **setContentIntent(PendingIntent)** will be fired when the user presses your **Notification** in the drawer. Calling **setAutoCancel(true)** tweaks that behavior a little bit. With **setAutoCancel(true)** set, your notification will also be deleted from the notification drawer when the user presses it.

Finally, you get an instance of **NotificationManagerCompat** from the current context (`NotificationManagerCompat.from(this)`) and call **NotificationManagerCompat.notify(…)**

to post your notification. The integer parameter you pass to **notify(...)** is an identifier for your notification. It should be unique across your application. If you post a second notification with this same ID, it will replace the last notification you posted with that ID. This is how you would implement a progress bar or other dynamic visuals.

And that is it. Run your app and turn polling on. You should eventually see a notification icon appear in the status bar. In the notification tray you will see a notification indicating that new photo results are available.

After you are satisfied that everything is working correctly, change your alarm constant to be something more sensible. (Using one of **AlarmManager**'s predefined interval constants ensures your app will get inexact repeating alarm behavior on pre-KitKat devices.)

Listing 26.18 Changing to a sensible alarm constant (`PollService.java`)

```
public class PollService extends IntentService {
    private static final String TAG = "PollService";

    public static final int POLL_INTERVAL = 1000 * 60; // 60 seconds
    private static final long POLL_INTERVAL = AlarmManager.INTERVAL_FIFTEEN_MINUTES;

    ...
}
```

Challenge: Notifications on Android Wear

Since you used **NotificationCompat** and **NotificationManagerCompat**, your notifications will automatically appear on an Android Wear device if the user has it paired with an Android device running your app. Users who receive the notification on a Wear device can swipe left to be presented with the option to Open the app on the connected handheld. Pressing **Open** on the Wear device will issue the notification's pending intent on the connected handheld device.

To test this out, set up an Android Wear emulator and pair it with a handheld device running your app. Details about how to do this can be found on `http://developer.android.com`.

For the More Curious: Service Details

We recommend using **IntentService** for most service tasks. If the **IntentService** pattern does not suit your architecture for a particular app, you will need to understand more about services to implement your own. Prepare for an infobomb, though – there are a lot of details and ins and outs to using services.

What a service does (and does not) do

A service is an application component that provides lifecycle callbacks, just like an activity. Those callbacks are even performed on the main UI thread for you, just like in an activity.

A service does *not* run any code on a background thread out of the box. This is the #1 reason we recommend **IntentService**. Most nontrivial services will require a background thread of some kind, and **IntentService** automatically manages the boilerplate code you need to accomplish that.

Let's see what lifecycle callbacks a service has.

A service's lifecycle

For a service started with **startService(Intent)**, life is fairly simple. There are three lifecycle callbacks.

- **onCreate(…)** – called when the service is created.

- **onStartCommand(Intent, int, int)** – called once each time a component starts the service with **startService(Intent)**. The two integer parameters are a set of flags and a start ID. The flags are used to signify whether this intent delivery is an attempt to redeliver an intent or if it is an attempt to retry a delivery which never made it to (or never returned from) **onStartCommand(Intent, int, int)**. The start ID will be different for every call to **onStartCommand(Intent, int, int)**, so it may be used to distinguish this command from others.

- **onDestroy()** – called when the service no longer needs to be alive. Often this will be after the service is stopped.

The **onDestroy()** callback is called when the service stops. This can happen in different ways, depending on what type of service you have written. The type of service is determined by the value returned from **onStartCommand(…)**, which may be Service.START_NOT_STICKY, START_REDELIVER_INTENT, or START_STICKY.

Non-sticky services

IntentService is a *non-sticky service*, so let's start there. A non-sticky service stops when the service itself says it is done. To make your service non-sticky, return either START_NOT_STICKY or START_REDELIVER_INTENT.

You tell Android that you are done by calling either **stopSelf()** or **stopSelf(int)**. The first method, **stopSelf()**, is unconditional. It will always stop your service, no matter how many times **onStartCommand(…)** has been called.

The second method, **stopSelf(int)**, is conditional. This method takes in the start ID received in **onStartCommand(…)**. This method will only stop your service if this was the most recent start ID received. (This is how **IntentService** works under the hood.)

So what is the difference between returning START_NOT_STICKY and START_REDELIVER_INTENT? The difference is in how your service behaves if the system needs to shut it down before it is done. A START_NOT_STICKY service will die and disappear into the void. START_REDELIVER_INTENT, on the other hand, will attempt to start up the service again later, when resources are less constrained.

Choosing between START_NOT_STICKY and START_REDELIVER_INTENT is a matter of deciding how important that operation is to your application. If the service is not critical, choose START_NOT_STICKY. In PhotoGallery, your service is being run repeatedly on an alarm. If one invocation falls through the cracks, it is not a big deal, so: START_NOT_STICKY. This is the default behavior for **IntentService**. To switch to using START_REDELIVER_INTENT, call **IntentService.setIntentRedelivery(true)**.

Sticky services

A *sticky service* stays started until something outside the service tells it to stop by calling **Context.stopService(Intent)**. To make your service sticky, return START_STICKY.

Once a sticky service is started it is "on" until a component calls **Context.stopService(Intent)**. If the service needs to be killed for some reason, it will be restarted again with a null intent passed in to **onStartCommand(...)**.

A sticky service may be appropriate for a long-running service, like a music player, which needs to stick around until the user tells it to stop. Even then, it is worth considering an alternative architecture using non-sticky services. Sticky service management is inconvenient, because it is difficult to tell whether the service is already started.

Bound services

In addition to all this, it is possible to bind to a service by using the **bindService(Intent, ServiceConnection, int)** method. This allows you to call methods on the service directly. **ServiceConnection** is an object that represents your service binding and receives all binding callbacks.

In a fragment, your binding code would look something like this:

```
private ServiceConnection mServiceConnection = new ServiceConnection() {
    public void onServiceConnected(ComponentName className,
            IBinder service) {
        // Used to communicate with the service
        MyBinder binder = (MyBinder)service;
    }

    public void onServiceDisconnected(ComponentName className) {
    }
};

@Override
public void onCreate(Bundle savedInstanceState) {
    super.onCreate(savedInstanceState);

    Intent i = new Intent(getActivity(), MyService.class);
    getActivity().bindService(i, mServiceConnection, 0);
}

@Override
public void onDestroy() {
    super.onDestroy();
    getActivity().unbindService(mServiceConnection);
}
```

On the service's side, binding introduces two additional lifecycle callbacks:

- **onBind(Intent)** – called every time the service is bound to. Returns the **IBinder** object received in **ServiceConnection.onServiceConnected(ComponentName, IBinder)**.

- **onUnbind(Intent)** – called when a service's binding is terminated.

Local service binding

So what does **MyBinder** look like? If the service is a local service, then it may be a simple Java object that lives in your local process. Usually this is used to provide a handle to directly call methods on your service:

```
private class MyBinder extends IBinder {
    public MyService getService() {
        return MyService.this;
    }
}

@Override
public void onBind(Intent intent) {
    return new MyBinder();
}
```

This pattern looks exciting. It is the only place in Android that enables one Android component to directly talk to another. However, we do not recommend it. Since services are effectively singletons, using them this way provides no major benefits over just using a singleton instead.

Remote service binding

Binding is more useful for remote services, because they give applications in other processes the ability to invoke methods on your service. Creating a remote service binder is an advanced topic and beyond the scope of this book. Check out the AIDL guide in the Android documentation or the **Messenger** class for more details.

For the More Curious: JobScheduler and JobServices

In this chapter, you saw how to use **AlarmManager**, an **IntentService**, and **PendingIntent**s to stitch together a periodically executing background task. In doing that, you had to do a few things manually:

- schedule a periodic task

- check whether that periodic task is currently running

- check whether the network is currently up

You might want to do more than that in the real world. For example, you might want to implement a backoff-and-retry policy if your request fails, or restrict network access to unmetered Internet access. What if you wanted to only check for new photos while the device was charging? These things are certainly possible, but they are not easy or obvious.

On top of that, there are some fundamental problems with how the implementation in this chapter is hooked up into the OS. For example, even if your service spins up and sees that there is nothing to do, it still has to spin up. There is no way to say, "Do not spin up my service in these circumstances." Another problem: you have to do extra work to make sure your job stays scheduled after a reboot. (You will see how that works in the next chapter, when you receive the BOOT_COMPLETED broadcast intent.)

We have presented this way of doing things because those are the APIs that are available in older versions of Android. In Lollipop (API 21), however, a new API was introduced that is designed to do exactly what your **PollService** does: the **JobScheduler** API. **JobScheduler** allows you to define services to run particular jobs, and then schedule them to run only when particular conditions apply.

Here is how it works. First, you create a service to handle your job. That is going to be some kind of **JobService** subclass. A **JobService** has two methods to override: **onStartJob(JobParameters)** and **onStopJob(JobParameters)**. (Do not enter this code anywhere. It is only a sample for purposes of this discussion.)

```
public class PollService extends JobService {
    @Override
    public boolean onStartJob(JobParameters params) {
        return false;
    }

    @Override
    public boolean onStopJob(JobParameters params) {
        return false;
    }
}
```

When Android is ready to run your job, your service will be started and you will receive a call to **onStartJob(…)** on your main thread. Returning false from this method means, "I went ahead and did everything this job needs, so it is complete." Returning true means, "Got it. I am working on this job now, but I am not done yet."

Unlike **IntentService**, **JobService** expects you to do your own threading, which is a minor hassle. You might do that with an **AsyncTask**:

```
private PollTask mCurrentTask;

@Override
public boolean onStartJob(JobParameters params) {
    mCurrentTask = new PollTask();
    mCurrentTask.execute(params);
    return true;
}

private class PollTask extends AsyncTask<JobParameters,Void,Void> {
    @Override
    protected Void doInBackground(JobParameters... params) {
        JobParameters jobParams = params[0];

        // Poll Flickr for new images

        jobFinished(jobParams, false);
        return null;
    }
}
```

When you are done with your job, you call **jobFinished(JobParameters, boolean)** to say that you are done. Passing in true for the second parameter means that you were not able to get the job done this time, and that the job should be rescheduled again for the future.

The **onStopJob(JobParameters)** callback is for when your job needs to be interrupted. Maybe you only want your job to run when a WiFi connection is available. If the phone moves out of WiFi range before you call **jobFinished(…)**, you will get a call to **onStopJob(…)**, which is your cue to drop everything immediately.

```
@Override
public boolean onStopJob(JobParameters params) {
    if (mCurrentTask != null) {
        mCurrentTask.cancel(true);
    }
    return true;
}
```

A call to **onStopJob(…)** is an indication that your service is about to be shut down. No waiting is allowed: you must stop your business immediately. Returning true here means that your job should be rescheduled to run again in the future. Returning false means, "Okay, I was done anyway. Do not reschedule me."

When you register your service in the manifest, you must export it and add a permission:

```
<service
    android:name=".PollService"
    android:permission="android.permission.BIND_JOB_SERVICE"
    android:exported="true"/>
```

Exporting it exposes it to the world at large, but adding the permission restricts it back down so that only **JobScheduler** can run it.

Once you have created a **JobService**, kicking it off is a snap. You can use **JobScheduler** to check on whether your job has been scheduled.

```
final int JOB_ID = 1;

JobScheduler scheduler = (JobScheduler)
    context.getSystemService(Context.JOB_SCHEDULER_SERVICE);

boolean hasBeenScheduled = false;
for (JobInfo jobInfo : scheduler.getAllPendingJobs()) {
    if (jobInfo.getId() == JOB_ID) {
        hasBeenScheduled = true;
    }
}
```

And if it has not, you can create a new **JobInfo** that says when you want your job to run. Hmm, when should **PollService** run? How about something like this:

```
final int JOB_ID = 1;

JobScheduler scheduler = (JobScheduler)
    context.getSystemService(Context.JOB_SCHEDULER_SERVICE);

JobInfo jobInfo = new JobInfo.Builder(
        JOB_ID, new ComponentName(context, PollService.class))
        .setRequiredNetworkType(JobInfo.NETWORK_TYPE_UNMETERED)
        .setPeriodic(1000 * 60 * 15)
        .setPersisted(true)
        .build();
scheduler.schedule(jobInfo);
```

This schedules your job to run every 15 minutes, but only on WiFi or another unmetered network. Calling **setPersisted(true)** also makes your job persisted: it will survive a reboot. Check out the reference documentation to see all the other ways you can configure a **JobInfo**.

For the More Curious: Sync Adapters

Yet another way to set up a regularly polling web service is to use a *sync adapter*. Sync adapters are not adapters like you have seen before. Instead, their sole purpose is to sync data with a data source (uploading, downloading, or both). Unlike **JobScheduler**, sync adapters have been around for a while, so you do not have to worry about which version of Android you are running on.

Like **JobScheduler**, sync adapters can be used as a replacement for the **AlarmManager** setup that you had in PhotoGallery. Syncs from multiple applications are grouped together by default, without you having to set flags a certain way. Furthermore, you do not have to worry about resetting the sync alarm across reboots because sync adapters handle this for you.

Sync adapters also integrate nicely with the OS from a user perspective. You can expose your app as a sync-able account that the user can manage through the Settings → Accounts menu. This is where users manage accounts for other apps that use sync adapters, such as Google's suite of apps (Figure 26.2).

Figure 26.2 Accounts settings

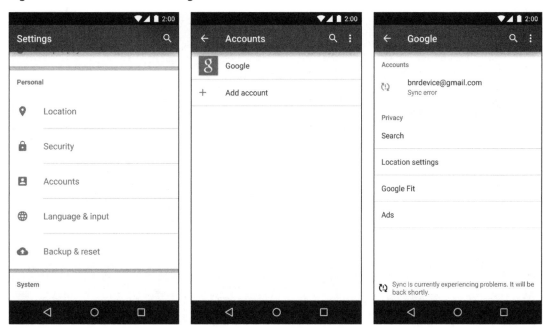

While using a sync adapter makes correct usage of scheduling repeating network work easier, and allows you to get rid of the alarm management and pending intent code, a sync adapter does require a bunch more code. First, a sync adapter does not do any of your web requests for you, so you still have to write that code (e.g., **FlickrFetchr**). Second, it requires a content provider implementation to wrap the data, account, and authenticator classes to represent an account on a remote server (even if the server does not require authentication), and a sync adapter and sync service implementation. It also requires working knowledge of bound services.

So if your application already uses a **ContentProvider** for its data layer and requires account authentication, using a sync adapter is a good option for you to consider. It is a big advantage that sync adapters integrate with the user interface provided by the OS, too. **JobScheduler** does not do that, either. If none of those considerations apply, the extra code required might not be worth it.

The online developer docs provide a tutorial on using sync adapters: https:// developer.android.com/training/sync-adapters/index.html. Check it out to learn more.

Challenge: Using JobService on Lollipop

For an additional challenge, create a second implementation of **PollService** that subclasses **JobService** and is run using **JobScheduler**. In your **PollService** startup code, check to see whether you are on Lollipop. If so, use **JobScheduler** to schedule your **JobService**. Otherwise, fall back on your old **AlarmManager** implementation.

27

Broadcast Intents

In this chapter you will polish PhotoGallery in two big ways. First, you will make the app poll for new search results and notify the user if new results are found, even if the user has not opened the application since booting the device. Second, you will ensure notifications about new results are posted only if the user is not interacting with the app. (It is annoying and redundant to both get a notification and see the results update in the screen when you are actively viewing an app.)

In making these updates, you will learn how to listen for *broadcast intents* from the system and how to handle such intents using a *broadcast receiver*. You will also dynamically send and receive broadcast intents within your app at runtime. Finally, you will use ordered broadcasts to determine if your application is currently running in the foreground or not.

Regular Intents vs. Broadcast Intents

Things are happening all the time on an Android device. WiFi is going in and out of range, packages are getting installed, phone calls and text messages are coming and going.

When many components on the system need to know that some event has occurred, Android uses a broadcast intent to tell everyone about it. Broadcast intents work similarly to the intents you already know and love, except that they can be received by multiple components, called broadcast receivers, at the same time (Figure 27.1).

Figure 27.1 Regular intents vs. broadcast intents

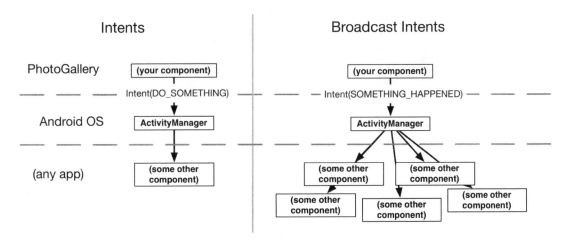

Activities and services should respond to implicit intents whenever they are used as part of a public API. In other circumstances, explicit intents are almost always sufficient. On the other hand, the entire reason broadcast intents exist is to send information to more than one listener. So while broadcast receivers *can* respond to explicit intents, they are rarely, if ever, used this way, because explicit intents have only have one receiver.

Receiving a System Broadcast: Waking Up on Boot

PhotoGallery's background alarm works, but it is not perfect. If the user reboots the device, the alarm will be forgotten.

Apps that perform an ongoing process for the user usually need to wake themselves up after the device is booted. You can detect when boot is completed by listening for a broadcast intent with the BOOT_COMPLETED action. The system sends out a BOOT_COMPLETED broadcast intent whenever the device is turned on. You can listen for it by creating and registering a standalone broadcast receiver that filters for the appropriate action.

Creating and registering a standalone receiver

A *standalone receiver* is a broadcast receiver that is declared in the manifest. Such a receiver can be activated even if your app process is dead. (Later you will learn about *dynamic receivers*, which can instead be tied to the lifecycle of a visible app component, like a fragment or activity.)

Just like services and activities, broadcast receivers must be registered with the system in order to do anything useful. If the receiver is not registered with the system, the system will not send any intents its way and in turn the receiver's **onReceive(…)** will not get executed as desired.

But before you can register your broadcast receiver, you have to write it. Create a new Java class called **StartupReceiver** that is a subclass of **android.content.BroadcastReceiver**.

Listing 27.1 Your first broadcast receiver (StartupReceiver.java)

```
public class StartupReceiver extends BroadcastReceiver{
    private static final String TAG = "StartupReceiver";

    @Override
    public void onReceive(Context context, Intent intent) {
        Log.i(TAG, "Received broadcast intent: " + intent.getAction());
    }
}
```

A broadcast receiver is a component that receives intents, just like a service or an activity. When an intent is issued to **StartupReceiver**, its **onReceive(…)** method will be called.

Next, open AndroidManifest.xml and hook up **StartupReceiver** as a standalone receiver:

Listing 27.2 Adding your receiver to the manifest (AndroidManifest.xml)

```xml
<manifest ...>

    <uses-permission android:name="android.permission.INTERNET"/>
    <uses-permission android:name="android.permission.ACCESS_NETWORK_STATE"/>
    <uses-permission android:name="android.permission.RECEIVE_BOOT_COMPLETED" />

    <application
        ...>
        <activity
            android:name=".PhotoGalleryActivity"
            android:label="@string/app_name">
            ...
        </activity>

        <service android:name=".PollService"/>

        <receiver android:name=".StartupReceiver">
            <intent-filter>
                <action android:name="android.intent.action.BOOT_COMPLETED"/>
            </intent-filter>
        </receiver>
    </application>

</manifest>
```

Registering a standalone receiver to respond to an implicit intent works just like registering an activity to do the same. You use the receiver tag with appropriate intent-filters within. **StartupReceiver** will be listening for the BOOT_COMPLETED action. This action also requires a permission, so you include an appropriate uses-permission tag as well.

With your broadcast receiver declared in your manifest, it will wake up any time a matching broadcast intent is sent – even if your app is not currently running. Upon waking up, the ephemeral broadcast receiver's **onReceive(Context, Intent)** method will be run, and then it will die, as shown in Figure 27.2.

Figure 27.2 Receiving BOOT_COMPLETED

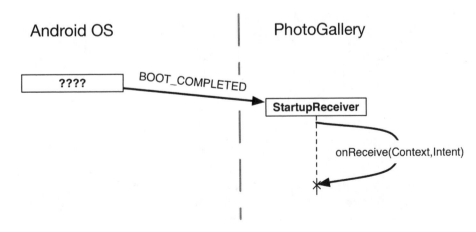

Time to verify that **StartupReceiver**'s **onReceive(…)** is executed when the device boots up. First, run PhotoGallery to install the most recent version on your device.

Next, shut down your device. If you are using a physical device, power it all the way off. If you are using an emulator, the easiest way to shut it down is to quit out of the emulator by closing the emulator window.

Turn the device back on. If you are using a physical device, use the power button. If you are using an emulator, either rerun your application or start the device using AVD Manager. Make sure you are using the same emulator image you just shut down.

Now, open the Android Device Monitor by selecting Tools → Android → Android Device Monitor.

(You may hear the Android Device Monitor called "Dalvik Debug Monitor Server" or "DDMS." Prior to KitKat (4.4), Dalvik was the only runtime system available on Android. Starting with KitKat, Android Runtime (ART) was included as an alternative; as of Lollipop (5.0), ART is the only runtime used. Android Device Monitor has been renamed accordingly, but the old name still lingers.)

Click on your device in Android Device Monitor's Devices tab. (If you do not see the device listed, try unplugging and replugging in your USB device, or restarting the emulator.)

Search the LogCat results within the Android Device Monitor window for your log statement (Figure 27.3).

Figure 27.3 Searching LogCat output

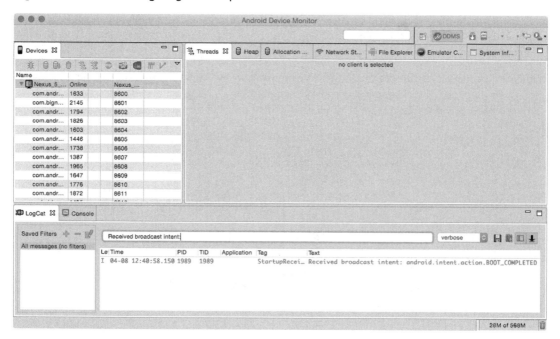

You should see a LogCat statement showing that your receiver ran. However, if you check your device in the Devices tab, you will probably not see a process for PhotoGallery. Your process came to life just long enough to run your broadcast receiver, and then it died again.

(Testing that the receiver executed can be unreliable when you are using LogCat output, especially if you are using an emulator. If you do not see the log statement the first time through the instructions above, try a few more times. Worst case, continue through the rest of the exercise. Once you get to the part where you hook up notifications you will have a more reliable way to check on whether the receiver is working.)

Using receivers

The fact that broadcast receivers live such short lives restricts the things you can do with them. You cannot use any asynchronous APIs, for example, or register any listeners, because your receiver will not be alive any longer than the length of **onReceive(Context, Intent)**. Also, because **onReceive(Context, Intent)** runs on your main thread, you cannot do any heavy lifting inside it. That means no networking or heavy work with permanent storage.

This does not make receivers useless, though. They are invaluable for all kinds of little plumbing code, such as starting an activity or service (so long as you do not expect a result back) or resetting a recurring alarm when the system finishes rebooting (as you will do in this exercise).

Your receiver will need to know whether the alarm should be on or off. Add a preference constant and convenience methods to **QueryPreferences** to store this information in shared preferences.

Listing 27.3 Adding alarm status preference (QueryPreferences.java)

```java
public class QueryPreferences {
    private static final String PREF_SEARCH_QUERY = "searchQuery";
    private static final String PREF_LAST_RESULT_ID = "lastResultId";
    private static final String PREF_IS_ALARM_ON = "isAlarmOn";

    ...

    public static void setLastResultId(Context context, String lastResultId) {
        ...
    }

    public static boolean isAlarmOn(Context context) {
        return PreferenceManager.getDefaultSharedPreferences(context)
                .getBoolean(PREF_IS_ALARM_ON, false);
    }

    public static void setAlarmOn(Context context, boolean isOn) {
        PreferenceManager.getDefaultSharedPreferences(context)
                .edit()
                .putBoolean(PREF_IS_ALARM_ON, isOn)
                .apply();
    }
}
```

Next, update **PollService.setServiceAlarm(…)** to write to shared preferences when the alarm is set.

Listing 27.4 Writing alarm status preference when alarm is set (`PollService.java`)

```java
public class PollService extends IntentService {
    ...

    public static void setServiceAlarm(Context context, boolean isOn) {
        ...

        if (isOn) {
            alarmManager.setInexactRepeating(AlarmManager.ELAPSED_REALTIME,
                    SystemClock.elapsedRealtime(), POLL_INTERVAL, pi);
        } else {
            alarmManager.cancel(pi);
            pi.cancel();
        }

        QueryPreferences.setAlarmOn(context, isOn);
    }

    ...
}
```

Then your **StartupReceiver** can use it to turn the alarm on at boot.

Listing 27.5 Starting alarm on boot (`StartupReceiver.java`)

```java
public class StartupReceiver extends BroadcastReceiver{
    private static final String TAG = "StartupReceiver";

    @Override
    public void onReceive(Context context, Intent intent) {
        Log.i(TAG, "Received broadcast intent: " + intent.getAction());

        boolean isOn = QueryPreferences.isAlarmOn(context);
        PollService.setServiceAlarm(context, isOn);
    }
}
```

Run PhotoGallery again. (You may want to change `PollService.POLL_INTERVAL` back to a shorter interval, such as 60 seconds, for testing purposes.) Turn polling on by clicking Start polling in the toolbar. Reboot your device. This time, your background polling should be restarted after you reboot your phone, tablet, or emulator.

Filtering Foreground Notifications

With that sharp corner filed down a bit, lets turn to another imperfection in PhotoGallery. Your notifications work great, but they are sent even when the user already has the application open.

You can fix this problem with broadcast intents, too. But they will work in a completely different way.

First, you will send (and receive) your own custom broadcast intent (and ultimately will lock it down so it can be received by components in your application only). Second, you will register a receiver for your broadcast dynamically in code, rather than in the manifest. Finally, you will send an ordered broadcast to pass data along a chain of receivers, ensuring a certain receiver is run last. (You do not know how to do all this yet, but you will by the time you are done.)

Sending broadcast intents

This part is easy: you need to send your own broadcast intent. Specifically, you will send a broadcast notifying interested components that a new search results notification is ready to post. To send a broadcast intent, create an intent and pass it in to **sendBroadcast(Intent)**. In this case, you will want it to broadcast an action you define, so define an action constant as well.

Add these items in **PollService**.

Listing 27.6 Sending a broadcast intent (PollService.java)

```java
public class PollService extends IntentService {
    private static final String TAG = "PollService";

    private static final long POLL_INTERVAL = AlarmManager.INTERVAL_FIFTEEN_MINUTES;

    public static final String ACTION_SHOW_NOTIFICATION =
            "com.bignerdranch.android.photogallery.SHOW_NOTIFICATION";

    ...

    @Override
    protected void onHandleIntent(Intent intent) {

        ...

        String resultId = items.get(0).getId();
        if (resultId.equals(lastResultId)) {
            Log.i(TAG, "Got an old result: " + resultId);
        } else {
            ...

            NotificationManagerCompat notificationManager =
                    NotificationManagerCompat.from(this);
            notificationManager.notify(0, notification);

            sendBroadcast(new Intent(ACTION_SHOW_NOTIFICATION));
        }

        QueryPreferences.setLastResultId(this, resultId);
    }

    ...
}
```

Now your app will send out a broadcast every time new search results are available.

Creating and registering a dynamic receiver

Now you need a receiver for your ACTION_SHOW_NOTIFICATION broadcast intent.

You could write a standalone broadcast receiver, like **StartupReceiver**, and register it in the manifest. But that would not be ideal in this case. Here, you want **PhotoGalleryFragment** to receive the intent only while it is alive. A standalone receiver declared in the manifest would always receive the intent and would need some other way of knowing that **PhotoGalleryFragment** is alive (which is not easily achieved in Android).

The solution is to use a *dynamic broadcast receiver*. A dynamic receiver is registered in code, not in the manifest. You register the receiver by calling **registerReceiver(BroadcastReceiver, IntentFilter)** and unregister it by calling **unregisterReceiver(BroadcastReceiver)**. The receiver itself is typically defined as an inner instance, like a button-click listener. However, since you need the same instance in **registerReceiver(…)** and **unregisterReceiver(…)**, you will need to assign the receiver to an instance variable.

Create a new abstract class called **VisibleFragment**, with **Fragment** as its superclass. This class will be a generic fragment that hides foreground notifications. (You will write another fragment like this in Chapter 28.)

Listing 27.7 A receiver of **VisibleFragment**'s own (VisibleFragment.java)

```java
public abstract class VisibleFragment extends Fragment {
    private static final String TAG = "VisibleFragment";

    @Override
    public void onStart() {
        super.onStart();
        IntentFilter filter = new IntentFilter(PollService.ACTION_SHOW_NOTIFICATION);
        getActivity().registerReceiver(mOnShowNotification, filter);
    }

    @Override
    public void onStop() {
        super.onStop();
        getActivity().unregisterReceiver(mOnShowNotification);
    }


    private BroadcastReceiver mOnShowNotification = new BroadcastReceiver() {
        @Override
        public void onReceive(Context context, Intent intent) {
            Toast.makeText(getActivity(),
                    "Got a broadcast:" + intent.getAction(),
                    Toast.LENGTH_LONG)
                .show();
        }
    };
}
```

Note that to pass in an **IntentFilter**, you have to create one in code. Your **IntentFilter** here is identical to the filter specified by the following XML:

```xml
<intent-filter>
    <action android:name="com.bignerdranch.android.photogallery.SHOW_NOTIFICATION" />
</intent-filter>
```

Any **IntentFilter** you can express in XML can also be expressed in code this way. Just call **addCategory(String)**, **addAction(String)**, **addDataPath(String)**, and so on to configure your filter.

When you use dynamically registered broadcast receivers, you must also take care to clean them up. Typically, if you register a receiver in a startup lifecycle method, you call **Context.unregisterReceiver(BroadcastReceiver)** in the corresponding shutdown method. Here, you register inside **onStart()** and unregister inside **onStop()**. If instead you registered inside **onActivityCreated(…)**, you would unregister inside **onActivityDestroyed()**.

(Be careful with **onCreate(…)** and **onDestroy()** in retained fragments, by the way. **getActivity()** will return different values in **onCreate(…)** and **onDestroy()** if the screen has rotated. If you want to register/unregister in **Fragment.onCreate(Bundle)** and **Fragment.onDestroy()**, use **getActivity().getApplicationContext()** instead.)

Next, modify **PhotoGalleryFragment** to be a subclass of your new **VisibleFragment**.

Listing 27.8 Making your fragment visible (PhotoGalleryFragment.java)

```
public class PhotoGalleryFragment extends FragmentVisibleFragment {
    ...
}
```

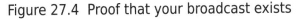

Run PhotoGallery and toggle background polling a couple of times. You will see a nice toast pop up in addition to your notification icon up top (Figure 27.4).

Figure 27.4 Proof that your broadcast exists

Limiting broadcasts to your app using private permissions

One issue with a broadcast like this is that anyone on the system can listen to it or trigger your receivers. You are usually not going to want either of those things to happen.

You can preclude these unauthorized intrusions into your personal business in a couple of ways. One way is to declare in your manifest that the receiver is internal to your app by adding an `android:exported="false"` attribute to your receiver tag. This will prevent it from being visible to other applications on the system.

Another way is to create your own permission by adding a `permission` tag to your `AndroidManifest.xml`. This is the approach you will take for PhotoGallery.

Declare and acquire your own permission in `AndroidManifest.xml`.

Listing 27.9 Adding a private permission (`AndroidManifest.xml`)

```
<manifest ...>

  <permission android:name="com.bignerdranch.android.photogallery.PRIVATE"
    android:protectionLevel="signature" />

  <uses-permission android:name="android.permission.INTERNET" />
  <uses-permission android:name="android.permission.ACCESS_NETWORK_STATE" />
  <uses-permission android:name="android.permission.RECEIVE_BOOT_COMPLETED" />
  <uses-permission android:name="com.bignerdranch.android.photogallery.PRIVATE" />

  <application
    ... >
    ...
  </application>

</manifest>
```

Notice that you define a custom permission with a *protection level* of `signature`. You will learn more about protection levels in just a moment. The permission itself is a simple string, just like intent actions, categories, and system permissions you have used. You must always acquire a permission to use it, even when you defined it yourself. Them's the rules.

Take note of the shaded constant value above, by the way. This string needs to appear in three more places and must be identical in each place. You would be wise to copy and paste it rather than typing it out by hand.

Now, use your permission by defining a corresponding constant in code and then passing it in to your **sendBroadcast(…)** call.

Listing 27.10 Sending with a permission (`PollService.java`)

```java
public class PollService extends IntentService {
    ...

    public static final String ACTION_SHOW_NOTIFICATION =
            "com.bignerdranch.android.photogallery.SHOW_NOTIFICATION";
    public static final String PERM_PRIVATE =
            "com.bignerdranch.android.photogallery.PRIVATE";

    public static Intent newIntent(Context context) {
        return new Intent(context, PollService.class);
    }

    ...

    @Override
    protected void onHandleIntent(Intent intent) {

        ...

        String resultId = items.get(0).getId();
        if (resultId.equals(lastResultId)) {
            Log.i(TAG, "Got an old result: " + resultId);
        } else {
            ...
            notificationManager.notify(0, notification);

            sendBroadcast(new Intent(ACTION_SHOW_NOTIFICATION), PERM_PRIVATE);
        }

        QueryPreferences.setLastResultId(this, resultId);
    }

    ...
}
```

To use your permission, you pass it as a parameter to **sendBroadcast(...)**. Using the permission here ensures that any application must use that same permission to receive the intent you are sending.

What about your broadcast receiver? Someone could create their own broadcast intent to trigger it. You can fix that by passing in your permission in **registerReceiver(...)**, too.

Listing 27.11 Permissions on a broadcast receiver (`VisibleFragment.java`)

```java
public abstract class VisibleFragment extends Fragment {
    ...

    @Override
    public void onStart() {
        super.onStart();
        IntentFilter filter = new IntentFilter(PollService.ACTION_SHOW_NOTIFICATION);
        getActivity().registerReceiver(mOnShowNotification, filter,
                PollService.PERM_PRIVATE, null);
    }

    ...
}
```

Now, your app is the only app that can trigger that receiver.

More about protection levels

Every custom permission has to specify a value for `android:protectionLevel`. Your permission's `protectionLevel` tells Android how it should be used. In your case, you used a `protectionLevel` of `signature`.

The `signature` protection level means that if another application wants to use your permission, it has to be signed with the same key as your application. This is usually the right choice for permissions you use internally in your application. Because other developers do not have your key, they cannot get access to anything this permission protects. Plus, because you *do* have your own key, you can use this permission in any other app you decide to write later.

Table 27.1 Values for `protectionLevel`

Value	Description
`normal`	This is for protecting app functionality that will not do anything dangerous like accessing secure personal data or sending data to the Internet. The user can see the permission before choosing to install the app, but is not explicitly asked to grant it. `android.permission.RECEIVE_BOOT_COMPLETED` uses this permission level, and so does the permission that lets your app vibrate the user's device.
`dangerous`	This is for everything you would not use `normal` for – accessing personal data, sending and receiving things from network interfaces, accessing hardware that might be used to spy on the user, or anything else that could cause real problems. The Internet permission, camera permission, and contacts permission all fall under this category. Android may ask the user for an explicit go-ahead before approving a `dangerous` permission.
`signature`	The system grants this permission if the app is signed with the same certificate as the declaring application, and denies it otherwise. If the permission is granted, the user is not notified. This is for functionality that is internal to an app – as the developer, because you have the certificate and only apps signed with the same certificate can use the permission, you have control over who uses the permission. You used it here to prevent anyone else from seeing your broadcasts. If you wanted, you could write another app that listens to them, too.
`signatureOrSystem`	This is like signature, but it also grants permission to all packages in the Android system image. This is for communicating with apps built into the system image. If the permission is granted, the user is not notified. Most developers do not need to use it.

Passing and receiving data with ordered broadcasts

Time to finally bring this baby home. The last piece is to ensure your dynamically registered receiver always receives the `PollService.ACTION_SHOW_NOTIFICATION` broadcast before any other receivers and that it modifies the broadcast to indicate that the notification should not be posted.

Right now you are sending your own personal private broadcast, but so far you only have one-way communication (Figure 27.5).

Figure 27.5 Regular broadcast intents

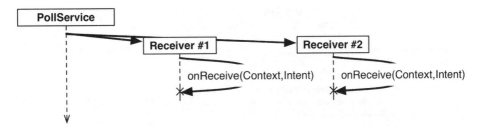

This is because a regular broadcast intent is conceptually received by everyone at the same time. In reality, because **onReceive(…)** is called on the main thread, your receivers are not actually executed concurrently. However, it is not possible to rely on their being executed in any particular order or to know when they have all completed execution. As a result, it is a hassle for the broadcast receivers to communicate with each other or for the sender of the intent to receive information from the receivers.

You can implement two-way communication using an *ordered broadcast intent* (Figure 27.6). Ordered broadcasts allow a sequence of broadcast receivers to process a broadcast intent in order. They also allow the sender of a broadcast to receive results from the broadcast's recipients by passing in a special broadcast receiver, called the *result receiver*.

Figure 27.6 Ordered broadcast intents

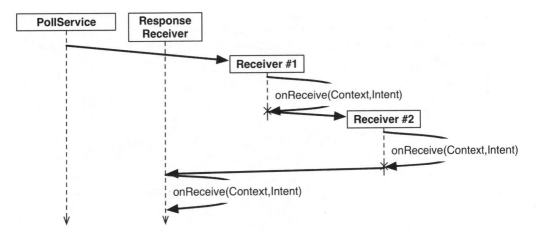

On the receiving side, this looks mostly the same as a regular broadcast. But you get an additional tool: a set of methods used to change the return value of your receiver. Here, you want to cancel the notification. This can be communicated by use of a simple integer result code. You will use the **setResultCode(int)** method to set the result code to Activity.RESULT_CANCELED.

Modify **VisibleFragment** to tell the sender of SHOW_NOTIFICATION whether the notification should be posted. This information will also be sent to any other broadcast receivers along the chain.

Listing 27.12 Sending a simple result back (`VisibleFragment.java`)

```
public abstract class VisibleFragment extends Fragment {
    private static final String TAG = "VisibleFragment";

    private BroadcastReceiver mOnShowNotification = new BroadcastReceiver() {
        @Override
        public void onReceive(Context context, Intent intent) {
            Toast.makeText(getActivity(),
                    "Got a broadcast:" + intent.getAction(),
                    Toast.LENGTH_LONG)
                .show();
            // If we receive this, we're visible, so cancel
            // the notification
            Log.i(TAG, "canceling notification");
            setResultCode(Activity.RESULT_CANCELED);
        }
    };

    ...
}
```

Because all you need to do is signal yes or no here, you only need the result code. If you need to return more complicated data, you can use **setResultData(String)** or **setResultExtras(Bundle)**. And if you want to set all three values, you can call **setResult(int, String, Bundle)**. Once your return values are set here, every subsequent receiver will be able to see or modify them.

For those methods to do anything useful, your broadcast needs to be ordered. Write a new method to send an ordered broadcast in **PollService**. This method will package up a **Notification** invocation and send it out as a broadcast. Update **onHandleIntent(…)** to call your new method and, in turn, send out an ordered broadcast instead of posting the notification directly to the **NotificationManager**.

Listing 27.13 Sending an ordered broadcast (`PollService.java`)

```
...
public static final String PERM_PRIVATE =
        "com.bignerdranch.android.photogallery.PRIVATE";
public static final String REQUEST_CODE = "REQUEST_CODE";
public static final String NOTIFICATION = "NOTIFICATION";
...

@Override
protected void onHandleIntent(Intent intent) {
    ...

    String resultId = items.get(0).getId();
    if (resultId.equals(lastResultId)) {
        Log.i(TAG, "Got an old result: " + resultId);
    } else {
        Log.i(TAG, "Got a new result: " + resultId);
        ...

        Notification notification = ...;

        NotificationManagerCompat notificationManager =
                NotificationManagerCompat.from(this);
        notificationManager.notify(0, notification);

        sendBroadcast(new Intent(ACTION_SHOW_NOTIFICATION), PERM_PRIVATE);
        showBackgroundNotification(0, notification);
    }

    QueryPreferences.setLastResultId(this, resultId);
}

private void showBackgroundNotification(int requestCode, Notification notification) {
    Intent i = new Intent(ACTION_SHOW_NOTIFICATION);
    i.putExtra(REQUEST_CODE, requestCode);
    i.putExtra(NOTIFICATION, notification);
    sendOrderedBroadcast(i, PERM_PRIVATE, null, null,
            Activity.RESULT_OK, null, null);
}

...
```

`Context.sendOrderedBroadcast(Intent, String, BroadcastReceiver, Handler, int, String, Bundle)` has five additional parameters beyond the ones you used in `sendBroadcast(Intent, String)`. They are, in order: a *result receiver*, a `Handler` to run the result receiver on, and then initial values for the result code, result data, and result extras for the ordered broadcast.

The result receiver is a special receiver that runs after all the other recipients of your ordered broadcast intent. In other circumstances, you would be able to use the result receiver to receive the broadcast and post the notification object. Here, though, that will not work. This broadcast intent will often be sent right before `PollService` dies. That means that your broadcast receiver might be dead, too.

Thus, your final broadcast receiver will need to be a standalone receiver, and you will need to enforce that it runs after the dynamically registered receiver by different means.

First, create a new `BroadcastReceiver` subclass called `NotificationReceiver`. Implement it as follows:

Listing 27.14 Implementing your result receiver (NotificationReceiver.java)

```java
public class NotificationReceiver extends BroadcastReceiver {
    private static final String TAG = "NotificationReceiver";

    @Override
    public void onReceive(Context c, Intent i) {
        Log.i(TAG, "received result: " + getResultCode());
        if (getResultCode() != Activity.RESULT_OK) {
            // A foreground activity cancelled the broadcast
            return;
        }

        int requestCode = i.getIntExtra(PollService.REQUEST_CODE, 0);
        Notification notification = (Notification)
                i.getParcelableExtra(PollService.NOTIFICATION);

        NotificationManagerCompat notificationManager =
                NotificationManagerCompat.from(c);
        notificationManager.notify(requestCode, notification);
    }
}
```

Next, register your new receiver and assign it a priority. To ensure **NotificationReceiver** receives the broadcast after your dynamically registered receiver (so it can check to see whether it should post the notification to **NotificationManager**), you need to set a low priority for **NotificationReceiver**. Give it a priority of –999 so that it runs last. This is the lowest user-defined priority possible (–1000 and below are reserved).

Also, since this receiver is only used by your application, you do not need it to be externally visible. Set android:exported="false" to keep this receiver to yourself.

Listing 27.15 Registering the notification receiver (AndroidManifest.xml)

```xml
<manifest ...>
  ...

  <application
    ... >
    ...
    <receiver android:name=".StartupReceiver">
      <intent-filter>
        <action android:name="android.intent.action.BOOT_COMPLETED" />
      </intent-filter>
    </receiver>
    <receiver android:name=".NotificationReceiver"
      android:exported="false">
      <intent-filter
        android:priority="-999">
        <action
            android:name="com.bignerdranch.android.photogallery.SHOW_NOTIFICATION" />
      </intent-filter>
    </receiver>
  </application>

</manifest>
```

Run PhotoGallery and toggle background polling a couple of times. You should see that notifications no longer appear when you have the app in the foreground. (If you have not already done so, change `PollService.POLL_INTERVAL` to 60 seconds so that you do not have to wait 15 minutes to verify that notifications still work in the background.)

Receivers and Long-Running Tasks

So what do you do if you want a broadcast intent to kick off a longer-running task than the restrictions of the main run loop allow?

You have two options. The first is to put that work into a service instead, and start the service in your broadcast receiver's small window of opportunity. This is the method we recommend. A service can take as long as it needs to service a request. It can queue up multiple requests and service them in order or otherwise manage requests as it sees fit.

The second is to use the `BroadcastReceiver.goAsync()` method. This method returns a `BroadcastReceiver.PendingResult` object, which can be used to provide a result at a later time. So you could give that `PendingResult` to an `AsyncTask` to perform some longer running work, and then respond to the broadcast by calling methods on `PendingResult`.

There is one downside to using the `goAsync` method: it is less flexible. You still have to service the broadcast within 10 seconds or so, and you have fewer architectural options than you do with a service.

Of course, `goAsync()` has one huge advantage: you can set results for ordered broadcasts with it. If you really need that, nothing else will do. Just make sure you do not take too long.

For the More Curious: Local Events

Broadcast intents allow you to propagate information across the system in a global fashion. What if you want to broadcast the occurrence of an event within your app's process only? Using an *event bus* is a great alternative.

An *event bus* operates on the idea of having a shared bus, or stream of data, that components within your application can subscribe to. When an event is posted to the bus, subscribed components will be activated and have their callback code executed.

EventBus by greenrobot is a third-party event bus library we use in our Android applications. Other alternatives to consider include Square's Otto, which is another event bus implementation, or using RxJava `Subjects` and `Observables` to simulate an event bus.

Android does provide a local way to send broadcast intents, called `LocalBroadcastManager`. But we find that the third-party libraries mentioned here provide a more flexible and easier-to-use API for broadcasting local events.

Using EventBus

In order to use EventBus in your application, you must add a library dependency to your project. Once the dependency is set up, you define a class representing an event (you can add fields to the event if you need to pass data along):

```
public class NewFriendAddedEvent { }
```

You can post to the bus from just about anywhere in your app:

```
EventBus eventBus = EventBus.getDefault();
eventBus.post(new NewFriendAddedEvent());
```

Other parts of your app can subscribe to receive events by first registering to listen on the bus. Often you will register and unregister activities or fragments in corresponding lifecycle methods, such as **onStart(...)** and **onStop(...)**:

```
// In some fragment or activity...
private EventBus mEventBus;

@Override
public void onCreate(Bundle savedInstanceState) {
    super.onCreate(savedInstanceState);
    mEventBus = EventBus.getDefault();
}

@Override
public void onStart() {
    super.onStart();
    mEventBus.register(this);
}

@Override
public void onStop() {
    super.onStop();
    mEventBus.unregister(this);
}
```

You specify what the subscriber should do when an event it is looking for is posted by implementing an **onEvent(...)** or **onEventMainThread(...)** method with the appropriate event type as input. Using **onEvent(...)** means the event will be processed on the same thread it was sent from. (You could implement **onEventMainThread(...)** to ensure the event is processed on the main thread if it happens to be issued from a background thread.)

```
// In some registered component, like a fragment or activity...
public void onEventMainThread(NewFriendAddedEvent event){
    Friend newFriend = event.getFriend();
    // Update the UI or do something in response to event...
}
```

Using RxJava

RxJava can also be used to implement an event broadcasting mechanism. RxJava is a library for writing "reactive"-style Java code. That "reactive" idea is broad, and beyond the scope of what we can cover here. The short story is that it allows you to publish and subscribe to sequences of events and gives you a broad set of generic tools for manipulating these event sequences.

So you could create something called a **Subject**, which is an object you can publish events to as well as subscribe to events on.

```
Subject<Object, Object> eventBus = new SerializedSubject<>(PublishSubject.create());
```

You can publish events to it:

```
Friend someNewFriend = ...;
NewFriendAddedEvent event = new NewFriendAddedEvent(someNewFriend);
eventBus.onNext(event);
```

And subscribe to events on it:

```
eventBus.subscribe(new Action1<Object>() {
    @Override
    public void call(Object event) {
        if (event instanceof NewFriendAddedEvent) {
            Friend newFriend = ((NewFriendAddedEvent)event).getFriend();
            // Update the UI
        }
    }
})
```

The advantage of RxJava's solution is that your eventBus is now also an **Observable**, RxJava's representation of a stream of events. That means that you get to use all of RxJava's various event manipulation tools. If that piques your interest, check out the wiki on RxJava's project page: https://github.com/ReactiveX/RxJava/wiki.

For the More Curious: Detecting the Visibility of Your Fragment

When you reflect on your PhotoGallery implementation, you may notice that you used the global broadcast mechanism to broadcast the SHOW_NOTIFICATION intent. However, you locked the receiving of that broadcast to items local to your app progress by using custom permissions. You may find yourself asking, "Why am I using a global mechanism if I am just communicating things in my own app? Why not a local mechanism instead?"

This is because you were specifically trying to solve the problem of knowing whether or not **PhotoGalleryFragment** was visible. The combination of ordered broadcasts, standalone receivers, and dynamically registered receivers you implemented gets the job done. There is not a more straightforward way to do this in Android.

More specifically, **LocalBroadcastManager** would not work for PhotoGallery's notification broadcast and visible fragment detection, for two main reasons.

First, **LocalBroadcastManager** does not support ordered broadcasts (though it does provide a blocking way to broadcast, namely **sendBroadcastSync(Intent intent)**). This will not work for PhotoGallery because you need to force **NotificationReceiver** to run last in the chain.

Second, **sendBroadcastSync(Intent intent)** does not support sending and receiving a broadcast on separate threads. In PhotoGallery you need to send the broadcast from a background thread (in **PollService.onHandleIntent(…)**) and receive the intent on the main thread (by the dynamic receiver that is registered by **PhotoGalleryFragment** on the main thread in **onResume(…)**).

As of this writing, the semantics of **LocalBroadcastManager**'s thread delivery are not well documented and, in our experience, are not intuitive. For example, if you call **sendBroadcastSync(…)** from a background thread, all pending broadcasts will get flushed out on that background thread regardless of whether they were posted from the main thread.

This is not to say **LocalBroadcastManager** is not useful. It is simply not the right tool for the problems you solved in this chapter.

28

Browsing the Web and WebView

Each photo you get from Flickr has a page associated with it. In this chapter, you are going to update PhotoGallery so that users can press a photo to see its Flickr page. You will learn two different ways to integrate web content into your apps, shown in Figure 28.1. The first works with the device's browser app (left), and the second uses a **WebView** to display web content within PhotoGallery (right).

Figure 28.1 Web content: two different approaches

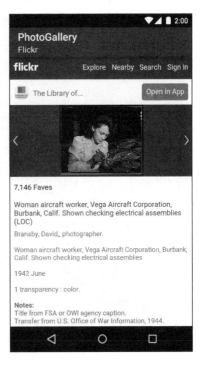

One Last Bit of Flickr Data

For both ways, you need to get the URL for a photo's Flickr page. If you look at the JSON you are currently receiving for each photo, you can see that the photo page is not part of those results.

```
{
  "photos": {
    ...,
    "photo": [
      {
        "id": "9452133594",
        "owner": "44494372@N05",
        "secret": "d6d20af93e",
        "server": "7365",
        "farm": 8,
        "title": "Low and Wisoff at Work",
        "ispublic": 1,
        "isfriend": 0,
        "isfamily": 0,
        "url_s":"https://farm8.staticflickr.com/7365/9452133594_d6d20af93e_m.jpg"
      }, ...
    ]
  },
  "stat": "ok"
}
```

You might think that you are in for some more JSON request writing. Fortunately, that is not the case. If you look at the "Web Page URLs" section of Flickr's documentation at http://www.flickr.com/services/api/misc.urls.html, you will see that you can create the URL for an individual photo's page like so:

> http://www.flickr.com/photos/*user-id*/*photo-id*

The photo-id seen here is the same as the value of the id attribute from your JSON. You are already stashing that in mId in **GalleryItem**. What about user-id? If you poke around the documentation, you will find that the owner attribute in your JSON is a user ID. So if you pull out the owner attribute, you should be able to build the URL from your photo JSON:

> http://www.flickr.com/photos/*owner*/*id*

Update **GalleryItem** to put this plan into action.

Listing 28.1 Adding code for photo page (`GalleryItem.java`)

```java
public class GalleryItem {
    private String mCaption;
    private String mId;
    private String mUrl;
    private String mOwner;

    ...

    public void setUrl(String url) {
        mUrl = url;
    }

    public String getOwner() {
        return mOwner;
    }

    public void setOwner(String owner) {
        mOwner = owner;
    }

    public Uri getPhotoPageUri() {
        return Uri.parse("http://www.flickr.com/photos/")
                .buildUpon()
                .appendPath(mOwner)
                .appendPath(mId)
                .build();
    }

    @Override
    public String toString() {
        return mCaption;
    }
}
```

Here, you create a new mOwner property here and add a short method called **getPhotoPageUri()** to generate photo page URLs as discussed above.

Now change **parseItems(…)** to read in the owner attribute.

Listing 28.2 Reading in owner attribute (`FlickrFetchr.java`)

```java
public class FlickrFetchr {

    ...

    private void parseItems(List<GalleryItem> items, JSONObject jsonBody)
            throws IOException, JSONException {

        JSONObject photosJsonObject = jsonBody.getJSONObject("photos");
        JSONArray photoJsonArray = photosJsonObject.getJSONArray("photo");

        for (int i = 0; i < photoJsonArray.length(); i++) {
            JSONObject photoJsonObject = photoJsonArray.getJSONObject(i);

            GalleryItem item = new GalleryItem();
            item.setId(photoJsonObject.getString("id"));
            item.setCaption(photoJsonObject.getString("title"));

            if (!photoJsonObject.has("url_s")) {
                continue;
            }

            item.setUrl(photoJsonObject.getString("url_s"));
            item.setOwner(photoJsonObject.getString("owner"));
            items.add(item);
        }
    }
}
```

Easy peasy. Now to have fun with your new photo page URL.

The Easy Way: Implicit Intents

You will browse to this URL first by using your old friend the implicit intent. This intent will start up the browser with your photo URL.

The first step is to make your app listen to presses on an item in the **RecyclerView**. Update **PhotoGalleryFragment**'s **PhotoHolder** to implement a click listener that will fire an implicit intent.

Listing 28.3 Firing implicit intent when item is pressed (PhotoGalleryFragment.java)

```java
public class PhotoGalleryFragment extends VisibleFragment {
    ...

    private class PhotoHolder extends RecyclerView.ViewHolder
            implements View.OnClickListener {
        private ImageView mItemImageView;
        private GalleryItem mGalleryItem;

        public PhotoHolder(View itemView) {
            super(itemView);

            mItemImageView = (ImageView) itemView
                .findViewById(R.id.fragment_photo_gallery_image_view);
            itemView.setOnClickListener(this);
        }

        public void bindDrawable(Drawable drawable) {
            mItemImageView.setImageDrawable(drawable);
        }

        public void bindGalleryItem(GalleryItem galleryItem) {
            mGalleryItem = galleryItem;
        }

        @Override
        public void onClick(View v) {
            Intent i = new Intent(Intent.ACTION_VIEW, mGalleryItem.getPhotoPageUri());
            startActivity(i);
        }
    }

    ...
}
```

Next, bind the **PhotoHolder** to a **GalleryItem** in **PhotoAdapter.onBindViewHolder(…)**.

Listing 28.4 Binding **GalleryItem** (PhotoGalleryFragment.java)

```java
...

private class PhotoAdapter extends RecyclerView.Adapter<PhotoHolder> {

    ...

    @Override
    public void onBindViewHolder(PhotoHolder photoHolder, int position) {
        GalleryItem galleryItem = mGalleryItems.get(position);
        photoHolder.bindGalleryItem(galleryItem);
        Drawable placeholder = getResources().getDrawable(R.drawable.bill_up_close);
        photoHolder.bindDrawable(placeholder);
        mThumbnailDownloader.queueThumbnail(photoHolder, galleryItem.getUrl());
    }

    ...
}
...
```

That is it. Start up PhotoGallery and press on a photo. Your browser app should pop up and load the photo page for the item you pressed (similar to the image on the left in Figure 28.1).

The Harder Way: WebView

Using an implicit intent to display the photo page is easy and effective. But what if you do not want your app to open the browser?

Often, you want to display web content within your own activities instead of heading off to the browser. You may want to display HTML that you generate yourself, or you may want to lock down the browser somehow. For apps that include help documentation, it is common to implement it as a web page so that it is easy to update. Opening a web browser to a help web page does not look professional, and it prevents you from customizing behavior or integrating that web page into your own user interface.

When you want to present web content within your own user interface, you use the **WebView** class. We are calling this the "harder" way here, but it is pretty darned easy. (Anything is hard compared to using implicit intents.)

The first step is to create a new activity and fragment to display the **WebView**. Start, as usual, by defining a layout file, using Figure 28.2.

Figure 28.2 Initial layout (res/layout/fragment_photo_page.xml)

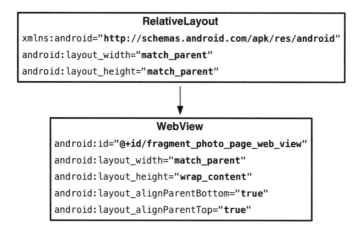

You may be thinking, "That **RelativeLayout** is pretty useless." True enough – for the moment. You will fill it out later in the chapter with additional "chrome."

Next, get the rudiments of your fragment set up. Create **PhotoPageFragment** as a subclass of the **VisibleFragment** class you created in the last chapter. You will need to inflate your layout file, extract your **WebView** from it, and forward along the URL to display as a fragment argument.

Listing 28.5 Setting up your web browser fragment (`PhotoPageFragment.java`)

```java
public class PhotoPageFragment extends VisibleFragment {
    private static final String ARG_URI = "photo_page_url";

    private Uri mUri;
    private WebView mWebView;

    public static PhotoPageFragment newInstance(Uri uri) {
        Bundle args = new Bundle();
        args.putParcelable(ARG_URI, uri);

        PhotoPageFragment fragment = new PhotoPageFragment();
        fragment.setArguments(args);
        return fragment;
    }

    @Override
    public void onCreate(Bundle savedInstanceState) {
        super.onCreate(savedInstanceState);

        mUri = getArguments().getParcelable(ARG_URI);
    }

    @Override
    public View onCreateView(LayoutInflater inflater, ViewGroup container,
                             Bundle savedInstanceState) {
        View v = inflater.inflate(R.layout.fragment_photo_page, container, false);

        mWebView = (WebView) v.findViewById(R.id.fragment_photo_page_web_view);

        return v;
    }
}
```

For now, this is just a skeleton. You will fill it out a bit more in a moment. But first, create the containing **PhotoPageActivity** class using good old **SingleFragmentActivity**.

Listing 28.6 Creating web activity (`PhotoPageActivity.java`)

```java
public class PhotoPageActivity extends SingleFragmentActivity {

    public static Intent newIntent(Context context, Uri photoPageUri) {
        Intent i = new Intent(context, PhotoPageActivity.class);
        i.setData(photoPageUri);
        return i;
    }

    @Override
    protected Fragment createFragment() {
        return PhotoPageFragment.newInstance(getIntent().getData());
    }
}
```

Switch up your code in **PhotoGalleryFragment** to launch your new activity instead of the implicit intent.

Listing 28.7 Switching to launch your activity (`PhotoGalleryFragment.java`)

```java
public class PhotoGalleryFragment extends VisibleFragment {
    ...

    private class PhotoHolder extends RecyclerView.ViewHolder
            implements View.OnClickListener{
        ...

        @Override
        public void onClick(View v) {
            Intent i = new Intent(Intent.ACTION_VIEW, mGalleryItem.getPhotoPageUri());
            Intent i = PhotoPageActivity
                .newIntent(getActivity(), mGalleryItem.getPhotoPageUri());
            startActivity(i);
        }
    }

    ...
}
```

And, finally, add your new activity to the manifest.

Listing 28.8 Adding activity to manifest (`AndroidManifest.xml`)

```xml
<manifest ... >
    ...

    <application
        ...>
        <activity
            android:name=".PhotoGalleryActivity"
            android:label="@string/app_name" >
            ...
        </activity>

        <activity android:name=".PhotoPageActivity" />

        <service android:name=".PollService" />

        ...
    </application>

</manifest>
```

Run PhotoGallery and press on a picture. You should see a new empty activity pop up.

OK, now to get to the meat and actually make your fragment do something. You need to do three things to make your **WebView** successfully display a Flickr photo page. The first one is straightforward – you need to tell it what URL to load.

The second thing you need to do is enable JavaScript. By default, JavaScript is off. You do not always need to have it on, but for Flickr, you do. (If you run Android Lint, it gives you a warning for doing this. It is worried about cross-site scripting attacks. You can suppress this Lint warning here by annotating **onCreateView(…)** with @SuppressLint("SetJavaScriptEnabled").)

Finally, you need to override one method on a class called **WebViewClient**, **shouldOverrideUrlLoading(WebView, String)**, and return false. We will discuss this class a bit more after you enter the code.

Listing 28.9 Loading URL into **WebView** (PhotoPageFragment.java)

```java
public class PhotoPageFragment extends VisibleFragment {
    ...

    @Override
    public View onCreateView(LayoutInflater inflater, ViewGroup container,
                             Bundle savedInstanceState) {
        View v = inflater.inflate(R.layout.fragment_photo_page, container, false);

        mWebView = (WebView) v.findViewById(R.id.fragment_photo_page_web_view);
        mWebView.getSettings().setJavaScriptEnabled(true);
        mWebView.setWebViewClient(new WebViewClient() {
            public boolean shouldOverrideUrlLoading(WebView view, String url) {
                return false;
            }
        });
        mWebView.loadUrl(mUri.toString());

        return v;
    }
}
```

Loading the URL has to be done after configuring the **WebView**, so you do that last. Before that, you turn JavaScript on by calling **getSettings()** to get an instance of **WebSettings** and calling **WebSettings.setJavaScriptEnabled(true)**. **WebSettings** is the first of the three ways you can modify your **WebView**. It has various properties you can set, like the user agent string and text size.

After that, you configure your **WebViewClient**. **WebViewClient** is an event interface. By providing your own implementation of **WebViewClient**, you can respond to rendering events. For example, you could detect when the renderer starts loading an image from a particular URL or decide whether to resubmit a POST request to the server.

WebViewClient has many methods you can override, most of which you will not deal with. However, you do need to replace the default **WebViewClient**'s implementation of **shouldOverrideUrlLoading(WebView, String)**. This method determines what will happen when a new URL is loaded in the **WebView**, like by pressing a link. If you return true, you are saying, "Do not handle this URL, I am handling it myself." If you return false, you are saying, "Go ahead and load this URL, **WebView**, I'm not doing anything with it."

The default implementation fires an implicit intent with the URL, just like you did earlier. Now, though, this would be a severe problem. The first thing Flickr does is redirect you to the mobile version of the website. With the default **WebViewClient**, that means that you are immediately sent to the user's default web browser. This is just what you are trying to avoid.

The fix is simple – just override the default implementation and return false.

Run PhotoGallery, press an item, and you should see the item's photo page displayed in the **WebView** (just like the image on the right in Figure 28.1).

Using WebChromeClient to spruce things up

Since you are taking the time to create your own **WebView**, let's spruce it up a bit by adding a progress bar and updating the toolbar's subtitle with the title of the loaded page. Crack open `fragment_photo_page.xml` and get started on these changes.

Listing 28.10 Adding title and progress (`fragment_photo_page.xml`)

```
<RelativeLayout ...>

    <ProgressBar
        android:id="@+id/fragment_photo_page_progress_bar"
        android:layout_width="match_parent"
        android:layout_height="wrap_content"
        android:layout_alignParentTop="true"
        android:visibility="gone"
        style="?android:attr/progressBarStyleHorizontal"
        android:background="?attr/colorPrimary"/>

    <WebView
        android:id="@+id/fragment_photo_page_web_view"
        android:layout_width="match_parent"
        android:layout_height="wrap_content"
        android:layout_height="match_parent"
        android:layout_alignParentTop="true" />
        android:layout_alignParentBottom="true"
        android:layout_below="@id/fragment_photo_page_progress_bar" />

</RelativeLayout>
```

To hook up the **ProgressBar**, you will use the second callback on **WebView**: **WebChromeClient**. **WebViewClient** is an interface for responding to rendering events; **WebChromeClient** is an event interface for reacting to events that should change elements of *chrome* around the browser. This includes JavaScript alerts, favicons, and of course updates for loading progress and the title of the current page.

Hook it up in **onCreateView(…)**.

Listing 28.11 Using **WebChromeClient** (PhotoPageFragment.java)

```java
public class PhotoPageFragment extends VisibleFragment {
    ...
    private WebView mWebView;
    private ProgressBar mProgressBar;

    ...

    @Override
    public View onCreateView(LayoutInflater inflater, ViewGroup container,
                              Bundle savedInstanceState) {
        View v = inflater.inflate(R.layout.fragment_photo_page, container, false);

        mProgressBar =
                (ProgressBar)v.findViewById(R.id.fragment_photo_page_progress_bar);
        mProgressBar.setMax(100); // WebChromeClient reports in range 0-100

        mWebView = (WebView) v.findViewById(R.id.fragment_photo_page_web_view);
        mWebView.getSettings().setJavaScriptEnabled(true);
        mWebView.setWebChromeClient(new WebChromeClient() {
            public void onProgressChanged(WebView webView, int newProgress) {
                if (newProgress == 100) {
                    mProgressBar.setVisibility(View.GONE);
                } else {
                    mProgressBar.setVisibility(View.VISIBLE);
                    mProgressBar.setProgress(newProgress);
                }
            }

            public void onReceivedTitle(WebView webView, String title) {
                AppCompatActivity activity = (AppCompatActivity) getActivity();
                activity.getSupportActionBar().setSubtitle(title);
            }
        });
        mWebView.setWebViewClient(new WebViewClient() {
            ...
        });
        mWebView.loadUrl(mUri.toString());

        return v;
    }
}
```

Progress updates and title updates each have their own callback method,
onProgressChanged(WebView, int) and **onReceivedTitle(WebView, String)**. The progress you
receive from **onProgressChanged(WebView, int)** is an integer from 0 to 100. If it is 100, you know
that the page is done loading, so you hide the **ProgressBar** by setting its visibility to View.GONE.

Run PhotoGallery to test your changes. It should look like Figure 28.3.

Figure 28.3 Fancy **WebView**

When you press on a photo, **PhotoPageActivity** pops up. A progress bar displays as the page loads and a subtitle reflecting the subtitle received in **onReceivedTitle(…)** appears in the toolbar. Once the page is loaded, the progress bar disappears.

Proper Rotation with WebView

Try rotating your screen. While it does work correctly, you will notice that the **WebView** has to completely reload the web page. This is because **WebView** has too much data to save it all out inside **onSaveInstanceState(…)**. It has to start from scratch each time it is re-created on rotation.

You may think the easiest way to resolve this problem would be to retain **PhotoPageFragment**. However, this would not work, because **WebView** is part of the view hierarchy and is thus still destroyed and re-created on rotation.

For some classes like this (**VideoView** is another one), the Android documentation recommends that you allow the activity to handle the configuration change itself. This means that instead of the activity being destroyed on rotation, it simply moves its views around to fit the new screen size. As a result, **WebView** does not have to reload all of its data.

To tell **PhotoPageActivity** to handle its own darned configuration changes, make the following tweak to AndroidManifest.xml.

Listing 28.12 Handling configuration changes yourself (`AndroidManifest.xml`)

```
<manifest ... >
    ...

    <activity
        android:name=".PhotoPageActivity"
        android:configChanges="keyboardHidden|orientation|screenSize" />

    ...
</manifest>
```

This attribute says that if the configuration changes because the keyboard was opened or closed, due to an orientation change, or due to the screen size changing (which also happens when switching between portrait and landscape after Android 3.2), then the activity should handle the change itself.

And that is it. Try rotating again, and admire how smoothly the change is handled.

Dangers of handling configuration changes

That is so easy and works so well that you are probably wondering why you do not do this all the time. It seems like it would make life so much easier. However, handling configuration changes on your own is a dangerous habit.

First, resource qualifiers no longer work automatically. You instead have to manually reload your view. This can be more complicated than it sounds.

Second, and more important, allowing the activity to handle configuration changes will likely cause you to not bother with overriding **Activity.onSavedInstanceState(…)** to stash transient UI states. Doing so is still necessary, even if the activity is handling configuration changes on its own, because you still have to worry about death and re-creation in low-memory situations. (Remember, the activity can be destroyed and stashed by the system at any time if it is not in the running state, as shown in Figure 3.13 on Page 71.)

For the More Curious: Injecting JavaScript Objects

In this chapter, you have seen how to use **WebViewClient** and **WebChromeClient** to respond to specific events that happen in your **WebView**. However, it is possible to do even more than that by injecting arbitrary JavaScript objects into the document contained in the **WebView** itself. Check out the documentation at `http://developer.android.com/reference/android/webkit/WebView.html` and scroll down to the **addJavascriptInterface(Object, String)** method. Using this, you can inject an arbitrary object into the document with a name you specify.

```
mWebView.addJavascriptInterface(new Object() {
    @JavascriptInterface
    public void send(String message) {
        Log.i(TAG, "Received message: " + message);
    }
}, "androidObject");
```

And then invoke it like so:

```
<input type="button" value="In WebView!"
    onClick="sendToAndroid('In Android land')" />

<script type="text/javascript">
    function sendToAndroid(message) {
        androidObject.send(message);
    }
</script>
```

Starting with API 17 (Jelly Bean 4.2) and up, only public methods annotated @JavascriptInterface are exported to JavaScript. Prior to that, all public methods in the object hierarchy were accessible.

Either way, this could be dangerous. You are letting some potentially strange web page fiddle with your program. So to be safe, it is a good idea to make sure you own the HTML in question – either that, or be extremely conservative with the interface you expose.

For the More Curious: KitKat's WebView Overhaul

WebView underwent a serious overhaul with the release of KitKat (Android 4.4, API 19). The new **WebView** is based on the Chromium open source project. It now shares the same rendering engine used by the Chrome for Android app, meaning pages should look and behave more consistently across the two. (However, **WebView** does not have all the features Chrome for Android does. You can see a good table comparing the two at https://developer.chrome.com/multidevice/webview/overview.)

The move to Chromium meant some really exciting improvements for **WebView**, like support for new web standards like HTML5 and CSS3, an updated JavaScript engine, and improved performance. From a development perspective, one of the most exciting new features is the added support for remote debugging of **WebView** using Chrome DevTools (which can be enabled by calling **WebView.setWebContentsDebuggingEnabled()**).

But what if your app supports pre-KitKat devices? It is important to note that some things behave very differently now. For example, interaction with content providers is no longer allowed from nonlocal web content (pages hosted on a server rather than your device), and custom URL schemes are handled in a more restrictive fashion.

If you set your target SDK to a value less than API 19, **WebView** will try to avoid the behavior changes introduced in API 19 while still attempting to provide the benefits of improved performance and web standards support. (This is called "quirks mode.") However, in some cases this is still not enough. For example, default zoom levels are not supported at all on API 19 and higher devices.

To make a long story short, if you are supporting pre-KitKat devices and rely on **WebView**, you will want to learn more about the differences between the pre- and post-KitKat versions. There is a great guide on migrating to the new **WebView** on the developer site http://developer.android.com/guide/webapps/migrating.html. Be prepared to test your **WebView** on both pre- and post-KitKat devices, and also know that some changes may have to happen to the web content itself.

Challenge: Using the Back Button for Browser History

You may have noticed that you can follow other links within the **WebView** once you launch **PhotoPageActivity**. However, no matter how many links you follow, the Back button always brings you immediately back to **PhotoGalleryActivity**. What if you instead want the Back button to bring users their browsing history within the **WebView**?

Implement this behavior by overriding the Back button method **Activity.onBackPressed()**. Within that method you can use a combination of **WebView**'s browsing history methods (**WebView.canGoBack()** and **WebView.goBack()**) to do the right thing. If there are items in the **WebView**'s browsing history, go back to the previous item. Otherwise, allow the Back button to behave as normal by calling through to **super.onBackPressed()**.

Challenge: Supporting Non-HTTP Links

If you poke around within **PhotoPageFragment**'s **WebView**, you may stumble upon non-HTTP links. For example, as of this writing, the photo detail page Flickr provides displays an Open in App button. Pressing this button is supposed to launch the Flickr app if it is installed. If it is not installed, the Google Play store should launch and offer the option to install the Flickr app.

However, if you press Open in App, the **WebView** instead displays error text, as shown in Figure 28.4.

Figure 28.4 Open in app error

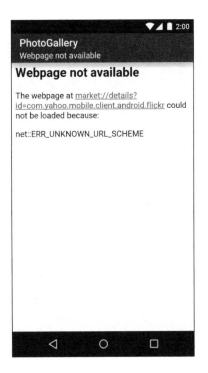

This is because you overrode **WebViewClient.shouldOverrideUrlLoading(…)** to always return false. In turn, the **WebView** always tries to load the URI into itself, even if the URI scheme is not supported by **WebView**.

To fix this, you want non-HTTP URIs to be handled by the application that is the best fit for that URI. Before a URI is loaded, check the scheme. If the scheme is not HTTP or HTTPS, issue an Intent.ACTION_VIEW for the URI.

29

Custom Views and Touch Events

In this chapter, you will learn how to handle touch events by writing a custom subclass of **View** named **BoxDrawingView**. The **BoxDrawingView** class will be the star of a new project named DragAndDraw and will draw boxes in response to the user touching the screen and dragging. The finished product will look like Figure 29.1.

Figure 29.1 Boxes drawn in many shapes and sizes

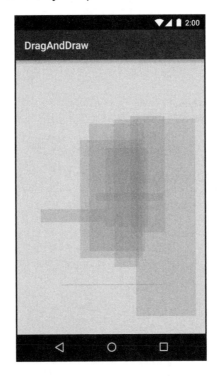

Setting Up the DragAndDraw Project

Create a new project named "DragAndDraw". Select API 16 as the minimum SDK and create a blank activity. Name the activity **DragAndDrawActivity**.

Setting up DragAndDrawActivity

DragAndDrawActivity will be a subclass of **SingleFragmentActivity** that inflates the usual single-fragment-containing layout. Copy SingleFragmentActivity.java and its activity_fragment.xml layout file into the DragAndDraw project.

In DragAndDrawActivity.java, make **DragAndDrawActivity** a **SingleFragmentActivity** that creates a **DragAndDrawFragment** (a class that you will create next).

Listing 29.1 Modifying the activity (DragAndDrawActivity.java)

```
public class DragAndDrawActivity extends AppCompatActivity SingleFragmentActivity {
    @Override
    protected void onCreate(Bundle savedInstanceState) {
        ...
    }

    @Override
    public boolean onCreateOptionsMenu(Menu menu) {
        ...
    }

    @Override
    public boolean onOptionsItemSelected(MenuItem item) {
        ...
    }

    @Override
    public Fragment createFragment() {
        return DragAndDrawFragment.newInstance();
    }
}
```

Setting up DragAndDrawFragment

To prepare a layout for **DragAndDrawFragment**, rename the activity_drag_and_draw.xml layout file to fragment_drag_and_draw.xml.

DragAndDrawFragment's layout will eventually consist of a **BoxDrawingView**, the custom view that you are going to write. All of the drawing and touch-event handling will be implemented in **BoxDrawingView**.

Create a new class named **DragAndDrawFragment** and make its superclass
android.support.v4.app.Fragment. Override **onCreateView(…)** to inflate
`fragment_drag_and_draw.xml`.

Listing 29.2 Creating the fragment (DragAndDrawFragment.java)

```
public class DragAndDrawFragment extends Fragment {

    public static DragAndDrawFragment newInstance() {
        return new DragAndDrawFragment();
    }

    @Override
    public View onCreateView(LayoutInflater inflater, ViewGroup container,
                            Bundle savedInstanceState) {
        View v = inflater.inflate(R.layout.fragment_drag_and_draw, container, false);
        return v;
    }
}
```

You can run DragAndDraw to confirm that your app is set up properly. It should look like Figure 29.2.

Figure 29.2 DragAndDraw with default layout

Creating a Custom View

Android provides many excellent standard views and widgets, but sometimes you need a custom view that presents visuals that are unique to your app.

While there are all kinds of custom views, you can shoehorn them into two broad categories:

simple	A simple view may be complicated inside; what makes it "simple" is that it has no child views. A simple view will almost always perform custom rendering.
composite	Composite views are composed of other view objects. Composite views typically manage child views but do not perform custom rendering. Instead, rendering is delegated to each child view.

There are three steps to follow when creating a custom view:

1. Pick a superclass. For a simple custom view, **View** is a blank canvas, so it is the most common choice. For a composite custom view, choose an appropriate layout class, such as **FrameLayout**.

2. Subclass this class and override the constructors from the superclass.

3. Override other key methods to customize behavior.

Creating BoxDrawingView

BoxDrawingView will be a simple view and a direct subclass of **View**.

Create a new class named **BoxDrawingView** and make **View** its superclass. In BoxDrawingView.java, add two constructors.

Listing 29.3 Initial implementation for **BoxDrawingView** (BoxDrawingView.java)

```
public class BoxDrawingView extends View {

    // Used when creating the view in code
    public BoxDrawingView(Context context) {
        this(context, null);
    }

    // Used when inflating the view from XML
    public BoxDrawingView(Context context, AttributeSet attrs) {
        super(context, attrs);
    }

}
```

You write two constructors because your view could be instantiated in code or from a layout file. Views instantiated from a layout file receive an instance of **AttributeSet** containing the XML attributes that were specified in XML. Even if you do not plan on using both constructors, it is good practice to include them.

Next, update your `fragment_drag_and_draw.xml` layout file to use your new view.

Listing 29.4 Adding **BoxDrawingView** to layout (`fragment_drag_and_draw.xml`)

```
<RelativeLayout xmlns:android="http://schemas.android.com/apk/res/android"
    xmlns:tools="http://schemas.android.com/tools"
    android:layout_width="match_parent"
    android:layout_height="match_parent"
    >

    <TextView
        android:layout_width="wrap_content"
        android:layout_height="wrap_content"
        android:layout_centerHorizontal="true"
        android:layout_centerVertical="true"
        android:text="@string/hello_world" />

</RelativeLayout>
<com.bignerdranch.android.draganddraw.BoxDrawingView
    xmlns:android="http://schemas.android.com/apk/res/android"
    android:layout_width="match_parent"
    android:layout_height="match_parent"
    />
```

You must use **BoxDrawingView**'s fully qualified class name so that the layout inflater can find it. The inflater works through a layout file creating **View** instances. If the element name is an unqualified class name, then the inflater looks for a class with that name in the android.view and android.widget packages. If the class lives somewhere else, then the layout inflater will not find it, and your app will crash.

So, for custom classes and other classes that live outside of android.view and android.widget, you must always specify the fully qualified class name.

Run DragAndDraw to confirm that all the connections are correct. All you will see is an empty view (Figure 29.3).

Figure 29.3 **BoxDrawingView** with no boxes

The next step is to get **BoxDrawingView** listening for touch events and using the information from them to draw boxes on the screen.

Handling Touch Events

One way to listen for touch events is to set a touch event listener using the following **View** method:

```
public void setOnTouchListener(View.OnTouchListener l)
```

This method works the same way as **setOnClickListener(View.OnClickListener)**. You provide an implementation of **View.OnTouchListener**, and your listener will be called every time a touch event happens.

However, because you are subclassing **View**, you can take a shortcut and override this **View** method:

```
public boolean onTouchEvent(MotionEvent event)
```

This method receives an instance of **MotionEvent**, a class that describes the touch event, including its location and its *action*. The action describes the stage of the event:

action constants	description
ACTION_DOWN	user's finger touches the screen
ACTION_MOVE	user moves finger on the screen
ACTION_UP	user lifts finger off the screen
ACTION_CANCEL	a parent view has intercepted the touch event

In your implementation of **onTouchEvent(…)**, you can check the value of the action by calling the **MotionEvent** method:

```
public final int getAction()
```

Let's get to it. In BoxDrawingView.java, add a log tag and then an implementation of **onTouchEvent(…)** that logs a message for each of the four different actions.

Listing 29.5 Implementing **BoxDrawingView** (BoxDrawingView.java)

```
public class BoxDrawingView extends View {
    private static final String TAG = "BoxDrawingView";

    ...

    @Override
    public boolean onTouchEvent(MotionEvent event) {
        PointF current = new PointF(event.getX(), event.getY());
        String action = "";

        switch (event.getAction()) {
            case MotionEvent.ACTION_DOWN:
                action = "ACTION_DOWN";
                break;
            case MotionEvent.ACTION_MOVE:
                action = "ACTION_MOVE";
                break;
            case MotionEvent.ACTION_UP:
                action = "ACTION_UP";
                break;
            case MotionEvent.ACTION_CANCEL:
                action = "ACTION_CANCEL";
                break;
        }

        Log.i(TAG, action + " at x=" + current.x +
                ", y=" + current.y);

        return true;
    }
}
```

Notice that you package your X and Y coordinates in a **PointF** object. You want to pass these two values together as you go through the rest of the chapter. **PointF** is a container class provided by Android that does this for you.

Run DragAndDraw and pull up LogCat. Touch the screen and drag your finger. You should see a report of the X and Y coordinate of every touch action that **BoxDrawingView** receives.

Tracking across motion events

BoxDrawingView is intended to draw boxes on the screen, not just log coordinates. There are a few problems to solve to get there.

First, to define a box, you need two points: the origin point (where the finger was initially placed) and the current point (where the finger currently is).

To define a box, then, requires keeping track of data from more than one **MotionEvent**. You will store this data in a **Box** object.

Create a class named **Box** to represent the data that defines a single box.

Listing 29.6 Adding **Box** (Box.java)

```java
public class Box {
    private PointF mOrigin;
    private PointF mCurrent;

    public Box(PointF origin) {
        mOrigin = origin;
        mCurrent = origin;
    }

    public PointF getCurrent() {
        return mCurrent;
    }

    public void setCurrent(PointF current) {
        mCurrent = current;
    }

    public PointF getOrigin() {
        return mOrigin;
    }
}
```

When the user touches **BoxDrawingView**, a new **Box** will be created and added to a list of existing boxes (Figure 29.4).

Figure 29.4 Objects in DragAndDraw

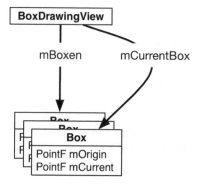

Back in **BoxDrawingView**, use your new **Box** object to track your drawing state.

Listing 29.7 Adding drag lifecycle methods (BoxDrawingView.java)

```java
public class BoxDrawingView extends View {
    public static final String TAG = "BoxDrawingView";

    private Box mCurrentBox;
    private List<Box> mBoxen = new ArrayList<>();

    ...

    @Override
    public boolean onTouchEvent(MotionEvent event) {
        PointF current = new PointF(event.getX(), event.getY());
        String action = "";

        switch (event.getAction()) {
            case MotionEvent.ACTION_DOWN:
                action = "ACTION_DOWN";
                // Reset drawing state
                mCurrentBox = new Box(current);
                mBoxen.add(mCurrentBox);
                break;
            case MotionEvent.ACTION_MOVE:
                action = "ACTION_MOVE";
                if (mCurrentBox != null) {
                    mCurrentBox.setCurrent(current);
                    invalidate();
                }
                break;
            case MotionEvent.ACTION_UP:
                action = "ACTION_UP";
                mCurrentBox = null;
                break;
            case MotionEvent.ACTION_CANCEL:
                action = "ACTION_CANCEL";
                mCurrentBox = null;
                break;
        }

        Log.i(TAG, action + " at x=" + current.x +
                ", y=" + current.y);

        return true;
    }
}
```

Any time an ACTION_DOWN motion event is received, you set mCurrentBox to be a new **Box** with its origin as the event's location. This new **Box** is added to the list of boxes. (In the next section, when you implement custom drawing, **BoxDrawingView** will draw every **Box** within this list to the screen.)

As the user's finger moves around the screen, you update mCurrentBox.mCurrent. Then, when the touch is canceled or when the user's finger leaves the screen, you null out mCurrentBox to end your draw motion. The **Box** is complete; it is stored safely in the list but will no longer be updated about motion events.

Notice the call to **invalidate()** in the case of ACTION_MOVE. This forces **BoxDrawingView** to redraw itself so that the user can see the box while dragging across the screen. Which brings you to the next step: drawing the boxes to the screen.

Rendering Inside onDraw(...)

When your application is launched, all of its views are *invalid*. This means that they have not drawn anything to the screen. To fix this situation, Android calls the top-level **View**'s **draw()** method. This causes that view to draw itself, which causes its children to draw themselves. Those children's children then draw themselves, and so on down the hierarchy. When all the views in the hierarchy have drawn themselves, the top-level **View** is no longer invalid.

To hook into this drawing, you override the following **View** method:

```
protected void onDraw(Canvas canvas)
```

The call to **invalidate()** that you make in response to ACTION_MOVE in **onTouchEvent(...)** makes the **BoxDrawingView** invalid again. This causes it to redraw itself and will cause **onDraw(...)** to be called again.

Now let's consider the **Canvas** parameter. **Canvas** and **Paint** are the two main drawing classes in Android:

- The **Canvas** class has all the drawing operations you perform. The methods you call on **Canvas** determine where and what you draw – a line, a circle, a word, or a rectangle.

- The **Paint** class determines how these operations are done. The methods you call on **Paint** specify characteristics – whether shapes are filled, which font text is drawn in, and what color lines are.

In BoxDrawingView.java, create two **Paint** objects in **BoxDrawingView**'s XML constructor.

Listing 29.8 Creating your paint (BoxDrawingView.java)

```java
public class BoxDrawingView extends View {
    private static final String TAG = "BoxDrawingView";

    private Box mCurrentBox;
    private List<Box> mBoxen = new ArrayList<>();
    private Paint mBoxPaint;
    private Paint mBackgroundPaint;

    ...

    // Used when inflating the view from XML
    public BoxDrawingView(Context context, AttributeSet attrs) {
        super(context, attrs);

        // Paint the boxes a nice semitransparent red (ARGB)
        mBoxPaint = new Paint();
        mBoxPaint.setColor(0x22ff0000);

        // Paint the background off-white
        mBackgroundPaint = new Paint();
        mBackgroundPaint.setColor(0xfff8efe0);
    }
}
```

Armed with paint, you can now draw your boxes to the screen.

Listing 29.9 Overriding **onDraw(Canvas)** (BoxDrawingView.java)

```java
public BoxDrawingView(Context context, AttributeSet attrs) {
    ...
}

@Override
protected void onDraw(Canvas canvas) {
    // Fill the background
    canvas.drawPaint(mBackgroundPaint);

    for (Box box : mBoxen) {
        float left = Math.min(box.getOrigin().x, box.getCurrent().x);
        float right = Math.max(box.getOrigin().x, box.getCurrent().x);
        float top = Math.min(box.getOrigin().y, box.getCurrent().y);
        float bottom = Math.max(box.getOrigin().y, box.getCurrent().y);

        canvas.drawRect(left, top, right, bottom, mBoxPaint);
    }
}
```

The first part of this code is straightforward: using your off-white background paint, you fill the canvas with a backdrop for your boxes.

Then, for each box in your list of boxes, you determine what the left, right, top, and bottom of the box should be by looking at the two points for the box. The left and top values will be the minimum values, and the bottom and right will be the maximum values.

After calculating these values, you call **Canvas.drawRect(…)** to draw a red rectangle onto the screen.

Run DragAndDraw and draw some red rectangles (Figure 29.5).

Figure 29.5 An expression of programmerly emotion

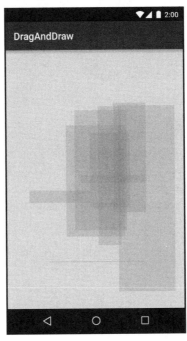

And that is it. You have now created a view that captures its own touch events and performs its own drawing.

Challenge: Saving State

Figure out how to persist your boxes across orientation changes from within your **View**. This can be done with the following **View** methods:

```
protected Parcelable onSaveInstanceState()
protected void onRestoreInstanceState(Parcelable state)
```

These methods do not work like **Activity** and **Fragment**'s **onSaveInstanceState(Bundle)**. First, they will only be called if your **View** has an ID. Second, instead of taking in a **Bundle**, they return and process an object that implements the **Parcelable** interface. We recommend using a **Bundle** as the **Parcelable** instead of implementing a **Parcelable** class yourself. (Implementing the **Parcelable** interface is complicated. It is better to avoid doing so when possible.)

Finally, you must also maintain the saved state of **BoxDrawingView**'s parent, the **View** class. Save the result of **super.onSaveInstanceState()** in your new **Bundle** and send that same result to the super class when calling **super.onRestoreInstanceState(Parcelable)**.

Challenge: Rotating Boxes

For a harder challenge, make it so that you can use a second finger to rotate your rectangles. To do this, you will need to handle multiple pointers in your **MotionEvent** handling code. You will also need to rotate your canvas.

When dealing with multiple touches, you need these extra ideas:

pointer index   tells you which pointer in the current set of pointers the event is for

pointer ID   gives you a unique ID for a specific finger in a gesture

The pointer index may change, but the pointer ID will not.

For more details, check out the documentation for the following **MotionEvent** methods:

```
public final int getActionMasked()
public final int getActionIndex()
public final int getPointerId(int pointerIndex)
public final float getX(int pointerIndex)
public final float getY(int pointerIndex)
```

Also look at the documentation for the ACTION_POINTER_UP and ACTION_POINTER_DOWN constants.

30

Property Animation

For an app to be functional, all you need to do is write your code correctly so that it does not crash. For an app to be a joy to use, though, you need to give it more love than that. You need to make it feel like a real, physical phenomenon playing out on your phone or tablet's screen.

Real things move. To make your user interface move, you *animate* its elements into new positions.

In this chapter, you will write an app that shows a scene of the sun in the sky. When you press on the scene, it will animate the sun down below the horizon, and the sky will change colors like a sunset.

Building the Scene

The first step is to build the scene that will be animated. Create a new project called Sunset. Make sure that your minSdkVersion is set to 16. Name your main activity **SunsetActivity**, and add SingleFragmentActivity.java and activity_fragment.xml to your project.

Now, build out your scene. A sunset by the sea should be colorful, so it will help to name a few colors. Add a colors.xml file to your res/values folder, and add the following values to it:

Listing 30.1 Adding sunset colors (res/values/colors.xml)

```xml
<?xml version="1.0" encoding="utf-8"?>
<resources>
    <color name="bright_sun">#fcfcb7</color>
    <color name="blue_sky">#1e7ac7</color>
    <color name="sunset_sky">#ec8100</color>
    <color name="night_sky">#05192e</color>
    <color name="sea">#224869</color>
</resources>
```

Rectangular views will make for a fine impression of the sky and the sea. But people will not buy a rectangular sun, no matter how much you argue in favor of its technical simplicity. So, in the res/drawable/ folder, add an oval shape drawable for a circular sun called sun.xml.

Listing 30.2 Adding sun XML drawable (res/drawable/sun.xml)

```xml
<?xml version="1.0" encoding="utf-8"?>
<shape xmlns:android="http://schemas.android.com/apk/res/android"
    android:shape="oval">
    <solid android:color="@color/bright_sun" />
</shape>
```

When you display this oval in a square view, you will get a circle. People will nod their heads in approval, and then think about the real sun up in the sky.

Next, build the entire scene out in a layout file. This layout will be used in **SunsetFragment**, which you will build in a moment, so name it fragment_sunset.xml.

Listing 30.3 Setting up the layout (res/layout/fragment_sunset.xml)

```xml
<?xml version="1.0" encoding="utf-8"?>
<LinearLayout xmlns:android="http://schemas.android.com/apk/res/android"
    android:orientation="vertical"
    android:layout_width="match_parent"
    android:layout_height="match_parent">
    <FrameLayout
        android:id="@+id/sky"
        android:layout_width="match_parent"
        android:layout_height="0dp"
        android:layout_weight="0.61"
        android:background="@color/blue_sky">
        <ImageView
            android:id="@+id/sun"
            android:layout_width="100dp"
            android:layout_height="100dp"
            android:layout_gravity="center"
            android:src="@drawable/sun"
            />
    </FrameLayout>

    <View
        android:layout_width="match_parent"
        android:layout_height="0dp"
        android:layout_weight="0.39"
        android:background="@color/sea"
        />
</LinearLayout>
```

Check out the preview. You should see a daytime scene of the sun in a blue sky over a dark blue sea. You may find yourself thinking about a trip you once took to the beach or aboard a boat.

Time to finally get this thing up and running on a device. Create a fragment called **SunsetFragment** and add a **newInstance(…)** method. In **onCreateView(…)**, inflate the fragment_sunset layout file and return the resulting view.

Listing 30.4 Creating **SunsetFragment** (SunsetFragment.java)

```java
public class SunsetFragment extends Fragment {

    public static SunsetFragment newInstance() {
        return new SunsetFragment();
    }

    @Override
    public View onCreateView(LayoutInflater inflater, ViewGroup container,
            Bundle savedInstanceState) {
        View view = inflater.inflate(R.layout.fragment_sunset, container, false);

        return view;
    }
}
```

Now turn **SunsetActivity** into a **SingleFragmentActivity** that displays your fragment.

Listing 30.5 Displaying **SunsetFragment** (SunsetActivity.java)

```
public class SunsetActivity extends SingleFragmentActivity {

    @Override
    protected void onCreate(Bundle savedInstanceState) {
        ...
    }

    @Override
    public boolean onCreateOptionsMenu(Menu menu) {
        ...
    }

    @Override
    public boolean onOptionsItemSelected(MenuItem item) {
        ...
    }

    @Override
    protected Fragment createFragment() {
        return SunsetFragment.newInstance();
    }

}
```

Take a moment to run Sunset to make sure everything is hooked up correctly before moving on. It should look like Figure 30.1. Ahhh.

Figure 30.1 Before sunset

Simple Property Animation

Now that you have the scene set up, it is time to make it do your bidding by moving parts of it around. You are going to animate the sun down below the horizon.

But before you start animating, you will want a few bits of information handy in your fragment. Inside of **onCreateView(…)**, pull out a couple of views into fields on **SunsetFragment**.

Listing 30.6 Pulling out view references (SunsetFragment.java)

```
public class SunsetFragment extends Fragment {

    private View mSceneView;
    private View mSunView;
    private View mSkyView;

    public static SunsetFragment newInstance() {
        return new SunsetFragment();
    }

    @Override
    public View onCreateView(LayoutInflater inflater, ViewGroup container,
                             Bundle savedInstanceState) {
        View view = inflater.inflate(R.layout.fragment_sunset, container, false);

        mSceneView = view;
        mSunView = view.findViewById(R.id.sun);
        mSkyView = view.findViewById(R.id.sky);

        return view;
    }
}
```

Now that you have those, you can write your code to animate the sun. Here is the plan: smoothly move mSunView so that its top is right at the edge of the top of the sea. You will do this by *translating* the location of the top of mSunView to the bottom of its parent.

The first step is to find where the animation should start and end. Write this first step in a new method called **startAnimation()**.

Listing 30.7 Getting top of views (SunsetFragment.java)

```
    @Override
    public View onCreateView(LayoutInflater inflater, ViewGroup container,
                             Bundle savedInstanceState) {
        ...
    }

    private void startAnimation() {
        float sunYStart = mSunView.getTop();
        float sunYEnd = mSkyView.getHeight();
    }
```

The **getTop()** method is one of four methods on **View** that return the *local layout rect* for that view: **getTop()**, **getBottom()**, **getRight()**, and **getLeft()**. A view's local layout rect is the position and

542

size of that view in relation to its parent, as determined when the view was laid out. It is possible to change the location of the view on screen by modifying these values, but it is not recommended. They are reset every time a layout pass occurs, so they tend not to hold their value.

In any event, the animation will start with the top of the view at its current location. It needs to end with the top at the bottom of mSunView's parent, mSkyView. To get it there, it should be as far down as mSkyView is tall, which you find by calling **getHeight()**. The **getHeight()** method returns the same thing as getTop() – getBottom().

Now that you know where the animation should start and end, create and run an **ObjectAnimator** to perform it.

Listing 30.8 Creating a sun animator (SunsetFragment.java)

```
private void startAnimation() {
    float sunYStart = mSunView.getTop();
    float sunYEnd = mSkyView.getHeight();

    ObjectAnimator heightAnimator = ObjectAnimator
            .ofFloat(mSunView, "y", sunYStart, sunYEnd)
            .setDuration(3000);

    heightAnimator.start();
}
```

Then hook up **startAnimation()** so that it is called every time the user presses anywhere in the scene.

Listing 30.9 Starting animation on press (SunsetFragment.java)

```
public View onCreateView(LayoutInflater inflater, ViewGroup container,
        Bundle savedInstanceState) {
    View view = inflater.inflate(R.layout.fragment_sunset, container, false);

    mSceneView = view;
    mSunView = view.findViewById(R.id.sun);
    mSkyView = view.findViewById(R.id.sky);

    mSceneView.setOnClickListener(new View.OnClickListener() {
        @Override
        public void onClick(View v) {
            startAnimation();
        }
    });

    return view;
}
```

Run Sunset and press anywhere on the scene to run the animation (Figure 30.2).

Figure 30.2 Setting sun

You should see the sun move below the horizon.

Here is how it works: **ObjectAnimator** is a *property animator*. Instead of knowing specifically about how to move a view around the screen, a property animator repeatedly calls property setter methods with different values.

The following method call creates an **ObjectAnimator**:

```
ObjectAnimator.ofFloat(mSunView, "y", 0, 1)
```

When that **ObjectAnimator** is started, it will then repeatedly call **mSunView.setY(float)** with values starting at 0 and moving up. Like this:

```
mSunView.setY(0);
mSunView.setY(0.02);
mSunView.setY(0.04);
mSunView.setY(0.06);
mSunView.setY(0.08);
...
```

...and so on, until it finally calls **mSunView.setY(1)**. This process of finding values in between a starting and ending point is called *interpolation*. Between each interpolated value, a little time will pass, which makes it look like the view is moving.

View transformation properties

Property animators are great, but with them alone it would be impossible to animate a view as easily as you just did. Modern Android property animation works in concert with *transformation properties*.

Your view has a local layout rect, which is the position and size it is assigned from the layout process. You can move the view around after that by setting additional properties on the view, called transformation properties. You have three properties to rotate the view (rotation, pivotX, and pivotY), two properties to scale the view vertically and horizontally (scaleX and scaleY), and two to move the view around the screen (translationX and translationY), as represented in Figure 30.3, Figure 30.4, and Figure 30.5.

Figure 30.3 View translation

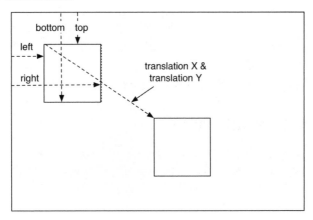

Figure 30.4 View rotation

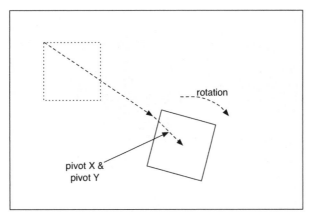

Figure 30.5 View scaling

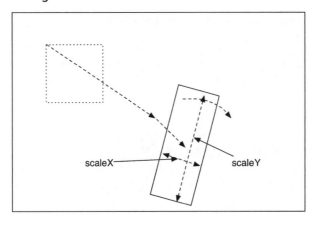

All of these properties have getters and setters. For example, if you wanted to know the current value of translationX, you would call **getTranslationX()**. If you wanted to set it, you would call **setTranslationX(float)**.

So what does the y property do? The x and y properties are conveniences built on top of local layout coordinates and the transformation properties. They allow you to write code that simply says, "Put this view at this X coordinate and this Y coordinate." Under the hood, these properties will modify translationX or translationY to put the view where you want it to be. That means that a call to mSunView.setY(50) really means this:

```
mSunView.setTranslationY(50 - mSunView.getTop())
```

Using different interpolators

Your animation, while pretty, is abrupt. If the sun was really sitting there perfectly still in the sky, it would take a moment for it to accelerate into the animation you see. To add this sensation of acceleration, all you need to do is use a **TimeInterpolator**. **TimeInterpolator** has one role: to change the way your animation goes from point A to point B.

Add a line of code to **startAnimation()** to make your sun speed up a bit at the beginning using an **AccelerateInterpolator**.

Listing 30.10 Adding acceleration (SunsetFragment.java)

```
private void startAnimation() {
    float sunYStart = mSunView.getTop();
    float sunYEnd = mSkyView.getHeight();

    ObjectAnimator heightAnimator = ObjectAnimator
            .ofFloat(mSunView, "y", sunYStart, sunYEnd)
            .setDuration(3000);
    heightAnimator.setInterpolator(new AccelerateInterpolator());

    heightAnimator.start();
}
```

Run Sunset one more time and press to see your animation. Your sun should now start moving slowly and accelerate to a quicker pace as it moves toward the horizon.

There are a lot of styles of motion you might want to use in your app, so there are a lot of different **TimeInterpolator**s. To see all the interpolators that ship with Android, look at the "Known Indirect Subclasses" section in the reference documentation for **TimeInterpolator**.

Color evaluation

Now that your sun is animating down, let's animate the sky to a sunset-y color. Inside of **onCreateView(…)**, pull all of the colors you defined in colors.xml into instance variables.

Listing 30.11 Pulling out sunset colors (SunsetFragment.java)

```
public class SunsetFragment extends Fragment {

    ...
    private View mSkyView;

    private int mBlueSkyColor;
    private int mSunsetSkyColor;
    private int mNightSkyColor;

    ...

    public View onCreateView(LayoutInflater inflater, ViewGroup container,
            Bundle savedInstanceState) {
        ...
        mSkyView = view.findViewById(R.id.sky);

        Resources resources = getResources();
        mBlueSkyColor = resources.getColor(R.color.blue_sky);
        mSunsetSkyColor = resources.getColor(R.color.sunset_sky);
        mNightSkyColor = resources.getColor(R.color.night_sky);

        mSceneView.setOnClickListener(new View.OnClickListener() {
            ...
        });

        return view;
    }
```

Now add an additional animation to **startAnimation()** to animate the sky from mBlueSkyColor to mSunsetSkyColor.

Listing 30.12 Animating sky colors (SunsetFragment.java)

```
    private void startAnimation() {
        float sunYStart = mSunView.getTop();
        float sunYEnd = mSkyView.getHeight();

        ObjectAnimator heightAnimator = ObjectAnimator
                .ofFloat(mSunView, "y", sunYStart, sunYEnd)
                .setDuration(3000);
        heightAnimator.setInterpolator(new AccelerateInterpolator());

        ObjectAnimator sunsetSkyAnimator = ObjectAnimator
                .ofInt(mSkyView, "backgroundColor", mBlueSkyColor, mSunsetSkyColor)
                .setDuration(3000);

        heightAnimator.start();
        sunsetSkyAnimator.start();
    }
```

This seems like it is headed in the right direction, but if you run it you will see that something is amiss. Instead of moving smoothly from blue to orange, the colors will kaleidoscope wildly.

The reason this happens is that a color integer is not a simple number. It is four smaller numbers schlupped together into one int. So for **ObjectAnimator** to properly evaluate which color is halfway between blue and orange, it needs to know how that works.

When **ObjectAnimator**'s normal understanding of how to find values between the start and end is insufficient, you can provide a subclass of **TypeEvaluator** to fix things. A **TypeEvaluator** is an object that tells **ObjectAnimator** what value is, say, a quarter of the way between a start value and end value. Android provides a subclass of **TypeEvaluator** called **ArgbEvaluator** that will do the trick here.

Listing 30.13 Providing **ArgbEvaluator** (SunsetFragment.java)

```java
private void startAnimation() {
    float sunYStart = mSunView.getTop();
    float sunYEnd = mSkyView.getHeight();

    ObjectAnimator heightAnimator = ObjectAnimator
            .ofFloat(mSunView, "y", sunYStart, sunYEnd)
            .setDuration(3000);
    heightAnimator.setInterpolator(new AccelerateInterpolator());

    ObjectAnimator sunsetSkyAnimator = ObjectAnimator
            .ofInt(mSkyView, "backgroundColor", mBlueSkyColor, mSunsetSkyColor)
            .setDuration(3000);
    sunsetSkyAnimator.setEvaluator(new ArgbEvaluator());

    heightAnimator.start();
    sunsetSkyAnimator.start();
}
```

Run your animation one more time, and you should see the sky fade to a beautiful orange color (Figure 30.6).

Figure 30.6 Changing sunset color

Playing Animators Together

If all you need to do is kick off a few animations at the same time, then your job is simple: call **start()** on them all at the same time. They will all animate in sync with one another.

For more sophisticated animation choreography, this will not do the trick. For example, to complete the illusion of a sunset, it would be nice to show the sky turning from orange to a midnight blue after the sun goes down.

This can be done by using an **AnimatorListener**. **AnimatorListener** tells you when an animation completes. So you could write a listener that waits until the end of the first animation, at which time you can start the second night sky animation. This is a huge hassle, though, and requires a lot of listeners. It is much easier to use an **AnimatorSet**.

First, build out the night sky animation and delete your old animation start code.

Listing 30.14 Building night animation (SunsetFragment.java)

```
private void startAnimation() {
    ...
    sunsetSkyAnimator.setEvaluator(new ArgbEvaluator());

    ObjectAnimator nightSkyAnimator = ObjectAnimator
            .ofInt(mSkyView, "backgroundColor", mSunsetSkyColor, mNightSkyColor)
            .setDuration(1500);
    nightSkyAnimator.setEvaluator(new ArgbEvaluator());

    heightAnimator.start();
    sunsetSkyAnimator.start();
}
```

And then build and run an **AnimatorSet**.

Listing 30.15 Building animator set (SunsetFragment.java)

```
private void startAnimation() {
    ...

    ObjectAnimator nightSkyAnimator = ObjectAnimator
            .ofInt(mSkyView, "backgroundColor", mSunsetSkyColor, mNightSkyColor)
            .setDuration(1500);
    nightSkyAnimator.setEvaluator(new ArgbEvaluator());

    AnimatorSet animatorSet = new AnimatorSet();
    animatorSet
            .play(heightAnimator)
            .with(sunsetSkyAnimator)
            .before(nightSkyAnimator);
    animatorSet.start();
}
```

An **AnimatorSet** is nothing more than a set of animations that can be played together. There are a few ways to build one, but the easiest way is to use the **play(Animator)** method you used above.

When you call **play(Animator)**, you get an **AnimatorSet.Builder**, which allows you to build a chain of instructions. The **Animator** passed in to **play(Animator)** is the "subject" of the chain. So the chain of calls you wrote here could be described as, "Play heightAnimator with sunsetSkyAnimator; also, play heightAnimator before nightSkyAnimator." For complicated **AnimatorSet**s, you may find it necessary to call **play(Animator)** a few times, which is perfectly fine.

Run your app one more time and savor the soothing sunset you have created. Magic.

For the More Curious: Other Animation APIs

While property animation is the most broadly useful tool in the animation toolbox, it is not the only one. Whether or not you are using them, it is a good idea to know about the other tools out there.

Legacy animation tools

One set of tools is the classes living in the android.view.animation package. This should not be confused with the newer android.animation package, which was introduced in Honeycomb.

This is the legacy animation framework, which you should mainly know about so that you can ignore it. If you see the word "animaTION" in the class name instead of "animaTOR", that is a good sign that it is a legacy tool you should ignore.

Transitions

Android 4.4 introduced a new transitions framework, which enables fancy transitions between view hierarchies. You might define a transition that explodes a small view in one activity into a zoomed-in version of that view in another activity.

The basic idea of the transitions framework is that you can define scenes, which represent the state of a view hierarchy at some point, and transitions between those scenes. Scenes can be described in XML layout files, and transitions can be described in animation XML files.

When an activity is already running, as in this chapter, the transitions framework is not that useful. This is where the property animation framework shines. However, the property animation framework is not good at animating a layout as it is coming onto the screen.

Take CriminalIntent's crime pictures as an example. If you were to try to implement a "zoom" animation to the zoomed in dialog of an image, you would have to figure out where the original image was and where the new image would be on the dialog. **ObjectAnimator** cannot achieve an effect like that without a lot of work. In that case, you would want to use the transitions framework instead.

Challenges

For the first challenge, add the ability to *reverse* the sunset after it is completed. So you can press for a sunset, and then press a second time to get a sunrise. You will need to build another **AnimatorSet** to do this – **AnimatorSet**s cannot be run in reverse.

For a second challenge, add a continuing animation to the sun. Make it pulsate with heat, or give it a spinning halo of rays. (You can use the **setRepeatCount(int)** method on **ObjectAnimator** to make your animation repeat itself.)

Another good challenge would be to have a reflection for the sun in the water.

Your final challenge is to add the ability to press to reverse the sunset scene while it is still happening. So if you press the scene while the sun is halfway down, it will go right back up again seamlessly. Likewise, if you press the scene while transitioning to night, it will smoothly transition right back to a sunrise.

31

Locations and Play Services

In this chapter, you will start writing a new app called Locatr that performs a Flickr geosearch. It will find your current location and then look for pictures nearby (Figure 31.1). Then, in the next chapter, you will show the picture on a map.

Figure 31.1 Locatr at the end of this chapter

It turns out that this simple job – finding your current location – is more interesting than you might expect. It requires integrating with Google's set of libraries that live outside the standard library set, called Google Play Services.

Locations and Libraries

To see why, let's talk a bit about what your average Android device can see and what tools Android gives you to see those things yourself.

Out of the box, Android provides a basic Location API. This API lets you listen to location data from a variety of sources. For most phones, those sources are fine location points from a GPS radio and coarse points from cell towers or WiFi connections. These APIs have been around for as long as Android itself. You can find them in the `android.location` package.

So the `android.location` APIs exist. But they fall short of perfection. Real-world applications make requests like, "Use as much battery as you can to get as much accuracy as possible," or "I need a location, but I would rather not waste my battery life." Rarely if ever do they need to make a request as specific as, "Please fire up the GPS radio and tell me what it says."

This starts to be a problem when your devices move around. If you are outside, GPS is best. If you have no GPS signal, the cell tower fix may be best. And if you can find neither of those signals, it would be nicer to get by with the accelerometer and gyroscope than with no location fix at all.

In the past, high-quality apps had to manually subscribe to all of these different data sources and switch between them as appropriate. This was not straightforward or easy to do right.

Google Play Services

A better API was needed. However, if it were added to the standard library, it would take a couple of years for all developers to be able to use it. This was annoying, because the OS had everything that a better API would need: GPS, coarse location, and so forth.

Fortunately, the standard library is not the only way Google can get code into your hands. In addition to the standard library, Google provides Play Services. This is a set of common services that are installed alongside the Google Play store application. To fix this locations mess, Google shipped a new locations service in Play Services called the Fused Location Provider.

Since these libraries live in another application, you must actually have that application installed. This means that only devices with the Play Store app installed and up to date will be able to use your application. This almost certainly means that your app will be distributed through the Play Store, too. If your app is *not* available through the Play store, you are unfortunately out of luck, and will need to use another location API.

For the purposes of this exercise, if you will be testing on a hardware device make sure that you have an up-to-date Play Store app. And what if you are running on an emulator? Never fear – we will cover that later in this chapter.

Creating Locatr

Now to get started. In Android Studio, create a new project called Locatr. Name your main activity **LocatrActivity**. As you have for your other apps, set your minSdkVersion to 16 and copy in **SingleFragmentActivity** and `activity_fragment.xml`.

You will also want some additional code from PhotoGallery. You will be querying Flickr again, so having your old query code will be handy. Open up your PhotoGallery solution (anything after Chapter 24 will do), select `FlickrFetchr.java` and `GalleryItem.java`, and right-click to copy them. Then paste them into your Java code area in Locatr.

In a minute, you will get started on building out your user interface. If you are using an emulator, though, read this next section so that you can test all the code you are about to write. If you are not, feel free to skip on ahead to the section called "Building out Locatr".

Play Services and Location Testing on Emulators

If you are using an AVD emulator, you must first make sure that your emulator images are up to date.

To do that, open up your SDK Manager (Tools → Android → SDK Manager). Go down to the version of Android you plan to use for your emulator and ensure that the Google APIs System Images are both installed and up to date. If an update is available, click the button to install the update and wait until it is ready to go before continuing (Figure 31.2).

Figure 31.2 Ensuring your emulator is up to date

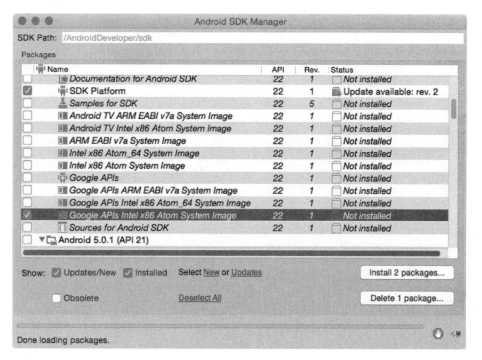

Your AVD emulator also needs to have a target OS version that supports the Google APIs. When you create an emulator you can identify these target OS versions because they will say "Google APIs" on the right. Choose one with an API level of 21 or higher, and you will be all set (Figure 31.3).

Figure 31.3 Choosing a Google APIs image

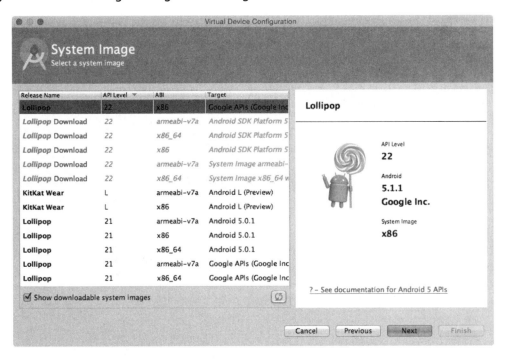

If you already have a suitable emulator, but you had to update your images through the SDK earlier, you will need to restart your emulator for it to work.

For these two chapters, if you are going to use an emulator, we recommend the built-in AVD emulator over a Genymotion emulator. It is possible to use either, but setting up the Genymotion emulator for use with this exercise is neither straightforward nor in the scope of this book. Explore the documentation on Genymotion's website for more information.

Mock location data

On an emulator you will also need some dummy (or mock) location updates to work with. Android Studio provides an Emulator Control panel that lets you send location points to the emulator. This works great on the old location services, but does nothing on the new Fused Location Provider. Instead, you have to publish mock locations programmatically.

We here at Big Nerd Ranch love to explain interesting things in minute detail. After the debacle that was *Snipe Hunting: The Big Nerd Ranch Guide*, though, we prefer to explain *useful* things. So instead of making you type out this mock location code, we have written it for you in a stand-alone app, called MockWalker. To use it, download and install the APK at this URL:

```
https://www.bignerdranch.com/solutions/MockWalker.apk
```

The easiest way to do that is to open the browser app in your emulator and type in the URL (Figure 31.4).

Figure 31.4 Typing in the URL

When it is done, press the download notification item in the toolbar to open the APK (Figure 31.5).

Figure 31.5 Opening the download

MockWalker will trigger a mock walk for you via a service that posts mock location data to Fused Location Provider. It will pretend to walk in a loop around the Kirkwood neighborhood in Atlanta.

While the service is running, any time Locatr asks Fused Location Provider for a location fix, it will receive a location posted by MockWalker (Figure 31.6).

Figure 31.6 Running MockWalker

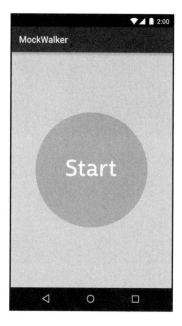

Run MockWalker and press Start. Its service will keep running after you exit the app. (Do not exit the emulator, however. Leave the emulator running while you work on Locatr.) When you no longer need those mock locations, open MockWalker again and press the Stop button.

If you would like to know how MockWalker works, you can find its source code in the solutions folder for this chapter (see the section called "Adding an Icon" in Chapter 2 for more on the solutions). It uses a few interesting things: RxJava and a sticky foreground service to manage the ongoing location updates. If those sound interesting to you, check it out.

Building out Locatr

Next, create your interface. First, add a string for your search button in res/values/strings.xml.

Listing 31.1 Adding search button text (res/values/strings.xml)

```
<resources>
    <string name="app_name">Locatr</string>

    <string name="hello_world">Hello world!</string>
    <string name="action_settings">Settings</string>
    <string name="search">Find an image near you</string>
</resources>
```

You will be using a fragment, as usual, so rename activity_locatr.xml to fragment_locatr.xml. Change out the insides of its **RelativeLayout** to have an **ImageView** to display the image you find

(Figure 31.7). (The padding attribute values come from the template code as of this writing. They are not important, so feel free to leave them out.)

Figure 31.7 Locatr's layout (res/layout/fragment_locatr.xml)

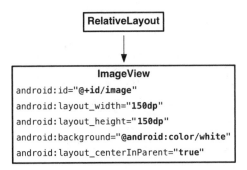

You also need a button to trigger the search. You can use your toolbar for that. Rename res/menu/ menu_locatr.xml to res/menu/fragment_locatr.xml and change its button to display a location icon. (Yes, this is the same filename as res/layout/fragment_locatr.xml. This is no problem at all: menu resources live in a different namespace.)

Listing 31.2 Setting up Locatr's menu (res/menu/fragment_locatr.xml)

```xml
<menu xmlns:android="http://schemas.android.com/apk/res/android"
      xmlns:app="http://schemas.android.com/apk/res-auto"
      xmlns:tools="http://schemas.android.com/tools"
      tools:context=".LocatrActivity">
    <item android:id="@+id/action_settings"
          android:title="@string/action_settings"
          android:orderInCategory="100"
          app:showAsAction="never"/>
    <item android:id="@+id/action_locate"
          android:icon="@android:drawable/ic_menu_compass"
          android:title="@string/search"
          android:orderInCategory="100"
          android:enabled="false"
          app:showAsAction="ifRoom"/>
</menu>
```

The button is disabled in XML by default. Later on, you will enable it once you are connected to Play Services.

Now create a **Fragment** subclass called **LocatrFragment** that hooks up your layout and pulls out that **ImageView**.

Listing 31.3 Creating **LocatrFragment** (LocatrFragment.java)

```java
public class LocatrFragment extends Fragment {
    private ImageView mImageView;

    public static LocatrFragment newInstance() {
        return new LocatrFragment();
    }

    @Override
    public View onCreateView(LayoutInflater inflater, ViewGroup container,
                             Bundle savedInstanceState) {
        View v = inflater.inflate(R.layout.fragment_locatr, container, false);

        mImageView = (ImageView) v.findViewById(R.id.image);

        return v;
    }
}
```

Hook up your menu item, too. Pull it out into its own instance variable so that you can enable it later on.

Listing 31.4 Adding menu to fragment (LocatrFragment.java)

```java
public class LocatrFragment extends Fragment {
    private ImageView mImageView;

    public static LocatrFragment newInstance() {
        return new LocatrFragment();
    }

    @Override
    public void onCreate(Bundle savedInstanceState) {
        super.onCreate(savedInstanceState);
        setHasOptionsMenu(true);
    }

    @Override
    public View onCreateView(LayoutInflater inflater, ViewGroup container,
                             Bundle savedInstanceState) {
        ...
    }

    @Override
    public void onCreateOptionsMenu(Menu menu, MenuInflater inflater) {
        super.onCreateOptionsMenu(menu, inflater);
        inflater.inflate(R.menu.fragment_locatr, menu);
    }
}
```

Now hook it up in **LocatrActivity**. Delete everything inside this class and replace it, like so:

Listing 31.5 Hooking up Locatr fragment (`LocatrActivity.java`)

```java
public class LocatrActivity extends SingleFragmentActivity {
    @Override
    protected Fragment createFragment() {
        return LocatrFragment.newInstance();
    }
}
```

With that, you should be ready to get into some trouble.

Setting Up Google Play Services

To get your location using the Fused Location Provider, you need to use Google Play Services. To get those up and running, you will need to add a few standard bits of boilerplate to your app.

First, you need to add the Google Play Services library dependency. The services themselves live in the Play app, but the Play Services library contains all the code to interface with them.

Open up your app module's settings (File → Project Structure). Navigate to its dependencies, and add a library dependency. Type in the following dependency name: `com.google.android.gms:play-services-location:7.3.0`. (As of this writing, this dependency will not show up in search results, so type carefully.) This is the location portion of Play Services.

Over time, the version number for this library will change. If you want to see what the most up-to-date version is, search the library dependencies for `play-services`. The `com.google.android.gms:play-services` dependency will appear, along with a version number. This is the dependency that includes everything in Play Services. If you want to use the latest version of the library, you can use the version number from `play-services` for the more limited `play-services-location` library, too.

Which version number should you use, though? In your own practice, it is best to use the most recent version you possibly can. But we cannot guarantee that the code in this chapter will work the same for future versions. So for this chapter, use the version we wrote this code for: `7.3.0`.

Next, you need to verify that Play Services is available. Since the working parts live in another app on your device, the Play Services library is not always guaranteed to be working. The library makes it easy to verify this. Update your main activity to perform this check.

Listing 31.6 Adding Play Services check (`LocatrActivity.java`)

```java
public class LocatrActivity extends SingleFragmentActivity {
    private static final int REQUEST_ERROR = 0;

    @Override
    protected Fragment createFragment() {
        return LocatrFragment.newInstance();
    }

    @Override
    protected void onResume() {
        super.onResume();

        int errorCode = GooglePlayServicesUtil.isGooglePlayServicesAvailable(this);

        if (errorCode != ConnectionResult.SUCCESS) {
            Dialog errorDialog = GooglePlayServicesUtil
                    .getErrorDialog(errorCode, this, REQUEST_ERROR,
                            new DialogInterface.OnCancelListener() {

                                @Override
                                public void onCancel(DialogInterface dialog) {
                                    // Leave if services are unavailable.
                                    finish();
                                }
                            });

            errorDialog.show();
        }
    }
}
```

Normally you would not use a bare **Dialog** like this. However, in this case there is no need to defend against rotation issues. The errorCode value will be the same if the user rotates, so the **Dialog** will be displayed again.

Location permissions

You will also need some location permissions for your app to work. There are two relevant permissions: android.permission.ACCESS_FINE_LOCATION, and android.permission.ACCESS_COARSE_LOCATION. Fine location is the GPS radio; coarse location is derived from cell towers or WiFi access points.

In this chapter, you will be requesting a high accuracy location fix, so you will definitely need ACCESS_FINE_LOCATION. But it is also a good idea to request ACCESS_COARSE_LOCATION. If the fine location provider is not available, this gives you permission to use the coarse provider as a backup.

Add these permissions to your manifest. Add an Internet permission while you are at it, too, so that you can query Flickr.

Listing 31.7 Adding permissions (`AndroidManifest.xml`)

```xml
<manifest xmlns:android="http://schemas.android.com/apk/res/android"
    package="com.bignerdranch.android.locatr" >

    <uses-permission
        android:name="android.permission.ACCESS_FINE_LOCATION" />
    <uses-permission
        android:name="android.permission.ACCESS_COARSE_LOCATION" />
    <uses-permission
        android:name="android.permission.INTERNET" />

    ...

</manifest>
```

Using Google Play Services

To use Play Services, you need to create a client. That client is an instance of the `GoogleApiClient` class. You can find the documentation for this class (and all the other Play Services classes you will be using in these two chapters) in the Play Services reference section: `http://developer.android.com/reference/gms-packages.html`.

To create a client, create a `GoogleApiClient.Builder` and configure it. At a minimum, you want to configure the instance with the specific APIs you will be using. Then call `build()` to create an instance.

Inside your `onCreate(Bundle)`, create an instance of `GoogleApiClient.Builder` and add the Location Services API to your instance.

Listing 31.8 Creating `GoogleApiClient` (`LocatrFragment.java`)

```java
public class LocatrFragment extends Fragment {
    private ImageView mImageView;
    private GoogleApiClient mClient;

    public static LocatrFragment newInstance() {
        return new LocatrFragment();
    }

    @Override
    public void onCreate(Bundle savedInstanceState) {
        super.onCreate(savedInstanceState);
        setHasOptionsMenu(true);

        mClient = new GoogleApiClient.Builder(getActivity())
                .addApi(LocationServices.API)
                .build();
    }
}
```

Once you do that, you need to connect to the client. Google recommends always connecting to the client in `onStart()` and disconnecting in `onStop()`. Calling `connect()` on your client will change what your menu button can do, too, so call `invalidateOptionsMenu()` to update its visible state. (You will call it one more time later: after you are told you have been connected.)

Listing 31.9 Connecting and disconnecting (LocatrFragment.java)

```
@Override
public View onCreateView(LayoutInflater inflater, ViewGroup container,
                         Bundle savedInstanceState) {
    ...
}

@Override
public void onStart() {
    super.onStart();

    getActivity().invalidateOptionsMenu();
    mClient.connect();
}

@Override
public void onStop() {
    super.onStop();

    mClient.disconnect();
}

@Override
public void onCreateOptionsMenu(Menu menu, MenuInflater inflater) {
    ...
```

If your client is not connected, your app will not be able to do anything. So for the next step, enable or disable the button depending on whether the client is connected.

Listing 31.10 Updating the menu button (LocatrFragment.java)

```
@Override
public void onCreateOptionsMenu(Menu menu, MenuInflater inflater) {
    super.onCreateOptionsMenu(menu, inflater);
    inflater.inflate(R.menu.fragment_locatr, menu);

    MenuItem searchItem = menu.findItem(R.id.action_locate);
    searchItem.setEnabled(mClient.isConnected());
}
```

Then add another call to **getActivity().invalidateOptionsMenu()** to update your menu item when you find out that you are connected. Connection state information is passed through two callback interfaces: **ConnectionCallbacks** and **OnConnectionFailedListener**. Hook up a **ConnectionCallbacks** listener in **onCreate(Bundle)** to invalidate your toolbar when you are connected.

Listing 31.11 Listening for connection events (`LocatrFragment.java`)

```
@Override
public void onCreate(Bundle savedInstanceState) {
    super.onCreate(savedInstanceState);
    getActivity().invalidateOptionsMenu();

    mClient = new GoogleApiClient.Builder(getActivity())
            .addApi(LocationServices.API)
            .addConnectionCallbacks(new GoogleApiClient.ConnectionCallbacks() {
                @Override
                public void onConnected(Bundle bundle) {
                    getActivity().invalidateOptionsMenu();
                }

                @Override
                public void onConnectionSuspended(int i) {

                }
            })
            .build();
}
```

If you are curious, you can hook up an **OnConnectionFailedListener** and see what it reports. But it is not necessary.

With that, your Google Play Services hookup is ready.

Flickr Geosearch

The next step is to add the ability to search for geographic locations on Flickr. To do this, you perform a regular search, but you also provide a latitude and longitude.

In Android, the location APIs pass around these location fixes in **Location** objects. So write a new **buildUrl(…)** override that takes in one of these **Location** objects and builds an appropriate search query.

Listing 31.12 New **buildUrl(Location)** (`FlickrFetchr.java`)

```
private String buildUrl(String method, String query) {
    ...
}

private String buildUrl(Location location) {
    return ENDPOINT.buildUpon()
            .appendQueryParameter("method", SEARCH_METHOD)
            .appendQueryParameter("lat", "" + location.getLatitude())
            .appendQueryParameter("lon", "" + location.getLongitude())
            .build().toString();
}
```

And then write a matching **searchPhotos(Location)** method.

Listing 31.13 New **searchPhotos(Location)** (FlickrFetchr.java)

```
public List<GalleryItem> searchPhotos(String query) {
    ...
}

public List<GalleryItem> searchPhotos(Location location) {
    String url = buildUrl(location);
    return downloadGalleryItems(url);
}
```

Getting a Location Fix

Now that you have everything set up, you are ready to get a location fix. Your window to the Fused Location Provider API is a class named, appropriately enough, **FusedLocationProviderApi**. There is one instance of this class. It is a singleton object that lives on **LocationServices** called FusedLocationApi.

To get a location fix from this API, you need to build a location request. Fused location requests are represented by **LocationRequest** objects. Create one and configure it in a new method called **findImage()**. (There are two **LocationRequest** classes. Use the one with the complete name of **com.google.android.gms.location.LocationRequest**.)

Listing 31.14 Building a location request (LocatrFragment.java)

```
    @Override
    public void onCreateOptionsMenu(Menu menu, MenuInflater inflater) {
        ...
    }

    private void findImage() {
        LocationRequest request = LocationRequest.create();
        request.setPriority(LocationRequest.PRIORITY_HIGH_ACCURACY);
        request.setNumUpdates(1);
        request.setInterval(0);
    }
}
```

LocationRequest objects configure a variety of parameters for your request:

- *interval* – how frequently the location should be updated

- *number of updates* – how many times the location should be updated

- *priority* – how Android should prioritize battery life against accuracy to satisfy your request

- *expiration* – whether the request should expire and, if so, when

- *smallest displacement* – the smallest amount the device must move (in meters) to trigger a location update

When you first create a **LocationRequest**, it will be configured for accuracy within a city block, with repeated slow updates until the end of time. In your code, you change this to get a single, high-accuracy location fix by changing the priority and the number of updates. You also set the interval to 0, to signify that you would like a location fix as soon as possible.

The next step is to send off this request and listen for the **Location**s that come back. You do this by adding a **LocationListener**. There are two versions of **LocationListener** you can import. Choose **com.google.android.gms.location.LocationListener**. Add another method call to **findImage()**.

Listing 31.15 Sending **LocationRequest** (LocatrFragment.java)

```java
public class LocatrFragment extends Fragment {
    private static final String TAG = "LocatrFragment";
    ...

    private void findImage() {
        LocationRequest request = LocationRequest.create();
        request.setPriority(LocationRequest.PRIORITY_HIGH_ACCURACY);
        request.setNumUpdates(1);
        request.setInterval(0);
        LocationServices.FusedLocationApi
                .requestLocationUpdates(mClient, request, new LocationListener() {
                    @Override
                    public void onLocationChanged(Location location) {
                        Log.i(TAG, "Got a fix: " + location);
                    }
                });
    }
```

If this were a longer-lived request, you would need to hold on to your listener and call **removeLocationUpdates(…)** later to cancel the request. However, since you called **setNumUpdates(1)**, all you need to do is send this off and forget about it.

Finally, to send this off you need to hook up your search button. Override **onOptionsItemSelected(…)** to call **findImage()**.

Listing 31.16 Hooking up search button (LocatrFragment.java)

```java
@Override
public void onCreateOptionsMenu(Menu menu, MenuInflater inflater) {
    ...
}

@Override
public boolean onOptionsItemSelected(MenuItem item) {
    switch (item.getItemId()) {
        case R.id.action_locate:
            findImage();
            return true;
        default:
            return super.onOptionsItemSelected(item);
    }
}
```

Run your app and press the search button. Remember to have MockWalker running if you are running on an emulator. (If you run into issues with the menu, flip back to Chapter 13 to integrate the AppCompat library.) You should see a line something like this logged out:

```
...D/libEGL: loaded /system/lib/egl/libGLESv2_MRVL.so
...D/GC: <tid=12423> OES20 ===> GC Version   : GC Ver rls_pxa988_KK44_GC13.24
...D/OpenGLRenderer: Enabling debug mode 0
...I/LocatrFragment: Got a fix: Location[fused 33.758998,-84.331796 acc=38 et=...]
```

This shows you the latitude and longitude, accuracy, and the estimated time of the location fix. If
you plug your lat-lon pair into Google Maps, you should be able to pull up your current location
(Figure 31.8).

Figure 31.8 Our current location

Find and Display an Image

Now that you have a location fix, it is time to use it. Write an async task to find a `GalleryItem` near
your location fix, download its associated image, and display it.

Put this code inside a new inner `AsyncTask` called `SearchTask`. Start by performing the search,
selecting the first `GalleryItem` that comes up.

Listing 31.17 Writing **SearchTask** (LocatrFragment.java)

```java
private void findImage() {
    ...
    LocationServices.FusedLocationApi
            .requestLocationUpdates(mClient, request, new LocationListener() {
                @Override
                public void onLocationChanged(Location location) {
                    Log.i(TAG, "Got a fix: " + location);
                    new SearchTask().execute(location);
                }
            });
}

private class SearchTask extends AsyncTask<Location,Void,Void> {
    private GalleryItem mGalleryItem;

    @Override
    protected Void doInBackground(Location... params) {
        FlickrFetchr fetchr = new FlickrFetchr();
        List<GalleryItem> items = fetchr.searchPhotos(params[0]);

        if (items.size() == 0) {
            return null;
        }

        mGalleryItem = items.get(0);

        return null;
    }
}
```

Saving out the **GalleryItem** here accomplishes nothing for now. But it will save you a bit of typing in the next chapter.

Next, download that **GalleryItem**'s associated image data and decode it. Then display it on mImageView inside **onPostExecute(Void)**.

Listing 31.18 Downloading and displaying image (LocatrFragment.java)

```
private class SearchTask extends AsyncTask<Location,Void,Void> {
    private GalleryItem mGalleryItem;
    private Bitmap mBitmap;

    @Override
    protected Void doInBackground(Location... params) {
        ...

        mGalleryItem = items.get(0);

        try {
            byte[] bytes = fetchr.getUrlBytes(mGalleryItem.getUrl());
            mBitmap = BitmapFactory.decodeByteArray(bytes, 0, bytes.length);
        } catch (IOException ioe) {
            Log.i(TAG, "Unable to download bitmap", ioe);
        }
        return null;
    }

    @Override
    protected void onPostExecute(Void result) {
        mImageView.setImageBitmap(mBitmap);
    }
}
```

With that, you should be able to find a nearby image on Flickr (Figure 31.9). Fire up Locatr and press your location button.

Figure 31.9 The final product

Challenge: Progress

This simple app could use some more feedback in its interface. There is no immediate indication when you press the button that anything has happened.

For this challenge, modify Locatr so that it responds immediately to a press by displaying a progress indicator. The **ProgressDialog** class can show a spinning progress indicator that will do the trick nicely. You will also need to track when **SearchTask** is running so that you can clear away the progress when that is appropriate.

32

Maps

In this chapter, you will go one step further with `LocatrFragment`. In addition to searching for a nearby image, you will find its latitude and longitude and plot it on a map.

Importing Play Services Maps

Before you get started, you need to import the mapping library. This is another Play Services library. Open your project structure and add the following dependency to your app module: `com.google.android.gms:play-services-maps:7.0.0`. As in the previous chapter, note that the actual version number will change over time. Use whatever the latest version number is for the plain `play-services` dependency.

Mapping on Android

As enjoyable as it is to have data that tells you where your phone is, that data begs to be visualized. Mapping was probably the first truly killer app for smartphones, which is why Android has had mapping since day one.

Mapping is big, complicated, and involves an entire support system of servers to provide base map data. Most of Android can stand alone as part of the Android Open Source Project. Maps, however, cannot.

So while Android has always *had* maps, maps have also always been separate from the rest of Android's APIs. The current version of the Maps API, version 2, lives in Google Play Services along with the Fused Location Provider. So in order to use it, the same requirements apply as you saw in the section called "Google Play Services" in Chapter 31: you have to either have a device with the Play Store installed or an emulator with the Google APIs.

If you are making something with maps and happen to flip to this chapter, make sure that you have followed the steps from the previous chapter before you start:

1. Ensure your device supports Play Services.

2. Import the appropriate Play Services library.

3. Use `GooglePlayServicesUtil` at an appropriate entry point to ensure that an up-to-date Play Store app is installed.

Maps API Setup

Let's move forward. In addition to the permissions configuration you did in the previous chapter, the Maps API requires adding more items to your manifest.

The first part of that is simply to add a few additional permissions. The Maps API needs to be able to do the following:

- download map data from the Internet (`android.permission.INTERNET`)

- query the state of the network (`android.permission.ACCESS_NETWORK_STATE`)

- write temporary map data to external storage (`android.permission.WRITE_EXTERNAL_STORAGE`)

The `INTERNET` permission was added in the previous chapter, so that is already taken care of. Add the other two permissions to your manifest.

Listing 32.1 Adding more permissions (`AndroidManifest.xml`)

```xml
<?xml version="1.0" encoding="utf-8"?>
<manifest xmlns:android="http://schemas.android.com/apk/res/android"
    package="com.bignerdranch.android.locatr" >

    <uses-permission
        android:name="android.permission.ACCESS_FINE_LOCATION" />
    <uses-permission
        android:name="android.permission.ACCESS_COARSE_LOCATION" />
    <uses-permission
        android:name="android.permission.INTERNET" />
    <uses-permission android:name="android.permission.ACCESS_NETWORK_STATE"/>
    <uses-permission android:name="android.permission.WRITE_EXTERNAL_STORAGE"/>
    ...
```

Getting a Maps API Key

Using the Maps API also requires you to declare an API key in your manifest. To do that, you have to go get your own API key. This API key is used to ensure that your app is authorized to use Google's mapping services.

To get an API key, you need to obtain a hash of your signing key and then use it to register for the Google Maps v2 API on the Google Developer Console. In the next section, we will show you how to use the Android tools to see what your signing key is. The Google Developer Console is beyond the scope of this book, however, so we will be pointing you to some documentation on the Web after that.

Getting an API key requires you to identify yourself by your signing key. A signing key is a mathematically inscrutable chunk of numbers that is yours and yours alone. Every app that is installed to an Android device is signed with a unique key so that Android knows who made that app.

You have not needed to worry about this so far, because it has been taken care of for you. Behind the scenes, Android Studio automatically created a default signing key for you, called a debug key. Every time it builds your app it signs your APK with that debug key before deploying it.

Your signing key

Gradle makes finding this signing key straightforward, but it does require you to do a little bit of work on the command line.

Open up a command line terminal in your OS and change your directory to your project directory by typing in a cd command. On OS X, your author would type in a command like this:

Listing 32.2 Changing directory to solution folder (terminal)

```
$ cd /Users/bphillips/src/android/Locatr
```

Then you use one of the gradle command line tools to get a signing report. For Linux or OS X, run the following command:

Listing 32.3 Signing report on Linux/OS X (terminal)

```
$ cd /Users/bphillips/src/android/Locatr
$ ./gradlew signingReport
```

If you are on Windows, on the other hand, use the Windows directory structure and run gradlew.bat instead:

Listing 32.4 Signing report on Windows (terminal)

```
> cd c:\users\bphillips\Documents\android\Locatr
> gradlew.bat signingReport
```

When you type in that command, you will get a printout of a report of what signing keys are used for different kinds of builds. It should look something like this:

```
$ ./gradlew signingReport
:app:signingReport
Variant: debug
Config: debug
Store: /Users/bphillips/.android/debug.keystore
Alias: AndroidDebugKey
MD5: XX:XX:XX:XX:XX:XX:XX:XX:XX:XX:XX:XX:XX:XX:XX:XX
SHA1: XX:XX:XX:XX:XX:XX:XX:XX:XX:XX:XX:XX:XX:XX:XX:XX:XX:XX:XX:XX
Valid until: Friday, May 16, 2042
----------
Variant: release
Config: none
----------
Variant: debugTest
Config: debug
Store: /Users/bphillips/.android/debug.keystore
Alias: AndroidDebugKey
MD5: XX:XX:XX:XX:XX:XX:XX:XX:XX:XX:XX:XX:XX:XX:XX:XX
SHA1: XX:XX:XX:XX:XX:XX:XX:XX:XX:XX:XX:XX:XX:XX:XX:XX:XX:XX:XX:XX
Valid until: Friday, May 16, 2042
----------

BUILD SUCCESSFUL

Total time: 4.354 secs
```

In your report, you will see hexadecimal numbers instead of XX for the MD5 and SHA1 values reported above. The debug SHA1 value shaded above will be the key you want to provide in a moment to get your API key.

Getting an API key

Once you have the SHA1 of your debug key, you are ready to get an API key. For instructions on how to finish that process, visit Google's documentation:

```
https://developers.google.com/maps/documentation/android/start
```

When you finish those instructions, you will be provided with an API key for your project that corresponds to your debug signing key. Add it to your manifest.

Listing 32.5 Adding API key to manifest (AndroidManifest.xml)

```
<application
    android:allowBackup="true"
    android:icon="@mipmap/ic_launcher"
    android:label="@string/app_name"
    android:theme="@style/AppTheme" >
    <meta-data
        android:name="com.google.android.maps.v2.API_KEY"
        android:value="XXXXXXXXXXXXXXXXXXXXXXXXXXXXXXXXXXXXXXXX"/>
    ...
</application>
```

With that, you are all ready to go.

Setting Up Your Map

Now that you have the Maps API set up, you need to create a map. Maps are displayed, appropriately enough, in a **MapView**. **MapView** is like other views, mostly, except in one way: for it to work correctly, you have to forward all of your lifecycle events, like this:

```
@Override
public void onCreate(Bundle savedInstanceState) {
    super.onCreate(savedInstanceState);

    mMapView.onCreate(savedInstanceState);
}
```

This is a huge pain in the neck. It is far easier to let the SDK do that work for you instead by using a **MapFragment** or, if you are using support library fragments, **SupportMapFragment**. The **MapFragment** will create and host a **MapView** for you, including the proper lifecycle callback hookups.

Your first step is to wipe out your old user interface entirely and replace it with a **SupportMapFragment**. This is not as painful as it might sound. All you need to do is switch to using a **SupportMapFragment**, delete your **onCreateView(…)** method, and delete everything that uses your **ImageView**.

Listing 32.6 Switching to **SupportMapFragment** (`LocatrFragment.java`)

```java
public class LocatrFragment extends SupportMapFragment Fragment{
    private static final String TAG = "LocatrFragment";

    private ImageView mImageView;
    private GoogleApiClient mClient;

    ...

    @Override
    public View onCreateView(LayoutInflater inflater, ViewGroup container,
                             Bundle savedInstanceState) {
        View v = inflater.inflate(R.layout.fragment_locatr, container, false);

        mImageView = (ImageView) v.findViewById(R.id.image);

        return v;
    }

    ...

    private class SearchTask extends AsyncTask<Location,Void,Void> {
        ...

        @Override
        protected void onPostExecute(Void result) {
            mImageView.setImageBitmap(mBitmap);
        }
    }
}
```

SupportMapFragment has its own override of **onCreateView(…)**, so you should be all set. Run Locatr to see a map displayed (Figure 32.1).

Figure 32.1 A plain old map

Getting More Location Data

To actually plot your image on this map, you need to know where it is. Add an additional "extra" parameter to your Flickr API query to fetch a lat-lon pair back for your **GalleryItem**.

Listing 32.7 Adding lat-lon to query (`FlickrFetchr.java`)

```
private static final String API_KEY = "XXXXXXXXXXXXXXXXXXXXXXXXXXXXXXXXXX";
private static final String FETCH_RECENTS_METHOD = "flickr.photos.getRecent";
private static final String SEARCH_METHOD = "flickr.photos.search";
private static final Uri ENDPOINT = Uri.parse("https://api.flickr.com/services/rest/")
        .buildUpon()
        .appendQueryParameter("api_key", API_KEY)
        .appendQueryParameter("format", "json")
        .appendQueryParameter("nojsoncallback", "1")
        .appendQueryParameter("extras", "url_s,geo")
        .build();
```

Now add latitude and longitude to **GalleryItem**.

Listing 32.8 Adding lat-lon properties (`GalleryItem.java`)

```java
public class GalleryItem {
    private String mCaption;
    private String mId;
    private String mUrl;
    private double mLat;
    private double mLon;

    ...

    public void setId(String id) {
        mId = id;
    }

    public double getLat() {
        return mLat;
    }

    public void setLat(double lat) {
        mLat = lat;
    }

    public double getLon() {
        return mLon;
    }

    public void setLon(double lon) {
        mLon = lon;
    }

    @Override
    public String toString() {
        return mCaption;
    }
}
```

And then pull that data out of your Flickr JSON response.

Listing 32.9 Pulling data from Flickr JSON response (`FlickrFetchr.java`)

```java
private void parseItems(List<GalleryItem> items, JSONObject jsonBody)
        throws IOException, JSONException {

    JSONObject photosJsonObject = jsonBody.getJSONObject("photos");
    JSONArray photoJsonArray = photosJsonObject.getJSONArray("photo");

    for (int i = 0; i < photoJsonArray.length(); i++) {
        JSONObject photoJsonObject = photoJsonArray.getJSONObject(i);

        GalleryItem item = new GalleryItem();
        item.setId(photoJsonObject.getString("id"));
        item.setCaption(photoJsonObject.getString("title"));

        if (!photoJsonObject.has("url_s")) {
            continue;
        }

        item.setUrl(photoJsonObject.getString("url_s"));
        item.setLat(photoJsonObject.getDouble("latitude"));
        item.setLon(photoJsonObject.getDouble("longitude"));

        items.add(item);
    }
}
```

Now that you are getting your location data, add some fields to your main fragment to store the current state of your search. Add one field to stash the **Bitmap** you will display, one for the **GalleryItem** it is associated with, and one for your current **Location**.

Listing 32.10 Adding map data (`LocatrFragment.java`)

```java
public class LocatrFragment extends SupportMapFragment {
    private static final String TAG = "LocatrFragment";

    private GoogleApiClient mClient;
    private Bitmap mMapImage;
    private GalleryItem mMapItem;
    private Location mCurrentLocation;

    ...
```

Next, save those bits of information out from within **SearchTask**.

Listing 32.11 Saving out query results (LocatrFragment.java)

```java
private class SearchTask extends AsyncTask<Location,Void,Void> {
    private Bitmap mBitmap;
    private GalleryItem mGalleryItem;
    private Location mLocation;

    @Override
    protected Void doInBackground(Location... params) {
        mLocation = params[0];
        FlickrFetchr fetchr = new FlickrFetchr();
        ...
    }

    @Override
    protected void onPostExecute(Void result) {
        mMapImage = mBitmap;
        mMapItem = mGalleryItem;
        mCurrentLocation = mLocation;
    }
}
```

With that, you have the data you need. Next up: making your map show it.

Working with Your Map

Your **SupportMapFragment** creates a **MapView**, which is, in turn, a host for the object that does the real work: **GoogleMap**. So your first step is to acquire a reference to this master object. Do this by calling **getMapAsync(OnMapReadyCallback)**.

Listing 32.12 Getting a **GoogleMap** (LocatrFragment.java)

```java
public class LocatrFragment extends SupportMapFragment {
    private static final String TAG = "LocatrFragment";

    private GoogleApiClient mClient;
    private GoogleMap mMap;
    private Bitmap mMapImage;
    private GalleryItem mMapItem;
    private Location mCurrentLocation;

    @Override
    public void onCreate(Bundle savedInstanceState) {
        super.onCreate(savedInstanceState);
        setHasOptionsMenu(true);

        mClient = new GoogleApiClient.Builder(getActivity())
                ...
                .build();

        getMapAsync(new OnMapReadyCallback() {
            @Override
            public void onMapReady(GoogleMap googleMap) {
                mMap = googleMap;
            }
        });
    }

    ...
```

SupportMapFragment.getMapAsync(…) does what it says on the tin: it gets a map object asynchronously. If you call this from within your **onCreate(Bundle)**, you will get a reference to a **GoogleMap** once it is created and initialized.

Now that you have a **GoogleMap**, you can update the look of that map according to the current state of **LocatrFragment**. The first thing you will want to do is zoom in on an area of interest. You will want a margin around that area of interest. Add a dimension value for that margin.

Listing 32.13 Adding margin (res/values/dimens.xml)

```
<resources>
    <!-- Default screen margins, per the Android Design guidelines. -->
    <dimen name="activity_horizontal_margin">16dp</dimen>
    <dimen name="activity_vertical_margin">16dp</dimen>
    <dimen name="map_inset_margin">100dp</dimen>
</resources>
```

Then add an **updateUI()** implementation to perform the zoom.

Listing 32.14 Zooming in (LocatrFragment.java)

```
private void findImage() {
    ...
}

private void updateUI() {
    if (mMap == null || mMapImage == null) {
        return;
    }

    LatLng itemPoint = new LatLng(mMapItem.getLat(), mMapItem.getLon());
    LatLng myPoint = new LatLng(
            mCurrentLocation.getLatitude(), mCurrentLocation.getLongitude());

    LatLngBounds bounds = new LatLngBounds.Builder()
            .include(itemPoint)
            .include(myPoint)
            .build();

    int margin = getResources().getDimensionPixelSize(R.dimen.map_inset_margin);
    CameraUpdate update = CameraUpdateFactory.newLatLngBounds(bounds, margin);
    mMap.animateCamera(update);
}

private class SearchTask extends AsyncTask<Location,Void,Void> {
    ...
```

Here is what you just did. To move your **GoogleMap** around, you built a **CameraUpdate**. **CameraUpdateFactory** has a variety of static methods to build different kinds of **CameraUpdate** objects that adjust the position, zoom level, and other properties around what your map is displaying.

Here, you created an update that points the camera at a specific **LatLngBounds**. You can think of a **LatLngBounds** as a rectangle around a set of points. You can make one explicitly by saying what the southwest and northeast corners of it should be.

More often, it is easier to provide a list of points that you would like this rectangle to encompass. **LatLngBounds.Builder** makes it easy to do this: simply create a **LatLngBounds.Builder** and call **.include(LatLng)** for each point your **LatLngBounds** should encompass (represented by **LatLng** objects). When you are done, call **build()**, and you get an appropriately configured **LatLngBounds**.

With that done, you can update your map in two ways: with **moveCamera(CameraUpdate)** or **animateCamera(CameraUpdate)**. Animating is more fun, so naturally that is what you used above.

Next, hook up your **updateUI()** method in two places: when the map is first received, and when your search is finished.

Listing 32.15 Hooking up **updateUI()** (LocatrFragment.java)

```
@Override
public void onCreate(Bundle savedInstanceState) {
    ...

    getMapAsync(new OnMapReadyCallback() {
        @Override
        public void onMapReady(GoogleMap googleMap) {
            mMap = googleMap;
            updateUI();
        }
    });
}

...

private class SearchTask extends AsyncTask<Location,Void,Void> {
    ...

    @Override
    protected void onPostExecute(Void result) {
        mMapImage = mBitmap;
        mMapItem = mGalleryItem;
        mCurrentLocation = mLocation;

        updateUI();
    }
}
```

Run Locatr and press the search button. You should see your map zoom in on an area of interest that includes your current location (Figure 32.2). (Emulator users will need to have MockWalker running to get a location fix.)

Figure 32.2 Zoomed map

Drawing on the map

Your map is nice, but a little vague. You know that you are in there somewhere, and you know that the Flickr photo is in there somewhere. But where? Let's add specificity with some markers.

Drawing on a map is not the same as drawing on a regular view. It is a little easier, in fact. Instead of drawing pixels to the screen, you draw features to a geographic area. And by "drawing," we mean, "build little objects and add them to your `GoogleMap` so that it can draw them for you."

Actually, that is not quite right, either. It is, in fact, the `GoogleMap` object that makes these objects, not you. Instead, you create objects that describe what you want the `GoogleMap` to create, called *options objects*.

Add two markers to your map by creating `MarkerOptions` objects and then calling `mMap.addMarker(MarkerOptions)`.

Listing 32.16 Adding markers (LocatrFragment.java)

```java
private void updateUI() {
    ...

    LatLng itemPoint = new LatLng(mMapItem.getLat(), mMapItem.getLon());
    LatLng myPoint = new LatLng(
            mCurrentLocation.getLatitude(), mCurrentLocation.getLongitude());

    BitmapDescriptor itemBitmap = BitmapDescriptorFactory.fromBitmap(mMapImage);
    MarkerOptions itemMarker = new MarkerOptions()
            .position(itemPoint)
            .icon(itemBitmap);
    MarkerOptions myMarker = new MarkerOptions()
            .position(myPoint);

    mMap.clear();
    mMap.addMarker(itemMarker);
    mMap.addMarker(myMarker);

    LatLngBounds bounds = new LatLngBounds.Builder()
    ...
}
```

When you call **addMarker(MarkerOptions)**, the **GoogleMap** builds a **Marker** instance and adds it to the map. If you need to remove or modify the marker in the future, you can hold on to this instance. In this case, you will be clearing the map every time you update it. As a result, you do not need to hold on to the **Marker**s.

Run Locatr, press the search button, and you should see your two markers show up (Figure 32.3).

Figure 32.3 Geographic looming

And with that, your little geographic image finder is complete. You figured out how to use two Play Services APIs, you tracked your phone's location, you registered for one of Google's many web services APIs, and you plotted everything on a map. Perhaps a nap is in order now that your app's map is in order.

For the More Curious: Teams and API Keys

When you have more than one person working an app with an API key, debug builds start to be a pain. Your signing credentials are stored in a keystore file, which is unique to you. On a team, everyone will have their *own* keystore file, and their own credentials. In order for anyone new to work on the app, you have to ask them for their SHA1, and then go and update your API key's credentials.

Or, at least, that is one option for how to manage the API key: manage all of the signing hashes in your project. If you want a lot of explicit control over who is doing what, that may be the right solution.

But there is another option: create a debug keystore specifically for the project. Start by creating a brand new debug keystore with Java's keytool program.

Listing 32.17 Creating a new keystore (terminal)

```
$ keytool -genkey -v -keystore debug.keystore -alias androiddebugkey \
-storepass android -keypass android -keyalg RSA -validity 14600
```

You will be asked a series of questions by keytool. Answer them honestly, as if no one were watching. (Since this is a debug key, it is OK to leave the default value on everything but the name if you like.)

```
$ keytool -genkey -v -keystore debug.keystore -alias androiddebugkey \
-storepass android -keypass android -keyalg RSA -validity 14600
What is your first and last name?
  [Unknown]:  Bill Phillips
...
```

Once you have that debug.keystore file, move it into your app module's folder. Then open up your project structure, select your app module, and navigate to the Signing tab. Click the + button to add a new signing config. Type in debug in the Name field and debug.keystore for your newly created keystore (Figure 32.4).

Figure 32.4 Configuring debug signing key

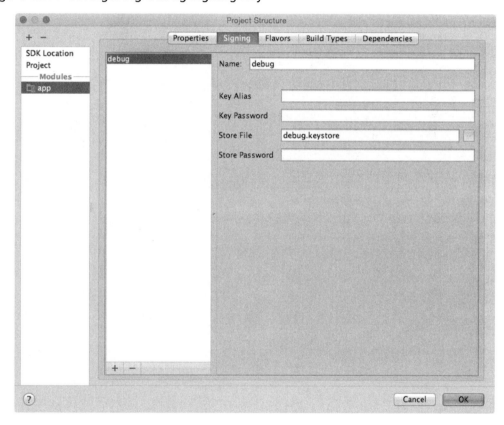

If you configure your API key to use this new keystore, then anyone else can use the same API key by using the same keystore. Much easier.

Note that if you do this, you need to exercise some caution about how you distribute this new debug.keystore. If you only share it in a private code repo, you should be fine. But do not publish this keystore in a public repo where anybody can get to it, because it will allow them to use your API key.

33

Material Design

The biggest change in Android 5.0 Lollipop was the introduction of a new design style: material design. This new visual language made a big splash and was accompanied by a wonderfully exhaustive style guide.

Of course, as developers we are usually only peripherally concerned with questions of design. Our job is to get it done, no matter what "it" is. However, material design introduces some new interface concepts in addition to design sensibilities. If you familiarize yourself with them, you will find it much easier to implement these new designs.

This final chapter is a little different from previous chapters. You can think of it as an enormous For The More Curious section. There is no example app to work through, and most of this information is not required reading.

For designers, material design emphasizes three big ideas:

- *Material is the metaphor*: The pieces of the app should act like physical, material objects.

- *Bold, graphic, and intentional*: App designs should jump off the page like they would in a well-designed magazine or book.

- *Motion provides meaning*: The app should animate in response to actions taken by the user.

The only one of these that our book has nothing to say about is *bold, graphic, and intentional*. This is a designer's responsibility. If you are designing your own app, check out the material design guidelines to see what they mean by that.

For the *material is the metaphor* part, designers need your help to build out the material surfaces. You will need to know how to position them in three dimensions using z-axis properties, and you will need to know how to use two new material widgets: floating action bars and snackbars.

Finally, to live up to the directive that *motion provides meaning*, you can learn a new set of animation tools: state list animators, animated state list drawables (yes, you read that right – they are different from state list animators), circular reveals, and shared element transitions. These can be used to add the visual interest that bold designers crave.

Material Surfaces

As a developer, the single most important idea you should be familiar with in material design is the idea of material surfaces. Designers think of these as 1dp thick bits of cardstock. These bits of cardstock act like magically changeable bits of paper and ink: they can grow, they can show animated pictures, they can show changing text (Figure 33.1).

Figure 33.1 An interface with two material surfaces

However, as magical as they may be they still behave like real pieces of paper. For example, one sheet of paper cannot move right through another. The same logic applies when you animate material surfaces: they cannot animate through one another.

Instead, surfaces exist and maneuver around one another in a three-dimensional space. They can move up toward your finger, or down and away (Figure 33.2).

Figure 33.2 A material design in 3-D space

To animate one surface across another, you move it up and across the other surface (Figure 33.3).

Figure 33.3 Animating one surface over another

Elevation and Z values

The most apparent way users will see the depth in your interface is by seeing how elements of your app cast shadows on one another. Some might think that a perfect world would be one where the designers worry about drawing those shadows and we developers go eat bagels. (Opinions differ on what a perfect world looks like.)

But doing that with a variety of surfaces in play – while animating, no less – is not possible for designers to do by themselves. Instead, you let Android take care of drawing the shadows by giving each of your **View**s an *elevation*.

Lollipop introduced a z-axis to the layout system, allowing you to specify where a view lives in 3-D space. Elevation is like the coordinates assigned to your view in layout: you can animate your view away from this position, but this is where it naturally lives (Figure 33.4).

Figure 33.4 Elevation on the Z plane

elevation: 2dp

To set the elevation value, you can either call the **View.setElevation(float)** method or set the value in your layout file.

Listing 33.1 Setting elevation on a view in a layout file

```xml
<?xml version="1.0" encoding="utf-8"?>
<Button xmlns:android="http://schemas.android.com/apk/res/android"
    xmlns:tools="http://schemas.android.com/tools"
    android:id="@+id/button"
    android:layout_width="wrap_content"
    android:layout_height="wrap_content"
    android:elevation="2dp"/>
```

Because this is intended to be your baseline Z value, using the XML attribute is preferred. It is also easier to use than **setElevation(float)**, because the elevation attribute is silently ignored on older versions of Android, so you do not need to worry about compatibility.

To change a **View**'s elevation, you use the translationZ and Z properties. These work exactly like translationX, translationY, X, and Y, which you saw in Chapter 30. Z's value is always elevation plus translationZ. If you assign a value to Z, it will do the math to assign the right value to translationZ (Figure 33.5).

Figure 33.5 Z and translationZ

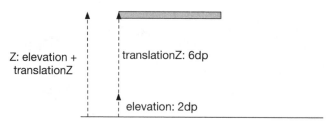

State list animators

Material applications are often designed with many animated user interactions. Press a button on Lollipop to see one example: the button will animate up on the z-axis to meet your finger. When you release your finger, it will animate back down.

To make implementing these animations easier, Lollipop introduced *state list animators*. State list animators are the animation counterpart to the state list drawable: instead of switching out one drawable for another, they animate the view into a particular state. To implement an animation that raises the button up when you press it, you can define a state list animator that looks like this in res/animator:

Listing 33.2 An example state list animator

```xml
<?xml version="1.0" encoding="utf-8"?>
<selector xmlns:android="http://schemas.android.com/apk/res/android">
    <item android:state_pressed="true">
        <objectAnimator android:propertyName="translationZ"
                        android:duration="100"
                        android:valueTo="6dp"
                        android:valueType="floatType"
                        />
    </item>
    <item android:state_pressed="false">
        <objectAnimator android:propertyName="translationZ"
                        android:duration="100"
                        android:valueTo="0dp"
                        android:valueType="floatType"
            />
    </item>
</selector>
```

This is great if you need to use a property animation. If you want to perform a framed animation, you need to use another tool: the *animated state list drawable*.

The name "animated state list drawable" is a little confusing. It sounds similar to "state list animator," but the purpose is totally different. Animated state list drawables allow you to define images for each state, like a normal state list drawable, but they also allow you to define frame animation transitions between those states.

Back in Chapter 21, you defined a state list drawable for BeatBox's sound buttons. If a sadistic designer (like our own Kar Loong Wong) wanted to have a multiframe animation each time the button was pressed, you could modify your XML to look like Listing 33.3. This version would need to live inside res/drawable-21 because this feature is not supported prior to Lollipop.

Listing 33.3 An animated state list drawable

```xml
<?xml version="1.0" encoding="utf-8"?>
<animated-selector xmlns:android="http://schemas.android.com/apk/res/android">
    <item android:id="@+id/pressed"
          android:drawable="@drawable/button_beat_box_pressed"
          android:state_pressed="true"/>
    <item android:id="@+id/released"
          android:drawable="@drawable/button_beat_box_normal" />

    <transition
        android:fromId="@id/released"
        android:toId="@id/pressed">
        <animation-list>
            <item android:duration="10" android:drawable="@drawable/button_frame_1" />
            <item android:duration="10" android:drawable="@drawable/button_frame_2" />
            <item android:duration="10" android:drawable="@drawable/button_frame_3" />
            ...
        </animation-list>
    </transition>
</animated-selector>
```

Here, each item in the selector gets an ID. You can then define a transition between different IDs to play a multiframe animation. If you want to provide an animation when you release the button, too, that requires an additional transition tag.

Animation Tools

Material design has many nifty new animations. Some of them can be achieved quickly. Others require more work, but Android provides some tools to help you out.

Circular reveal

The circular reveal animation is used in material design to look like an ink flood-fill. A view or piece of content is progressively revealed outward from a point of interaction, usually a point pressed by the user. Figure 33.6 gives you an idea of what a circular reveal can bring to the party.

Figure 33.6 Circular reveal from pressing an item in BeatBox

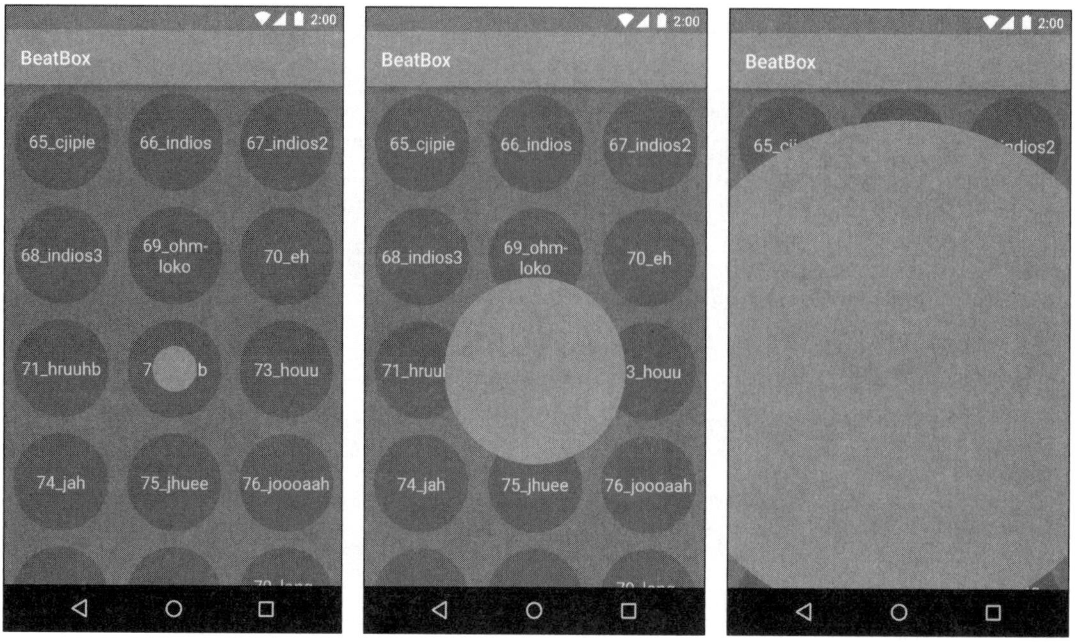

You may remember using a simple version of this way back in Chapter 6, where you used it to hide a button. Here we will talk about another way to use circular reveal that is slightly more involved.

To create a circular reveal animation, you call the **createCircularReveal(…)** method on **ViewAnimationUtils**. This method takes in quite a few parameters:

```
static Animator createCircularReveal(View view, int centerX, int centerY,
        float startRadius, float endRadius)
```

The **View** passed in is the **View** you would like to reveal. In Figure 33.6, this view is a solid red view that is the same width and height of the **BeatBoxFragment**. If you animate from a startRadius of 0 to a large endRadius, this view will start out being completely transparent, and then slowly be revealed as the circle expands. The circle's origin (in terms of the **View**'s coordinates) will be centerX and centerY. This method returns an **Animator**, which works exactly like the **Animator** you used back in Chapter 30.

The material design guidelines say that these animations should originate from the point where the user touched the screen. So your first step is to find the screen coordinates of the view that the user touched, as in Listing 33.4.

Listing 33.4 Finding screen coordinates in a click listener

```
@Override
public void onClick(View clickSource) {
    int[] clickCoords = new int[2];

    // Find the location of clickSource on the screen
    clickSource.getLocationOnScreen(clickCoords);

    // Tweak that location so that it points at the center of the view,
    // not the corner
    clickCoords[0] += clickSource.getWidth() / 2;
    clickCoords[1] += clickSource.getHeight() / 2;

    performRevealAnimation(mViewToReveal, clickCoords[0], clickCoords[1]);
}
```

Then you can perform your reveal animation (Listing 33.5).

Listing 33.5 Making and executing a reveal animation

```
private void performRevealAnimation(View view, int screenCenterX, int screenCenterY) {
    // Find the center relative to the view that will be animated
    int[] animatingViewCoords = new int[2];
    view.getLocationOnScreen(animatingViewCoords);
    int centerX = screenCenterX - animatingViewCoords[0];
    int centerY = screenCenterY - animatingViewCoords[1];

    // Find the maximum radius
    Point size = new Point();
    getActivity().getWindowManager().getDefaultDisplay().getSize(size);
    int maxRadius = size.y;

    if (Build.VERSION.SDK_INT >= Build.VERSION_CODES.LOLLIPOP) {
        ViewAnimationUtils.createCircularReveal(view, centerX, centerY, 0, maxRadius)
                .start();
    }
}
```

Important note: the **View** must already be in the layout for this method to work.

Shared element transitions

Another kind of animation that is new to material design is the *shared element transition*, or *hero transition*. This transition is meant for a specific situation: where two screens display some of the same things.

Think back to your work on CriminalIntent. In that application, you had a thumbnail view of a picture you took in **CrimeDetailFragment**. In one of the challenges, you were asked to construct another view that zoomed in to a full-size visual of that picture. Your solution might have looked something like Figure 33.7.

Figure 33.7 A zoomed-in picture view

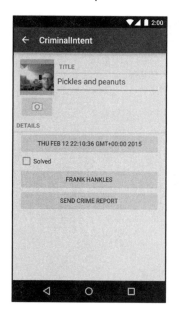 

This is a common interface pattern: you press one element and the next view provides more detail for that element.

A shared element transition is an animation for any situation where you are transitioning between two screens that are displaying some of the same elements. In this case, both the big image on the right and the small one on the left are displaying the same picture. The picture, in other words, is a *shared element*.

In Lollipop, Android provides techniques for accomplishing a transition between activities or between fragments. Here, we will show you how it works with activities. The middle of the animation looks like Figure 33.8.

Figure 33.8 Shared element transition

For activities, the basic implementation is a three-step process:

1. Turn on activity transitions.

2. Set transition name values for each shared element view.

3. Start your next activity with an **ActivityOptions** that will trigger the transition.

First, you have to turn on activity transitions. If your activity uses the AppCompat theme used elsewhere in the book, then you can skip this step. (AppCompat inherits from the Material theme, which turns on activity transitions for you.)

In our example, we gave our activity a transparent background by using @android:style/ Theme.Translucent.NoTitleBar. This theme does not inherit from the Material theme, so it does not have activity transitions turned on. They have to be turned on manually, which can happen in either of two ways. One option is to add a line of code to the activity, as in Listing 33.6.

Listing 33.6 Turning on activity transitions in code

```
@Override
public void onCreate(Bundle savedInstanceState) {
    getWindow().requestFeature(Window.FEATURE_ACTIVITY_TRANSITIONS);
    super.onCreate(savedInstanceState);

    ...
}
```

The other way is to tweak the style the activity uses and set the android:windowActivityTransitions attribute to true.

Listing 33.7 Turning on activity transitions in a style

```
<resources>
    <style name="TransparentTheme"
        parent="@android:style/Theme.Translucent.NoTitleBar">
        <item name="android:windowActivityTransitions">true</item>
    </style>

</resources>
```

The next step in the shared element transition is to tag each shared element view with a transition name. This is done in a property on **View** introduced in API 21: transitionName. You can set it in either XML or in code; depending on the circumstance, one or the other might be appropriate. In our case, we set the transition name for the zoomed-in image by setting android:transitionName to image in our layout XML, as in Figure 33.9.

Figure 33.9 Zoomed-in image layout

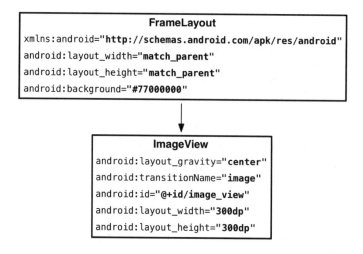

Then we defined a static method **startWithTransition(…)** (Listing 33.8) to set the same transition name on a view to animate from.

Listing 33.8 Start with transition method

```
public static void startWithTransition(Activity activity, Intent intent,
  View sourceView) {
    ViewCompat.setTransitionName(sourceView, "image");
    ActivityOptionsCompat options = ActivityOptionsCompat
        .makeSceneTransitionAnimation(activity, sourceView, "image");

    activity.startActivity(intent, options.toBundle());
}
```

`ViewCompat.setTransitionName(View, String)` is there to help out on older versions of Android, where `View` will not have a `setTransitionName(String)` implementation.

In Listing 33.8, you can see the final step, too: making an `ActivityOptions`. The `ActivityOptions` tells the OS what the shared elements are and what `transitionName` value to use.

There is a lot more to know about transitions and shared element transitions. They can also be used for fragment transitions, for example. For more information, check out Google's documentation for the transitions framework: `https://developer.android.com/training/transitions/overview.html`.

View Components

Lollipop's new material design guidelines specify a few new kinds of view components. The Android team provides implementations of many of these components. Let's take a look at a few of the views you are likely to run into.

Cards

The first new widget is a frame for other widgets: *cards* (Figure 33.10).

Figure 33.10 Cards

A card is a container for other kinds of content. It is elevated slightly, with a shadow behind it, and its corners are slightly rounded.

This is not a design book, so we cannot provide advice on when and where to use cards. (See Google's material design documentation on the web if you are curious: http://www.google.com/design/spec.) We can tell you how to make them, though: by using **CardView**.

CardView is a class provided in its own v7 support library, much like **RecyclerView**. You can include it in your project by adding a dependency on com.android.support:cardview-v7 to your module.

Once you do that, you can use **CardView** like any other **ViewGroup** in a layout. It is a **FrameLayout** subclass, so you can use any of **FrameLayout**'s layout params for **CardView**'s children.

Listing 33.9 Using CardView in a layout

```
<LinearLayout xmlns:android="http://schemas.android.com/apk/res/android"
              xmlns:tools="http://schemas.android.com/tools"
              android:layout_width="match_parent"
              android:layout_height="match_parent"
              android:orientation="vertical"
              tools:context=".MainActivity">
    <android.support.v7.widget.CardView
        android:id="@+id/item"
        android:layout_width="match_parent"
        android:layout_height="200dp"
        android:layout_margin="16dp"
        >
        ...
    </android.support.v7.widget.CardView>

</LinearLayout>
```

Because **CardView** is a support library class, it gives you some nice compatibility features on older devices. Unlike other widgets, it will always project a shadow. (On older versions, it will simply draw its own – not a perfect shadow, but close enough.) See **CardView**'s documentation for other minor visual differences, if you are interested.

Floating action buttons

Another component you will often see is the *floating action button*, or FAB. You can see one in Figure 33.11.

Figure 33.11 A floating action button

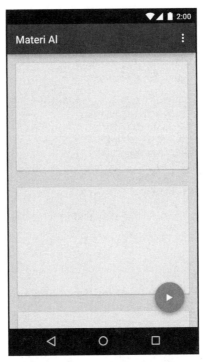

An implementation of the floating action button is available in Google's design support library. You can include this library in your project with this dependency on your module: `com.android.support:design:22.2.0`.

Floating action buttons are little more than a solid-color circle with a custom circular shadow, provided by an **OutlineProvider**. The **FloatingActionButton** class, a subclass of **ImageView**, takes care of the circle and shadow for you. Simply place a **FloatingActionButton** in your layout file and set its **src** attribute to the image that you want to display in your button.

While you could place your floating action button in a **FrameLayout**, the design support library also includes the clever **CoordinatorLayout**. This layout is a subclass of **FrameLayout** that changes your floating action button's position based on the movement of other components. Now, when you display a **Snackbar**, your FAB will move up so that the **Snackbar** does not cover it. This will look like Listing 33.10.

Listing 33.10 Laying out a floating action button

```
<android.support.design.widget.CoordinatorLayout
            xmlns:android="http://schemas.android.com/apk/res/android"
            xmlns:tools="http://schemas.android.com/tools"
            xmlns:app="http://schemas.android.com/apk/res-auto"
            android:layout_width="match_parent"
            android:layout_height="match_parent">
    [... main content here ...]
    <android.support.design.widget.FloatingActionButton
        android:id="@+id/floating_action_button"
        android:layout_width="wrap_content"
        android:layout_height="wrap_content"
        android:layout_gravity="bottom|right"
        android:layout_margin="16dp"
        android:src="@drawable/play"/>
</android.support.design.widget.CoordinatorLayout>
```

This code will place the button over the rest of the content in the bottom right, without interfering with any of it.

Snackbars

Snackbars are a bit more involved than floating action buttons. They are little interaction components that appear at the bottom of the screen (Figure 33.12).

Figure 33.12 A snackbar

Snackbars animate up from the bottom of the screen. After a certain period of time, or after another interaction on the screen, they automatically animate back down. Snackbars are similar in purpose to

Toasts, but unlike **Toast**s they are a part of your app's own interface. A **Toast** appears above your app and will stick around even if you navigate away. Also, snackbars let you provide a button so that the user can take immediate action.

Like floating action buttons, Android provides an implementation of snackbars in the design support library.

Snackbars are constructed and displayed in a similar way as **Toast**s (Listing 33.11).

Listing 33.11 Having a snack(bar)

```
Snackbar.make(container, R.string.munch, Snackbar.LENGTH_SHORT).show();
```

When constructing a **Snackbar**, pass in the view where the snackbar will be displayed, the text to display, and the length of time that the snackbar should be visible for. Finally, call **show()** to display the snackbar.

Snackbars can optionally provide an action on the right side. This is handy if the user performs a destructive action, like deleting a crime, and you want to provide a way for the user to undo that action.

More on Material Design

In this chapter, we presented what amounts to a big grab bag of tools. Those tools are hardly any fun if you let them sit and gather dust. So keep an eye out for ways to spiff up your application with some depth or new animations.

One great place to look for inspiration is the material design specification itself, which is full of great ideas: `http://www.google.com/design/spec/material-design/introduction.html`. You can also look in Google Play to see what other apps are doing, and ask yourself: How would I do that in my own app? You might end up with a niftier program than what you initially imagined.

34
Afterword

Congratulations! You are at the end of this guide. Not everyone has the discipline to do what you have done, to learn what you have learned. Take a quick moment and give yourself a pat on the back.

This hard work has paid off: you are now an Android developer.

The Final Challenge

We have one last challenge for you: become a *good* Android developer. Good developers are each good in their own way, so you must find your own path from here on out.

Where might you start, then? Here are some places we recommend:

Write code. Now. You will quickly forget what you have learned here if you do not apply it. Contribute to a project, or write a simple application of your own. Whatever you do, waste no time: write code.

Learn. You have learned a little bit about a lot of things in this book. Did any of them spark your imagination? Write some code to play around with your favorite thing. Find and read more documentation about it, or an entire book if there is one. Also, check out the Android Developers YouTube channel and listen to the Android Developers Backstage podcast for Android updates from Google.

Meet people. Local meetups are a good place to meet like-minded developers. Lots of top-notch Android developers are active on Twitter and Google Plus. Attend Android conferences to meet other Android developers (and maybe even us!).

Explore the open source community. Android development is exploding on `http://www.github.com`. When you find a cool library, see what other projects its contributors are committing to. Share your own code, too – you never know who will find it useful or interesting. We find the Android Weekly mailing list to be a great way to see what is happening in the Android community (`http://androidweekly.net/`).

Shameless Plugs

You can find all of us on Twitter. Bill is `@billjings`, Chris is `@cstew`, Brian is `@lyricsboy`, and Kristin is `@kristinmars`.

If you enjoyed this book, check out other Big Nerd Ranch Guides at `http://www.bignerdranch.com/books`. We also have a broad selection of week-long courses for developers, where we make it easy to learn this amount of stuff in only a week of time. And of course, if you just need someone to write great code, we do contract programming, too. For more, go to our website at `http://www.bignerdranch.com`.

Thank You

Without readers like you, our work would not exist. Thank you for buying and reading our book.

Index

Symbols

A

Android

Visual Reference Guide

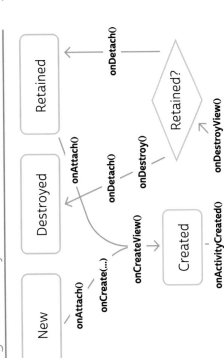

Android Versions

Version	Name	API Level
2.2	Froyo	8
2.3.3 - 2.3.7	Gingerbread	10
4.0.3 - 4.0.4	Ice Cream Sandwich	15
4.1.x	Jelly Bean	16
4.2.x	Jelly Bean	17
4.3	Jelly Bean	18
4.4	KitKat	19
5.0	Lollipop	21
5.1	Lollipop	22

Java

```
// inline array init
new String[] {"Quick", "Brown", "Fox"}

// constructible enum
public enum Planet {
    MERCURY(4, 7.0),
    VENUS(3, 8.0),
    EARTH(2, 9.0);

    private final int mMass;
    private final double mRadius;

    Planet(int mass, double radius) {
        mMass = mass;
        mRadius = radius;
    }

    public double getMass() {
        return mMass;
    }

    public double getRadius() {
        return mRadius;
    }
}
```

Activity Lifecycle

Non-existent

— onDestroy() ← Finished or destroyed

— Launch
onCreate(...) →

Stopped (not visible)

— onStop() ← No longer visible

— Visible to user
onStart() →

Paused (visible)

— onPause() ← Leaves foreground

— Enters foreground
onResume() →

Running (visible & in foreground)

www.bignerdranch.com

Fragment Lifecycle

New

onAttach()
onCreate(...) →

Retained

← onDetach()

Retained?

Destroyed

onAttach()
onDetach()
onDestroy()

onCreateView() →

Created

onActivityCreated() →

onDestroyView()

Stopped!

— onStop() ←

onStart() →

Paused!

— onPause() ←

onResume() →

Running!

Big Nerd Ranch

We Teach   We Develop   We Write

Android Studio

Visual Reference Guide

Find

⌘ ⇧ A	Find Action / Shortcut	
⌘ ⇧ F	Search Entire Project for String	
⇧ ⇧	Search for Method, Variable, File, or Class	
⌥ F7	Find all Usages within Project	
⌃ H	Display Call Hierarchy	
⌘ ⇧ F7	Find Occurrences within File	
⌘ ⌥ O	Find Symbol (e.g., method name)	
⌘ E	Open Recent	

Generate / Autocomplete

⌘ ⇧ ENTER	Complete Statement	
⌘ P	Show Method Arguments	
⌘ ⌥ I	Format Code	
⌃ SPACE	Autocomplete	
⌃ ⇧ SPACE	Smart Autocomplete	
⌘ N	Generate	

Refactor

⇧ F6	Rename all Occurrences	
⌘ F6	Change Signature	
F6	Move File or Method	
⌘ DELETE	Delete Entire Line	
⇧ /	Comment / Uncomment Line	

Run

⌃ R	▷	Run
⌃ D	🐞	Debug

Navigate

⌘ Click		Go to Definition
⌃ (hold) Tab		Switcher (switch between all open files / Android studio panes)
⌘ [or]		Navigate backward or forward through previous previous cursor locations

Jump to...

→		Next Character
⌥ →		Next Word
⌘ →		End of Line
Hold ⇧		Highlight
↑		Move Backward

Basics

⌘ C	Copy	
⌘ X	Cut	
⌘ V	Paste	
⌘ Z	Undo	

Misc

⌘ ⇧ + or -	Expand / Collapse	
	All Methods	

Key

⌘	Command
⇧	Shift
⌥	Option
⌃	Control

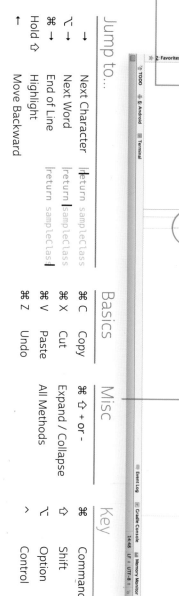